Social Resilience in the Neoliberal I

What is the impact of three decades of nec and individual lives? What are the sources of social resilience? This book offers a sweeping assessment of the effects of neoliberalism, the dominant feature of our times. It analyzes the ideology in unusually wide-ranging terms as a movement that not only opened markets but also introduced new logics into social life, integrating macro-level analyses of how neoliberal narratives made their way into international policy regimes with micro-level analyses of how individuals responded to the challenges of the neoliberal era. The book introduces the concept of social resilience and explores how communities, social groups, and nations sustain their well-being in the face of such challenges. The product of ten years of collaboration among a distinguished group of scholars, it integrates institutional and cultural analysis to understand neoliberalism as a syncretic social process and to explore the sources of social resilience across communities in the developed and developing worlds.

Peter A. Hall is Krupp Foundation Professor of European Studies at Harvard University, where he has also served at various times as director of the Minda de Gunzburg Center for European Studies, director of Graduate Studies in Government, and associate dean of the Faculty of Arts and Sciences. He is co-director of the Successful Societies Program for the Canadian Institute for Advanced Research. He is an editor of *Changing France: The Politics that Markets Make*; *Varieties of Capitalism: The Institutional Foundations of Comparative Advantage*; *The Political Power of Economic Ideas: Keynesianism across Nations*; *Developments in French Politics I and II*; and *European Labor in the 1980s* and the author of *Governing the Economy*, which won the Woodrow Wilson Award for the best book in political science published in 1986. He has published more than eighty articles on European politics and public policymaking and comparative political economy and serves on the editorial boards of many scholarly journals and on advisory boards at Sciences Po, Paris; the Free University of Berlin; and the University of Birmingham.

Michèle Lamont is a Fellow of the Canadian Institute for Advanced Research and is co-director of its research program on Successful Societies. She taught at Princeton University for fifteen years before moving to Harvard in 2003. She has published on the topics of inequality, culture, race, immigration, knowledge, theory, qualitative methods, and comparative sociology. She is the author of more than eighty articles and a dozen books and edited volumes, including *How Professors Think: Inside the Curious World of Academic Judgment*; *The Dignity of Working Men: Morality and the Boundaries of Race, Class, and Immigration* (winner of the C. Wright Mills Award from the Society for the Study of Social Problems); and *Money, Morals and Manners: The Culture of the French and the American Upper-Middle Class*. Past responsibilities include chair of the Council for European Studies (2005–2009) and senior advisor on Faculty Development and Diversity, Faculty of the Arts and Sciences, Harvard (2008–2010).

This book is dedicated to Chaviva Hošek – visionary for a better society

Social Resilience in the Neoliberal Era

Edited by
PETER A. HALL AND MICHÈLE LAMONT

CAMBRIDGE
UNIVERSITY PRESS

CAMBRIDGE UNIVERSITY PRESS
Cambridge, New York, Melbourne, Madrid, Cape Town,
Singapore, São Paulo, Delhi, Mexico City

Cambridge University Press
32 Avenue of the Americas, New York, NY 10013-2473, USA

www.cambridge.org
Information on this title: www.cambridge.org/9781107659841

© Cambridge University Press 2013

First published 2013

Printed in the United States of America

A catalog record for this publication is available from the British Library.

Library of Congress Cataloging in Publication data

Social resilience in the neoliberal era / edited by Peter A. Hall, Michèle Lamont.
    pages   cm
ISBN 978-1-107-03497-6 (hardback) – ISBN 978-1-107-65984-1 (paperback)
1. Social policy.   2. Social history.   3. Neoliberalism.   I. Hall, Peter A., 1950– editor of
compilation.   II. Lamont, Michèle, 1957– editor of compilation.
HN17.5.S617   2013
361.2'5 – dc23   2012035325

ISBN 978-1-107-03497-6 Hardback
ISBN 978-1-107-65984-1 Paperback

Contents

Contributors

Marcos Ancelovici is a professor in the Department of Sociology at the Université du Québec à Montréal. He holds a PhD in political science from MIT, and his doctoral thesis won the 2008 George Lavau Dissertation Award from the American Political Science Association. In 2009–10, he was a Junior Fellow in the Successful Societies Program of the Canadian Institute for Advanced Research (CIFAR). He works on social movements, labor politics, globalization, and the sociology of Pierre Bourdieu, and is currently studying anti-austerity protests.

Jonathan Arac is Andrew W. Mellon Professor of English and founding director of the Humanities Center at the University of Pittsburgh. He also serves on the *boundary* 2 editorial collective. From 2002 until 2012, he chaired the Advisory Committee for the Successful Societies Program of the CIFAR.

Lucy Barnes is a prize postdoctoral research Fellow in politics at Nuffield College, Oxford. She received her PhD in political economy and government from Harvard University in 2010.

Dr. Alan Bernstein, president and CEO of CIFAR, previously served as executive director of the Global HIV Vaccine Enterprise and founding president of the Canadian Institutes of Health Research. He has published more than 200 papers on stem cells, cancer research, and science and public policy and is the recipient of numerous awards and honorary degrees, including the Gairdner Wightman Award and the Order of Canada.

Gérard Bouchard is a member of the Royal Society of Canada and holder of a Canada research chair in collective imaginaries. He is a sociologist and a historian teaching in the Department of Human Sciences at the Université du Québec à Chicoutimi. Over the past forty years, he has published widely in the field of social and cultural history. He now specializes in the comparative study of social myths and collective imaginaries.

James R. Dunn is an associate professor in the Department of Health, Aging and Society at McMaster University and a scientist at the Centre for Research on Inner City Health at St. Michael's Hospital. Dr. Dunn holds a chair in Applied Public Health from the Canadian Institutes of Health Research and the Public Health Agency of Canada.

Peter B. Evans is professor of sociology emeritus at Berkeley and a senior Fellow at the Watson Institute for International Studies at Brown University. He is best known for his research on the role of the state in industrial transformation in the Global South and is now working on "counter-hegemonic globalization" with a focus on the global labor movement.

Crystal M. Fleming, a cultural sociologist, is an assistant professor of sociology at SUNY Stony Brook in New York. She graduated from Wellesley College with degrees in sociology and French and earned her AM (2007) and PhD (2011) in sociology from Harvard University. Her work explores how subjective constructions of identity and collective memory contribute to the making and unmaking of ethnoracial boundaries in France and the United States. Her doctoral thesis on the representation of French Atlantic slavery won the 2012 Georges Lavau award for the best dissertation on contemporary French politics.

Peter A. Hall is Krupp Foundation Professor of European Studies at the Minda de Gunzburg Center for European Studies and a faculty member in the Department of Government at Harvard University as well as co-director of the Program on Successful Societies for the CIFAR. His publications include *Successful Societies* (with Michèle Lamont), *Varieties of Capitalism* (with David Soskice), and more than eighty articles on politics and policymaking in Europe.

Dr. Clyde Hertzman is director of the Human Early Learning Partnership, Canada Research Chair in Population Health and Human Development, and professor in the School of Population and Public Health at the University of British Columbia. He is a Fellow of the Experience-Based Brain and Biological Development Program and the Successful Societies Program of the CIFAR, as well as the Royal Society of Canada and the Canadian Academy of Health Sciences.

Jane Jenson is a professor of political science and has held the Canada Research Chair in Citizenship and Governance at the Université de Montréal since 2001. In 2005, she was named a Fellow of the Trudeau Foundation and has been a member of the Successful Societies Program of CIFAR since 2004. Her research focuses on comparative social policy and European politics as well as social movements.

Dr. Daniel Keating is professor of psychology, psychiatry, and pediatrics and research professor at the Survey Research Center, Institute for Social Research, University of Michigan. His most recent book (*Nature and Nurture in Early*

Child Development, Cambridge, 2011) integrates research across multiple disciplines in developmental science. His research program focuses on the connections between population developmental health and underlying developmental and biodevelopmental mechanisms.

Will Kymlicka is the Canada Research Chair in political philosophy at Queen's University in Kingston, Canada. His work explores how countries address issues of ethnic, racial, and religious diversity, with a focus on the theory and practice of multicultural citizenship. He is the author of seven books published by Oxford University Press, including *Liberalism, Community, and Culture*; *Multicultural Citizenship*; and *Multicultural Odysseys: Navigating the New International Politics of Diversity*.

Michèle Lamont is the Robert I. Goldman Professor of European Studies and professor of sociology and African and African American Studies at Harvard University. She is also a Fellow of the CIFAR, where she co-directs the Program on Successful Societies. Her recent research concerns the cultural dimensions of inequality, the transformation of racial and ethnic boundaries, everyday responses to stigmatization, definitions of excellence in higher education, and evaluation processes.

Ron Levi holds the George Ignatieff Chair of Peace and Conflict Studies at the University of Toronto and is an associate professor of Global Affairs and Sociology. His research includes global justice regimes, the sociology of state power, and diasporic experiences of law and the state.

Quynh Nguyen received her MSPH (2009) and PhD (2011) in epidemiology from the University of North Carolina at Chapel Hill. She received her BA in human biology from Stanford University in 2005. Her research focuses on adolescent health, health disparities, chronic diseases, and international comparisons of health outcomes across developed countries. An overarching career goal is to examine factors that enable (and prohibit) success of at-risk youth.

William H. Sewell, Jr., is the Frank P. Hixon Distinguished Service Professor Emeritus of political science and history at the University of Chicago. He is the author most recently of *Logics of History: Social Theory and Social Transformation* (2005). He is currently working on the cultural consequences of capitalist development in eighteenth-century France.

Arjumand Siddiqi is assistant professor at the University of Toronto Dalla Lana School of Public Health and adjunct assistant professor at the University of North Carolina, Chapel Hill. She is interested in the role that societal conditions play in shaping inequities in population health and human development. Dr. Siddiqi received her doctorate in social epidemiology from Harvard University.

Leanne S. Son Hing is an associate professor in the Department of Psychology at the University of Guelph. She specializes in social justice issues from an organizational and social psychological perspective. In particular, she examines the interplay among prejudice, discrimination, inequality, and beliefs about meritocracy as well as their consequences for well-being and social policy attitudes.

Ann Swidler is professor of sociology at the University of California, Berkeley. Her most recent book is *Talk of Love: How Culture Matters* (University of Chicago Press, 2001). Her current research explores how culture shapes institutions by analyzing global and local responses to the AIDS epidemic in sub-Saharan Africa.

Jessica S. Welburn is a Presidential postdoctoral Fellow at the University of Michigan. Her research interests include race and ethnicity, cultural sociology, the sociology of the family, and qualitative methodology. She is currently working on a book exploring how African Americans from middle-class households conceptualize their social mobility prospects.

Foreword

Alan Bernstein

The Canadian Institute for Advanced Research (CIFAR) brings together some of the world's most extraordinary thinkers to form global research networks that frame and answer important questions for humanity at the frontiers of human knowledge.

Most often, these exciting questions lie at the boundaries between disciplines. Accordingly, CIFAR research networks are deliberately made up of a diverse array of exceptional individuals who work together in an environment that encourages collegiality, collaboration, respect, trust, meaningful engagement, and vigorous debate and discussion.

Today, CIFAR's global research networks are addressing some of the most interesting and pressing questions of our time. Their work has the potential to improve human health and the environment, transform technology, build strong societies, understand human culture, and chart the universe. The results are as unpredictable as they are exciting, leading to new ways of thinking and addressing central questions that confront humanity.

CIFAR has three programs that fall under the theme of Building Strong Societies. Researchers in these programs are creating new frameworks to understand how our economies, institutions, and communities are best structured to serve their citizens. Their work is intended to inform and guide political and economic leaders around the world in setting new policies to improve the quality of human life.

The research in CIFAR's Building Strong Societies cluster is especially relevant today as movements such as the Arab Spring, the Occupy Movement, and the 2012 student protests in Québec grab international headlines. The twentieth century witnessed extraordinary improvements in living standards around the world, yet disparities within countries and between nations continue to grow, threatening to undermine the very progress that has been achieved over the past few generations.

Within this cluster, CIFAR's Program in Successful Societies unites epidemiologists, economists, sociologists, historians, political scientists, philosophers, psychologists, lawyers, criminologists, and geographers. Together, they are shedding new light on how social and cultural processes intertwine to advance or limit a society's collective well-being.

Most recently, these researchers in Canada and the United States have been studying two interconnected questions: How have three decades of intensified market competition changed people's life situations, group identities, and concepts of themselves? How has their capacity for social resilience allowed them to respond to new policy regimes based on neoliberal ideals?

This book shares their collective and intensive investigation into these questions. Combining two approaches that are usually divided by disciplines, this book provides a unique and deep understanding of the cultural frameworks within which groups create meaning in societies, integrated with analyses of the institutional frameworks shaping key social, economic, and political outcomes.

Social Resilience in the Neoliberal Era offers new ways of understanding the sweeping, long-term effect of neoliberal policies and the sources for social resilience as a creative and evolving response. From Africa to France to Canada and the United States, these essays provide a broad historical and geographical context and deep cultural analysis.

CIFAR's Program in Successful Societies was inspired by the accomplishments of CIFAR's programs in Population Health and Human Development, which concluded in 2003. These programs significantly advanced our understanding of social and economic determinants of health and how early childhood experiences affect well-being throughout life.

CIFAR's Program in Successful Societies picked up where these programs left off – to better understand the roots of social inequalities and the role of social, economic, and cultural institutions in fostering well-being.

In 2009, program members published their first collective volume titled *Successful Societies: How Institutions and Culture Affect Health*. The book offered new perspectives on inequalities in well-being. Stressing the contribution that institutional practices and cultural repertoires make to population health, the book explored issues of health and human development from multiple perspectives. This earlier volume laid a solid foundation upon which this most recent book has evolved.

I would like to congratulate all of the members of CIFAR's Program in Successful Societies on this landmark volume. In particular, I would like to recognize the extraordinary leadership that Peter A. Hall and Michèle Lamont, both of Harvard University, have provided as co-directors of CIFAR's Program in Successful Societies. Together, they have ensured that the very best of each program member informs the collective work of research, vigorous discussion, and the development of new frameworks of understanding that have the potential to inform real social change.

I also thank CIFAR's exceptional community of individuals; foundations; corporations; the Government of Canada; and the provincial governments of Alberta, British Columbia, and Ontario. Most notably, I would like to express my appreciation to the Alva Foundation, BMO Financial Group, and Max

Bell Foundation, which provide designated support to CIFAR's Program in Successful Societies.

Together, the nearly 400 researchers at 103 institutions in sixteen countries who make up CIFAR's networks are creating the knowledge that leads to entirely new understandings of the world we live in. Such insights and discoveries will inevitably enrich all of our lives.

Dr. Alan Bernstein, O.C., FRSC
President and CEO
Canadian Institute for Advanced Research
June 2012

Prologue

Jonathan Arac

This extraordinary volume arises from a remarkable matrix, the Successful Societies Program (SSP) of the Canadian Institute for Advanced Research (CIFAR). Since its founding in the 1980s, CIFAR has been committed to cutting-edge, long-term collaborative projects, which have helped to form new objects of knowledge and fields of research. The SSP itself arose from the intersection of two long-term CIFAR programs, one in population health and one in human development. Between the macro scale of demography and the micro scale of ontogeny, researchers realized there was a missing piece: call it society. Over several years of exploratory meetings and debates led by the president of CIFAR, Chaviva Hošek, this group of distinguished, innovative scholars emerged. They're a team of academic X-Men: each has a special super-power, and together they work wonders.

Their second collaborative book charts the contours of neoliberalism in relation to the issue of social resilience. The capacity to bounce back from trauma helps to define a society's success, but this book distinguishes itself because it focuses not on the larger unit but on the well-being of the individuals who comprise it, not simply the capacity of a state to maintain its power, which has too often been a default definition.

The SSP, under the leadership of this volume's editors, Peter A. Hall and Michèle Lamont, has gathered a group of scholars so diverse in their specializations that it might have seemed impossible to form a truly interactive conversation: criminology, cultural sociology, developmental psychology, epidemiology, history, political economy, political philosophy, political science, political sociology, social psychology, and urban geography. CIFAR's commitment to blue-sky exploration, with no obligation to deliverables, allowed for years of open conversation, in which the members of the group learned each other's perspectives, grasped and advanced the problematics and skills associated with their colleagues, and gained confidence that distinguished senior scholars could bring their work to new levels by joining other similarly distinguished, but differently skilled, researchers in a collaboration with no predefined goals.

What would we mean by a "successful society"? Scale defines one problem area: as Keynes memorably insisted, "In the long run we are all dead." From the point of view of the universe, we know that before our sun is extinguished, it will expand to a giant that consumes the planet Earth, so no society will look very successful from that perspective. Was the Roman Empire successful? Perhaps yes, until it declined and fell. The scale, then, must be relatively short term, and success is never absolute, only relative. By what measure do we call some societies more successful than others? The SSP collaborators look beyond the most common current metric of social success, the growth of gross domestic product (GDP) per capita. Studies of population health had demonstrated that after a certain point, increases in GDP do not lead to better results for life expectancy or health, as the United States demonstrates. Further studies had suggested that levels of social equality more sensitively correlated with changes in mortality and morbidity: the more equal, the better health. As the art critic and radical economic thinker John Ruskin argued in the nineteenth century, "The only wealth is life."

For their first book, then, *Successful Societies: How Institutions and Culture Affect Health* (2009), the SSP group undertook to explore social success using health and well-being as relatively uncontroversial measures of success. Not all cultures at all times have agreed that long life and health override other measures of success. The classical Greek myths of Achilles and Hercules, for instance, both tell of young men who choose lives that are short but glorious, giving up the chance for a longer life without glory. Such aristocratic values do not suit our democratic sensibilities, but the cases illustrate the difficulty of reaching any simple consensus. Yet the SSP stands with Achilles and Hercules in one crucial respect: even though the group works with population-level data, the measure of success registers in the lives of individual human beings. It is not "the society" that succeeds by successfully reproducing itself, so that a system of governance or a religion or a set of stated values persists over time. Rather, societies succeed insofar as they afford individual people opportunities for better lives.

This new book on "resilience" likewise focuses on the possibilities for fruitful, active lives by individuals. Social resilience does not mean that a society faces challenges and recovers unchanged nor that it is better to be as little changed as possible. The methodological and the evaluative focus falls on persons even when viewed collectively for analytic purposes. This collaborative project operates within a liberal scheme of value. As the collaborators argue, liberal values have persisted without having been incorporated into neoliberalism. Social resilience contributes to successful societies by making it more possible for the people living in societies to lead good lives despite the challenges posed by a newly overriding emphasis on the market.

This volume performs a remarkable feat with the buzzword "neoliberalism." It cleans up the term and also makes it more interesting. The term is generally used by those who oppose it. People do not call themselves neoliberal; instead, they tag their enemies with the term. The contributors definitely think that the neoliberal age, starting in the later 1970s, has posed severe challenges, but they make the term descriptively analytic. Evans and Sewell, for example, locate the term in four areas: in technical economics, as a political ideology, as a guide for policy, and as a "social imaginary." Even those who know nothing of the technical arguments of Milton Friedman may believe that whatever a government does, it does inefficiently or, more largely, that an entrepreneur always does more for others than does a bureaucrat. This book does not argue that the economic theorists have defined an essence of neoliberalism that then expresses itself ever more widely and diffusely through three further phases. No simple chronological or causal relationship holds among these four aspects. This perspective on the key conception that the book addresses explains what Hall and Lamont, in their Introduction, mean by characterizing neoliberalism as a "syncretic process." The term *neoliberalism* brings together divergent practices and meanings, which require exploration by distinct techniques. In the now quaint language of Freud, this would be called "overdetermined," like a neurotic symptom. This book assembles worthy analysts to tease apart the layers and to delineate the new possibilities for life that show through.

Acknowledgments

This volume is the result of an interdisciplinary collaboration among a group of fifteen scholars who met three times a year over a ten-year period to develop shared questions and original ways to address them. Our goal was to tackle problems on the research frontier that are not readily tractable using the analytical tools of a single discipline. *Social Resilience in the Neoliberal Age* is our second collective endeavor and it builds on our first, published in 2009 by Cambridge University Press as *Successful Societies: How Institutions and Culture Affect Health*.

None of this work would have been possible without the material and moral support of the Canadian Institute for Advanced Research (CIFAR) and its president, Chaviva Hošek, who has been an unwavering champion of the Program on Successful Societies since its inception. On the landscape of research foundations, CIFAR stands out for its unique vision and ability to bring together large interdisciplinary teams to shape new domains of human and scientific inquiry. We have been fortunate to be able to work with the Institute's administrative team, Pekka Sinervo, Denis Thérien, and Penny Codding. Along the way, Sue Schenk, CIFAR's program director, has offered unique guidance, and as program coordinator, Susan Leclaire has efficiently facilitated many of our meetings. At Harvard, Travis Clough provided crucial support for our collaborative work.

We thank the members of our advisory committee, Peter Gourevitch, Danielle Juteau, Biju Rao, and Richard Simeon, as well as its chair, Jonathan Arac, for important intellectual contributions and sage advice as this book developed. We also benefited from the comments of the junior Fellows in the program. Two are contributors to this volume, Marcos Ancelovici and Arjumand Siddiqi, and the others are Josh Evans, Chris McLeod, and Nathan Fosse. Three scholars took time from busy schedules to provide feedback on sizable portions of the manuscript: Nitsan Chorev, Richard Fantasia, and Carol Greenhouse. We thank them, as well as the reviewers who read the book for Cambridge University Press. We have benefited greatly from their insights. We are also deeply grateful to all the colleagues from a wide range of disciplines, countries, and institutions who discussed their work at program meetings as this book was taking shape. They will find traces of their ideas and comments throughout the pages of this volume. Many of those presentations inspired defining moments in this collaboration. For shepherding this work to publication, we are also grateful to the efficient team at Cambridge University Press and, in particular, to Lew Bateman, a great editor.

Last but not least, we want to acknowledge our *compagnons de route*, the members of this research program who have been an exceptional source of stimulation and a unique long-distance intellectual community for the past ten years. To all: thank you!

Introduction

Social Resilience in the Neoliberal Era[1]

Peter A. Hall and Michèle Lamont

This book is an effort to assess developments in a neoliberal era spanning the past three decades of global history. Although social science examines many phenomena, it looks only rarely at what Pierson (2003) calls "big, slow-moving processes." We are often not aware of the sands shifting beneath our feet as events change the character of the times in diffuse ways. Beginning in the 1980s, the growing influence of market-oriented ideas constituted just such a process, global in scope, pervasive in effects. We want to know what consequences neoliberal ideas and policies had for social, economic, and political life. But even more central to this inquiry is a desire to understand the process whereby neoliberal ideas worked their way into the policies of governments, the operation of organizations, and the lives of ordinary people. In that respect, this volume is an investigation into the dynamics of social change.

Compared with many studies, this one involves a shift in optics. Neoliberalism is often analyzed as a set of policy reforms reflecting a class politics that ranges capital against labor (Duménil and Lévy 2004; Harvey 2005). Although that approach has some validity, such perspectives tend to treat a multidimensional set of developments in largely economic terms and sometimes overemphasize the negative effects of neoliberalism. Perspectives that treat neoliberalism as a cultural phenomenon offer a useful corrective but often overstate the domination of neoliberal ideas over social life. In this volume, we try to integrate economic, political, and cultural analyses of neoliberalism, and instead of seeing it as a development with homogenous effects across space and time, we view it as a more open-ended stimulus that provoked a diversity of responses.

[1] For their comments and suggestions, we thank the members of the Successful Societies program, particularly William Sewell, Jr., as well as Mary Brinton, Paul Leduc Browne, Mazen Elfakhani, Robert Fishman, Marion Fourcade, François Harelimana, Devesh Kapur, Robert Sampson, Jennifer Silva, and Martin Schröder.

Developments associated with neoliberalism, such as the opening of markets and new policy regimes, put important constraints on many people, usually linked to their social positions. But it also offered opportunities and new tools from which a response to such developments could be fashioned. In short, one of the core arguments of this book is that neoliberalism brought forth various types of creative responses. The results were far from similar across populations and national settings, not only because neoliberal initiatives were more intense in some times and places but also because people responded to them differently, drawing upon cultural and institutional resources distinctive to those settings. The effects of neoliberalism must be seen as the product of syncretic social processes that engaged many actors mobilizing multiple instruments in the social, economic, and political environment.

This is also a book about social resilience. Although neoliberal initiatives improved the lives of some people, it also posed profound challenges to the well-being of many groups, communities, and individuals as more intense market competition reallocated resources and market logics worked their way into ever more spheres of social life. We are interested in the ways in which groups sustained their well-being in the face of such challenges, and we see this as a problem of social resilience. We use the term "social resilience" to refer to the capacity of groups of people bound together in an organization, class, racial group, community, or nation to sustain and advance their well-being in the face of challenges to it. Although our focus here is on the response to neoliberalism, we conceptualize social resilience broadly to encompass the capacities of societies to cope with many kinds of challenges.

Social resilience is an essential characteristic of what we call successful societies – namely, societies that provide their members with the resources to live healthy, secure, and fulfilling lives. We are especially interested in understanding the sources of social resilience, and we look for them in the *institutional* and *cultural* resources that groups and individuals mobilize to sustain their well-being. In that respect, this book builds on our previous endeavor, *Successful Societies: How Institutions and Culture Affect Health* (Hall and Lamont 2009), which was also concerned with the resources that sustain people's capabilities for coping with challenges. Both books are the product of intensive intellectual collaboration over several years among a group of scholars drawn from a wide range of disciplines.

Our approach to social resilience can be contrasted with influential perspectives that emphasize the psychological qualities needed to cope with various types of shocks. We are less interested in individual traits than in the social and cultural frameworks underpinning resilience, and we are skeptical about the efforts of some governments to find in individual resilience the solution to social problems.[2] Even though many working class Americans believe they should find within themselves the psychological energy and resources to deal

---

[2] On resilience as an object of government policy and sponsored research, see http://www.cabinetoffice.gov.uk/ukresilience and http://www.amiando.com/WLVKYLQ.html.

with structural insecurity and rising inequality (e.g., Silva 2012; Sharone 2013), we look for the institutional and cultural resources that underpin resilience in the wider social environment.

Studying social resilience entails making linkages between the micro, meso, and macro levels of inquiry. Therefore, drawing on a range of analytical and disciplinary tools, we integrate accounts of the shifts in macro and meso contexts associated with neoliberalism with an examination of the impact those shifts had on what is perceived, conceived, and experienced at the individual level (Lefebvre 1974). Although the emphasis of each chapter varies, our focus is not only on the institutional and cultural changes structuring the contexts in which people live but on self-concepts, orders of worth and criteria of evaluation linked to the social dynamics of inclusion and exclusion (Lamont 1992, 2000; Boltanski and Thévenot 2006; Foucault 2008).

The Challenges and Impact of the Neoliberal Era

The past three decades, which we term the "neoliberal era," have seen profound economic, political, and cultural changes with global reach. We are most interested in those associated with neoliberalism, understood as a wide-ranging shift in prevalent ideas and social relationships privileging more intense market competition, less state intervention, and an entrepreneurial orientation to action (Harvey 2005). To some extent, of course, these are longstanding features of capitalism, whose prominence has ebbed and flowed over time (Sewell 2008). But we see the recent period as one in which they have come to the fore again with a new intensity.

Although there are important economic dimensions to these developments, including heightened competition in more open markets for goods, capital, and labor, at their heart was a series of shifts in thinking and discourse among ordinary citizens and elites. Some of these developments are bound up with globalization, but even the opening of global markets was contingent on changes in policy inspired by neoliberal paradigms. Therefore, we group a wide range of developments together under the rubric of neoliberalism.[3] Many are described in more detail in the next chapter by Peter Evans and William Sewell, which also describes the historical emergence of neoliberalism, initially as an economic ideology and then as a social and political phenomenon inspired, at least in part, by the economic crises of the 1970s. However, we begin with a brief summary of what we mean by the term.

Neoliberalism

The defining feature of the neoliberal age has been the rise of market ideologies that, at their apogee, approached the "market fundamentalism" Somers (2008) has described. They were marked by a resurgent faith in the power of markets

---

[3] Of course, many elements of neoliberalism are closely tied to the history of capitalism itself (see Harvey 2005; Jobert and Théret 1994; and Centeno and Cohen 2012).

to secure efficient outcomes, whose corollary was declining confidence in the capacity of states to allocate resources efficiently. As such ideologies gained traction in domestic politics and the international sphere, they called into question the principles used to justify many kinds of state intervention, forcing governments to reconsider how they delivered public services and the division of labor between the public and private sectors (Blyth 2002; Prasad 2006).

Such issues are central to the collective imaginary of a society. We use the term "collective imaginary" to describe the overarching narratives that tell people what their society is about, what its past embodies and its future portends, who belongs to it, and what kinds of behavior merit social respect. Although there are distinctive features to every national imaginary, the latter also draw on international imaginaries, considered in chapters by Will Kymlicka, Jane Jenson, and Ron Levi on human rights, social rights, and multiculturalism. In line with other analyses, we see the neoliberal era as one defined, not only by a new set of policy regimes but also by a collective reimagining of communities (Anderson 1983). The effects were far reaching and multifaceted. Governments and international agencies were called upon to rethink their missions, and individuals faced profound redefinitions in the criteria for social worth as economic performance and market status became more central markers for social and cultural membership.[4]

This process of change was never simple or seamless. Even in the most settled of times, people subscribe with varying degrees of enthusiasm to some elements in the collective imaginary while rejecting others. As neoliberal narratives came to prominence, they were taken up with fervor by some groups and stoutly resisted by others. Neoliberalism did not impose a new framework of ideas so much as set in motion a series of contests over ideological and material resources – inside societies and states. It shifted the context in which everyone had to operate, generating new opportunities and constraints that are the focal points of our analysis.

One reason we emphasize the neoliberal imaginary is the range of its import. In their most familiar forms, neoliberal ideas endorsed the value of market competition. They called for a rearrangement of state-market relations and, in some guises, for a shift to more robust civil societies that could perform the tasks at which states were no longer thought to be efficient. Where others had once seen families or communities, growing numbers of economists and policymakers began to posit congeries of economic actors driven by a market calculus. In some instances, market competition was deliberately extended to new spheres, including the delivery of health care and public services. In others, the growing popularity of market logics altered the *modus operandi* of organizations through ancillary processes, such as the adoption of ranking systems that promote competitive behavior (Espeland and Sauder 2007).

These developments can be seen as a contemporary manifestation of the dictum that different historical periods typically authorize different modes of action. Ours is a period that has authorized self-interested market behavior in

---

4 On social and cultural membership, see Lamont (1992, 2000) and Ong (2006)

settings where it might once not have been legitimate. That in turn has inspired some reconfiguration in social relationships. If never freeing people completely from the restraining bonds of moral sentiment, neoliberal ways of thinking often led to a decline in the respect accorded to norms of communal solidarity (Streeck 2009). In many parts of the world, the growth of markets in goods for which people once depended on local patrons or personal relationships could be liberating (Kapur et al. 2010). People's choices often increased, although with redistributive consequences as the availability of some goods became more dependent on income. In some cases, such developments may be altering local social orders by shifting people's willingness to invest in certain kinds of communal relationships.

In much the same way, neoliberalism inspired changes in the dominant scripts of personhood toward ones more focused on a person's individuality and productivity (Greenhouse 2009). It promoted new criteria of worth that encouraged many people to approach their lives as if they were "projects" (Boltanski and Chiapello 2007). As more value was attached to the capacity to prosper on competitive markets, people who had once derived self-respect from being "hard workers" found that was no longer enough: one now had to be a worker with high productivity deploying skills validated by the market, signaling worth and social membership through consumption (Lamont and Molnár 2001). Developments such as these have a bearing on the terms in which social recognition is granted and self-concepts formed. Over time, the narratives people used to describe themselves changed, with implications for what they thought they could do and how they saw themselves as acting in the world (Abelmann 2003; Polletta et al. 2011). Socioeconomic status, often intertwined with notions of moral status, became more central to the matrix through which individuals conceived their self-worth – although with notable cross-national variations (Lamont 1992, 2000).

In some cases, these developments may have been emancipatory and in others not. Although it is difficult to establish how far reaching such changes have been, some of the most consequential aspects of neoliberalism lie in its implications for human subjectivities (Greenhouse 2009; Ong 2006).[5] Again, however, these changes cannot be understood as the imposition of neoliberal modes of thinking on entirely plastic individuals. People responded to neoliberal values with varying degrees of enthusiasm and resistance, and many people turned neoliberal ideas to their own purposes (to establish racial equality, for instance, as noted in Chapter 4 by Lamont, Welburn, and Fleming on African Americans' responses to stigmatization). There is wide variation in the extent to which neoliberalism inspired new visions of agency.

Neoliberal Reform in the Economic and Political Realms
The concrete impact of neoliberal ideas is most obvious, of course, in the political realm, where they altered prevailing views about the appropriate relationship between the public and private sectors. In Chapter 1, Evans and Sewell

---

[5] On the gendered dimensions of subjectivity promoted by neoliberalism, see Walkerdine (2003).

provide a sweeping survey of these developments notable for its attention to the cultural as well as the political plane. Mainstream party platforms moved in neoliberal directions on both sides of the political spectrum and in many parts of the developed and developing world (Iversen 2006; Mudge 2011). As a result, the cultural matrix defining the "center of gravity" of political discourse was transformed. In the United States, for instance, the term "liberal" took on a negative valence, as the success of neoconservative movements altered the terms in which even their opponents characterized their own positions (Gross, Medvetz, and Russell 2011).[6] Encouraged by international agencies, governments across the world privatized public services (including public utilities, highways, prisons, schools, and hospitals) and "deregulated" markets with a view to promoting competition (Vogel 1996). Welfare programs were reconfigured into "workfare" programs to push recipients into employment under the guise of making them more "self-reliant" (Miller and Rose 2008; Duvoux 2009; Guetzkow 2010).

Jane Jenson and Ron Levi (in Chapter 2) see the political significance of neoliberalism in three developments affecting many spheres of policymaking. These include a shift in scale, as functions formerly performed by national states were passed to lower levels of government or to international regimes (Brenner, Peck, and Theodore 2010). Policies put a new emphasis on the individualization of risk, responsibility, and reward, and governments pursued a "new public management" that built market competition into the delivery of public services accompanied by "technologies of performance" based on monitoring, ranking, and benchmarking (Lascoumes and Le Galès 2004; Miller and Rose 2008).

Corresponding economic developments have been equally consequential. Accelerated by technological developments and rising demand for services, the opening of world markets, made possible by neoliberal policies, shifted relative prices and the feasibility of producing some kinds of goods in particular countries. The results were a shift in the economic opportunity structures facing many workers, rising levels of national income inequality, and rapid rates of growth in many parts of the developing world.

However, liberalization was not a monolithic process. One of the striking observations of Evans and Sewell (in Chapter 1) is that governments embraced neoliberal policies with widely varying degrees of enthusiasm and implemented them in terms adapted to local contexts. The form of neoliberal policies also changed over time (Peck and Tickell 2002). The picture that emerges from this study is not one in which neoliberal discourse achieves complete dominance but one in which countercurrents are engaged wherever neoliberal initiatives are proposed, often producing a fragmentation of discourses and diversities in policy. Hall and Thelen (2009) underline this point when they note that many of the initiatives often described as "neoliberal" have very different effects

---

[6] In the United States, the positions we characterize as neoliberal were often adopted by organizations described there as neoconservative. See Vaïsse (2010).

and that the effects even of similar policies vary by national context (see also Fourcade-Gourinchas and Babb 2002).

Much the same can be said about the impact of neoliberal policies on overall economic well-being. Evans and Sewell (see Chapter 1) observe that the economic effects of neoliberal reform varied with the context into which it was introduced. In countries where markets had been highly restricted, as in China and the postcommunist states of Eastern Europe, neoliberal reform brought real benefits, such as increased trade and greater access to consumption goods. By contrast, such reforms rarely inspired the high rates of growth once promised in the developed economies. The most favorable aggregate effects seem to have come in the developing world. Rapid economic growth in the emerging economies of Asia, Latin America, and Eastern Europe owes much to neoliberal policies. Economic reform provided new opportunities to many people otherwise earning a subsistence living in rural communities (Collier and Dollar 2002: 49). International trade brought them new markets and products, and global communication opened up new vistas on life. People locked into traditional communities found in market logics a new basis from which to mount claims for equality, much as eighteenth-century Europeans once had (Kapur et al. 2010; Sewell 2010). In terms of its aggregate economic and political effects, neoliberalism has been far from a purely negative phenomenon.

New Inequalities

However, neoliberal reform has also had profound distributive effects. When markets are made more open or competitive, the opportunity structure changes and some people gain, but others lose. In general, those with the resources and skills to prosper on competitive markets do well, but those lacking in such resources are disadvantaged even if they had the right skill sets for a previous era. This redistribution of opportunity has been reflected in rising levels of income inequality in both developed and developing countries. Thus, neoliberal reform has posed stringent challenges to specific social groups.

How widespread these challenges are varies by national context. In the emerging economies where neoliberal reform inspired rapid rates of growth, new markets have offered opportunities to many people aspiring to middle-class positions (Ravallion 2009; Kharas 2010). By contrast, in most of the developed democracies, even the middle class has seen its well-being stagnate in recent decades, as Lucy Barnes and Peter Hall note in Chapter 7. Large gains at the top of the earnings distribution have not been matched in the lower half (Fischer et al. 1996; Piketty and Saez 2003; Bartels 2008). The result has been an unprecedented concentration of wealth in the hands of the corporate class in the United States and United Kingdom and rising intergenerational inequality in many countries (Hacker and Pierson 2010; Chauvel 2010).

Other dimensions of neoliberal policy also imposed hardships on people in the lower socioeconomic strata. Initiatives that weakened the labor movement undercut the organizations best placed to defend these people (Fantasia and Voss 2004). Changes to the benefit levels, duration, and eligibility requirements of social benefits reduced the level of social protection available to them, and ancillary developments privatized risk (Smith 2002; Uchitelle 2006; Hacker 2008; Jacobs and Newman 2008). Growing numbers of people have been forced into precarious positions marked by low pay and minimal social benefits, from which it is difficult to escape (Gautié and Schmitt 2010). In some countries, these developments have deepened social divisions, notably between labor-market insiders and outsiders (Palier and Thelen 2010). Despite the labor activation schemes that have been a hallmark of the neoliberal era, there are durable differences between those engaged in social networks through work and those suffering from insecurity and social isolation as a result of poverty or unemployment that limits their access to income, sociability, and in some cases even health care (Paugam, Gallie, and Jacob 2003; Palier et al. 2012). Many societies are now better described by frameworks of social exclusion than of social capital (Silver 1994; Castel 1995; Paugam 1996; Daly and Silver 2008).

Moreover, the effects of such developments are by no means entirely economic. The shifts in relative prices that accompany the opening of markets induce corresponding shifts in social status even when they enrich the community as a whole. The status of those with skills in higher demand increases, but people whose status was based on outmoded skills or older institutional orders are threatened, for instance, as the jobs they held move to the global South. Effects of this sort stretch into the family, where women called upon to work to support the household sometimes gain, but underemployed men who might once have been the principal breadwinners lose stature. In both developed and developing economies, therefore, the more intense market competition characteristic of the neoliberal age gives rise to heightened status anxieties.

As various forms of social protection, both traditional and modern, have fallen, rising levels of material insecurity have threatened everyone. Even affluent members of the middle class have developed new concerns about reproducing their class position. Growing numbers of middle-class parents are devoting increasing amounts of resources to improving the prospects for their children (Lareau 2003; Aurini, Dierkes, and Davies forthcoming). For ordinary workers already under pressure to demonstrate self-reliance in a neoliberal world, the presence of the poor in public spaces keeps alive a "fear of falling," and rising competition for jobs intensifies people's concerns about losing ground vis-à-vis lower status groups (Ehrenreich 1989; Newman 1989; Duvoux 2009). The result has been rising xenophobia and declining support for poor relief (Art 2011; Skocpol and Williamson 2012).

Developments such as these have implications not only for individuals but also for national communities. Chauvel (2010) suggests, for instance, that long-term effects are likely to follow from the widespread fears market insecurity has induced in the younger generations. These fears are not only affecting self-concepts and levels of social engagement; they are also affecting their shared representations of the symbolic community (who cares for whom) in terms likely to be durable over the coming years (see also Brinton 2011). In much the same way, the shifts in self-concept associated with neoliberalism have political implications. Neoliberalism generally leads people to think of themselves as governed less by others and more by themselves (Greenhouse 2009). Although that has advantages for some individuals, it tends to feed declining levels of trust in the public authorities. Moreover, those suffering most from rising levels of inequality are most prone to distrust government and to doubt their capacities to influence it (Lascoumes and Bezes 2009). A self-perpetuating cycle is then set in motion as declining levels of civic engagement among these groups reduce electoral pressure on governments to redistribute resources (Anderson and Beramendi 2012).

Growing social divisions between insiders and outsiders also weaken the capacity of the public authorities to legitimate policies based on appeals to social solidarity (Palier et al. 2012). As we have noted, more intense competition for jobs and associated status anxieties feed a growing hostility toward immigrants. In France, for example, where southern European migrants were once regarded as contributors to the French economy (Noiriel 2006), non-European migrants are now more often resented as intruders (Bail 2008). In Chapter 5, Leanne Son Hing identifies a set of psychological dynamics that connect more intense market competition with more prejudice against outgroups; in Chapter 7, Barnes and Hall find more hostility to immigrants where the gap in well-being between the upper and lower middle class is larger. Although the meritocratic values promoted by neoliberalism should lead, in principle, to less discrimination, Son Hing notes that people primed by such values are more likely to express prejudice and people exposed to prejudice are more likely to suffer adverse effects if they subscribe to neoliberal values: they are more likely to blame themselves for their fate than to recognize structural discrimination. We see here that some of the most important effects of neoliberalism emerge from complex dynamics in which economic and political developments interact with shifting views of cultural membership and community.

To take another classic example, in many countries, rising levels of economic inequality have been accompanied by increasing spatial segregation in housing between income and ethnic groups (Massey and Denton 1994; Préteceille 2009). That segregation then narrows prevailing definitions of the symbolic community (namely, those with whom we feel a sense of solidarity or responsibility as part of "us"), which in turn encourages further segregation (Lamont 2000). Neoliberal schemata also encourage people to be more mobile in social and spatial terms (Jasper 2002) and thus more disconnected from any particular community (McPherson, Smith-Lovin, and Brashears 2006, but cf. Fischer 2011). Although that might promote intergroup interchanges, it can also make people feel more vulnerable and defensive vis-à-vis other social groups.

Our broad point is that the redistribution of advantage and disadvantage associated with neoliberalism follows not only from how markets reallocate resources but from how neoliberalism shifts discursive structures. Of central importance are the categories people use to assess worth. Neoliberal ideas promote particular frames used by people to define how they should live their lives, what they are capable of, and for what they can hope. These are constitutive elements of horizons of possibility and of the contours of symbolic communities. A discourse that elevates market criteria of worth tends to classify people who are affluent into a bounded community and to marginalize those with fewer economic resources. Corresponding ideas about productivity are often used to draw rigid moral boundaries around people who are unemployed, low skilled, or low paid, thereby narrowing the circle of people to whom citizens feel a sense of responsibility. Moreover, by defining worth in terms of levels of income or productivity they can never attain, neoliberal schemata can be disabling for people with low levels of income or skill. They come to be defined (and often self-define) as "losers" – especially in societies that do not support varied matrices of worth based on morality, solidarity, or other attributes unrelated to income (Lamont 2000).

The precise impact of developments such as these is hard to assess, of course, and they are to some extent part of an older story about capitalism. Over history, as markets expanded, consumption came to be viewed more widely as a marker of cultural membership, often in competition with notions grounding cultural membership in citizenship rights (Marshall 1950). Galbraith (1958) and Marcuse (1964) saw such processes at work in the 1950s, but they may have been intensified under the influence of a highly commercial media during the 1980s and 1990s (Schor 1998; Comaroff and Comaroff 2001). Commercial considerations are certainly penetrating more deeply into spheres of life once construed as autonomous from them (Zelizer 2010). Such tendencies are especially marked in countries such as China (Davis 2000; Hanser 2008) and Russia (Shevchenko 2001), which moved from command to market economies. However, Boltanski and Chiapello (2007) argue that even long-established market economies have seen the rise of a new model of individuality that views the most valued social actor as a networking entrepreneur developing his or her human capital for the purpose of achieving individual success. Barnes and Hall find some evidence for such shifts in attitudes (see Chapter 7), and, in Chapter 6, James Dunn charts changes in housing policy based on corresponding shifts in premises about how actors will behave.

A Syncretic Social Process

Neoliberalism must not be seen, however, as a blanket laid over the world. The process whereby neoliberal schemas acquired influence over policymaking and popular beliefs is ultimately best described as a syncretic social process. Neoliberal schemas had significant effects on the course of events: they were not simply a smokescreen behind which a politics driven by material or ideal interests went on exactly as before. But their social impact was inflected by the creativity with which political actors used them and conditioned by the contexts into which they were introduced. In many cases, actors devoted to a particular cause found they could pursue it by adopting the language made widely available in the neoliberal era (with references to benchmarking, return on investment, social entrepreneurship, best practices, and the like). By framing their demands in new terms, many groups could advance longstanding purposes. Over time, however, these shifts in strategy often affected the character of politics and what it secured. In that regard, neoliberal schemas changed the course of events in ways reminiscent of how new institutions change the outcomes of strategic interaction. Even when they did not change underlying preferences, they often altered what actors could achieve.

This characterization is borne out in the chapters by Will Kymlicka (Chapter 3) and Jane Jenson and Ron Levi (Chapter 2). They consider the impact of neoliberalism on international regimes and find, for the most part, that, influential though they were, neoliberal ideas did not significantly blunt the force of regimes promoting multiculturalism or human rights (see also Dezalay and Garth 2002). Although regimes for social protection shifted dramatically, they left social safety nets in place in the developed democracies. Similar to the gnarled pines to which Jenson and Levi refer, these regimes bent with the wind to survive relatively intact. *adopted the framework/language of neoliberalism to survive*

There is some variation across these regimes. The international human rights regime was always the most congruent with neoliberal ideals, and after initial opposition in the United States, many neoliberals came to see the promotion of markets and of human rights as complementary endeavors. Advocates for multiculturalism initially met neoliberal opposition but were able to adjust their appeals to fit a "liberal multiculturalism" that could be used to advance minority rights, especially where multicultural principles were already institutionalized. Welfare regimes changed more radically over these decades in directions that privileged means testing and tied benefits to participation in the workforce, and as Chapter 10 by Clyde Hertzman and Arjumand Siddiqi indicates, some of these reforms had adverse effects on working families. But regimes of social protection were redesigned and reinterpreted as "social investment" to accommodate a neoliberal logic – and survived.

These chapters describe a process in which the advocates for particular regimes accommodated themselves to a neoliberal imaginary by turning it to their own purposes. Immigrant groups seeking political recognition, such as some south Asian communities in Canada, began to present themselves less as ethnic groups seeking rights and more as transnational entrepreneurs capable of leveraging their foreign contacts in the service of national economic success. Human rights activists exploited the systems of ranking and monitoring favored by neoliberals to develop more effective ways of enforcing the regime, and in the name of social investment, social spending could sometimes be increased.

In all spheres, the process whereby neoliberal schemas acquired influence was marked by dissonance and active negotiation, as multiple actors sought to turn those ideas to their purposes but others resisted in the name of alternative values. Resistance was a recurrent feature of the syncretic processes at work here, and the development of counter-narratives was empowering for some groups. What emerged in each society was distinctive, based on how the response to developments was negotiated within its symbolic community. Similar initiatives were greeted quite differently, for instance, in the United

States and France. Although both countries experienced waves of neoliberal reform, there was little public mobilization against them in the United States until the Occupy movement emerged after the financial crisis of 2008 to 2009. However, France experienced repeated protests against neoliberal policies over three decades, undertaken in the name of social solidarity (Storey 2011). Just as globalization failed to produce the transnational convergence in culture that many expected, the reaction to neoliberalism in national political communities remains diverse (Norris and Inglehart 2009).

The Sources of Social Resilience

If one objective of this book is to analyze the effects of neoliberalism, the other is to develop an understanding of how individuals, communities, and societies secured their well-being in the face of its challenges. We think of this as a problem of understanding the bases for social resilience.

Socioeconomic change on this scale inevitably poses challenges to the groups and individuals facing it. Reforms that accelerated the reorganization of the economy exposed large groups of people to social dislocation and had profound redistributive effects. In the developed political economies, they altered the basis for social protection and increased economic insecurity especially at the bottom of the socioeconomic ladder (Hacker et al. 2010). We have also noted that neoliberalism affected self-concepts and criteria of worth in terms that were challenging for many people. Even when the ultimate effect of neoliberal initiatives was to increase opportunities, the need to devise new personal strategies to cope with them could be daunting.[7] Thus, we think it makes good sense to ask how people sustained their well-being in the face of the challenges of the neoliberal era.

The Meaning of Social Resilience

The term "resilience" features most prominently in three literatures – on ecology, developmental psychology, and the response to disaster (e.g., Cottle 2001; Masten 2010).[8] In the literature on ecology, resilience is generally seen as the property of a system, understood as an ecology of closely linked parts. The early literature was concerned primarily with ecologies of the natural world, but a growing body of work sees social relations as fundamental components of such systems (Adger, Kelly, and Ninh 2001). In the first instance, resilience

---

[7] There is variation, of course, across people and contexts in how challenging any given development is. Even the death of a child is experienced differently, depending on whether such deaths are exceptional or routine in one's environment (Scheper-Hughes 1993), and the intensity of the shock posed by unemployment, for instance, may depend on the extent to which individuals define their worth through their professional selves (Sharone 2013).

[8] There is also a growing literature on organizational resilience. See Sutcliffe and Vogus (2003). In a different vein, see also Wright (2010) on human flourishing and research efforts on the aftermath of Hurricane Katrina (http://katrinaresearchhub.ssrc.hub).

was understood as a property that allows the system to recover its prior state after suffering a shock, but ecologists have recently begun to see resilience in more dynamic terms, much as we do, emphasizing adaptation or transformation over return to an earlier state. In one pioneering formulation, Folke (2006: 259) notes that:

Resilience is currently defined in the literature as the capacity of a system to absorb disturbance and re-organize while undergoing change so as to still retain essentially the same function, structure, identity and feedbacks. . . . But resilience is not only about being persistent or robust to disturbance. It is also about the opportunities that disturbance opens up in terms of recombination of evolved structures and processes, renewal of the system and emergence of new trajectories. In this sense, resilience provides adaptive capacity. . . .

In developmental psychology, the term "resilience" is generally used to describe an outcome, characterized by satisfactory performance (academic or otherwise) after an individual has been exposed to factors that put this performance at risk, such as poverty or the loss of a parent (Schoon 2006). Studies link this kind of resilience to the availability of close attachments or a supportive and disciplined environment. Resilience is usually seen as a characteristic of the individual associated with better coping skills, multiple domains of the self, or stress-response characteristics that mitigate the negative effects of risk factors. However, sociologically oriented psychologists have developed related formulations, such as the concept of self-efficacy proposed by Bandura (1977, 1982), to understand how people feel empowered or constrained by their social world. This literature has also inspired influential social analyses, such as the study by Furstenburg et al. (1999) and others of successful parenting strategies among low-income families in Philadelphia (see also Carlson and England 2011).

We draw on the insights of these literatures but define resilience somewhat differently. Our principal concern is with well-being broadly defined and how it is secured by groups of people more or less bound together in an organization, class, racial group, community, or country. Accordingly, we use the term "social resilience" to denote an outcome in which the members of a group sustain their well-being in the face of challenges to it. We define "well-being" broadly to include physical and psychological health, material sustenance, and the sense of dignity and belonging that comes with being a recognized member of the community (Taylor 1994). We avoid specifying a precise hierarchy of needs or self-actualization as the goal because current research suggests that the value attached to these varies across populations and contexts (cf. Sen 1993). We see resilience in dynamic terms, not as the capacity to return to a prior state but as the achievement of well-being even when that entails significant modifications to behavior or to the social frameworks that structure and give meaning to behavior. At issue is the capacity of individuals or groups to secure favorable outcomes (material, symbolic, emotional) under new circumstances and, if need be, by new means.

Social Resilience as a Process

We are most interested in exploring the sources of social resilience. What confers social resilience? To what extent did developments during the neoliberal era bring such factors to the fore? Or did neoliberalism erode the factors on which resilience depends?

We look in particular at how the institutional structures and cultural repertoires available to people by virtue of how they are embedded in various sets of social relations enhance their capacities to sustain their well-being in challenging circumstances. In that respect, these chapters build on the formulations of our previous collective work, *Successful Societies* (Hall and Lamont 2009), which argued that well-being is conditioned by the balance between the life challenges people face and their capabilities for coping with them. We suggested that capabilities depend on access not only to economic resources but also to cultural and social resources embodied in networks, social hierarchies, and cultural repertoires. This book can be read as an effort to extend the concept of social resources and to analyze their role in contexts of social change.

The chapters that follow find that people fashion responses to challenges from resources found in multiple spheres nested inside one another – ranging from the family, neighborhood, and local community to the region, nation-state, and transnational regimes (e.g., Sampson, Morenoff, and Earls 1999). Indeed, one feature of the contemporary era is the interdependence visible between these levels, as the media carry national and international tropes into the heart of the family and local communities depend on national states or transnational organizations for crucial forms of support. The prospects of immigrants within a local community, for instance, cannot be understood without taking into account the recognition given minorities by national symbolic communities, the multicultural principles to which they might appeal, and the concrete resources and services provided by national policies (Bloemraad 2006; Kymlicka 2007). Even international regimes are relevant by virtue of how they support human rights and transnational linkages among migrant groups (Soysal 1994; Merry and Levitt 2009). Thus, to understand the situation of vulnerable groups, we need to consider not only the groups themselves but also the institutional and cultural scaffolding surrounding them, with an eye to the opportunities it offers and forecloses (Lamont 2009).

One of our conclusions is that social resilience is the result of active processes of response. Groups do not simply call passively on existing sets of resources. Social resilience is the product of much more creative processes in which people assemble a variety of tools, including collective resources and new images of themselves, to sustain their well-being in the face of social change. In some instances, those tools are features of existing context; in others, they are made available by neoliberalism itself. In many respects, this is another story about "culture in action" (Swidler 1986), as meaning making that occurs in the course of everyday interaction and collective political endeavor.

Marcos Ancelovici's study of the response of French trade unions to developments in the neoliberal era underlines this point (see Chapter 12). Contemporary analyses often treat "globalization" and "neoliberalism" as if they were exogenous shocks of homogenous character. But Ancelovici shows that organizations experienced neoliberalism as a series of developments unfolding in time that had to be interpreted, and these interpretations were filtered through the matrix of concerns preoccupying each actor. Thus, French trade unions *experienced* "globalization" and "neoliberalism" as an *organizational* challenge manifested in declining levels of membership, and their response was oriented to this problem. When neoliberalism is understood at the level of lived realities, it becomes apparent that how the problem is perceived varies across contexts and that responses are constructed from available cultural repertoires and previous experiences (Lamont and Thévenot 2000). In an analysis with resonance for other types of agents, Ancelovici breaks down this response into processes of narration, learning, and institutionalization. He finds that organizations with more heterogeneous repertoires and leaders with more organizational autonomy devised a more resilient response.

The Role of States and Social Organizations

As Polanyi (1944) observed some years ago, states have long been the most important potential counterweight to markets: their regulations shape market competition; they are the source for public goods that markets do not supply and for measures mitigating the adverse effects of markets on vulnerable groups. Therefore, states should have been important sources of social resilience during the neoliberal era, and our findings confirm that they often were. Evans and Sewell (see Chapter 1) note that aggregate well-being was sustained more effectively in countries where neoliberal initiatives were accompanied by substantial new efforts at social protection, as in France, Brazil, Taiwan, and South Korea. From a neoliberal perspective, it may seem antithetical for governments to increase social spending and market competition in tandem, but they often did so with salutary effects.

In parallel terms, Barnes and Hall (see Chapter 7) find that the lower-middle class has been better off where governments did not simply increase social spending but targeted it on redistribution, and Chapter 8 by Keating, Siddiqi, and Nguyen attributes better developmental health outcomes in Canada, compared with the United States, to higher levels of public provision and policies that decoupled access to basic goods such as health care and education from income (see also Zuberi 2006). They argue that investment in basic goods such as education can mediate the long-term effects of neoliberal initiatives on adolescent health and development. These findings resonate with a literature attributing the economic success of the "small states" of northern Europe to the ways in which they linked flexible responses to world markets to significant levels of social protection (Katzenstein 1985; cf. Rodrik 1997).

However, states do not automatically operate as factors of social resilience. In many instances, governmental initiatives were central to the intensification of market competition, and the levels of social protection they provided varied dramatically across countries. Similar to societies, states were sites for competition between advocates of neoliberal reform and those attempting to limit its effects, and much depended on the balance of power between them (Mudge 2008).

Relevant here is the finding of Barnes and Hall (see Chapter 7) that the well-being of the working class is better where trade unions are stronger. Some analysts see trade unions as part of the economic problem rather than the solution, and neoliberal initiatives have sent many unions into serious decline. But trade unions emerge as one of the organizations most central to the well-being of people in the lower socioeconomic strata, in particular, because of their political role as advocates for those people. Barnes and Hall find that a person's well-being is more strongly affected by the density of trade union membership in the country as a whole than by whether he or she is a member of a union. Trade unions seem to contribute to social resilience by shifting the balance of power between advocates and opponents of social protection. In this context, dramatic declines in union membership are one of the most durable and deleterious legacies of the neoliberal era (Western and Rosenfeld 2011).

However, social resilience also has roots in other forms of social organization, and, in the case of Québec, Gérard Bouchard explores a classic example (see Chapter 9). For most of the past twenty years, aggregate well-being has been sustained more effectively in Québec than in the other provinces of Canada. Bouchard attributes much of this success to the ways in which the province has nurtured a "social economy" marked by large numbers of cooperatives, enterprises supported by quasi-public organizations, and some notable deliberative processes. Public policies helped sustain this model, but it was built on networks of social organizations. In these respects, Québec resembles the regions of northern Italy and Germany that flourished in competitive world markets by forsaking highly competitive market relations at home for more collaborative interfirm relationships built on dense social networks supporting a culture of cooperation (Piore and Sabel 1984; Herrigel 1996; Streeck 1991).

Social networks underpin social resilience in other ways as well. A large literature suggests that ties to families, friends, and acquaintances constitute social resources on which people can draw to cope with many kinds of challenges (Berkman 1997; Berkman and Glass 2000; Sampson, Morenoff, and Gannon-Rowley 2002; Liebenberg and Unger 2009). From such connections, people secure information, logistical, and emotional support. Barnes and Hall (see Chapter 7) find that these types of social connectedness were important during the neoliberal era. Over the past three decades, people with closer ties to family and friends reported consistently higher levels of subjective well-being, and, as analysts of social capital posit, well-being was higher in countries with denser networks of civic engagement (Putnam 2000). Social connectedness in the form of direct ties between people is a source of social resilience and is likely to be even more powerful when accompanied by forms of social recognition that define a wide range of individuals as valued members of the community (Fraser and Honneth 2003; Barnes, Hall, and Taylor 2008).[9]

The Role of Collective Imaginaries

Other forms of social connectedness can also contribute to social resilience. Societies are bound together not only through social ties but also through collective imaginaries. As we have noted, these imaginaries embody narratives about the past and future of the community, who belongs to it, and what its chief qualities are (Bouchard 2003 and Chapter 9 of this volume). As such, they often stand in a mutually reinforcing relationship with the social organizations and policies that promote social resilience. Bouchard shows that longstanding myths about the character and history of Québec underpinned social solidarity there, sustaining both its social economy and social safety net. We see a similar phenomenon in the Nordic countries, where, despite neoliberal reforms, collective imaginaries that promote a sense of shared social responsibility have provided crucial support for the social organizations and policies that contribute to social resilience (Berman 2006; Offe 2011). In parallel terms, Keating, Siddiqi, and Nguyen (see Chapter 8) attribute better outcomes in Canada not only to differences between Canadian and American policies but also to the ways in which neoliberal scripts were filtered through their collective imaginaries.

Collective imaginaries can also be direct sources of resilience for individuals and groups by virtue of how they specify and support collective identities and who they define as valued members of the community. In Chapter 4, Michèle Lamont, Jessica Welburn, and Crystal Fleming show that the strategies deployed by members of stigmatized groups to counter racism draw heavily on national collective myths. African Americans often rely, for instance, on principles of equality central to the American creed, which empower them to confront racism. They also draw on repertoires associated with neoliberalism (e.g., those that attach value to individual effort and personal consumption) to buttress their sense of social belonging in the face of racist stereotyping. These strategies of confrontation are quite different from their counterparts in Brazil (where celebrating racial mixing prevails) and Israel (where Ethiopian Jews and Mizrahis tend to downplay discrimination and emphasize their shared Jewishness and belonging to the Zionist nation). In such contexts, the collective identities developed by minority groups are also important. Evidence indicates that attachment to a strong collective identity bolsters self-concepts and reduces the adverse psychological impact of experiences of immigration or racial discrimination (e.g., Feliciano 2005; Oyserman, Bybee, and Terry 2006). Such strategies are made possible by available cultural repertoires that make

---

[9] On the relationship between social capital, networks, and meaning, see Fishman (2009) and Pachucki and Breiger (2010).

some approaches to gaining recognition more successful than others (Lamont and Thévenot 2000).

These analyses are the tip of an important iceberg. The shared cultural references, myths, and narratives embodied in collective imaginaries can buttress an individual's sense of self and capabilities in many ways. People depend on the cultural tools such imaginaries provide to make sense of challenges and to imagine solutions to them (Small, Harding, and Lamont 2010; Swidler 1986). At stake are the possible selves and the futures people imagine and pursue for themselves and their communities (Markus and Nurius 1986). Chandler and Lalonde (1998) show, for instance, that differences in suicide rates across first-nation communities in British Columbia are conditioned by the community's ability to transmit to its younger members a sense of pride in its collective identity and history. Particularly important are broader narratives about recognition and dignity, often conveyed by school policies about the display of group-distinctive ways of dressing, speaking, and demonstrating collective identity (Carter 2012).

Alongside these collective imaginaries are a range of ancillary cultural structures likely to be consequential for social resilience. Because people find strategies for action by observing the behavior of those around them, many aspects of local cultural orders can be important for social resilience. Young (2006) shows, for instance, how marginalized black men imagine paths to upward mobility in interaction with their environment. Cultural frameworks specific to particular ethnic groups may be enabling or disabling. African Americans are less likely than Latinos, for example, to recommend co-ethnics for jobs, partly because widespread stereotypes about welfare dependency among African Americans encourage them to invest more strongly in notions of self-reliance (Smith 2010). Exploring what cultural repertoires contribute to recognition and social resilience should be an important item on contemporary research agendas.

However, neoliberalism may have effects of its own on collective imaginaries, and these also deserve more exploration. Because neoliberal ideals privilege market criteria for assessing worth, they should bolster the self-concepts of skilled market players but threaten people who lack marketable resources. The resilience of the latter may depend on whether they have at their disposal alternative repertoires for evaluating themselves (e.g., moral repertoires) so that they are not entirely dependent on the dominant standards for status (Lamont 2000). However, some societies support such repertoires better than others (Lamont 2000), and the influence of neoliberal narratives may have narrowed the availability of alternative repertoires.

Chapter 6 by James Dunn illustrates how complex the effects of neoliberalism are. He notes many ways that housing sustains resilience at the micro-level; in particular, it has developmental value for children and serves as a source of ontological security for adults. But access to supportive housing is dependent on conditions at multiple scales, ranging from the housing policies of the locality to the terms on which international markets supply finance. Because of interdependencies across these planes, it is difficult to determine the net effect of neoliberal developments on housing, but this is clearly a case in which the fate of an important source of resilience at the micro level depends on meso- and macro-level processes that proceed without much regard for the ultimate implications for social resilience.

Collective Capacities: The Interplay of Culture and Institutions

Social resilience depends not only on the features of society on which individuals draw to enhance their capabilities but also on the capacity of communities to mount collective responses to challenges. We have already noted the roles that states can play in this process, which turn on their capacities to redistribute resources, supply public goods on terms independent of income, and encourage forms of social organization that maintain employment and social solidarity. However, several chapters of this book identify collective capacities that are important at the local level and explore the conditions that sustain them. They point, in particular, to the importance of capacities to supply collective goods, understood as something more than standard public goods.

In Chapter 10, Clyde Hertzman and Arjumand Siddiqi note that efforts to foster early childhood development, crucial for the entire community's long-term well-being, cannot be understood simply as a matter of providing public goods. Thinking of early childhood development as a public good fails to capture the fact that fostering it requires active cooperation from multiple actors in the local community, ranging from school superintendents to parents and local business people. To convey this, Hertzman and Siddiqi describe early childhood development as a "collective-implementation good" – a term that can also be applied to other endeavors central to the social resilience of a community – seeing it as the product of government policy but one that can be produced only with the sustained involvement of durable, intersectoral coalitions.

In a different setting, Ann Swidler examines a similar problem, namely, how collective goods are supplied in African villages (see Chapter 11). Collective goods are goods that improve the well-being of the community and would not be supplied by markets because their benefits are nonexcludable, but similar to collective-implementation goods, they are supplied only through active forms of cooperation.[10] Capacities to provide such goods are crucial to a community's ability to maintain its well-being in the face of challenges. Therefore, understanding how they are generated is important for understanding social resilience.

Swidler's findings highlight the contributions that appropriate institutions and cultural frameworks make to such capacities. In the villages of Malawi, she finds that the institution of the local chief is crucial to the provision of collective goods, and she sees the "chief" as a culturally constituted institution made

---

[10] For parallel discussion of such problems in the case of common pool resources, see Ostrom (2005).

possible by the shared narratives of the community. These narratives accord chiefs a position from which they can seek the cooperation of the members of the community in collective endeavors. Their authority is bolstered by traditional control over symbolic resources, of the sort embodied in participation at a funeral, and by control over the allocation of some minor material resources, such as coupons for fertilizer. However, it is the culturally embedded role of the chief that is crucial to the supply of collective goods. By eliciting cooperation and ensuring everyone knows that the costs of contributing to the collectivity are being equally shared, chiefs provide assurances that encourage cooperation. They are the keystone for an arch of interdependencies that reaffirms the value attached to the collectivity.

This analysis has implications beyond African villages. Similar to Tsai's (2006) work on public goods in China, it suggests that a desire for status often motivates actors' contributions to collective goods and that collective goods are more likely to be supplied where shared narratives, reinforced by ritual, emphasize the value of the collectivity. Hertzman and Siddiqi observe that similar narratives support complex interdependencies in modern communities, and evidence indicates that the search for recognition within local status orders may motivate public-spirited action even inside institutional hierarchies (Willer 2009). In short, markets and hierarchies are not the only instruments available for organizing collective endeavor, and the contribution formal institutions make to the social resilience of a community often depends on their interplay with extant cultural frameworks (cf. Williamson 1985; Dobbin 1994; Ostrom 2005). Cultural and institutional structures can either reinforce or undercut one another, as they do in schools where peer-based status orders collide with teacher-driven status orders (Carter 2005; Warikoo 2010).

These observations have special pertinence for developments during the neoliberal era. As neoliberal ideas – about entrepreneurial behavior, for example – became more popular, they often shifted the cultural frameworks underpinning institutional practices, giving rise to new forms of behavior. Schröder (2011) shows, for example, that the willingness of companies to offshore production to low-cost countries was not driven entirely by clear-cut economic circumstances but often influenced by managers' embrace of neoliberal narratives. By the same token, market-oriented initiatives to improve the well-being of local communities in the developing world have had mixed success partly because many have not been attentive enough to local cultural contexts (Vollan 2008). Where such experiments ignore the social resources embedded in local cultural practices, they may destroy rather than create collective capacities (Rao and Walton 2004; Swidler and Watkins 2009).

However, resilience is not given by a static set of cultural frameworks. As we have noted, resilient outcomes usually demand active processes to engage and sustain the appropriate frameworks. Swidler emphasizes how ritualized activities reaffirm the value attached to the collectivity. Bouchard notes the importance of collective consultation, in the Estates General, to the successes of Québec politics. Hertzman and Siddiqi find that durable intersectoral coalitions for early childhood development depend on processes of concerted mobilization, and Ancelovici sees active processes of learning and institutionalization in the *Confédération française démocratique des travailleurs'* (CFDT's) response to neoliberalism. Social resilience ultimately depends on what might be called "cultural frameworks in action" and the use actors make of the "strategic capacities" for concerted response to challenges that institutions confer on them.

After the Crisis...

The global economic crisis that began in 2008 can be seen as the culmination of the neoliberal era. Indeed, its roots lie in the relaxation of government regulation and a blind faith in markets that encouraged unparalleled expansion of the financial sector and a vast increase in debt in many countries (Tett 2009; Rajan 2010). In addition to recession, the legacy is likely to be a politics of austerity lasting many years (Schaefer and Streeck 2013). One feature of this politics has been a growing sense of grievance, as unemployment rises in some countries and citizens wonder why banks were bailed out when they were not. That has increased support for parties and factions on the radical right and left, some explicitly opposed to neoliberal policies. In the developing world, the crisis has discredited doctrines based on an overweening faith in markets and stimulated a resurgence of interest in the developmental state (Bresser-Pereira and Oreira 2012). But the hopes of some that the crisis will sound the death knell for neoliberal ideas seem likely to be disappointed in anything but the very long term.

Neoliberal narratives and practices are now so deeply embedded at multiple levels in the economy, polity, and society that they are difficult to dislodge (Mudge 2008; Centeno and Cohen 2012). Although the doctrine of "efficient markets" has been discredited and Keynesian prescriptions for economic growth occasionally revived, few alternatives to the principles that became central to mainstream economics during the neoliberal era have gained traction (Hall 2013). Moreover, neoliberal practices have been so deeply institutionalized by governments and other organizations that they will be difficult to roll back. Some banks have been nationalized and modest efforts made to stiffen financial regulation, but even governments that would like to pursue alternative policies are constrained by the internationalization of finance, which grants credit on the basis of how well they conform to neoliberal practices. In the public sphere, the crisis has sparked a reaction, most visible in the Occupy movements that appeared in many countries, but it has inspired a competition for jobs and resources that tends to reinforce the *sauve qui peut* patterns of behavior characteristic of the neoliberal era (Ancelovici 2012).

In this context, there is more reason than ever to be concerned about social resilience. Many groups are facing straitened circumstances. In the United States, Hacker et al. (2010) estimate that the level of economic insecurity has almost doubled since the 1980s, and Fischer (2012) cites estimates that about half of all Americans will have some experience of poverty between the ages of 25 and 75 years. In southern Europe, the situation is dramatically worse and taking a deep toll on all aspects of people's well-being. In Greece, for instance, population health has deteriorated, and suicides increased by more than 50 percent between 2007 and 2012 (Kentikelenis et al. 2011). Conditions such as these strain the capacity of social groups to sustain their well-being and make it even more urgent to identify the sources of social resilience.

Conclusion

No single volume can do full justice to the big, slow-moving process associated with neoliberalism or to the sources of social resilience. However, the chapters in this volume provide an unusually multidimensional account of these phenomena. To appreciate the complexity of a sweeping macro-level process, we have tried to see it from the inside out as well as from the outside in, with an eye to the ways in which organized actors and ordinary people adopt new sets of categories and turned them to their own purposes (Bourdieu 1998). We see the unfolding of neoliberalism as a syncretic social process marked by adjustment, resistance, and creative transformation. It took place in a multilayered social space replete with institutional frameworks and cultural repertoires out of which actors constructed responses to the opportunities and challenges of this era.

We have paid special attention to these challenges in order to advance understandings of social resilience defined as the capacity of groups to sustain their well-being. That entails charting the ways in which institutional practices and cultural repertoires are constitutive of the sources of social resilience. But we have also argued that social resilience is more than a matter of calling upon existing resources. Instead, it is an active process that mobilizes people with loyalties and attachments promoted by particular cultural frameworks – French trade union leaders, African chiefs, Canadian school superintendents, and members of stigmatized groups. These processes of adjustment often shade, in turn, into creative endeavor, as actors find new ways to deploy existing institutions or cultural repertoires and exploit the new categories and opportunities generated by a neoliberal age. A reflexivity absent in physical systems plays an important role in these processes as memories rooted in the shared history of communities are mobilized to imagine future paths and construct new grammars of action.

Our goal has been to advance a larger research agenda. Social resilience is a key characteristic of successful societies, seen as ones that perform well on indicators for population health, social inclusion, and social justice. In such societies, many groups have at their disposal the cultural and institutional resources needed to respond to successive challenges. If we are to understand what makes societies successful, we need to know more about how social resilience is constituted and operates. Moreover, as an optic, social resilience casts old issues into a new light. As a framework for approaching issues of social justice, it is an alternative to traditional right–left debates about threatened welfare states, the virtues and dangers of individualism, or the evils of government intervention. It transcends traditional disciplinary frameworks to consider how institutions work in tandem with cultural repertoires to constitute collective capabilities, and it considers issues of recognition and cultural membership in tandem with questions about the distribution of resources.

Our hope is that the studies in this volume will open up new agendas and provide inspiration for further research into the effects of neoliberalism and the sources of social resilience. At the core of inquiries into social resilience must be the macro–meso-micro link. At the macro level, there is room for further modeling of adjustment to shocks (Bronfenbrenner 1979; Wuermli et al. 2012). At the meso level, we need a better understanding of how to keep institutions robust and cultural repertoires resonant. At the micro level, we need deeper explorations of the connections between cultural repertoires, institutional frameworks, and individual resilience of the sort indicated, for instance, by the finding that minority students with the best educational outcomes are typically "straddlers" endowed with a strong group identity but also with capacities to engage the majority culture (Carter 2005; Oyserman et al. 2006). One route into this would be through studies of the social processes that support "possibilities and hopes" understood as the institutional and cultural practices that allow individuals to negotiate new environments in flexible and ambitious ways.

Similarly, there is room for further investigation of the ways in which developments during the neoliberal era have affected the sources of social resilience. We have made a number of observations about this but not undertaken a systematic assessment of which resources were eroded or augmented over the past thirty years; and more specific case studies will be needed to develop a fine-grained understanding of such issues. Moreover, the recessions that many countries experienced in the wake of the global financial crisis have posed new challenges for social groups that could fruitfully be analyzed within this framework. We see many opportunities for following up the formulations introduced in this book.

References

Abelmann, Nancy. 2003. *The Melodrama of Mobility: Women, Talk, and Class in Contemporary South Korea*. Honolulu: University of Hawaii Press.

Adger, W. Neil, P. Mick Kelly, and Nguyen Huu Ninh. 2001. *Living with Environmental Change: Social Vulnerability, Adaptation and Resilience in Vietnam*. London: Routledge.

Ancelovici, Marcos. 2012. "Le mouvement Occupy et la question des inégalités: Ce que le slogan 'Nous sommes les 99%' dit et ne dit pas." In *Par dessus le marché! Réflexions critiques sur le capitalisme*, edited by F. Dupuis-Déri. Montreal: Écosociété.

Anderson, Benedict. 1983. *Imagined Communities*. London: Verso.

Anderson, Christopher J., and Pablo Beramendi. 2012. "Left Parties, Poor Voters and Electoral Participation in Advanced Industrial Societies." *Comparative Political Studies* 45 (6): 714–46.

Art, David. 2011. *Inside the Radical Right: The Development of Anti-Immigrant Parties in Western Europe*. New York: Cambridge University Press.

Aurini, Janice, Julian Dierkes, and Scott Davies, eds. Forthcoming. *Out of the Shadows: What Is Driving the International Rise of Supplementary Education*. London: Springer Press.

Bail, Christopher. 2008. "The Configuration of Symbolic Boundaries Against Immigrants in Europe." *American Sociological Review* 73 (February): 37–59.

Bandura, Albert. 1977. *Social Learning Theory*. Englewood Cliffs, NJ: Prentice-Hall.

Bandura, Albert. 1982. "Self-Efficacy Mechanism in Human Agency." *American Psychologist* 37: 122–147.

Barnes, Lucy, Peter A. Hall, and Rosemary C. R. Taylor. 2008. "The Social Sources of the Gradient: A Cross-National Analysis of the Pathways Linking Social Class to Population Health." Paper presented at the Annual Meeting of the American Political Science Association, Boston.

Bartels, Larry. 2008. *Unequal Democracy: The Political Economy of the New Gilded Age*. Princeton, NJ: Princeton University Press.

Berkman, Lisa F. 1997. "Looking beyond Age and Race: The Structure of Networks, Functions of Support, and Chronic Stress." *Epidemiology* 8 (September): 469–70.

Berkman, Lisa F. and Thomas Glass. 2000. "Social Integration, Social Networks, Social Support and Health." In *Social Epidemiology*, edited by Lisa F. Berkman and Ichiro Kawachi. New York: Oxford University Press: 137–74.

Berman, Sheri. 2006. *The Primacy of Politics: Social Democracy and the Making of Europe's Twentieth Century*. New York: Cambridge University Press.

Blyth, Mark. 2002. *Great Transformations: Economic Ideas and Institutional Change in the Twentieth Century*. New York: Cambridge University Press.

Bloemraad, Irene. 2006. *Becoming a Citizen: Incorporating Immigrants and Refugees in the United States and Canada*. Berkeley: University of California Press.

Boltanski, Luc and Eve Chiapello. 2007. *The New Spirit of Capitalism*. London: Verso.

Boltanski, Luc and Laurent Thévenot. 2006. *On Justification: Economies of Worth*. Princeton, NJ: Princeton University Press.

Bouchard, Gérard. 2003. *Raison et Contradiction: Le Mythe au Secours de la Pensée*. Québec: Éditions Nota bene/Cefan.

Bourdieu, Pierre. 1998. *Acts of Resistance: Against the Tyranny of the Market*. New York: The New Press.

Brenner, Neil, Jamie Peck, and Nick Theodore. 2010. "Variegated Neoliberalization: Geographies, Modalities, Pathways." *Global Networks* 10: 1.

Bresser-Pereira, Luiz Carlos and José Luis Oreira. 2012. "A Theoretical Framework for a Structuralist Development Economics." Paper presented at a Conference on Financial Stability and Growth, Sào Paulo, March.

Brinton, Mary C. 2011. *Lost in Transition: Youth, Education, and Work in Postindustrial Japan*. Cambridge, UK: Cambridge University Press.

Bronfenbrenner, Urie. 1979. *The Ecology of Human Development: Experiments by Nature and Design*. Cambridge, MA: Harvard University Press.

Carlson, Marcia and Paula England, eds. 2011. *Changing Families in an Unequal Society*. Stanford: Stanford University Press.

Carter, Prudence. 2005. *Keepin' It Real: School Success Beyond Black and White*. New York: Oxford University Press.

Carter, Prudence. 2012. *Stubborn Roots. Race, Culture and Inequality in US and South Africa Schools*. New York: Oxford University Press.

Castel, Robert. 1995. *Les métamorphoses de la question sociale*. Paris: Gallimard.

Centeno Miguel A. and Joseph N. Cohen. 2012. "The Arc of Neoliberalism." *Annual Review of Sociology* 38: 317–40.

Chandler, Michael and Christopher Lalonde. 1998. "Cultural Continuity as a Hedge Against Suicide in Canada's First Nations." *Journal of Transcultural Psychology* 35/2: 191–219.

Chauvel, Louis. 2010. *Le destin des generations structure sociale et cohortes en France du XXè siècle aux années*. Paris: Presses Universitaires de France.

Collier, Paul and David Dollar. 2002. *Globalization, Growth and Poverty: Building an Inclusive World Economy*. Washington, DC: The World Bank.

Comaroff, Jean and John L. Comaroff. 2001. *Millennial Capitalism and the Culture of Neoliberalism*. Durham, NC: Duke University Press.

Cottle, Thomas J. 2001. *Hardest Times: The Trauma of Long-Term Unemployment*. Westport, Conn: Praeger Publishers.

Daly, Mary, and Hilary Silver. 2008. "Social Exclusion and Social Capital." *Theory and Society* 37 (April): 537–66.

Davis, Deborah S, ed. 2000. *The Consumer Revolution in Urban China*. Berkeley, CA: University of California Press.

Dezalay, Yves and Bryant G. Garth. 2002. *The Internationalization of Palace Wars: Lawyers, Economists and the Contest to Transform Latin American States*. Chicago: University of Chicago Press.

Dobbin, Frank. 1994. "Cultural Models of Organization: The Social Construction of Rational Organizing Principles." In *The Sociology of Culture: Emerging Theoretical Perspectives*, edited by Diana Crane. Hoboken, NJ: Wiley-Blackwell: 117–41.

Duménil, Gérard and Dominique Lévy. 2004. *Capital Resurgent: Roots of the Neoliberal Revolution*. Cambridge, MA: Harvard University Press.

Duvoux, Nicolas. 2009. *L'autonomie des assistés*. Paris: Presses Universitaires de France.

Ehrenreich, Barbara. 1989. *Fear of Falling: The Inner Life of the Middle Class*. New York: Pantheon Books.

Espeland, Wendy and Michael Sauder. 2007. "Rankings and Reactivity: How Public Measures Recreate Social Worlds." *American Journal of Sociology* 113: 1–40.

Fantasia, Rick and Kim Voss. 2004. *Hard Work: Remaking the American Labor Movement*. Berkeley: University of California Press.

Feliciano, Cynthia. 2005. "Does Selective Migration Matter? Explaining Ethnic Disparities in Educational Attainment among Immigrants' Children." *International Migration Review* 39(4): 841–71.

Fischer, Claude, Michael Hout, Martin Sanchez Jankowski, Samuel R. Lucas, Ann Swidler, and Kim Voss. 1996. *Inequality by Design: Cracking the Bell Curve Myth*. Princeton: Princeton University Press.

Fischer, Claude. 2011. *Still Connected: Family and Friends in America Since 1970*. New York: Russell Sage.

Fischer, Claude. 2012. "How to Be Poor." *Boston Review* May/June. http://www.bostonreview.net.

Fishman, Robert M. 2009 "On the Costs of Conceptualizing Social Ties as Social Capital." In *Social Capital: Reaching Out, Reaching In*, edited by Vina Ona Bartkus and James H. Davis. Northampton, MA: Edward Elgar: 66–86.

Folke, Carl. 2006. "Resilience: The Emergence of a Perspective for Social-Ecological Systems Analysis." *Global Environmental Change* 16: 253–67.

Foucault, Michel. 2008. *The Birth of Biopolitics: Lectures at the Collège de France 1978–1979.* London: Palgrave.

Fourcade-Gourinchas, Marion and Sylvia Babb. 2002. "The Rebirth of the Liberal Creed: Paths to Neoliberalism in Four Countries." *American Journal of Sociology* 108(3): 533–79.

Fraser, Nancy and Axel Honneth. 2003. *Redistribution or Recognition? A Political-Philosophical Exchange.* London: Verso.

Furstenburg, Frank F. Jr., Thomas D. Cook, Jacquelynne Eccles, Glen H. Elder Jr., and Arnold Sameroff. 1999. *Managing to Make It: Urban Families and Adolescent Success.* Chicago: University of Chicago Press.

Galbraith, John Kenneth. 1958. *The Affluent Society.* Boston: Houghton Mifflin.

Gautié, Jérome and John Schmitt, eds. 2010. *Low Wage Work in the Wealthy World.* New York: Russell Sage Foundation.

Greenhouse, Carole J. 2009. *Ethnographies of Neoliberalism.* Philadelphia: University of Pennsylvania Press.

Gross, Neil, Thomas Medvetz, and Ruppert Russel. 2011. "The Contemporary American Conservative Movement." *Annual Review of Sociology* 37: 325–54.

Guetzkow, Joshua. 2010. "Beyond Deservingness: Congressional Discourse on Poverty, 1964–1999." *The Annals of the American Academy of Political and Social Science* 629: 173–97.

Hacker, Jacob. 2008. *The Great Risk Shift: The New Economic Insecurity and the Decline of the American Dream.* Oxford: Oxford University Press.

Hacker, Jacob S. and Paul Pierson. 2010. *Winner Take All Politics: How Washington Made the Rich Richer – And Turned Its Back on the Middle Class.* New York: Simon and Schuster.

Hacker, Jacob S., Gregory A. Huber, Philipp Rehm, Mark Schelsinger, and Rob Valletta. 2010. *The Economic Security Index: A New Measure of the Economic Security of American Workers and Their Families.* New York: Rockefeller Foundation.

Hall, Peter A. 2013. "The Political Origins of Our Economic Discontents: Contemporary Adjustment Problems in Historical Perspective." In *Politics in the New Hard Times,* edited by Miles Kahler and David Lake. Ithaca, NY: Cornell University Press.

Hall, Peter A. and Michèle Lamont. 2009. *Successful Societies: How Institutions and Culture Affect Health.* Cambridge, UK: Cambridge University Press.

Hall, Peter A. and Kathleen Thelen. 2009. "Institutional Change in Varieties of Capitalism." *Socio-Economic Review* 7: 7–34.

Hanser, Amy. 2008. *Service Encounters: Class, Gender, and the Market for Social Distinction in Urban China.* Stanford: Stanford University Press.

Harvey, David. 2005. *A Brief History of Neoliberalism.* Oxford: Oxford University Press.

Herrigel, Gary. 1996. *Industrial Constructions: The Sources of Germany's Industrial Power.* New York: Cambridge University Press.

Iversen, Torben. 2006. "Class Politics Is Dead! Long Live Class Politics! A Political Economy Perspective on the New Partisan Politics." *APSA-CP Newsletter* 17 (Summer): 1–6.

Jacobs, Elizabeth and Katherine S. Newman. 2008. "Rising Angst? Change and Stability in Perceptions of Economic Insecurity." In *Laid Off, Laid Low: Political and Economic Consequences of Employment Insecurity,* edited by K. S. Newman. West Sussex: Columbia University Press.

Jasper, James M. 2002. *Restless Nation: Starting Over in America*. Chicago: University of Chicago Press.

Jobert, Bruno and Bruno Théret. 1994. *Le tournant néo-libéral en Europe*. Paris: L'Harmattan.

Kapur, Devesh, Chandra Bhan Prasad, Lant Pritchett, and D. Shyam Babu, 2010. "Rethinking Inequality: Dalits in Uttar Pradesh in the Market Reform Era." *Economic and Political Weekly* CLV, 35 (August 28): 39–49.

Katzenstein, Peter. 1985. *Small States in World Markets*. Ithaca, NY: Cornell University Press.

Kentikelenis, Alexander, Marina Karanikolos, Irene Papanicolas, Sanjay Basu, Martin McKee, and David Stuckler. 2011. "Health Effects of Financial Crisis: Omens of a Greek Tragedy." *Lancet* 378 (9801): 1457–8.

Kharas, Homi. 2010. "The Emerging Middle Class in Developing Countries." *OECD Development Centre Working Paper* No. 285.

Kymlicka, Will. 2007. *Multicultural Odysseys: Navigating the New Global Politics of Diversity*. New York: Oxford University Press.

Lamont, Michèle. 1992. *Money, Morals, and Manners; The Culture of the French and the American Upper-Middle Class*. Chicago: University of Chicago Press.

Lamont, Michèle. 2000. *The Dignity of Working Men: Morality and the Boundaries of Race, Class, and Immigration*. Cambridge, MA: Harvard University Press.

Lamont, Michèle. 2009. "Responses to Racism, Health, and Social Inclusion as a Dimension of Successful Societies." In *Successful Societies: How Institutions and Culture Affect Health*, edited by Peter A. Hall and Michèle Lamont. Cambridge, UK: Cambridge University Press: 151–68.

Lamont, Michèle and Viràg Molnár. 2001. "How Blacks Use Consumption to Shape Their Collective Identity: Evidence from African-American Marketing Specialists." *Journal of Consumer Culture* 1: 31–45.

Lamont, Michèle and Laurent Thévenot. 2000. *Rethinking Comparative Cultural Sociology: Politics and Repertoires of Evaluation in France and the United States*. Cambridge, UK: Cambridge University Press.

Lareau, Annette. 2003. *Unequal Childhoods: Class, Race, and Family Life*. Berkeley: University of California Press.

Lascoumes, Pierre and Philippe Bezes. 2009. Les formes de jugement du politique. Principes moraux, principes d'action et registre légal. *Année sociologique* 59: 109–47.

Lascoumes, Pierre and Patrick Le Galès. 2004. *Gouverner par les Instruments*. Paris: Presses de Sciences PO.

Lefebvre, Henri. 1974. *The Production of Space*. Malden, MA: Blackwell Publishing.

Liebenberg, Linda and Michael Ungar. 2009. *Researching Resilience*. Toronto: University of Toronto Press.

Marcuse, Herbert. 1964. *One Dimensional Man: Studies in the Ideology of Advanced Industrial Society*. Boston: Beacon Press.

Markus, Hazel and Paula Nurius. 1986. "Possible Selves." *American Psychologist* 41: 954–69.

Massey, Douglas S. and Nancy Denton. 1994. *American Apartheid: Segregation and the Making of the Underclass*. Cambridge. MA: Harvard University Press.

Marshall, T. H. 1950. *Citizenship and Social Class and Other Essays*. Cambridge, UK: Cambridge University Press.

Masten, Ann S. 2010. "Ordinary Magic: Lessons from Research on Resilience in Human Development." *Education Canada* 49: 28–32.

McPherson, Miller, Lynn Smith-Lovin, and Matthew Brashears. 2006. "Social Isolation in America: Changes in Core Discussion Networks over Two Decades." *American Sociological Review* 71 (3): 353–75.

Merry, Sally Engle and Peggy Levitt. 2009. "Vernacularization on the Ground: Local Uses of Global Women's Rights in Peru, China, India and the United States." *Global Networks* 9: 441–61.

Miller, Peter and Nikolas Rose. 2008. *Governing the Present*. Cambridge: Polity Press.

Mudge, Stephanie Lee. 2008. "What Is Neoliberalism?" *Socio-Economic Review* 6: 703–31.

Mudge, Stephanie Lee. 2011. "What's Left of Leftism? Neoliberal Politics in Western Party Systems 1945–2004." *Social Science History* 35 (3): 337–80.

Newman, Katherine S. 1989. *Falling From Grace: Downward Mobility in the Age of Affluence*. Berkeley: University of California Press.

Noiriel, Gérard. 2006. *Le creuset français: Histoire de l'immigration*. Paris: Points Histoire.

Norris, Pippa and Ronald Inglehart. 2009. *Cosmopolitan Communication: Cultural Diversity in a Globalized World*. New York: Cambridge University Press.

Offe, Claus. 2011. "Shared Social Responsibility: The Need for and Supply of Responsible Patterns of Action." *Trends in Social Cohesion* 23: 15–34.

Ong, Aihwa. 2006. *Neoliberalism as Exception*. Durham. NC: Duke University Press.

Osterman, Paul. 2012. "Job Quality in America: The Myths That Block Action." In *Are Bad Jobs Inevitable*? edited by Françoise Carré, Chris Warhurst, Patricia Findlay, and Chris Tilly. London: Palgrave: 45–60.

Ostrom, Elinor. 2005. *Understanding Institutional Diversity*. Princeton, NJ: Princeton University Press.

Oyserman, Daphna, Deborah Bybee, and Kathy Terry. 2006. "Possible Selves and Academic Outcomes: How and When Possible Selves Impel Action." *Journal of Personality and Social Psychology* 91: 188–204.

Pachucki, Mark and Ronald L. Breiger. 2010. "Cultural Holes: Beyond Relationality in Social Networks and Culture." *Annual Review of Sociology* 36: 205–24.

Palier, Bruno, Patrick Emmenegger, Silja Häusermann, and Martin Seeleib-Kaiser, eds. 2012. *The Age of Dualization: The Changing Face of Inequality in Deindustrializing Societies*. Oxford: Oxford University Press.

Palier, Bruno and Kathleen Thelen. 2010. "Institutionalizing Dualism: Complementarities and Change in France and Germany." *Politics and Society* 38: 119–48.

Paugam, Serge. 1996. "Poverty and Social Disqualification: A Comparative Analysis of Cumulative Social Disadvantages in Europe" *Journal of European Social Policy* 6: 287–303.

Paugam, Serge, Duncan Gallie, and Sheila Jacobs. 2003. "Unemployment, Poverty and Social Isolation: Is There a Vicious Circle of Social Exclusion?" *European Societies* 5: 1–32.

Peck, Jamie and Adam Tickell. 2002. "Neoliberalizing Space." *Antipode* 34 (3): 380–404.

Pierson, Paul. 2003. "Big, Slow-Moving and Invisible . . . Macrosocial Processes in the Study of Comparative Politics." In *Comparative Historical Analysis in the Social Sciences*, edited by James Mahoney and Dietrich Rueschemeyer. New York: Cambridge University Press: 177–207.

Piketty, Thomas and Emmanuel Saez. 2003. "Income Inequality in the United States, 1913–1998." *Quarterly Journal of Economics* 118: 1–39.

Piore, Michael and Charles Sabel. 1984. *The Second Industrial Divide: Possibilities for Prosperity*. New York: Basic Books.

Polletta, Francesca, Pang Ching, Bobby Chen, Beth Gharrity Gardner, and Alice Mottes. 2011. "The Sociology of Storytelling." *Annual Review of Sociology* 37: 109–30.

Polanyi, Karl. 1944. *The Great Transformation: The Political and Economic Origins of Our Time*. Boston: Beacon Press.

Prasad, Monica. 2006. *The Politics of Free Markets: The Rise of Neoliberal Economic Policies in Britain, France, Germany and the United States*. Chicago: University of Chicago Press.

Préteceille, Edmond. 2009. "La ségrégation ethnoraciale dans la métropole parisienne." *Revue française de sociologie* 50: 489–519.

Putnam, Robert D. 2000. *Bowling Alone: The Collapse and Revival of American Communities*. New York: Simon and Schuster.

Rajan, Raguran. 2010. *Fault Lines: How Hidden Fractures Still Threaten the World Economy*. Princeton, NJ: Princeton University Press.

Rao, Vijayendra and Michael Walton, eds. 2004. *Culture and Public Action*. Stanford: Stanford University Press.

Ravallion, Martin. 2009. "The Developing World's Bulging (but Vulnerable) Middle Class." *Policy Research Working Paper 4816*. Washington, DC: The World Bank.

Rodrik, Dani. 1997. *Has Globalization Gone Too Far?* Washington, DC: Institute for International Economics.

Sampson, Robert J., Jeffrey Morenoff, and Felton Earls. 1999. "Beyond Social Capital: Spatial Dynamics of Collective Efficacy for Children." *American Sociological Review* 64: 633–60.

Sampson, Robert J., Jeffrey D. Morenoff, and Thomas Gannon-Rowley. 2002. "Assessing Neighborhood Effects: Social Processes and New Directions in Research." *Annual Review of Sociology* 28: 443–78.

Scheper-Hughes, Nancy. 1993. *Death Without Weeping: The Violence of Everyday Life in Brazil*. Berkeley: University of California Press.

Schaefer, Armin and Wolfgang Streeck, eds. 2013. *Politics in an Age of Austerity*. Cambridge, UK: Polity Press.

Schoon, Ingrid. 2006. *Risk and Resilience: Adaptations in Changing Times*. Cambridge, UK: Cambridge University Press.

Schor, Juliet B. 1998. *The Overspent American: Why We Want What We Don't Need*. New York: Perseus.

Schröder, Martin. 2011. *Die Macht Moralischer Argumente*. Wiesbaden: VS Verlag.

Sen, Amartya. 1993. "Capability and Well-Being." In *The Quality of Life*, edited by Martha Nussbaum and Amartya Sen. New York: Oxford Claredon Press: 30–53.

Sewell, William H. Jr. 2008. "The Temporalities of Capitalism." *Socio-Economic Review* 6(3): 517–37.

Sewell, William H. Jr. 2010. "The Empire of Fashion and the Rise of Capitalism in Eighteenth-Century France." *Past and Present* 206 (February): 81–120.

Sharone, Ofer. 2013. *Unemployment Experiences: Job Searching, Interpersonal Chemistry, and Self-Blame*. Chicago: University of Chicago Press.

Shevchenko, Olga. 2001. "Between the Holes: Emerging Identities and Hybrid Patterns of Consumptions in Post-Socialists Russia." *Europe-Asia Studies* 54: 841–66.

Silva, Jennifer. 2012. "Constructing Adulthood in an Age of Uncertainty." *American Sociological Review* 78: 505–522.

Silver, Hilary. 1994. "Social Exclusion and Social Solidarity: Three Paradigms." *International Labour Review* 133: 531–78.

Skocpol, Theda and Vanessa Williamson. 2012. *The Tea Party and the Remaking of American Conservatism*. New York: Oxford University Press.

Small, Mario, David Harding, and Michèle Lamont. 2010. "Introduction: Reconsidering Culture and Poverty." *Annals of the American Academy of Political and Social Sciences* 629: 6–27.

Smith, Sandra Susan. 2010. "A Test of Sincerity: How Black and Latino Service Workers Make Decisions about Making Referrals." *The Annals of the American Academy of Political and Social Science* 629 (May): 30–52.

Smith, Vicky. 2002. *Crossing the Great Divide: Worker Risk and Opportunity in the New Economy*. Ithaca, NY: Cornell University Press.

Somers, Margaret R. 2008. *Genealogies of Citizenship: Markets, Statelessness, and the Right to Have Rights*. Cambridge, UK: Cambridge University Press.

Soysal, Yasemin N. 1994. *The Limits of Citizenship: Migrants and Postnational Membership in Europe*. Chicago: University of Chicago Press.

Storey, Andy. 2011. "The Ambiguity of Resistance: Opposition to Neoliberalism in Europe." *Capital and Class* 35: 55–85.

Streeck, Wolfgang. 1991. "On the Institutional Conditions of Diversified Quality Production." In *Beyond Keynesianism: The Socio-Economics of Production and Employment*, edited by Egon Matzner and Wolfgang Streeck. London: Edward Elgar: 21–61.

Streeck, Wolfgang. 2009. *Re-Forming Capitalism: Institutional Change in the German Political Economy*. Oxford: Oxford University Press.

Sutcliffe, Kathleen M. and Timothy J. Vogus. 2003. "Organizing for Resilience." In *Positive Organizational Scholarship: Foundation of a New Discipline*, edited by Kim S. Cameron, Jane E. Dutton, and Robert E. Quinn. San Francisco: Berrett-Koehler Publishers: 94–110.

Swidler, Ann. 1986. "Culture in Action: Symbols and Strategies." *American Sociological Review* 51: 273–86.

Swidler, Ann and Susan Cott Watkins. 2009. "Teach a Man to Fish? The Sustainability Doctrine and Its Social Consequences." *World Development* 37 (7): 1182–96.

Taylor, Charles, with commentary by K. Anthony Appiah, Jurgen Habermas, Steven C. Rockefeller, Michael Walzer, Susan Wolf. Edited and introduced by Amy Gutman. 1994. *Multiculturalism: Examining the Politics of Recognition*. Princeton, NJ: Princeton University Press.

Tett, Gillian. 2009. *Fool's Gold*. New York: Free Press.

Tsai, Lily. 2006. *Accountability Without Democracy: Solidarity Groups and Public Goods Provision in Rural China*. New York: Cambridge University Press.

Uchitelle, Louis. 2006. *The Disposable American: Layoffs and Their Consequences*. New York: Vintage Books.

Vaïsse, Justin. 2010. *Neoconservatism: The Biography of a Movement*. Cambridge, MA: Harvard University Press.

Vogel, Stephen. 1996. *Freer Markets, More Rules: Regulatory Reform in Advanced Industrial Countries*. Ithaca, NY: Cornell University Press.

Vollan, Björn. 2008. "Socio-ecological Explanations for Crowding-Out Effects from Economic Field Experiments in Southern Africa." *Ecological Economics* 67 (4): 560–73.

Walkerdine, Valerie 2003. "Reclassifying Upward Mobility: Femininity and the Neoliberal Subject." *Gender and Education* 15 (3): 237–47.

Warikoo, Natasha. 2010. *Balancing Act: Youth Culture in the Global City.* Berkeley: University of California Press.

Western, Bruce and Jake Rosenfeld. 2011. "Unions, Norms and the Rise in American Wage Inequality." *American Sociological Review* 76: 513–37.

Willer, Robb. 2009. "Groups Reward Individual Sacrifice: The Status Solution to the Collective Action Problem." *American Sociological Review* 74: 23–43.

Williamson, Oliver. 1985. *The Economic Institutions of Capitalism.* New York: Free Press.

Wright, Erik Olin. 2010. *Envisioning Real Utopias.* New York: Verso.

Wuermli, Alice, Rainer Silbereisen, Mattias Lundberg, Michèle Lamont, Jere R. Behrman, and Lawrence Aber. 2012. "A Conceptual Framework." In *Economic Crisis and the Next Generation: Protecting and Promoting Young People's Development*, edited by A. Wuermli. Washington, DC: The World Bank: 29–102.

Young. Alford A., Jr. 2006. *The Mind of Marginalized Black Men: Making Sense of Mobility, Opportunity, and Future Life Chance.* Princeton, NJ: Princeton University Press.

Zelizer, Viviana A. 2010. *Economic Lives: How Culture Shapes the Economy.* Princeton, NJ: Princeton University Press.

Zuberi, Dan. 2006. *Differences that Matter: Social Policy and the Working Poor in the United States and Canada.* Ithaca, NY: Cornell University Press.

PART I

NEOLIBERALISM

Effects on Policy Regimes and International Regimes

I

Neoliberalism

Policy Regimes, International Regimes, and Social Effects

Peter B. Evans and William H. Sewell, Jr.

In the final three decades of the twentieth century, the world's political economic framework underwent a far-reaching transformation from a state-centric to a neoliberal form (Sewell 2005). In the years following World War II, economies in all areas of the world had been governed by state-centered regulatory regimes. In the wealthy countries of North America, Western Europe, Japan, Australia, and New Zealand, economies were based on free markets and private property, but they were carefully steered and regulated by democratic Keynesian welfare states. In the communist countries, almost all economic activity took place in authoritarian state institutions. And in most of the major countries of Africa, Asia, and Latin America, governments imposed ambitious schemes of state-led development. Over the course of the 1970s, state-led regulatory regimes entered into crisis. By the 1990s, the communist regimes had fallen or had been thoroughly transformed from within by introducing markets and privatizing production. The advanced capitalist countries had dismantled or watered down their regulatory states by privatizing publicly owned enterprises, lifting capital controls, deregulating markets, and, more selectively, paring back welfare guarantees. And the vast majority of developing countries in Asia, Africa, and Latin America had abandoned important elements of their nationalist development strategies and opened their borders to global flows of capital and goods – some on their own volition and others under the coercive urging of the International Monetary Fund (IMF) and the World Bank. All of these countries had become part of a rapidly integrating world market regulated by global rules administered by economic governance institutions such as the World Trade Organization and disciplined by instantaneous global exchanges for currencies, securities, and bonds.

This new regulatory framework of the world economy is commonly referred to as neoliberalism. The term "neoliberalism" seems apt. As in classical economic liberalism, the new economic order is envisioned as primarily governed, both within and between states, by market relations. But this is a "neo" or revised liberalism because it followed a long period during which markets had been highly constrained by states and because economic liberalism had to be altered to fit a landscape of states, firms, and economic actors very different from those of the nineteenth-century world in which liberalism had initially flourished. The new economic landscape was populated by giant firms with monopoly power, and the states, at least in the industrialized West, were democratic states with a commitment to social welfare rather than absolutist regimes or constitutional monarchies with limited suffrage. Using classic liberal formulas to construct political programs and policies in a mid-twentieth-century political economy had implications that eighteenth- or early-nineteenth-century liberals could hardly have foreseen.

To characterize the current era as neoliberal or the regulatory regime of the current world economy as neoliberalism is, of course, to emphasize the ideological dimension of the transformation. As we see it, the rise of a market-oriented world economic regime over the past three decades is not some inevitable outcome of technological or economic forces, although such forces certainly set limits to the possible outcomes. We believe that the current global order has been importantly shaped by the political and intellectual ascendancy of neoliberal ideas and policy blueprints – as opposed, for example, to Keynesianism or social democracy or communism or nationalist developmentalism, which shaped the diverse political economies of the previous period. In this chapter we attempt to clarify the concept of neoliberalism and to sketch the historical process by which neoliberalism rose to ascendancy. But we also trace out some of the deviations from full-fledged neoliberal policies that have emerged in various regions of the world – deviations that are common even in states that have adopted a wide range of apparently neoliberal reforms. We argue that the different political dynamics surrounding neoliberal reforms in different countries has meant that the social effects of neoliberalism are far from uniform.

What Is Neoliberalism?

If "neoliberalism" is an apt term for the current world economic regime, it is also a troublesome one. Neoliberalism has a wide range of meanings in current discourse and a strong left-leaning political inflection. It is used far more often by those who criticize the current economic order than by those who favor it. Indeed, "neoliberalism" all too often serves more as an epithet than as an analytically productive concept. We make no pretense to laying down some neutral and "scientific" definition of a concept that is essentially contested and will certainly remain so. But we consider it useful to distinguish four facets of the neoliberal phenomenon: neoliberalism as economic theory, neoliberalism as political ideology, neoliberalism as policy paradigm, and neoliberalism as social imaginary. At the same time, we would like to signal certain usages of the term that we regard as unhelpful or misleading.

Neoliberal economic theory stresses the welfare-maximizing consequences of market exchange. It does so with a level of technical finesse and erudition that makes it available mainly to professional economists with the appropriate mathematical skills. The high intellectual quality of this work, attested by numerous Nobel Prizes, has lent considerable luster to neoliberal ideology in general. In addition to these relatively inaccessible academic economic ideas, neoliberalism can denote a much more widely disseminated political ideology that extols the superiority of market allocation of goods and services over public provision and that favors lowering taxes, disempowering labor unions, suppressing state regulations of economic activity, and cutting public spending but that also embraces formal democracy and the rule of law. Milton Friedman's extraordinarily successful popular book *Capitalism and Freedom* (2002 [1962]) is a good example of how the economic arguments of neoliberalism can be translated into popular political ideology. Margaret Thatcher and Ronald Reagan were probably the most gifted purveyors of neoliberalism as political ideology. "Market fundamentalism" (Stiglitz 2002; Somers 2008) and "the personal responsibility crusade" (Hacker 2006) are efforts to describe its content.

Neoliberalism in the sense of a policy paradigm is a set of interrelated policies intended, generally speaking, to increase the role of markets in regulating economic life – policies that range from privatization of public enterprises, reduced controls on capital movements, so-called shock therapy, and global free-trade agreements to deregulation of credit or labor markets, IMF conditionalities, and new regimes of intellectual property. Neoliberalism as a policy paradigm is probably best symbolized by the much-publicized "Washington Consensus" of the late 1980s and early 1990s.[1] It is important to recognize that many such policies have been adopted by states that maintain a certain distance from neoliberalism as political ideology. Countries such as Sweden, France, and Germany, which have prided themselves on maintaining generous and comprehensive welfare states, have nevertheless adopted a whole range of measures that fit the neoliberal policy paradigm. One of our tasks in this chapter is to sort out the adoption of policies in the broad neoliberal mode – which have in effect become the price of admission to the contemporary global capitalist marketplace – from acceptance of a full-scale neoliberal ideology. It is above all the very widespread adoption of a neoliberal policy paradigm by states all over the world that emboldens us to speak of the past few decades as a "neoliberal era."

Neoliberalism as theory, ideology, and policy has also had diffuse but powerful effects on the global social imaginary. The neoliberal social imaginary extols entrepreneurship, self-reliance, and sturdy individualism; equates untrammeled

---

[1] The term "Washington Consensus," usually credited to John Williamson (1990), refers to the set of policy prescriptions considered to be "best practice" for developing economies by the "Washington" institutions – the World Bank and the International Monetary Fund. It was subsequently applied to a range of neoliberal prescriptions beyond Williamson's original formulation becoming an epithet in the same way that neoliberal neoliberalism became an epithet (see Williamson 1999).

pursuit of self-interest and consumer satisfaction with human freedom; glorifies personal wealth; sees volunteerism as the appropriate way to solve social problems; and associates government programs with inefficiency, corruption, and incompetence. The neoliberal social imaginary shapes individual goals and behavior while simultaneously making neoliberal political ideology and policy paradigms seem "natural" (see Somers 2008). The prevalence of this social imaginary, even among those whose welfare has been undercut by neoliberal policies, helps reinforce the political power of neoliberalism as ideology and policy paradigm.

Neoliberalism defined as economic theory, political ideology, policy paradigm, and social imaginary has also had consequences for the political economy of the neoliberal era. Although the actually existing structures of political and economic power during the neoliberal era are often quite distant from what neoliberal theory and ideology would prescribe, it is nevertheless true that their evolution over the past three decades cannot be understood without taking the effects of neoliberal theory and ideology into account.

In addition to assessing the effects of neoliberalism, in its several senses, on contemporary societies, we also wish to deny certain effects that are frequently alleged. Too often, phenomena whose etiologies are only tangentially related to the spread of neoliberal ideas or policies are attributed to neoliberalism, usually in order to denounce them. It is important to recognize that political agendas or policies drawing on elements of classical liberal ideology are not necessarily consequences of neoliberalism. After all, most modern emancipatory ideologies contain important elements derived from liberal thought. Hence, political and intellectual movements making prominent use of terms such as "individualism," "freedom," "human rights," and "democracy" should not automatically be tarred with the brush of neoliberalism because they are at least as likely to be derived from a broad liberal heritage as from neoliberalism per se. Second, we must resist attributing all the distinctive socioeconomic trends of contemporary global capitalism to neoliberalism. It is certainly the case that processes such as the expansion of world trade, the financialization of economic activity, globalized outsourcing, the rise of flexible production regimes, or worldwide currency arbitrage are consonant with neoliberal ideology and policy. Indeed, when neoliberalism is used in public discourse, it is often this whole socioeconomic package that is being invoked. But we should be careful not to presume that these trends and processes are causal effects of neoliberal ideology or policy because some may have quite other causes – for example, changes in international competitiveness or in the technology of communications and transportation. In fact, such trends have sometimes predated the rise of neoliberalism and may be as much causes of neoliberalism as policy or ideology as they are effects. Neoliberalism and the major trends of contemporary global capitalism are certainly intertwined, but it is important to sort out the mutual spiral of cause and effect among ideology, policy, and economic trends rather than attributing the whole to an amorphously defined neoliberalism.

The Rise of a Neoliberal Ideology

The beginnings of a neoliberal ideology go back to before World War II. Neoliberalism initially took form as a countermovement to the increasing sympathy for state regulation of economic life within the economics profession in the 1930s. By contrast, the early neoliberal economists (or, as they generally called themselves, simply "liberals") retained a commitment to the nineteenth-century tradition of classical liberalism. Dominant during the period of British hegemony of the middle decades of the nineteenth century, economic liberalism was already on the wane as a policy paradigm by the late nineteenth century, when many of the leading capitalist states erected high tariff barriers and massive cartelization of industry threatened to undermine the domestic basis of liberal competition. From World War I forward, states assumed a growing role in economies, a role enhanced in the 1930s by attempts to solve the catastrophic economic crisis of the Great Depression. Between the wars, state control over the economy took a wide range of forms: Soviet communism, the U.S. New Deal, the French Popular Front reforms, Swedish social democracy, and a wide variety of fascist regimes. The consensus among economists, even in the previous liberal stronghold of Britain, had moved very far from the ideals of classical liberalism by the 1930s. F. A. Hayek, one of neoliberalism's founding fathers, who taught at the London School of Economics in the 1930s and 1940s, wrote *The Road to Serfdom* because he was convinced that his colleagues "completely misconceived" the nature of the communist and fascist economic experiments on the continent and that it was "obvious that England herself was likely to experiment after the war" with socialistic policies of some description (2007 [1944], 39–40). He was right. Indeed, William Beveridge, Hayek's former director at the London School of Economics, was the author of the famous report that launched the British postwar welfare state (Caldwell 2007, 13). It is this rejection of nineteenth-century market ideology that Karl Polanyi (2001 [1944]) referred to as the "great transformation" of the mid-twentieth century.

The precise form of these postwar policies varied considerably across the industrialized Western democracies, but all established expansive welfare regimes and strong state regulation of the economy. Some nationalized important industries, but all retained private ownership and free enterprise as the principal form of economic activity. Public policy and public institutions protected citizens from the risks and volatility of markets while supplying welfare-enhancing collective goods – such as housing, health care, old-age pensions, or unemployment insurance – that were otherwise undersupplied by markets. In the ideal type of this "welfare capitalism," the market was no longer "self-regulating" but was aligned with social priorities by means of state action. In Polanyian terms, markets were "embedded" in a set of politically defined social priorities implemented by the state (cf. Polanyi 2001 [1944]). These embedded liberal regimes were based on a class compromise between capital and labor – indeed, on a wider democratic pluralism that afforded clout to a whole range of social and economic interests. In all advanced capitalist countries, unions were legally recognized, and labor relations were regulated by the state – although the particular form of labor relations differed considerably from one country to another. As Ruggie (1982) has pointed out, domestic social protection was a key element in making possible a revival of the open international trade that industrialized countries had abandoned during the Great Depression. Welfare capitalism was combined with a new international economic regime agreed to at Bretton Woods at the end of World War II, which notably included a pegged-rate currency regime. This international regime was enforced largely by the unchallenged political and economic hegemony of the United States, a hegemony much enhanced by a war that had destroyed much of the other belligerents' economic infrastructure but had greatly increased American productive capacity and financial power. The outbreak of the Cold War between the capitalist and communist blocks at the end of the 1940s provided a strong continuing incentive for coordination of economic policies within the capitalist block. In these political circumstances, the potential appeal of communism to the working class – an appeal made very real by the continuing electoral strength of mass Communist Parties in Italy and France – enhanced capitalists' preference for peaceful labor relations and their willingness to share the benefits of prosperity with their workforces.

Mid-twentieth-century welfare capitalism had a long and remarkably prosperous run. The extended boom from 1947 through 1973 has been dubbed the "Golden Age" of capitalism (Hobsbawm 1994). The class-compromise politics of the Golden Age fostered increases in productivity by supporting social infrastructure such as education and health delivery as well as investment in physical infrastructure and research and development. It was a period of economic growth unparalleled in the history of capitalism and of high profits, rising wages, and rising levels of welfare benefits. The more equal income distribution that resulted from the postwar political balance of the Golden Age also promoted economic growth by fostering unprecedented increases in the demand for manufactured goods and housing. This was the period that introduced the advanced countries of the world to high mass consumption – a socioeconomic regime in which ordinary people could afford such consumer goods as automobiles, refrigerators, washing machines, vacuum cleaners, and televisions – a condition achieved before the war solely by the masses in the United States and only incompletely. The advanced capitalist countries – the United States, Western Europe, Japan, Canada, Australia, and New Zealand – seemed, during this Golden Age, locked into an ever-ascending virtuous spiral of rising productivity, which enabled rising wages, growing demand, high profits, and rising investment, which in turn ensured further rises in productivity.

Nor was postwar prosperity confined to the advanced capitalist world. The developing countries of Asia, Africa, and Latin America, many of them recently freed from restrictive colonial economic policies, experienced historically high rates of growth as well, based on strong demand for their products from the advanced countries as well as the beginnings of industrialization internally.

In the countries of the Soviet sphere, where the command economies concentrated investment in heavy industry, rates of growth were roughly equal to those in the capitalist countries in the postwar period, although Soviet-sphere citizens experienced nothing like the Western cornucopia of consumer goods. In China, the victory of the communists in 1949 ended a decades-long period of civil warfare; economic growth was substantial despite disruptions during the disastrous "Great Leap Forward" from 1958 to 1960 and the Cultural Revolution in late 1960s and early 1970s.

In the 1970s, however, the great postwar economic boom finally fizzled out. The very successes of the past two decades, especially in Western Europe and Japan, had resulted in intensified competition and falling profits in many of the leading industries that had initially been dominated by the United States – for example, in automobiles, steel, shipbuilding, and home appliances (cf. Brenner 1998). Inflation pressures increased throughout the 1960s as wage demands from strong labor movements mounted while profits began to decline. The problem of inflation was particularly severe in the United States, where President Johnson attempted to fund his Great Society programs at the same time he was escalating the Vietnam War. This eventually threw the international monetary system into disarray, because the system's stability had depended on responsible American leadership (and on Fort Knox gold, which was rapidly diminishing). Between 1971 and 1973, the Bretton Woods system was bit by bit dismantled, and currencies henceforth floated on the international market. Then the Arab oil boycott, after the Yom Kippur War in the autumn of 1973, caused a jump in energy prices, pushing overall inflation across the capitalist world to crisis levels. This led to a stock market crash and a deep recession from late 1973 to 1975.

The economic crisis that began in 1973 was not just another periodic downturn like those of 1958, 1961, or 1970 but a general crisis of capitalism, one that was not resolved until the early 1980s. It featured a decline in heavy industries such as coal mining, steel, and shipbuilding in the advanced capitalist economies, eventually creating permanent "rust belts" in these countries' former industrial heartlands. Meanwhile, the floating of currencies, the rise of new electronic trading technologies, and recycling of the vast wealth created by high oil prices in the Middle East created new opportunities for financial speculation of all kinds, especially in London's "City" and on Wall Street. When put together with stagnating industrial production, this speculative activity made finance into the leading "industry" of the United States and United Kingdom by the mid 1980s. Perhaps the most distinctive mark of the deep capitalist crisis of the 1970s was the phenomenon of "stagflation," a puzzling and troubling combination of persistently high unemployment and persistently high inflation that seemed immune to the remedies on offer from the then dominant Keynesian economics. The conundrum of stagflation threw the economic policies of the major capitalist states into disarray.

Economic disarray was not confined to the advanced countries. The experiences of different countries in the global South began to diverge sharply in this period. On the one hand, the policies of import substitution faltered in Latin America and failed to gain momentum in Africa. On the other hand, the 1970s saw the emergence of a new form of developmentalist state, one based on subsidizing export industries rather than industries producing for the domestic market. Following in the footsteps of Japan's earlier developmentalist miracle, the economies of South Korea, Taiwan, Singapore, and Hong Kong, soon dubbed the East Asian "Tigers," grew rapidly through state-promoted shifts from import-substituting to export-oriented industrialization (see Evans 1995). Meanwhile, African and Latin American countries tried to keep their own developmental states afloat by borrowing heavily but at very low real interest rates from the big Wall Street and London banks, which during the 1970s were awash in so called "petrodollars" created by high oil prices and saw little profit to be gained by lending to the stagnating Western economies. It was when interest rates rose sharply in the early 1980s that the debtor countries were thrown into crisis by their suddenly unmanageable debt burdens.

In the communist countries, the 1970s was a decade of palpable stagnation, economically, politically, and in population health. In the Soviet Union, Brezhnev surrounded himself with grey bureaucrats who pursued stability at all costs; meanwhile, the Soviet suppression of the Prague Spring in 1968 had destroyed the hopes for reform in Eastern Europe. The Soviet-type economies limped along until 1989 but no longer seemed a promising model either to the European working class or to the people or politicians of poor countries in the Global South.

The late 1960s and the 1970s were also a period of cultural and political crisis, at least in the advanced capitalist world. Indeed, the cultural and political crisis predated the economic crisis by a half-decade or so. This was a period of much disillusionment with the status quo and of widespread experimentation with new political options and lifestyle choices. The vibrant youth and student movements of the late 1960s mounted a critique of the corporate social order and the bureaucratic state, one that (rather incoherently) combined socialist, egalitarian, bohemian, and libertarian strains. The late 1960s and the 1970s were marked by intensified labor activism but also by the struggles of minority racial and ethnic groups, women, gays, and lesbians. And it was in this period that a new environmental awareness raised doubts about the desirability – even the possibility – of unlimited economic growth as a sociopolitical ideal. When the cultural and political crisis was compounded by an economic crisis in the early 1970s, the apparently stable state-centered synthesis of the postwar political and economic world began to come apart at the seams.

It is important to realize that after the more revolutionary hopes of the 1960s movements had evaporated, the individualist and anti-state bias so characteristic of the era provided a fertile ground for a revival of a wide variety of liberal political ideas. Multiculturalism, which originated as a response to struggles for minority group rights, was articulated as a new liberal ideal in the 1970s (see Chapter 3). Meanwhile, the obvious stagnation of the communist countries, together with the blatant crushing of the democratic movement in Czechoslovakia and the continuing flow of revelations regarding Stalinist atrocities (e.g., Solzhenitsyn 1974), caused a widespread revulsion with communism among many former Marxists and socialists, many of whom began to explore liberal alternatives. As Samuel Moyn (2010) has recently argued, it was also in this period that the utopia of universal human rights – inspired in part by the revulsion against Stalinism – became a major international cause and movement. This era of crisis for the state-centric political economy was, in short, also a moment of efflorescence for new political ideas with liberal roots, on the left, in the center, and on the right.

It was in this period of widespread strife and confusion, anemic economic performance, persistently high inflation, and mounting liberal suspicion of overweening states, that neoliberal economic and political ideology came to the fore in public and political debate. The states of advanced capitalist countries initially responded to the economic crisis of the 1970s with initiatives that were variants of existing state-centric policies – for example, fiscal stimulus programs, extension of social spending, or income policies. The fact that these initiatives were generally judged failures did much to tarnish the reputation of Keynesianism and of state-centered initiatives (Hall forthcoming). The apparent failure of Keynesian economic policies, together with the evident stagnation of the socialist economies, undermined Polanyi's great transformation and created an opening for the previously heterodox ideas of the neoliberals. The neoliberalism that emerged as an ideology and policy paradigm in the 1970s drew on classical liberalism and on the efforts of theorists such as Hayek and Friedman to modernize classical liberalism, but in the process of moving to political dominance, some crucial elements of neoliberal theorizing were lost. Hayek distinguished his version of liberalism from the laissez-faire doctrine characteristic of the nineteenth-century liberals. It was, according to Hayek, a mistake to think that the state should do as little as possible. Rather, it should be the role of the state to intervene actively in economic life to ensure free competition under the rule of law. According to Hayek, various state regulations of economic activities, such as those limiting working hours or the use of noxious substances – or, for that matter, the provision of "an extensive system of social services" – might be countenanced so long as any regulations fell equally and predictably on all actors and did not restrict price competition. Rather than a night-watchman state, the liberal state should be an active state guided by sound economic analysis and the rule of law (Hayek 2007 [1944], 85–7, 118).

At the same time, neoliberalism's most crucial departure from classical liberalism was retained. Unlike classical liberalism, neoliberalism was not concerned about great concentrations of private wealth and power. Classical liberals had a decided antipathy toward trusts and cartels, which they saw as undermining the institutional basis of economic competition and as amassing too much power, both economic and political, in the hands of a few giant firms. But Hayek did not see private monopolies as particularly menacing; he blamed the

evident monopolistic tendencies of the twentieth century on mistaken government policies rather than on intrinsic tendencies of modern industrial technology or overweening corporate power (91–4; see also Friedman 2002 [1962];
Van Horn 2009). For Hayek and Friedman, only overweening government
activity threatened liberty. Indeed, Friedman blithely asserted that capitalism
"promotes political freedom because it separates economic power from political power" (2002 [1962], 9).

In the 1970s, the pioneering efforts of Hayek and Friedman were reinforced
by the rise to prominence within the economics profession of the doctrines of
such economists as George Stigler, James Buchanan, and Gary Becker, with
Friedman's Nobel Prize in 1976 perhaps the most obvious mark of neoliberalism's entry into the mainstream. In the 1970s, neoliberal think tanks and
foundations such as the American Enterprise Institute and the Heritage Foundation in the United States and the Institute for Economic Affairs and the Centre
for Policy Studies in the United Kingdom grew in size and influence – thanks
in large part to the munificence of their corporate donors. The right wings of
the Republican Party in the United States and the Conservative Party in Britain
were increasingly receptive to the neoliberal ideas put into circulation by these
think tanks and began to wrest control of their parties from moderates.

The decisive neoliberal breakthroughs came at the very end of the 1970s.
In the spring of 1979, Margaret Thatcher, a strong advocate of neoliberalism,
became prime minister of the United Kingdom. In November 1980, Ronald
Reagan was elected president of the United States. The successive victories of
Thatcher and Reagan meant that the world's hegemonic capitalist power and
its two leading financial centers, Wall Street and the City of London, came to
be dominated by neoliberal ideologies and policies. Already in the fall of 1979,
Paul Volker, the head of the Federal Reserve under U.S. President Jimmy Carter,
had publicly abandoned Keynesian policies for monetarism and had drastically
raised interest rates. The purpose of this "Volker shock," as it was called, was to
push the economy into a recession that would sharply increase unemployment
and definitively wring high inflation out of the system. Henceforth, monetary
stability was consistently favored over the Keynesian ideal of full employment. In the United States, this new policy induced the deepest recession since
the 1930s, one that stretched, with a brief intermission, from 1980 through
1982.

Margaret Thatcher, who was more ideologically consistent than Reagan,
immediately launched a neoliberal makeover of British economic policies, res-
olutely attacking the trade unions, cutting taxes, and privatizing nationalized
industries and the United Kingdom's extensive stock of public housing. She
denounced the "nanny state" and lectured sternly about the value of hard
work, self-reliance, and entrepreneurial risk taking. Her attacks on the National
Health System were stoutly resisted, however, and her efforts to slash other
aspects of the welfare state met with mixed results – it turned out that the
British people were more attached to their welfare benefits than Thatcher
had imagined (Pierson 1994). Ronald Reagan, too, made major changes in

economic policies, including deregulating industries, privatizing services, turning the National Labor Relations Board into an ally of union-busting corporations, and slashing taxes. Similar to Thatcher, he extolled entrepreneurialism and sturdy individualism; indeed, the effects of his rhetoric on public discourse probably ran ahead of his policy changes. His efforts to cut social security and Medicare, however, went nowhere – Americans, too, appreciated their welfare entitlements (Pierson 1994).

The elections of Thatcher and Reagan had an impact not only on the United States and the United Kingdom but also on the entire capitalist world. Because the United States was the world's hegemonic power, its turn to neoliberalism in the early 1980s put the issue of neoliberal reforms on the political agenda in all the noncommunist countries – which were all, in any case, searching for policies that might lift them out of the era's extended economic crisis. In fact, most politicians in the advanced capitalist powers remained quite skeptical of Thatcher's and Reagan's ideological zeal. But if zealous neoliberal ideology hardly swept the field, monetarist and Chicago School economics and arguments for market-based reforms made significant headway in policy circles virtually everywhere. Throughout the 1980s and 1990s, a variety of market-based policies – for example, deregulation, privatization, and free trade agreements – were adopted, generally piecemeal and pragmatically, by all of the capitalist states. In Europe, much of the initiative was taken by the European Union, which, because it was buffered from popular political control, could impose market-friendly policies that its members would have found difficult to enact on their own.

When the Reagan administration took control of Washington, it quickly tried to fashion the IMF and the World Bank into what Joseph Stiglitz calls "missionary institutions" for neoliberalism (2002). As interest rates shot up after the Volker shock, rolling over or refinancing debt at the new rates became impossible for many Latin American and African states, and they could escape bankruptcy only by means of IMF and World Bank loans. But these loans now came with drastic conditions. Borrowing countries were forced to cut domestic inflation; end import substitution policies; open their capital markets to the financial institutions of the wealthy countries; and slash domestic spending, even on education and health care, so as to balance budgets. In the worst cases, mostly in Africa, already weak states essentially collapsed, resulting in domestic chaos. For Latin America and Africa, neoliberal reforms, whether imposed or adopted voluntarily, helped to turn the 1980s into a "lost decade." But in East and Southeast Asia, things were very different. The original Tigers; a reformed China; and newer export-led successes such as Malaysia, Thailand, and Indonesia began to pull away from the rest of the Global South. Indeed, South Korea, Taiwan, Singapore, and Hong Kong were increasingly assimilated to the wealthy capitalist countries by the 1990s.

It was, of course, in the 1980s and 1990s that the communist world collapsed. In Poland, the Solidarity trade union posed a continual threat to communist control from 1980 forward. In the Soviet Union, Mikhail Gorbachev assumed power in 1985 and attempted to liberalize both public discourse by means of *glasnost* and the political and economic sphere by means of *perestroika*. The fall of the Berlin Wall in 1989 was the death knell of Soviet communism, although the Soviet Union itself subsisted until 1991. The former communist countries of central and eastern Europe generally adopted neoliberal policies, sometimes including the famous "shock therapy," for a double reason: not only were they abjectly dependent on the IMF and other Western institutions after the collapse of communism, but neoliberalism's hostility to the state and celebration of individual freedom were also profoundly appealing to people who had long been oppressed by corrupt and overweening states (Bockman and Eyal 2002; Bockman 2011). By 1989, there was already a core of convinced neoliberals in many of the former communist countries, many of whom became important figures in the post-revolutionary states. In China, the Communist Party retained its grip on power despite the chaos of the cultural revolution, but by the early 1980s, Deng Xiaoping was gradually steering the regime away from collectivism and toward a more market-based economy. By the early 1990s, it was clear that a neoliberal sea change had taken place in the dominant assumptions of economic theory, political ideology, and policy paradigms. The collapse of communism (or in the case of China, its internal transformation) had seemed to prove the permanent superiority of the free market system. The long slump from 1973 to 1982 had given way to an equally long if not particularly vigorous upturn punctuated but hardly stopped by the brief and shallow recession of 1991 to 1992. Nonetheless, the conviction that that adopting neoliberal policies would reinvigorate economic growth turned out to be ill grounded. Using Angus Maddison's (2008) calculations, which exclude the effects of the 2008 economic crisis, the absence of reinvigorating effects among the developed countries of the North during the neoliberal era is striking. As Figure 1-1 indicates, even if we use the relative low point of the 1978 to 1983 quinquennium as the starting point for the neoliberal era, no sustained recovery in growth rates can be observed in either the United States or Western Europe during the subsequent quarter of a century.

If the failure of neoliberalism to revitalize growth in Europe and the United States was already evident when the 2008 financial crisis struck, the crisis underscored the disconnect between neoliberal policies and growth. The performance of the United States economy was far worse than the growth rates in the 1970s that had been used to justify the shift to neoliberal policies; the countries less affected were those that had resisted full-blown neoliberalism, such as Sweden and Finland in the North and China, Brazil, and India in the South.[2]

[2] See Shane, Matthew. "Real Historical Gross Domestic Product (GDP) Per Capita and Growth Rates of GDP Per Capita for Baseline Countries/Regions (in 2005 dollars) 1969–2011." Economic Research Service International Macroeconomic Data Set. U.S. Department of Agriculture. http://www.ers.usda.gov/datafiles/International_Macroeconomic_Data/Historical_Data_Files/HistoricalRealGDPValues.xls.

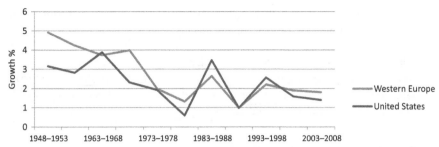

FIGURE I-I. Western Europe includes 30 countries and territories: Andorra, Austria, Belgium, Cyprus, Denmark, Faeroe Islands, Finland, France, Germany, Gibraltar, Greece, Greenland, Guernsey, Iceland, Ireland, Isle of Man, Italy, Jersey, Liechtenstein, Luxembourg, Malta, Monaco, the Netherlands, Norway, Portugal, San Marino, Spain, Sweden, Switzerland, and the United Kingdom. (*Source*: Maddison, Angus. (2008) "Statistics on World Population, GDP and Per Capita GDP, 1 AD -2008 AD." Groningen, the Netherlands: Groningen Growth and Development Center. http://www.ggdc.net/maddison/.)

Neoliberalism has actually been more successful as a means of shifting the balance of class political power than as an instrument for reinvigorating capitalist growth. Although overall economic growth rates have not actually increased, the proliferation of neoliberal policies has helped to funnel much of what growth there was into profits, particularly in the financial sector. There was, moreover, little dissent about economic policy. Deregulation, greater freedom of trade, encouraging entrepreneurship by lowering taxes, privatization of government services, encouraging financial innovation, freeing up of labor markets, enforcement of restrained monetary policies, pursuit of "shareholder value" as the goal of business – over the course of the 1980s and 1990s, these neoliberal goals became common sense across the capitalist world. Although Bill Clinton and then Tony Blair, who were critical of the excesses of Reagan and Thatcher, came to power in the United States and Britain, respectively, it was during their heyday that a thoroughgoing neoliberal international policy regime was codified and organizationally instantiated in bodies such as the World Trade Organization (Brenner, Peck, and Theodore 2010).

Yet if the 1990s were the pinnacle of neoliberal dominance, this was also the decade in which signs of fracture began to emerge. By the end of the decade, the Washington consensus was already being called "the Washington confusion," and the East Asian financial crisis and the fiasco of economic liberalization in Russia were being used by prestigious economists such as Joseph Stiglitz (2002) to discredit the policy paradigm used by the IMF and the World Bank. At the same time, as the analysis of Barnes and Hall (see Chapter 7) suggests, popular support for certain neoliberal propositions was beginning to decline. For example, World Values Survey data show that throughout the 1990s, there was a fall in the proportion of respondents who thought that competition was more helpful than harmful or that governments should take less rather than more responsibility for taking care of people.

A decade later, after the financial crisis of 2008 and the deep recession that has followed, neoliberalism's global ascendancy as economic theory, political ideology, and policy paradigm is under renewed challenge. Nevertheless, inertia and path dependence are likely to prolong neoliberalism's effects on the social imaginary and the structure of political and economic power for years to come.

Divergent Regional Strategies in the Neoliberal Era

Neoliberalism's global impact is undeniable, but its advocates fell far short of imposing a homogeneous development model around the globe. Distinctive national and regional histories and political institutions produced diverse trajectories despite global pressures to "harmonize" policies. In the discussion that follows, we illustrate the range of variation through synoptic snapshots of four regions: North America, Europe, Latin America, and East Asia. We anchor each regional snapshot with a brief analysis of an individual country: the United States, France, Brazil, and China.

We will start with the region that has most thoroughly embraced the neoliberal model – North America. We will then move to Europe and Latin America. Both adopted "market reforms" but ended up with policy mixes that looked more like efforts to recuperate or reinvent the social democratic model of the post–World War II "Golden Age" than like the full blown North American model of neoliberalism. Finally, we will turn to East Asia, the region that is universally acknowledged to have been most economically successful during the neoliberal era but whose development strategies have been, ironically, less an expression of neoliberalism than an alternative to it. This regional tour leaves out huge swathes of the world but demonstrates the fundamental importance of variation.

North America, The Neoliberal Epicenter

North America is the best illustration of how neoliberal ideological and policy paradigms can not only become embedded in concrete policy formulation but also reshape the contours of political power. The United States has been neoliberalism's most consistently enthusiastic proponent and adopter. It now appears that Canadian policies are following in the wake of the U.S. model, turning North America into the epicenter of neoliberalism. In the 1990s, European politicians often argued for increasing the role of markets in their own countries by ascribing the more rapid American growth rates of that decade to neoliberalism. But the relatively slow growth of the U.S. economy in the 2000s, capped by the economic crisis of 2008, have quieted such arguments. The United States has not only shared Europe's inability to recapture anything approaching the growth levels of the Golden Age, but, at least initially, did worse. U.S. average annual growth for the 2001 to 2010 decade was just over half the average growth rates in Europe in the same period.[3]

Politics, rather than some kind of structural economic logic, explain why the United States became a neoliberal bastion. The "Reagan Revolution" remains a lodestar for American politicians on the right and is still considered too popular to be challenged seriously by politicians of any stripe. Indeed, one might argue that neoliberal ideological tropes have become shibboleths, considered definitive of the American national identity by large segments of the political class. Despite the important historical role actually played by state in fostering the growth of the U.S. economy, a role that has continued surreptitiously throughout the neoliberal era (Block and Keller 2010), advocates of an explicit state role in promoting economic transformation are currently beleaguered. And despite a historical tradition of state intervention on behalf of social protection (Skocpol 1992), the legitimacy of efforts to protect ordinary citizens against the negative effects of markets seems increasingly precarious.

Although there are clear affinities between neoliberalism and longstanding anti-statist traditions in American political culture (Evans 1997), this tradition had been effectively marginalized between the 1930s and the middle 1970s. It was only the political upheavals of the 1960s and 1970s that enabled its revival. We have noted that Keynesian policies failed to resolve the economic woes of the 1970s, making neoliberal doctrines seem more plausible. Meanwhile, the upheavals of the civil rights and women's movements alienated the "Solid South" and a sizeable proportion of the white male working class from the Democratic Party. This provided an opening for the Republicans, who used appeals to "traditional values" and "the American way" to enlist a winning coalition of disgruntled men, conservative Christians, neoliberal ideologists, and erstwhile white supremacists along with its longstanding base in the capitalist class. These apparently strange bedfellows formed the social basis of the "Reagan Revolution" and have continued to provide its bedrock of support.

The adoption of neoliberal ideology and policies by the Reagan administration facilitated major shifts in the structure of American politics. Neoliberalism, always unconcerned about the potential political power of private economic elites, has effectively disabled arguments for checking corporate influence. An ideologically diverse set of analysts, ranging from Marxists such as Harvey (2005) and dissenting economists such as Simon Johnson (2009) to political scientists such as Hacker and Pierson (2010a, 2010b) and Bartels (2008) agree that the increasing political power of corporate capital, especially finance capital, has constituted a dramatic shift in the structure of U.S. politics – with profound consequences for policy and hence for American society. Ian Johnson (2009) puts it most starkly, asserting that "the finance industry has effectively captured our government." Hacker and Pierson (2010a, 2010b) provide a detailed exposition of the process by which this has happened. Journalists and

---

[3] 0.62% per year as opposed to 1.02% per year for 27 European countries. See references in footnote 2.

TABLE 1-1. *U.S. Inequality: The Golden Age versus the Neoliberal Era Golden Age*

Income Share	1976	1998	Approximate Change
Top 0.01%	0.56%	2.57%	+500%
Top 0.1%	2%	6%	+300%
Top 1%	8%	15%	+100%
Income Share	1947	1973	Approximate Change
Top 0.01%	0.90%	0.56%	−45%
Top 0.1%	3%	2%	−33%
Top 1%	11%	8%	−27%

Adapted from Piketty and Saez 2003.

social scientists alike chronicle the ability of politically well-placed corporations, especially those in the financial sector, to shift tax and regulatory rules in ways that increase their profits.

If a shifting balance of political power and corresponding changes in tax and regulatory policy are the most striking features of the politics of the neoliberal era in the United States, rising income inequality is the most prominent feature of its social effects. Inequality has skyrocketed in the United States since the mid 1970s. Real wages have stagnated, and the share of income going to the top tenth of one percent has quintupled since 1973. The now classic 2003 analysis by Piketty and Saez (2003) captures nicely the dramatic change in U.S. inequality during the neoliberal era (Table 1-1). The contrast between the evolution of income inequality during the Golden Age of embedded liberalism and the neoliberal era could hardly be more striking. The Golden Age continued the "great compression" of U.S. wage inequality that began before World War II (see Goldin and Margo 1992). The neoliberal era reversed it, taking inequality back to levels not seen since World War I.[4]

The social effects of inequality are broad, variegated, and well documented. The rising incidence of risk among the middle and working classes (Hacker 2006) and the erosion of social protection may well be more profound and socially corrosive than the shifts of income inequality per se. Frank, Levine, and Dijk (2010) provide a nice quantitative analysis of the secondary effects on inequality. Comparing high- and low-inequality jurisdictions in the United States, they find that high-inequality situations are associated with a tendency to "live beyond one's means" and therefore experience financial distress as measured by levels of bankruptcy. Their data also confirm the less obvious argument that "financial distress may increase the level of stress in personal

---

[4] It should be underlined that the contrast between the two periods involves no "growth-inequality trade-off." U.S. citizens were not compensated for getting a smaller share of the pie by being able to enjoy a faster growing pie. To the contrary, the pie grew more slowly while the rich took a bigger share.

relationships, thus increasing the likelihood of marriages ending in divorce" (2010:17).

The connection between the policy paradigm associated with neoliberalism and the rise of inequality in the United States is not hard to make. Efforts to find alternative explanations in market forces and technological change fall short, as Hacker and Pierson 2010b:34–40) explain nicely, leaving, as they put it, "the usual suspect: American Politics." Tax policy is the most obvious link between neoliberalism and increased inequality. Harvey (2005:26) points out the divergent impact of changing tax policy on rich and poor during the neoliberal era in the United States. Although the tax rate for the highest bracket was more than cut in half between the Golden Age and 2005, the rate in the lowest bracket was higher than it had been at the eve of World War II. Hacker and Pierson (2010b:49) estimate that three decades of tax cuts for the top 0.1 percent of income earners has almost doubled the increase in their share of national income.[5] Tax cuts are only the most obvious path from neoliberal policies to increased inequality. Changes in social provision and policies toward workers' rights have also had profound effects. Zuberi (2006) provides a compelling illustration of the consequences of differences in social provision and labor rights by comparing the lives of low-wage hotel workers in the Pacific Northwest on either side of the U.S.–Canadian border. Better wages and greater job security associated with higher rates of unionization, together with more social provision (particularly with regard to health care) in Canada, generated dramatic differences, not just in the individual lives of these workers but also in the comparative quality of the communities in which they lived.[6]

In his more recent book, Zuberi (2010) extends the analysis of the effects of different labor regimes by examining the changes over time in the working conditions of low-wage workers in Canadian hospitals. Here he shows how the reorganization of work and degrading of the employment relation under neoliberalism has ramifications beyond the deteriorating circumstances of low-wage workers. He carefully documents the connections between the degradation of working conditions among hospital cleaning and support staff and the alarming rate of deaths from hospital-acquired infections.[7] As Zuberi (2010:327) puts it, "Decent employment conditions are also a central cornerstone of public health and consumer safety." Zuberi thus provides an important complementary vision of the chain of causation leading from neoliberal policies to negative social effects.

The fact that Zuberi did not have to leave Vancouver to examine the effects of neoliberal labor policies in his more recent research meshes nicely with

---

[5] A flood of recent books make similar connections between shifts in the balance of political power and the rise of inequality in the U.S. (e.g. Bartels 2008; Kelly 2009).

[6] See also the discussion of these results by Herztman and Siddiqi in Hall and Lamont 2009.

[7] In the United States, hospital-acquired infections, 30 to 50 percent of which are preventable, lead to almost 2 million people sickened, just under 100,000 deaths, and $7 billion in treatment costs (Zuberi 2010:2).

Hertzman and Siddiqi's analysis (see Chapter 10) of the social effects of the increasing predominance of neoliberal policies in Canada. Examining U.S.–Canadian differences earlier in the neoliberal era, Hertzman and Sidiqqi (2009) showed that higher levels of social provision and social protection led to Canada's catching up to and surpassing the United States in terms of social indicators such as life expectancy over the initial decades of the neoliberal era. But Hertzman's and Siddiqi's more recent analysis (see Chapter 10) shows how Canada's shift toward more neoliberal policies in the mid-1990s has undermined the Canadian advantage. Although Bouchard (see Chapter 9) argues that resistance to neoliberalism as ideology and policy paradigm in Quebec has helped preserve and even extend previous levels of social protection up until the recent past, there is reason to worry that Canada's overall social trajectory will follow that of the United States.

The full-blown efforts to instantiate neoliberal ideology as policy in the United States from the beginning of the neoliberal era and more recently in Canada have had disturbingly negative social effects. The path of change leads from neoliberal ideology to politics and policies that sharpen economic inequalities. Rising inequalities in turn erode not just the relative economic status of the poor but also the social relations that knit together poor communities and connect them to the society at large, producing negative reverberations in the communities in which the poor live and in society at large. But although the United States case is a crucial one, it would be an error to assume that the United States is the archetype for social transformation in the neoliberal era. Some regions of the world experienced increased economic growth rather than stagnation during the neoliberal era, and some countries have witnessed impressive social progress as well. Divergent effects make sense when divergent trajectories of political and policy choices are taken into account.

Europe: The Persistence of Social Democratic Institutions

As we have already chronicled, Europe was strongly affected by neoliberal ideology and policy paradigms during the 1980s and 1990s. But with the exception of Thatcher's United Kingdom, the European trajectory was hardly an unambiguous triumph of neoliberalism. All Western European countries liberalized their markets – indeed, liberalization was required by membership in the European Union. But continental European countries also retained the protective social democratic institutions built during the "Golden Age."

Nor did this mixture of market-enhancing reforms with strong social protection condemn European social democratic regimes to slow growth and high rates of unemployment, as neoliberals claimed it would. Gross domestic product (GDP) growth between 1979 and 2005 was nearly identical in the European Union and the United States: 60.5 percent and 61.5 percent, respectively. And GDP per hour of work actually grew more rapidly in Europe than in the United States (Hacker and Pierson, 2010b:159, 198). Careful empirical analysis also demonstrated that "labor-market flexibility, US-style," did not hold up as a remedy for European unemployment (cf. Freeman 1994). Instead, European countries that adopted policies of labor activation and investment in human capital had employment levels higher than did European countries not adopting such policies (see Bradley and Stephens 2007; Huo, Nelson, and Stephens 2008; Iversen and Stephens 2008).

France provides a good illustration of the persistence of social democratic institutions in the face of an apparent "neoliberal turn." In the early 1980s, France seemed the obvious counterexample to the rapid advance of neoliberalism in the United Kingdom and the United States. In 1981, socialist François Mitterand was elected president, and a coalition of the socialist and communist parties won a large majority in the National Assembly. France already had a large state sector and a strong *dirigiste* state that featured extensive economic planning, tight regulation, and state-provided credit for private firms in key industrial sectors. This strong state had propelled very rapid economic growth in France during the Golden Age. In 1981, the left coalition further strengthened the state's hand by nationalizing a large number of industrial corporations and nearly all of the big banks. It also increased state spending with the explicitly Keynesian goal of lifting the country out of the deep recession of those years. But these measures increased the state debt, provoked capital flight, and plunged the country into a balance of payment crisis. When successive devaluations failed to solve the problem, France was threatened with expulsion from the European Monetary System. Mitterand, forced to chose between Europe and the left's program, unhesitatingly chose Europe. He made a U-turn in economic policy in 1983, sharply raising taxes and cutting the budget to reduce inflation (Hall 1987; Fourcade-Gourinchas and Babb 2002).

The U-turn entailed a far-reaching transformation of state industrial policy and hence of the French economy. Although the state continued to provide capital to industry, the availability of capital was now stringently conditioned on making firms internationally competitive, both within and beyond Europe. Hence the state, which had previously attempted to foster full employment, instead encouraged downsizing, subcontracting, shedding of unprofitable lines, and reorganization of production to increase productivity – which resulted in massive layoffs (Hancké 2001:316–7). It also changed regulations so as to give firms greater freedom to raise capital in national and international stock and bond markets and introduced greater flexibility into labor markets (Levy 2005:106). When the right gained a majority in the National Assembly in 1986, it began to privatize the state-owned companies, a policy that, partly because it raised considerable state revenue, was continued subsequently by both right and left governments. By 2000, it was only firms engaged in transportation, energy production, and weapons manufacture that remained in state hands (Levy 2005:106). By then leading French companies had become highly competitive in international markets and had indeed made considerable acquisitions both in Europe and in North America. In short, in the two decades after Mitterand's U-turn in 1983, the French state withdrew from its previous leading role in the economy and firms came to be governed increasingly by market forces. In retrospect, this was an absolutely breathtaking liberalization of what had been the most state-dominated economy in Western Europe.

These far-reaching changes were justified not by neoliberal doctrine but as a necessary and pragmatic modernization of the French economy. As J. D. Levy puts it, this was a "liberalization without liberals" (2005:122). This can be seen with particular clarity in the realm of social policy. The governments that imposed these reforms were concerned about their negative social effects, above all high unemployment, which in fact hovered around ten percent for most of the 1980s, 1990s, and 2000s. Both socialists and Gaullists responded by enacting compensatory social policies. Much of the unemployment that resulted from corporate downsizing was offset by new programs for early retirement. The state also offered extensive job training for workers who were made redundant, offered incentives for hiring young workers, and authorized part-time employment. Welfare programs – for example, in health care, childcare, and housing – were expanded to help cushion the hardships incumbent on marketization. By 1999, France was spending 29.5 percent of its GDP on social expenditures, the highest proportion of any European country outside Scandinavia. In the United States, the proportion was 15 percent (Levy 2005:107–10; Palier 2005). Far from adopting the entire neoliberal package of marketization and cuts in welfare spending, France compensated for aggressive marketization by equally aggressive and carefully targeted new welfare spending. One consequence of France's compensatory policies is that it is one of the few capitalist countries in which income inequality has failed to rise over the past thirty years. As Thomas Pickety has shown, French incomes, as was the case in most Organisation for Economic Co-operation and Development (OECD) countries, became steadily more equal through the mid 1970s, but, unlike elsewhere, French incomes were still as equal at the end of the twentieth century as they had been in 1973 (Figure 1-2). This is in sharp contrast to the United States, where the proportion of income going to the very wealthy has skyrocketed (and also in contrast to Canada, which has followed the U.S. trend with about a ten-year lag).

This result was achieved despite the liberalization of the product, capital, and labor markets described above, which indeed had the effect of increasing profits in industry and decreasing the share of labor in value added. The maintenance of relative income equality in France was mainly a consequence of postmarket redistribution, that is, of sharply progressive taxes that funded robust social programs (Piketty 2003:1022, 1027–33; Levy 2005:106–7). Contemporary France has its share of social problems. It has chronically high rates of unemployment that reach crushing levels among poor young men of immigrant extraction in the banlieux of its major cities, and it has serious problems of racial and ethnic discrimination and considerable populist rage against immigration. As in other countries that have undergone extensive economic liberalization, job security has declined sharply, and the labor market is increasingly divided into a secure primary and insecure secondary sector (Palier and Thelen 2010). But France has managed a transition to market-centered global

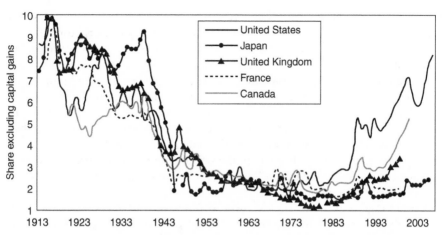

FIGURE 1-2. Top 0.1% income shares: United States, France, and Canada. (From Mishel, Lawrence, Jared Bernstein, and Heidi Shierholz. 2009. *The State of Working America 2008/2009*. Ithaca, NY: ILR Press, an imprint of Cornell University Press.)

capitalism that has substantially mitigated negative effects on social well-being. One could tell quite distinct yet essentially parallel stories about other West European countries such as Germany, the Netherlands, or Sweden. This widespread continental European pattern indicates that a pragmatic adoption of an extensive range of distinctly "neoliberal" economic reforms can in fact be combined with welfare-enhancing public policies.

The effects of the great financial crisis of 2008 have put this European compromise between neoliberalism and social democracy under considerable pressure. Euro-zone states suffering from serious public deficits, especially Greece, Ireland, Spain, Portugal, and Italy, have been forced by the European Union to adopt severe austerity policies that will undoubtedly require cutbacks in social programs. Indeed, nearly all European states have embraced austerity, either voluntarily or under duress. Yet the continuing popularity of social programs and the continuing strength of social democratic parties in most continental European countries make any wholesale abandonment of the current compromise between neoliberalism and social democracy extremely unlikely even under the terrible fiscal pressures of the present.

Latin America's Rediscovery of Social Democracy

If Pinochet's Chile made Latin America look like a U.S.-dominated laboratory for the imposition of neoliberal policies at the very beginning of the neoliberal era, the effects of neoliberalism in Latin America look quite different thirty years later. The wave of democratization that has swept through Latin America since the 1980s makes it the best arena for examining how the political effects of the classically liberal political thread that is entwined in neoliberal ideology interacts with the economic policy paradigms legitimated by neoliberal economic theories. Latin America, more obviously than any other region of the globe, has been the beneficiary of neoliberalism's rhetorical insistence on freedom and democracy. Many Latin American democratic movements of the 1980s and 1990s drew on global neoliberal tropes both to gain local legitimation and to attract allies in the North. Their success in unseating authoritarian regimes changed the tenor of Latin American politics. These political changes supported new efforts at social protection that arguably brought key Latin American countries closer to the social democratic model than they had been during the post–World War II Golden Age of capitalism.

In the Golden Age, the benefits of the welfare state in Latin America were a privilege reserved for the elite minority with stable formal sector jobs. Institutions of social protection were weak, and inequality was more extreme than in any other region of the world (de Ferranti, Ferreira, and Walton 2004). Given the weak institutional foundations for social protection in Latin America, it is all the more impressive that after initial setbacks in the 1970s and 1980s, social democratic politics began to revive in the 1990s. In the first decade of the twenty-first century, the effects of democratization were intensified with the election of a series of "pink tide" political leaders, from Luiz Inacio "Lula" da Silva in Brazil to Evo Morales in Bolivia, who were brought to power by popular mobilization and left parties. The shifts in inequality accompanying democratization in Latin America are the mirror image of the shifts associated with the increasing political power of capital in the United States. According to economist Nora Lustig (2009:1): "Inequality in Latin American countries has declined in twelve out of the seventeen countries for which there is comparable data at an average rate equal to 1.1 percent a year." Lustig (2009:19) adds that "average reductions in poverty and extreme poverty were roughly between two and three times greater (or even more in the case of extreme poverty) in those countries governed by the left."

The policy effects of the shift to more democratic politics have occurred despite conformity to important elements of the neoliberal policy paradigm. Brazil illustrates the point. On the one hand, democratization has taken place not just at the national level in the form of free elections and a new constitution but also at the local level in an effervescent combination of mobilization and innovative democratic institutional forms (Baiocchi, Heller, and Silva 2011). On the other hand, democratic Brazil has, similar to Europe, adopted consequential elements of neoliberal economic policy. Despite the size and diversity of the Brazilian economy, chronic international indebtedness and corresponding balance of payments problems have made conformity with the fiscal dictates of neoliberalism essential to economic survival. Nor was the shift toward more neoliberal economic policies simply a matter of external pressure. As in Europe, advocates of reform could easily claim that rigidities resulting from regulation and a heavy state presence in the economy were hindering economic growth. Equally important, 400 years as an economy firmly integrated into global markets had nurtured a local elite that believed deeply in the value of capitalism. For them, as for many elites in the Global South, powerful global actors urging the adoption of neoliberal policies were welcome allies. Despite pragmatic and ideological support for neoliberal policies, however, the influence of neoliberalism was tempered by powerful nationalist traditions and weaker, but still appreciable, socialist currents. For the left, national aspirations included the necessity of leaving behind Brazil's colonial legacy of gross inequality and poverty encompassing most of the rural population. Both the left and right agreed that Brazil should take its rightful place in the world as a major power and that this required a diversified local economy with a substantial degree of local control over resources. Brazilian elites never fully embraced the anti-statist assumptions of Anglo-Saxon–style neoliberalism. Authoritarian generals and democratic socialists were both happy to use the state alongside markets to make sure that the Brazilian economy continued to diversify and that Brazil's trajectory of growth was not primarily shaped by the priorities of capital and governments in the North (see Evans 1995).

The combination of democratic pressures and nationalist economic traditions led to a hybrid set of policies that melded an increased openness to global markets with a continued economic role for the state and systematic efforts at social protection. F. H. Cardoso, who served as president of Brazil in the 1990s, reduced protections for local industrialists and used the sale of state-owned industry as a source of hard currency. But despite reductions in the state's presence in the economy under Cardoso, Brazil continued to rely on the state to play a strategic role.[8] Equally important, Cardoso built institutional foundations for a more socially oriented development. Lula, Cardoso's successor, was the leader of the Worker's Party, which had strong Marxist socialist traditions. But after being elected in 2002, he put officials acceptable to global finance in charge of financial policy and kept real interest rates at high levels. Similar to Cardoso, he earned the epithet "neoliberal" on the Brazilian left. In fact, neither Cardoso nor Lula was a neoliberal despite their recognition that financial conformity was an inescapable consequence of life in a neoliberal era. Nor were their social and developmental strategies those that would be predicted on the basis of a generic neoliberal paradigm. Indeed, Brazil appeared to be experimenting with a new "social development" policy paradigm (Kerstenetzky, 2010). Taxes and public employment expanded rather than contracting (see Kerstenetzky 2009:14). Rather than a deteriorating social safety net, Brazilians experienced a gradually improving one during the neoliberal era. *Bolsa Familia*, Brazil's conditional transfer program, was small in terms of overall expenditures but transformed the lives of tens of millions of poor Brazilians, almost a quarter of the entire population. Access to health care and education expanded. Brazil relinquished its claim to being the world champion of inequality. Instead of growth bringing greater inequality as it had

---

[8] The trajectory of Petrobrás, the state-owned oil company, illustrates the point. Petrobrás is now officially a private company, but the state retains enough ownership to continue to use Petrobrás as an instrument of national policy, including, most dramatically, in the discovery of huge new offshore oil reserves that should fundamentally change Brazil's balance of payments situation.

under the military in the 1970s, it was "accompanied by rising average earnings, more formal employment, greater social protection for the population as
a whole, greater equality in household income and wages, and a reduction in
poverty" (Kerstenetzky 2009:15).

Contrary to neoliberalism's claims that the welfare state undercuts economic
dynamism, Lula's social policies proved to be growth policies as well as social
policies (cf. Evans 2010). Brazil weathered the 2008 economic crisis very well.
In the 2008 to 2011 period of crisis, Brazil's growth rates were double or triple
those of the United States and Europe.[9] The combination of increasing formal
employment and public support for the incomes of the poorest helped sustain growth. As Kerstenetzky (2009:33) summarizes the outcome, "The recent
social developmentalist experiment has combined growth with equity and (still
marginal) capability gains in Sen's sense." Brazilian policymakers' ability to
produce such salutary results, despite its economic elite's thorough commitment to capitalism and its relatively precarious position *vis a vis* international
financial markets, again underlines the importance of politics. However, the
explanation for Brazil's ability to combine growth with greater social protection
is not purely political. Increased demand from China for Brazil's agricultural
and mineral exports, as well as for a select range of local manufactured products
(Castro 2007, 2008) counterbalanced the negative effects of globally dictated
high interest rates and helped sustain growth. Nonetheless, the basic story of
Brazil's development strategy remains the political choices that flowed out of
democratization, popular mobilization, and the new structure of democratic
competition that they produced.

Other major Latin American countries had their own distinctive trajectories,
but by the turn of the century, these strategies could not be considered as shaped
primarily by the embrace of neoliberal ideology and policy paradigms. In Chile,
Ricardo Lagos and Michelle Bachelet worked to subvert the institutional constraints inherited from Pinochet's politically illiberal version of neoliberalism.
In Argentina, efforts at complete conformity to neoliberalism led to economic
collapse and to a new search for alternatives. In Venezuela, oil revenues supported Latin America's most avowedly socialist regime outside of Cuba, and
in Bolivia, socialist ideology is combined with a new ethnic politics to create a
redistributive political agenda (see Chapter 3; also see Lucero 2008). Although
Brazil has been especially successful in its rediscovery of social democracy, the
economic benefits of continued social investment are evident throughout the
continent. Latin American social democratic regimes have managed economic
growth rates far higher than those they achieved in the 1980s. Twenty-first
century Latin America continues to face serious social challenges, but (outside
of finance) its strategies are not being dictated by imposed neoliberal policy
paradigms, nor do they emanate from an active embrace of neoliberal ideology. Indeed, the contemporary Latin American vision might be characterized

[9] See footnote 2 for sources.

as a nascent quest to build a "globalized social democracy" (Cardoso 2009; Evans 2009).

East Asian Developmentalism

If Latin America best illustrates the complexity of political dynamics in the neoliberal era, East Asia is the obvious place to explore the dynamics of economic success. Rapid post–World War II East Asian development began with Japan's experience in the 1950s and 1960s, spread to Korea and Taiwan in the 1970s, and was then adopted in altered form by China in the 1980s. The shift in East Asia's position in the global hierarchy of wealth and productive capacity during the neoliberal era is historically unprecedented in its magnitude and rapidity. Indeed, when future historians look back at the late twentieth-century political economy, East Asia's vertiginous rise may well eclipse neoliberalism as the main story. East Asia's developmental success is clear. What it tells us about the effects of neoliberalism as ideology or policy paradigm is less clear. Although East Asia's success included increased engagement with global markets, regional practices stood largely in contrast to neoliberalism both as economic theory and as political practice. From the East Asian Tigers to the "communist capitalism" of China, East Asia in the late twentieth century is the home of the "developmental state," an anathema from the point of view of neoliberal economic theory. China's three decades of rapid development is the most important single case, but the ways in which trajectories of Korea and Taiwan have diverged from China's are an essential complement for assessing social effects.

China's combination of market logic with a panoply of structural and ideological features that diverge sharply from neoliberal prescriptions is the single most glaring example of the variations possible within the global paradigm of neoliberalism. The increasing role of markets was crucial to China's rapid economic growth. Centralized control over the allocation of economic resources by an opaque political apparatus restrained by few political or economic checks was mitigated after the late 1970s by an increased role for market allocation. This helped decentralize economic decisions and increased efficiency, particularly in agricultural markets.

Calling Deng Xiao Ping, the architect of these changes, a "neoliberal," as David Harvey (2005) does, may be a useful rhetorical device, but it obscures the continued central and powerful role of state and party in the allocation of resources and the formulation of economic strategy. China's ability to turn the increased role of markets into an engine of growth was predicated on the persistence of a pervasive role of the state and specifically of the Chinese Communist Party in the economy (Johnson 2010). Despite the collapse of the communist-era state-owned enterprises, new corporations wholly or partially owned by the state continue to dominate the most advanced sectors of the Chinese economy, and smaller enterprises owned by local units of government are also ubiquitous. The state determines the grand outlines of industrial policy, provides much of the financing of enterprises, and stringently oversees infusions of foreign capital.

The trajectory of social effects that has accompanied China's development also makes it tempting to apply the "neoliberal" label. Despite embedding markets in a complex, state-dominated system of political control, Chinese society has suffered from sharply rising income inequality and a massive withdrawal of social protections (see Davis and Wang, 2009). "Communist capitalism" has erased the exceptionally low levels of inequality and relatively high levels of social protection that had characterized China in the socialist period. China's trajectory in this regard stands in sharp contrast to the Brazilian case, which suggests that the absence of institutionalized mechanisms for bringing political demands from below to bear on the state is the culprit behind the negative social effects. Chinese politics are nonetheless still a far cry from neoliberal politics as epitomized by the United States. To be sure, a burgeoning local capitalist class has already co-opted enough party officials to affect policy formation, but the Chinese Communist Party remains a formidable political actor. The Party state still appears able and willing to reshape market rules when restructuring is considered necessary to preserve social stability. Hu Jintao's "harmonious society" platform, which included pushing labor law reform through in the face of opposition from foreign capital, illustrates the point. For the present, when the interests of capital appear to conflict with national interests as defined by the Communist Party, the Party appears able to prevail (see Arrighi 2007). Striking workers and protesting peasants reinforce these tendencies by feeding the Party's preoccupation with social stability and strengthening the hand of those who prioritize stability. On the other hand, unrest also tends to reinforce the Party's resistance to democratization – which, to judge from the Brazilian case, would be expected to increase the demand for social protection.

Two basic lessons might be extracted from the Chinese case. Both are consistent with the lessons we drew from the analysis of Brazil, despite the sharp contrast between the trajectories of Latin America and East Asia during the neoliberal era. First, economic success appears to depend on preserving the state's capacity to play a strategic economic role. Second, it appears that unless the democratic voice of ordinary citizens can be institutionalized, it will be difficult to avoid potentially negative consequences of the expanded role of markets.

Looking at Korea and Taiwan reinforces both lessons. Beginning in the 1970s, they combined active and authoritarian developmental states with engagement in global markets to produce rates of growth unprecedented in the histories of Europe or the United States. But in the later decades of the neoliberal era, both Korea and Taiwan moved toward democratization and began a notable expansion of social protection (see Wong 2004; Peng and Wong 2008; Dostal 2010; McGuire 2010). In Taiwan and Korea, the past quarter century has been a period of sociopolitical transformation that looks more like an effort construct a version of the post–World War II Golden Age in Asia than like the application of a neoliberal template. Siddiqi and Hertzman (2001:331) sum up the lessons of the Asian Tigers as follows, "The Tiger economies of Southeast Asia seem to be an example of economic growth and increasing parity in income distribution occurring together over time, concurrent with a dramatic improvement in population health." Between 1985 and 1995, at the height of neoliberalism in Europe and the United States, state expenditures as a percentage of GDP increased by 25% in Korea and more than 30% in Taiwan, largely because of increased welfare programs. Joseph Wong (2004), who chronicles the shift toward greater public expenditures on health, argues for a strong connection between extension of welfare spending and democratization. Three-fourths of Wong's elite respondents in the two countries endorsed the statement, "In Taiwan/Korea, there would be no improvement in social welfare without transition to democracy." McGuire (2010:300) notes that a network of "progressive doctors, academics, and former democracy advocates lobbied successfully for the introduction of single-payer national health insurance" in Korea in the early 1990s. Dostal (2010:165) highlights "democratization and political mobilization" as the most significant factors in expanding social provision in both Korea and Taiwan.

Even more clearly than Europe and Latin America, East Asia illustrates the importance of looking at trajectories of change during the neoliberal era as driven by a complex mix of global opportunities and pressures on the one hand and distinctive national and regional political and institutional traditions on the other. East Asia also reinforces the idea that it is worth distinguishing the effects of neoliberal policy paradigms from the effects of shifts in political institutions. Markets were useful tools for East Asian regimes precisely because these regimes did not relinquish the institutional capacity to make political decisions on how markets should be used. The cases of Taiwan and Korea also reinforce the idea, which emerged in our analysis of both Europe and Latin America, that the attraction of traditional social democratic strategies remains powerful even thirty years into the neoliberal era. When preferences for social democratic practices are effectively institutionalized, they mitigate the perverse social effects of neoliberal policy paradigms. The two cases – China and the United States – that show least evidence of social democratic tendency are strange bedfellows. China's explicitly illiberal politics produce social effects that parallel the inegalitarian evolution of the United States, where rhetorical loyalty to classical liberal principles is assumed to make the fusion of economic with political power unproblematic.

Conclusion

What have been the overall consequences of neoliberalism's emergence as the dominant theoretical and ideological framework for the global political economy? Any answer to this question must first acknowledge the limits of neoliberalism's success. Creating a uniform neoliberal global economy and homogenizing national institutions (see Evans 2004) proved a more difficult project than advocates of neoliberalism imagined. National politics have turned out to be far more resistant than either proponents or critics of neoliberalism are wont to acknowledge. From inside the Anglo-Saxon world, particularly from inside the United States, the transformative effects of neoliberalism seem overwhelming. Seen from the region that has emerged as most successful in the neoliberal era – East Asia – neoliberalism is only one element in an array of eclectic ideological constructions that include statist developmental strategies, and that, in the case of China, also feature profoundly illiberal politics. From the perspective of other regions – Europe and Latin America – the persistence and even revitalization of pre-neoliberal social democratic traditions is as striking as the effects of neoliberalism itself. But despite these sweeping caveats, neoliberalism has had powerful effects, not just in the United States but also around the world.

If the neoliberal era has seen no increase in economic growth rates, it has seen a remarkable transformation of the institutional structure and dynamics of the world economy. It has, in most countries of the world, decreased the power of organized labor and increased the power of capital. In all but a few countries, this has meant increasing inequality of incomes. These changes have followed from the enhanced role of markets, including global markets, in the allocation of resources. Increased "globalization" of economic activity has certainly been one of the most prominent features of the neoliberal era. World trade has grown rapidly, and corporations have become much more international in their financing, sales, and internal division of labor. In part, this is attributable to technological changes such as containerization of transport; the generalization and improvement of commercial airline service; and the development of high-speed communications via satellite, fiberoptic cables, and the internet. These technologies, which have drastically increased the speed and cut the costs of long-distance transportation and communication, were, of course, primarily the result of technological changes quite independent of neoliberal policies and would probably have led to increased internationalization of the economy had neoliberalism never attained hegemony. But the increasing ease and decreasing costs of world trade and communication certainly helped to make the neoliberals' push for freeing international trade more alluring to corporate interests and more plausible to the general public. In turn, the worldwide consolidation of a neoliberal institutional framework for international exchange fostered ever more rapid and "frictionless" global circulation. Neoliberalism hence figures as both cause and effect of the exceptionally rapid global time–space compression of the past three decades (Harvey 1991).

The undoubted rise of global trade in the neoliberal era should not, however, be glossed as simply the rise of "free markets." Despite their professed belief in open markets, the rich countries of the North continue to follow neomercantilist strategies to a degree that belies their rhetorical pronouncements. Agricultural policies are the most blatant cases, but close examination of any "free trade agreement" yields myriad less obvious examples. Likewise, the rules that govern global markets are, in large measure, the result of carefully orchestrated political action on the part of the corporate capital whose profits depend on how these rules are written. Finally, of course, the United States (and other countries in slightly more subtle ways) continues to engage in old-fashioned efforts to gain political and economic control over other countries by political and military means. It is a more globalized world but not a world in which markets have been freed from politics.

Another important economic transformation of the neoliberal era has been a tremendous rise in the importance and economic weight of finance, both nationally and globally. Again, financialization figures as both cause and effect of the rise of neoliberalism. The collapse of the Bretton Woods system of pegged exchange rates opened the way to new forms of financial intermediations based on newly fluctuating currency values in the 1970s. By the early 1980s, the pressure of international financial speculators was often instrumental in forcing or inducing countries to adopt neoliberal policies as a means of countering runs on their currency (see, e.g., Fourcade-Gourinchas and Babb 2002). Meanwhile, the increasingly wealthy financial institutions mounted effective political campaigns for loosening or dismantling of regulations, campaigns that were legitimated by neoliberal ideology. The resulting policy changes led to a proliferation of new financial "products," the growing international reach of finance, and the increasing reliance by firms of all sorts on financial benchmarks in judging success. This financialization of the economy also contributed importantly to the rising instability both of the micro-economy by fostering buy-outs, downsizing, and bankruptcies and of the macro-economy by increasing the incidence of national, regional, or global crises. This instability has resulted in increasing insecurity for ordinary people and capitalists alike, which is among the most important and problematic social effects of the neoliberalization of the world economy.

Just as the structure of the global political economy has shifted, the social imaginary that neoliberalism fosters seems to have been assimilated very broadly across the world despite differences in the policy mixes and policy discourses of national environments. As a result of global neoliberalism, the language and the institutional model of the market appear to have seeped into nearly all aspects of contemporary life. The media and popular culture have absorbed the notion that we should have entrepreneurial selves, that we must be constantly ready to retool ourselves for new opportunities, that seeking individual interest is natural, and that vast riches are the just reward for innovators.

If Friedrich Hayek could return and view the world that his intellectual efforts helped to make, he might take great satisfaction in some parts of the transformation, but he might also find some consequences of neoliberalism's success disconcerting. Although neoliberalism may claim some credit for having helped check the power of oppressive state officials, it would be hard for Hayek to ignore the magnified power of private elites that it has indubitably abetted. Although neoliberalism has increased the role of markets, it has also increased the ability of capital to reap unfair returns by writing the rules that determine how those markets work. And Hayek surely would have been disappointed in the lack of economic dynamism exhibited by the countries that hewed most closely to neoliberal doctrines.

For those of a more Polanyian bent, who value equity and community and consider the self-regulating market a dangerous utopia, the failure of the great transformation and the rise of neoliberalism is a bitter confirmation of their theoretical presuppositions, as well as a suggestion that they too should have been more worried about the ability of private elites to capture political power. Where it has been systematically put in place, neoliberalism has not just exposed families and communities to the volatility and irrationality of the market but has also enabled the rich to use public policy to shift resources in their favor while undermining the public institutions that support ordinary citizens' efforts to live fruitful and productive lives. These changes have sharply intensified the problem of social resilience in the age of neoliberalism.

References

Arrighi, Giovanni. 2007. *Adam Smith in Beijing: Lineages of the Twenty-First Century*. London: Verso.

Baiocchi, Gianpaolo, Patrick Heller, and Marcelo K. Silva. 2011. *Bootstrapping Democracy: Transforming Local Governance and Civil Society in Brazil*. Stanford: Stanford University Press.

Bartels, Larry. 2008. *Unequal Democracy: The Political Economy of the Gilded Age*. Princeton, NJ: Princeton University Press.

Block, Fred and Matthew Keller, eds. 2010. *The Invisible Hand of Government: Innovation Policy in the U.S.* Boulder, CO: Paradigm Publishers.

Bockman, Johanna. 2011. *Markets in the Name of Socialism: The Left-Wing Origins of Neoliberalism*. Stanford: Stanford University Press.

Bockman, Johanna K. and Gil Eyal. 2002. "Eastern Europe as a Laboratory for Economic Knowledge: The Transnational Roots of Neoliberalism." *American Journal of Sociology* 108: 310–52.

Bradley, David H. and John D. Stephens. 2007. "Employment Performance in OECD Countries: A Test of Neoliberal and Institutionalist Hypotheses." *Comparative Political Studies* 40 (12): 1486–1510.

Brenner, Neil, Jamie Peck and Nik Theodore. 2010. "Variegated Neoliberalism: Geographies, Modalities, Pathways." *Global Networks* 10: 1–41.

Brenner, Robert. 1998. "The Economics of Global Turbulence" (Special Issue). *New Left Review* May–June: 1–265.

Caldwell, Bruce. 2007. "Introduction." In F. A. Hayek, *The Road to Serfdom*, ed. Bruce Caldwell. Chicago: University of Chicago Press, pp. 1–33.

Cardoso, F. H. 2009. "New Paths: Globalization in Historical Perspective." *Studies in Comparative International Development* 44: 296–317.

Castro A. B. 2007. "No espelho da China" Rio de Janeiro: Universidade Federal do Rio de Janeiro: unpublished manuscript.

Castro A. B. 2008. "From Semi-Stagnation to Growth in a Sino-Centric Market." *Brazilian Journal of Political Economy [Revista de Economia Política]* 28 (1): 3–27.

Davis, Deborah, and Feng Wang, eds. 2009. *Creating Wealth and Poverty in Post-Socialist China*. Stanford: Stanford University Press.

de Ferranti, David, Guillermo E. Perry, Francisco H. G. Ferreira, and Michael Walton. 2004. *Inequality in Latin America: Breaking with History?* Washington: the World Bank.

de Janvry, A., and Sadoulet, E. 2005. *Conditional Cash Transfer Programs for Child Human Capital Development: Lessons Derived from Experience in Mexico and Brazil.* Washington, DC: World Bank Development Economics Research Group.

Dostal, Jörg Michael. 2010. "The Developmental Welfare State and Social Policy: Shifting From Basic to Universal Social Protection." *The Korean Journal of Policy Studies* 25 (3): 147–72.

Evans, Peter. 1995. *Embedded Autonomy: States and Industrial Transformation.* Princeton, NJ: Princeton University Press.

Evans, Peter. 1997. "The Eclipse of the State? Reflections on Stateness in an Era of Globalization." *World Politics* 50 (October): 62–87.

Evans, Peter. 2004. "Development as Institutional Change: The Pitfalls of Monocropping and Potentials of Deliberation." *Studies in Comparative International Development* 38 (4): 30–53.

Evans, Peter. 2009. "From Situations of Dependency to Globalized Social Democracy." *Studies in Comparative International Development* 44: 318–36.

Evans, Peter. 2010. "Constructing the 21st century Developmental State: Potentialities and Pitfalls." In *Constructing a Democratic Developmental State in South Africa: Potentials and Challenges*, edited by Omano Edigheji. Capetown, South Africa: HSRC Press.

Fairbrother, Malcolm. 2003. "The Freedom of the State? Recent NDP Governments and a Reply to the Globalization Skeptics." *Canadian Review of Sociology and Anthropology* 40 (3): 311–29.

Fourcade-Gourinchas, Marion, and Sarah Babb. 2002. "The Rebirth of the Liberal Creed: Paths to Neoliberalism in Four Countries." *American Journal of Sociology* 108 (3): 533–79.

Frank, Robert H, Adam Seth Levine, and Oege Dijk. 2010. "Expenditure Cascades." Unpublished working paper, available electronically at Social Science Research Network.

Freeman, Richard 1994. "Doing It Right? The U.S. Labor Market Response to the 1980s/1990s." Paper presented at the *Egon-Sohmen-Foundation Symposium on Fighting Europe's Unemployment in the 1990s*, Salzburg, Austria, August 27–28.

Friedman, Milton. 2002 [1962]. *Capitalism and Freedom.* Chicago: University of Chicago Press.

Goldin, Claudia and Robert Margo. 1992. "The Great Compression: The Wage Structure in the United States at Mid-Century." *Quarterly Journal of Economics* 108: 1–34.

Hacker, Jacob S. 2006. *The Great Risk Shift: The Assault on American Jobs, Families, Health Care, and Retirement and How You Can Fight Back.* New York: Oxford University Press.

Hacker, Jacob and Paul Pierson. 2010a. "Winner-Take-All Politics: Public Policy, Political Organization, and the Precipitous Rise of Top Incomes in the United States." Paper presented at conference sponsored by *Politics & Society*.

Hacker, Jacob and Paul Pierson. 2010b. *Winner Take-All Politics: How Washington Made the Rich Richer and Turned Its Back on the Middle Class.* New York: Simon and Schuster.

Hall, Peter A. 1987. "The Evolution of Economic Policy under Mitterrand." In *The Mitterrand Experiment: Continuity and Change in Modern France*, edited by George Ross, Stanley Hoffmann, and Sylvia Malzacher. New York: Oxford University Press.

Hall, Peter A. Forthcoming. *Politics in the New Hard Times: The Great Recession in Comparative Perspective*, edited by Miles Kahler and David Lake.

Hall, Peter A. and Michèle Lamont, eds. 2009. *Successful Societies: How Institutions and Culture Affect Health*. Cambridge: Cambridge University Press.

Hancké, B. 2001. "Revisiting the French Model: Coordination and Restructuring in French Industry." In *Varieties of Capitalism: The Institutional Foundations of Comparative Advantage*, edited by Peter A. Hall and David Soskice. Oxford: Oxford University Press.

Harvey, David. 1991. *The Conditions of Postmodernity: An Enquiry into the Origins of Cultural Change*. Oxford: Blackwell.

Harvey, David. 2005. *A Brief History of Neoliberalism*. Oxford: Oxford University Press.

Hayek, F. A. 2007 [1944]. *The Road to Serfdom: Text and Documents*, edited by Bruce Caldwell. Chicago: University of Chicago Press.

Hertzman, Clyde, and Arjumand Sidiqqi. 2009. "Population Health and the Dynamics of Collective Development." In Hall and Lamont (eds.) *Successful Societies: How Institutions and Culture Affect Health*, edited by Peter A. Hall and Michèle Lamont. Cambridge: Cambridge University Press: 23–53.

Hobsbawm, E. J. 1994. *The Age of Extremes: A History of the World, 1914–1991*. New York: Vintage.

Huo, Jingjing, Moira Nelson, and J. D. Stephens. 2008. "Decommodification and Activation in Social Democratic Policy: Resolving the Paradox." *Journal of European Social Policy* 18 (1): 5–20.

Iversen, Torben and J. D. Stephens. 2008. "Partisan Politics, the Welfare State, and Three Worlds of Human Capital Formation." *Comparative Political Studies* 41 (4/5): 600–37.

Johnson, Ian. 2010. "The Party: Impenetrable, All Powerful." *New York Review of Books* LVII (14): 69–72.

Johnson, Simon. 2009. "The Quiet Coup." *Atlantic Monthly*. May. http://www.theatlantic.com/magazine/archive/2009/05/the-quiet-coup/7364/.

Kelly, Nathan. 2009. *The Politics of Income Inequality in the United States*. Cambridge, UK: Cambridge University Press.

Kerstenetzky, Celia Lessa. 2009. "The Brazilian Social Developmental State: A Progressive Agenda in a (Still) Conservative Political Society." Unpublished manuscript.

Kerstenetzky, Celia Lessa. 2010. "Social Development in Latin America?" Discussion Paper No. 26 – July. Niteroi, RJ, Brazil: Center for Studies on Inequality and Development, Universidade Federal Fluminense.

Levy, J. D. 2005. "Redeploying the State: Liberalization and Social Policy in France." In *Beyond Continuity: Institutional Change in Advanced Political Economies*, edited by Wolfgang Streeck and Kathleen Thelen. Oxford: Oxford University Press.

Lucero, José Antonio. 2008. *Struggles of Voice: The Politics of Indigenous Representation in the Andes*. Pittsburgh: University of Pittsburgh Press.

Lustig, N. 2009. *Poverty, Inequality and the New Left in Latin America. Democratic Governance and the "New Left."* Washington, DC: Woodrow Wilson International Center for Scholars, Latin American Program.

McGuire, James W. 2010. *Wealth, Health, and Democracy in East Asia and Latin America*. Cambridge: Cambridge University Press.

Mirowski, Philip and Dieter Plehwe, eds. 2009. *The Road From Mount Pelerin: The Making of the Neoliberal Thought Collective*. Cambridge, MA: Harvard University Press.

Moyn, Samuel. 2010. *The Last Utopia: Human Rights in History*. Cambridge, MA: Harvard University Press.

Palier, Bruno. 2005. "Ambiguous Agreement, Cumulative Change: French Social Policy in the 1990s." In *Beyond Continuity: Institutional Change in Advanced Political Economies*, edited by Wolfgang Streeck and Kathleen Thelen. Oxford: Oxford University Press.

Palier, Bruno and Kathleen Thelen (2010) "Institutionalizing Dualism: Complementarities in Germany and France." *Politics and Society* 38 (1): 119–48.

Peng, Ito and Joseph Wong, 2008. "Institutions and Institutional Purpose: Continuity and Change in East Asian Policy." *Politics and Society* 36: 61

Pierson, Paul. 1994. *Dismantling the Welfare State? Reagan, Thatcher and the Politics of Retrenchment*. Cambridge: Cambridge University Press.

Piketty, Thomas. 2003. "Income Inequality in France, 1901–1998." *Journal of Political Economy* 111 (5): 1004–42.

Piketty, Thomas and Emmanel Saez. 2003. "Income Inequality in the United States, 1913–1998." *Quarterly Journal of Economics* 118 (1): 1–39.

Polanyi, Karl. 2001 [1944]. *The Great Transformation: The Political and Economic Origins of Our Time*. Boston: Beacon Press.

Ruggie, John Gerard. 1982. "International Regimes, Transactions and Change: Embedded Liberalism in the Postwar Economic Order." *International Organization* 36: 379–97.

Sewell, William H., Jr. 2009. "From State-Centrism to Neoliberalism: Macro-Historical Contexts of Population Health Since World War II." In *Successful Societies: Institutions, Cultural Repertories, and Health*, edited by Peter A. Hall and Michèle Lamont. Cambridge: Cambridge University Press.

Siddiqi, A. & Hertzman, C. 2001. "Economic Growth, Income Equality and Population Health among the Asian Tigers." *International Journal of Health Services* 31: 323–34.

Skocpol, Theda. 1992. *Protecting Soldiers and Mothers: The Political Origins of Social Policy in the United States*, Cambridge, MA: The Belknap Press of Harvard University Press.

Solzhenitsyn, Aleksandr. 1974. *The Gulag Archipelago: An Experiment in Literary Investigation*, translated by Thomas P. Whitney. New York: Harper and Row.

Somers, Margaret R. 2008. *Genealogies of Citizenship: Markets, Statelessness, and the Right to Have Rights*. New York: Cambridge University Press.

Stiglitz, Joseph E. 2002. *Globalization and Its Discontents*. New York: W. W. Norton.

Van Horn, Rob. 2009. "Reinventing Monopoly and the Role of Corporations: The Roots of Chicago Law and Economics." In *The Road From Mount Pelerin: The Making of the Neoliberal Thought Collective*, edited by Philip Mirowski and Dieter Plehwe. Cambridge, MA: Harvard University Press.

Williamson, John. 1990. "What Washington Means by Policy Reform." In *Latin American Adjustment: How Much Has Happened?* edited by John Williamson. Washington, DC: Institute for International Economics.

Williamson, John. 1999. "What Should the World Bank Think About the Washington
    Consensus?" Paper prepared as a background to the World Bank's World Develop-
    ment Report 2000.
Wong, Joseph. 2004. *Healthy Democracies: Welfare Politics in Taiwan and South
    Korea.* Ithaca, NY: Cornell University Press.
Zuberi, Dan. 2006. *Differences that Matter: Social Policy and the Working Poor in the
    United States and Canada.* Ithaca, NY: Cornell University Press/ILR Press.
Zuberi, Dan. 2010. *Outsourced: Neoliberalism and the Fate of Our Hospitals, Health
    Care Systems, and Societies.* Book manuscript in progress.

2

Narratives and Regimes of Social and Human Rights

The Jack Pines of the Neoliberal Era

Jane Jenson and Ron Levi

The Jack pine (*pin gris* in French) is an icon of Canadian art. It anchors the thin soil of the Canadian Shield even as it is subjected to harsh and howling winds. For some, its bent and twisted form is a sign of deformity. For others, it is a symbol of endurance. The social and human rights regimes are currently much like this Jack pine. Evaluated by some as deformed by neoliberalism, they are dismissed as incapable of promoting the values with which they were originally imbued. For others, these regimes continue to offer social resources to buffer neoliberal challenges. We see them as the equivalent of the Jack pine: through successive encounters with neoliberal institutions and actors, they have evolved, sometimes in dramatic ways, and in the process each developed new ways to anchor capacities for social resilience.

The history of these regimes is important for any consideration of the neoliberal era. International human rights are a central resource for social inclusion and well-being. They promise universal and inalienable protection of individuals and groups' dignity, key freedoms, and rights to fair treatment as well as participation. Any country's capacity to move these rights from paper to reality provides a resource for social resilience just as lack of respect for basic human rights curtails capabilities and life chances. Similarly, social rights and social protection are a fundamental resource on which people have drawn for more than a century. The direction that each regime has taken in the neoliberal era is thus essential to assessing the resources available to cope with the challenges coming from profound changes in social, economic, and political environments and in the narratives of social inclusion and recognition available to people.[1]

These are also regimes that share a long common history, including an overlapping understanding of their contributions to social resilience. Both human rights and social rights regimes emerged with the post-1945 construction of institutions intended to avoid the horrors of the interwar years. When the overarching document of the human rights regime was adopted in Paris in

---

[1] See Lamont, Welburn and Fleming, and Bouchard chapters (Chapters 4 and 9, respectively).

1948, the *Universal Declaration of Human Rights* incorporated articles 22 through 26 that gestured to the social rights that many industrialized countries were simultaneously engaged in extending to their citizens. In the 1960s, the international human rights regime centered on the United Nations (UN) was extended; this institutionalization brought the *International Covenant on Economic, Social and Cultural Rights*, voted by the General Assembly in 1966. The timing of this specification of the content of rights such those to social security, to form and join trade unions, to an adequate standard of living, and to education and health continued to track and correspond in historical time to the consolidation of welfare regimes in many countries. The first half of the 1960s was in many ways the zenith of social citizenship rights and the welfare regimes that housed them.[2] Then, just as their expansion had tracked each other, each regime was threatened by the discourse and politics of the neoliberal era.

When describing the cultural complex they call the new spirit of capitalism, Luc Boltanski and Ève Chiapello remind us "criticism is a catalyst for changes" and "enemies" are those who " ... provide it with the moral foundation that it lacks, and who enable it to incorporate justice-enhancing mechanisms whose relevancy it would not otherwise have to acknowledge" (2005: 163).[3] A similar dynamic is observable with respect to the cultural and political content of neoliberalism, conceptualized here (following Evans and Sewell in Chapter 1) as a broad range of cultural and political narratives and practices. Similar to Ancelovici (see Chapter 12) and Kymlicka (see Chapter 3), we examine the strategies of institutions as they respond to a changed universe of political discourse and institutional configuration.

Our claim is that as the two regimes encountered the institutions and ideologues of neoliberal politics, many of the actors who were their promoters learned to construct a new common sense, eventually mapping their own goals and concerns onto neoliberalism's broad cultural narrative. They developed accounts of individual and societal resilience, and this new common sense then helped actors shape understandings of their own mission and support for well-being. Indeed, we argue that as the regimes and their institutions evolved, they promoted new definitions of individual and societal resilience, echoing neoliberal discourses themselves.

Part I identifies three features of neoliberalism, present from its earliest years and going well beyond a simple economic analysis. Parts II and III then document the encounter of each regime with neoliberal institutions and ideas

---

[2] By the term "regime," we suggest two things: that discourses and practices have some stability over time and that elements exist in an ordered relation to each other as institutional arrangements, rules, and understandings that guide and shape problem definition, policy decisions, and claims making by citizens (Jenson 2008: 535). The literature identifies a "human rights regime" (Donnelly 1986). We also sometimes use the more widespread terminology of "welfare regime" to capture the congeries of narratives, practices, and institutions that form the social rights regime.

[3] This is an English summary of their book *Le nouvel esprit du capitalisme* published in 1999.

and the ways their cultural as well as political work allowed them to continue their mission. We find that in both, after an initial period of uncertainty about how to respond, key actors deployed strategies that mapped onto the cultural logics of neoliberal policy. Nonetheless, this process was not simply one of adoption, nor can the trajectories of these regimes be reduced to underlying structural mechanisms or to the mere force of neoliberal ideas. Instead, actors within these regimes adapted their practices and discourse to the changing political context in contingent fashion as they encountered dominant neoliberal institutions and actors. These regime actors opened new avenues for promoting social resilience. In the process, each regime conserved essential elements while actively redefining social resilience along dimensions that mapped onto the prevailing narratives of the neoliberal era.

Rights Regimes and Narratives of Neoliberalism

Neoliberalism targeted these two regimes. Neoliberals sought to ensure that the social and economic rights of the 1966 *Covenant* would not gain traction while initially seeking to limit commitments to individual human rights so as to give free rein to foreign policy. Neoliberals also identified what they saw as the disruptive effects of social protection for markets and individuals. Indeed, social policy was accused of creating dependency and undermining the resilience of individuals and families.

Yet both regimes fared better than such initial targeting would have predicted. Eventually, the international human rights regime enlarged its scope, gaining institutionalized leverage in areas that were previously unthinkable (e.g., punishing war crimes and genocide), and achieved significant institutionalization of economic, social, and cultural rights. Nor did the contraction of welfare regimes advocated by neoliberals occur: there is little evidence of reduced spending on social policy. Instead, they have been redesigned around new choices about rights and protections for vulnerable populations (Castles 2007: 2–3; Jenson 2010).

How might we understand these outcomes? For welfare regimes, a much-cited early explanation was that 30 or more years of government provision of pensions, social security, health care, and other social rights had generated stakeholders who mobilized politically in opposition to cuts, thereby mitigating them (Pierson 1998). It would be difficult, however, to apply such a generic explanation to the most recent redesigns in which there have been significant reduction of rights in some areas – especially pensions – but there have been significant new investments in other domains. Nor is a claim about powerful stakeholders acting to insulate and protect "their" human rights convincing, since beneficiaries rarely access the international institutions that oversee the human rights regime.

Our goal is to provide an alternative interpretation. We start from the position that neoliberalism provided a narrative of social and political relations. As Evans and Sewell make clear in describing neoliberals' social imaginary (see Chapter 1), it was not simply a critique of post-1945 economic policies. Margaret Thatcher summarized well the social relations and sources of social resilience imagined by early neoliberals: "By 'the healthy society' I mean a society in which the vast majority of men and women are encouraged, and helped, to accept responsibility for themselves and their families, and to live their lives with the maximum of independence and self-reliance."[4] In other words, neoliberals denigrated the notion that "... the state was both orchestrator and guarantor of the well-being of society and those who inhabited it ... " (Rose, O'Malley, and Valverde 2006: 91–2).

In place of the state, neoliberals advocated an alternative assemblage of techniques, experts, and institutions. Enthusiasm for local communities as more authentic than national states, for new instruments of governing focused on outcomes rather than inputs, and for the individualization of life risks, were neither randomly deployed nor limited to one policy domain. Nor were they a specific story of a particular country. Rather, they constitute an interconnected collection of ideas promoted by neoliberals domestically and internationally. We identify three central features of this assemblage as it had taken form by the 1990s.

A Shift in Scale and Sector

The neoliberal narrative discredited the national state's role and worked two shifts in scale, with responsibilities and authority moving both up and down the chain of governance. There was a scaling upward toward the *transnational* and *supranational*. Yet there was a parallel scaling downward toward the *local*, including an emphasis on the voluntary sector and on the role of "community."

One of the most visible results of the scaling upward was the consolidation of the supranational European Union with pooled sovereignty and an Economic and Monetary Union setting limits on member states' room for maneuver in public spending. Governments on several continents also concluded free trade agreements, thereby limiting their own actions in the name of freer markets. International economic institutions, such as the International Monetary Fund (IMF) and the World Bank actively intervened via their structural adjustment programs and imposed conditionality, thereby shaping the social as well as macroeconomic policies of national governments.

As supranational and international institutions were being built and strengthened, the *local* scale and sector were also, and sometimes by these same organizations, vaunted as the most legitimate scale of action.[5] Families, communities, schools, local governments, and nongovernmental organizations (NGOs) were identified as the ideal first responders. Certainly, the most common and well-known dimension of this shift in scale was the emergence of

---

[4] Speech to Social Services Conference Dinner, December 2, 1976. http://www.margaretthatcher. org/speeches/displaydocument.asp?docid=103161. In this same speech, she describes "industry, the basic social service," and the roles of the voluntary sector and self-help.

[5] On the European Union's support for the local scale, see, for example, Bradford (2004: 42–3).

a notion of "community" in the sense that " ... community is not simply the territory of government, but a *means* of government: its ties, bonds, forces, and affiliations are to be celebrated, encouraged, nurtured, shaped and instrumentalized in the hope of producing consequences that are desirable for all and for each" (Rose 1996: 355). The ambiguity of "community" provided much of its rhetorical and programmatic strength: sometimes emphasizing locality, sometimes stressing primordial bonds of affiliation, and still other times extolling a community of volunteers.

For decades, the voluntary sector with its multitudinous associations as well as trade unions and churches has been involved in the delivery of state-funded as well as private services. With the scale shift of neoliberalism, however, these relationships changed significantly, as " ... governments – in the UK, the USA and across much of Western Europe – have attempted to shift the focus towards various forms of co-production with other agencies and with citizens themselves through partnerships, community involvement and strategies of 'responsibilisation'" (Newman et al. 2004: 204). As the discourse about the inherent value of "community" gained ground, a new balance of political power followed; large national-level organizations as well as the state were displaced in favor of smaller, local (and less powerful) groups. This was as much the case in international politics – where there was an explosion of transnational NGOs that often bypassed national governments in favor of substate and local initiatives – as in countries where national governments made the scale shift themselves.

This turn to the local and to community-based organizations had consequences. One was the invention of a range of policy instruments such as compacts and alliances with the voluntary sector (White 2005). These were applied to relationships with NGOs in the Global South as well as the North. Another was the emergence of neighborhoods and villages as a primary locale of intervention, again in the South as well as the North. A third was devolution or "downloading" to lower levels of government, such as municipalities and other local authorities, often with insufficient resources (Levi and Valverde 2006). And fourth was the widespread enthusiasm for social capital.[6] Being essentially privately generated and often presented as an antidote to overly invasive states, communities "rich in social capital" were assumed capable of everything from providing better democratic government to fostering healthy neighborhoods and "opportunities for mutually beneficial collective action" in the poorest communities of the Global South (Woolcock 1998: 153 and passim).

Individualization of Risk, Reward, and Responsibility

A second cultural and political feature of neoliberalism is its narrative of the individual (see Evans and Sewell, Chapter 1). The image of the citizen in the

---

[6] For an overview of the enthusiasm for this discourse of social capital in the World Bank and its external and internal critiques, including the accusation it is "antipolitics," see Bebbington et al. (2002: 36ff.).

post-1945 decades drew extensively on tropes of social solidarity drawn from notions of either class solidarity or religious duty and sometimes both. By the 1970s, however, the uniformity of treatment these narratives had generated led to a revolt in the name of diversity and space for self-expression.

This critique of the state from the left opened a breach that neoliberals easily widened. They could transform 1960s and 1970s notions of "self-help" into their preferred vision of *entrepreneurial* citizens responsible for seeking out opportunities and avoiding risks for themselves, their families, and their communities (Evers 2009: 248). This entrepreneurialism and privatized risk management became "duties" of neoliberal citizenship: as Rose (1999: 145) describes the neoliberal position, "one can best fulfill one's obligations to one's nation by most effectively pursuing the enhancement of the economic well-being of oneself, one's family, one's firm, business or organization."

The citizen-consumers of neoliberalism were urged to actively actualize their life plans (Clarke et al. 2007). "Within this new regime of the actively responsible self, individuals are to fulfill their national obligations not through their relations of dependency and obligation to one another, but through seeking to *fulfil themselves* through a variety of micro-moral domains or 'communities' – families, workplaces, schools, leisure associations, neighbourhoods" (Rose 1999: 145). Whether by taking responsibility for their retirement pensions, avoiding the risks posed by cigarette smoking, or engaging in active aging, individuals were assigned not only moral but also financial responsibilities. This entrepreneurial but careful citizen was also exhorted, however, not to be too self-absorbed and to engage in volunteerism. Citizens were expected to play a part in ensuring the well-being of their communities.

New Governance: Alternative Expertise, Targets, and Measures

Greater recognition, acceptance, and indeed insistence on new types of experts and forms of expertise also characterized the neoliberal era. As ideas about "new public management" took hold, governments shed state employees in favor of consultants hired from the private sector to inculcate supposedly businesslike practices or financial management in government departments (Saint-Martin 1998). Cadres of consultants moved between contracts with the public sector, with NGOs, and with a variety of community groups. In addition, and following on notions of both self-help and the "entrepreneurial" citizen, citizens themselves saw their claims for expertise validated in the practices of community involvement.

Techniques of standardization and of transparency (labeled "technologies of performance" by Dean 1999: 168) underpinned enthusiasm for indicators and benchmarking and for forms of oversight such as audits (Power 1994). Performance indicators and benchmarking shift attention from *how* an output is achieved (e.g., public or private service, respect for rules, dignity of citizens, participation in decision making) to ask *whether* the outcome has been achieved. This question requires common metrics and notions of commensurability (Sauder and Espeland 2009). Audits, for their part, became essential as public funds were transferred to the private and third sector in the name of community and the public sector was enjoined to become more businesslike.

Of course, these strategies and instruments are by no means new, yet they proliferated and extended to new domains during the neoliberal era. Moreover, they have become discursive and organizational weapons to undermine Weberian-style state bureaucracies, characterized as hierarchal rather than flexible (as consultants supposedly are) or rule and procedure bound rather than outcome oriented (as indicators, benchmarking, and audits supposedly encourage). Thus, these techniques go hand in hand with – indeed, are essential to – general critiques of the state.

This assemblage has profoundly shaped the two regimes analyzed here. The next two sections examine each regime in these terms.

The Human Rights Regime and the Neoliberal Conjuncture

The human rights regime gained significant momentum before the neoliberal era. This was an effect of decolonization and the entry of new states into the UN (Clapham 2007: 49), and by powerful western states' growing enthusiasm, as signaled in President Carter's (1977) inaugural address, proclaiming that "our commitment to human rights must be absolute."

Given their emphasis on individual choice and rights-bearers, classically liberal human rights have obvious ideological compatibilities with neoliberalism (Merry 2006:103). Yet the neoliberal era opened with a conservative thrust, with anticommunist neoliberals such as Secretary of State Alexander Haig (*The New York Times* 28 January 1981: A10), Elliot Abrams as assistant secretary of state for Human Rights and Humanitarian Affairs (Neier 2003: 186), and Jeane Kirpatrick as U.S. Ambassador to the UN, launching attacks on human rights as hamstringing U.S. foreign policy (Kirkpatrick 1979: 34; 1981: 331–32). This conservatism soon gave way, however, with human rights being adopted as a tool for Soviet containment (Jacoby 1986: 1067). Yet this early resistance had effects. Support for human rights was redefined as an instrument for democracy promotion and other foreign policy goals (Guilhot 2005). Elliot Abrams termed it a "human rights policy that people could believe in as Reaganites" (Sikkink 2004: 156).

Neoliberals, furthermore, were consistently opposed to economic, social, and cultural rights, making a sharp distinction between them and the civil and political rights they were willing to accept.[7] Such opposition brought more precariousness throughout the 1980s (Alston 1990: 374), and except for isolated instances, U.K. and U.S. skepticism over economic and social rights persisted throughout the neoliberal era (Alston 2009).[8]

---

[7] This built on classic liberal divisions of the nineteenth century but stood in contrast to the Universal Declaration of Human Rights that defines all rights as "indivisible" (Donnelly 2003: 28).

[8] Canadian support for human rights was "one of timidity and often appalling indifference" (Gordon 1983: 8).

Internationally, the broad project of human rights was also disputed during the neoliberal era. The regime's norms were challenged by developing countries, which denigrated them as culturally specific and inextricably linked with colonialism (Donnelly 2003: chapter 6). The first Human Rights Conference since 1968 convened in 1993 in Vienna and was marked by Asian and developing states' accusations of Western cultural imperialism. The conference heard concerns that the West "sought to use human rights as a stalking horse to achieve global economic dominance over the developing and poorer world" (Boyle 1995: 84).

Yet during this same period, the human rights regime grew, with an expansion of human rights norms, a proliferation of NGOs and institutions monitoring human rights compliance, and the shift from a declaratory regime to increasing enforcement (Donnelly 2003: Figure 8.1). Prominent examples include Human Rights Watch, which began as Helsinki Watch in 1978, and Americas Watch during the Reagan administration in 1981; the UN Office of the High Commissioner for Human Rights (OHCHR) in 1993; and the emergence in 1993 of international tribunals to prosecute atrocities, the first since the Nürnberg and Tokyo War Crimes Tribunals. Prominent media also increased their attention to human rights, with an expansion of institutions and individuals working in the field expanded during the neoliberal heyday of the 1980s. Further growth followed the Cold War (Elliott 2008; Hafner-Burton and Ron 2009).

The human rights regime thus saw "monumental" change during the neoliberal era (Moyn 2010: 218–19). Next we trace how the regime expanded while coming to match the cultural logic of neoliberalism and how these changes have also come to provide somewhat greater resources for social inclusion and the capacity for delivering well-being.

Individualization of Risk, Reward, and Responsibility

The human rights regime is founded on a premise of liberal individual rights bearers. But over the past 20 years, there has been a shift to assigning individuals *responsibility* for managing their risks and rewards as rights holders. Perhaps unexpectedly, this match to neoliberalism's cultural logic supports the regime's expansion into previously blocked domains, most notably by underwriting the link between human rights and development and by assigning criminal liability to individuals for human rights violations.

An Active Rights Claimer for Development

Discussion of a "right to development" began as decolonization brought new states into the UN (Kirchmeier 2006: 8). At the Tehran Conference on Human Rights in 1968, attention turned on consequences of development failures for human rights, but in the 1980s, neoliberal governments opposed making links between rights and development. The Reagan administration rejected it as an attempt to produce a New International Economic Order (Marks 2004: 143), to legitimate economic, social, and cultural rights and as the "antithesis of a large part of its foreign policy" in Eastern Europe and the Third World (Alston 1988: 22). Nonetheless, in 1986, a right to development was affirmed by the General Assembly with the United States dissenting, and in the late 1980s, advocates opened dialogue over the human rights implications of structural adjustment measures (Alston 1988: 16–17).

For neoliberals, the focus was on civil and political rights within developing countries.[9] In 1991, the UN Development Program Administrator, William Draper (1991)[10] said to the General Assembly:

We have defined human development as 'a process of enlarging the range of people's choices.' Income is only one of those choices. . . . The most basic choice for any individual is the freedom to make a choice. Freedom is thus an integral part of the concept of human development. If a society represses its people, it also represses their creativity and motivation and thus its growth rate and its human progress. It is not surprising, therefore, that there is a close link – with very few exceptions, between human development and human freedom.

The possible synergies between development and human rights seemed limited, with different actors working within each field (Jonsson 2005: 47; Robinson 2007: 301–02). Yet even the most enthusiastic neoliberal institutions were recasting the link between human rights, poverty, and development. In 1991, the World Bank's General Counsel asserted "its staff increasingly realize that human needs are not limited to the material 'basic needs' often emphasized in the 1970s" and that "no balanced development can be achieved without the realization of a minimum degree of all human rights" (Shihata 1991: 133), a position maintained under James Wolfensohn's presidency of the World Bank (Sarfaty 2009: 660). The United Nations Development Program (UNDP) (2000) considered the language of rights provided development arguments with greater "moral legitimacy," with Amartya Sen writing the conceptual framework on "human rights and human development" (Frankovitz 2006: 19).

Expertise and knowledge generated in the development field traveled to human rights (Sarfaty 2009). Publications presented a framework of rights-holders who made *claims* (Sengupta 2000). Former UN High Commissioner for Human Rights Mary Robinson referred to "convergence of thinking between the human rights agenda and the World Bank agenda. The bridge is built" (Robinson 2007: 307). The UN Committee on Economic, Social and Cultural Rights emphasized the importance of "active and informed participation" by the poor (United Nations Economic and Social Council 2001) as did the High

---

[9] During the Cold War, there was whole-scale opposition to human rights in the development context (Donnelly 2003: 196–8).

[10] During the Reagan administration, Draper headed the U.S. Export-Import Bank (Margolis 1986).

Commissioner who emphasized the link between rights, empowerment, and poverty reduction (Robinson 2007: 130).

The result has been some traction, even if limited, on a right to development. Although the content of this right has never been well-defined (Kirchmeier 2006), the United States no longer objects, although it interprets it as "each individual should enjoy the right to develop his or her intellectual or other capacities to the maximum extent possible through the exercise of the full range of civil and political rights" (Commission of Human Rights 2005).

The OHCHR has more recently provided intellectual scaffolding linking human rights to development. Its position is that "a rights-based development outlook views people as active claimants of their rights, rather than passive beneficiaries of charitable works or government services" (OHCHR 2010), further quoting an NGO activist stating that "rights enshrined in national and international laws and treaties are not automatically enforced, they are realized through the actions of citizens" (OHCHR 2008: 34).

Overall, we thus see the building of a right to development through an emphasis on active citizens who demand and set the terms of their rights, resonating with and calling forth responsibilized and entrepreneurial citizens of neoliberalism.[11]

Human Rights and Criminalization

Perhaps the most significant change in international human rights is the emphasis on human rights *enforcement* through individual criminal responsibility. This turn to individuals rather than states includes the 1998 arrest of Augusto Pinochet in London; the first indictment of a sitting head of state, Slobodan Milošević, in 1999; and the creation of the International Criminal Court in 2002. Emphasizing criminal liability demonstrates a shift in thinking about war and atrocities toward a model of individual accountability rather than group conflict or state violence. As stated in the first annual report of the International Criminal Tribunal for the Former Yugoslavia (1994: 12), "If responsibility for the appalling crimes perpetrated in the former Yugoslavia is not attributed to individuals, then whole ethnic and religious groups will be held accountable for these crimes...."

Criminalizing individuals for human rights violations certainly predates the neoliberal era, with the current "justice cascade" linked to trials that began in domestic jurisdictions in mid-1970s Latin America, taking off from 1987 onward (Lutz and Sikkink 2001; Sikkink and Walling 2007). Yet during the neoliberal era, NGO groups such as Human Rights Watch were critical

---

[11] This resonates with an emphasis on individual "human rights defenders" since the 1990s. When Liu Xiaobo was awarded the 2010 Nobel Peace Prize, the presentation said "the human rights activists in China are defenders of the international order and the main trends in the global community."

promoters of this international turn to criminalization (Dezalay and Garth 2006: 248; Korey 1998: 309).

The notion of criminal accountability increases access to the domain of human rights during conflict. The perception that the human rights regime is powerless, which was particularly acute in the wake of atrocities in the Balkans and Rwanda, is declining (Sikkink 2009: 122–4). Thus, when learning of the indictment of Sudanese President Omar al-Bashir, the UN Secretary-General said it would "have very serious consequences for peacekeeping operations including the political process. I'm very worried, but nobody can evade justice" (Blair 2008).

Performance Indicators and Target-Based Government

As with global governance generally (Davis, Kingsbury, and Merry 2010), the past twenty years witnessed "an emerging market in human rights indicators" (Rosga and Satterthwaite 2009: 255). During the Carter administration, there was research on how to produce rights data for foreign policy efforts (de Neufville 1982: 385; Barsh 1993: 98). This continued through the 1980s, appearing in World Bank Reports, U.S. State Department country reports, and institutions such as Freedom House (Sano and Lindholt 2000: 58). These methods traveled from the U.S. policy realm to neoliberal actors in the international human rights regime: in 1991, the UNDP produced a "Human Freedom Index" in its *Human Development Report* followed by the World Bank's *World Development Report* that relied on a human rights index to articulate the relationship between freedom and growth (UNDP 1991; World Bank 1991).

The UNDP (1991: 21) concluded that "political freedom seems to have unleashed the creative energies of the people – and led to ever higher levels of income and social progress." This Human Freedom Index unleashed a firestorm because it identified the poorest countries as the least free. Speaking on behalf of the Group of 77 developing countries, the Ambassador for Ghana railed against supposedly universal standards of human rights that were culturally specific and Western. The Group of 77 questioned the very attempt to produce standardization and rankings, and the political motivation for the UNDP's claim that "the lack of political commitment, not of financial resources, is often the real cause of human neglect" (Barsh 1993: 88). Faced with a General Assembly Resolution suggesting that the UNDP reconsider its efforts, these indicators were replaced by narrower "political freedom indicators," and country scores and rankings were replaced with simple aggregations of countries into groups (Barsh 1993: 89–90).

For its part, however, the Committee on Economic, Social and Cultural Rights began to *emphasize* indicators of economic and social rights. Fearing state backlash that they could not afford the cost of such rights, in advance of the 1993 Vienna Conference, the Committee suggested states should monitor their own progress. States might argue that they could not afford to fully guarantee positive rights, but they were barred from arguing they could not afford to monitor their progress. It thereby imposed on states a duty to monitor their own progress rather than generating standard measures. Secondly, because there was concern that social and economic rights were too indeterminate for quantitative indicators, the model shifted from standardized *indicators* to a focus on progress and *benchmarking* (Rosga and Satterthwaite 2009: 272–3). The Committee, in turn, took on the second-order role of monitoring state-level progress rather than developing universal indicators of how the rights should be enjoyed (Merry 2009).

This approach was soon paralleled by others. The UNDP (2000) ventured back into human rights measurement in its 2000 Report *Human Rights and Human Development* (Sano and Lindholt 2000: 61). In contrast to the early 1990s, the measures now included economic and social as well as civil and political rights. Mirroring the Committee on Economic, Social and Cultural Rights, the UNDP suggested that the way forward was to focus on national measures of human rights compliance. Countries would be less politically resistant to nationally driven reports, and the UNDP (2000: 113) further noted that external measurements largely ignore economic and social rights and thus "can distort the reality of human rights struggles" by "making human rights appear to be an issue of the 'West versus the rest.'" In place of country rankings, it emphasized benchmarks for states to assess *progress* on rights. Indicators would underlie benchmarks, but the focus would shift away from determining whether a right was protected toward incremental process and context.

Benchmarking is now taken up as a general approach. To assist states in this process, the OHCHR (2006) is developing illustrative indicators for all types of rights – civil, political, economic, social, and cultural – stressing in turn their *indivisibility and interdependence*. Importing a model developed for the right to health (Hunt 2003), states provide data on their *commitment* and their *efforts*, as well as the *results* achieved. This allows states to produce "a kind of 'performance profile' that reflects its context, efforts and outcomes," and allows treaty bodies to rely on them "for monitoring compliance of State parties with international human rights instruments" (OHCHR 2006: 13). Key to the OHCHR's approach is that it explicitly rejects comparing countries and simply provides *illustrative* indicators for each right. In this way, the lens is increasingly focused on a "progressive realization" of rights that is historically identified with economic, social, and cultural rights rather than an absolutist view of rights compliance (Green 2001: 1070–1).

The reemergence of human rights indicators has thus produced benchmarking for states and greater monitoring capacity for treaty bodies. The argument that human rights are inherently incapable of translation into meaningful indicators has been largely abandoned, and benchmarking now produces an incremental approach to achieving rights rather than a formal legalistic one. There is greater agreement that at minimum, illustrative indicators can be distilled; that states have a duty to monitor progress; and that this monitoring encompasses economic and social rights and civil and political rights.

A Shift in Scale and Sector

The human rights regime has experienced two separate but complementary shifts in scale. At the level of compliance there has been a scalar shift upward, with centralization of human rights oversight, monitoring of national legislation and practices, and the strengthening of international legal enforcement. There has also been a scalar shift downward for human rights promotion toward the nongovernmental sector. These scalar shifts have underwritten significant change in the international human rights regime.

At the international level, the regime is strengthened. Where in the 1970s it was largely "promotional," it now seeks to monitor practices, enforce binding legal norms, and sanction human rights violations (Donnelly 2003: Table 8.1). One sign of this shift is that human rights treaty bodies gained enforcement and implementation capacities during the neoliberal era (Buergenthal 1997), adopting through the 1980s and 1990s a more adjudicative and quasi-judicial stance in "general comments" and "concluding observations" that provide an analysis and elaboration of by the Committee regarding treaty obligations (Steiner 2000: 50).

The scalar shift upward is also apparent in the 1993 creation of the Office of the High Commissioner for Human Rights, meant to remove obstacles worldwide to the realization of human rights (UN General Assembly 1993; Robinson 2007). The Office is the UN's central authority on human rights, intended to play an active role in preventing human rights violations, and the High Commissioner is "at the apex of the United Nations Human Rights system" (Flood 1998: 119).

This scalar shift is further apparent in regional human rights regimes. Created in 1959, the European Court of Human Rights (ECHR) had rendered only 17 decisions by 1977 (Gearty 1993: 90), from which states could exempt themselves (Donnelly 2003: 139). Judges of the ECHR delivered landmark decisions through the late 1970s and early 1980s that took advantage of the changing geopolitics of the era to entrench the European human rights regime (Madsen 2007). Through the 1980s and 1990s, the ECHR's caseload grew rapidly, and it became a supervisory court for all European contracting parties. Procedures were changed, allowing individuals to apply to the ECHR directly. Receiving nearly 60,000 applications and issuing more than 1,500 binding annual rulings (Council of Europe 2010), the ECHR has become "the most active rights-protecting jurisdiction in the world" (Stone Sweet 2009: 4).

Accompanying this upward movement is increased reliance on international and transnational NGOs. NGOs were part of the UN human rights regime from the outset (Charnowitz 1996; Korey 1999: 152–3) but through the 1970s were viewed with antipathy by member states across the political spectrum (Pei-Heng 1981: 193). Even at the 1993 Vienna Conference on Human Rights, Arab and Asian states sought to exclude NGOs from official sessions (Otto 1996: 119).

Yet human rights NGOs flourished in the neoliberal era, spurred by neoliberal narratives. NGOs were "championed by numerous international actors as the voice of the people and vehicles of private initiative," and NGOs were increasingly regarded as necessary "to be a properly functioning free market and democratic nation" (Reimann 2006: 59). The number of human rights organizations grew by more than 300 percent between 1973 and 1993, with the plurality of transnational social movement organizations focusing on human rights (Smith 1997: 47). In the 1990s, the cumulative number of times NGOs were mentioned in official human rights instruments surpassed other organizations (Elliott 2008: 155). By marshalling their position as outside of state structures, NGOs have successfully articulated new norms such as the Convention on the Rights of the Child (Korey 1998: 228), and become partners in committees such as the Economic and Social Council (Willetts 2000). The Human Rights Committee, the oldest treaty monitoring body in the UN, has relied heavily on the work of human rights NGOs from the late 1980s. This included signal briefings by the Lawyers Committee for Human Rights and Amnesty International on human rights violations in Colombia in the mid 1990s and quieter initiatives by Amnesty International addressing human rights in peacekeeping operations (Korey 1998: 270, 300). By the early 1990s, "nongovernmental organisations essentially serve[d] as unofficial researchers to [treaty body] committee members, rendering invaluable aid in place of the understaffed, poorly-financed secretariat" (Gaer 1995: 394).

Political change in Europe also allowed NGOs to gain greater recognition. In the wake of post–Cold War political change, the Organization for Security and Co-operation in Europe (OSCE) worked with organizations such as Amnesty International and Human Rights Watch (Wangborg 1995: 395–9). Already identified as important in the 1990 Charter of Paris for a New Europe, by 1999 the Istanbul Charter for European Security noted that "non-governmental organizations (NGOs) can perform a vital role in the promotion of human rights, democracy and the rule of law.... We pledge ourselves to enhance the ability of NGOs to make their full contribution to the further development of civil society and respect for human rights and fundamental freedoms" (OSCE 2007: 47–8).

Complementing this shift toward NGOs, the human rights regime now emphasizes country-based field offices for rights promotion and protection. This began in El Salvador in 1991, and the OHCHR now maintains a presence in more than 50 countries to monitor human rights and build local capacity for rights reforms (Horowitz 2010: 30; O'Flaherty 2007: 8; O'Flaherty and Ulrich 2010: 5). The OHCHR (2009) thus emphasizes work done with local governments, civil society groups, and regional and subregional institutions.

From Retrenchment to Social Investment: Narratives of Social Rights

Welfare regimes were also a priority target of neoliberals, who castigated them as overly generous and blamed them for excessive state spending and budget deficits. But neoliberals' greatest wrath was reserved for their supposed cultural effects.

This was a clear change from the interwar and post-1945 years, when theorists and advocates of social programs (e.g., T. H. Marshall, Alma and Gunnar Myrdal, and Lord Beveridge as well as trade unions and left-wing and Christian Democratic political parties) had seen liberating possibilities in social rights. State-supported health coverage, public pension regimes, universal secondary and tertiary education, and family allowances would provide citizens with protection from life risks by limiting hardship and increasing well-being (Goodin et al. 1999: chapter 1). Thus, social rights were interpreted as fostering the resilience of individuals and families. Moreover, a postwar consensus shared by Keynesian economists and social policy experts described a virtuous circle in the relationship among economic growth, expanding social rights, and democratic politics: "In the era of the 'Keynesian consensus' there was no perceived trade-off between social security and economic growth, between equality and efficiency" (Esping-Andersen 1999: 3). Societal resilience was thereby considered to be enhanced by the existence of social rights.

Neoliberals turned these claims on their head. In addition to the familiar critiques of interference with the market and the inefficiencies and lack of productivity of public bureaucracies, neoliberals sketched a set of cultural effects. Social programs, whether social assistance, disability pensions, or early retirement, were accused of sapping the work ethic, generating "a cycle of dependence" rather than individual responsibility, and promoting submission to bureaucratic fiat and social control rather than citizens' autonomy.[12]

A third source of difficulty for advocates of standard post-1945 welfare regimes in the face of neoliberal critiques was, of course, the political economy of those same decades. Monetarism began to displace Keynesianism and by the 1980s had gained particular political resonance with neoliberal political forces such as the British Conservatives (Hall 1993) and international institutions promoting structural adjustments. High rates of inflation as well as the portion of gross domestic product going to public social spending in some European countries seemed to give credence to analyses that acquired social rights were a threat to a sound political economy. Cutbacks were promised in national political campaigns across Europe as well as in North America and were promoted by international organizations such as the Organisation for Economic Cooperation and Development (OECD), the World Bank, and the IMF in what became known as the Washington Consensus of the 1980s and 1990s.

In this context, certain analysts identified retrenchment and permanent austerity as the only real options. They observed that popular political support for welfare regimes continued to be high *and* institutional "stickiness" existed (this was the influential argument of Pierson 1998: 551ff). At the same time, however, other experts were painting a somewhat different portrait of the situation. They had begun to observe the emergence, by the mid 1990s, of a

---

[12] Pierson (1991: 48) summarizes six theses of neoliberalism that critiqued welfare regimes. See also Evans and Sewell (Chapter 1) and Bouchard (Chapter 9).

social policy response to standard neoliberalism, one they labeled the "social investment perspective," and that could contribute to rebuilding capacities for social resilience.[13]

This perspective on the conditions individuals, families, and societies need in order to be resilient gained traction within some of the very institutions that had been the most vociferous and early supporters of neoliberalism. The OECD, for example, was a fervent proponent of neoliberal style interventions in the 1980s and early 1990s but by mid-decade began to be very concerned about social cohesion, instability, and the social and political costs of its proposals for structural adjustments. The 1996 high-level conference, *Beyond 2000: The New Social Policy Agenda*, concluded with a call for a "new framework for social policy reform," labeled a "social investment approach," in which "the challenge was to ensure that return to social expenditures were maximised, in the form of social cohesion and active participation in society and the labour market" (OECD, 1997: 5–6). Similarly, the 1997 *World Development Report* refocused the World Bank's attention, innovating in its systematic and comprehensive attempt to show that an "effective – not minimal – state" was vital for economic development, enabling markets *and* addressing social issues.[14] National governments, such as Britain's after the 1997 election of New Labour, as well as the European Union engaged in preparing the Lisbon Agenda of 2000, sidelined standard neoliberalism, claiming instead that social spending was a productive factor rather than simply an economic burden (Jenson 2010: 72). At the international level, the United Nations Children's Fund (UNICEF) confronted the Washington Consensus head on in the name of social investments and children.[15] It advanced its analyses of the effect of policy choices by tracing rising poverty under neoliberalism for children in both rich countries and the developing world (UNICEF 2000).[16]

Over time, there was a rising popularity of policies and instruments, such as childcare, human capital investments, and active labor market policy, all identified as useful for tamping down some of the inequality that had emerged during the neoliberal era. As Esping-Andersen wrote (1999: 3):

Critics insist that the associated social costs of the American route [to high employment with high inequality] are too high in terms of polarization and poverty. They suggest a "social investment" strategy as an alternative. Rather than draconian roll-backs,

---

[13] For discussions of the emergence of this perspective, see Jenson and Saint-Martin (2006). For an overview, see Morel, Palier, and Palme (2012).

[14] http://siteresources.worldbank.org/INTWDRS/Resources/WDR_Summaries_4DC3.pdf, p. 4.

[15] The UN agency that many thought could – and should – confront the Washington Consensus was the United Nations Development Programme (UNDP), but it chose not to do so. "UNDP's low profile left the job of directing the public battle of ideas to UNICEF" (Murphy 2006: 227; also 223ff.).

[16] UNICEF documented a huge rise in child poverty in the United Kingdom during the Thatcherist years. As it wrote at the end of the 1990s: "A fifth of Britain's children lived in poverty in the 1990s. . . . And while child poverty has remained stable or risen only slightly in most industrial nations over the last 20 years, it tripled in Britain" (UNICEF 2000: 21).

the idea is to redirect social policy from its current bias in favour of passive income maintenance towards active labour market programmes that "put people back to work," help households harmonize work and family obligations, and train the population in the kinds of skills that postindustrial society demands.

This social investment perspective deploys the three narrative features of the neoliberal assemblage but reworks them to serve ends other than simple market protection and family responsibility. The next subsections describe the move from standard neoliberalism's critiques of social rights toward the responses by advocates of modernized social rights. The reworking and matching with neoliberalism generated by these responses has become a major factor in ensuring the resilience of the regimes themselves, saving them from the wrath of voters as well as neoliberal politicians and providing the kind of social supports that allow several categories of individuals and families to maintain or even increase their well-being.

Individualization of Risk, Reward, and Responsibility

Social rights were a particular target of neoliberals who developed strong critiques. In liberal welfare regimes, including Britain, Canada, and the United States, social assistance was a key and visible expression of social rights, and it quickly came under attack from those who claimed that it created "welfare traps" that both discouraged work effort and provided little real help to the poor.[17]

But political parties and public administrations in corporatist and social-democratic welfare regimes also undertook a neoliberal cure. Perhaps most interesting, given the high level of commitment to universalism in post-1945 decades, was the move in Sweden in the 1980s towards emphasizing individual rather than collective choice and public responsibility for benefit levels, termed the "choice revolution" (Blomqvist 2004). These efforts, often implemented by Social Democrats, resulted in the so-called Third Road approach, explicitly defined as a route "between Keynesian reflation and Thatcherite austerity policies" (Stephens 1999: 44). For example, more of the "risk" of ageing, traditionally covered in welfare regimes by pensions, was reassigned to individuals, whose own past contributions and savings would determine their income after retirement. Although a basic – and quite generous – public pension remained, Sweden's pension system was radically overhauled, clearly assigning responsibility for the total level of pension benefit to one's own contributions over a life of employment. "This marks a move away from Sweden's tradition of allocating benefits as a matter of rights relatively independent of contributions...." (Esping-Andersen 1999: 13–14; see also Stephens 1999: 43–51). Nonetheless, this Third Road approach proposed by Sweden's Social Democrats differed

---

[17] For a comparative overview of Canada and the United States during the height of neoliberalism, see Myles (1999).

from standard neoliberalism, in which the virtual elimination of publicly provided pensions was the objective.

Social democratic welfare regimes also sought to raise employment rates by
lowering tax rates and redesigning labor policy to foster and support individuals' employability and job seeking. This was a sign that advocates of the social
investment perspective were in many ways matching their policy prescriptions
to the ideas of neoliberalism, albeit proposing less hard-nosed and more supportive ways of promoting "work for all." For example, the "work approach"
was developed to replace passive benefits in Norway. Also in this category is the
much vaunted "flexicurity" of Denmark, whose Social Democratic–led government beginning in 1994 undertook widespread reform of all aspects of labor
markets, from benefits to training. "This activation orientation implies that
the public sector is responsible for giving the unemployed more opportunities
for work and training, and the unemployed are obliged to accept these offers"
(Kosonen 2001: 166–7). This approach has been taken up by the European
Commission as appropriate across the Union.[18]

A policy instrument that became particularly popular within the social
investment perspective is the in-work benefit.[19] In essence, governments recognize that the labor market is incapable of generating sufficient income to
combat poverty and that the number of working poor is on the rise. "Any job"
was not good enough to keep families, especially those with children, above the
poverty line. Therefore, and in the name of investing in children, governments
in the late 1990s and 2000s innovated by providing supplements to earned
income, usually in the form of tax credits. Sometimes, as in Canada and the
United States, they were targeted to families with children and provided the
most support to families with some level of earned income.[20] Sometimes all
low-income workers might receive the transfers as in Britain's Working Tax
Credit or France's in-work benefit.

In the Global South, policymakers adhering to the social investment perspective promoted a new policy instrument, the conditional cash transfer (CCT).
Their focus was on providing extreme poor and poor households with a minimum consumption floor, conditional on using education and health services

---

[18] According to the European Union, "Flexicurity is an integrated strategy for enhancing, at the
same time, flexibility and security in the labour market. It attempts to reconcile employers' need
for a flexible workforce with workers' need for security – confidence that they will not face long
periods of unemployment." See http://ec.europa.eu/social/main.jsp?catId=102&langId=en.

[19] "In-work benefits (also called employment-conditional benefits) are a central element in 'Making Work Pay' strategies, which can be seen as efforts to tailor employment-friendly social policies with aims of simultaneously alleviating family poverty and boosting employment.... these
benefits are paid only to persons who have taken up a full-time or part-time job. The IWB
programs are established primarily with a view to reduce benefit dependency and increase
employment" (Leppik 2006: 2).

[20] These were the tax credits associated with the National Child Benefit in Canada and the Earned
Income Tax Credit in the United States.

for children.[21] "Putting cash in the hands of poor people (especially families and women) we are told, is an effective means to use resources to build human capital and prevent the generational transmission of poverty" (St-Clair 2009: 177). This instrument actually provides families with some certainty and therefore the capacity to manage risk responsibly, in contrast to forms of aid that tended to be driven by contingent events, such as food crises or the availability of donors.

As other social policies and programs, CCTs are meant to increase resilience via the notion of "co-responsibility." Individuals must be "responsible risk takers," whether in their work life, family life, or managing their health (Evers 2009: 255). But the responsibility is not one way. CCTs impose "conditionalities [that] are meant to ensure household investment in schooling and health care, and co-responsibilities of service providers to reduce exclusion" (Barrientos 2009: 166). This notion that resilience must be supported via state action distinguishes the social investment approach to the individualization of risk and responsibility from that of the standard liberalism of the 1980s. As noted, neoliberals acknowledge little role for the state in supporting self-reliance. In contrast, in 2002, Tony Blair summarized his social investment strategy as directed toward aiding those lacking sufficient training and skills (e.g., lone parents, long-term unemployed individuals, and people with disabilities), but in the Prime Minister's view, if government programs provided support for learning and childcare, it also became individuals' responsibility to accept basic skill training if they needed it and then to look for work.[22] Co-responsibility became the norm, reflecting the uptake and reworking of an important trope of the neoliberal narrative.

A Shift in Scale and Sector

As part of their rejection of the state – and especially the "nanny state" so vilified by British Conservatives – neoliberals singled out the community and voluntary sector to fill the gap and provide support for those in need. The voluntary sector in the North and NGOs in the Global South working in and with local communities were often enthusiastically identified as better able to deliver social services than the state. This emphasis on decentralization and community was retained as the social investment perspective took shape. One good example is from the practices of Britain's New Labour after 1997. *Sure Start* was a neighborhood-based program for poor children and their mothers intended to end the intergenerational transmission of poverty. Notions of social investment led to ideas about the advantages of targeting places of

---

[21] For the details of CCT programs worldwide through 2008, see Fizbein and Schady (2009: 214ff). For a more critical view see Molyneux (2006).

[22] "PM Speech on welfare reform," available at http://webarchive.nationalarchives.gov.uk/20091006031459/number10.gov.uk/page1716. Consulted on 24 September 2010.

disadvantage for older children as well. Educational Action Zones were instituted as public–private partnerships to provide alternative approaches to learning, and Excellence in Cities targeted funds to teachers and welfare workers,
that is "joined-up governing" in inner cities (Dobrowolsky and Jenson 2005:
212).[23]

Retaining neoliberalism's focus on the local scale has consequences for the
social investment perspective. There has been a reconfiguration of responsibility among levels of government and sectors (public, private, and third sectors,
sometimes termed NGOs). Between 1998 and 2001, six national governments
signed formal accords with their voluntary sectors to organize the involvement
of the voluntary sector in service delivery as well as governance (White 2005).
These were all part of an effort to normalize the relationship rather than simply "downloading" new responsibilities on voluntary associations. New governance arrangements were both proposed and instituted based on networks,
partnerships, deliberative forums, and government efforts to activate broad
alliances (Evers 2009: 255).

One example among many is the Toronto City Summit Alliance, which
serves an umbrella for public–private cooperation. Its *Strong Neighbourhood
Task Force* was launched by the city in partnership with United Way and
called for collaboration of all three levels of government with the voluntary
sector, targeting social service improvements in neighborhoods with growing
needs. The resulting strategy advocated "a system to take all publicly owned
facilities and real estate into consideration for strengthening the social service
infrastructure of investment neighbourhoods, including common public assets
like school buildings for after-hour programs."[24]

Approaches to poverty and to social cohesion with a model of multilevel
governance and "convening the community" are also found in the European
Union's governance practices (Bradford 2004). Scale shift can be both down
to the community and up to the supranational, the latter shift often calling
forth a whole series of transnational actors, such as the European Anti-Poverty
Network and others whose scale of action for matters of social investment is
the supranational (Zeitlin and Pochet 2005: chapter 10).

Scale shift and reliance on several sectors is not unique to the North. In
the Global South as well, themes of community focus and community control
resonate. In Brazil, for example, the administration of the CCT involves multiple scales. The creation of a unified federal information system as a central
registry organized by the federal government made the *Bolsa Família* possible.
Municipal social workers enter families into the registry, and the computerized data are available to them. In other countries with more fragile public

---

[23] Another innovative approach to emphasizing the local context of interventions for child development is found in British Columbia (Guhn, Janus, and Hertzman 2007; see also Chapter
10).

[24] See http://www.torontoalliance.ca/tcsa_initiatives/strong_neighbourhoods/, consulted 24 September 2010. For other examples see Bradford (2004).

administrations, local administrators rely on local knowledge to identify beneficiaries. Cambodia's program "... dispenses with the cadre of field worker/social workers who often administer the instrument. Instead, students fill out the program application/proxy means test form in school. Then the teacher reads the information aloud and the classmates help verify/certify that it is correct" (Fizbein and Schady 2009: 71). As important as the involvement of the private sector; many CCTs are deposited in beneficiaries' bank accounts, and they are encouraged to rely on up-to-date technology, such as micro-chip cards, which the banks must agree to distribute to them. One effect is to increase the amount of money in circulation in smaller villages and regions, thereby supporting the local commerce and small businesses.

Changing Governance of the Social: Alternative Expertise, Targets, and Measures

This third narrative feature of neoliberalism, adopted and adapted by regimes of social rights as they incorporate the social investment perspective, involves a redefinition of governance practices in the realm of the social. Traditional welfarism was criticized from both the right and left for its emphasis on top-down and rigid bureaucratic forms. Discourses of empowerment developed in the 1970s often gave rise to user committees of various sorts (social housing residents, disability rights, social assistant recipients, and so forth) that sought to displace bureaucratic authority and emphasize the capacities of users for making their own decisions. It was then easy for neoliberals to take up such tropes, stressing the expertise of the users of services over the bureaucratic providers: "the various meanings of empowerment shifted from issues of 'voice' to issues of 'choice'" (Evers 2009: 253). Such criticisms then helped anchor neoliberalism's emphasis on market choices as the most legitimate way for meeting social needs. Citizen-consumers were called on to exercise their own capacity for choice in selecting services, whether provided privately, by NGOs, or by the state. The neoliberal movement in the Global South as much as the North, as Cornwall and Gaventa (2000) say, promoted "users and choosers."

The new public management so popular among neoliberals called for governments to *steer*, not *row*, using forms for service delivery such as contracting out, partnerships, privatization, and so on. The preference for "less state" encouraged governments to shed policy capacity, seeking to replace it with the input of both *expert* (consultants) and *experiential* knowledge (voluntary organizations and citizens).[25] The push for increased accountability was translated by an emphasis on outcome measurement and an explosion of auditing of third-party contracts and contribution agreements. In theory, such accountability might provide a role for citizens as watchdogs, but as Orsini and Phillips

---

[25] The literature on the citizen jury, citizen forum, citizen engagement, and various other modes of citizen involvement in policy choice is large. For one overview see Orsini and Phillips (2004).

(2004: 5) observed of this "audit explosion," sometimes audit reports communicate little but the fact that the audit was done.

Nonetheless, and despite initial skepticism, new forms of knowledge and experts are part of the social investment perspective within which consultations, audits, and benchmarking are popular. Participatory budgeting is one example of this move toward more responsive state action after experiencing neoliberal market excesses. Begun in Porto Alegre, Brazil, at the beginning of the 1990s, it " ... aimed at guaranteeing popular participation in preparing and carrying out the municipal budget, hence in the distribution of resources and definition of investment priorities" (Santos 1998: 464). The notion is that political decisions about municipal investments, even the most technical, can be understood and therefore made, by citizens in possession of sufficient information. The practice has spread widely from Brazil to other continents, including numerous cities in Western and Eastern Europe, often promoted by progressives interested in promoting Habermasian-style deliberative democracy or leftists seeking a tool for social struggles (Sintomer, Herzberg, and Rocke 2008: 165). Social investments in schools and services are a frequent topic for deliberation.

A similar repositioning of experts and expertise was originally intended for the open method of coordination (OMC), the European Union's policy tool for coordinating social policy outcomes across the Union after 2000 (Zeitlin and Pochet 2005). As it evolved, the OMC brought shifts in definitions of authority and expertise, with growing attention to common indicators, best practices, and common outcomes. Now social inclusion, pensions, and health care are monitored via common indicators across the 27 member states of the EU. These common processes involve production of and reliance on detailed indicators that are meant to measure outcomes in target groups and benchmarks against which member states can measure their own performance. They have been applied in particular in the areas of human capital and child poverty that are central to the European Union's social investment position (Marlier et al. 2006).

Of course, national states too have turned to policymaking using indicators and that measure "outcomes" in a wide range of social fields.[26] Child outcomes in health and development, best practices in early childhood education, the return to investments in human capital, the results over the life course of interventions at different key moments – all became the dominant vocabulary of social rights communities.

Indeed, this shift marks significant changes in post–neoliberal governance. If the Weberian state concerned itself above all with monitoring the "inputs" of policy – costs especially but also the careful selection of employees who would provide the services – and if neoliberalism delegitimized the state, the social investment perspective for governing social rights regimes legitimated its own actions differently. Its authority and expertise did not reside in its

---

[26] In Canada, the political momentum toward the National Child Benefit and attendant programs was deeply imbued with this governance discourse.

capacity for controlling the inputs but rather for ensuring that its outputs led to the outcomes it sought. In turn, at the front end of the policy process, as just described, non-experts – that is, citizens – were invited to participate in the design of the policy and program. This marks a shift in the social rights regime. It also indicates its capacity to adapt to the critiques of neoliberals about hierarchal and ultimately inefficient bureaucracy by essentially redesigning its role.

Conclusion

The status of these two regimes was in flux at the beginning of the neoliberal era. In the human rights regime, economic and social rights were dismissed as unattainable, and an autonomous or independent regime was said to unduly hamper foreign policy efforts and strengthen the hand of communist states. The social rights regime was vilified as interfering with the market and generating a cycle of dependence among citizens.

In their encounter with institutions, events, and actors of the neoliberal era, these regimes have changed their form. We see a shift in scale toward both supranational and subnational actors (including a sectoral shift toward communities and NGOs), an integration of new forms of expertise and a reliance on indicator-driven decision making, and an emphasis on a narrative of active individuals said to be responsible for charting their own course. Both regimes have, in other words, taken on the central cultural and political narratives of neoliberalism.

It is far more complex to assess whether these changes have rendered the international human rights regime more efficacious at enhancing the social resilience of individuals and societies. Research on the effects of human rights is often murky (Hafner-Burton and Ron 2009). Yet available studies suggest that recent changes in the human rights regime are likely to enhance social inclusion and prevent future abuses. Criminal trials for human rights violations produce a salutary effect on human rights protections within transitional countries and may deter human rights violations in neighboring countries (Kim and Sikkink 2010). Similarly, human rights treaties improve domestic practices in partially democratic states (Simmons 2009). Furthermore, the increasing relevance of NGOs appears central to human rights successes: the strength of international NGO membership has positive effects for domestic human rights protections, particularly within repressive states (Hafner-Burton and Tsutsui 2005). And although decisions of the ECHR are at times met with hostility by Russia and Turkey, for European liberal democracies, there is a "compliance pull" with conformity to adverse judgments (von Staden 2009).

Any assessment of the effects of redesigned social rights, even under the influence of efforts to make social investments, is difficult. This is not because, as many authors argued in the 1980s and 1990s, of "permanent austerity" and retrenchment. Levels of state spending have been less cut back than redirected, with the result that there are now different "winners" and new "losers."

Certainly acquired rights to publicly and universal pensions have been retracted in many countries. Yet even in Chile where the neoliberal "Chicago boys" had had their greatest effects on public pensions, Michelle Bachelet's government created new basic pension rights for the previously unprotected (Rofman, Fajnzylber, and Herrera 2008: 26ff.). Across Europe as well, cost-containment efforts struck heavily at publicly financed pensions everywhere (Bonoli and Natali forthcoming). Yet at the same time, new spending in alternative areas such as childcare, employment services, in-work benefits, and other instruments of the social investment perspective has been observed (Castles 2007). This has meant that there is now some support available for lone parents, young families, and young people in general to help weather bouts of employment difficulty or a labor market that no longer generates as many good jobs as during the *trente glorieuses*. On the other hand, fewer workers will have the guarantee of generous public pensions than earlier; only those who earned enough to save enough will be in that situation. On the other hand, the new spending in alternative areas, particularly on childcare services and in-work benefits, also allow more women, even with young children, a degree of personal autonomy in their life choices, and investments in education permit them to increase their human capital.

As the Jack pines of the neoliberal era, the human and social rights regimes have shown themselves to be supple and able to adjust to new contexts by adapting their practices for supporting social resilience. The transformation of the regimes has been contingent, as actors within each faced critiques derived from neoliberal theory and institutions. This encounter has led to significant changes, with actors within these regimes building new approaches to social resilience by mapping as much as possible their own priorities, vocabularies, and institutions onto the political and cultural narratives of neoliberalism.

References

Alston, P. 1988. "Making Space for New Human Rights: The Case of the Right to Development." *Harvard Human Rights Yearbook* 1 (3): 6–40.

Alston, P. 1990. "US Ratification of the Covenant on Economic, Social, and Cultural Rights: the Need for an Entirely New Strategy." *American Journal of International Law* 84: 365–93.

Alston, P. 2009. *Putting Economic, Social, and Cultural Rights Back on the Agenda of the United States*. New York University School of Law, Public Law Research Working Paper No. 09–35.

Barrientos, A. 2009. "Understanding Conditions in Income Transfer Programmes." *Global Social Policy* 9: 165–7.

Barsh, J. 1993. "Measuring Human Rights: Problems of Methodology and Purpose." *Human Rights Quarterly* 15: 87–121.

Bebbington, A., S. Guggenheim, E. Olson, and M. Woolcock. 2002. "Exploring Social Capital Debates at the World Bank." *Journal of Development Studies* 45: 33–64.

Blair, D. 2008. "Sudan Dictator Omar al-Bashir 'Committed Darfur Genocide.'" *The Telegraph*: July 14.

Blomqvist, P. 2004. "The Choice Revolution: Privatization of Swedish Welfare Services in the 1990s." *Social Policy & Administration* 38: 139–55.

Boltanski, L. and È. Chiapello. 2005. "The New Spirit of Capitalism." *International Journal of Cultural Sociology* 18: 161–88.

Bonoli, G. and D. Natali. Forthcoming. "The Politics of the 'New' Welfare State: Key Routes to Reforms and their Consequences." In *The Politics of the New Welfare State*, edited by G. Bonoli and D. Natali. Oxford: Oxford University Press.

Boyle, K. 1995. "Stock-Taking on Human Rights: The World Conference on Human Rights, Vienna, 1993." *Political Studies* 43: 79–95.

Bradford, N. 2004. "Place Matters and Multi-Level Governance: Perspectives on a New Urban Policy Paradigm." *Policy Options* 25 (2): 39–44.

Buergenthal, T. 1997. "The Normative and Institutional Evolution of International Human Rights." *Human Rights Quarterly* 19: 703–23.

Carter, J. 1977. "Inaugural Address of President Jimmy Carter, January 20, 1977." *Inaugural Addresses of the Presidents of the United States*. http://www.bartleby.com/124/pres60.html.

Castles, F., ed. 2007. *The Disappearing State. Retrenchment Realities in an Age of Globalisation*. Cheltenham: Edward Elgar.

Charnowitz, S. 1996. "Two Centuries of Participation: NGOs and International Governance." *Michigan Journal of International Law* 18: 183–286.

Clapham, A. 2007. *Human Rights: A Very Short Introduction*. Oxford: Oxford University Press.

Clarke, J., J. Newman, N. Smith, E. Vidler, and L. Westmarland. 2007. *Creating Citizen-Consumers: Changing Publics and Changing Public Services*. London: Sage.

Commission of Human Rights. 2005. *Commission Starts General Debate on Right to Development, Discusses Report of Working Group on Development*. HR/CN/05/17, 22 March.

Cornwall, A. and J. Gaventa. 2000. "From Users and Choosers to Makers and Shapers. Repositioning Participation in Social Policy." *Institute for Development Studies (IDS) Bulletin* 31 (4): 50–62.

Council of Europe. 2010. *50 Years of Activity: The European Court of Human Rights. Some Facts and Figures*. http://www.echr.coe.int/NR/rdonlyres/ACD46A0F-615A-48B9–89D6–8480AFCC29FD/0/FactsAndFigures_EN.pdf.

Davis, K. E., B. Kingsbury, and S. Merry. 2010. *Indicators as a Technology of Global Governance*. IILJ Working Paper 2010/2: Institute for International Law and Justice.

Dean, M. 1999. *Governmentality: Power and Rule in Modern Society*. London: Sage.

de Neufville, J. Innes. 1982. "Social Indicators of Basic Needs: Quantitative Data for Human Rights Policy." *Social Indicators Research* 11: 383–403.

Dezalay, Y. and B. Garth. 2006. "From the Cold War to Kosovo: The Rise and Renewal of the Field of International Human Rights." *Annual Review of Law and Social Science* 2: 231–55.

Dobrowolsky, A. and J. Jenson. 2005. "Social Investment Perspectives and Practices: A Decade in British Politics." In *Social Policy Review*, edited by M. Powell, L. Bauld, and K. Clarke. Bristol, UK: The Policy Press, 203–30.

Donnelly, J. 1986. "International Human Rights: A Regime Analysis." *International Organization* 40: 599–642.

Donnelly, J. 2003. *Universal Human Rights in Theory and Practice.* Ithaca, NY: Cornell University Press.

Draper, W. H. 1991. *Response by William H. Draper III Administrator of the United Nations Development Programme to the General Debate.* New York: United Nations Development Programme: June 12.

Elliot, M. A. 2008. *A Cult of the Individual for a Global Society: The Development and Worldwide Expansion of Human Rights Ideology.* Ph.D. dissertation, Emory University.

Esping-Andersen, G., ed. 1999. *Welfare States in Transition.* London: Sage.

Evers, A. 2009. "Civicness and Civility: Their Meanings for Social Services." *Voluntas* 20: 239–59.

Fizbein, A. and N. Schady. 2009. *Conditional Cash Transfers. Reducing Present and Future Poverty.* Washington, DC: World Bank Policy Research Report.

Flood, J. P. 1998. *The Effectiveness of UN Human Rights Institutions.* Westport, CT: Praeger.

Frankovitz, A. 2006. *The Human Rights Based Approach and the United Nations System.* Paris: UNESCO.

Gaer, F. 1995. "Reality Check: Human Rights Nongovernmental Organizations Confront Governments at the United Nations." *Third World Quarterly* 16: 389–404.

Gearty, C. A. 1993. "The European Court of Human Rights and the Protection of Civil Liberties: An Overview." *Cambridge Law Journal* 52: 89–127.

Goodin, R. E., B. Headey, R. Muffels, and H.-J. Driven. 1999. *The Real Worlds of Welfare Capitalism.* Cambridge, UK: Cambridge University Press.

Gordon, S. E. 1983. "The Canadian Government and Human Rights Abroad." *International Perspectives* November–December: 8–10.

Green, M. 2001. "What We Talk About When We Talk About Indicators: Current Approaches to Human Rights Measurement." *Human Rights Quarterly* 23: 1062–97.

Guilhot, N. 2005. *The Democracy Makers: Human Rights and International Order.* New York: Columbia University Press.

Guhn, M., M. Janus, and C. Hertzman. 2007. "The Early Development Instrument: Translating School Readiness Assessment into Community Actions and Policy Planning." *Early Education & Development* 18: 369–74.

Hafner-Burton E. and J. Ron. 2009. "Seeing Double: Human Rights Impact through Qualitative and Quantitative Eyes." *World Politics* 61: 360–401.

Hafner-Burton, E. and K. Tsutsui. 2005. "Human Rights in a Globalizing World: The Paradox of Empty Promises." *American Journal of Sociology* 110: 1373–411.

Hall, P. 1993. "Policy Paradigms, Social Learning, and the State: The Case of Economic Policymaking in Britain." *Comparative Politics* 25: 275–96.

Horowitz, J. 2010. "OHCHR Pre-deployment Human Rights Training: Adapting to the Evolving Roles, Responsibilities, and Influence of UN Human Rights Officers." *Journal of Human Rights Practice* 2: 28–48.

Hunt, P. 2003. "The Right of Everyone to Enjoy the Highest Attainable Standard of Physical and Mental Health." United Nations General Assembly, 58th Session, *Human Rights Situations and Reports of Special Rapporteurs and Representatives.*

International Criminal Tribunal for the Former Yugoslavia. 1994. "Report of the International Tribunal for the Prosecution of Persons Responsible for Serious Violations of International Humanitarian Law Committed in the Territory of the Former

Yugoslavia Since 1991. Note by the Secretary-General." Forty-ninth Session, Item 152 of the Provisional Agenda, August 29.

Jacoby, T. 1986. "The Reagan Turnaround on Human Rights." *Foreign Affairs* 64(5): 1066–86.

Jenson, J. 2008. "Getting to Sewers and Sanitation: Doing Public Health within Nineteenth-Century Britain's Citizenship Regime." *Politics & Society* 36 (4): 532–56.

Jenson, J. 2010. "Diffusing Ideas for After Neoliberalism: The Social Investment Perspective in Europe and Latin America." *Global Social Policy* 10: 59–84.

Jenson, J. and D. Saint-Martin. 2006. "Building Blocks for a New Social Architecture: The LEGO™ Paradigm of an Active Society." *Policy & Politics* 34 (3): 429–51.

Jonsson, U. 2005. "A Human-Rights Based Approach to Programming." In *Reinventing Development: Translating Rights-Based Approaches from Theory Into Practice*, edited by P. Gready and J. Ensor. London: Zed Books: 47–62.

Kim, H. and K. Sikkink. 2010. "Explaining the Deterrence Effect of Human Rights Prosecutions for Transitional Countries." *International Studies Quarterly* 54: 939–63.

Kirkpatrick, J. 1979. "Dictatorships and Double Standards." *Commentary* November: 34–45.

Kirkpatrick, J. 1981. "U.S. Security & Latin America." *Commentary* 71 (January): 29–40.

Kirchmeier, F. 2006. "The Right to Development: Where do we stand? The State of the Debate on the Right to Development." *Dialogue on Globalization* (Occasional Papers) 23. Geneva: Fridrich Ebert Stiftung.

Korey, W. 1998. *NGOs and the Universal Declaration of Human Rights: A Curious Grapevine*. New York: St. Martin's.

Korey, W. 1999. "Human Rights NGOs: The Power of Persuasion." *Ethics and International Affairs* 13: 151–74.

Kosonen, P. 2001. "Globalization and the Nordic Welfare States." In *Globalization and European Welfare States: Challenges and Change*, edited by R. Sykes, B. Palier, and P. Prior. New York: Palgrave, 153–72.

Leppik, L. 2006. "In-Work Benefits. A Literature Review." http://siteresources.worldbank.org/INTECONEVAL/Resources/IWBliteratureReviewFinal.pdf.

Levi, R. and M. Valverde. 2006. "Freedom of the City. Canadian Cities and the Quest for Governmental Status." *Osgoode Hall Law Journal* 44: 409–61.

Lutz, E. and K. Sikkink. 2001. "The Justice Cascade: The Evolution and Impact of Foreign Human Rights Trials in Latin America." *Chicago Journal of International Law* 2: 1–33.

Madsen, M. 2007. "From Cold War Instrument to Supreme European Court: The European Court of Human Rights at the Crossroads of International and National Law and Politics." *Law & Social Inquiry* 32: 137–159.

Margolis, J. 1986. "Chink Found in Bush Armor as Conservatives Watch, Kemp Grabs Lance." *Chicago Tribune* March 3: 4.

Marlier, É., T. Atkinson, B. Cantillon, and B. Nolan. 2006. *The EU and Social Inclusion: Facing the Challenge*. Cambridge, UK: Polity.

Marks, S. 2004. "The Human Right to Development: Between Rhetoric and Reality." *Harvard Human Rights Journal* 17: 139–68.

Merry, S. E. 2006. *Human Rights and Gender Violence: Translating International Law into Local Justice*. Chicago: University of Chicago Press.

Merry, S. E. 2009. "Measuring the World: Indicators, Human Rights, and Global Governance." *Proceedings of the Annual Meeting (American Society of International Law)* 103 (March 25–28): 239–43.

Molyneux, M. 2006. "Mothers at the Service of the New Poverty Agenda: *Progresa/Oportunidades*, Mexico's Conditional Transfer Programme." *Social Politics & Administration* 40: 425–49.

Morel, N., B. Palier, and J. Palme, eds. 2012. *Towards a Social Investment Welfare State? Ideas, Policies and Challenges*. Bristol, UK: Policy Press.

Moyn, S. 2010. *The Last Utopia: Human Rights in History*. Cambridge, MA: Harvard University Press.

Murphy, C. 2006. *The United Nations Development Programme. A Better Way?* Cambridge, UK: Cambridge University Press.

Myles, J. 1999. "When Markets Fail. Social Welfare in Canada and the United States." In *Welfare States in Transition*, edited by G. Esping-Andersen. London: Sage: 116–40.

Neier, A. 2003. *Taking Liberties: Four Decades in the Struggle for Rights*. Cambridge, MA: Public Affairs.

Newman, J., M. Barnes, H. Sullivan, and A. Knops. 2004. "Public Participation and Collaborative Governance." *Journal of Social Policy* 33: 203–23.

The New York Times. 1981. "Excerpts from Haig's Remarks at First News Conference as Secretary of State." January 28: A10.

O'Flaherty, M. 2007. "Case Study: The United Nations Human Rights Field Operation in Sierra Leone." In *The Human Rights Field Operation: Law, Theory and Practice*, edited by M. O'Flaherty. Hampshire, UK: Ashgate: 287–316.

O'Flaherty, M. and G. Ulrich. 2010. "The Professionalization of Human Rights Field Work." *Journal of Human Rights Practice* 2: 1–27.

OECD. 1997. "Beyond 2000: The New Social Policy Agenda." *OECD Working Papers*, V: 43. Paris: OECD.

OHCHR. 2006. "International Human Rights Instruments. Report on Indicators for Monitoring Compliance with International Human Rights Instruments." Twentieth Meeting of Chairpersons of the Human Rights Treaty Bodies: May 11.

OHCHR. 2008. *Claiming the Millennium Development Goals: A Human Rights Approach*. New York/Geneva: United Nations Human Rights.

OHCHR. 2009. *2009 Report: Activities and Results*. New York/Geneva: United Nations Human Rights.

OHCHR. 2010. "Rights and Goals." http://www.ohchr.org/EN/NEWSEVENTS/Pages/RightsandGoals.aspx.

Orsini, M. and S. D. Phillips. 2004. *Mapping the Links: Citizen Involvement in Policy Processes*. Ottawa: CPRN. http://www.cprn.org.

OSCE. 2007. *Human Rights Defenders in the OSCE Region: Challenges and Good Practices*. Office for Democratic Institutions and Human Rights. http://www.osce.org/odihr/documents/35652.

Otto, D. 1996. "Nongovernmental Organizations in the United Nations System: The Emerging Role of International Civil Society." *Human Rights Quarterly* 18: 107–41.

Pei-Heng, C. 1981. *Non-Governmental Organizations at the United Nations: Identity, Role, and Function*. New York: Praeger.

Pierson, C. 1991. *Beyond the Welfare State? The New Political Economy of Welfare*. University Park, PA: Pennsylvania State University Press.

Pierson, P. 1998. "Irresistible Forces, Immovable Objects: Post-industrial Welfare States Confront Permanent Austerity." *Journal of European Social Policy* 5: 539–60.

Power, M. 1994. *The Audit Explosion*. London: Demos.

Reimann, K. 2006. "A View from the Top: International Politics, Norms and the Worldwide Growth of NGOs." *International Studies Quarterly* 50: 45–67.

Robinson, M. 2007. *A Voice for Human Rights*. Philadelphia: University of Pennsylvania Press.

Rofman, R., E. Fajnzylber, and G. Herrera. 2008. *Reforming the Pension Reforms. The Recent Initiatives and Actions on Pensions in Argentina and Chile*. SP Discussion Paper #0831. Washington, DC: World Bank.

Rose, N., P. O'Malley, and M. Valverde. 2006. "Governmentality." *Annual Review of Law and Social Science* 2: 83–104.

Rose, N. 1996. "The Death of the Social? Refiguring the Social Territory of Government." *Economy and Society* 25: 327–56.

Rose, N. 1999. *Powers of Freedom: Reframing Political Thought*. Cambridge, UK: Cambridge University Press.

Rosga, A. and M. L. Satterthwaite. 2009. "Trust in Indicators: Measuring Human Rights." *Berkeley Journal of International Law* 27: 253–315.

Saint-Martin, D. 1998. "The New Managerialism and the Policy Influence of Consultants in Government: An Historical-Institutionalist Analysis of Britain, Canada and France." *Governance: An International Journal of Policy and Administration* 11: 319–56.

Sano, H. and L. Lindholt. 2000. *Human Rights Indicators 2000. Country Data and Methodology*. Copenhagen: Danish Institute of Human Rights.

Santos, B. de Sousa. 1998. "Participatory Budgeting in Porto Alegre. Towards a Redistributive Democracy." *Politics & Society* 26 (4): 461–510.

Sarfaty, G.A. 2009. "Why Culture Matters in International Institutions: The Marginality of Human Rights at the World Bank." *American Journal of International Law* 103: 647–83.

Sauder, M. and W. Espeland. 2009. "The Discipline of Rankings: Tight Coupling and Organizational Change." *American Sociological Review* 74: 63–82.

Sengupta. A. 2000. "Realizing the Right to Development." *Development and Change* 31: 553–78.

Shihata, I. F. I. 1991. *The World Bank in a Changing World*. Dordrecht, Netherlands: M. Nijohff Publishers.

Sikkink, K. 2004. *Mixed Signals: US Human Rights Policy and Latin America*. Ithaca, NY: Cornell University Press.

Sikkink, K. 2009. "From State Responsibility to Individual Criminal Accountability: A New Regulatory Model for Core Human Rights Violations." In *The Politics of Global Regulation*, edited by W. Mattli and N. Woods. Princeton, NJ: Princeton University Press: 121–50.

Sikkink, K. and C. B. Walling. 2007. "The Justice Cascade and the Impact of Human Rights Trials in Latin America." *Journal of Peace Research* 44: 427–45.

Simmons, B. 2009. *Mobilizing for Human Rights: International Law in Domestic Politics*. New York: Cambridge University Press.

Sintomer, Y., C. Herzberg, and A. Rocke. 2008. "Participatory Budgeting in Europe: Potentials and Challenges." *International Journal of Urban and Regional Research* 32: 164–78.

Smith, J. 1997. "Characteristics of the Modern Transnational Social Movement Sector." In *Transnational Social Movements and Global Politics: Solidarity Beyond the State*, edited by J. Smith, C. Chatfield, and R. Pagnuccio. Syracuse, NY: Syracuse University Press: 42–58.

St-Clair, A. 2009. "Conditional Cash Transfers: The Need for an Integrated and Historical Perspective." *Global Social Policy* 9: 17–179.

Steiner, H. J. 2000. "Individual Claims in a World of Massive Violations: What Role for the Human Rights Committee?" In *The Future of UN Human Rights Treaty Monitoring*, edited by P. Alston and J. Crawford. Cambridge, UK: Cambridge University Press: 14–54.

Stephens, J. 1999. "The Scandinavian Welfare States: Achievements, Crisis and Prospects" In *Welfare States in Transition*, edited by G. Esping-Andersen. London: Sage.

Stone Sweet, A. 2009. "On the Constitutionalisation of the Convention: The European Court of Human Rights as a Constitutional Court." *Faculty Scholarship Series*. Paper 71.

UNDP. 1991. *Human Development Report 1991*. Human Development Report Office. Oxford: Oxford University Press.

UNDP. 2000. *Human Development Report 2000*. Human Development Report Office. Oxford: Oxford University Press.

United Nations Economic and Social Council. 2001. "Poverty and the International Covenant on Economic, Social and Cultural Rights." Committee on Economic, Social, and Cultural Rights, Twenty-fifth Session, Geneva, May 10.

United Nations General Assembly. 1993. *Address by the High Commissioner for the Promotion and Protection of All Human Rights*. 85th plenary meeting: December 20.

UNICEF. 2000. *The League Tables of Child Poverty in Rich Nations*. Florence: UNICEF Innocenti Research Centre.

von Staden, A. 2009. *Shaping Human Rights Policy in Liberal Democracies: Assessing and Explaining Compliance with the Judgments of the European Court of Human Rights*. Ph.D. dissertation, Princeton University.

Wangborg, M. 1995. "The OSCE at 20: Breakthrough for 'citizen diplomacy'? Towards closer OSCE-NGO interaction?" *European Security* 4 (3): 393–99.

White, D. 2005. "State-third sector partnership frameworks: From administration to participation." In *Administering Welfare Reform: International Transformations in Welfare Governance*., edited by P. Henman and M. Fenger. Bristol, UK: Policy Press, 45–72.

Willetts, P. 2000. "From 'Consultative Arrangements' to 'Partnership': The Changing Status of NGOs in Diplomacy at the UN." *Global Governance* 6: 191–212.

Woolcock, M. 1998. "Social Capital and Economic Development: Toward a Theoretical Synthesis and Policy Framework." *Theory and Society* 27: 151–208.

World Bank. 1991. *World Development Report 1991: The Challenge of Development*. Report 9696. Oxford: Oxford University Press.

Zeitlin, J. and P. Pochet. 2005. *The Open Method of Co-ordination in Action. The European Employment and Social Inclusion Strategies*. Brussels: PIE-Peter Lang.

3

Neoliberal Multiculturalism?[1]

Will Kymlicka

The era of neoliberalism is often defined as a set of changes in economic policy and in economic relationships, many of which created new challenges and insecurities for individuals. But it also reshaped the structure of social relationships, including relationships in the family, workplace, neighborhood, and civil society. It may even have reshaped people's subjectivities – their sense of self, their sense of agency, and their identities and solidarities (Brown 2003). According to its most severe critics, the cumulative impact of these changes is a radical atomization of society. In the name of emancipating the autonomous individual, neoliberalism has eroded the social bonds and solidarities upon which individuals depended, leaving people to fend for themselves as "companies of one" in an increasingly insecure world (Lane 2011).

Yet the modern world is hardly devoid of social bonds and collective identities. Wherever neoliberal reforms have been implemented, they have operated within a dense field of social relationships that conditions the impact of neoliberalism. If neoliberalism has shaped social relations, it is equally true that those relations have shaped neoliberalism, blocking some neoliberal reforms entirely while pushing other reforms in unexpected directions, with unintended results. In the process, we can see social resilience at work as people contest, contain, subvert, or appropriate neoliberal ideas and policies to protect the social bonds and identities they value.

This chapter explores these themes through the lens of ethnic relations. Ethnic identities and ethnic differentiations are an enduring feature of modern societies despite the predictions of 1950s modernization theory. Ethnicity remains an important (although by no means the only) basis of personal identity, informal networks, social status, cultural meanings, and political mobilization. Indeed, far from disappearing as a result of modernization, sociologists

[1] Thanks to Iain Reeve for research assistance; to Matt James for helpful comments; and to the members of the Successful Societies program, particularly Peter Evans and Peter Hall, for illuminating discussions.

talk about the "ethnic revival" in the contemporary world (Smith 1981). Ethnicity seems to flourish in an era of civil rights, nondiscrimination, democratic freedoms, and global communications and mobility. For many minorities in the past, their ethnic identity was a source of stigma and disadvantage to be denied or hidden. But in our postcolonial and post–civil rights era, the racialist and supremacist ideologies that stigmatized minorities have been delegitimized, and democratic freedom and global networks facilitate ethnic self-organization and mobilization. The result has been a flourishing of ethnic projects, including the struggle of indigenous peoples such as the Maya and Inuit for land and self-government, the demands of substate national minorities such as the Welsh or Catalans for language rights and regional autonomy, or the demands of immigrant groups such as the Indian and Chinese diaspora for multicultural accommodations.[2]

As a result, ethnic identities are part of the field of social relations that neoliberal projects encountered, setting the stage for potential conflict. Just as neoliberalism sought to transform the structure of ethnic relations, so too members of ethnic groups have drawn upon the social resources generated by their ethnic identities and relations to contest neoliberalism. For critics who see neoliberalism as an all-encompassing hegemonic force, this was an unequal struggle that resulted in the "social destructuration" of ethnic groups (Magord 2008: 134), eviscerating them of any collective capacity to challenge the dictates of market fundamentalism (Hale and Millaman 2005).

I will argue that the story is more complex and less one sided. Some ethnic groups have managed to resist aspects of the neoliberal project or even to turn neoliberal reforms to their advantage. When neoliberal projects ran up against preexisting ethnic projects, the results were not a foregone conclusion.

One might be inclined to interpret the resilience of ethnic projects as evidence of the primordial power of ethnicity, as if attachments to "blood and soil" are deeper in the human psyche than the material and political resources deployed by neoliberal actors. But this too would be a misreading. The capacity of ethnic actors to contest neoliberal projects depends in large part, I will argue, not on their ability to tap primordial attachments to blood and soil but on the extent to which their ethnic projects were already embedded in public institutions and in national narratives, typically through discourses of "multiculturalism" and the legal recognition of minority rights. As we will see, neoliberal projects encountered not only a field of preexisting ethnic relations but also a field of laws and policies that institutionalized certain ethnic projects, according them social acceptance and political resources.

As a result, insofar as neoliberal reformers sought to transform the structure of ethnic relations, they had to target the politics of multiculturalism that affirmed and sheltered those ethnic projects. As James puts it, "multiculturalism has been a particularly important target of neoliberal change" (2013)

---

[2] By "ethnic projects," I refer to cases in which political actors appeal to ethnic identities as a basis for political mobilization and legal claims. I discuss how the civil rights revolution and democratic reforms enabled such projects in Kymlicka (2007).

because it helps to define the terms of belonging and citizenship. And indeed, neoliberalism has had a marked impact on multiculturalism around the world. But it has been an uneven and unpredictable impact, and moreover, it has been a reciprocal impact, changing neoliberalism as much as it has changed multiculturalism. The story of the resilience of ethnicity is, therefore, at least in part, the story of the resilience of multiculturalism and of the picture of belonging and citizenship it offers. That is the story I want to trace in this chapter.

Multiculturalism Before Neoliberalism

To explore the impact of neoliberalism on ethnic relations, we first need to understand the rise of multiculturalism. Ethnic differentiations are an enduring feature of societies, but the idea that the state should adopt policies to affirm and shelter minority ethnic projects is relatively novel. Historically, nation-states have been distrustful of minority ethnic political mobilization, which they stigmatized as disloyal, backward, and balkanizing. The history of state-minority relations throughout most of the nineteenth and twentieth centuries is one of constant pressure for assimilation, combined with animosity towards, if not prohibition of, minority political mobilization.

Starting in the 1960s, however, we see a shift toward a more multicultural approach to state-minority relations. The public expression and political mobilization of minority ethnic identities is no longer seen as an inherent threat to the state but is accepted as a normal and legitimate part of a democratic society. In many cases, these mobilizations were not just tolerated but were politically effective. Across the Western democracies, we see a trend toward the increasing recognition of minority rights, whether in the form of land claims and treaty rights for indigenous peoples; strengthened language rights and regional autonomy for substate national minorities; and accommodation rights for immigrant-origin ethnic groups.[3] For this chapter, I will call all of these "multiculturalism policies" (or MCPs for short).

This term covers a wide range of policies, but what they have in common is that they go beyond the protection of the basic civil and political rights guaranteed to all individuals in a liberal-democratic state to also extend some level of public recognition and support for minorities to express their distinct identities and practices. The rise of MCPs therefore goes beyond the broader politics of civil rights and nondiscrimination. Until the 1950s and 1960s, many Western states explicitly discriminated against certain racial or religious groups, denying them the right to immigrate or to become citizens or subjecting them to discrimination or segregation in access to public education, housing, or employment. This sort of explicit state-sanctioned discrimination has been repudiated, and most countries have also adopted measures to tackle discrimination by non-state actors such as private employers or landlords. The adoption of such

[3] For a statistical measure of such policies across the OECD, see the "Multiculturalism Policy Index" introduced by Banting and Kymlicka (2006) and updated through 2010 at http://www.queensu.ca/mcp.

antidiscrimination measures is often discussed as a form of multiculturalism or minority rights because minorities are the beneficiaries.

As I am using the term, however, multiculturalism is not just about ensuring the nondiscriminatory application of laws but also about changing the laws and regulations themselves to better reflect the distinctive needs and aspirations of minorities. For example, the logic of antidiscrimination required extending the vote to Aboriginal individuals in Canada in 1960, but it was a different logic that extended rights of self-government to Aboriginal communities in the 1980s through the devolution of power to Aboriginal councils. Similarly, the logic of antidiscrimination requires that Sikhs be hired based on merit in the police force, but changing police dress codes so that Sikhs can wear a turban is a positive accommodation. Self-government rights for Aboriginals and accommodation rights for Sikhs are paradigm examples of multiculturalism because the relevant policies are being deliberately redefined to fit the aspirations of members of minority groups. Although the adoption of positive MCPs has been more controversial than antidiscrimination, we see a clear trend across the Western democracies toward the strengthening of both antidiscrimination and MCPs since the 1960s.

The rise of MCPs was a response to the organized mobilization of minority groups reinforced by the specter of more radical movements. States were willing to negotiate with moderate and democratic minority actors, partly to blunt challenges from more revolutionary and violent movements, such as the Black Panthers and American Indian Movement in the United States or the Front de libération du Québec in Canada.

In this way, multiculturalism emerged out of the emancipatory social movements of the 1960s, although the ultimate outcome was shaped as much by the imperatives of state control as by the objectives of social movements. MCPs helped to define a new "system of interest intermediation" that gave organized ethnic groups a seat at the table of public decision making while also giving states a means to shape and discipline those groups to ensure their compliance with overarching state needs for social peace and effective state regulation of economic and political life (James 2013).

Commentators debate the relative balance of "emancipation" versus "control" in the resulting settlements. For a critic such as Katharyne Mitchell, the form of multiculturalism that emerged was fundamentally an instrument of control: "a broad technology of state control of difference, and as one of many capillaries of disciplinary power/knowledge concerning the formation of the state subject." Multiculturalism was a "tool of domestication" to bring everyone into a shared national narrative, and hence "a strategic partner in the growth and expansion of a Fordist capitalist regime of accumulation" (Mitchell 2004: 92, 119, 123–4).

But it is important to remember not only that multiculturalism arose in response to mobilization by minorities themselves (Hinz 2010) but also that it gives them an ongoing seat at the table of public decision making that they have used to some effect. In the Canadian case, for example, multiculturalism was invoked in the 1980s to strengthen equality rights in the Canadian Charter, strengthen hate-speech laws, strengthen employment equity legislation, and lobby for historical redress agreements (e.g., for the internment of Japanese Canadians) (James 2006: 79–82, 104–6). If multiculturalism was a "tool of domestication" by the state, it was also "a tool of civic voice for historically excluded and oppressed people," and "equality-seeking movements invoked the official commitment to multiculturalism to buttress their claims for inclusion and respect" (James 2013).

One way to reconcile these contradictory views of multiculturalism is to attend to the nature of the "national citizen" and "state subject" being created. Mitchell views multiculturalism as a tool by which states seek to contain difference within national boundaries, by constituting "nationally oriented multicultural selves" (Mitchell 2003: 399), and by "inculcating a sense of tolerance as part of a citizen's obligation toward national social coherence" (Mitchell 2004: 87). But as she acknowledges, the "national social coherence" being constituted was defined in progressive "social liberalism" terms that sought to redress disadvantages: "as a socially liberal philosophy and policy, Canadian multiculturalism invoked a complex mix of tolerance of differences, social equity, opportunity and nationalism" (Mitchell 2004: 87–88).

This complex mix took root in part because it is attractive to both members of minorities and state elites. This mix of nationalism and social liberalism created space for minorities to contest disadvantage and to renegotiate the terms of belonging while reassuring state officials that it is still "Canada" to which all citizens belong and to which all citizens wish to contribute.

Put another way, multiculturalism's mix of nationalism and social liberalism can be seen as a process of citizenization.[4] Historically, ethnic relations have been defined in illiberal and undemocratic ways – including relations of conqueror and conquered, colonizer and colonized, settler and indigenous, racialized and unmarked, normalized and deviant, orthodox and heretic, civilized and backward, ally and enemy, master and slave. The task for all liberal democracies has been to turn this catalogue of uncivil relations into relationships of liberal-democratic citizenship, both in terms of the vertical relationship between the members of minorities and the state and the horizontal relationships among the members of different groups.

---

[4] I take the term "citizenization" from Tully (2001). As Tully emphasizes, citizenization is not just about extending formal citizenship to minorities because this can be done in a unilateral and paternalistic way. (This is how Canadian citizenship was extended to Aboriginal peoples in 1960.) Citizenization, rather, involves a willingness to negotiate as equals the terms of belonging with the goal of reaching consent. In the case of indigenous peoples, this may include the willingness to consider challenges to the state's legitimacy and jurisdiction, which were initially imposed by force on colonized groups. In that sense, citizenization is not only more than formal citizenship; it can also include challenges to state citizenship, as when some Aboriginal leaders insist they never consented to being Canadian citizens. As long as the goal is to replace coercion and paternalism with democratic consent and to replace hierarchy with nondomination, then we have citizenization.

In the past, it was widely assumed that the only way to engage in this process of citizenization was to impose a single undifferentiated model of citizenship on all individuals. But multiculturalism starts from the assumption that this complex history inevitably generates group-differentiated ethnopolitical claims – that is, claims for MCPs, not just for antidiscrimination. The key to citizenization is not to suppress these differential claims but rather to frame them through the values of social liberalism. This is what liberal multiculturalism seeks to do, whether in the form of land claims and self-government for indigenous peoples, language rights and regional autonomy for substate national groups, or accommodation rights for immigrant groups. All seek to convert older hierarchies into new relations of liberal democratic citizenship.[5]

The idea that multiculturalism can serve as a vehicle for deepening relations of liberal-democratic citizenship is contested. But we now have 40 years of experience with liberal multiculturalism, and there is growing evidence that it can serve this function.

Citizenization is a complex idea, with at least three dimensions: effective political participation, equal economic opportunities, and social acceptance. On all three dimensions, evidence suggests that MCPs contribute to citizenization. It would take too long to review all of the evidence here, so I will focus on the immigrant case, partly because it is the most controversial.

I will start with the Canadian case, which was the first Western country to adopt an official multiculturalism policy towards immigrant-origin ethnic groups, and remains the only country in which multiculturalism is enshrined in the constitution. It therefore provides a good first test case for the impact of MCPs. The evidence to date shows that:

- In terms of political participation, compared with other Western democracies, immigrants in Canada are more likely to become citizens (Bloemraad 2006), to vote and to run for office (Howe 2007), and to be elected to office (Adams 2007), partly because voters in Canada do not discriminate against such candidates (Black and Erickson 2006; Bird 2009). There are many factors that explain this, including the fact that Canada tends to select more highly skilled immigrants than other countries. But scholars who study the political participation of immigrants in Canada in comparison with other countries concur that multiculturalism has enhanced their participation (Bloemraad 2006).
- In terms of economic opportunity, opportunity has two key dimensions: first, to acquire skills; and second, to translate those skills into jobs that are commensurate. In both cases, Canada outperforms other Western democracies. The children of immigrants have better educational outcomes in Canada than in other Western democracies (Organisation for Economic

---

5 Other examples of citizenization include the claims of women, gays, and people with disabilities. They have a similar trajectory starting in the 1960s, seeking to replace earlier uncivil relations of dominance and intolerance with newer relations of democratic citizenship. All of these struggles borrowed arguments and strategies from each other.

Co-operation and Development [OECD] 2006), and in terms of acquiring employment; although immigrants in all Western societies suffer from an "ethnic penalty" in translating their skills into jobs, the size of this ethnic penalty is lowest in Canada (Heath 2007). Here again, several factors explain this comparative record, but there are good reasons to think that MCPs play a role, partly because of the way they help children acculturate (Berry et al. 2006).

- In terms of social acceptance, compared with other Western democracies, Canadians are more likely to say that immigration is beneficial (Focus Canada 2006; Laczko 2007), and whereas ethnic diversity has been shown to erode social capital in other countries, there appears to be a "Canadian exceptionalism" in this regard (Kazemipur 2009). Here again, many factors are at work, but researchers argue that the presence of multicultural norms has played an important role, helping to "normalize" diversity and making it part of Canadian national identity (Harell 2009; Kazemipur 2009).

So, growing evidence indicates that in the Canadian case, MCPs contribute to citizenization. A skeptic might respond that Canada is an outlier and that we cannot generalize from one case. So let us set aside the Canadian case, and ask which country comes *second* in cross-national studies of immigrant political participation, equal opportunity, and mutual respect. The answer typically is Australia, which is the country that most quickly and closely followed Canada in adopting an MCP.

A skeptic might retreat further and argue that Canada and Australia are both New World "countries of immigration" and that evidence from those countries cannot be applied to Europe. But if we ask which *European* country does best on these criteria, it is often Sweden, which has been one of the strongest and most consistent proponents of a multicultural approach. Sweden outperforms those countries that never embraced multiculturalism (France, Germany) or that have retreated from earlier commitments (Netherlands).[6]

So countries with strong and consistent policies of immigrant multiculturalism seem to outperform other Western democracies. This is still just three countries, and perhaps all three are exceptional. But insofar as we have cross-national data, the evidence suggests that the beneficial effects of MCPs are more generalized. For example, a cross-national study of 13 countries shows that children are psychologically better adapted in countries with MCPs (Berry et al. 2006); a cross-national study of diversity and social capital in 19 countries shows that MCPs have a positive impact on political participation and social capital (Kesler and Bloemraad 2010); a cross-national study of prejudice shows that multiculturalism has a positive effect on reducing prejudice (Weldon 2006); and earlier cross-national work that I conducted with Keith Banting suggested that MCPs may have a positive effect on redistribution (Banting and Kymlicka, 2006; see also Crepaz 2006).

---

[6] For documentation on the points in this and preceding paragraphs, see Kymlicka (2010).

I believe that a similar story can be told about the impact of MCPs for indigenous peoples and substate national groups. For example, on a wide range of measures, indigenous peoples fare better in countries with stronger indigenous rights policies (Kauffman 2004), and this result is confirmed by case studies from within individual countries, including the United States (Cornell and Kalt 2000), Canada (Chandler and Lalonde 1998), and New Zealand (Ringold 2005).

Much of this research focuses on large-scale statistical comparisons and does not yet specify the causal mechanisms by which MCPs contribute to citizenization. More work is needed to "drill down" to see how MCPs affect people's circumstances and choices. The answer, I suspect, will center primarily on how MCPs shape the social identities, networks, narratives, and cultural resources available to individuals and groups or indeed to society as a whole. The amount of money spent on multiculturalism is tiny in most countries, and if MCPs have significant effects, it is not primarily by directly putting more money in anyone's hands, but rather by changing people's sense of what is possible, of what is legitimate, of who belongs, of who we can trust, of what we can take pride in from the past (and what we can hope for in the future), and of what we owe each other. I think these effects arise at multiple levels – from informal interactions in neighborhoods and workplaces to formal institutional rules of participation – and cumulatively affect the magnitude and distribution of social resources in society.

There is surprisingly little evidence on these social effects, partly because there are very few evaluations of MCPs (Marc 2009; Reitz 2009: 13). But the problem is not simply the lack of studies but also the level of analysis. Most existing attempts to evaluate multiculturalism operate at the level of discrete programs – such as introducing a new multicultural component to a particular school curriculum and then evaluating its effect on student performance in that grade or introducing a new culturally sensitive mode of health delivery in hospitals and then evaluating its effect on patient recovery. But this misses the potentially significant effects of MCPs on broader social identities and narratives. If hospitals in Vancouver train their nurses to be sensitive to the cultural needs of Chinese patients, the most significant result may not be better health for a particular patient but rather a stronger sense among the Chinese community generally that they are accepted and welcomed by public institutions in Canada. Seeing a family member treated respectfully in hospitals may make someone more likely to trust the police, join a political party, or get involved in the local school. The benefits of MCPs may therefore show up in strengthened feelings of trust in one's co-citizens and in public institutions and strengthened feelings of belonging and membership.[7] The cross-national evidence suggests

---

[7] These feelings of belonging and participation may in turn have beneficial health outcomes given the well-known indirect effects of stigmatization on health (Williams 1999). In this way, MCPs may indirectly promote health in addition to whatever direct effects arise for an individual patient from (for example) more culturally sensitive health care.

that MCPs are indeed having these sorts of effects, but existing studies of policy impacts do not get at them effectively.

We can learn here from similar debates about anti-poverty strategies. One way to evaluate an anti-poverty policy is to examine its immediate effect on a beneficiary's material resources – that is, putting money into a needy person's pocket. But the framing of anti-poverty policies also has powerful long-term effects on people's sense of identity, community, and solidarity, reconstructing shared definitions of "us" and "them" and of who is valued and "deserving" (e.g., Guetzkow 2010) – effects that over time can either sustain or erode the moral commitments that underpin anti-poverty policies in the first place. We need comparable studies of the impact of MCPs, not just on individual beneficiaries but on social identities and cultural narratives as well.

From Social Liberal to Neoliberal Multiculturalism

When neoliberalism emerged as a powerful force in the early 1980s, it emerged into societies that were being transformed in a multicultural direction. One of the first questions confronting neoliberal reformers was how to respond to this new social reality. Because at the time multiculturalism was clearly rooted in a social liberalism and was an outgrowth of 1960s progressive social movements, the initial reaction of most neoliberal actors was one of hostility. Indeed, the first wave of neoliberals in the United States, United Kingdom, Canada, and Australia were uniformly critical of multiculturalism, which they viewed as a prime example of unjustified intervention in the market in response to "special interests" caused by the capture of state power by ethnic entrepreneurs and their rent-seeking allies in the bureaucracy. The result, neoliberals argued, was both the distortion of the proper use of state power and the unhealthy dependence of civil society on government funds. Indeed, the close links between advocacy groups and the state built up under multiculturalism represented precisely the sort of "nanny state" that they aimed to demolish. Neoliberals opposed on principle the idea of state support for ethnic projects and opposed most of the reforms that followed in multiculturalism's trail, such as the employment equity laws that minorities demanded in the name of multiculturalism. In short, neoliberals viewed multiculturalism as embodying the sort of welfare state liberalism they opposed.[8]

This neoliberal attack on multiculturalism took both an institutional and a symbolic form. Institutionally, neoliberals severed the links between the state and progressive advocacy groups, slashing funding and political access for such groups. Symbolically, neoliberals delegitimized multiculturalism by contrasting "ordinary" hard-working tax-paying citizens against the "special interests" represented by "ethnic lobbies." As James puts it, neoliberals invoked discourses that "valorized the so-called 'ordinary Canadian', figured as a

[8] See Kim (2010) on Thatcher's opposition to multiculturalism and Abu-Laban and Gabriel (2002) on neoliberal opposition in Canada.

taxpayer and consumer, to delegitimize group experiences and identities as positive considerations in civic deliberation and debate" (James 2013).

And yet multiculturalism survived this initial onslaught of neoliberalism. Indeed, multiculturalism has not only endured in the era of neoliberalism but expanded. Based on the Multiculturalism Policy Index we devised to measure the diffusion of MCPs across the OECD countries, there has been a steady trend toward an increasing adoption of MCPs in the period after 1980.[9] Despite talk about the "retreat from multiculturalism," only the Netherlands shows a real retreat from MCPs; most other countries actually strengthened their commitment to MCPs.[10]

In part, this can be seen as evidence of the resilience of the coalitions that generated MCPs in the first place. Confronted with neoliberal opposition, minority groups and their allies mobilized to sustain the programs they had initially fought for and to defend the image of belonging these programs promoted. Faced with this opposition, many neoliberal actors sheathed their swords against multiculturalism, judging that it was not worth the fight (James 2013). Viewed this way, multiculturalism persists as an island of social liberalism in a sea of neoliberal change.

---

[9] See the Appendix for our measure of the increasing level of MCPs across the OECD. In a separate study, Koopmans, Michalowski, and Waibel (2012) have also identified a clear trend toward the increasing adoption of MCPs for immigrant groups in Europe, with the Netherlands as the obvious exception. This may surprise readers accustomed to high-profile declarations about the "death" or "retreat" of multiculturalism, particularly in Europe. But the evidence suggests this "retreat" is more rhetorical than real. Politicians in many countries have decided not to use "the 'm' word" and to talk instead about, say, "diversity," "pluralism," "intercultural dialogue," "civic integration," or "community cohesion," but these changes in wording have not necessarily affected actual policies on the ground. As Vertovec and Wessendorf note, although the word multiculturalism "has mostly disappeared from political rhetoric," this "has not emerged with the eradication, nor even much to the detriment, of actual measures, institutions and frameworks of minority cultural recognition" (Vertovec and Wessendorf 2010: 18; see also McGhee 2008: 85). Talk of a "wholesale retreat" (Joppke 2004: 244) is therefore misleading. Of course, the fact that politicians are retreating from the rhetoric of multiculturalism may well be undermining the benefits of the policies. Insofar as MCPs work by publicly expressing a more inclusive sense of identity and belonging, rhetoric may be an essential component of their success.

[10] There have been important policy changes across the West in the field of immigration, but the main change has not been the abandonment of MCPs but rather changes to settlement and naturalization policies. In many Western countries, immigrants are required to pass new or strengthened tests of their knowledge of the country's official language and of its laws and institutions in order gain citizenship or even to renew their residency. Although these "civic integration" reforms are often described as a retreat from multiculturalism, they do not directly affect any preexisting MCPs. Moreover, if we examine the conceptions of citizenship promoted within the new citizenship tests, they tend to mirror the preexisting commitment to multiculturalism. Countries with strong MCPs promote a multiculturalist conception of citizenship in their citizenship tests (see the comparison of Canadian and Danish tests in Adamo [2008]; for a broader attempt to measure the ethnic exclusiveness of naturalization policies, see Koning 2011). Citizenship tests are not an alternative to multiculturalism but rather are one more forum in which countries manifest their commitment (or lack of commitment) to multiculturalism. For further discussion of the relationship between multiculturalism polices and new civic integration policies, see Kymlicka (2012).

But this is hardly the full story. Many neoliberal actors have not only tolerated multiculturalism but positively embraced it and became agents for its diffusion. The same international organizations that championed neoliberalism – such as the World Bank, the OECD, or the European Union[11] – have also pushed multiculturalism. For example, the World Bank requires developing countries to comply with indigenous rights norms to qualify for loans. The European Union requires countries seeking to join the Union to respect the rights of national minorities. In these and other cases, neoliberal actors have promoted multiculturalism in countries that had little experience of them.

Clearly, neoliberal actors saw something in multiculturalism that they found useful. If at first glance neoliberals saw multiculturalism as a pathology of the interventionist welfare state, on a sober second glance, they saw certain elective affinities that could be built upon. They saw, in short, the potential for something like "neoliberal multiculturalism."

The overriding concern of neoliberals in the field of ethnic relations is with integrating minorities into global markets and with the contribution they can make to economic competitiveness. If social liberalism was fundamentally about citizenization – about the creation of relations of democratic citizenship – neoliberalism is fundamentally about creating effective market actors and competitive economies. This need not lead to support for multiculturalism. Indeed, in the past, the attachment of minorities to their languages and cultures was seen as a hindrance to effective market participation. But the defining feature of neoliberal multiculturalism is the belief that ethnic identities and attachments can be assets to market actors and hence that they can legitimately be supported by the neoliberal state. And this is precisely what many neoliberals have come to believe.

In some contexts, ethnicity is a market asset in the very tangible form of cultural artifacts that can be marketed globally (music, art, fashion). But in most cases, ethnicity is seen as a market asset because it is a source of "social capital" that successful market actors require. Consider the following description of the World Bank's commitment to "ethnodevelopment" for indigenous peoples in Ecuador:

Social exclusion, economic deprivation, and political marginalization are sometimes perceived as the predominant characteristic of Ecuador's indigenous peoples. But as they often remind outsiders, indigenous peoples are also characterized by strong positive attributes, particularly their high levels of social capital. Besides language and their own sense of ethnic identity, the distinctive features of indigenous peoples include solidarity and social unity (reflected in strong social organizations), a well-defined geographical concentration and attachment to ancestral lands, a rich cultural patrimony, and other customs and practices distinct from those of Ecuador's national society.... The [World Bank] project aims to mobilize this social capital, based on these characteristics, as a platform for ethnodevelopment (van Nieuwkoop and Uquillas 2000: 18).

[11] All of these organizations eventually backed away from neoliberalism, but they were all participants in the "hegemonic globalization" that characterized the neoliberal era.

Or consider this quote from Shelton Davis, one of the driving forces behind the World Bank's indigenous policy:

Until recently, a local culture has been seen as a hindrance to development, whereas today we must rather look upon culture as an asset, as a driving force for self-development... one might argue that more culture is more wealth, that having more know-how, more languages, and more centres of interest enriches indigenous peoples as well as enriching in the process the rest of a country's citizens and some segment of humanity as well (Davis and Ebbe 1993: 8).

In short, a neoliberal multiculturalism is possible because ethnicity is a source of social capital, social capital enables effective market participation, and governments can promote this market-enhancing social capital through MCPs that treat minorities as legitimate partners.[12]

The way in which ethnicity facilitates market participation varies from group to group. In the case of immigrants, social capital does not flow from "a well-defined geographical concentration and attachment to ancestral lands" – immigrants are precisely uprooted from their ancestral lands. But from a neoliberal perspective, this uprooting is itself a potential asset because it enables transnational linkages that native-born citizens lack. Immigrant transnationalism, then, is an asset in an increasingly global marketplace – it facilitates global trade – exemplified by the commercial linkages in the Indian and Chinese diasporas. Insofar as multiculturalism legitimates the ethnic identities that underpin these transnational links, it can be seen as good for the economies of both sending and receiving countries.

We see this version of multiculturalism emerging in Australia and Canada in the 1980s as neoliberal governments adopted the discourse of "productive multiculturalism" and organized conferences with titles such as "Multiculturalism Means Business" and cities marketed themselves as the multicultural home of transnational entrepreneurs.[13]

So the neoliberal vision of transnational multiculturalism for immigrant groups is different from their vision of ethnodevelopment for indigenous peoples (which is different yet again from the neoliberal vision of the market role of substate national groups).[14] But in each case, neoliberals have found a way

---

[12] "Social capital" in this context is a broader notion than found in Putnam's influential work (2000), where it refers primarily to generalized interpersonal trust. It is being used here as a label for any social or cultural feature that supports effective community development.

[13] See Murphy, O'Brien, and Watson (2003) on the neoliberal marketing of multicultural Sydney; Abu-Laban and Gabriel (2002) and Mitchell (2004: 100–1) on Vancouver and Toronto; and Glick-Schiller (2011) on Manchester, New Hampshire. This valorizing of immigrant transnationalism as a source of economic competitiveness is related to, but distinct from, the more general claim that ethnic diversity in the workplace or in corporate boards increases productivity or profits (Herring 2009). This latter idea was another trope in the neoliberal reframing of multiculturalism.

[14] Granting autonomy to groups like the Catalans and Scots has been supported by some neoliberals as a potential site for a more innovative and entrepreneurial culture, sustained by higher levels of social cohesion (Keating 2001).

to legitimize ethnicity, to justify MCPs that shelter those ethnic projects, and to reinterpret these policies in line with neoliberalism's core ideas (enhancing economic competitiveness and innovation, shifting responsibility from the state to civil society, promoting decentralization, deemphasizing national solidarity in favor of local bonds or transnational ties, viewing cultural diversity as an economic asset or commodity in a global market).

In the process, the meaning of multiculturalism has clearly changed. As we saw, multiculturalism originally was rooted in both social liberalism (committed to remedying disadvantages) and nationalism (building good citizens who can work across differences for the good of the nation), both of which shaped the underlying idea of citizenization. The neoliberal vision of multiculturalism, by contrast, is largely indifferent to both the progressive equality-seeking component of multiculturalism and its national boundedness. The goal of neoliberal multiculturalism is not a tolerant national citizen who is concerned for the disadvantaged in her own society but a cosmopolitan market actor who can compete effectively across state boundaries. I will discuss below the extent to which these two images of tolerant national citizen and effective global market actor can be combined, but the main impulse of the neoliberal reform of multiculturalism was to displace the former with the latter. Mitchell captures this in her account of changes to multicultural education in the United States, United Kingdom, and Canada under the influence of neoliberalism:

There is no longer much need for the multicultural subject interested in working towards harmony across the differences of race or class, one able to find points of convergence in the general spirit of a nexus of production and consumption benevolently regulated by the state. The spirit of harmonious accumulation, for the capitalist, the worker and the nation, is gone, and the multicultural self is no longer the ideal state citizen.... In this neoliberal vision of education, educating a child to be a good citizen is no longer synonymous with constituting a well-rounded, nationally oriented, multicultural self, but rather about attainment of the "complex skills" necessary for individual success in the global economy (Mitchell 2003: 392, 399).[15]

Focusing specifically on the Canadian case, Mitchell summarizes the shift from social liberal to neoliberal multiculturalism this way:

Multiculturalism [in its social liberal form] operated effectively as an instrument of state formation on a number of levels: as a national narrative of coherence in the face of British-French and then immigrant "difference," as a broad technology of state control of difference, and as one of many capillaries of disciplinary power/knowledge concerning the formation of the state subject. In all of this, but especially in the constitution of national citizens able and willing to work through difference for the nation, the socially liberal philosophy and practice of multiculturalism was a strategic partner in the growth and expansion of a Fordist capitalist regime of accumulation. However, with the rise of transnational lives, deterritorialized states, and neoliberal pressures in the past two decades, this type of state subject has been increasingly irrelevant. The

---

[15] According to Resnik (2009), the resulting new spirit of multicultural education is "Good for Business but not for the State."

particular form of what I have termed "liberal multiculturalism" – one jointly bound up in the constitution of the nation, the tolerant national self, and the formation of a regime of accumulation regulated by the state – is evolving into something qualitatively different. Liberal multiculturalism, a spatially specific ethos of tolerance contingent on the history and geography of a city and a nation, is now rapidly morphing into neoliberal multiculturalism, the "progressive process of planetary integration." It reflects a logic of pluralism on a global scale, and a strategic, outward-looking cosmopolitanism (Mitchell 2004: 123–4).

The shift toward a neoliberal conception of multiculturalism has entailed a dramatic narrowing of the scope of political contestation. In the case of immigrants, old-style multiculturalism opened up space to raise issues of structural inequalities in racialized societies, leading to programs such as employment equity. But the new multiculturalism replaces this with ideas of "managing diversity" for competitive success:

The diversity within the "managing diversity" model that has supplanted employment equity in important ways suggests that all individual differences are important and that firms and sectors that fail to acknowledge this will not be able to compete effectively in a global market. This vision of diversity is also narrow insofar as it fails to problematize structural inequalities that exist between groups of people (Abu-Laban and Gabriel 2002: 173).

Neoliberal multiculturalism for immigrants affirms – even valorizes – ethnic immigrant entrepreneurship, strategic cosmopolitanism, and transnational commercial linkages and remittances but silences debates on economic redistribution, racial inequality, unemployment, economic restructuring, and labor rights.

In the case of indigenous peoples, neoliberal multiculturalism has sought to divide Indians into "safe" and "radical" and seeks to accommodate the former – the *indio permitodo* ("permitted Indian"), in Hale's phrase – through a range of multicultural rights. These rights are deemed acceptable as long as (a) they do not contradict the long-term economic development model of moving toward free-market service- and manufacturing-based economies and (b) the resulting level of political clout does not pass a certain line where existing authorities are seriously challenged. Neoliberal multiculturalism thereby gives state and business elites the "ability to restructure the arena of political contention, driving a wedge between cultural rights and the assertion of the control over resources necessary for those rights to be realized" (Hale 2005: 13). The "cultural project of neoliberalism" accords rights to indigenous peoples but only "to help them compete in the rigors of globalized capitalism or, if this is deemed impossible, to relegate them to the sidelines, allowing the game to proceed unperturbed" (Hale and Millamen 2005: 301). And as McNeish notes, this cultural project is not just about limiting indigenous demands but also about restructuring indigenous subjectivities:

Indians are recognized as citizens by governing elites as long as they do not question or threaten the integrity of the existing regime of productive relations, especially in the sectors most closely connected to the global markets. As such . . . the ultimate goal of neoliberalism is not just radical individualism, but rather the creation of subjects who govern themselves in accordance with the logic of globalized capitalism (McNeish 2008: 34).[16]

Viewed this way, the persistence of multiculturalism in the face of neoliberalism is a Pyrrhic victory, obscuring its fundamental transformation. The original aims of multiculturalism – to build fairer terms of democratic citizenship within nation-states – have been replaced with the logic of diversity as a competitive asset for cosmopolitan market actors, indifferent to issues of racial hierarchy and structural inequality.

Indeed, the ability of neoliberalism to appropriate the discourse of multiculturalism has been so great that many people assume multiculturalism was a neoliberal invention. Zizek famously stated that multiculturalism emerged as the "cultural logic of multinational capitalism" (Zizek 1997). The historic link between multiculturalism and national projects of social liberalism has been erased from memory, washed away by the hegemonic forces of neoliberal change.

Locating Resilience

So far, so bad. We are back to the view of neoliberalism as a hegemonic force that "destructures" any ethnic projects that seek to resist it. The persistence of multiculturalism in the neoliberal era, it seems, is not evidence of social resilience but is simply one more manifestation of the "cunning of imperialist reason" (Bourdieu and Wacquant 1999; cf. Melamed 2006).

And yet, this story of multiculturalism's transubstantiation is too neat and misses important moments of resilience. Neoliberal reformers may have hoped that minorities would use MCPs only for "safe" demands, but if so, they miscalculated because minorities have demonstrably refused to contain their ethnic projects within the boundaries of neoliberalism. Indeed, some commentators have argued that insofar as neoliberal multiculturalism was a cultural project aiming to change people's subjectivities and political aspirations, it has simply failed. Neoliberalism may have tried to create "subjects who govern themselves in accordance with the logic of globalized capitalism" (McNeish 2008: 34), but Sawyer argues that this effort "backfired" and instead produced new "transgressive political subjects" (Sawyer 2004: 15) who invoke multiculturalism for their own purposes relating to democratic citizenship and self-determination.

We can see three different aspects to this resilience. First, in some cases, neoliberal reformers simply lacked the capacity to displace earlier socially liberal forms of multiculturalism, which therefore endured over time. This is most

---

[16] See also the description of how neoliberal reforms aimed to reshape indigenous subjectivities in Macdonald and Muldoon (2006: 218–19) (on Australia) and Ratner, Carroll, and Woolford (2003) (on Canada).

apparent in contexts where earlier multicultural settlements have been constitutionalized, rendering them immune from the vagaries of everyday politics. In
their study comparing the impact of neoliberalism on Francophone minorities
in Canada with the Welsh minority in Britain, Cardinal and Denault (2007)
note the crucial role played by the constitutional protection of French language rights in Canada compared with the merely administrative protection
of Welsh. In the former case, because of the preexisting constitutional commitments, neoliberal reforms (e.g., techniques of New Public Management)
changed the means used to administer minority rights but could not change
their underlying goals or core mission.[17] Macdonald and Muldoon (2006)
tell a similar story about the impact of neoliberalism on the Maori in New
Zealand compared with Aboriginals in Australia. Because the basic terms of
the state–Maori relationship are defined by a constitutional treaty (the Treaty
of Waitangi), the preexisting commitment to self-determination was relatively
immune to neoliberal reform, which was largely limited to matters of administrative technique. By contrast, the absence of constitutional protection of
Aboriginal rights in Australia left Aboriginal peoples exposed to a harsh form
of neoliberal restructuring that cut deeply into the basic terms of Aboriginal
citizenship.[18]

Even where earlier settlements were not constitutionalized and hence were
vulnerable to neoliberal reform, they sometimes endured because of concerted
political efforts to preserve them. Abu-Laban and Gabriel (2002: 22) and Joshee
(2004: 144–50) argue that neoliberal reforms to immigrant multiculturalism in
Canada were partially blocked by effective lobbying, generating a hybrid mix
of social liberal and neoliberal programs and discourses.

Second, even where neoliberal reforms have taken place, they have not
always had the effects that were intended by their advocates. In many cases,
neoliberal reforms gave a seat at the table to groups that used their voice to
contest neoliberalism. For example, Bolivia was widely cited in the literature
as the paradigm case of neoliberal multiculturalism and its associated ideals
of the "permitted Indian." But it was precisely these neoliberal multicultural
reforms that made possible the election of the radical indigenist regime of Evo

[17] For a similar analysis, see Heller (2010), who notes that the preexisting constitutional and statu-
tory protection of Francophone minorities meant that "the state's general neoliberal strategies,
focused on individual worker skills development and privatization, were modified to accommodate commitments to 'linguistic duality' in the form of programs supporting 'community
economic development'" (Heller 2010: 115), empowering Francophone communities to shape
their collective development.

[18] See also Davidson and Schejter's (2005) analysis of neoliberal multiculturalism in Israel, where
media privatization was rhetorically justified on the grounds that it would better serve minorities. In practice, however, the Arab minority lacked the political standing to influence the
licensing process and therefore remains excluded from both public and private media. Neoliberal multiculturalism in Israel, they argue, has been "a rhetoric that champions the cultural and
economic rights of minorities and the disadvantaged while masking a policy stance that negates
these very rights" by defending "the preservation of existing political power blocs" from which
Arabs were excluded (Davidson and Schejter 2011: 15, 17).

Morales. Neoliberals in Bolivia instituted reforms to implement their image of neoliberal good governance (i.e., decentralization, delegation to civil society), but anti-neoliberal indigenous groups were able to capture these new political opportunities and use them as a stepping stone to take over the central state itself (Lucero 2008: 141). The social capital that neoliberals hoped indigenous peoples would use to turn themselves into better market actors was instead used to turn themselves into effective political citizens who captured the opportunities created by neoliberal innovations and used them for their own anti-neoliberal purposes.

Nor is this a unique case. Wherever neoliberal multiculturalism has been adopted, its limits have been contested by minority actors and its institutions used for purposes that were not intended by their neoliberal designers. Speaking of Ecuador, Lucero notes that "despite worries over the [depoliticizing effects] of multiculturalism, the dynamism of indigenous politics remains unextinguished. Multicultural neoliberalism, either as a strategy of governance or development, cannot once and for all impose rigid limits on indigenous political subjectivities" (Lucero 2008: 151). Speaking of Latin America generally, Fischer notes that although neoliberalism offers only a "confined multiculturalism," indigenous peoples have been "able to use these manageable categories to make further demands and redefine the terms of relations between the state and civil society and indigenous peoples" (Fischer 2007: 11; see also Van Cott 2006).

These first two forms of resilience suggest a picture of opposition between social liberal and neoliberal multiculturalism, with resilience taking the form of either blocking neoliberal reforms from taking place (the first form of resilience) or capturing and subverting neoliberal reforms when they do take place (the second form). In each case, the assumption is that the advocates for ethnic projects are indifferent to, or actively opposed to, the neoliberal preoccupation with turning minorities into effective actors in global markets. But there is a third form of resilience in which minority ethnic actors embrace the logic of global competitiveness and integrate this with their earlier commitments to democratic citizenization. On this view, minorities can adopt neoliberal multiculturalism, not in place of a social liberal multiculturalism that aspires to citizenization but as a supplement to it and indeed as a way of extending it.

This raises complex issues about the relationship between our status as democratic citizens and our status as market actors. In much of the critical literature on neoliberalism, it is assumed that these operate in a zero-sum relationship: the neoliberal emphasis on expanding the scope of the market comes at the expense of shrinking the scope of citizenship (e.g., Somers 2008). This may indeed be true for many members of dominant groups, who have historically used the nation-state effectively to affirm their citizenship and for whom neoliberalism has eroded the protections that national citizenship offered. But for minority groups, the centralized nation-state has rarely been a benign protector of citizenship – it has rather been a vehicle for assimilation or exclusion. And this exclusion has both an economic and a political dimension: minorities have been disadvantaged within national labor markets and property regimes, as well as within national political systems. As a result, neoliberal reforms that open up markets while delegating state power may be seen by minorities not as replacing citizenship with markets but as enhancing their status as both market actors and democratic citizens.[19]

Of course, enhancing one's status as a democratic citizen requires that there be sites for the exercise of political agency. And here we return to the earlier point about the significance of preexisting settlements establishing forms of multicultural citizenship before the introduction of neoliberalism. Recall that in the case of Francophone minorities in Canada and Maori in New Zealand, these constitutionalized settlements protected social liberal multiculturalism from neoliberal erosion. But in fact, where these constitutional protections existed, neoliberal reforms may actually empower minorities to make fuller use of their multicultural citizenship. Neoliberal reforms helped these groups to more fully enact the rights that first emerged from socially liberal multiculturalism.

According to Macdonald and Muldoon, for example, neoliberalism "did not always work against attempts by indigenous people to obtain greater control over their lives. Provided there was an effective treaty or underlying commitment to self-determination in place, the introduction of neo-liberal systems of governance in New Zealand and Australia could create opportunities for indigenous people to extend the scope of self-determination" (Macdonald and Muldoon 2006: 221). The constitutional commitment to Maori self-determination not only blocked certain neoliberal reforms – for example, plans to privatize state property were blocked by Maori claims that they had vested rights in that property – but also meant that the Maori were in a position to take advantage of the reforms that did take place. Before neoliberal reforms, Maori affairs (and the delivery of public services to the Maori) were monopolized by one (paternalistic) department of government, but neoliberal reforms allowed Maori organizations to contract with various government departments to provide a wide range of services to Maori and indeed to non-Maori people. The techniques of neoliberal New Public Management "released a myriad of political possibilities that Maori seized with both hands," strengthening their ability to shape the future of their communities.[20] Neoliberal reforms also allowed Maori communities more direct access to global markets, which in turn allowed them to "stand tall" in negotiating with the state (ibid., 216, 212–13).

It is crucial to emphasize that indigenous politics is not driven by neoliberal motivations. As Lucero puts it, "the rise of indigenous politics is about

---

[19] Speaking of francophone minorities in Canada, Heller describes the impact of neoliberalism this way: "The only thing the state had ever made of their Frenchness was to construct it as a problem that somehow had to be resolved. Now, the state, at various levels, regards it as something to sell" (Heller 2010: 149). Critics may bemoan this framing of cultural difference as a commodity, but it is surely better than framing difference as a "problem" to be "resolved." The former opens up both political and economic possibilities that the latter forecloses.

[20] For a similar argument about neoliberalism's effects on indigenous self-determination in Canada, see Slowey (2008). For a more skeptical view, see Friedel (2011).

nothing less than the finding of a democratic route toward decolonization, and a decolonizing route toward democracy" (Lucero 2008: ix). The point, rather, is that where these democratic and decolonizing impulses have gained political recognition – where forms of multicultural citizenship are in place – then indigenous people are capable of taking advantage of neoliberal reforms to enhance their status as market actors *and to use their enhanced status as market actors to further strengthen their ethnic projects of indigenous self-determination*. This is a theme that recurs repeatedly, if sotto voce, in the literature on neoliberal multiculturalism. The dominant motif in the literature is Hale's claim that neoliberalism has reduced space for indigenous political projects to the "safe" confines of the "permitted Indian." The contrapuntal theme is that neoliberalism's promotion of market participation for indigenous peoples has strengthened their capacity to pursue "a democratic route toward decolonization." In at least some circumstances, "indigenous groups can find tools and resources in neo-liberal programs" (Fischer 2007: 11).

A similar story applies to the case of immigrants and national minorities. Where a threshold level of democratic citizenization was established before neoliberalism, the introduction of neoliberal reforms could sometimes benefit rather than harm minorities. For example, Cardinal and Denault (2007) argue that new forms of neoliberal governance helped to empower francophone minorities in Canada to extend their language rights. Similarly, Mitchell (2004) argues that Chinese immigrants were able to deploy neoliberal commitments, such as the valorizing of transnational entrepreneurship, to challenge exclusionary aspects of national identity in Canada.[21] And Harney (2011) argues that the shift to a more entrepreneurial model of nongovernmental organization advocacy was seen as by some activists as a way of enhancing their effectiveness without undermining their core mission.[22] In all of these cases, a commitment to multicultural citizenship was already institutionalized, and neoliberal reforms provided new opportunities to advance that goal.

I am not suggesting that *only* neoliberalism could have secured these benefits or that neoliberalism did not have offsetting negative effects.[23] Free trade

---

[21] For the complexities of "acceptable Asianness" in an era of neoliberal multiculturalism, see Park (2011).

[22] According to Harney's ethnography of a multicultural organization in Ontario, the staff adapted to, and embraced, the logic of financialization and entrepreneurship while retaining their commitment to a "pre-neoliberal ethos of solidarity and democratic pluralism." As he puts it, "This is not to suggest that workers did not find their now flexible labour positions more precarious, the long-term stability of the institution more unclear nor that they did not begin to think of themselves as human capital or entrepreneurs of the self" but nonetheless they "maintained their solidaristic pre-neoliberal conception of multiculturalism even as they experimented with a sociality dominated by market exchange" and indeed "envisaged that some of these specific features of neoliberal practice might enhance the prior localised practices and ethics" (Harney 2011).

[23] Macdonald and Muldoon (2006) say that neoliberalism "released global forces that devastated the social and economic worlds of Maori," including a massive jump in unemployment. Yet they argue that the political gains made by Maori under neoliberalism mean that "Maori have

agreements and deregulated markets should not be necessary to give indigenous peoples greater self-determination, to give Francophone minorities more
autonomy, or to give Chinese immigrants more respect. Keynesian welfare
states should have been able to do so. Unfortunately, in many cases, they did
not, partly because they served majorities better than they served minorities,
and hence some minorities were able to see neoliberal reforms as strengthening
both their market participation and their political standing.

This suggests that multiculturalism is most effective when it attends both to
people's citizenship status and to their market status. Either, on its own, may
be inadequate. On the one hand, social liberal forms of multiculturalism may
fail if they leave their intended beneficiaries excluded from effective market
access. This is (part of) Koopmans's analysis for the failure of multiculturalism
in the Netherlands compared with its apparent success in countries such as
Canada, Australia, and the United States (Koopmans 2010). Although Dutch
multiculturalism provided political recognition to immigrant groups and generous social rights, it did not give them effective access to Dutch labor markets,
leading to a situation of social segregation and political stigmatization. The
problem was not poverty because the Dutch welfare system is reasonably generous. The problem, rather, is that participating in markets and making an
economic contribution is a source of many intangible social resources – bridging and bonding networks, identities, narratives of belonging – from which
immigrants were excluded. In Koopman's view, the older model of Dutch multiculturalism neglected the importance of market participation.

On the other hand, neoliberal reforms that expose minorities to market
reforms will also fail if minorities lack a robust citizenship standing that enables
their effective political agency. This is the story of the neoliberal destructuring
of Aboriginal communities in Australia, in which neoliberalism undermined the
fragile forms of Aboriginal self-government and replaced them with a "range
of new initiatives that interpellate Indigenous people as a collection of failed
liberal individuals who need to be encouraged (by 'carrots and sticks') into
taking greater responsibility for themselves" (Macdonald and Muldoon 2006:
218–19).

There is rich material here for reflecting on the nature of social resilience.
If we are indeed moving into a post-neoliberal age in which we are trying to
reintegrate democratic citizenship and markets, multiculturalism might provide
some instructive cases of how they can (or cannot) be combined.

However, it is premature to draw conclusions from these cases, and more
work is needed to clarify how different forms of multiculturalism affect people's resources and capacities. As a starting point, we might predict that social
liberal multiculturalism has quite different impacts from neoliberal multiculturalism – the former contributing to citizenization and the latter to market

reconfigured their citizenship to such an extent that they have reduced the structural inequalities
that existed prior to the globalisation of the economy" (Macdonald and Muldoon 2006: 212,
216).

access at the expense of citizenship. But we do not yet have systematic evidence for such predictions. I noted earlier that there was compelling evidence that MCPs have contributed to citizenization. But none of the studies I cited there distinguish between social liberal and neoliberal MCPs, and we do not yet have reliable evidence to disentangle the effects of these different forms of multiculturalism. Nor is it clear that we can make this distinction in practice. Real-world MCPs are always hybrids, not ideal types, reflecting multiple interests and path-dependent influences. Moreover, social liberal multiculturalism in the West was always capitalist, so a background of market relations was taken for granted even if not highlighted in the same way as in the era of neoliberalism. And conversely neoliberalism – similar to any form of liberalism – is not just about markets but also about the liberal civil and political rights that are essential to citizenship. So even as ideal types, it is inaccurate to say that social liberalism is about citizenship, not markets, or that neoliberalism is about markets, not citizenship. These are differences in emphasis, not bright lines. In seems unlikely, therefore, that we will be able to devise large-scale studies that would systematically test the differential effects of social liberal MCPs compared with neoliberal MCPs. In any event, no one has yet undertaken such a project.

Similarly, it would be premature to claim that the prior existence of social liberal multiculturalism is a precondition for minorities to be able to effectively resist or adapt neoliberal reforms. That is one possible conclusion of the case studies mentioned earlier, but they are a small sample, and other factors are likely to play a significant role. I believe it is important that minority actors be able to draw upon a discourse and practice of multicultural citizenship when resisting or adapting neoliberalism, but in today's world, that discourse circulates globally. Ideas of multicultural citizenship are pervasive within the globalized policy networks and transnational advocacy networks that play such a prominent role in contemporary debates and indeed are codified in various international conventions.[24] In that sense, minority actors everywhere can draw upon global norms and global networks of multicultural citizenship even in countries that lack their own history of MCPs. A full analysis of the preconditions for minorities to effectively resist or adapt neoliberal reforms would require a more multilevel analysis than I have given here.

In the absence of such evidence, I have made a more modest argument. I have disputed the easy assumption that a hegemonic neoliberalism operated to destructure ethnic groups – to disable their collective capacities and political projects – and have suggested instead that the impact of neoliberalism depended on the extent to which groups were able to rely on preexisting multicultural settlements that ensured their effective political agency. To make further progress, we will need to find new ways to explore the interactions between our status as citizens and as market actors.

---

[24] On the international diffusion of ideas of multicultural citizenship, see Kymlicka (2007).

Appendix: Immigrant Multiculturalism Policy Scores, 1980–2010

	Total Score (out of a possible 8)		
	1980	2000	2010
Canada	5	7.5	7.5
Australia	4	8	8
Austria	0	1	1.5
Belgium	1	3	5.5
Denmark	0	0.5	0
Finland	0	1.5	6
France	1	2	2
Germany	0	2	2.5
Greece	0.5	0.5	2.5
Ireland	1	1.5	3
Italy	0	1.5	1
Japan	0	0	0
Netherlands	2.5	5.5	2
New Zealand	2.5	5	5.5
Norway	0	0	3.5
Portugal	1	2	3.5
Spain	0	1	3.5
Sweden	3	5	7
Switzerland	0	1	1
United Kingdom	2.5	5.5	5.5
United States	3	3	3
Average	**1.29**	**2.71**	**3.52**

Source: Multiculturalism Policy Index, http://www.queensu
.ca/mcp/.

Note

Countries could receive a total score of eight, one for each of the following
eight policies:

1. Constitutional, legislative or parliamentary affirmation of multiculturalism at the central and/or regional and municipal levels and the existence
   of a government ministry, secretariat or advisory board to implement
   this policy in consultation with ethnic communities.
2. The adoption of multiculturalism in school curriculum.
3. The inclusion of ethnic representation/sensitivity in the mandate of public
   media or media licensing.
4. Exemptions from dress codes.
5. Allowing of dual citizenship.
6. The funding of ethnic group organizations or activities.
7. The funding of bilingual education or mother-tongue instruction.
8. Affirmative action for disadvantaged immigrant groups.

References

Abu-Laban, Yasmeen and Christina Gabriel. 2002. *Selling Diversity: Immigration, Multiculturalism, Employment Equity and Globalization*. Peterborough, Ontario: Broadview.

Adams, Michael. 2007. *Unlikely Utopia: The Surprising Triumph of Canadian Pluralism*. Toronto: Viking.

Adamo. Silvia. 2008. "Northern Exposure: The New Danish Model of Citizenship Test." *International Journal on Multicultural Societies* 10 (1): 10–28.

Banting, Keith and Will Kymlicka. 2006. "Multiculturalism and the Welfare State: Setting the Context." In *Multiculturalism and the Welfare State*, edited by Keith Banting and Will Kymlicka. Oxford: Oxford University Press.

Berry, John, Jean Phinney, David Sam, and Paul Vedder. 2006. *Immigrant Youth in Cultural Transition*. Mahwah, NJ: Lawrence Erlbaum.

Bird, Karen. 2009. "Running Visible Minority Candidates in Canada: The Effects of Voter and Candidate Ethnicity and Gender on Voter Choice." Paper presented at conference on Diversity and Democratic Politics: Canada in Comparative Perspective, Queen's University, Kingston, ON.

Black, Jerome and Lynda Erickson. 2006. "Ethno-racial Origins of Candidates and Electoral Performance." *Party Politics* 12 (4): 541–61.

Bloemraad, Irene. 2006. *Becoming a Citizen: Incorporating Immigrants and Refugees in the United States and Canada*. Berkeley: University of California Press.

Brown, Wendy. 2003. "Neo-liberalism and the End of Liberal Democracy." *Theory and Event* 7 (1). http://muse.jhu.edu/journals/theory_&_event/.

Bourdieu, Pierre and Loïc Wacquant. 1999. "On the Cunning of Imperialist Reason." *Theory, Culture & Society* 16 (1): 41–58.

Cardinal, Linda and Anne-Andre Denault. 2007. "Empowering Linguistic Minorities: Neo-liberal Governance and Language Policies in Canada and Wales." *Regional & Federal Studies* 17 (4): 437–56.

Chandler, Michael and Christopher Lalonde. 1998. "Cultural Continuity as a Hedge Against Suicide in Canada's First Nations." *Journal of Transcultural Psychiatry* 35 (2): 191–219.

Cornell, Stephen and Joseph Kalt. 2000. "Where's the Glue? Institutional Bases of American Indian Economic Development." *Journal of Socio-Economics* 29: 443–70.

Crepaz, Markus. 2006. "'If you are my brother, I may give you a dime!' Public Opinion on Multiculturalism, Trust and the Welfare State." In *Multiculturalism and the Welfare State: Recognition and Redistribution in Contemporary Democracies*, ed. Keith Banting and Will Kymlicka. Oxford: Oxford University Press.

Davidson, Roei and Amit Schejter. 2011. "Their Deeds are the Deeds of Zimri; but They Expect a Reward Like Phineas: Neoliberal and Multicultural Discourses in the Development of Israeli DTT Policy." *Communication, Culture Critique* 4 (1): 1–22.

Davis, Shelton and Katrinka Ebbe. 1993. Traditional Knowledge and Sustainable Development: Environmentally Sustainable Development Proceedings Series No. 4, Washington, DC: World Bank.

Fischer, Edward. 2007. "Indigenous Peoples, Neo-liberal Regimes, and Varieties of Civil Society in Latin America." *Social Analysis* 51 (2): 1–18.

Focus Canada. 2006. *Canadians' Attitudes toward Muslims*. Toronto: Environics.

Friedel, Tracy. 2011. "Enduring Neoliberalism in Alberta's Oil Sands: The Troubling Effects of Private-Public Partnerships for First Nation and Métis Communities." *Citizenship Studies* 15 (6): 815–35.

Glick-Schiller, Nina. 2011. "Localized Neoliberalism, Multiculturalism and Global Religion: Exploring the Agency of Migrants and City Boosters." *Economy and Society* 40 (2): 211–38.

Guetzkow, Joshua. 2010. "Beyond Deservingness: Congressional Discourse on Poverty, 1964–1996." *Annals of the American Academy of Political and Social Science.* 629: 173–97.

Hale, Charles. 2005. "Neoliberal Multiculturalism." *POLAR: Political and Legal Anthropology Review* 28 (1): 10–28.

Hale, Charles and Rosamel Millaman. 2005. "Cultural Agency and Political Struggle in the Era of Indio Permitido." In *Cultural Agency in the Americas*, edited by Doris Sommer. Durham, NC: Duke University Press.

Harell, Allison. 2009. "Minority-Majority Relations in Canada: The Rights Regime and the Adoption of Multicultural Values." Paper presented at the Canadian Political Science Association Annual Meeting, Ottawa.

Harney, Nicholas. 2011. "Neoliberal Restructuring and Multicultural Legacies: The Experiences of a Mid-Level Actor in Recognizing Difference." *Ethnic and Racial Studies* 34 (11): 1913–32.

Heath, Anthony. 2007. "Crossnational Patterns and Processes of Ethnic Disadvantage." In *Unequal Chances: Ethnic Minorities in Western Labour Markets*, edited by Anthony Heath and Sin Yi Cheung. Oxford: Oxford University Press.

Heller, Monica. 2010. *Paths to Post-Nationalism*. Oxford: Oxford University Press.

Herring, C. 2009. "Does Diversity Pay? Race, Gender and the Business Case for Diversity." *American Sociological Review* 74 (2): 208–24.

Hinz, Bronwyn Ann. 2010. "The Untold Story of Australian Multiculturalism: How It Was Shaped from Below by Ethnic Communities." Paper presented to Midwest Political Science Association 68th Annual Conference, Chicago.

Howe, Paul. 2007. "The Political Engagement of New Canadians: A Comparative Perspective." In *Belonging? Diversity, Recognition and Shared Citizenship in Canada*, edited by Keith Banting, Thomas J. Courchene and F. Leslie Seidle. Montreal: Institute for Research on Public Policy.

James, Matt. 2006. *Misrecognized Materialists: Social Movements in Canadian Constitutional Politics*. Vancouver: UBC Press.

James, Matt. 2013. "Neoliberal Heritage Redress." In *Reconciling Canada: Critical Perspectives on the Culture of Redress*, edited by Jennifer Henderson and Pauline Wakeham. Toronto: University of Toronto Press.

Joppke, Christian. 2004. "The Retreat of Multiculturalism in the Liberal State: Theory and Policy." *British Journal of Sociology* 55 (2): 237–57.

Joshee, Reva. 2004. "Citizenship and Multicultural Education in Canada." In *Diversity and Citizenship Education*, edited by James Banks. San Francisco: Jossey-Bass.

Kauffman, Paul. 2004. "Diversity and Indigenous Policy Outcomes: Comparisons Between Four Nations." *International Journal of Diversity in Organizations, Communities and Nations*, 3: 159–80.

Kazemipur, Abdolmohammad. 2009. *Social Capital and Diversity: Some Lessons from Canada*. Bern: Peter Lang.

Keating, Michael. 2001. *Nations Against the State: The New Politics of Nationalism in Quebec, Catalonia and Scotland*. Basingstoke: Palgrave.

Kesler, Christel and Irene Bloemraad. 2010. "Does Immigration Erode Social Capital? The Conditional Effects of Immigration-Generated Diversity on Trust, Membership, and Participation Across 19 Countries, 1981–2000." *Canadian Journal of Political Science* 43 (2): 319–47.

Kim, Nam-Kook. 2010. "Revisiting New Right Citizenship Discourse in Thatcher's Britain." *Ethnicities* 10 (2): 208–35.

Koning, E. A. 2011. "Ethnic and Civic Dealings with Newcomers: Naturalization Policies and Practices in 26 Immigration Countries." *Ethnic and Racial Studies* 34 (11): 1974–94.

Koopmans, Ruud. 2010. "Trade-Offs Between Equality and Difference: Immigrant Integration, Multiculturalism and the Welfare State in Cross-National Perspective." *Journal of Ethnic and Migration Studies* 36 (1): 1–26.

Koopmans, Ruud, Ines Michalowski, and Stine Waibel. 2012. "Citizenship Rights for Immigrants: National Political Processes and Cross-National Convergence in Western Europe, 1980–2008." *American Journal of Sociology* 117 (4): 1202–45.

Kymlicka, Will. 2007. *Multicultural Odysseys: Navigating the New International Politics of Diversity*. Oxford: Oxford University Press.

Kymlicka, Will. 2010. "Testing the Liberal Multiculturalist Hypothesis: Normative Theories and Social Science Evidence." *Canadian Journal of Political Science* 43 (2): 257–71.

Kymlicka, Will. 2012. *Multiculturalism: Success, Failure, and the Future*. Washington, DC: Migration Policy Institute.

Laczko, Leslie. 2007. "National and Continental Attachments and Attitudes towards Immigrants: North America and Europe Compared." Paper presented at the Annual Meeting of the Canadian Sociology Association, Saskatoon.

Lane, Carrie. 2011. *A Company of One: Insecurity, Independence, and the New World of White-Collar Unemployment*. Ithaca, NY: Cornell University Press.

Lucero, Jose Antonio. 2008. *Struggles of Voice: The Politics of Indigenous Representation in the Andes*. Pittsburgh: University of Pittsburgh Press.

Macdonald, Lindsay Te Ata O Tu, and Paul Muldoon. 2006. "Globalisation, Neo-Liberalism, and the Struggle for Indigenous Citizenship." *Australian Journal of Political Science* 41 (2): 209–23.

Magord, Andre. 2008. *The Quest for Autonomy in Acadia*. Bern: Lang.

Marc, Alexandre. 2009. *Delivering Services in Multicultural Societies*. Washington, DC: World Bank.

McGhee, Derek. 2008. *The End of Multiculturalism? Terrorism, Integration and Human Rights*. Maidenhead: Open University Press.

McNeish, John-Andrew. 2008. "Beyond the Permitted Indian? Bolivia and Guatemala in an Era of Neo-Liberal Developmentalism." *Latin American and Caribbean Ethnic Studies* 3: 33–59.

Melamed, Jodi. 2006. "The Spirit of Neoliberalism: Racial Liberalism to Neoliberal Multiculturalism." *Social Text* 24 (4): 1–24.

Mitchell, Katharyne. 2003. "Educating the National Citizen in Neoliberal Times: From the Multicultural Self to the Strategic Cosmopolitan." *Transactions of the Institute of British Geographers, New Series* 28 (4): 387–403.

Mitchell, Katharyne. 2004. *Crossing the Neoliberal Line: Pacific Rim Migration and the Metropolis*. Philadelphia: Temple University Press.

Murphy, P. B. O'Brien and S. Watson. 2003. "Selling Australia, Selling Sydney: The Ambivalent Politics of Entrepreneurial Multiculturalism." *Journal of International Migration and Immigration* 4: 471–98.

OECD. 2006. *Where Immigrant Students Succeed: A Comparative Review of Performance and Engagement in PISA 2003*. Paris: OECD, Program for International Student Assessment.

Park, Hijin. 2011. "Being Canada's National Citizen: Difference and the Economics of Multicultural Nationalism." *Social Identities* 17 (5): 643–63.

Putnam, Robert D. 2000. *Bowling Alone: The Collapse and Revival of American Communities*. New York: Simon and Schuster.

Ratner, R. S., William Carroll, and James Woolford. 2003. "Wealth of Nations: Aboriginal Treaty Making in the Era of Globalization." In *Politics and the Past: On Repairing Historical Injustices*, edited by John Torpey. Lanham: Rowman and Littlefield: 217–48.

Reitz, Jeffrey. 2009. "Assessing Multiculturalism as a Behavioural Theory." In *Multiculturalism and Social Cohesion: Potentials and Challenges of Diversity*, edited by Raymond Breton, Karen Dion, and Kenneth Dion. New York: Springer.

Resnik, Julia. 2009. "Multicultural Education – Good for Business But Not for the State? The IB Curriculum and Global Capitalism." *British Journal of Education Studies* 57/3: 217–44.

Ringold, Dena. 2005. "Accounting for Diversity: Policy Design and Maori Development in New Zealand." Working paper prepared for World Bank conference on "New Frontiers of Social Policy: Development in a Globalizing World." Arusha, Tanzania, December.

Sawyer, Suzana. 2004. *Crude Chronicles: Indigenous Politics, Multinational Oil, and Neoliberalism in Ecuador*. Durham: Duke University Press.

Slowey, Gabrielle. 2008. *Navigating Neoliberalism: Self-Determination and the Mikisew Cree First Nation*. Vancouver: UBC Press.

Smith, Anthony. 1981. *The Ethnic Revival in the Modern World*. Cambridge, UK: Cambridge University Press.

Somers, Margaret. 2008. *Genealogies of Citizenship: Markets, Statelessness, and the Right to have Rights*. Cambridge, UK: Cambridge University Press.

Tully, James. 2001. "Introduction." In *Multinational Democracies*, edited by Alain Gagnon and James Tully. Cambridge, UK: Cambridge University Press.

Van Cott, Donna Lee. 2006. "Multiculturalism against Neoliberalism in Latin America." In Keith Banting and Will Kymlicka, eds. *Multiculturalism and the Welfare State*. Oxford: Oxford University Press.

van Nieuwkoop, Martien and Jorge Uquillas. 2000. *Defining Ethnodevelopment in Operational Terms: Lessons from the Ecuador Indigenous and Afro-Ecuadoran Peoples Project*. LCR Sustainable Development Working Paper No. 6, Environmentally and Socially Sustainable Development Sector Management Unit, Latin American and Caribbean Regional Office, World Bank.

Vertovec, Steven and Susan Wessendorf, eds. 2010. *The Multiculturalism Backlash: European Discourses, Policies and Practices*. London: Routledge.

Weldon, Steven. 2006. "The Institutional Context of Tolerance for Ethnic Minorities: A Comparative Multilevel Analysis of Western Europe." *American Journal of Political Science* 50 (2): 331–49.

Williams, David. 1999. "Race, Socioeconomic Status and Health: The Added Effects of Racism and Discrimination." *Annals of the New York Academy of Sciences* 896: 173–188.

Zizek, Slavoj. 1997. "Multiculturalism, or the Cultural Logic of Multinational Capitalism." *New Left Review* 225: 28–51.

PART II

THE SOCIAL SOURCES OF INDIVIDUAL RESILIENCE

4

Responses to Discrimination and Social Resilience Under Neoliberalism

The United States Compared[1]

Michèle Lamont, Jessica S. Welburn, and
Crystal M. Fleming

Members of stigmatized groups often live with the expectation that they will be overscrutinized, overlooked, underappreciated, misunderstood, and disrespected in the course of their daily lives. How do they interpret and respond to this lived reality? What resources do they have at their disposal to do so? How are their responses shaped by neoliberalism? How can responses to stigmatization foster social resilience?

This chapter enriches our understanding of social resilience by considering whether and how stigmatized groups may be empowered by potentially

[1] This research developed in the context of an international research project. Conversations with our collaborators Joshua Guetzkow, Hanna Herzog, Nissim Mizrachi, Elisa Reis, and Graziella Silva de Moraes fed our thinking in multiple ways. Our chapter also benefitted from the input of the members of the Successful Societies Program and the support of the Canadian Institute for Advanced Research, as well as from comments from Kathleen Blee, Robert Castel, Anthony Jack, Carol Greenhouse, and Andreas Wimmer. The research was presented in a number of settings where the reactions of the audience broadened our thinking: the Institut Marcel Mauss; Ecole des Hautes études en sciences sociales; the Centre Maurice Halbwachs; Ecole normale supérieure; the Obervatoire sociologique du changement, Sciences Po; the seminar "Cities are Back in Town," Sciences Po; the Humanities Center, University of Pittsburg; the Departments of Sociology at Yale University, Boston University, Brandeis University, and Brown University; the Faculty of Social Sciences and History of the Diego Portales University, Santiago de Chile; the POLINE conference on Perceptions of Inequality, Sciences Po (Paris, May 2011); the Nordic Sociological Association meetings (Oslo, August 2011); the Adlerbert Research Foundation Jubilee Conference on "Creating Successful and Sustainable Societies" (Gothenburg, November 2011); and the meetings of the Association for the Study of Ethnicity and Nationalism (London, March 2012). Funding for the comparative study of responses to stigmatization and for data gathering in Brazil was provided by a faculty grant and a Weatherhead Initiative grant from the Weatherhead Center for International Affairs, Harvard University. Research on African American responses to stigmatization was funded by a grant from the National Science Foundation (# 701542). Research on Israeli responses to stigmatization was funded by a grant from the US-Israeli Binational Science Foundation. Michèle Lamont acknowledges the generous support of the Canadian Institute for Advanced Research. We thank Travis Clough for his technical assistance.

contradictory contextual forces – more specifically, by cultural repertoires that enable their social inclusion. We consider repertoires to be social scripts, myths, and cultural structures and that the content of these repertoires varies to some extent across national contexts (Lamont and Thévenot 2000).[2] We also consider that certain repertoires can foster resilience by feeding the capacity of individuals to maintain positive self-concepts; dignity; and a sense of inclusion, belonging, and recognition.[3] We argue that societies provide individuals with different means for bolstering their identity and building resilience. This is accomplished by making available repertoires that are fed by national ideologies, neoliberalism, and narratives concerning the collective identity of their groups.[4]

Considering repertoires is an essential macro complement to the generally more micro approaches to resilience and responses to stigma. It shifts the focus on social resilience conceived as a feature of groups as opposed to a feature of individuals. It also brings to light neglected conditions for recognition and social inclusion, which are essential dimensions of successful societies (Hall and Lamont 2009). For instance, Wright and Bloemraad (2012) show that societies that adopt multicultural narratives about collective identity and multicultural policies (i.e., that score high on the multiculturalism index) signal to immigrants that they value their contributions to the host society. These societies not only provide recognition to immigrants but also foster their emotional and cognitive engagement in this host society as manifested for instance in their greater political participation. This means that repertoires matter. Also, while stigmatization and discrimination toward particular groups is a universal feature of societies, national histories of group boundaries, conflict, and reconciliation vary. Societal trajectories of group relations shape the opportunities and resources individuals have at their disposal for understanding and dealing with stigmatization and thus affect their resilience.

Although this chapter concerns primarily the United States, we adopt a comparative approach and also describe responses to stigmatization in Brazil and Israel, countries where the boundaries separating the main stigmatized group from other groups differ in their degree of permeability and porousness

---

[2] On repertoires, see Swidler (1986), and Tilly (2006). Although collective imaginaries provide to a group a sense of shared past and future, as well as shared identity (see the introduction to this volume), the term "repertoire" can be apply to such collective imaginaries, as well as to other relatively stable schemas or cultural structure.

[3] On recognition, see Taylor (1992), Honneth (1996), and Fraser and Honneth (2003). Walton and Cohen (2011) have shown that social belonging increases self-reported well-being among African American college students. In future research, we will consider how various types of responses to stigmatization influences subjective well-being. On collective imaginaries and health, see Bouchard (2009).

[4] Other repertoires may be more relevant in other societies and historical periods. We take Jenkins' (1996) theory concerning social identity as a point of departure: we understand it as resulting from both self-identification (e.g., what it means for African Americans to belong to this group) and group categorization (the meaning given to this group by outgroup members; see also Cornell and Hartman 1997 and Brubaker and Cooper 2000).

(Lamont and Bail 2005). In the three national settings under consideration, we focus on responses to stigmatization among members of groups that are marked on different bases and with different intensities, that is: (a) African Americans in the New York metropolitan area; (b) Afro-Brazilians in Rio de Janeiro; and (b) Ethiopian Jews, second-generation of Mizrahi Jews, and Arab citizens of Israel in greater Tel Aviv. Whereas the first three groups have historically been stigmatized based on phenotype, Mizrahis are discriminated against based on ethnicity – although they are a majority group in Israel. For their part, Arab Israelis are primarily stigmatized because of their ethno-religious identity – that is, as Arabs and non-Jews.[5]

The comparison is informed by interviews conducted with large samples of "ordinary" middle class and working class men and women in each of these three national contexts (with 150 interviews in the United States, 160 in Brazil, and 125 in Israel).[6] These individuals are ordinary in the sense that they are not characterized by, nor selected on the basis of, their involvement in social movements related to identity politics (unlike Moon 2012). They were selected as research participants generally randomly based on criteria such as place of residence, occupations, and level of education (see Appendix for details). This approach is most appropriate for documenting the whole range of responses to stigmatization found in a population without privileging social actors who are most politicized. This is necessary because we are concerned with how the consolidation of collective identity may affect everyday responses to stigmatization.[7]

The empirical focus of our interviews is accounts of rhetorical and strategic tools deployed by individual members of stigmatized groups to respond to perceived stigmatization (a broad term that includes or accompanies perceived assaults on dignity, blatant racism, and discrimination). Responses to

---

[5] Bases of stigmatization are historically contingent, with (for instance) biological racism being replaced by cultural racism in the so-called "post-racialism" era in the United States (Bobo 2011).

[6] This research was conducted by three groups of social scientists who have engaged in a collaborative study since 2005. We adopted a comparative approach with parallel research designs and data collection procedures. Core collaborators in Israel are Joshua Guetzkow (Department of Anthropology and Sociology, Hebrew University), Hanna Herzog, and Nissim Mizrachi (Department of Anthropology and Sociology, Tel Aviv University). For Brazil, collaborators are Elisa Reis and Graziella Silva (Interdisciplinary Center for the Study of Inequality, Federal University of Rio). For the United States, the core team consists of Crystal Fleming (Department of Sociology, State University of New York at Stony Brook), Michèle Lamont (Department of Sociology and Department of African and African American Studies, Harvard University), and Jessica Welburn (Department of Sociology and Department of African-American Studies, University of Michigan). The U.S. team benefitted from the assistance of Monica Bell, Mellisa Bellin, Steven Brown, Moa Bursell, Nathan Fosse, Nicole Hirsch, Veronique Irwin, Anthony Jack, Michael Jeffries, and Cassi Pittman.

[7] The notion of "everyday response to stigmatization" is inspired by Essed (1991)'s notion of everyday racism as "... integration of racism into everyday situations through practices that activate underlying power relations" (50). It also expands on Aptheker (1992)'s definition of anti-racism as rhetoric aimed at disproving racial inferiority. For a discussion of everyday anti-racism, see Pollock (2008). On stigma, see Goffman (1963).

stigmatization can be individual or collective, and they take a variety of forms such as confronting, evading or deflating conflict, claiming inclusion or superiority, educating or reforming the ignorant, attempting to conform to majority culture or affirming distinctiveness, wanting to "pass" or denouncing stereotyping, and engaging in boundary work toward undesirable "others" when responding to stigmatization. They also include "exit" strategies, such as "limiting contacts," "absorbing it," "ignoring the racists," and "managing the self" (Fleming, Lamont, and Welburn 2012). These responses (including decisions to not respond) occur both in private (when individuals ruminate about past experiences and try to make sense of them) and in public (when they interact with others while reacting to specific events or incidents) (see Bickerstaff 2012 on public and private responses).

As we explored responses to stigmatization, we paid special attention to interviewees' references to national histories and scripts and to collective myths, as well as to their views concerning what grounds cultural membership and belonging – criteria ranging from economic success to morality and cultural similarities (Lamont 2000). In doing so, we aimed to capture what repertoires respondents drew on in describing situations of stigmatization and how they dealt with them. We also gathered information on their beliefs about, and explanations for, equality and differences between human groups.[8] Although comparative studies of race relations are generally focused on political ideology and state structures (e.g., Marx 1998; Lieberman 2009) or elite discourse (e.g., Van Dijk 1993; Eyerman 2002),[9] we connect such ideologies to individual narratives about daily experiences, intergroup relationships, and group boundaries.[10]

Our topic is particularly significant at the present juncture and this is for two reasons: First, to the extent that neoliberalism is often associated with individualization, depoliticization, and a flight away from social justice movements (Lazzarato 2009; Greenhouse 2011), we need to better distinguish between responses to stigma that aim to correct the situation of the individual versus that of the group (see also Ancelovici [Chapter 12] on French responses to class domination). Second, in the current period of growing economic inequality, members of stigmatized groups are often more vulnerable (Pierson and Hacker 2010; also Welburn 2012 on the downwardly mobile African American middle class).[11] In this period of increased insecurity, it is particularly urgent to

---

[8] This approach is developed in Lamont (2000). Drawing on the sociology of science, it focuses specifically on how ordinary people construct facts on the nature of human groups based on various types of evidence. See also Morning (2009) on racial conceptualizations and Roth (2012) on racial schemas.

[9] Space limitation precludes a comparison of our approach with the influential critical discourse analysis approach to racism (e.g., Wodak 2001) or to more political studies of white and black anti-racism (Feagin and Sikes 1994; Picca and Feagin 2007; for a review, see O'Brien 2007).

[10] On groupness and ethno-racial boundaries, see Zolberg and Wong (1999); Lamont (2000); Lamont and Molnar (2002); Todd (2004); Wimmer (2006); Pachucki, Lamont, and Pendergrass (2006); Bail (2008); Brubaker (2009); Alba (2009); and Massey and Sanchez (2010).

[11] In May 2012, the Bureau of Labor Statistics reported that 7.4 percent of whites were currently unemployed compared with 13.6 percent of African Americans. Research has also consistently

better understand which resources (cultural and others) enable the development of their social resilience and the lessening of vulnerabilities.

Our concern is subjectivities in the neoliberal age. The growing literature on the neoliberal subjectivities has focused primarily on the transformation of middle and upper-middle class selves under late capitalism (e.g., Hearn 2008), described alternatively (under the influence of Giddens 1991, Boltanski and Chiafello 1999, and others) as having self-actualizing, networked, branded, and cosmopolitan selves. Social scientists have generally neglected the national scripts or myths made available to "ordinary" working class people, who make up half of our respondents and more than the majority of the American population. This group is also neglected in studies of everyday responses to racism – despite a huge literature on African Americans' responses to racism, particularly through social movements (but for a few exceptions, e.g., Frederick [2010] on African Americans' aspirations to be millionaires).

The paper opens with two examples of experiences and responses to stigmatization by African American men. It discusses what most African American interviewees believe is the best way to respond to racists: confrontation. It also explores how this response is shaped by American national histories and myths. Second, drawing on the collective work of our collaborators in Brazil and Israel (as presented in a special issue of *Ethnic and Racial Studies* by Lamont and Mizrachi 2012), we sketch how responses to stigmatization in these countries are also shaped by national collective myths, including those that concern the history, place, and salience of ethno-racial minorities in the polity. Third, we take a closer look at the American case to examine how responses to stigmatization are shaped by (a) repertoires about matrices of human worth that are connected to neoliberalism and that emphasize competition, consumption, individualization, and personal achievement and (b) repertoires tied to African American collective identity, its tradition of resilience, and its distinctive criteria of worth. Information on research design, selection, interviews, and data collection and analysis are available in the Appendix.

Drawing only on questions we asked interviewees concerning their ideal or "best" approaches to responding to stigmatization, the chapter highlights the responses to stigmatization in Brazil, Israel, and the United States. We found that the most popular response among African Americans we talked to is confronting racism (Fleming et al. 2011), which is motivated by a national history of *de jure* racial exclusion and fed by the lasting legacy of the civil rights movement. In contrast, most Afro-Brazilian interviewees assert the centrality of racial mixture (variously defined) in their society, including the notion that

shown that African Americans have considerably less wealth than whites, which includes lower homeownership rates, less saving, and few investments (e.g., Conley 1999; Oliver and Shapiro 2006; Pew Charitable Trust Foundation 2011). For example, Shapiro and Oliver (2005) find that African Americans control only ten cents for every dollar whites control. A 2011 report by the Pew Charitable Trust Foundation shows that the wealth gap has only grown since the 2008 global recession.

"we are all a little black." In this context, they promote accommodation over confrontation (Silva and Reis 2011) as more compatible with national identity and culture (with reference to the notion of racial democracy). For their part, interviewees from stigmatized Jewish groups in Israel emphasize shared religion over ethno-racial identity and respond to stigmatization by asserting the Jewish identity they share with the majority group (Mizrachi and Herzog 2012). Finally, in the face of strong ethnic and religious discrimination, Arab Israelis respond by evoking the universal respect of human dignity. They also avoid making claims based on group rights (Mizrachi and Zawdu 2012). We suggest that in each case, these responses are facilitated by widely available cultural myths about national belonging – more specifically, by the American dream, the myth of Brazilian racial democracy, and Israeli Zionism.

A closer look at the American case reveals that African Americans draw on two additional repertoires in responding to stigmatization. First, they use a repertoire made more readily available by neoliberalism, which focuses on scripts that value competition, consumption, individualization (Bourdieu 1998), and personal achievements (in line with market fundamentalism) (Somers 2008). These scripts of response go hand in hand with individualist explanations of low achievement, poverty, and unemployment, which are often associated with poor moral character (laziness, lack of self-reliance), as opposed to market and structural forces.[12] Second, they use a repertoire that is connected to group identity and that celebrates shared culture and experiences. These narratives are sources of pleasure and comfort that can act as a counterweight to feelings of isolation and powerlessness, and as such, enable social resilience. These repertoires also emphasize moral strength and a history of survival that mitigate self-blaming and may also act as a resource for social resilience. Finally as Lamont (2000) argued based on interviews conducted in 1993, we also find an alternative moral matrix of evaluation that allows African Americans to not measure themselves by the dominant standard of socioeconomic success.[13] These alternative repertoires can potentially act as sources of social resilience by broadening the criteria of social inclusion.

Widely available narratives that stress the American history of racism and fight against racial domination (of the type associated with the American civil rights movement and with African American social movements, such as the Black Panthers) and representations of shared African American collective identity characterized by resilience can enable collective responses oriented toward confrontation. But scripts central to neoliberalism may also primarily favor individualist responses to stigma, particularly the pursuit of individual

---

[12] Similarly, Greenhouse (2011) argues that the moral construction of African Americans and poverty has been profoundly transformed under neoliberalism – with a stronger stigmatization of welfare dependency and celebration of a neoliberal self. This means that the tools with which African Americans respond to racism are themselves the product of neoliberalism.

[13] This is one of the three elements of definition of social resilience at the center of this collective volume. The two other dimensions are ability to imagine better futures that are within one's reach and the ability to resist discrimination, exploitation, and exclusion.

mobility. Addressing whether individual or collective responses have positive or negative association with social resilience is beyond the scope of this chapter. However, we point out ways in which the various repertoires respondents draw on may affect social resilience. For instance, although a focus on personal achievement may encourage African Americans to escape stigma through an agentic and universalist logic (as one respondent puts it, "get the skills to get the job – may the best man win"), it may also limit the appeal of alternative matrixes of evaluation (e.g., the notion that blacks have a caring self and solidarity) (Lamont 2000) that emphasizes morality, downplays socioeconomic success, and thus sustains positive self-images despite low social status.

This chapter builds directly on *Successful Societies: How Institutions and Culture Affect Health*, which focused on the capability of individuals and groups to respond to the challenges they encounter and on how institutions and shared cultural repertoires serve as resources and buffers against the "wear and tear of inequality" that epidemiologists address (Clark, Clark, and Williams 1999; Hertzman and Boyce 2010). National identity, scripts provided by neoliberalism, and scripts about collective identity, are some of the main repertoires or toolkits on which individuals draw to gain recognition and respond to the challenges they face (Lamont 2009). Thus, resilience is maintained not only by inner moral strength and resourcefulness or by social support (often emphasized in popular and scholarly writings) but also through the repertoires that sustain recognition or the institutionalization and circulation of positive conceptions of individual or collective selves. From this perspective, members of stigmatized groups vary with regard to their ability to reshape group relations in ways that allow for the widespread adoption of representations and narratives asserting the dignity and worth of their group.

This argument complements social psychological approaches to resilience. Social psychologists typically focus on the psychological orientations that foster individual resilience, such as privileging the in-group as a reference group (Crocker, Major, and Steele, 1998)[14] and having a strong racial identification or biculturalism (Oyserman and Swim 2001). They also consider the impact of cognitive ability, positive self-perception, and emotional regulation on resilience, as well as the broader environment, generally network and community support (see Son Hing, Chapter 5).[15] In contrast, again, our analysis centers on the cultural supply side of the equation, that is, on cultural repertoires

---

[14] See also Pinel (1999) on "stigma consciousness" and Clark et al. (1999) on how minority groups cope psychologically with the "perceived stressor" of racism and prejudice. Also Son Hing 2012. See Link and Phelan (2000) for a broader review of the literature on stigma, which is most often concerned with the stigma of "stressors" such as mental illness and physical disabilities and their impact on health.

[15] Son Hing (Chapter 5) considers that "protective factors (i.e., strengths or capabilities) may reside within the individual (e.g., emotional regulation, self-enhancement), the family (e.g., secure attachments, authoritative parenting), or the community or environment (e.g., community resources, programming)." Cultural repertoires are not part of the protective factors they have paid attention to.

and the relative availability of alternative ways of understanding social reality (also Harding, Lamont, and Small 2010).

It is important to note that institutional and structural forces also play a crucial role in shaping responses and diffusing repertoires. Indeed, a large literature addresses the role of public policies in defining the conditions of reception for minority groups, including how they understand their place in the polity (e.g., Kastoryano 2002; Ireland 2004; Koopmans et al. 2005; Wimmer and Min 2006). These topics are beyond the scope of this chapter, so we leave them aside. For the most part, we also leave aside the important questions of how repertoires diffuse, why individuals or groups are more likely to draw on one script rather than another (see, e.g., Lamont 1992; Schudson 1988), and variations in the salience of ethno-racial identities across groups.[16]

African Americans Experiencing and Responding to Stigmatization

How does it feel to be outside of a boundary? Most of the African American men and women we interviewed perceive themselves as being underestimated, distrusted, overscrutinized, misunderstood, feared, overlooked, avoided, or plainly discriminated against due to their ethnoracial belonging at some point in their lives. This perception can be persistent for some respondents and situational for others. Two examples provide suitable illustrations. They both concern two strikingly similar narratives in which an African American man finds himself inside an elevator with outgroup members.[17]

In the first case, Marcus, a black court employee, enters an elevator in which there is a middle-aged Indian woman who also works at the court.[18] He describes the situation thus: "She clutches her purse. I almost fainted. I almost fainted.... It devastated me. But it's happened to brothers before. Welcome to the Black race, brother. You've got it. I've got it." Her reactions prompt Marcus's anger and humiliation because, as he explains, he often feels that people think he does not belong in the court building. For instance, he

---

[16] Of the three groups of African descent, African Americans are most likely to self-define through their racial identity, and they are more likely to label an interaction or a person as "racist." Afro-Brazilians and Ethiopian Jews have racial identities that are less salient or that are expressed primarily through class (in Brazil) or religious (in Israel) frames. Thus, national contexts make various kinds of historical scripts, myths, or repertoires more or less readily available to social actors to make sense of their reality (Lamont and Thévenot 2000; see also Swidler 1986; Mizrachi, Drori, and Anspach 2007.) Along with Wimmer (2008) and Brubaker (2009), we analyze not only social identity but also identification processes and the development of group-ness. However, unlike these scholars, we are centrally concerned not only with cognition but also with the role of emotion (particularly anger, pain, pride, and other feelings directly associated with identity management; see Archer 2003; Summers-Effler 2002). And we also connect the drawing of group boundaries to everyday morality (e.g., Lamont [2000] and Sayer [2005] in the case of class).

[17] For a discussion of the place of our argument in the literature on African American anti-racism (e.g., in relation to the work of Karyn Lacy, Joe Feagin, and others), see Fleming et al. (2012).

[18] We use "African American" and "black" interchangeably to reflect the use of these terms by our respondents.

is routinely questioned about whether he truly works at the court and knows others who work there. Marcus has to carefully consider how he should respond to the situation. Should he ignore the slight and let it go? Should he confront the woman, and if so, how? And what will be the costs of confrontation (emotional, interactional, potentially legal)? Marcus wants to maintain his image of professionalism *and* stand up for himself. How can he do both? He explains that these are the questions that often emerge when he experiences stigmatization. The repeated experience of such an internal dialogue can take a toll and contribute to the "wear and tear of everyday life" that results in huge disparities in the health and well-being of ethno-racial groups in the United States and elsewhere.

In a second example, Joe, a recreation specialist, faces a more blatant racist situation. His account viscerally expresses perceptions of the health impact of anger in the experience of stigmatization (see Mabry and Kiecolt 2005). He finds himself alone with several white men in an elevator. He recalls the scene thus:

One made a joke about Blacks and monkeys. I said, "Man, listen, I ain't into jokes." . . . His demeanor changed, my demeanor changed. All of the positive energy that was in there was being sucked out because the racial part. And the other guys, you could actually see them shrinking up in the corner because they didn't want no parts of it. . . . [I told myself] get out of it because if I stay in it, I'm going to be in that circle and [won't be able to] get out. . . . The stress level rose. My tolerance was getting thin, my blood pressure peaking and my temper rising. By the grace of God, thank you Jesus, as I stepped off the elevator, there was a Black minister walking past. I said, "Can I speak to you for a minute because I just encountered something that I got to talk about because I'm this far [to exploding]. . . . " I had been at the job for a week. This is all I need to get me fired. He said, "You're a better man than me." [Now] I'm trying to get through the affair [to decide] if I was to go to the city [to complain].

Joe knows that anger and impulse control are imperative if he wants to keep his job. He has to manage his emotions and finds an outlet when a chance encounter with an African American pastor offers relief – or a buffer – from a fellow group member who can relate to his situation. Similar to the majority of our interviewees, Joe factors in pragmatic considerations when weighing various courses of action (Fleming et al. 2012). But his normative response is that one needs to confront racism. This gap between ideal responses and situational constraints may have consequences for the emotional well-being of our respondents.

When probed about the "best approach" for dealing with racism (using an open-ended question format), three quarters of the 112 African American interviewees who addressed this question focused on how to respond (what we call "modalities" of responses): half of them (47 percent) favored confronting or challenging racism and discrimination. They prefer to "name the problem," "openly discuss the situation," and "make others aware that their action makes me uncomfortable." This compares to a third (32 percent) who prefer conflict-deflecting strategies – believing that it is best to ignore, accept, forgive, manage anger, or walk away (Fleming et al. 2012). The rest favor a mixed strategy, choosing to "pick their battles" or to "tolerate." Two thirds (65 percent) focused not on "modalities" but on what they consider to be the specific "tools" for responding to discrimination.[19] For one third of them (37 percent), the best approach is educating stigmatizers and (in some cases) fellow blacks about tolerance, diversity, and the lives and culture of African Americans. For one fifth of them (17 percent), the best tool is to increase formal education for African Americans to improve mobility outcomes for members of the group.[20]

An illustration of the desire to confront is provided by a prison instructor. When asked how we should deal with racism, he responds:

Confront it. 'Cuz people will try to tell you that it doesn't exist and it does exist... confront it. Not in a negative way, but just bring it up, discuss it. White folks will try to act like it doesn't exist and then they'll try to reverse it on you.

This is typical of the responses voiced by many interviewees. Their shared belief in the legitimacy of confrontation as a response is bolstered by the widespread availability of national scripts about the racist history of the United States, to which they often make reference in the context of the interviews (whether they talk about the history of chattel slavery, Jim Crow, or the experiences of their parents growing up in the South). Equally important is their awareness of the civil rights movements (including the struggles around school desegregation, the Newark Riots, the marches on Washington) and their current experiences with discrimination at work or elsewhere. More specifically, among 302 mentions of landmark historical events made during the course of the interviews, 30 percent concerned slavery, 16 percent concerned the 2008 elections, 15 mentioned the civil rights movement, and 11 mentioned race riots. For instance, one interviewee explains that "my wife's father had a black garage in South Carolina. The Ku Klux Klan burned it down. That's why they moved up here, to get away from it. A lot of older people, they don't even like to talk about it.... We just had to deal with it."

As suggested by the examples of Marcus and Joe (and as observed by social psychologists), the ideal of confronting racism is tempered by pragmatic consideration concerning costs (material, symbolic, or emotional). Individual strategies are constrained by what respondents believe is possible and doable given their needs and dependency on resources. In the presence of obstacles to confronting, a majority of middle class African American respondents focus on hard work and achievement as the key to challenging racial inequality (also Welburn and Pittman 2012) –[21] essential to the pursuit of the American

---

[19] Some respondents mentioned both modalities and tools in their response to the "best approach" for responding to discrimination.

[20] A number of other tools (e.g., gaining information) were mentioned by only a few respondents and thus are not reported here. Some respondents mentioned more than one "best approach" for dealing with racism.

[21] The forty five African-American middle class respondents interviewed by Welburn and Pittman (2012) more frequently explain racial inequality by motivational than by structural problems. These authors find 79 mentions of the former in interviews (e.g., decline in values and morality,

dream. Many embrace this crucial national collective myth (Hochschild 1995), through educational and economic achievement, and through the consumption it enables (as one respondent, a network technician, puts it: "You need to do something positive with your life. The American dream is out there; all you got to do is grab it and run with it."). We will see that this individualist response coexists with a more collectivist strategy grounded in a shared African American identity.

The continued commemoration of the African American history of discrimination and courage (e.g., through the institutionalization of Black History Month, the existence of African American studies as an academic discipline, as well as important aspects of black popular culture) enables interviewees to believe that it is legitimate to denounce and confront racism and discrimination. This orientation is less frequent among respondents in Brazil and Israel (Silva and Reis 2012; Mizrachi and Herzog 2012).

National Responses Compared

Israel

Similar to the African Americans we spoke with, Israelis anchor their responses to stigmatization in national history and myths. Indeed, Mizrachi and Zawdu (2012) show that ordinary Ethiopian Jews use the Zionist national narrative to neutralize the stigma associated with blackness – unlike political activists who have attracted the attention of the Israeli media in 2011. They downplay their phenotypical markings (e.g., skin tone) and define their identity as "just another group of immigrants," similar to other Jewish immigrant groups who eventually assimilate and prosper in Israel (often referring to the Russian Jews who preceded them en masse in the 1990s). This identification as "Jewish immigrants" grounded in the Zionist narrative serves as an equalizer: it legitimates their participation in the larger society. Similarly, the Mizrahis mobilize an assimilationist state ideology as a cultural tool for gaining recognition – an ideology that defines all Jews, regardless of regional, phenotypical, or other characteristic, as members of the polity. Both groups find in this ideology empowering repertoires of religious citizenship that make their responses to stigmatization possible (Dieckhoff 2003). These accounts contrast with the responses to stigmatization by Arab Israelis, which appeal to universal human dignity, as opposed to shared religion (Mizrahi and Herzog 2012). Members of this group attempt to depoliticize social difference by avoiding the use of a language of human rights and mobilize Jews in their social network in their defense (ibid.). Their ethno-religious identity, however, remained explicit and firmly differentiated from that of the Jews.

Brazil

When interviewing middle class and working class Afro-Brazilians about their views on the best approach for responding to stigmatization, Silva and Reis

lack of efforts, making excuses) compared with 65 mentions of the latter ("fewer opportunities for African American males," "racism and discriminations," and so on).

(2012) find that they most frequently embrace a dialogical and fuzzy "racial mixture" script as a response. This term is used to describe the multiracial character of the Brazilian population ("we are all a little black") and its hybrid culture and identity, as much as the notion that everyone, independently of phenotype, can be fully committed to a multiracial society. Racial mixture is a crucial collective myth for the Brazilian nation (along with the myth of racial democracy), and it acts as a more inclusive and less politically loaded cultural basis for cultural membership than does shared religion in the Israeli case.[22] Silva and Reis remark that few interviewees consistently used one single concept of racial mixing throughout the interview, switching between meanings according to context (p. 396). In a recent review of the literature on racial mixture, Telles and Sue (2009) suggest that in Latin America especially, the centrality of mixed racial categories does not translate into a decline in racial inequality. Marx (1998) also analyzes the role of the state in creating racial boundaries and hierarchies. Governments feed collective imaginaries by defining rules of membership across a number of policy areas that have a direct impact on those who experience exclusion as well as on shared conceptions of cultural membership (alternatively, ethnic boundaries also shape state action – see also Lieberman [2009] for a cross-national illustration concerning state responses to aids in Brazil, India, and South Africa).

This analysis suggests that some strategies are more likely to be found in some contexts than others (e.g., promoting racial mixture in Brazil and confronting in the United States). However, the use of repertoires is linked not only to their availability but also to proximate and remote determinants that make some individuals more or less likely to use certain repertoires than others (Lamont 1992). A more detailed look at the interaction between repertoires, social resources, situational cost, and opportunity structure will be the object of future analysis. For now, suffice to restate that national ideologies do not push individuals toward a single strategy – they simply make strategies more or less likely across contexts, enabling and constraining them.

The United States: Other Repertoires

Neoliberalism

We now provide a closer look at African American responses enabled by neoliberalism, that is, responses that emphasize (a) self-reliance and autonomy (connected to individualization and the privatization of risk [Sharone 2013]), (b) competitiveness and educational and economic achievement, and (c) the

---

[22] Silva and Reis (2012) identify four uses of the term "racial mixture:" (a) to describe whitening among blacks; (b) to celebrate Brazilian negritude (which is defined as mixed); (c) to describe Brazilian national identity; and (d) to describe a personal experience or non-racist strategy for responding to racism, that is, "non-essentialist racialism" which can be mobilized by whites as well. Although the last two frames are used by more than 50 percent of the respondents, the last one is the most popular (being used by 66 percent of the 160 respondents), and the first one is the least popular (being used by 17 percent only).

signaling of social status through consumption. These individualist responses may be an alternative to, and often threaten, collective responses, such as social movement and political mobilization (Bourdieu 1998; see below).

It may be objected that these responses exist independently of neoliberalism because they are central to the tenets of the American creed (as described by Hochschild 1995; also see Fischer 2010). However, their centrality and availability are likely to be accentuated in the neoliberal era because the two types of repertoires (the American dream and neoliberalism) become intertwined under the influence of market fundamentalism (see Greenhouse 2011; also Richland 2009). In the neoliberal era, the American dream is less about individual freedom and equality and more about individual success, performance, competition, and economic achievement.

Although there is great variation in how African Americans interpret the "American dream," some defining it as nightmare, many of our interviewees believe that the best response of racism is for blacks to work to get ahead through education and that they should persevere regardless of persistent discrimination (also Welburn and Pittman 2012 based on data on African Americans living in New Jersey). Moreover, the desire to "make it big" is very salient in interviews, and a large number of the individuals we talked to dream of starting their own business; they mention the distance from racists that being self-employed can provide together with the advantage of financial security (also Frederick 2010). They also value hard work and its most important outcome, financial independence. It is worth quoting one working class man who is a particularly vocal advocate of economic achievement. He describes the people he likes as "hustlers" who, like him, hold several jobs and are willing to do anything to make money. He talks about his friend Thomas, who he says: "does landscaping in the morning for a company. Then he has his own contracts in the middle of the day, sleeps and goes to work for FedEx at night.... I like to see hustlers because that's something that I do: just hustling. No laws are being broke, no one is being hurt."

Respondents also put a great emphasis on self-reliance for themselves and others. In so doing, they may want to mark distance toward the stereotype of low-income African Americans who depend on others for their subsistence and "don't want to pull their own weight." For instance, a woman who works for a dry-cleaning business and a grocery store and who admits to struggling financially says:

I don't like beggars. I don't like anybody's looking for a handout, I like people that want to get out and do something for themselves and help themselves.... I just can't deal with beggars.

This script, which is found in many interviews, is embraced by white and black American working class men alike (Lamont 2000; also Pattillo-McCoy 1999). It is reinforced by the script of privatization of risk central to neoliberalism (Hacker 2006) and is embodied in the Personal Responsibility and

Work Opportunity Act of 1996, which implicitly defined the poor as lazy and immoral (Guetzkow 2010).

Similar responses are found among middle class respondents, with a focus on professional achievement and improving their social and economic status. The majority of the respondents in this class category describe themselves as strongly committed to such goals. They also often define themselves by their ability to "do the job" as well as or better than whites, and they conceive of competence as an important anti-racist strategy (Lamont and Fleming 2005). Others celebrate the virtue of competition and define African American culture as embracing it (as a transit technician puts it, "We love to compete. Anything you put us in that's athletic, we just excel. [We] love to compete."). These respondents say they want to hire other African Americans when possible but that incompetence defines the limits of racial solidarity (as one respondent says: "You fuck up and I am done with you.") The conditions for cultural memberships that are imposed on middle-class African Americans may put limitations on their racial solidarity toward low-income blacks if achievement and economic success are *sine qua non* for cultural membership (Lamont and Fleming 2005).

Formal education and individual educational attainment are viewed by many as essential in a highly competitive neoliberal climate, especially for African Americans who have experienced greater job market instability than members of other racial groups in recent years. Accordingly, when asked about the best way to respond to racism, the pursuit of education is frequently mentioned. As one of them puts it, speaking of young African Americans:

You can't take a diploma from them.... It's recorded.... They are African-Americans so...there are some strikes. Get all the education so when you're sitting down with the competition, at least you know [what it's like]. He has it, your competition has it. You're going to get it. I'll go in debt to get my sons the education money.... You can take sports away, but you can't take a diploma away.

Echoing this interviewee, a writer also celebrates education as a tool for gaining inclusion while noting its limitation. She also stresses the importance of financial independence and points the importance of "being on top":

My mother said, "Girl, go to school. Get your education. They can't take it out of your head...you'll get the job. You'll get fair treatment." So that's what I expected from a job. But that's not what it's all about.... Go get your education, but don't make that everything. Have you some side something going on.... When the cards fall, as they will, you have to decide you want to be on top. And the only way you can be on top is if you get something for yourself.

Along similar lines, a teacher explains the importance of education for autonomy, the utility of separatism, and the self-reliance of African Americans in a context of pervasive racism:

Even though we will never be integrated fully, we will never be accepted, as long as we can educate a number of our people, we can challenge these different cultures that we face each and every day. Or we can have our own hospitals, our banks, our own, be our and have our own so we don't have to be subjected with negativity each and every day.

Although getting a formal education is not exclusive of collective solutions (as getting education may contribute to "lifting the race") and of collective empowerment ("to put our people in place... to create a future for us"), the prime beneficiary of a college degree is its holder. One interviewee, a property manager, emphasizes that collective empowerment is more important than individual success when he says (after stating "you need the monetary flow... if you want to make your own rules"):

I don't believe in pursuing in the American dream by just having physical things. It's more important that we establish the institutions that would give our people longevity and empowerment in the future. The American dream tells us to be successful as individuals, where[as] everybody else comes here and is successful as a group. Our American dream is an illusion because most of our dreams are through credit... which makes us sharecroppers.

He asserts the importance of collective empowerment over the simple accumulation of goods and individual achievement for fighting racism. Nevertheless, of the respondents who discussed formal education when we questioned them about the best tool for responding to stigmatization, a third spoke of its importance for the improvement of the group, and two thirds referred to its importance for the individual. This is in line with the neoliberal emphasis on the privatization of risk and with the related question of how African Americans explain their fate (as resulting from individual effort or linked fate). Recent research demonstrates that African Americans have become more individualist in their explanation of inequality over the past few decades (Bobo et al. 2012; Welburn and Pittman 2012).

As a correlate of the emphasis put on economic and educational achievement, some African American respondents also emphasize consumption as a means to providing proofs of cultural citizenship. Some respondents define their success in terms of what they are able to afford to buy – whether a house, a car, or an education for their children. Being able to use money as an equalizer (e.g., by shopping at brand stores, sporting professional attire, or driving a nice car) is often seen as a fool-proof means of demonstrating that one belongs and that one has achieved a middle class status that lessens, to some extent, the stigma of being black in contemporary America (Lamont and Molnar 2002; Pittman 2012).[23] Although the literature emphasizes conspicuous consumption of luxury goods among African Americans (ibid.), we find that our respondents are most concerned with consuming items that are associated with a "decent" or "normal" middle or working class lifestyle. For instance, the dry-cleaner and

---

[23] These behaviors had already been noted for the black middle class in Franklin Frazier's 1957 *Black Bourgeoisie*, and in reaction to Wilson's (1978) writing on the spatial and cultural isolation of the black middle class.

grocery store employee expresses regrets: "I wish I had my own condo, a decent car to drive. . . . take a vacation and sit at home." Also, many interviewees value having the means to support themselves, to buy health insurance, and to have "a little cushion." But as is the case for elite African Americans (Lamont and Fleming 2005), using access to economic resources as a criterion for cultural membership excludes all low-income African Americans.

It would be important to ascertain whether and how neoliberalism has transformed African American understandings of the conditions for gaining cultural membership and whether economic achievement looms larger in these scripts today than it did a few decades ago, reinforcing themes central to the national scripts centered on achievement and individualism (Sears, Sidanius, and Bobo 2000). This is not an easy task because the spread of neoliberalism occurred concurrently with economic, educational, political, and legal gains for African Americans, which led some to believe in the advent of a "post-racial America," especially in the wake of Barack Obama's presidential election in 2008. Although racial discrimination persists, it is equally diffi-cult to ascertain the relative impact of neoliberalism on stigmatized groups in other countries. However, given the relative significance of governmental efforts to promote neoliberal policies and to protect workers from its impact across advanced industrial societies, one can presume that this impact has been particularly important in the United States.[24] More than ever, many African Americans may have become convinced that self-reliance, economic success, individual achievement, and consumption are the best responses to stigmati-zation. However, many of our respondents are nostalgic about a time when black collective movements were dynamic, and they have vivid memories of the systematic dismantling of radical collective movements, such as the Black Power movement, by the state. Thus, it is not surprising that there is a clash between individualist responses inspired by neoliberalism and other responses enabled by repertoires celebrating collective identity, as we suggest in the next section.

African American Collective Identity

The collective identity and vision of a common past serves as a buffer against stigmatization for a number of African Americans. This is accomplished through (a) a shared narrative of "we-ness" that can act as a source of comfort and pleasure; (b) an awareness of a shared tradition of resilience in the context of continued discrimination, which helps individuals make sense of their expe-rience; and (c) an identity defined in opposition to that of whites that reinforces non-economic matrices of worth. We gathered evidence on these questions by

---

[24] This is confirmed by Greenhouse's (2011) ethnographic analysis of the entanglements of politics and identity in the major American legislation of the 1990s. See also Chauvel (2010) on the impact of the welfare state on the economic instability of youth across advanced industrial societies.

probing interviewees on what it means for them to be African American, what makes their group distinctive, and related questions.

In the context of interviews, a large number of individuals explained that African Americans have a common culture and social experience or a shared "background" that provides them a sense of pleasure. This sense of "cultural intimacy" (Herzfeld 1996) is described by one middle-aged African man:

That's what I like about our people. Good or bad, we're coming together.... We all got an uncle somewhere that chases young girls, and a grandmother somewhere who has certain sayings.... Or an aunt who can cook a sweet potato pie.... You put us together in a restaurant and we'll walk out of there laughin' because it's going to be something that we have in common. And that's just our people; it's just the way it is. I haven't met anybody that didn't have a grandmother like my grandmother. Or an aunt. Somebody.

Similarly, one interviewee describes African Americans as "having a bond," as being "on the same frequency," and another explains that African Americans generally know where other blacks "are coming from." It is noteworthy that this sense of cultural intimacy is also salient in discussions of interracial relationships, where the absence of shared experiences of discrimination is described as a major challenge. This is illustrated by one middle class interviewee who discards white romantic partners after one negative experience. Referring to his former girlfriend, he explains that "she can't get the joy out of watching Mandela walk out of jail.... She can't understand when three white police officers shoot two black males for nothing. She could say 'they shouldn't have been out there.' See, I'd have to choke her.... "

When probing interviewees about the distinctive characteristics of African Americans, we find that the notion of "a shared culture" is frequently mentioned spontaneously, *ex aequo* with similar responses that all point to other aspects of "cultural sameness:" morality, the importance of religion, the importance of caring, the richness of black culture, and black aesthetics and popular culture (each received 11 percent of the 307 responses given to this probe). These figures support the relatively high salience of shared culture in "folk" or "racial" conceptualization of blackness among African Americans (Morning 2009; Silva 2012).

Psychologists have shown that shared identity provides feelings of comfort and of being understood that can act as buffers or provide solace when one fears being underestimated, distrusted, overscrutinized, misunderstood, feared, overlooked, avoided, or discriminated against (e.g., Neblett, Shelton, and Sellers 2004). As such, widely available repertoires presenting and making salient African American shared identity and culture can act as resources that sustain social resilience. Such repertoires are crucial sources for recognition that have been neglected by social psychologists who tend to focus on networks, family, and community as environmental sources of resilience (as summarized by Son Hing in Chapter 5). If they are absent, individuals are more likely to find themselves vulnerable, isolated, and less able to respond to assaults on their sense of dignity – as was the case for Joe before he ran into a black minister when exiting an elevator in the incident related earlier. Such repertoires are likely to be more widely available in societies that support multiculturalism (see Kymlicka 2007; Wright and Bloemraad 2012) and adopt institutional structures that mitigate a clear ingroup–outgroup demarcation (Emmenegger et al. 2011).

In describing what African Americans have in common, a number of respondents often mention resilience and a tradition of overcoming barriers. Indeed, when probing interviewees about the distinctive characteristics of African Americans, we find that, respectively, 15 percent and 12 percent of the responses concern "resilience" and a shared history of overcoming racial barriers. Accordingly, respondents refer with respect and admiration to the stories their parents have told them about their past experiences with combating or dealing with racism. These stories make salient shared identity and past struggles. They also provide individuals standardized tools for making sense of their individual experiences and for avoiding internalizing negative messages. As such, they do contribute to the social resilience of their group. However, a number of respondents also mentioned what they perceive to be the more negative features of African Americans: self-destructiveness, lack of solidarity, lack of self-respect, the use of Ebonics, hip hop fashion, and the prevalence of youth violence – for a total 12 percent of the characteristics mentioned. Thus, collective identity can be a source of collective shame as well as a source of pleasure and pride.

African American social resilience is also likely to be strengthened by a widely available repertoire that defines blacks in opposition to whites and puts their "caring self" above the "disciplined self" of whites. Based on interviews conducted in 1993, Lamont (2000) argued that the African American working class men she talked with perceived themselves as more caring and accepting, as "having the spirit" or "soul" or as more in contact "with the human thing" than whites. Some contrasted this portrayal with a view of whites as materialist, power obsessed ("he who has the gold makes the rules"), arrogant, and self-serving – as manifested in the "illusion of white superiority." Lamont (2000) argued that by defining themselves as more moral than whites, African Americans promoted a matrix of evaluation that counterbalanced the emphasis on economic achievement promoted by neoliberalism. This matrix functions as an alternative measuring stick and enables low to middle income earners to cultivate a sense of dignity and self-pride despite their lower socioeconomic status. These observations appear to hold for the respondents we interviewed in 2012 (a topic to be explored in future publications.)[25]

Awareness of the need to cultivate alternative matrices of evaluation is strong among some respondents. A few emphasize the importance of celebrating a range of achievements by African Americans and of cultivating knowledge of black culture and tradition (knowing "their roots") among young

---

[25] For a complementary perspective, see Stephens, Fryberg, and Markus (2012).

people. They also lament the weak sense of black pride in their community. For instance, a property manager explains:

Most of our problems as Black people stem from the fact that we do not have our connection to our roots.... We don't look back to our story for any type of strength or encouragement.... We don't have a village where there are elders who direct the youth.

This man stresses the importance of giving black children a sense of purpose and pride by reconnecting them with their group identity (also Bouchard 2009). He wants to broadcast an alternative collective narrative about the group's past and future that may bolster social resilience – in lieu of scripts of consumerism and individual achievement that are enabled and made more salient by neoliberalism. Strengthening the connection with the past could provide a way for low-income blacks to gain a sense of cultural membership despite their being low on the totem pole of individual achievement – a way not to be a "loser" in an increasingly dominant neoliberal competition.

Conclusion: What Confers Social Resilience?

In examining the question "How can responses to stigmatization confer social resilience?" this chapter has focused on social resources that may sustain recognition by focusing on the cultural repertoires on which African Americans draw to consider their the ideal responses to racism. We have suggested that these repertoires act as resources that sustain social resilience, conceived as features of groups. Such repertoires are part of an environment that feeds the sense of empowerment and worth of group members. They may be unevenly available across social contexts, depending on the success of mobilization efforts enacted by the stigmatized as well as their allies and the extent to which societies support multiculturalism or other means of creating more porous boundaries between various types of ingroups and outgroups.

In the preceding section, we have argued that exposure to cultural repertoires that make salient and celebrate a shared culture has positive effects on social resilience. This complements findings from social psychology described by Son Hing (see Chapter 5) that strong ingroup (racial) identification fosters resilience for those who experience lower levels of discrimination. Indeed, among ethnic minority youth in Scotland, the more girls experienced collective self-esteem, the lower their depression and their anxiety (Cassidy, Howe, and Warden 2004). Similarly, Asian American children experiencing discrimination from their peers have higher self-esteem if they feel more positively toward their ethnic group (Rivas-Drake, Hughes, and Way 2008). This work suggests that the mere fact of partaking in a similar experience and of sharing a similar narrative may provide a buffer in the form of social support. Although psychologists are generally not concerned with the cultural sources of such strong group identities, our chapter illuminates this part of the puzzle.

Future research should explore which of the three types of repertoires considered here – national myths, neoliberalism, and collective identity and history – have the most positive impact on social resilience. However, this cannot be an easy task for several reasons: (a) although social actors generally privilege a repertoire, they often alternate between them across situations and over time, making it difficult to establish a direct causal relationship between types of repertoires, social resilience, and well-being; (b) the three types of repertoires may be becoming increasingly braided, especially under the growing influence of neoliberalism; and (c) neoliberal themes may have simultaneously beneficial and pernicious effects on social resilience. Indeed, they may promote self-blaming for failure (see Chapter 5), encourage African Americans to escape stigma through a universalist logic (e.g., compete to "get the skills to get the job" according to the principle of "the best man for the job"), and limit the appeal of alternative moral matrices of evaluation that may allow low-status individuals to fare better. To complicate matters further, neoliberalism may also encourage stigmatized group to make claims based on human rights (also see Chapters 2 and 3) while undercutting in practice collective claims by promoting individualization. Finally, neoliberalism may promote competition with members of other stigmatized groups and thus affect negatively the potential for collective mobilization.[26]

There is also the possibility that individuals are using repertoires differently under neoliberalism: they may be increasingly skeptical of collective projects and collective myths and find refuge in their private lives. For example, this is suggested in the paradoxical fact that in early 2011, the French were found to be more pessimistic about the future than most other national groups being compared yet were producing more children.[27] Privatization may be more likely in a context where individuals have few resources to realize their dream and yet are asked to deploy entrepreneurialism and other neoliberal virtues.

It is too early to determine whether patterns in responses to stigmatization are converging across the national cases we are considering and whether, overall, African Americans are better off (e.g., in terms of subjective well-being) than their Brazilian or Israeli counterparts. Also, more comparative analysis is needed before we can draw conclusions on the relative impact of neoliberalism on social resilience for African Americans compared with Afro-Brazilians and stigmatized groups in Israel. Nevertheless, we venture to predict that the former are less culturally buffered from the pernicious effects of neoliberalism than their counterparts in Brazil and Israel, given the centrality of individualism and economic achievement in the collective myth of the American dream. Moreover, the fact that in the United States, the "losers" of market

---

[26] Future research should draw on ethnographic observation to assess how accounts of responses to stigmatization compare with actual responses. This is essential to better understand the relationship between interaction and available grammars of action – two deeply intertwined aspects of social life, which each gives us only a partial view of human action.

[27] The annual BVA–Gallup international survey revealed the French to be the "world champions of pessimism." It found that 61 percent of French thought that 2011 would bring economic difficulties compared with an average of 28 percent in the 53 countries surveyed (http://www. bva.fr/fr/sondages/les_perspectives_economiques_2011.html).

fundamentalism (as measured by unemployment rate and other indicators) are disproportionately symbolic "outsiders" (immigrants and African Americans) can also increase the legitimacy of neoliberal themes in this national context. Although the "American dream" empowers many, it often leaves those who cannot achieve it without hopes. This is both the grandeur and the tragedy of the American collective imaginary.

Methodological Appendix

Case Selection

Our countries of comparison were selected to maximize differences in frequency of perceived discrimination across cases, the latter being an indicator of the strength or permeability of boundaries across national contexts. The selection was based on a comparison by Lamont and Bail (2005) of the relative strength of social boundaries in various realms (labor market, spatial segregation, and so on), as well as that of symbolic boundaries (pertaining to collective identity) across half a dozen countries. We had hypothesized that *overall*, perceived discrimination, and by extension, the range and salience of anti-racist strategies, would be greater for Muslim Palestinian citizens of Israel than for *Negros* in Brazil, for whom interracial sociability and interracial sexual relationships are relatively frequent. We originally viewed the American case as an intermediary one, one in which racism would be very salient, but also one in which intergroup boundaries would be weaker than in Israel, with different patterns of response. Of course, as data collection proceeded, we became increasingly aware of the complexity of the comparison, which would be far less linear and more multidimensional than we had anticipated.

Research Design

The research designs for the three national cases were largely parallel in each site. We conducted interviews with a relatively large number of respondents (by the standards of qualitative methods), with the goals of reaching saturation and of systematically comparing anti-racist strategies across populations. The data collection consisted of open-ended two-hour interviews with working and middle class men and women. In the United States, we conducted interviews in the New York metropolitan area, which presents a full spectrum of social classes for both majority and minority groups. In Brazil and Israel, we chose as major metropolitan centers Rio de Janeiro and Tel Aviv because, similar to New York, they are mixed cities where relationships between members of various ethno-racial groups are frequent and highly routinized without the clear predominance of one particular group (on mixed cities, see Monterescu and Rabinowitz 2007). These metropolises should not be viewed as representative of the national population because there are large regional variations in the spatial distribution of ethno-racial groups in each of the three countries under consideration.

Selection of Respondents

Respondents were limited to native-born interviewees (with the exception of Ethiopian immigrants to Israel). The samples comprise males and females in roughly comparable numbers for each site. Middle class respondents have a two- or four-year college degree and are typically professionals or managers. The working class respondents have a high school degree (or equivalent) but no college degree. The age range is between 20 and 70 years, with small variations across the three countries.

Sampling

Methods for sampling respondents varied slightly cross-nationally in response to the specific challenges associated with locating respondents from various class and racial groups across sites given the local patterns of social and spatial segregation and concentration and cultural factors.

In the United States, middle and working class respondents were recruited using two primary techniques. First, we used a survey research company to recruit participants. The company used census track and marketing data to identify potential participants who met a number of criteria. Then the company mailed letters announcing the study to these randomly sampled African Americans living in northern New Jersey and called potential participants to encourage participation and confirm their eligibility for the study. Second, to increase our sample size, we used snowball sampling techniques, with no more than three referrals per participant. This method was particularly fruitful for recruiting working class respondents and men, who were less likely to respond to requests from our survey research company. Respondents were paid $20 for their participation.

In the case of Brazil, sampling procedures were as follows. Because the number of black middle class individuals remains limited, we identified respondents through firms (e.g., in the sectors of oil and telecommunication), networks (i.e., Facebook for black professionals), and professional associations in addition to some snowball sampling from a wide network of contacts (with up to three referees per respondent). Working class respondents were identified by a survey firm and paid for their participation (this was not the case for the middle class because we anticipated that this would not create a good context of exchange for the interview).

Finally, in Israel, the sample was constructed through multi-entry snowballing. Interviewers reached out to individuals meeting our various sampling criteria in a large range of settings. They aimed to diversify the composition of the sample in terms by occupation.

Interviews and Data Analysis

In the three sites, most respondents were interviewed by an ethno-racial (but not a class) ingroup member (for all but a few exceptions). The interviews were confidential, conducted in a location of the respondent's choosing, and were recorded with the interviewee's consent. Respondents were questioned on a range of issues concerning what it means to be an "X" (e.g., African American), similarities and differences between them and other ethno-racial groups, their views on social mobility and inequality, past experiences with racism, what they have learned in their family and at school about how to deal with exclusion, and so on. Discourse was elicited by asking respondents to describe past, most recent, and general experiences with racism and discrimination; relationships with coworkers, neighbors, family members, and community members involving discrimination; and the strategies they used for handling these situations.

The interview schedule, first developed for the American case, was carefully adapted to the Brazilian and Israeli cultural contexts. Most importantly in the Brazil case, instead of explicitly asking questions about racial identity, we waited for it to emerge spontaneously in the context of the interview. If it did not, we asked questions on this topic at the end of the interview – the salience of racial identity being one of the key foci of the project.[28] In Israel, we were particularly interested in the articulation between various types of stigmatized identities (blackness, Arab identity, and the backwardness that are often likened in views about the Mizrahis).

The interviews were fully transcribed and systematically coded by a team of research assistants with the help of the qualitative data analysis software Atlas.ti. The coding scheme was developed iteratively by the three national teams of coders, with the American coders taking the lead. This coding scheme includes more than 1,500 entries. A substantial portion of the interviews were coded by more than one person. Codes and a list of interviewees are available upon request.

Studying Responses to Stigmatization

In the three countries, we documented responses to stigmatization by asking interviewees about ideal or "best approach" for dealing with racism, independently of context, their responses to specific racist incidents, the lessons they teach their children about how to deal with racism, their views on the best tools their group has at its disposal to improve their situation, and their reactions to a list of specific strategies. We also considered how these responses vary with a number of social and cultural indicators (including gender, class, age; whether individuals live in integrated or segregated environments; whether racist incidents occurred in public or private spaces and entailed violence, assaults against one's dignity, or institutional discrimination).

References

Alba, Richard. 2009. *Blurring the Color Line: The New Chance for a More Integrated America*. Cambridge, MA: Harvard University Press.

---

[28] We initially postponed mentioning the centrality of race in our project in our interviews with African Americans, but this created awkward situations because most respondents expected the study to be concerned with this topic.

Aptheker, Herbert. 1992. *Anti-Racism in U.S. History: The First Two Hundred Years.* Westport, CT: Greenwood Press.

Archer, Margaret. 2003. *Structure, Agency and the Internal Conversation.* New York: Cambridge University Press.

Bail, Christopher. 2008. "The Configuration of Symbolic Boundaries against Immigrants in Europe." *American Sociological Review* 73 (1): 37–59.

Bickerstaff, Jovonne. 2012. "Ethnic Versus Racial Identification: Variation in the Antiracist Responses of First Generation French Blacks." *Du Bois Review: Social Science Research on Race* 9 (1): 107–31.

Bobo, Lawrence D. 2011. "Somewhere between Jim Crow and Post-Racialism: Reflections on the Racial Divide in America Today." *Daedalus* 140 (2): 11–31.

Bobo, Lawrence D., Camille Z. Charles, Maria Krysan, and Alicia D. Simmons. forthcoming "The Real Record on Racial Attitudes." In *Social Trends in the United States 1972–2008: Evidence from the General Social Survey*, edited by Peter V. Marsden. Princeton, NJ: Princeton University Press: 38–83.

Boltanski Luc and Eve Chiapello. 1999. *Le nouvel esprit du capitalisme.* Paris: Gallimard.

Bouchard, Gérard. 2009. "Collective Imaginaries and Population Health." In *Successful Societies: How Institutions and Culture Affect Health*, edited by Peter A. Hall and Michèle Lamont. New York: Harvard University Press: 169–200.

Bourdieu, Pierre. 1998. "The Essence of Neo-liberalism." *Le Monde Diplomatique.* http://mondediplo.com/1998/12/08bourdieu.

Brubaker, Rogers. 2009. "Ethnicity, Race, and Nationalism." *Annual Review of Sociology* 35: 21–42.

Brubaker, Rogers and Frederic Cooper. 2000. "Beyond 'Identity.'" *Theory and Society* 29: 1–47.

Cassidy, O'Connor, Christine Howe, and David Warden. 2004. "Perceived Discrimination and Psychological Distress: The Role of Personal and Ethnic Self-Esteem." *Journal of Counseling Psychology* 51 (3): 329–39.

Chauvel, Louis. 2010. *Le destin des générations structure sociale et cohortes en France du XXè siècle aux années 2000.* Paris: Presses Universitaires de France.

Clark, R., Anderson, N. B., Clark, V. R., and Williams, D. R. 1999. "Racism as a Stressor for African Americans: A Biopsychosocial Model." *American Psychologist* 54 (10): 805–16.

Conley, D. 1999. *Being Black, Living in the Red. Race, Wealth, and Social Policy in America.* Berkeley, CA: University of California Press.

Cornell, Stephen and Douglas Hartman. 1997. *Ethnicity and Race. Making Identity in a Changing World.* Thousand Oaks, CA: Pine Forge Press.

Crocker, Jennifer, Brenda Major, and Claude Steele. 1998. "Social Stigma." In *Handbook of Social Psychology*, edited by Daniel T. Gilbert, Susan T Fiske, and Gardner Lindzey. Boston: McGraw-Hill.

Dieckhoff, Alain. 2003. *The Invention of a Nation: Zionist Thought and the Making of Modern Israel.* New York: Columbia University Press.

Emmenegger, Patrick, Silja Häusermann, Bruno Palier, and Martin Seeleib-Kaiser. 2011. *The Age of Dualization: The Changing Face of Inequality in De-industrializing Societies.* New York: Oxford University Press.

Essed, Philomena. 1991. *Understanding Everyday Racism: An Interdisciplinary Theory.* London: Sage Publications.

Eyerman, Ron. 2002. *Cultural Trauma: Slavery and the Formation of African American Identity.* Cambridge, UK: Cambridge University Press.

Feagin, Joe. R. and Melvin P. Sikes. 1994. *Living with Racism: The Black Middle Class Experience.* Boston: Beacon.

Fischer, Claude. 2010. *Made in America. A Social History of American Character and Culture.* Berkeley: California University Press.

Fleming, Crystal, Michèle Lamont, and Jessica Welburn. 2012. "Responding to Stigmatization and Gaining Recognition: Evidence from Middle Class and Working Class African-Americans." *Ethnic and Racial Studies* 35 (3): 400–17.

Fraser, Nancy and Axel Honneth. 2003. *Redistribution or Recognition? A Political-Philosophical Exchange.* London: Verso.

Frazier, Franklin. 1957. *The Black Bourgeoisie: The Book That Brought the Shock of Self-Revelation to Middle-Class Blacks in America.* New York: Free Press Paperbacks.

Frederick, Marla. 2010. "Rags to Riches. Religion, the Media and the Performance of Wealth in a Neoliberal Age." In *Ethnographies of Neo-liberalism*, edited by Carol Greenhouse. Philadelphia: University of Pennsylvania Press: 221–37.

Giddens, Anthony. 1991. *Modernity and Self-Identity: Self and Society in the Late Modern Age.* Cambridge, UK: Polity Press.

Goffman, Erving. 1963. *Stigma.* New York: Simon and Schuster.

Greenhouse, Carol. 2009. *Ethnographies of Neo-liberalism.* Philadelphia: University of Pennsylvania Press.

Greenhouse, Carol. 2011. *The Paradox of Relevance: Citizenship and Ethnography in the United States.* Philadelphia: University of Pennsylvania Press.

Guetzkow, Joshua. 2010. "Beyond Deservingness: Congressional Discourse on Poverty, 1964–1996." *Annals of the American Academy of Political and Social Sciences* 629: 173–99.

Hacker, Jacob. 2006. *The Great Risk Shift.* New York: Oxford University Press.

Hall, Peter A. and Michèle Lamont, eds. 2009. *Successful Societies: How Institutions and Culture Matter for Health.* New York: Cambridge University Press.

Harding, David, Michèle Lamont, and Mario Small. 2010. "Reconsidering Culture and Poverty." Special Issue of *Annals of the American Academy of Political and Social Sciences* 629: 6–27.

Hearn, Alison. 2008. "Meat, Mask, and Burden: Probing the Contours of the Branded 'Self.'" *Journal of Consumer Culture* 8 (2): 197–217.

Hertzman, Clyde and Tom Boyce, 2010. "How Experience Gets Under the Skin to Create Gradients in Developmental Health." *Annual Review of Public Health* 31: 329–47.

Herzfeld, Michael. 1996. *Cultural Intimacy: Social Poetics in the Nation State.* London: Routledge.

Hochschild, Jennifer. 1995. *Facing Up to the American Dream: Race, Class, and the Soul of the Nation.* Princeton, NJ: Princeton University Press.

Honneth, Alex. 1996. *The Struggle for Recognition: The Moral Grammar of Social Conflicts.* London: Polity Press.

Ireland, Patrick R. 2004. *Becoming Europe: Immigration, Integration, and the Welfare State.* Pittsburgh: University of Pittsburgh Press.

Jenkins, Richard. 1996. *Social Identity.* London: Routledge.

Kastoryano, Riva. 2002. *Negotiating Identities: States and Immigrants in France and Germany.* Princeton, NJ: Princeton University Press.

Koopmans, Rudd, Paul Statham, Marco Giugni, and Florence Passy. 2005. *Contested Citizenship: Immigration and Cultural Diversity in Europe.* Minneapolis: University of Minnesota Press.

Krysan, Maria. 2012. "From Color Caste to Color Blind? Contemporary Era Racial Attitudes, 1976–2004." In *The Oxford Handbook of African American Citizenship*, edited by Henry Louis Gates, Claude Steele, Lawrence D. Bobo, Michael C. Dawson, Gerald Jaynes, Lisa Crooms-Robinson, and Linda Darling-Hammond. New York: Oxford University Press: 235–78.

Kymlicka, Will. 2007. *Multicultural Odysseys: Navigating the New Global Politics of Diversity*. New York: Oxford University Press.

Lamont, Michèle. 1992. *Money, Morals, and Manners; the Culture of the French and the American Upper-Middle Class*. Chicago: University of Chicago Press.

Lamont, Michèle. 2000. *The Dignity of Working Men: Morality and the Boundaries of Race, Class, and Immigration*. Cambridge, MA: Harvard University Press.

Lamont, Michèle. 2009 "Responses to Racism, Health, and Social Inclusion as a Dimension of Successful Societies." In *Successful Societies: How Institutions and Culture Matter for Health*, edited by Peter A. Hall and Michèle Lamont. New York: Cambridge University Press: 151–168.

Lamont, Michèle and Christopher Bail. 2005. "Sur les Frontières de la Reconnaissance. Les Catégories Internes et Externes de l'Identité Collective." *Revue Européenne De Migrations Internationales* 21 (2): 61–90.

Lamont, Michèle and Crystal Fleming. 2005. "Everyday Anti-Racism: Competence and Religion in the Cultural Repertoire of African-American Elite and Working Class." *Du Bois Review* 2 (1): 29–43.

Lamont, Michèle and Nissim Mizrachi. 2012. "Ordinary People Doing Extraordinary Things, One Step at the Time: Responses to Stigmatization in Comparative Perspective." *Ethnic and Racial Studies* 35 (3): 365–81.

Lamont, Michèle and Virag Molnar. 2002. "The Study of Boundaries in the Social Sciences." *Annual Review of Sociology* 28: 167–95.

Lamont, Michèle and Laurent Thévenot. 2000. *Rethinking Comparative Cultural Sociology: Repertoires of Evaluation in France and the United States*. London: Cambridge University Press and Paris: Presses de la Maison des Sciences de l'Homme.

Lazzarato, Maurizio. 2009. "Neoliberalism in Action: Inequality, Insecurity, and the Reconstitution of the Social." *Theory, Culture and Society* 26 (6): 109–33.

Lieberman, Evan. 2009. *Boundaries of Contagion: How Ethnic Politics Have Shaped Governmental Responses to Aids*. Princeton, NJ: Princeton University Press.

Link, Bruce. G. and Jo Phelan. 2000. "Evaluating the Fundamental Cause Explanation for Social Disparities in Health." *Handbook of Medical Sociology*, edited by Chloe E. Bird, Peter Conrad, and Allen M. Fremont. Nashville: Vanderbilt University Press: 33–46.

Mabry, B. and J. K Kiecolt. 2005. "Anger in Black and White: Race, Alienation, and Anger." *Journal of Health and Social Behavior* 46 (85): 1–101.

Marx, Anthony. 1998. *Making Race and Nation: A Comparison of South Africa, the United States and Brazil*. Cambridge, UK: Cambridge University Press.

Massey, Douglas S. and Magaly Sánchez R. 2010. *Brokered Boundaries: Creating Immigrant Identity in Anti-Immigrant Times*. New York: Russell Sage Foundation.

Mizrachi, Nissim, I. Drori, and Renee Anspach. 2007. "Repertoires of Trust: The Practice of Trust in a Multinational Organization Amid Political Conflict." *American Sociological Review* 72: 143–65.

Mizrachi, Nissim and Hanna Herzog. 2012. "Participatory Destigmatization Strategies among Palestinian Citizens of Israel, Ethiopian Jews and Mizrahi Jews." *Ethnic and Racial Studies* 35 (3): 418–35.

Mizrachi, Nissim and Adane Zawdu. 2012. "Between Global Racial and Bounded Identity: Choice of Destigmatization Strategies among Ethiopian Jews in Israel." *Ethnic and Racial Studies* 35 (3): 436–52.

Moon, Dawn. 2012. "Who am I and Who are We? Conflicting Narratives of Collective Selfhood in Stigmatized Groups." *American Journal of Sociology* 117 (5): 1336–70.

Monterescu, Daniel and Dan Rabinowitz. 2007. *Mixed Towns/Trapped Communities: Historical Narratives, Spatial Dynamics and Gender Relations in Jewish-Arab Mixed Towns in Israel/Palestine*. London: Ashgate Publishing.

Morning, Ann. 2009. "Toward a Sociology of Racial Conceptualization for the 21st Century." *Social Forces* 87 (3): 1167–92.

Neblett, Enrique. W., J. Nicole Shelton, and Robert. M. Sellers. 2004. "The Role of Racial Identity in Managing Daily Racial Hassles." In *Racial Identity in Context: The Legacy of Kenneth Clark*, edited by G. Philogene. Washington, DC: American Psychological Association Press: 77–90.

O'Brien, Eileen. 2007. "Antiracism." *Handbook of the Sociology of Racial and Ethnic Relation*, edited by Herman Vera and Joe Feagin. New York: Springer.

Oliver, Melvin L. and Thomas M. Shapiro. 2006. *Black Wealth/White Wealth: A New Perspective on Racial Inequality*. New York: Routledge.

Oyserman, Daphne and J. K. Swim. 2001. "Social Stigma: An Insider's View." *Journal of Social Issues* 57 (1): 1–14.

Pachucki, Mark, Michèle Lamont, and Sabrina Pendergrass. 2006. "Boundary Processes: Recent Theoretical Developments and New Contributions." *Poetics* 35 (6): 331–51.

Pattillo-McCoy, Mary. 1999. *Black Picket Fences. Privileges and Perils Among the Black Middle Class*. Chicago: University of Chicago Press.

Pew Charitable Trust Foundation. 2011. "Wealth Gaps Rise to Record Highs Between Whites, Blacks and Hispanics." Retrieved from http://www.pewsocialtrends.org/2011/07/26/wealth-gaps-rise-to-record-highs-between-whites-blacks-hispanics/.

Picca, L. H. and Joe R. Feagin. 2007. *Two-Faced Racism. White in the Backstage and Frontstage*. New York: Routledge.

Pierson, Paul and Jacob Hacker. 2010. *Winner-Take-All Politics*. New York: Simon and Schuster.

Pinel, E. C. 1999. "Stigma Consciousness: The Psychological Legacy of Social Stereotypes." *Journal of Personality and Social Psychology* 76 (1): 114–28.

Pittman, Cassi. 2012. *Race, Class, and Social Context: an Examination of the Impact of Race on the Consumption Preferences and Practices of Middle and Working Class African American*. Unpublished dissertation, Department of Sociology, Harvard University.

Pollock, Mica. 2008. *Everyday Antiracism: Getting Real About Race*. New York: The New Press.

Richland, Justin B. 2009. "On Neoliberalism and Other Social Diseases: The 2008 Sociocultural Anthropology Year in Review." *American Anthropologist* 110 (2): 170–76.

Rivas-Drake, Deborah, Diane Hughes, and Niobe Way. 2008. "A Closer Look at Peer Discrimination, Ethnic Identity, and Psychological Well-Being Among Urban Chinese Sixth Graders." *Journal of Youth and Adolescence* 37 (1): 12–21.

Roth, Wendy. 2012. *Race Migrations: Latinos and the Cultural Transformation of Race*. Stanford, CA: Stanford University Press.

Sayer, Andrew. 2005. *The Moral Significance of Class*. New York: Cambridge University Press.

Schudson, Michael. 1988. "How Culture Works." *Theory and Society* 18: 153–180.

Sears, David O., James Sidanius, and Lawrence Bobo, eds. 2000. *Racialized Politics: The Debate about Racism in America*. Chicago: University of Chicago Press.

Shapiro, Thomas M. and Melvin L. Oliver. 2006. *Black Wealth, White Wealth, A New Perspective on Racial Inequality*. London: Routledge.

Sharone, Ofer. 2013. *Unemployment Experiences: Job Searching, Interpersonal Chemistry, and Self-Blame*. Chicago: University of Chicago Press.

Silva, Graziella Moraes D. 2012. "Folk Conceptualizations of Racism and Antiracism in Brazil and South Africa." *Ethnic and Racial Studies* 35 (3): 506–22.

Silva, Graziella Moraes D. and Elisa Reis. 2012. "The Multiple Dimensions of Racial Mixture: From Whitening to Brazilian Negritude." *Ethnic and Racial Studies* 35 (3): 382–99.

Somers, Margaret. 2008. *Genealogies of Citizenship*. New York: Cambridge University Press.

Son Hing, Leanne. 2012. "Responses to Stigmatization: The Moderating Roles of Primary and Secondary Appraisals." *Du Bois Review* 9 (1): 149–68.

Stephens, Nicole M, Stephanie A. Fryberg, and Hazel Rose Markus. 2012. "It's Your Choice: How the Middle Class Model of Independence Disadvantages Working Class Americans." In *Facing Social Class*, edited by Susan T. Fiske and Hazel Rose Markus. New York: Russell Sage Foundation: 87–106.

Summers-Effler, Erika. 2002. "The Micro Potential for Social Change: Emotion, Consciousness and Social Movement Formation." *Sociological Theory* 20: 21–60.

Swidler, Ann. 1986. "Culture in Action: Symbols and Strategies." *American Sociological Review* 51: 273–86.

Taylor, Charles, with commentary by K. Anthony Appiah, Jurgen Habermas, Steven C. Rockefeller, Michael Walzer, Susan Wolf. Edited and introduced by Amy Gutman et al. 1994. *Multiculturalism: Examining the Politics of Recognition*. Princeton, NJ: Princeton University Press.

Telles, Edward E. and Christina A. Sue. 2009. "Racial Mixture: Boundary Crossing in Comparative Perspectives." *Annual Review of Sociology* 35: 129–46.

Tilly, Charles. 2006. *Regimes and Repertoires*. Chicago: University of Chicago Press.

Todd, Jennifer. 2004. "Social Transformation, Collective Categories and Identity Change." *Theory and Society* 34 (4): 429–63.

Van Dijk, Teun A. 1993. *Elite Discourse and Racism*. Newbury Park, CA: Sage.

Walton, Gregory M. and Geoffrey L. Cohen. 2011. "A Brief Social-Belonging Intervention Improves Academic and Health Outcomes for Minority Students." *Science* 331 (6023): 1447–51.

Welburn, Jessica. 2011. *Managing Instability: Conceptions of Opportunity and Success among African Americans from Middle-Income Households*. PhD dissertation, Harvard University.

Welburn, Jessica and Cassi Pittman. 2012. "Stop Blaming 'The Man': Perceptions of Inequality and Opportunities for Success in the Obama Era Among Middle Class African-Americans." *Ethnic and Racial Studies* 35 (3): 523–40.

Wilson, William Julius. 1978. *The Declining Significance of Race*. Chicago: University of Chicago Press.

Wimmer, Andreas. 2008. "The Making and Unmaking of Ethnic Boundaries: A Multi-Level Process Theory." *American Journal of Sociology* 113 (4): 970–1022.

Wimmer, Andreas and B. Min. 2006. "From Empire to Nation-States. Explaining Wars in the Modern World." *American Sociological Review* 71 (6): 267–97.

Wodak, Ruth. 2001. "The Discourse-Historical Approach." In *Methods of Critical Discourse Analysis*, edited by Ruth Wodak and M. Meyer. London: Sage.

Wright, Matthew and Irene Bloemraad. 2012. "Is There a Trade-Off between Multi-culturalism and Socio-Political Integration? Policy Regimes and Immigrant Incorporation in Comparative Perspective." *Perspectives on Politics* 10: 77–95.

Zolberg, Aristide and L. L. Woon. 1999. "Why Islam is Like Spanish: Cultural Incorporation in Europe and the United States." *Politics and Society* 27 (1): 5–38.

5

Stigmatization, Neoliberalism, and Resilience[1]

Leanne S. Son Hing

This chapter applies the theories and tools of contemporary psychology to explore the relationship between neoliberalism understood as a set of values and socioeconomic conditions and various aspects of intergroup relations. My focus is on the sources and effects of prejudice or stigmatization and on the factors that confer resilience in the face of discrimination. There are significant puzzles here. Important contemporary social debates about immigration, racial equality, and aboriginal rights center on intergroup relations and such debates are now conditioned by neoliberal ideas (see Chapters 2 and 3). Does the prevalence of neoliberal beliefs increase the incidence of prejudice, as some suspect, or render it less likely by bringing meritocratic values to the fore (Becker 1957)? How might the popularity of neoliberal beliefs affect the resilience of people who experience discrimination? These are issues on which contemporary psychological research can shed light (e.g., Son Hing et al. 2011).

After considering the forms that prejudice can take, I begin by reviewing the changes in prejudice that have taken place during the neoliberal era. Second, drawing on literatures in psychology that associate prejudice with experiences of psychological threat, I explore how societal changes linked to neoliberal policies, practices, and narratives might have increased the incidence of prejudice. Finally, I review psychological research, including my own, that examines the relationship between attitudes that reflect prejudice and beliefs associated with neoliberalism.

[1] Paper prepared for "Social Resilience in the Age of Neoliberalism," edited by Peter Hall and Michèle Lamont. My research discussed here was supported by funding from the Canadian Institute for Advanced Research. Thank you to Vishi Gnanakumaran for assistance with the General Social Survey data; to Susan Pankiw for assistance with manuscript preparation; to Dustin Burt and Homan Allami for assistance with researching the literature; to Mark Zanna for his feedback on this chapter; and to my Canadian Institute for Advanced Research colleagues, particularly Nyla Branscombe, Donna Garcia, Peter Hall, Michèle Lamont, and Ron Levi, for their help in developing this chapter.

In this chapter, I draw predominantly on psychological studies of North Americans and Western Europeans, conducted mostly with undergraduate students, but I also consider research conducted around the globe and with adult samples published mainly between the mid 1980s and 2010. Some findings may be valid only for specific time periods and settings, but the basic processes are likely to be more general. Whether the results of any study generalize to a different sample, location, or historical period is an empirical question.

The Nature of the Problem: Prejudice, Stereotyping, and Discrimination

The consequences of stigmatization for members of a group that is devalued can be adverse: the more members anticipate being stigmatized, perceive their group to be stigmatized, or experience stigmatization themselves, the worse their physical and mental health, well-being, and performance (Williams and Williams-Morris 2000; Pascoe and Smart Richman 2009). Three aspects of stigmatization are widely studied in social psychology: prejudice, stereotypes, and discrimination. Prejudice can be defined as negative overall evaluation of, or attitude toward, outgroups marked by cognitions (e.g., stereotypes), affects or emotions (e.g., antipathy), and behavioral intentions (e.g., to discriminate; Zanna and Rempel 1988). Stereotypes are beliefs about what typical outgroup members are like. Discrimination involves the treatment of ingroup (vs. outgroup) members that results in unfair, illegitimate, or negative outcomes. Both prejudice and stereotypes can be explicit (i.e., controlled and deliberate) or implicit (i.e., automatic and uncontrollable). Whereas explicit processes can be assessed with self-report surveys, implicit processes are assessed with computerized split-second response time tasks. For instance, people with more implicitly prejudiced attitudes are quicker than those with less implicitly prejudiced attitudes to associate negative stimuli with outgroups and positive stimuli with ingroups because such associations are well practiced and well formed in the brain. Explicit and implicit prejudice are only weakly related (Hofmann et al. 2005), and implicit attitudes and stereotypes predict discriminatory behavior better than explicit attitudes and stereotypes (Rudman 2004; Greenwald et al. 2009). Now that stigmatization is defined, let us turn to the issue of how neoliberalism might be related to it.

Neoliberal Beliefs and Types of Prejudice at the Macro Level

One way to explore the link between neoliberalism and stigmatization is to look at how the nature of prejudice has changed during the neoliberal era compared with earlier periods. I will focus on longitudinal research conducted in the United States on Whites' attitudes toward Blacks. Changes in prejudice cannot be conclusively attributed to the influence of the prevailing neoliberal discourse, but it is possible to explore how expressions of prejudice altered as neoliberal ideology rose to dominance in the United States during the early 1980s.

The literature in psychology distinguishes among different types of racism. Traditional racism is characterized by bigotry, antipathy, beliefs in race-based superiority, and a desire for racial segregation. Reports of traditional, blatant racism have decreased steadily over time (Firebaugh and Davis 1988). For example, the percentage of White Americans who favor laws against racial intermarriage decreased from 39 percent in 1972, to 33 percent in 1982, to 19 percent in 1993, to 10 percent in 2002 (author's compilation of General Social Survey data). When asked why Blacks have worse jobs, income, and housing compared with Whites, the percentage of White Americans who attribute these outcomes to the inborn and lower abilities of Blacks to learn decreased from 26 percent in 1972, to 19 percent in 1989, to 10 percent in 1998, to 8 percent in 2006 (author's compilation of General Social Survey data). Thus, traditional prejudice has declined. Furthermore, the predictive validity of traditional prejudice measures has waned over the neoliberal era (McConahay 1983; Pettigrew and Meertens 1995).

Over time, however, White Americans' sympathy for corrective measures has also declined, in tandem with changes in their beliefs about why inequality exists. When asked why Blacks have worse jobs, income, and housing compared with Whites, the percentage of White Americans who attribute these racial differences to internal causes (e.g., a lack of motivation) versus external causes (e.g., discrimination against Blacks) has increased over time (Bobo 2001). The percentage of Whites who believe that Blacks just need to try harder increased from 70 percent in the 1970s to approximately 80 percent by the mid 1980s (Bobo 2001), and Whites have become less concerned with the unfair treatment of minority groups. The percentage of young Whites expressing apathy about racial issues increased from 10 percent in 1976, to 13 percent in 1988, to 16 percent in 1998, and to 18 percent in 2000 (Forman 2004).[2] The percentage of White Americans who believe that the government has an obligation to improve Blacks' living standards has decreased from 11 percent in 1975 to 4 to 5 percent in 1986, 1996, and 2006 (author's compilation of General Social Survey data). Interestingly, the more Whites perceive Blacks to be worse off financially, the more negatively they stereotype Blacks as lazy (Brezina and Winder 2003). The 1990 General Social Survey revealed that 44 percent of White Americans perceived Blacks to be lazy, and 56 percent perceived them to prefer to live off welfare (Davis, Smith, and Marsden 2007). Taken together, these figures reveal that Whites have become less likely to see structural barriers against Blacks, more likely to attribute their disadvantaged status to laziness, and thus be less concerned with social justice and government assistance for them. How can we account for such changes in the attitudes associated with prejudice? Is there a relationship here to neoliberal ideas?

During the 1980s, two social psychological theories were introduced to explain the changing nature of prejudice toward Blacks in the United States – those associated with "modern racism" (McConahay 1986) and "symbolic

---

[2] Generalized apathy, in contrast, has held steady over time at 10 to 11 percent (Forman 2004).

racism" (Kinder and Sears 1981).[3] In keeping with the data I have just reported, both theories assert that only a small proportion of racists hold the attitudes described as "traditional prejudice." Since the 1980s, the majority of racists are said to hold attitudes characteristic of modern or symbolic racism, which are less blatantly prejudiced and stem from a blend of antipathy to Blacks and strongly individualistic values. Because the two theories are very similar (symbolic racism theory places a stronger emphasis on individualism), I will use the term "modern racism" to refer to both.

Modern racists justify their racial antipathy on the grounds that Blacks violate traditional American ideals such as the Protestant work ethic (Kinder 1986; Sears and Henry 2003). Measures for modern racism tap the beliefs that discrimination no longer exists, that Blacks' demands for special treatment are unfair, and that Blacks fail to get ahead because of a lack of hard work and self-reliance (Henry and Sears 2002). These theories of modern racism reflect the fact that neoliberal values have provided narratives that allow some individuals to articulate racial prejudice in less blatant ways. For example, we have found that the higher people score on modern racism and modern sexism scales, the more likely they are to oppose affirmative action – specifically on the grounds that it will assist women and minorities, whom they see as less deserving (Bobocel et al. 1998). Thus, people whose attitudes reflect what is widely seen as modern prejudice discriminate based on concerns with meritocracy.

However, it is important to note that not all people became modern racists during the neoliberal era. Another theory, associated with aversive racism and also proposed in the mid 1980s, has been developed to identify and explain prejudiced attitudes held by politically progressive Whites (Gaertner and Dovidio 1986). Aversive racists value fairness and espouse egalitarian values yet unconsciously hold negative feelings toward outgroup members (Gaertner and Dovidio 1986). Because they explicitly denounce prejudice, aversive racists are said to discriminate only in situations in which they can appear nonprejudiced, that is, ones in which there are no clear standards for non–racially based behavior or in which there is a non–race-related excuse to respond negatively. Participants affiliated with progressive (liberal) political parties have shown this pattern of discriminatory behavior (Dovidio and Gaertner 2004). Thus, racial prejudice is found on the political left.

Moreover, a theory of principled conservatism has been advanced to show that political conservatives are not all prejudiced (Sniderman and Tetlock 1986). Its proponents argue that many conservatives are misclassified because measures for modern racism often confound racism and conservatism. Principled conservatives are said to be those with right-wing policy preferences, which have negative implications for group equality (e.g., opposition to affirmative action) but who are motivated by non-racial principles (e.g., concerns with meritocracy). When presented with clear evidence of the deservingness of a claimant for unemployment assistance, for instance, principled conservatives

---

[3] The theory of modern racism has since been extended to other groups.

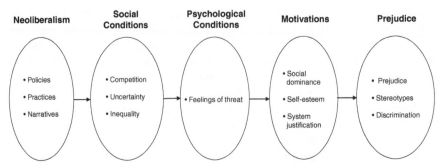

FIGURE 5-1. Indirect Relation Between Neoliberalism and Prejudice.

do not discriminate against Black claimants (Sniderman and Piazza 1993).[4]
Thus, conservatives do not always discriminate against subordinate groups.

In sum, although research into modern racism provides some evidence that
neoliberal beliefs are closely associated with prejudice, it is important to emphasize that a left–right political and economic orientation does not map perfectly
onto prejudice. There are a number of aversive racists on the political left who
are prejudiced and principled conservatives on the right who are not particularly prejudiced.

Neoliberal Initiatives as an Indirect Factor Behind Prejudice

Alongside the direct links between neoliberal beliefs and prejudice, there is a
second channel through which developments during the neoliberal era might
have led indirectly to higher levels of prejudice. In recent decades, changes in
attitudes associated with multiculturalism, human rights, and the civil rights
movements have likely led to some decline in prejudice. However, neoliberal
policies, practices, and narratives have also created specific social conditions
(i.e., more intense competition over resources, uncertainty about the future, and
greater inequality) that have the potential to increase the incidence of prejudice.
Significant literatures in psychology suggest that social conditions of this sort
often have psychological effects (notably, increased feelings of threat), which
stimulate psychologically based mechanisms (based on social dominance, self-
esteem, and system justification) that are known to give rise to prejudice (see
Fig. 5-1).

This model moves from the macro to the micro level, and there may be
complex interaction effects here. For instance, individual-level prejudice could
be used to rally support for neoliberal policies. Consequently, this model should
be seen only as a starting point from which to develop a fuller understanding
of the links between neoliberalism and prejudice, but I will outline a few of the
potential paths in the model for illustrative purposes (see Fig. 5-1).

---

[4] In fact, they show a preference for black versus white claimants, likely because the former have
violated their expectations and thus appear particularly deserving (i.e., a "shifting standards"
phenomenon).

Neoliberal policies and practices, which open markets and reduce regulation, often lead to increased competition among individuals. Other social changes during the neoliberal era (associated with globalization, immigration, and the increased participation of women in the labor force) may also have led to greater intergroup contact and competition (e.g., for jobs, promotions). In parallel, a neoliberal discourse, which emphasizes how individuals facing competition need to maximize their "human capital" and marketability, reinforce this sense of more intense competition.

That context of greater competition should lead, in turn, to increases in feelings of threat, which can lead to prejudice – particularly when people perceive themselves to be in competition with outgroup members. The perception of competition is a major source of the feelings of threat from outgroup members that result in intergroup conflict (Campbell 1965). People can perceive outgroup members to be a threat based on competition over resources or over more symbolic goods, such as values (Stephan and Stephan 2000). Correlational research reveals that perceptions of threat account for 30 to 71 percent of the variance in prejudice toward immigrants in the United States, Israel, and Spain (Stephan and Renfro 2002). Thus, where neoliberalism inspires increased competition, it may lead to greater feelings of threat and prejudice.

Feelings of threat lead to prejudice through various socio-cognitive mechanisms (see Fig. 5-1). One of the most prominent is social dominance orientation (SDO), a set of attitudes that reflect the degree to which people believe that hierarchy among social groups is good for society (Pratto et al. 1994; Sidanius and Pratto 1999). There is strong empirical evidence, for instance, that increases in threat lead to higher social dominance motives, which in turn lead to greater prejudice. In one study, non–Asian Americans who were experimentally threatened by inducing a sense of competition with Asian Americans (i.e., primed with the idea that Asians are taking over America) reported higher levels of SDO than those in the control condition (Morrison and Ybarra 2008). The effects of threat on SDO are particularly strong for people who belong to groups of higher status (Morrison, Fast, and Ybarra 2009).

Greater feelings of threat can also lead to prejudice because they motivate people to bolster their self-esteem (Branscombe and Wann 1994), and people often engage in downward social comparisons with outgroups to enhance the status of their ingroup and their self-evaluations (Tajfel and Turner 1986). After threat, the more people derogate an outgroup member, the higher their self-esteem (Fein and Spencer 1997). When Whites are threatened via negative feedback from an outgroup member (e.g., a Black evaluator), they automatically activate negative stereotypes more quickly than when they are not threatened (Sinclair and Kunda 1999). But even when people are threatened (e.g., receive failure feedback) *by an ingroup member*, they apply stereotypes more in their judgments of outgroup members compared with when they are not threatened (Fein and Spencer 1997). Another mechanism operates through system justification. When people are threatened, experience fear, or face uncertainty, they become more strongly motivated to rationalize their social system as just or fair (Jost, Banaji, and Nosek 2004). For instance, when people's system justification motives are activated by threatening the legitimacy of their society, participants later rate powerful people as more intelligent and independent and people without power as less intelligent and independent compared with those in a no-threat condition (Kay, Jost, and Young, 2005; see also Kay et al. 2009). Thus, increases in economic insecurity and in income inequality that are a hallmark of the neoliberal age may lead people to engage in system justification in which they evoke stereotypes speaking to subordinate groups' lower levels of competence and deservingness.

How Neoliberal Economic Beliefs and Stigmatization Are Related at the Micro Level

Are people who are more prejudiced more likely to endorse neoliberalism? Before I draw on the psychological research pertinent to this issue, I must note that psychologists do not study "neoliberalism." Typically, they study people's political and economic beliefs conceptualized along a traditional left–right continuum. Of course, many of the results are relevant to capitalist societies in general, but some have direct bearing on the relationship between neoliberal beliefs and prejudice. First, let us consider the explicit prejudices people may have. A small but consistent literature indicates that people who more strongly endorse neoliberal economic beliefs tend to hold more explicitly prejudiced attitudes.[5] The more strongly European American students believe that economic inequality is legitimate (e.g., agree that "Laws of nature are responsible for differences in wealth in society"), the more racist they are (Jost and Thompson 2000). The more positively Belgians evaluate capitalism, private initiative, unrestricted competition, income differences among people, for instance, and trade unions and government intervention into the economy negatively, the more racist they are ($r = .33$; Van Hiel, Pandelaere, and Duriez 2004). Materialist attitudes are also directly related to racist attitudes ($r = .22$; Roets, Van Hiel, and Cornelis 2006). Among Australians, a stronger self-identification with the group "Capitalists" is associated with more negative attitudes toward women's rights (Heaven and St. Quintin 1999). Studies conducted in the United States and Sweden found that the more participants support free market capitalism (i.e., positive attitudes toward capitalism and negative attitudes toward socialism and nationalization of corporations), then the more racist they were. This is the case for Americans toward Blacks ($r = .25$) and Swedes toward immigrants ($r = .38$) (Sidanius and Pratto 1993; cf., Leeson and Heaven 1999). Thus, investigations in multiple countries during the 1990s and early 2000s indicate the presence of a positive but weak relation between neoliberal economic beliefs and explicit prejudice.

Much of the research on this topic uses only a few items to measure economic beliefs, and these measures were not validated. To better assess the relationship

---

[5] This is true regardless of the form of explicit prejudice studied: traditional, modern, or negative affect.

between neoliberal economic beliefs and prejudice, my collaborator, Suzanne Kiani, and I developed a 25-item measure of neoliberal economic beliefs, which includes attitudes toward free market capitalism, competition and the merito-cratic ideal, and privatization and limits on regulation (Son Hing and Kiani 2008).[6] The topics examined do not cover all neoliberal beliefs, nor are they necessarily exclusive to a neoliberal worldview. Yet they have strong internal consistency or coherence for our participants.

My collaborators and I found that, among a community sample of Whites from the American South ages 20 to 69 years, endorsement of neoliberal-ism was positively associated with holding modern racist attitudes toward Blacks ($r = .35$; $p = .001$; Son Hing et al. 2012). By contrast, neoliberalism was marginally and inversely associated with implicit prejudice toward Blacks ($r = -.19$; $p = .06$). When we controlled for the participant's age, the negative relationship between neoliberalism and implicit prejudice becomes significant (partial $r = -.24$; $p = .03$). Thus, when using a better measure of participants' neoliberal economic beliefs, we find that the more people endorse such beliefs, the more likely they are to be explicitly prejudiced. However, the more peo-ple endorse neoliberalism, the less likely they are to have negative automatic or uncontrollable biases. It appears that, when Southern Whites have positive automatic reactions toward Blacks, they are less likely to endorse competition, merit-based rewards, and unrestricted markets.

In a parallel study of Canadian university men, we found that endorsement of neoliberal beliefs was positively, if moderately, associated with their levels of modern sexism ($r = .55$; $p < .001$). By contrast, we found no relation between men's levels of neoliberalism and their implicit prejudice (i.e., automatic asso-ciations of competence with men and incompetence with women; $r = -.09$, not significant).[7] Thus, the more inclined men are to endorse neoliberal beliefs, the more explicitly – but not implicitly – sexist they are.

Why Neoliberals Tend to Be More Explicitly Prejudiced

Why is it that people who more strongly endorse neoliberalism also tend to have attitudes that are more explicitly – but not implicitly – prejudiced? I want to suggest that within social contexts marked by group inequality and a history of capitalism, explicit *prejudice and neoliberal economic beliefs should be linked because they are part of a cluster of ideologies that serves to legitimize a hierarchical status quo*. In contrast, implicit prejudice is not related to neoliberal beliefs because the kind of automatic responses driven by paired associations

---

[6] The neoliberalism scale demonstrates predictive validity, in that stronger neoliberal beliefs pre-dict self-reported voting in the 2008 presidential race (American sample) and evaluations of a fictitious conservative political candidate (Canadian sample).

[7] Interestingly, among women, the more they endorse neoliberalism, the less implicitly sexist they are ($r = -.21$; $p = .03$). It is perhaps the case that the more women automatically associate competence with men, the less positive they are toward competition and merit-based outcomes. However, it is important to note that this is not an issue of prejudice.

that this type of prejudice reflects is based on repeated experience – not on a well-articulated ideology.

The particular socioeconomic or political beliefs that people adopt may well be driven, in part, by their endorsement of two broader sociopolitical ideologies: SDO and conservatism (Duckitt 2001; Jost et al. 2003). As I have noted, SDO reflects the degree to which people believe that hierarchy among social groups is good for society (Sidanius and Pratto 1999). Conservatism reflects the degree to which people support common conventions and the status quo (Stangor and Leary 2006), and it can refer to political conservatism (i.e., left–right identification) or to social conservatism (e.g., attitudes toward morality, traditional family). If the levels of SDO or conservatism that people display conditions both their attitudes to neoliberalism and explicit prejudice, then these overarching orientations may explain the empirical link between the two. If it is the case that SDO drives the relation between explicit prejudice and neoliberalism, then SDO should be positively related to both and, in general, it is. People higher in SDO are more sexist, racist (e.g., toward Blacks, aboriginals, Indians, Arabs, Asians), prejudiced toward immigrants, lesbians, gay men, feminists, housewives, and physically disabled people (e.g., Altemeyer 1998; Duckitt 2001) compared with people lower in SDO. Moreover, experimental studies reveal that inducing an increase in SDO gives rise to higher levels of explicit prejudice (Guimond et al. 2003). It is also likely that people who display higher levels of SDO should endorse key aspects of neoliberal ideology more strongly (e.g., marketization, privatization of risk). Our research finds that Canadian men who more strongly endorse neoliberal beliefs score higher in SDO ($r = .50$; $p < .001$). Thus, SDO can plausibly drive the relationship between neoliberal economic beliefs and explicit prejudice.

Much the same can be said of conservatism. If conservatism is the driver behind the relationship between explicit prejudice and neoliberalism, then conservatism should be positively related to both. And, indeed, people who are more politically conservative tend to be more racist (Van Hiel et al. 2004). The relationship is even stronger for those who are more socially conservative. Moreover, our Canadian research found that undergraduate men who endorse neoliberal beliefs more strongly also endorse political conservatism ($r = .35$; $p < .001$) and social conservatism ($r = .30$; $p < .001$) more strongly. The relationship is even stronger among a sample of White Americans in the South: those who more strongly endorse neoliberal beliefs more strongly endorsed political conservatism ($r = .53$; $p < .001$) and social conservatism ($r = .49$; $p < .001$).[8] These data support the notion that neoliberal economic beliefs and explicit prejudice can, *in some social contexts*, serve as hierarchy-legitimizing ideologies.

---

[8] Given that the United States is more neoliberal than Canada, it is interesting to note that neoliberal economic beliefs are more strongly related to social and political conservatism in the United States.

Structural equation modeling techniques reveal that the relation between explicit racism and right-wing economic beliefs can stem from SDO (Sidanius and Pratto 1993; Van Hiel et al. 2004; Cornelis and Van Hiel 2006) or from political conservatism (Sidanius and Pratto 1993). So which of SDO or conservatism is the more important causal link between neoliberalism and explicit prejudice? There is reason to believe that the answer should depend on the perceived status and conventionality of the outgroup of interest because SDO predicts explicit prejudice, particularly toward groups with low status (e.g., Blacks), but conservatism predicts explicit prejudice particularly toward groups (e.g., gays) whose values are seen to threaten social conventions (Duckitt 2006). Therefore, whereas SDO is likely a causal link between neoliberal beliefs and explicit prejudice toward low-status outgroups, conservatism is more likely to provide the causal link between neoliberalism and explicit prejudice toward an unconventional outgroup.

Thus far I have looked at implicit and explicit attitudes separately. Next let us consider how implicit and explicit prejudices operate in tandem and how they relate to neoliberal beliefs. Previously it was impossible to differentiate "modern racists" from "political conservatives" (because of a confounded measure) and to differentiate "aversive racists" from people with truly little prejudice (because of self-reporting problems). But my colleagues and I have proposed and tested a two-dimensional model of prejudice that disambiguates prejudice from left–right orientations (Son Hing et al. 2008). We use the distinction between explicit and implicit prejudice to classify people into one of four prejudice profiles (Fig. 5-2). Truly low-prejudiced people are low in modern racism and low in implicit prejudice. Aversive racists are low in modern racism but high in implicit prejudice. Principled conservatives are high in modern racism and but low in implicit prejudice. Modern racists are high in modern racism and high in implicit prejudice.

Our studies of Canadians and Americans validate this classification and reveal the types of beliefs endorsed by those who display each form of prejudice. We found that principled conservatives are the most identified with the social groups "capitalist" and "conservative" and most strongly endorse neoliberal economic beliefs. Whereas modern racists are the next most right-leaning on our measures of political conservatism and neoliberalism, aversive racists are the most left leaning. In a study of prejudice toward Asians among White Canadians, we found that modern racists scored the highest on the two best predictors of generalized prejudice (SDO and social conservatism); whereas the truly low-prejudiced participants scored the lowest, aversive racists and principled conservatives fell in the middle (Son Hing and Zanna 2010).

Consistent with this theory (Gaertner and Dovidio 1986), we found that the discriminatory behavior of aversive racists and modern racists depended on the situation (Son Hing et al. 2008). Participants either evaluated an outgroup member who was a well-qualified job applicant (i.e., the no-excuse-to-discriminate condition) or an outgroup member whose qualifications were

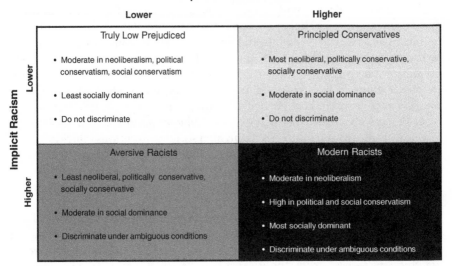

Explicit Modern Racism

Darker shading indicates more stigmatizing attitudes and behaviors.

FIGURE 5-2. The Relations Between the Four Prejudice Profiles and Neoliberalism.

ambiguous (i.e., the excuse-to-discriminate condition). In the no-excuse-to-discriminate condition, in which discriminatory behavior would be obvious, aversive and modern racists avoided it; but in the excuse-to-discriminate condition, they evaluated an outgroup member as less hirable than a matched ingroup member. Neither the truly low-prejudiced nor principled conservatives discriminated even when there was an excuse to do so (Son Hing et al. 2008). In sum, the relationship between neoliberal beliefs and prejudice is not monotonic. The people who were the most racist and likely to discriminate (i.e., modern racists) were not the strongest endorsers of neoliberalism, and the people who were the least racist and discriminatory (truly low-prejudiced people) were not the biggest opponents of neoliberalism. Moreover, the people who are most neoliberal, the principled conservatives, were not the most prejudiced in terms of their underlying ideologies, and they never took the opportunity to discriminate against an outgroup member.

The Experience and Effect of Stigma

Now that we have a sense of how prejudice, stereotyping, and discrimination are related to neoliberalism, let us turn to the other side of the issue, namely to the question of how neoliberalism might affect the experience of stigmatization and resilience to it.

People are stigmatized when one or more of their attributes is associated with devalued social status in a particular context (Crocker, Major, and Steele

1998). Stigmatization has many negative effects on people's life circumstances, the stressors they face, the resources on which they can draw, and ultimately on their health and life expectancy (Williams et al. 1997). For instance, systemic (i.e., institutional) or personal (individual) discrimination can raise barriers in employment, housing, education, and health care (Sidanius and Pratto 1999). In the workplace, discrimination affects the advancement and salary of devalued group members. White supervisors rate their Black employees' performance significantly lower than Black supervisors rate these same employees (Mount et al. 1997). When controlling for actual performance evaluations (as well as age, tenure, and part-time status), women experience lower salary growth compared with men, and Blacks experience lower salary growth and a higher likelihood of layoffs compared with Whites (Elvira and Zatzick 2002; Castilla 2008).

Health is another important outcome on which we can compare stigmatized and nonstigmatized groups. In the United States, there is a Black–White life expectancy gap (advantaging Whites) of approximately 6.5 years for men and 4.5 years for women (Harper et al. 2007). Compared with nonstigmatized group members, stigmatized group members endure more daily stressors and have fewer resources on which they can draw (Williams et al. 1997). Chronic experiences of stress can deregulate the stress response, which impairs immune functioning, leading to illness such as heart disease and cancer (Glaser and Kiecolt-Glaser 2005; Miller and Blackwell 2006).

Group comparisons of this sort, of course, do not allow one to establish the extent to which group differences are directly attributable to stigmatization. But the issue of causality has been addressed with experimental studies. Stigmatization experiences are manipulated in the lab by exposing devalued group members to prejudice by reminding them of past experiences of discrimination, of their stigmatized group status, of negative stereotypes about their group, and so on. These investigations reveal that the experience of stigmatization (vs. no stigmatization) results consistently in greater physiological reactivity, such as cardiovascular reactivity with moderate to large effect sizes (Blascovich et al. 2001; Murphy et al. 2007; Williams and Mohammed 2009). And experimentally induced stigmatization leads to worse psychological well-being among the members of devalued groups (Crocker, Cornwell, and Major 1993). However, it should be noted that survey-based assessments suggest that the effects of stigmatization are not as universally harmful as one might expect. For instance, a recent meta-analysis revealed that self-reported experiences of discrimination are only weakly associated with stress responses ($r = -.11$), with physical health ($r = -.13$; Pascoe and Smart Richman 2009), and with later mental health ($r = -.28$; Pavalko, Mossakowski, and Hamilton 2003; Mak et al. 2007). Many studies reveal conditional effects, and the research literature yields at best mixed results, which suggest that perceiving oneself to be stigmatized is harmful but the effects are weak (Son Hing 2012). This discrepancy may be explained at least partly by the fact that compared with experimental manipulation, subjective experiences of stigmatization in the world may often be ambiguous – especially because racism is likely to be implicit rather than explicit. Both modern and aversive racists are likely to discriminate only when there is a non–race-related excuse for doing so. Thus, from the perspective of the stigmatized, it is not entirely clear whether one is the target of prejudice, stereotyping, or discrimination. Moreover, those who encounter stigmatization or discrimination can often adopt a variety of strategies to cope with it and to sustain their resilience; it is to that subject that I now turn.

Resilience, Stress, and Coping

Psychologists approach resilience as an inferential construct: when an individual does better than expected given challenging circumstances, resilience is inferred (Masten 2001). Psychological conceptualizations of resilience differ, but many definitions include (a) the presence of serious threats to development (e.g., low socioeconomic status, trauma, or stressful life events) and (b) the achievement of positive outcomes based on societal expectations for well-being (Masten 2001; Armstrong, Birnie-Lefcovitch, and Ungar 2005).[9]

What are the sources of resilience according to psychologists? One perspective suggests that that relevant resources (i.e., assets or protective factors) may reside within the individual (e.g., emotional regulation; self-efficacy, i.e., a belief that one can successfully navigate one's environment), the social or family context (e.g., secure attachments, authoritative parenting), or the community (e.g., a safe environment; religious, spiritual, and cultural affiliations). Cross-cultural research (Ungar 2008) indicates that although some protective factors are culturally dependent (e.g., self-esteem), others are universally important (e.g., supportive family and friends, educational and employment opportunities).

Although early conceptualizations presumed that resilience was rare, today it is understood to be a common outcome of multiple, normal human adaptive processes (Masten 2001). This does not mean that all people display resilience. Resilience is least likely when risk factors threaten adaptive systems, which include cognitive development, emotional and behavioral regulation, and a motivation for learning and engaging in the environment (Werner and Smith 1992; Masten et al. 1999). Consequently, those at the highest level of risk are unlikely to develop the personal assets that foster resilience (Vanderbilt-Adriance and Shaw 2008). Resilience is neither exceptional nor guaranteed.

To provide some insight into how resilience actually works, I will use the transactional model of stress and coping (Folkman and Lazarus 1980). According to this model, to experience stress, a person must assess the stressor as self-relevant and harmful, and she or he must believe that she or he does not

---

[9] Others think of resilience as a process of successful adaptation to (i.e., change in response to) an acute or chronic stressful event (Bonanno 2004). Yet others conceptualize resilience as a dynamic process derived from repeated interactions between a person and favorable contextual variables (Luthar and Zelazo 2003). Thus, for resilience to be demonstrated, supportive contexts must be created.

have the capacity to cope with the threat given the resources in the environment (Folkman and Lazarus 1985). If individuals perceive themselves as able to cope, they experience the stimulus as a challenge rather than a stressor. An individual's personal resources (e.g., material goods) and his or her access to resources in the environment (e.g., social support) affect this cognitive appraisal process (Folkman and Lazarus 1985). In keeping with this, I contend that having more individual, social, or institutional resources can reduce the likelihood that people will see potential stressors as ones with which they do not have the ability to cope, rendering them less susceptible to stress and other related negative outcomes. In short, there is some potential for people to demonstrate resilience when confronted with challenges.

When a potential stressor is appraised as a threat, the experience of stress involves physiological, cognitive, emotional, and behavioral responses (Holahan, Moos, and Schaefer 1996). Some of these responses are involuntary (e.g., physiological arousal and anger), and some are voluntary, such as coping responses (i.e., cognitive and behavioral efforts to manage the demands of the stressful encounter; Compas et al. 2001). For those who engage in more effective coping responses, stress is less likely to lead to psychological, physical, and behavioral strain (e.g., depression, illness) (Miller 2006). Thus, people with more resources are more resilient because they have a broader array of coping responses to draw on and are more likely to use effective ones.

Resilience and Coping with Stigma

Let us now consider how the concepts of risks, resilience, resources, stress, and coping come into play for those experiencing stigmatization. The experience of stigmatization (i.e., stereotyping, prejudice, and discrimination) can be conceptualized as a social stressor – and one of the most harmful kinds: ambiguous, uncontrollable, and unpredictable (Carter 2007). How people respond to stigmatization depends on how they construe it. People are less resilient to stigmatization when they construe it to be more self-relevant and more harmful. People are more resilient to stigmatization if they have greater resources available on which they can draw to cope with stigmatization. These assets might exist at the level of the individual, the social, or the institutional.

Individual-level resources can foster resilience to discrimination. Among people with a weak sense of control over themselves and their environment, for instance, experiences of discrimination are associated with more negative effect, but this effect is greatly mitigated among those with a stronger sense of control over themselves and their environment (Jang, Chiriboga, and Small 2008). A study of Chinese Canadians living in Toronto found that among those low in hardiness (i.e., with a weak sense of control and low in self-esteem), the more they had personally experienced discrimination in the past, the more psychological symptoms they reported (Dion, Dion, and Pak 1992). However, among those high in hardiness, experienced discrimination gave rise to no psychological symptoms.

Social assets can also foster resilience, especially when they foster positive evaluations of or identification with one's ingroup. A study of ethnic minority girls in Scotland found that the more positively they evaluated their ingroup, the lower was the incidence of depression and anxiety among them (Cassidy et al. 2004). Positive evaluations of the ingroup can buffer the negative effects of experiences of discrimination. Among African American children, experiencing more discrimination from their peers is associated with higher levels of depression, but this effect is weaker for those who feel more positively about their ethnic group (Rivas-Drake, Hughes, and Way 2008). For African American youth, the typical effect of greater (vs. fewer) experiences of discrimination on felt stress is entirely mitigated for those who have been socialized by their parents to value Black culture, to be aware of discrimination, and to believe in racial equality (Neblett et al. 2008). These effects appear to operate through stress processes (Neblett et al. 2008). It seems likely that when people are threatened by stigmatization, those who value their ingroup can draw on this positive identity to provide a sense of self-worth that offers resilience in the face of discrimination (Tajfel and Turner 1986).

Identifying with one's ingroup seems to have similar effects. Among African Americans, a stronger ingroup identification is associated with higher self-esteem and fewer negative emotions (Branscombe, Schmitt, and Harvey 1999). The more African American youth experience discrimination at school, the worse their academic self-concept and school achievement; however, this effect is weaker for those with a strong connection to their ethnic group (Wong, Eccles, and Sameroff 2003).[10] Even the experience of discrimination may play some role here. Among both African American men and women, perceiving more discrimination against one's group leads to greater ingroup identification, which mitigates negative responses to perceived discrimination (Schmitt and Branscombe 2002).

These effects may operate through several mechanisms. Those who identify with their ingroup are more likely to appraise themselves as having the resources needed to cope with stigma compared with those who are less identified (Rusch et al. 2009). Ingroup identification may promote access to cultural repertoires that provide alternate sources of group recognition (Lamont and Mizrachi forthcoming); and it may engender a sense of belonging or acceptance, which is a critically important human motive (Baumeister and Leary 1995). Finally, ingroup identification might go hand in hand with having a better social network to draw on for important coping resources (Schmitt and Branscombe 2002).

Finally, institutional factors can also be sources of resilience. Among a predominantly Hispanic sample of MBA students, the more participants perceived that they had been discriminated against at work, the less just they believed

---

[10] It appears that a strong ingroup identification can help foster resilience for those experiencing lower levels of discrimination. However, those who faced more extreme threats are not protected (Yoo and Lee 2005).

their treatment at work was; however, this effect was weaker for those working in organizations that had taken steps to support diversity by sponsor-
ing workshops on diversity and so on (Triana and Garcia 2009). For HIV-
positive, gay, Hispanic men who are not active in HIV or gay organizations,
the more personal discrimination they have experienced, the lower their self-
esteem (Ramirez-Valles et al. 2005). However, for those active in either form
of organization, the effects of experienced discrimination on self-esteem are
buffered. For African Americans, the adverse effects of perceived discrimination on negative affect are buffered by religious attendance (Bierman 2006).
These findings all suggest that participating in institutions that provide a sense
of belonging help to create resilience to stigmatization.

Neoliberal Beliefs and Resilience

From the perspective of this volume, the implications for resilience of holding neoliberal beliefs are especially interesting. Endorsing aspects of neoliberal
ideologies (e.g., beliefs that meritocracy exists, that inequality is legitimate)
seem to render the members of devalued social groups more, rather than less,
vulnerable in the face of stigmatization or discrimination. For instance, the
more strongly African Americans believe that economic inequality is legitimate,
the more they experience negative affect (Jost and Thompson 2000). Among
African American men, the more strongly they endorse individualism, competition, and materialism, the higher their blood pressure (Daniels et al. 2001).
Finally, among African and Latino Americans who are strongly identified with
their ingroup, the more they believe that the world is just, that individual mobility is possible, and that status differences are legitimate, then the worse their
self-esteem and the greater their depression (O'Brien, and Major 2005). By contrast, for the members of dominant groups, endorsement of neoliberal beliefs is
either unrelated or positively related to well-being (Jost and Thompson 2000;
O'Brien, and Major 2005).

Why might holding neoliberal beliefs be harmful for members of devalued social groups? In a nutshell, it seems likely that those beliefs impair the
ability of members of such groups to activate a normal defense mechanism:
externalizing negative feedback. When confronted with adverse experiences,
such as negative feedback about one's work performance, attributing that to
discrimination (rather than to one's own performance) can be self-protective
(Crocker and Major 1989). Women who can attribute negative feedback from
a male experimenter to his sexism rather than to their own abilities report
higher self-esteem, for instance, than do women in a setting where no cues are
given about the prejudices of the experimenter (Major, Quinton, and Schmader
2003). When the cues provided regarding stigmatization are ambiguous, the
likelihood of making self-protective attributions to discrimination for negative signals or treatment received from dominant group members varies across
individuals and social groups. On the whole, when facing ambiguous discrimination, Blacks are generally able to make self-protective attributions (Major

et al. 1998), but only women who are highly identified with their ingroup are able to do so (Major et al. 2003). This difference may stem from the higher levels of awareness of discrimination found among Blacks than among women, and that in turn has implications for the impact of neoliberal ideas.

In general, beliefs in the meritocratic ideals of neoliberalism are inversely related to beliefs about discrimination. When receiving negative feedback from a dominant group member, devalued group members who strongly endorse the beliefs that individual mobility is possible and hard work brings success are less likely to perceive discrimination against themselves (Major et al. 2002) or against their group (Major et al. 2007). Experimental evidence reveals that priming meritocratic beliefs leads to a denial of discrimination (McCoy and Major 2007). In lab-based experiments, when women, African Americans, and Hispanic Americans who receive negative feedback from a White man believe strongly that individual mobility is possible for all, then they are less likely to attribute their treatment to discrimination and more likely to blame themselves for the rejection (Major et al. 2002). In short, devalued group members who endorse beliefs associated with neoliberalism view negative outcomes as more self-relevant and more harmful and thus are less likely to be resilient in the face of them.

Opportunities for Coping and Resilience

Seen from a broader perspective, the research I have reviewed here suggests that members of groups that are socially devalued often display surprising levels of resilience. Indeed, the members of devalued groups tend to have better mental health (e.g., depression, anxiety disorders), greater well-being (self-esteem, positive affect, life satisfaction), and more positive evaluations of the ingroup, than do members of groups that are not devalued (Crocker et al. 1994; Twenge and Crocker 2002; Ryff and Hughes 2003; cf., Diener and Diener 1995). How do the members of such groups summon up such high levels of resilience on dimensions of mental health and well-being but demonstrate such poor outcomes on dimensions of physiological stress and physical health?

An important clue to the answer can be found by considering the processes by which stigmatization has its affects. Physical health is a domain in which stigmatization leads to processes that are involuntary (i.e., automatic, uncontrollable) that compound over time, making resilience less likely. For instance, when people experience stigmatization, the sympathetic nervous system creates the "fight or flight response" (e.g., physiological arousal); chronic experiences of stress can deregulate this stress response, which impairs immune functioning, leading to illness (Glaser and Kiecolt-Glaser 2005; Miller and Blackwell 2006). Thus, the effects of stigmatization on physical health are involuntary and can be chronic (Mays, Cochran, and Barnes 2007). In sum, in domains where the response to stigmatization is involuntary, uncontrollable, and cumulative in its effects, members of devalued groups are highly vulnerable.

In contrast, in domains more liable to voluntary coping responses, such as mental health and well-being, resilience is much more likely. This suggests, as I have argued, that resilience is closely associated with coping responses that involve cognitive restructuring (i.e., redefinitions of meaning). Cognitive restructuring or making personal meaning out of adverse events is a typically adaptive coping response (Gottlieb 1997). Thus, it seems reasonable to conclude that when responses to stigmatization can be mediated through a process of cognitive restructuring, there are real possibilities for resilience. Moreover, people make use of the resources they find in their cultural and institutional environments to effect this restructuring. Thus, we find that the members of devalued groups who are high in self-esteem, strongly identified with their ingroup, and actively engaged in supportive institutions are most likely to draw on those assets to make meaning out of their experiences with stigmatization and demonstrate a resulting resilience. This directs our attention, in turn, to the quality of the resources available to such people and to the ways in which they make use of them for these purposes (see Chapter 4).

Conclusion

In this chapter, I have explored the relations between prejudice, stereotyping, and discrimination and developments associated with the neoliberal era. I have noted that there are different types of prejudice or racism, including explicit and implicit racism, and that the incidence of each seems to have changed in recent decades. In particular, traditional, explicit racism has given way to implicit racism, modern racism, and aversive racism, especially in North America. Drawing on my own research as well as the existing literature, I have identified four types of racism (see Fig. 5-2). When we examine the relations between these types and neoliberal beliefs, we find a complex relationship. Those who evince neoliberal beliefs most strongly are more likely than others to express explicit, modern racist views, but when multiple forms of racism are considered, they are generally not the group most likely to discriminate, and some who are unsympathetic to neoliberal beliefs nonetheless do so, when circumstances allow them to without being blatant about it. Nevertheless, I also find evidence of a relationship between neoliberal beliefs and explicit racism that seems to be driven by the overarching belief systems associated with an SDO and conservatism. Drawing on the relevant literatures in psychology, I have also argued there are good reasons for thinking that the higher levels of competition and uncertainty associated with many neoliberal initiatives are likely to trigger threats to status that are typically associated with the stigmatization of others.

I have also looked at the ways in which the members of stigmatized groups summon up resilience in the face of discrimination and the role that neoliberal ideas might play in that process. In general, a review of the literature reveals that the members of stigmatized groups in North America are able to summon up substantial levels of resilience, and I have suggested that they do so via an active coping process involving cognitive restructuring and meaning making in which they draw on a wide range of resources at the individual, social, and institutional levels. In general, those with positive evaluations of their own group and strong group identification are able to withstand the emotional

challenges of discrimination better than others, although they remain susceptible to its physical effects. In this context, however, strong beliefs in the meritocratic values advanced by neoliberalism increase the vulnerability of members
of devalued groups to experiences of discrimination. People with those beliefs
are less able to discount those experiences by blaming them on others and more
inclined to blame themselves.

Given the limitations on the data available, it is impossible to reach precise
conclusions about the impact of the neoliberal initiatives or ideas that have
been so prominent in recent years on the nature or incidence of prejudice. It
is clear that despite the hopes of some exponents, the rise of neoliberalism
has not done away with prejudice (cf. Becker 1957), although, in tandem with
developments associated with the movements for civil rights, human rights,
and multiculturalism, it may have contributed to a decline in blatant or explicit
racism while rendering many more vulnerable to the effects of discrimination
that often stem from subtle and implicit racism. The larger lesson here, however, is that key features of social and cultural context can have important
effects, operating through well-known psychological mechanisms. Neoliberal
ideas are not irrelevant to the likelihood that someone will discriminate or to
the effects of such discrimination, and many other elements in the wider cultural and institutional environment also contribute to the resilience that people
can muster in contexts of prejudice or discrimination.

References

Altemeyer, B. 1998. "The Other 'Authoritarian Personality.'" *Advances in Experimental
Social Psychology* 30: 47–92.

Armstrong, M. I., S. Birnie-Lefcovitch, and M. T. Ungar. 2005. "Pathways Between
Social Support, Family Well Being, Quality of Parenting, and Child Resilience: What
We Know." *Journal of Child and Family Studies* 14 (2): 269–81.

Baumeister, R. F. and M. R. Leary. 1995. "The Need to Belong: Desire for Interpersonal
Attachments as a Fundamental Human Motive." *Psychological Bulletin* 117 (3): 497–
529.

Becker, G. A. 1957. *The Economics of Discrimination.* Chicago, IL: University of
Chicago Press.

Bierman, A. 2006. "Does Religion Buffer the Effects of Discrimination on Mental
Health? Differing Effects by Race." *Journal for the Scientific Study of Religion* 45
(4): 551–65.

Blascovich, J., S. J. Spencer, D. Quinn, and C. Steele. 2001. "African Americans and
High Blood Pressure: The Role of Stereotype Threat." *Psychological Science* 12 (3):
225–9.

Bobo, L. D. 2001. *Racial Attitudes and Relations at the Close of the Twentieth Century.
In America Becoming: The Growing Complexity of America's Racial Mosaic,* edited
by N. J. Smelser, W. J. Wilson, and F. Mitchell. Santa Monica, CA: Rand.

Bobocel, D. R., L. S. Son Hing, L. M. Davey, D. J. Stanley, and M. P. Zanna. 1998.
"Justice-Based Opposition to Social Policies: Is It Genuine?" *Journal of Personality
and Social Psychology* 75 (3): 653–69.

Bonanno, G. A. 2004. "Loss, Trauma, and Human Resilience: Have We Underestimated the Human Capacity to Thrive After Extremely Aversive Events?" *American
Psychologist* 59 (1): 20–8.

Branscombe, N. R., M. T. Schmitt, and R. D. Harvey. 1999. "Perceiving Pervasive Discrimination Among African Americans: Implications for Group Identification and Well-Being." *Journal of Personality and Social Psychology* 77: 135–49.

Branscombe, N. R. and D. L. Wann. 1994. "Collective Self-Esteem Consequences of Outgroup Derogation When a Valued Social Identity Is on Trial." *European Journal of Social Psychology* 24: 641–57.

Brezina, T. and K. Winder. 2003. "Economic Disadvantage: Status Generalization and Negative Racial Stereotyping by White Americans." *Social Psychology Quarterly* 66: 402–18.

Campbell, D. T. 1965. *Ethnocentric and Altruistic Motives.* Lincoln, NE: University of Nebraska Press.

Carter, R. T. 2007. "Racism and Psychological and Emotional Injury: Recognizing and Assessing Race-Based Traumatic Stress." *The Counseling Psychologist* 35 (1): 13–105.

Cassidy, C., R. C. O'Conner, C. Howe, and D. Warden. 2004. "Perceived Discrimination and Psychological Distress: The Role of Personal and Ethnic Self-Esteem." *Journal of Counseling Psychology* 51 (3): 329–39.

Castilla, E. J. 2008. "Gender, Race, and Meritocracy in Organizational Careers." *American Journal of Sociology* 113 (6): 1479–1526.

Castilla, E. J. and S. Bernard. 2010. "The Paradox of Meritocracy in Organizations." *Administrative Science Quarterly* 55: 543–76.

Compas, B. E., J. K. Connor-Smith, H. Saltzman, A. H. Thomsen, and M. E. Wadsworth. 2001. "Coping with Stress During Childhood and Adolescence: Problems, Progress, and Potential in Theory and Research." *Psychological Bulletin* 127: 87–127.

Cornelis, I. and A. Van Hiel. 2006. "The Impact of Cognitive Styles on Authoritarianism Based Conservatism and Racism." *Basic and Applied Social Psychology* 28 (1): 37–50.

Crocker, J. and B. Major. 1989. "Social Stigma and Self-Esteem: The Self-Protective Properties of Stigma." *Psychological Review* 96 (4): 608–30.

Crocker, J., B. Cornwell, and B. Major. 1993. "The Stigma of Overweight: Affective Consequences of Attributional Ambiguity." *Journal of Personality and Social Psychology* 64 (1): 60–70.

Crocker, J., R. Luhtanen, B. Blaine, and S. Broadnax. 1994. "Collective Self-Esteem and Psychological Well-Being Among White, Black, and Asian College Students." *Personality and Social Psychology Bulletin* 20 (5): 503–13.

Crocker, J., B., Major, and C. Steele. 1998. "Social Stigma." In *Handbook of Social Psychology,* edited by D. T. Gilbert, S. T. Fiske, and G. Lindzey. New York: McGraw-Hill: 503–53.

Daniels, I. N., J. P. Harrell, L. J. Floyd, and S. R. Bell. 2001. "Hostility, Cultural Orientation, and Causal Blood Pressure Readings in African Americans." *Ethnicity and Disease* 11 (4): 779–87.

Davis, J. A., T. W. Smith, and P. V. Marsden. 2007. "General Social Surveys 1972–2006." National Opinion Research Center.

Diener, E. and M. Diener. 1995. "Cross-Cultural Correlates of Life Satisfaction and Self-Esteem." *Journal of Personality and Social Psychology* 68 (4): 653–63.

Dion, K. L., K. K. Dion, and A. Pak. 1992. "Personality-Based Hardiness as a Buffer for Discrimination-Related Stress in Members of Toronto's Chinese Community." *Canadian Journal of Behavioural Science* 24 (4): 517–36.

Dovidio, J. F. and S. L. Gaertner. 2004. "Aversive Racism." In *Advances in Experimental Social Psychology* (Vol. 36), edited by M. P. Zanna. San Diego: Academic Press: 1–52.

Duckitt, J. 2001. "A Dual-Process Cognitive-Motivational Theory of Ideology and Prejudice." *Advances in Experimental Social Psychology* 33: 41–113.

Duckitt, J. 2006. "Differential Effects of Right Wing Authoritarianism and Social Dominance Orientation on Outgroup Attitudes and Their Mediation by Threat from and Competitiveness to Outgroups." *Personality and Social Psychology Bulletin* 32 (5): 684–96.

Elvira, M. M. and C. D. Zatzick. 2002. "Who's Displaced First? The Role of Race in Layoff Decisions." *Industrial Relations* 41 (2): 329–61.

Fein, S. and S. J. Spencer. 1997. "Prejudice as Self-Image Maintenance: Affirming the Self Through Derogating Others." *Journal of Personality and Social Psychology* 73 (1): 31–44.

Firebaugh, G. and K. E. Davis. 1988. "Trends in Antiblack Prejudice, 1972–1984: Region and Cohort Effects." *American Journal of Sociology* 94 (2): 251–72.

Folkman, S. and R. S. Lazarus. 1980. "An Analysis of Coping in a Middle-Aged Community Sample." *Journal of Health and Social Behavior* 21 (3): 219–39.

Folkman, S. and R. S. Lazarus. 1985. "If It Changes It Must Be a Process: Study of Emotion and Coping During Three Stages of College Examination." *Journal of Personality and Social Psychology* 48 (1): 150–70.

Folkman, S., R. S. Lazarus, R. J. Gruen, and A. DeLongis. 1986. "Appraisal, Coping, Health Status, and Psychological Symptoms." *Journal of Personality and Social Psychology* 50 (3): 571–9.

Forman, T. A. 2004. "Color-Blind Racism and Racial Indifference: The Role of Racial Apathy in Facilitating Enduring Inequalities." In *The Changing Terrain of Race and Ethnicity*, edited by Kryson, M. and A. Lewis. New York: Russell Sage.

Gaertner, S. L. and J. F. Dovidio. 1986. *The Aversive Form of Racism*. San Diego: Academic Press.

Glaser, R. and J. K. Kiecolt-Glaser. 2005. "Stress-Induced Immune Dysfunction: Implications for Health." *Nature Reviews Immunology* 5: 243–51.

Gottlieb, B. 1997. *Coping with Chronic Stress*. New York: Plenum Press.

Greenwald, A. G., T. A. Poehlman, E. L. Uhlmann, and M. R. Banaji. 2009. "Understanding and Using the Implicit Association Test: III. Meta-Analysis of Predictive Validity." *Journal of Personality and Social Psychology* 97 (1): 17–41.

Guimond, S., M. Dambrun, N. Michinov, and S. Duarte. 2003. "Does Social Dominance Generate Prejudice? Integrating Individual and Contextual Determinants of Intergroup Cognition." *Journal of Personality and Social Psychology* 84 (4): 697–721.

Harper, S., J. Lunch, S. Burris, and G. D. Smith. 2007. "Trends in the Black-White Life Expectancy Gap in the United States, 1983-2003." *The Journal of the American Medical Association* 297 (11): 1224–32.

Harrell, J. O., S. Hall, and J. Taliaferro. 2003. "Physiological Responses to Racism and Discrimination: An Assessment of the Evidence." *American Journal of Public Health* 93 (2): 243–48.

Heaven, P. C. L. and D. St. Quintin. 1999. "Personality Factors Predict Prejudice." *Personality and Individual Difference* 34: 625–34.

Henry, P. J. and D. O. Sears. 2002. "The Symbolic Racism 2000 Scale." *Political Psychology* 23 (2): 253–83.

Hofmann, W., B. Gawronski, T. Gschwendner, H. Le, and M. Schmitt. 2005. "A Meta-Analysis on the Correlation Between the Implicit Association Test and Explicit Self-Report Measures." *Personality and Social Psychology Bulletin* 3: 1369–85.

Holahan, C. J., R. H. Moos, and J. A. Schaefer. 1996. "Coping, Stress Resistance, and Growth: Conceptualizing Adaptive Functioning." In *Handbook of Coping*, edited by Zeidner, M. and S. Endler. New York: John Wiley and Sons: 24–43.

Jang, Y., D. A. Chiriboga, and B. J. Small. 2008. "Perceived Discrimination and Psychological Well-Being: The Mediating and Moderating Role of Sense of Control." *The International Journal of Aging and Human Development* 66 (3): 213–27.

Jost, J. T., M. T. Banaji, and B. A. Nosek. 2004. "A Decade of System Justification Theory: Accumulated Evidence of Conscious and Unconscious Bolstering of the Status Quo." *Political Psychology* 25 (6): 881–919.

Jost, J. T., J. Glaser, A. W. Kruglanski, and F. Sulloway. 2003. "Political Conservatism as Motivated Social Cognition." *Psychological Bulletin* 129: 339–75.

Jost, J. T. and E. P. Thompson. 2000. "Group-Based Dominance and Opposition to Equality as Independent Predictors of Self-Esteem, Ethnocentrism, and Social Policy Attitudes Among African Americans and European Americans." *Journal of Experimental Social Psychology* 36 (3): 209–32.

Kay, A. C., D. Gaucher, J. M. Peach, K. Laurin, J. Friesen, M. P. Zanna, and S. J. Spencer. 2009. "Inequality, Discrimination, and the Power of the Status Quo: Direct Evidence for a Motivation to See the Ways Things Are as the Way They Should Be." *Journal of Personality and Social Psychology* 97: 421–34.

Kay, A. C., J. T. Jost, and S. Young. 2005. "Victim Derogation and Victim Enhancement as Alternate Routes to System Justification." *Psychological Science* 16 (3): 240–6.

Kinder, D. R. 1986. "The Continuing American Dilemma: White Resistance to the Racial Change 40 Years after Myrdal." *Journal of Social Issues* 42 (2): 151–71.

Kinder, D. R. and D. O. Sears. 1981. "Prejudice and Politics: Symbolic Racism Versus Racial Threats to the Good Life." *Journal of Personality and Social Psychology* 40 (3): 414–31.

Lamont, Michèle and Nissim Mizrachi. 2012. "Ordinary People Doing Extraordinary Things, One Step at the Time: Responses to Stigmatization in Comparative Perspective." *Ethnic and Racial Studies* 35 (3): 365–81.

Leeson, P. and P. C. L. Heaven. 1999. "Social Attitudes and Personality." *Australian Journal of Psychology* 51 (1): 19–24.

Luthar, S. S. and L. B. Zelazo. 2003. "Research on Resilience: An Integrative Review." In *Resilience and Vulnerability: Adaptation in the Context of Childhood Adversities*, edited by S. S. Luthar. New York: Cambridge University Press: 510–49.

Major, B., R. H. Gramzow, S. K. McCoy, S. Levine, T. Schmader, and J. Sidanius. 2002. "Perceiving Personal Discrimination: The Role of Group Status and Legitimizing Ideology." *Journal of Personality and Social Psychology* 82 (3): 269–82.

Major, B., C. R. Kaiser, L. T. O'Brien, and S. K. McCoy. 2007. "Perceived Discrimination as Worldview Threat or Worldview Confirmation: Implications for Self-Esteem." *Journal of Personality and Social Psychology* 92 (6): 1068–86.

Major, B., W. J. Quinton, and T. Schmader. 2003. "Attributions to Discrimination and Self-Esteem: Impact of Group Identification and Situational Ambiguity." *Journal of Experimental Social Psychology* 39 (3): 220–31.

Major, B., S. Spencer, T. Schmader, C. Wolfe, and J. Crocker. 1998. "Coping with Negative Stereotypes about Intellectual Performance: The Role of Psychological Disengagement." *Personality and Social Psychology Bulletin* 24 (1): 34–50.

Mak, W. W. S., C. Y. M. Poon, L. Y. K. Pun, and, S. F. Cheung. 2007. "Meta-Analysis of Stigma and Mental Health." *Social Science and Medicine* 65 (2): 245–61.

Masten, A. S. 2001. "Ordinary Magic: Resilience Processes in Development." *American Psychologist* 56 (3): 227–38.

Masten, A. S., J. J. Hubbard, S. D. Gest, A. Tellegen, M. Garmezy, and M. Ramirez. 1999. "Competence in the Context of Adversity: Pathways to Resilience and Maladaptation from Childhood to Late Adolescence." *Developmental and Psychopathology* 11 (1): 143–69.

Mays, V. M., S. D. Cochran, and N. W. Barnes. 2007. "Race, Race-Based Discrimination, and Health Outcomes Among African Americans." *Annual Review of Psychology* 58: 201–25.

McConahay, J. B. 1983. "Modern Racism and Modern Discrimination: The Effects of Race, Racial Attitudes and Context on Simulated Hiring Decisions." *Personality and Social Psychology Bulletin* 9 (4): 551–58.

McConahay, J. B. 1986. *Modern Racism, Ambivalence, and the Modern Racism Scale.* Orlando, FL: Academic Press.

McCoy, S. K. and B. Major. 2003. "Group Identification Moderates Emotional Responses to Perceived Prejudice." *Personality and Social Psychology Bulletin,* 29 (8): 1005–17.

Miller, C. T. 2006. "Social Psychological Perspectives on Coping with Stressors Related to Stigma." In *Stigma and Group Inequality: Social Psychological Perspectives,* edited by S. Levin and C. van Laar. Mahwah, NJ: Lawrence Erlbaum Associates: 21–44.

Miller, G. E. and E. Blackwell. 2006. "Turning Up the Heat: Inflammation as a Mechanism Linking Chronic Stress, Depression, and Heart Disease." *Current Directions in Psychological Science* 15 (6): 269–72.

Morrison, K. R., N. J. Fast, and O. Ybarra. 2009. "Group Status, Perceptions of Threat, and Support for Social Inequality." *Journal of Experimental Social Psychology* 45 (1): 204–10.

Morrison, K. R. and O. Ybarra. 2008. "The Effects of Realistic Threat and Group Identification on Social Dominance Orientation." *Journal of Experimental Social Psychology* 44 (1): 156–63.

Mount, M. K., M. R. Sytsma, J. Fisher Hazucha, and K. E. Holt. 1997. "Rater-Ratee Race Effects in Developmental Performance Ratings of Managers." *Personnel Psychology* 50 (1): 51–69.

Murphy, M. C., C. M. Steele, and J. Gross. 2007. "Signaling Threat: How Situational Cues Affect Women In Math, Science, and Engineering Settings." *Psychological Science* 18 (10): 879–85.

Neblett Jr., E. W., R. L. White, K. R. Ford, C. L. Phillip, H. X. Nguyen, and R. M. Sellers. 2008. "Pattern of Racial Socialization and Psychological Adjustment: Can Parental Communications About Race Reduce the Impact of Racial Discrimination?" *Journal of Research Adolescence* 18 (3): 477–515.

O'Brien, L. T. and B. Major. 2005. "System-Justifying Beliefs and Psychological Well-Being: The Roles of Group Status and Identity." *Personality and Social Psychology Bulletin* 31 (12): 1718–29.

Pascoe, E. A. and L. Smart Richman. 2009. "Perceived Discrimination and Health: A Meta-Analytic Review." *Psychological Bulletin* 135 (4): 531–54.

Pavalko, E. K., K. N. Mossakowski, and V. J. Hamilton. 2003. "Does Perceived Discrimination Affect Health? Longitudinal Relationship Between Work Discrimination and Women's Physical and Emotional Health." *Journal of Health and Social Behavior* 44 (1): 18–33.

Pettigrew, T. F., O. Christ, U. Wagner, and J. Stellmacher. 2007. "Direct and Indirect Intergroup Contact Effects on Prejudice: A Normative Interpretation." *International Journal of Intercultural Relations* 31 (4): 411–25.

Pettigrew, T. F. and R. W. Meertens. 1995. "Subtle and Blatant Prejudice in Western Europe." *European Journal of Social Psychology* 25: 57–75.

Pratto, F., J. Sidanius, L. M. Stallworth, and B. F. Malle. 1994. "Social Dominance Orientation: A Personality Variable Predicting Social and Political Attitudes." *Journal of Personality and Social Psychology* 67 (4): 741–63.

Ramirez-Valles, J., S. Fergus, C. A. Reisen, J. Poppen, and M. C. Zea. 2005. "Confronting Stigma: Community Involvement and Psychological Well-Being Among HIV-Positive Latino Gay Men." *Hispanic Journal of Behavioral Sciences* 27 (1): 101–19.

Rivas-Drake, D., D. Hughes, and N. Way. 2008. "A Closer Look at Peer Discrimination, Ethnic Identity, and Psychological Well-Being Among Urban Chinese Sixth Graders." *Journal of Youth and Adolescence* 37 (1): 12–21.

Roets, A., A. Van Hiel, and I. Cornelis. 2006. "Does Materialism Predict Racism? Materialism as a Distinctive Social Attitude and a Predictor of Prejudice." *European Journal of Personality* 20 (2): 155–68.

Rudman, L. A. 2004. "Sources of Implicit Attitudes." *Current Directions in Psychological Science* 13 (4): 79–82.

Rusch, N., P. W. Corrigan, A. Wassel, P. Michaels, M. Olschewski, S. Wilkmiss, and K. Batia. 2009. "A Stress-coping Model of Mental Illness Stigma: 1. Predictors of Cognitive Stress Appraisal." *Schizophrenia Research* 110 (1–3): 59–64.

Ryff, C. K. and D. Hughes. 2003. "Status Inequalities, Perceived Discrimination, and Eudaimonic Well-Being: Do the Challenges of Minority Life Hone Purpose and Growth?" *Journal of Health and Social Behavior. Special Issue: Race, Ethnicity and Mental Health* 44 (3): 275–91.

Schmitt, M. T. and N. R. Branscombe. 2002. "The Meaning and Consequences of Perceived Discrimination in Disadvantaged and Privileged Social Groups." *European Review of Social Psychology* 12: 167–99.

Sears, D. O. and P. J. Henry. 2003. "The Origins of Symbolic Racism." *Journal of Personality and Social Psychology* 85 (2): 259–75.

Sidanius, J. and F. Pratto. 1993. "Racism and Support of Free-Market Capitalism: A Cross-Cultural Analysis." *Political Psychology* 14 (3): 381–401.

Sidanius, J. and F. Pratto. 1999. *Social Dominance: An Intergroup Theory of Social Hierarchy and Oppression.* New York: Cambridge University Press.

Sinclair, L. and Z. Kunda. 1999. "Reactions to a Black Professional: Motivated Inhibition and Activation of Conflicting Stereotypes." *Journal of Personality and Social Psychology* 77 (5): 885–904.

Sniderman, P. M. and T. Piazza. 1993. *The Scar of Race.* Cambridge, MA: Harvard University Press.

Sniderman, P. M. and P. E. Tetlock. 1986. "Reflections on American Racism." *Journal of Social Issues* 42 (2): 173–87.

Son Hing, L. S. 2012. "Responses to Stigmatization: The Moderating Roles of Primary and Secondary Appraisals." *The Dubois Review* 9 (1): 149–68.

Son Hing, L. S., D. R. Bobocel, M. P. Zanna, D. M. Garcia, S. Gee, and K. Orazietti. 2011. "The Merit of Meritocracy." *Journal of Personality and Social Psychology* 101 (3): 433–50.

Son Hing, L. S., G. A. Chung-Yan, L. K. Hamilton, and M. P. Zanna. 2008. "A Two-Dimensional Model That Employs Explicit and Implicit Attitudes to Characterize Prejudice." *Journal of Personality and Social Psychology* 94 (6): 971–87.

Son Hing, L. S. and S. Kiani. 2008. "Political, Economic, and Social Conservatism: Relations to Explicit/Implicit Prejudice?" Paper presented at the meeting of the Society for the Psychological Study of Social Issues. Chicago, IL.

Son Hing, L. S. and M. P. Zanna. 2010. "Individual Differences in Prejudice." In *The SAGE Handbook of Prejudice, Stereotyping, and Discrimination*, edited by J. Dovidio, P.M. Hewstone, P. Glick, and V. Esses. London: Sage: 163–78.

Son Hing, L. S., M. P. Zanna, P. Nail, and P. Zuniuk. 2011. *Conservatism, Modern Racism, and Implicit Prejudice Against Blacks in the South*. Research in progress.

Stangor, C. and S. P. Leary 2006. "Intergroup Beliefs: Investigations from the Social Side." *Advances in Experimental Social Psychology* 38: 243–81.

Stephan, W. G. and C. L. Renfro. 2002. "The Role of Threat in Intergroup Relations." In *From Prejudice to Intergroup Emotions: Differentiated Reactions to Social Groups*, edited by D. M. Mackie and E. R. Smith. New York: Psychology Press: 191–207.

Stephan, W. G. and C. W. Stephan. 2000. *An Integrated Threat Theory of Prejudice*. Mahwah, NJ: Lawrence Erlbaum.

Tajfel, H. and J. C. Turner. 1986. *The Social Identity Theory of Intergroup Behaviours*. Chicago: Nelson-Hall.

Triana, M. C. and M. F. Garcia. 2009. "Valuing Diversity: A Group-Value to Understanding the Importance of Organizational Efforts to Support Diversity." *Journal of Organizational Behavior* 30 (7): 941–62.

Twenge, J. M. and J. Crocker. 2002. "Race and Self-Esteem: Meta-Analyses Comparing Whites, Blacks, Hispanics, Asians, and American Indians" and Comment on Gray-Little and Hafdahl. 2000 *Psychological Bulletin* 128 (3): 371–408.

Ungar, M. 2008. "Resilience Across Cultures." *British Journal of Social Work* 38 (2): 218–35.

Vanderbilt-Adriance, E. D. and S. Shaw. 2008. "Protective Factors and the Development of Resilience in the Context of Neighborhood Disadvantage." *Journal of Abnormal Child Psychology* 36 (6): 887–901.

Van Hiel, A., M. Pandelaere, and B. Duriez. 2004. "The Impact of Need for Closure on Conservative Beliefs and Racism: Differential Mediation by Authoritarian Submission and Authoritarian Dominance." *Personality and Social Psychology Bulletin* 30 (7): 824–37.

Werner, E. E. and R. S. Smith 1992. *Overcoming the Odds: High Risk Children from Birth to Adulthood*. Ithaca, NY: Cornell University Press.

Williams, D. R. and S. A. Mohammed. 2009. "Discrimination and Racial Disparities in Health: Evidence and Research Needed." *Journal of Behavioral Medicine* 32 (1): 20–47.

Williams, D. R. and R. Williams-Morris. 2000. "Racism and Mental Health: The African American Experience." *Ethnicity & Health* 5 (3–4): 243–68.

Williams, D. R., Y. Yu, J. S. Jackson, and N. B Anderson. 1997. "Racial Differences in Physical and Mental Health: Socio-Economic Status, Stress, and Discrimination." *Journal of Health Psychology* 2 (3): 335–51.

Wong, C. A., J. S. Eccles, and A. Sameroff. 2004. "The Influence of Ethnic Discrimination and Ethnic Identification of African American Adolescents' School and Socioemotional Adjustment." *Journal of Personality* 71 (6): 1197–1232.

Yoo, H. C. and R. M. Lee. 2005. "Ethnic Identity and Approach-Type Coping as Moderators of the Racial Discrimination/Well-Being Relations in Asian Americans." *Journal of Counseling Psychology* 52 (4): 497–506.

Zanna, M. P. and J. K. Rempel. 1988. "Attitudes: A New Look at an Old Concept." In *The Social Psychology of Knowledge*, edited by Bar-Tal, D. and A. W. Kruglanski. New York: Cambridge University Press: 315–34.

6

Security, Meaning, and the Home

Conceptualizing Multiscalar Resilience in a Neoliberal Era

James R. Dunn

Introduction

To say that one's home is a significant contributor to social resilience may seem self-evident. Indeed, housing is fundamental to so many areas of social life as to make its importance nearly tautological. Housing and home are a site for and constitutive of crucial social phenomena that include gender, family, child development, health, social relationships, wealth, identity, ethnicity, culture, aging, and many other indicators and determinants of resilience. Indeed, its embeddedness within so many spheres of social life makes its importance challenging to distinguish, leaving it to be taken for granted.

The housing sector has arguably been a critical sector for the unfolding of neoliberalism, although relatively few aspects of this relationship have been examined in the mainstream literature on neoliberalism. Notable neoliberal transformations in the housing sector include the selling off of nearly one-third of Council housing stock in the United Kingdom in the late 1980s and early 1990s under the Right to Buy policy (Ginsburg 2005; Mullins and Murie 2006), the effective elimination of new investments in public housing in Canada in the name of deficit reduction starting in 1993 (Wolfe 1998; Hulchanski 2004), and the stealthy retrenchment from its role as a public landlord by U.S Department of Housing and Urban Development in the United States in favor of a voucher-based system with delivery of housing units by the private rental sector (Schwartz 2010). These represent an important means by which neoliberal governments shrank the state in the 1980s and 1990s consistent with neoliberal doctrine. Although some of these changes could be viewed as part of a continuous evolution of liberal doctrine (especially the Right to Buy policy as a continuation of a historical thrust toward more home ownership), changes in public housing provision to market delivery mechanisms in many countries, including the United States and Germany, signal a neoliberal shift. Most importantly, the establishment and growth of large, publicly funded and publicly managed physical housing stocks and related programs in the early part of the twentieth century has been progressively reversed in the neoliberal era. Moreover, all of these changes can be seen as examples of the "privatization of risk" (Hacker 2008), a pillar of neoliberal transformations.

At the same time, housing has become socially and culturally shrouded in such virtuous goals as increasing home ownership rates (Rohe and Watson 2007; Vale 2007), although some argue that this is merely the sociocultural manifestation of a project to generate economic activity in the financial sector in such a way that little risk is borne by investors but substantial risk is borne by home owners. Such activity is aided by a series of neoliberal practices such as low central bank rates, financial deregulation, and increasing creativity in various credit instruments (i.e., mortgage-backed securities). These represent tools in the perpetuation of economic activity founded on fictitious capital (Marx 1894; Harvey 1982) and amounts to what Walks (2010) calls "ponzi capitalism." These developments, which depend on the exploitation and manipulation of the cultural myth of home ownership ("the American dream" or Great Britain as a "Nation of Home-Owners" – Saunders 1984; Rohe and Watson 2007) to attract people at the margins of the market into it in order to expand the market for mortgage-backed paper, have become hallmarks of the extremes of neoliberalism for their role in the economic crisis.

The initial premise of this chapter is that the social distribution of resilience is a reflection of the social distribution of a number of dimensions of the basic security systems of individuals and that according to this view, social policy – and specifically housing policy – should be (much more) concerned (than it currently appears to be) with ways to reinforce the basic security systems of individuals at multiple scales. This will not, however, lead to a romantic return to the traditional welfare state even though it was capable of providing a high level of security to large populations. This basic premise about security, resilience, and their social distribution is illustrated through a concrete example: the experience of housing and home in the neoliberal era. Housing and home, I argue, are fundamental to the development and maintenance of individuals', households', communities', and societies' basic security systems and societal resilience and have been at the center of a number of important transformations in the neoliberal era, some of which have important implications for the future. The latter part of the chapter "scales up" from the household level to assess contemporary housing systems at the neighborhood, metropolitan, and nation-state levels. Central to this discussion are the mixed and often contradictory directions that have been taken in the neoliberal era. Consequently, although housing systems have probably declined in their overall ability to provide the material bases for security and resilience, this is not universal nor without contradictions.

Housing, Urban Development, and Neoliberalism

Neoliberalism is a recurrent theme in the housing and urban studies literature over the past 20-plus years, but in the mainstream literature on neoliberalism, the housing sector has been arguably understudied. The housing and urban studies literature has grappled with some of the same definitional issues for neoliberalism that this book does (see Introduction chapter). Hackworth and Moriah (2006), however, provide a useful reduction of the various approaches to neoliberalism encountered in the housing and urban studies literature. The first approach eschews analyses based on ideal-type neoliberalism in favor of a more contingent, place- and time-specific understanding along with appreciation that neoliberalism is not a wholly "top-down" process. Wilson (2004) describes neoliberalism as a political project that is "anything but a 'top-down,' brute, de-sensitized imposition on cities" and prefers to think of the neoliberal project as "a series of differentiated, keenly negotiating, processual, and space-mobilizing constructions in new political and economic times..." that are "...constituted and re-constituted through the vagaries of the situated: social hierarchies, situated knowledges, meanings and politics..." that "...define contemporary problems, villains, victims, salvationists, solutions, and programmatic responses" (p.780). A second approach focuses on the internal inconsistency of neoliberalism, noting that one of the basic premises – a minimalist state – requires state intervention to implement and maintain (Brenner and Theodore 2002). A third approach recognizes that transformations related to housing and urban form are seldom "purely" driven by neoliberal principles and that other forces are usually present, including, according to Jessop (2002), neocorporatism, neocommunitarianism, and neostatism. The final approach suggests that the term "neoliberalism" is "used to encapsulate a set of processes that are either so different or loosely connected to the liberal project that they have rendered the term meaninglessly broad" (Hackworth and Moriah 2006: 513). Interestingly, all of these challenges to ideal-type neoliberalism can be seen in an analysis of developments in housing and urban studies.

Definitional issues aside, it is most important to note that analyses of changes in housing and urban studies from a neoliberal perspective have emphasized two key themes: (a) changes in the housing sector as a part of broader changes to the welfare state and (b) the emphasis of the co-optation of the state, in the neoliberal era into the task of "extracting value" from the city. The most important framework for the first theme has been the distinction between "roll-back" neoliberalism (state retrenchment and shrinkage) and "roll-out" neoliberalism. Many aspects of these changes in housing have been analyzed as a part of broader neoliberal welfare state transformations and retrenchment (e.g., Peck and Tickell 2002; Dodson 2006). In the second major theme, urban studies research has emphasized how state regulation of land markets and land development are increasingly aimed at the extraction of value from land in the interests of capital and at the expense of poor and marginalized groups (Weber 2002). Although this is not superficially different from the urban political economy literature of 20 to 40 years ago (e.g., Badcock 1984; Harvey 1973, 1985), the neoliberal perspective takes a critical perspective and suggests that the state, and often the local state, has taken a more active and open stance toward supporting such activities, including the sale of state-owned land and other assets and other kinds of public–private partnerships (Weber 2002).

But relatively little of this work addresses the experience of individuals and households and the impact of such broad transformations on their security and resilience. The next sections of this chapter attempt to conceptualize such linkages through the experience of housing and home. Arguably, the reason for having housing policies and state-organized housing systems is to ensure the basic material security of households and to support them to be resilient in the face of unexpected life challenges. Next, I "scale up" the basic conceptual model linking housing experience to security and well-being to consider the implications for other geographic scales before concluding with a final assessment.

A Conceptualization of Human Socio-Emotional Security Systems for the Neoliberal Era

After the postmodern turn, the social sciences came to eschew any effort to define dimensions of "human nature" or even basic properties of human social being in order to avoid "essentializing discourses." Although the avoidance of essentializing discourses was a positive development in many respects, it may have been an overcorrection because it has left something of a knowledge vacuum for guiding policy decisions in a variety of institutions (including governments, firms, and so on). As Daniel Pink (2009) suggests, for example, there are a number of unexamined, common (although contestable) presuppositions about human motivation that guide most management practices, and similar heuristics arguably exist, at least implicitly, for public policymakers as well. Moreover, an assessment of social resilience in the neoliberal era also needs such a heuristic.

Giddens (1991) provides a set of relatively simple but fundamental concepts that help to fill this gap but largely avoids essentialism in so doing.[1] These key concepts are existential anxiety, ontological security, self-identity, reflexive project of the self, and colonization of the future. After defining these terms and explaining their interconnections, I consider more fully how housing is important to these concepts and to multiscalar resilience in the neoliberal era.

Existential Anxiety and Ontological Security

According to Giddens (1991) social being necessarily implies that individuals encounter and must deal with "**existential questions,**" which are "queries about

---

[1] Coincidentally (or not?), Giddens is both the author of this compelling notion of the basic parameters of social being and was an important advisor to Tony Blair in the development of the "Third Way," a significant part of the neoliberal turn. It could be argued that Giddens' concern with ontological security in his scholarly writings was not translated into the policies of his employer, Tony Blair. This connection does underscore, however, that public policy does require such heuristics to make and implement policy.

basic dimensions of human existence, in respect of human life as well as the material world," that people 'answer' in the course of the routinized daily activity (p. 243). The ongoing ability to answer such questions is a fundamental part of an individual's ability to maintain a sense of "**ontological security**," which Giddens defines as a "sense of continuity and order in events, including those not directly within the perceptual environment of the individual" (1991: 243).

According to this view, the site at which ontological security is produced and reproduced is in the routinized daily activity of individuals (of which housing is unquestionably a critical component, given its centrality to routine human activity). Although ontological security is an indication of the extent to which the individual has bracketed existential questions, it depends on more than just the individual's personal skills for generating it. The ability to generate ontological security also depends on a certain orderliness of day-to-day life that Giddens describes as "a miraculous occurrence" (1991: 52). But this orderliness is "not one that stems from outside intervention; it is brought about as a continuous achievement on the part of everyday actors in an entirely routine way" (ibid.). These routine actions, in turn, depend on myriad material structures, institutionalized social practices, and technologies that exist at multiple scales of human existence.

The failure to successfully answer existential questions, on Giddens' view, can lead to the experience of existential anxiety, not only in specific situations but also as a fundamental character of everyday life: "[A]nxiety has to be understood in relation to the overall security system the individual develops, rather than only as a situationally specific phenomenon connected to particular risks and dangers," and as such "anxiety is a generalised state of the emotions of the individual" (1991: 43). Furthermore, "[S]ince anxiety, trust and everyday routines of social interaction are so closely bound up with one another, we can readily understand the rituals of day-to-day life as coping mechanisms" (1991: 46).

Reflexive Project of the Self, Narrative Identity, and Colonization of the Future

From the individual standpoint, the ability to maintain a coherent self-identity is a fundamental part of an individual's ability to maintain ontological security (Giddens 1991). The notions of self-identity and the reflexive project of the self imply that "[E]ach of us not only 'has', but *lives* a biography reflexively organized in terms of flows of social and psychological information about possible ways of life" (1991: 14). Any individual possesses a notion of him- or herself as separate and distinct from their environment, Giddens claims, and that "self" is "reflexively understood by the individual in terms of his or her biography" (1991: 244). In fact, Giddens argues that humans are inevitably engaged in a "reflexive project of the self," which he defines as "the process whereby self-identity is constituted by the reflexive ordering of self-narratives" (1991: 244).

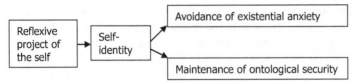

FIGURE 6-1. Reflexive Project of the Self, Existential Anxiety, and Ontological Security.

One of the more compelling arguments in Giddens' version of self-identity is that *the future* of the self is also organized according to self-narratives. Through his or her reflexive project of the self, an individual must engage in "*colonization of the future*" using narratives and actively creating "future territories of possibilities" (Giddens 1991: 242). The narratives used may be of the individual's own making, made from some choice of existing cultural repertoires (Lamont 2000), or drawing on collective imaginaries (Bouchard 2009). Part of the reflexive project of the self, therefore, concerns developing a sense of control and ontological security about the future – a sense of stability and orderliness that can be expected for the future. Stable housing, it would seem, is a potentially important site for the creation of "future territories of possibilities" and colonizing the future (ibid.). I will return to this point again shortly.

Drawing on Giddens, these concepts can be understood to be simplistically linked in the manner shown in Figure 6-1. Although Giddens's (1991) conceptualization of identity is a simplistic and partial one, compared, for instance with the work of Sewell (1992), Ashmore and Jussim (1997), Archer (2000), and Sayer (2005), it does provide the basis for a useful heuristic for understanding how resilience is achieved and maintained and gives us a glimpse into how experiences of housing could contribute to it. In the following section, I explain the ways in which the material bases of everyday life, similar to housing, intersects with this understanding of the basic socio-emotional security systems of the self.

Housing, Home, and Basic Socio-Emotional Security Systems of the Self Over the Life Course

Dunn et al. (2004) have developed a conceptual model for linking attributes of housing and home to health and well-being that provides the basis for a discussion of the attributes of housing that contribute to the socio-emotional security system. In economics, housing is often referred to as a "multi-attribute phenomenon" and therefore, efforts to link it to human well-being demand that the attributes of importance and potential pathways to such outcomes be identified. In this section, I draw on selected elements of that model but modify it to consider the broader notion of socio-emotional security systems of the self described above.

Box 6-1: Attributes of Housing Affecting Health and Well-Being

Biological, chemical, and physical exposures in the home
Physical design of housing
Psychological attributes of housing
Social attributes of housing
Financial attributes of housing
Locational aspects of housing

The six elements of the model appear in Box 6-1, but the most important aspects for this discussion, the psychological and financial attributes of housing, are described in detail below. Biological, chemical, and physical exposures in the home are certainly important to health, and institutions exist to establish and maintain building codes, environmental protection measures, regulations regarding home insurance, and so on. These are part of the institutional bedrock of well-functioning societies that help to deliver a level of orderliness of day-to-day life fundamental to ontological security, but these are no less or more important in the neoliberal era. Similarly, the physical design of housing allows for experiences that enhance ontological security, such as privacy, refuge, and so on (within the dwelling) and wayfinding, surveillance, legibility, and so on (in the surrounding landscape or within a neighborhood) (Dunn et al. 2004). Additionally, it is well established that the physical design of dwellings structures gender and family relations (Hayden 2002; Kern 2007). In terms of its social attributes, there is great sociological significance attributed to the boundary between the inside of the home and the outside world, and this is common to almost all cultures. To invite someone into your home as a guest is a symbol of escalating a relationship, making it closer. The home is an important site for the development and maintenance of social relationships, both with household members and others, and these relationships are significant contributors to ontological security. The locational dimensions of housing are important to well-being because the home acts as a focal point for everyday activity. So in addition to being an important site for the narratives of self-identity, the home and its immediate locality can be central in creating a sense of ontological security – a sense of stability and orderliness in the basic dimensions of human experience.

Two main psychological attributes of housing are being transformed in the neoliberal era. First is the importance of the home as a site for the exercise of control. Housing provides material stability, permitting the exercise of control. Notwithstanding personality differences in the need for control (Lachman and Weaver 1998), of all the sites in our everyday life, the home is the only place where we are socially – and in many ways, legally – sanctioned to have complete control. Where this control is chronically lacking, life is almost invariably going to be stressful. Indeed, numerous perspectives on the meaning of home (e.g., Sixsmith 1986; Madigan, Munro, and Smith 1990; Despres 1991; Smith 1994; Mallett 2004) also suggest that related concepts such as permanence, continuity, and security are also essential features of housing. These also intersect importantly with the reflexive project of the self and ontological security. Saunders (1990), moreover, has argued that home is a place "where people feel in control of their environment, free from surveillance, free to be themselves and at ease, in a world that might at times be experienced as threatening and uncontrollable" (361), linking clearly with the notion of ontological security.

The other element of the psychological attributes of housing derives from the fact that the home is one of the most important sites for the investment of meaning in people's lives and is also an important site for the inscription of self-identity. In all cultures, there are significant myths, rituals, symbols, and meanings ascribed to housing and home, almost as a human universal. The best evidence for the importance of the meaning of home is the real estate pages of the Saturday newspaper – they are not selling bricks and mortar; instead, they are selling an identity and the opportunity for life satisfaction – buy this house and be this kind of person (Eyles 1987).

A significant part of an individual's basic security system is arguably the ability to construct meaning about one's life, within the context of larger societal myths and cultural repertoires by means of the reflexive project of the self. Housing and home is critically important in, and perhaps even a universal concrete medium through which, we structure our identities and therefore becomes an important part of the construction of the basic security system at another level. Many of our culture's central themes concern hopes, aspirations, and dreams pertaining to houses and homes. According to Csikszentmihalyi and Rochberg-Halton (1981),

... home is much more than a shelter, it is a world in which a person can create a material environment that embodies what he or she considers significant. In this sense, the home becomes the most powerful symbol of the self of the inhabitant who dwells within it. (Csikszentmihalyi and Rochberg-Halton 1981: 123)

This is further illustrated by the semiotic construction of the "dream home" in housing advertisements (Eyles 1987). The notion of the "dream home" implies a colonization of the future and the answering of existential questions pertaining to one's self-identity. Individual biographies and self-identity are frequently organized according to the homes and places in which people have lived (Gutting 1996). The intersection of housing and the autobiographical dimensions of self-identity are illustrated by Saegert, who claims that

[G]iven the strong emotional tone of most people's recollections of their childhood homes, it seems likely that the significance of the home in children's personal and social development goes much beyond the meager body of literature on the topic. (Saegert 1985: 293)

Related to this, it is often said that the home is an important medium of self-expression and personal identity (Smith 1994). According to this view, home is a symbol of both how people see themselves and how they want others to see them. The home can also be a medium for personalization or a surface for inscribing self-identity, as in the example of personal objects and home decorations that communicate information about the owner(s) (Smith 1994: 32–3; see also Cooper Marcus 1995).

Finally, the financial attributes of housing have always been critical to resilience but perhaps even more so in the neoliberal era. It is well-established that housing markets are powerful engines of inequality (Harvey 1973; Badcock 1984) and continue to be so in the neoliberal era (Hackworth and Moriah 2006; Hackworth 2008). Several well-understood mechanisms work to redistribute wealth and income in a highly regressive fashion. In Anglo-American societies, the key fulcrum on which this redistribution hinges is the distinction between owner-occupiers and renters of housing (Badcock 1984). Indeed, there are several well-understood (but seldom tracked) pathways by which income and wealth are redistributed from renters to owners (e.g., capital gains tax exemption for the primary residence; other tax deductions, subsidies for home ownership, and the nontaxability of imputed rents – see Badcock 1984). Effectively, these mechanisms have the effect of transferring income from renters (the people with the least security) to owners (the people with the greatest security). Ironically, however, although home ownership is a housing tenure that provides high levels of security and resilience, it also carries with it risks and threats to security and resilience (Nettleton and Burrows 1998; Colic-Peisker and Johnson 2010), especially at the margins of the market in the neoliberal era (Saegert, Fields, and Libman 2009).

Arguably, the financial aspects of housing have become increasingly more important to well-being for more households over the past 50 to 60 years with the movement in Anglo-American societies toward greater home ownership as a public policy goal (Colic-Peisker and Johnson 2010). This has long been the goal in North America and Australia but was a more recent development in the United Kingdom, where the roughly one third of Council housing stock was sold to occupants during the Thatcher era.[2] But the experience of the United Kingdom showed that merely changing the tenure status of a large segment of the population did not erase inequalities; indeed, many of them became owners of virtually worthless properties, but others fared very well. This is just one example showing that although the home ownership policy paradigm carries with it considerable potential for financial rewards for a greater number and diversity of households, it also carries with it significantly greater levels of

---

[2] It is worth noting that even after the Thatcher-era sell-off of Council housing, there were still 22 percent of U.K. households that received their housing from the public sector, a decline from 33 percent before Thatcher. In the Netherlands, more than 40 percent of households receive their housing from the public sector; in Canada, this figure has never eclipsed 6 percent (Hackworth and Moriah 2006).

financial risk and vulnerability to exploitation for households on the margins of the home ownership market.

This is ironic, of course, because many of the so-called "winners" in the housing market have arguably been sold a false bill of goods, as the dream of home ownership has become a nightmare on the other side of the housing bubble, while global financial capitalism has flourished, but for a few hiccups (Saegert et al. 2009; Colic-Peisker and Johnson 2010). The evidence for this became all too clear during the 2008 to 2010 credit crisis. Such households are squeezed by a variety of pressures to accept such privatized risks, including participation in collective imaginaries related to the citizenship and status that home ownership carries with it, the lack of stable and affordable rental housing alternatives, the significant tax advantages and incentives related to home ownership, and the prospect of accumulating wealth (perhaps savings is a more accurate term) through housing even if it may be illusory. Indeed, in the aftermath of the credit crisis and its ensuing recession, the solution adopted by many governments has been quantitative easing (Saft 2010), gives homeowners the impression that they are getting wealthier because their homes are going up in value, ideally prompting them to spend. Of course, those on the margins of the home ownership market – that is those who could only buy under the most favorable of circumstances – are most affected.

In this respect, the financial and ontological security of many millions of homeowners across many nation-states is dependent on an array of national and international financial regulations and statutes that affect the functioning and stability of international credit markets and national mortgage markets. These, similar to other institutions, can be fragile, obviously, and their management is also a hotly contested issue in the relationship between the global financial industry (which has grown significantly in importance during the neoliberal era – Harvey 1989, 2009) and national governments that are trying to foster recovery and growth in an industry that has contributed greatly to growth rates in recent decades. The losers in these neoliberal gambles, however, are some of the least resilient and most vulnerable individuals in affluent societies, and the impacts of the crisis are going to be seen in generations of lost ontological security for many millions of households and their descendants.

Housing, Ontological Security, and Resilience in Life-Course Development

Giddens' arguments about ontological security, existential anxiety, reflexive project of the self, and colonization of the future resonate strongly with a number of strands of research in developmental psychology, notably about emotional self-regulation, executive function, and attachment. These related concepts represent the early-life roots of capacities for stress management, health behavior, arguably through colonization of the future and its role in ontological security. Attention to the connection between the concepts related to ontological security and developmental psychology, in the concrete areas of sectors such as housing, is an important new direction. It appears, in other words, that there may be a reasonably clear biological component to people's capabilities to engage in a reflexive project of the self and achieve ontological security that is rooted in early life experiences.

Self-regulation refers to processes that "enable an individual to guide his/her goal-directed activities over time and across changing circumstances," such as regulation or modulation of "thought, affect, behavior, or attention via deliberate or automated use of specific mechanisms and supportive meta-skills" (Karoly 1993). Similarly, executive functions include identifying problems, making decisions, planning, staying focused on a task, adapting flexibly to changing situations, controlling impulses, and regulating emotions and behavior. Executive functions are important for moment-to-moment activities and for activities that take place over longer periods (Zelazo et al. 1997). "Attachment" simply refers to an emotional bond to another person, theorized to arise from interactions in infancy and early childhood. Psychologist Mary Ainsworth and ethologist John Bowlby were the first attachment theorists (Ainsworth and Bowlby 1954) and described attachment as a "lasting psychological connectedness between human beings" (Bowlby 1969: 194). It is widely acknowledged that the earliest bonds formed by children with their caregivers have a tremendous impact that continues throughout life. A central premise of attachment theory in childhood is that caregivers who are available and responsive to their infant's needs establish a sense of security for the child. The infant knows that the caregiver is dependable, which creates a secure base for the child to then explore the world. In adulthood, arguably, relationships with others and stability of both the material and symbolic world are important contributors to ontological security.

Problems of self-regulation, executive function, and attachment are patterned by socioeconomic status, with children of lower socioeconomic status, and poor housing, more likely to have deficits in these processes (Farah et al. 2006). This suggests that the experience of the stress of low socioeconomic status and the outcomes of those stressful circumstances may have deep roots early in life and should be considered an essential part of the development of resilience in contemporary society. In this way, the observed socioeconomic gradient both in stress responses to environmental stimuli like relative poverty are also likely expressions of people's development early in life and their capacities for self-regulation (critical to having a reflexive project of the self and maintaining ontological security). These findings are consistent with previous comprehensive reviews of the social determinants of "developmental health" (Keating and Hertzman 1999; Keating 2009).

The home is a critical site for the exercise of control in our society, as argued earlier. But what it means to have control (and to develop executive function) *literally depends on our experience of the home as children* as Williams (1987) argues. If an individual's home does not act as a site for the exercise of control, it is likely to be a significant source of stress and represent a gap in the spectrum of developmental stimuli needed to ensure development of self-regulation and executive function and ultimately the development of resilience. Williams (1987) sums up the importance of control in housing and home for life-course development succinctly when he says,

[T]he home, in a variety of ways, penetrates deeply into the core of our social being. Our notions of privacy, freedom and choice are, for example, centred in part upon conceptions of the home as a location (both physical and social) where these ideas may be exercised (156).

Further evidence of the importance of housing to the development of executive function comes from an unpacking of the term "hard to house." This refers to people who have difficulty in maintaining residence in a home. Its use suggests that the act of "dwelling" or "to dwell" is a set of skilled activities that are part of human social development but seldom recognized as such. There is evidence now that roughly 75 percent of homeless people in a longitudinal cohort of homeless individuals in Toronto have a history of traumatic brain injury . . . an injury that is often located in the prefrontal cortex, the same brain region responsible for executive function (Hwang et al. 2008), reinforcing the contention that there is a bidirectional relationship between "dwelling" and brain development.

It follows from this that the underlying capacity to engage successfully in a reflexive project of the self and therefore develop self-regulation, attachment, and executive function may in fact depend on and be enhanced by the lifelong experience of housing and home. Through what is known as "developmental cascades," early experiences of lack of control and security have an enduring impact (Yates, Obradović, and Egeland 2010).

Scaling Up: Housing, Socio-Spatial Inequality, National Policy, and Global Finance

In this final substantive section of the chapter, I attempt to scale up from the household level to assess contemporary housing systems at the neighborhood, metropolitan, and nation-state levels. Interestingly, the housing and urban studies literatures have found that rather than being a consistent force for liberalization, deregulation, and privatization, neoliberalism's "actually existing" (Brenner and Theodore 2002) implementation is mixed and often contradictory. But first I tackle the issue of changes to the housing sector in the neoliberal era. On the whole, because a secular roll-back of state involvement in the housing sector, housing systems have probably declined in their overall ability to provide the material bases for security and resilience, but this is not universal nor without contradictions, and numerous examples of roll-out neoliberalism also exist in the housing sector.

Neoliberalism and the Housing Sector
As mentioned previously, the housing sector provides a great deal of evidence that neoliberalism was not a monolithic movement toward state retrenchment

and marketization of public services but rather more differentiated and variegated. Dodson (2006) argues that varying degrees of roll-back and roll-out neoliberalism were evident in the housing and welfare sectors of different countries. Overall, he suggests that despite perceptions of a weakening state presence in housing assistance in Australia, New Zealand, the United Kingdom, and the Netherlands, state influence remains strong, although clearly transformed. In the United Kingdom, for example, despite an initial roll-back of the state in the sell-off of thousands of units of Council housing in the Right to Buy scheme, the new Labour government in the late 1990s and 2000s envisions a continuing role for the state, although delivery of housing services and the conception of the tenant have been neoliberalized. As Dodson (2006) articulates it, "tenants have been transformed from passive recipients of state beneficence to rational choice-oriented housing consumers who select among a range of alternative sources of housing that which most closely matches their self-identified needs and purchasing capacity . . . signifying a neoliberal governmentality in operation" (230). A similar reconceptualization of the tenant is seen in the Netherlands. On the delivery side, the U.K. government established entities independent from but accountable to the state to deliver housing, namely housing associations. In New Zealand, one of the chief objectives was to make the social housing sector operate with more of a market orientation and to stimulate the housing market, but housing assistance remained quite strong. These examples, rather than representing a withering of the state, really more accurately reflect a variegated transformation of the state's positioning of itself, tenants, and the market in the social housing sector. Forrest and Hirayama (2009) make a similar argument about the variegated nature of neoliberal transformations in the housing sectors of the United Kingdom and Japan. Emblematic of the transition is the change in name of this sector in most jurisdictions: from the public housing sector to the social housing sector.

In addition to this cross-national comparison, the housing sector provides one of the most compelling examples of the double-edged sword of neoliberalism, notably through changes in the societal treatment of people with severe mental illness in the most affluent countries. Although the specifics differ somewhat among countries, the general trend is the same. After the development of the modern class of antipsychotic drugs in the middle of the twentieth century, a movement to deinstitutionalize psychiatric patients began to emerge in the 1960s on humanitarian grounds, arguably based on principles from liberalism. The (correct) belief was that patients who were managing their symptoms well could succeed living in the community with the assistance of community-based support services. There were, however, early currents of thought similar to neoliberalism that saw such developments as a way of shrinking the welfare state's significant investment in psychiatric institutions and the costs of care of people with severe mental illness more generally. As such, the community supports, income supports, and housing opportunities that were imagined by some proponents of deinstitutionalization never materialized (and still have not), arguably leading to the neoliberal era phenomenon of homelessness (along with other factors, such as post-Fordist industrial restructuring) (Dear and Wolch 1987).

Interestingly, at the same time that the neoliberal transformations in housing assistance were occurring, which arguably made assisted housing more difficult to obtain, this raised much less widespread societal concern than has homelessness. In the late neoliberal era, this concern has prompted some innovations that may not have been possible without neoliberalism, notably the "housing first" movement. In the early years of deinstitutionalization, it was believed that ex-psychiatric patients needed to move from institutions into communal, supervised housing situations in the community before moving onto more independent housing. Indeed, many programs were based on the premise that client-tenants needed to demonstrate "housing readiness" before moving to more independent housing. But homelessness was still prevalent and many people did not do well in this model. Moreover, the costs of these and other models with uneven effectiveness began to be appreciated. In a noteworthy article in the *New Yorker* in 2006, Malcolm Gladwell documented how a homeless man named Murray consumed more than $1 million in social, health and other public services in a year, far more than it would cost to provide him with housing and supports. In so doing, Gladwell argued that homelessness was too complex to manage and much easier to solve (i.e., via housing). This kind of logic has led to "housing first," the new prominent model, whereby people with mental illness in housing need go direct to independent housing and have customized, flexible housing and mental illness supports. The cost-effective pragmatism, "consumer choice," and enlightened self-interest elements of the approach fit well within neoliberal principles, and when implemented well, it is definitely better than the alternatives for at least a major subset of people who are hard to house (Tsemberis, Gulcur, and Nakae 2004). In this sense, this example shows the double-edged nature of neoliberalism in the housing sector.[3]

From Housing to Neighborhoods to Nation-States

In Anglo-American society, a large number of policies and also cultural narratives provide support for home ownership (Basolo 2007). Home ownership is supposed to be virtuous for the individual and the household, providing such things as self-esteem, perceived control over life, security of tenure, life satisfaction for having achieved this rite of passage, and ontological security (Saunders 1990; Rohe et al. 2001; Hiscock et al. 2001). At the community

---

[3] Consistent with this, in 2008, the Government of Canada established the Mental Health Commission of Canada, the chief activity of which is to conduct a pan-Canadian demonstration project of the effects of housing first approaches on people with mental illness who are at risk for homelessness. The project is ongoing, with intake having just been completed in mid 2011, but funding for the housing and support services for the demonstration project have only been committed for two years, and it remains to be seen how the results will be received by the Conservative government in Canada and what reaction it will prompt.

level, home ownership is supposed to be a stabilizing force, partly because homeowners move less frequently than renters, but longer tenure "along with greater economic investment in their homes, is thought to cause homeowners to take better care of their properties..." which may lead to "...both the overall attractiveness of the area and local property values" (Rohe et al. 2001: 11). In addition, "homeownership is also thought to lead to higher levels of participation in local voluntary organizations and political activities as homeowners seek to protect their economic and emotional investments in their communities" (Rohe et al. 2001: 11).

Although the overall evidence suggests that there are positive associations between homeownership and well-being, this is crucially dependent on the affordability of the home to its owners. Unaffordable housing, particularly if it reaches the point of mortgage arrears or foreclosure, severely compromises well-being (Nettleton and Burrows 1998; Saegert et al. 2009). At the community level, the evidence of an association between homeownership and community stability and participation could well be completely spurious – people who are inclined to residential stability are also inclined to homeownership. Additionally, although it is certainly true that homeownership is considered a rite of passage in a person's biography and a rite of citizenship in Anglo-American societies, in continental Europe, where homeownership is much less common, social stability and security of tenure are achieved through renting. The virtues, both personal and societal, are arguably overstated (Rohe et al. 2001; Stern 2011) and the risks understated (Saegert et al. 2009; Walks 2010). Nevertheless, the strong emphasis on homeownership has continued in the neoliberal era, perhaps not so coincidentally with the increasing financialization of the economy, the importance of debt markets, and the roll-back of state supported housing.

At the neighborhood level, it is interesting to note that the early neoliberal era also coincided with a decline in the importance of "community" (after a rich history in the early Chicago School of Sociology) as a spatially bound concept in the scholarly literature followed by a more recent revival through research on neighborhoods and well-being (Sampson 1999; Sampson, Morenoff, and Gannon-Rowley 2002). In a seminal 1979 article, for example, Wellman and Leighton followed on Webber's (1964) introduction of the term "community without propinquity" and argued that neighborhoods had ceased to be the central unit for supportive, non–familial-based social relationships; rather, they had been supplanted by non–geographically organized social networks (community "unbound" as they put it – see also Sampson 1999). The territorial basis for community life, in other words, was no longer bounded by a geographical neighborhood; it instead took the form of a social network. This view fits well with emphases on contemporary globalization, which have largely coincided with the liberal area. Ironically, however, much of the implementation of neoliberal principles in the area of governance have been characterized by a number of different instances of "re-scaling of governance" (Brenner 2004), a key feature of which has been "downloading" of responsibilities previously held by centralized welfare states to smaller units of governance, such as municipalities and regions according to the argument that "community" level governance is more effective (Harvey 1997). It is at this level, where the social costs of macro-scale neoliberal transformations is most visible, of course, through homelessness, decline of public services, and so on, that spatially defined "communities" and neighborhoods have become more important (as reflected by the use of the term 'glocalization' – Mendis 2007), something that is reflected in the research literature. "Communities" at this level have had to mobilize to fill the gaps in the welfare state and to maintain a quality of life and a sense of ontological security in their localities (see Chapter 2).

Although there has long been recognition of the sociospatial differentiation that occurs to sort people of similar socioeconomic status into similar parts of the city (Harvey 1973; Badcock 1984), during the early neoliberal era, these processes continued unchecked, fuelled in the United States by "white flight" to the suburbs and the social distance between the problematic inner cities and the suburbs. Concentrated urban poverty, by a number of accounts, clearly appears to undermine resilience and security. More recent trends have seen a return of the upper and middle classes to the inner city, and critics argue that this is aided by state-sanctioned gentrification policies and practices. More recently, partly because of rescaling of governance, there is much more interest in the negative societal impacts of concentrated urban poverty and disadvantage, and one of the suggested, arguably neoliberal remedies is so-called "place-based" policy to reduce concentrated urban poverty and its negative consequences. Although it is possible that this is little more than a balm to try to minimize the effects of inequality, even the Organisation for Economic Co-operation and Development (OECD) has identified concentrated urban poverty as an important issue for member states because of its potentially negative impact on growth (Bradford 2008). Ironically, therefore, late neoliberalism is attempting to provide the solution to problems exacerbated by early neoliberalism.

Another common solution to the problem of concentrated urban poverty and disadvantage is the encouragement of "social mix" in neighborhoods. This often occurs with passive assistance from the local state (ignoring displacement of low-income, marginalized people from gentrified neighborhoods) and often with active assistance, too, in the form of socially mixed public housing redevelopment. The latter has been implemented in numerous cities in the United Kingdom, Canada, Australia, and the United States. Despite the virtues of reducing concentrated urban poverty, many have criticized this (Darcy 2010) as state-sanctioned gentrification (Smith 2002), denying people the "right to the city" (Duke 2009). Certainly, where socially mixed redevelopment has displaced people or made them worse off in some other way, it is not acceptable, but in some cases, people are better off, so the criticism may not be universally valid. What the local turn in neoliberalism has done to basic socio-emotional security systems, ontological security, however, is again mixed and contradictory.

Scaling up to the level of the nation state, I revisit the OECD's interest in remedying pockets of concentrated urban poverty because they pose a threat to economic growth (Bradford 2007). But, of course, the converse of this concern is that spatially concentrated poverty is an important part of the process of creative destruction in land markets (Harvey 1973) that devalues capital embodied in the built environment only to create a large rent gap (Smith 1987), opening these areas up for new rounds of investment and profit taking.

In the context of neoliberalism, the stakes for housing and neighborhoods in this process have been heightened significantly, with the financialization of the economy in the neoliberal era. According to Walks (2010), "the entire global-ized and neoliberalized economy has evolved into a giant ponzi system, in that flows of new investment are increasingly not used for technological innovation or new production facilities, but to pay off earlier speculators." He notes Har-vey's (2005, 2006) description of how liberalism differs from neoliberalism. In the former, the lenders and investors took the losses, but in the neoliberal era, investors and lenders are bailed out, and borrowers are forced to compensate them for the losses. The response of nation-states to the global financial crisis was to use "public policy to resuscitate this system, and in doing so, are repro-ducing highly contradictory and unsustainable, but self-reinforcing, dynamics (doom-looping) that imperil future social and economic sustainability" (Walks 2010: 54). He further argues that financial elites depending on ponzi finance are "not likely to support systemic reforms that reduce their power in the name of investments in the productive economy, but instead to advocate for extension of the system in order to maintain their positions and access remain-ing sources of potential profit," which, except for some modest reforms and controls imposed, was largely achieved (Walks 2010: 64).

With this resetting of the global financial system, questions that had previ-ously been raised about the impact of neoliberal influences on housing and neighborhood dynamics are renewed. Kern (2007), in her examination of the intersections between neoliberalism, condominium development, gentrifica-tion, and gender, argues that there have been and will continue to be "pervasive and longterm consequences of a massive wave of condominium development on social, political, and economic relations" (658). She argues that the traditional ways of conceptualizing the development of neoliberal urbanism "leave little space to explore the impacts of residential intensification and the expansion of homeownership in the central city as crucial moments in the redefinition of urban community and urban citizenship" because they are primarily concerned with privatization, roll-back of the welfare state, and roll-out neoliberal prac-tices. Again, with the resetting of the global financial system more or less the way it was before the global financial crisis, the question is how neoliberalism will support security and resilience for all. Kern raises such issues when she argues

As dominant discourses and strategies position homeownership, intensification, and private redevelopment as natural, inevitable, necessary, and good, the needs and desires of gentrifiers are legitimated and prioritized. When the needs of city dwellers are assumed to be centered on security, privacy, leisure, consumption, and profit, the relationship between people and place is manipulated in ways that are congruent with the neoliberal philosophy of market-run, privatized space and services. If a person's relationship to the city is redefined as one of consumer, spectator, and client, the city is no longer obligated to be a provider of social services, a promoter of difference, or an engineer of social justice. The reshaping of urban space through residential intensification alters the ways that rights claims are constituted and legitimated. The process of urban citizenship, of staking a claim to the city and asserting a sense of belonging in the city, may increasingly rest in the hands of those who can assert that claim privately through the market (675–76).

These issues raise further questions about ontological security and resilience for whom? If indeed the next chapter in the neoliberal era is to likely to involve more state support for, and focus on, housing intensification, condominium development, and the reduction of concentrated urban poverty, greater security and resilience may have been achieved by some segments of the population, but low-income, marginalized households will continue to fare poorly.

What It Means for Assessing Social Resilience in the Neoliberal Era

Debates and critiques about state-sanctioned gentrification as an instrument for implementing the neoliberal agenda are a side show to the more important issue of how the housing sector and urban development policies can be used, in conjunction with other sectors, to produce housing conditions that offer more security and resilience under the conditions of neoliberalism. Despite its inconsistencies and contradictions, neoliberalism is a powerful force, so it should be expected that there will be changes to housing and cities that reflect that. But it is also necessary to acknowledge that the spatial concentration of poverty and marginalization is untenable and contrary to the well-being of affected populations and society at large. Local state actors have few levers to address more than just the symptoms of broader problems, and there are many local state, quasi-state, and private sector actors who have implemented great innovations that have improved the security and resilience people derive from their housing.

The broader problem, however, is the secular roll-back in the housing sector and the financialization of housing more generally, both outgrowths of neoliberalism. Despite Raham Emmanuel's warning to "never let a crisis go to waste," according to Walks (2010), the conditions for crisis have simply been renewed in the aftermath of the global financial crisis, and the global financial system is as vulnerable as ever (Saegert et al. 2009).

Given the financialization of housing, the narratives of home ownership and citizenship, and the market freedom rhetoric that still prevails, the immediate outlook for housing is status quo. Despite its importance for social resilience and security in the neoliberal era, as argued earlier, it will likely not become a strategic sector for enhancing social resilience as we enter the late neoliberal era. Rather, it will remain a potential vehicle for niche programs to protect "deserving," vulnerable populations from incurring too many costs to other public sector programs and as an instrument of the ongoing financialization of the global economy. Although this former is laudable, it represents a missed opportunity to make broader societal gains, as does the failure to take a more examined approach to the latter.

References

Ainsworth, M. D. and J. Bowlby. 1954. "Research Strategy in the Study of Mother-Child Separation." *Courrier* 4: 105–31

Archer, M. 2000. *Being Human: The Problem of Agency.* Cambridge, UK: Cambridge University Press.

Ashmore, R. J. and L. J. Jussim. 1997. "Towards a Second Century of the Scientific Analysis of Self and Identity." In *Self and Identity: Fundamental Issues*, edited by R. J. Ashmore and L. J. Jussim. Oxford: Oxford University Press.

Badcock, B. 1984. *Unfairly Structured Cities.* London: Blackwell.

Basolo, V. 2007. "Explaining the Support for Homeownership Policy in US Cities: A Political Economy Perspective." *Housing Studies* 22 (1): 99–119.

Bowlby, J. 1969. *Attachment and Loss, Vol. 1: Attachment.* New York: Basic Books.

Bouchard, G. 2009. "Collective Imaginaries and Population Health: How Health Data Can Highlight Cultural History. In *Successful Societies How Institutions and Culture Affect Health*, edited by P. A. Hall and M. Lamont. Cambridge, UK: Cambridge University Press.

Bradford, N. 2007. "Placing Social Policy? Reflections on Canada's New Deal for Cities and Communities." *Canadian Journal of Urban Research* 16 (2): 1–26.

Bradford, N. 2008. "The OECD's Local Turn: "Innovative Liberalism" for the Cities? In *The OECD and Transnational Governance*, edited by R. Mahon and S. McBride. Vancouver: UBC Press.

Brenner, N. 2004. *New State Spaces: Urban Governance and the Rescaling of Statehood.* Oxford: Oxford University Press.

Brenner, N. and N. Theodore. 2002. "Cities and the Geographies of Actually Existing Neo-Liberalism." *Antipode* 34 (3): 349–78.

Colic-Peisker, V. and G. Johnson. 2010. "Security and Anxiety of Homeownership: Perceptions of Middle-Class Australians at Different Stages of their Housing Careers." *Housing, Theory & Society* 27 (4): 351–71.

Cooper Marcus, C. 1995. *House as Mirror of Self: Exploring the Deeper Meaning of Home.* Berkeley, CA: Conari Press.

Csikszentmihalyi, M. and E. Rochberg-Halton. 1981. *The Meaning of Things: Domestic Symbols and the Self.* Cambridge, UK: Cambridge University Press.

Darcy, M. 2010. "De-concentration of Disadvantage and Mixed Income Housing: A Critical Discourse Approach." *Housing, Theory and Society* 27 (1): 1–22.

Dear, M. and J. Wolch. 1987. *Landscapes of Despair: From Deinstitutionalization to Homelessness.* Princeton, NJ: Princeton University Press.

Despres, C. 1991. "The Meaning of Home: Literature Review and Directions for Future Research and Theoretical Development." *Journal of Architectural and Planning Research* 8 (2): 96–115.

Dodson, J. 2006. "The 'Roll' of the State: Government Neo-Liberalism and Housing Assistance in Four Advanced Economies." *Housing Theory & Society* 23 (4): 224–43.

Duke, J. J. 2009. "Mixed Income Housing Policy and Public Housing Residents' 'Right to the City.'" *Critical Social Policy* 29 (1): 100–20.

Dunn, J. R., M.V. Hayes, D. Hulchanski, S.W. Hwang, and L. Potvin. 2004. "Housing as a Socio-Economic Determinant of Health: A Canadian Research Framework." In *Housing & Health: Research, Policy and Innovation*, edited by P. Howden-Chapman and P. Carrol. Wellington, NZ: Steele Roberts: 12–39.

Eyles, J. 1987. "Housing Advertisements as Signs: Locality Creation and Meaning-Systems." *Geografiska Annaler* 69B (2): 93–105.

Farah, M. J., D. M. Shera, J. H. Savage, L. Betancourt, J. M. Giannetta, N. L. Brodsky, E. K. Malmud, and H. Hurt. 2006. "Childhood Poverty: Specific Associations with Neurocognitive Development." *Brain Research* 1110: 166–74.

Forrest, R. and Y. Hirayama. 2009. "The Uneven Impact of neo-Liberalism on Housing Opportunities." *International Journal of Urban and Regional Research* 33 (4): 998–1013.

Giddens, A. 1991. *Modernity and Self-Identity: Self and Society in the Late Modern Age*. Stanford, CA: Stanford University Press.

Ginsburg, N. 2005. "The Privatization of Council Housing." *Critical Social Policy* 25(1): 115–35.

Gladwell, M. 2006. "Million-Dollar Murray." *The New Yorker* February 13: 96.

Gutting, D. 1996. "Narrative Identity and Residential History." *Area* 28 (4): 482–90.

Hacker, J. 2008. *The Great Risk Shift: The New Economic Insecurity and the Decline of the American Dream*. Oxford: Oxford University Press.

Hackworth, J. 2008. "The Durability of Roll-Out Neo-Liberalism Under Centre-Left Governance: The Case of Ontario's Social Housing Sector." *Studies in Political Economy* 81: 7–26.

Hackworth, J. and A. Moriah. 2006. "Neo-liberalism, Contingency, and Urban Policy: The Case of Social Housing in Ontario." *International Journal of Urban and Regional Research* 30 (3): 510–27.

Harvey, D. 1973. *Social Justice and the City*. Baltimore: Johns Hopkins University Press.

Harvey, D. 1982. *Limits to Capital*. Chicago: University of Chicago Press.

Harvey, D. 1985. *The Urbanization of Capital*. Baltimore: Johns Hopkins University Press.

Harvey, D. 1989. *The Condition of Postmodernity*. Cambridge: Blackwell.

Harvey, D. 1997. "The New Urbanism and the Communitarian Trap." *Harvard Design Magazine* Winter/Spring (1): 1–3.

Harvey, D. 2005. *A Brief History of Neo-liberalism*. Oxford: Oxford University Press.

Harvey, D. 2006. *Space of Global Capitalism*. London: Verso.

Harvey, D. 2009. "Reshaping Economic Geography: The World Development Report 2009." *Development & Change* 40 (6): 1269–77.

Hayden, D. 2002. *Redesigning The American Dream: Gender, Housing and Family Life* (revised and updated). New York: WW Norton.

Hiscock, R., A. Kearns, S. Macintyre, and A. Ellaway. 2001. "Ontological Security and Psycho-Social Benefits from the Home: Qualitative Evidence on Issues of Tenure." *Housing Theory & Society* 18 (1–2): 50–66.

Hulchanski, J. D. 2004. "How Did We Get Here? The Evolution of Canada's 'Exclusionary' Housing System." In *Finding Room: Policy Options for a Canadian Rental*

Housing Strategy, edited by J. Hulchanski and M. Shapcott. Toronto: University of Toronto Press.

Hwang, S. W., A. Colantonio, S. Chiu, G. Tolomiczenko, A. Kiss, L. Cowan, D. Redelmeier, and W. Levinson. 2008. "The Effect of Traumatic Brain Injury on the Health of Homeless People." *Canadian Medical Association Journal* 179 (8): 779–84.

Jessop, R. 2002. "Liberalism, neo-Liberalism, and Urban Governance: A State-Theoretical Perspective." *Antipode* 34: 452–72.

Karoly, P. 1993. "Mechanisms of Self-Regulation: A Systems View." *Annual Review of Psychology* 44: 23–52.

Keating, D. P. 2009. "Social Interactions in Human Development: Pathways to Health and Capabilities." In *Successful Societies: How Institutions and Culture Affect Health*, edited by P. Hall and M. Lamont. Cambridge, UK: Cambridge University Press.

Keating, D. P. and C. Hertzman. 1999. "Modernity's Paradox." In *Developmental Health and the Wealth of Nations. Social, Biological, and Educational Dynamics*, edited by D. P. Keating and C. Hertzman. New York: Guilford Press.

Kern, Leslie. 2007. "Reshaping the Boundaries of Public and Private Life: Gender, Condominium Development and the Neo-Liberalization of Urban Living." *Urban Geography* 28 (7): 657–81.

Lachman, M. E. and S. L. Weaver. 1998. "The Sense of Control as a Moderator of Social Class Differences in Health and Well-Being." *Journal of Personality and Social Psychology* 74 (3): 763–73.

Lamont, M. 2000. *The Dignity of Working Men: Morality and the Boundaries of Race, Class, and Immigration*. New York: Russell Sage Foundation.

Madigan, R., M. Munro, and S. J. Smith. 1990. "Gender and the Meaning of the Home." *International Journal of Urban and Regional Research* 14 (4): 625–47.

Mallett, S. 2004. "Understanding Home: A Critical Review of the Literature." *The Sociological Review* 52(1): 62–89.

Marx, K. 1894. *Capital* (vol. III). New York: Penguin.

Mendis, P. 2007. *Glocalization: The Human Side of Globalization as If the Washington Consensus Mattered*. Morrisville, NC: Lulu Pres.

Mullins, D. and A. Murie. 2006. *Housing Policy in the UK*. New York: Palgrave Macmillan.

Nettleton, S. and R. Burrows. 1998. "Mortgage Debt, Insecure Home Ownership and Health: An Exploratory Analysis." *Sociology of Health and Illness* 20 (5): 731–58.

Peck, J. and A. Tickell. 2002. "Neo-Liberalizing Space." *Antipode* 34 (3): 380–440.

Pink, D. 2009. *Drive: The Surprising Truth About What Motivates Us*. New York: Knopf Doubleday Publishing Group.

Rohe, W. M. and H. Watson, eds. 2007. *Chasing the American Dream: New Perspectives on Affordable Housing*. Ithaca, NY: Cornell University Press.

Rohe, W. M., S. Van Zandt, and G. McCarthy. 2001. *The Social Benefits and Costs of Homeownership: A Critical Assessment of the Research*. Cambridge, MA: Joint Center For Housing Studies, Harvard University, LIHO-01.12, October 2012.

Saegert, S. 1985. "The Role of Housing in the Experience of Dwelling." In *Home Environments*, edited by I. Altman and C. Werner. Milwaukee: Plenum Press.

Saegert, S., D. Fields, and K. Libman. 2009. "Deflating the Dream: Radical Risk and the Neo-Liberalization of Homeownership." *Journal of Urban Affairs* 31 (3): 297–317.

Saft J. 2010. "Fed's Plan Would Create Paper Wealth." *International Herald Tribune* October 8: 23.

Sampson, R. J. 1999. "What 'Community' Supplies." In *Urban Problems and Community Development*, edited by R. F. Ferguson and W. T. Dickens. Washington, DC: Brookings Institution Press.

Sampson, Robert J., Jeffrey D. Morenoff, and Thomas Gannon-Rowley. 2002. "Assessing 'Neighborhood Effects': Social Processes and New Directions in Research." *Annual Review of Sociology* 28: 443–78.

Saunders, P. 1984. "Beyond Housing Classes: The Sociological Significance of Private Property Rights in Means of Consumption." *International Journal of Urban and Regional Research* 8 (2): 202–27.

Saunders, P. 1990. *A Nation of Home Owners*. London: Unwin Hyman.

Sayer, A. 2005. "Class, Moral Worth and Recognition." *Sociology* 39 (5): 947–63.

Schwartz, A. 2010. *Housing Policy in the United States*, 2nd ed. New York: Routledge.

Sewell W. H., Jr. 1992. "Introduction: Narratives and Social Identities." *Social Science History* 16: 479–88.

Sixsmith, J. 1986. "The Meaning of Home: An Exploratory Study of Environmental Experience." *Journal of Environmental Psychology* 6 (4): 281–98.

Smith, N. 1987. "Gentrification and the Rent-Gap." *Annals of the Association of American Geographers* 77 (3): 462–5.

Smith, N. 2002. "New Globalism, New Urbanism: Gentrification as a Global Urban Strategy." *Antipode* 34: 428–50.

Smith, S. G. 1994. "The Essential Qualities of a Home." *Journal of Environmental Psychology* 14: 31–46.

Stern, S. 2011. "Reassessing the Citizen Virtues of Homeownership." *Columbia Law Review* 100 (2): 101–51.

Tsemberis, S., L. Gulcur, and M. Nakae. 2004. "Housing First, Consumer Choice, and Harm Reduction for Homeless Individuals with a Dual Diagnosis." *American Journal of Public Health* 94 (4): 651–6.

Vale, L. 2007. "The Ideological Origins of Affordable Homeownership Efforts." In *Chasing the American Dream: New Perspectives on American Homeownership*, edited by W. M. Rohe and H. L. Watson. Ithaca, NY: Cornell University Press: 15–40.

Walks, A. 2010. "Bailing out the Wealthy: Responses to the Financial Crisis, Ponzi Neo-Liberalism, and the City." *Human Geography* 3 (3): 54–84.

Weber, R. 2002. "Extracting Value from the City: Neo-liberalism and Urban Redevelopment." *Antipode* 34 (3): 519–40.

Webber, M. M. 1964. "The Urban Place and the Non-Place Urban Realm." In *Explorations into Urban Structure*, edited by M. M. Webber. Philadelphia: Pennsylvania University Press.

Wellman, B. and B. Leighton. 1979. "Networks, Neighborhoods, and Communities: Approaches to the Study of the Community Question." *Urban Affairs Quarterly* 14 (3): 363–90.

Williams, P. 1987. "Constituting Class and Gender: A Social History of the Home, 1700–1901." In *Class and Space: The Making of Urban Society*, edited by N. Thrift and P. Williams. London: Routledge & Kegan Paul.

Wilson, D. 2004. "Toward a Contingent Urban neo-Liberalism." *Urban Geography* 25 (8): 771–83.

Wolfe, J. 1998. "Canadian Housing Policy in the Nineties." *Housing Studies* 13 (1): 121–33.

Yates, T. M., J. Obradović, and B. Egeland. 2010. "Transactional Relations Across Contextual Strain, Parenting Quality, and Early Childhood Regulation and Adaptation in a High-Risk Sample." *Developmental Psychopathology* 22 (3):539–55.

Zelazo, P. D., A. Carter, J. S. Resnick, and D. Frye. 1997. "Early Development of Executive Function: A Problem-Solving Framework." *Review of General Psychology* 1 (2): 198–226.

PART III

SOCIAL RESILIENCE ON A MACRO SCALE

7

Neoliberalism and Social Resilience in the Developed Democracies

Lucy Barnes and Peter A. Hall

History flows in streams that overlap and sometimes shift direction. From the early 1980s, just such a shift was discernible in the history of the developed democracies. For thirty years after World War II, their states took on greater roles in the allocation of resources as governments anxious to avoid the social conflicts of the inter-war years adopted activist economic policies and generous social benefits to construct a Keynesian welfare state (Offe 1983; Eichengreen 2007). However, economic recession and slower rates of growth during the 1970s gave rise to widespread disillusionment with existing modes of policymaking. In reaction, policymakers began to argue that employment was the responsibility of markets rather than governments and growth could be restored only by expanding the ambit and competitiveness of markets (Hall 1993; McNamara 1998: Blyth 2002).

The pioneering steps were taken by governments elected under Margaret Thatcher in 1979 and Ronald Reagan in 1980. In the context of widespread fears about national decline, they promised to restore the prosperity of the nation by enhancing the role of markets vis-à-vis the state in the economy (Krieger 1986). Paradoxically, the initial requirement was a more assertive state (Gamble 1988). The two administrations initiated legislation to reduce the power of trade unions and fought high-profile battles with British miners and American air controllers. In the name of deregulation, they privatized national enterprises, contracted out public services, tightened social benefits, and made many markets more competitive (King 1987; Vogel 1998; Prasad 2006).

On the European continent and in Asia, the move to the market came more slowly. The Wende that Helmut Kohl promised Germany in 1984 proved more rhetorical than real, and a socialist government under François Mitterrand tried to revive French dirigisme before beginning a string of market-oriented reforms in 1983 (Hall 1986; Wood 2001). Other governments were often slower to act. With the adoption of the Single European Act of 1986, the European Community committed itself to more intense market competition and turned

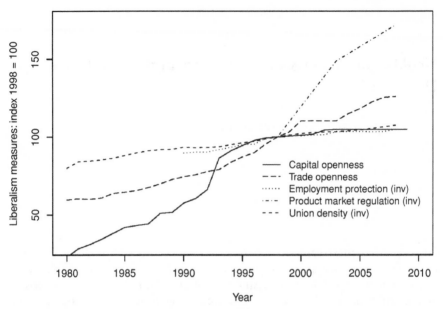

FIGURE 7-1. Movement in indicators of liberalization, 1980 to 2010. *Notes:* Indices are constructed from Organisation for Economic Co-operation and Development measures for product market regulation, employment protection, percent of the labor force in trade unions, and exports and imports as a share of gross domestic product.

its Commission into an agent for market liberalization. By the early 1990s, markets were being liberalized in all of the Organisation for Economic Co-operation and Development (OECD) countries, and liberalization continued until the global financial crisis of 2008.

In short, the past thirty years have been a neoliberal era marked by the opening of international markets, the intensification of market competition, and the growing influence of markets over the allocation of resources. In labor markets, liberalization has featured initiatives to reduce employment protection, make part-time and temporary employment more feasible, tighten eligibility and replacement rates for unemployment or sickness benefits, and weaken trade unions. In markets for corporate governance, neoliberal initiatives reduced impediments to foreign direct investment, made corporate takeovers more feasible, and increased the power of shareholders relative to stakeholders. In markets for goods and services, analogous initiatives reduced barriers to trade, privatized public enterprises, encouraged the contracting out of public services, and opened markets to new competitors. Although these initiatives were more intense in some countries than others, as Peter Evans and William Sewell note in Chapter 1, Figure 7-1 indicates that the OECD countries moved broadly in these directions (cf. Hall and Thelen 2009).

The object of this chapter is to examine the effects of this turn toward more intense market competition on ordinary people in the developed democracies.

We are especially interested in the distribution of well-being and the sources of social resilience sustaining it in the neoliberal era. How have people fared in the context of this neoliberal era? Are they generally better or worse off? Which groups have benefited, and which have lost in the face of these developments?

The answers to these questions are not obvious. On the one hand, there is a sound rationale in economic theory for expecting intensified market competition to improve economic performance and aggregate well-being by stimulating trade, encouraging innovation, and reducing consumer prices. On the other hand, intensified competition is likely to have restrained wages and made some jobs less secure, and the tightening of social benefits disadvantages those in precarious labor-market positions. Whether liberalization improved the overall well-being of all groups in society resists ex ante specification.

Even if we construe well-being in entirely material terms, measurable by income or wealth, the outcome remains unclear. On average, the OECD countries saw modest increases in national income and in income inequality during the 1980s and 1990s (OECD 2008). However, there is wide cross-national variation in the extent to which income inequality has increased as well as in the income ranges and types of income affected. In some countries, the distribution of earned income is not much more unequal today than it was at the beginning of the 1980s. In others, increases in earnings inequality have been offset by redistributive taxes and transfers. In general, inequality across households has increased less than across individuals. Thus, it is difficult to assess well-being on the basis of aggregate figures for income inequality (Gottschalk and Smeeding 1997; Pontusson 2005; Kenworthy and Pontusson 2005; Pontusson and Rueda 2009).

Moreover, income is not synonymous with well-being, and market liberalization has effects that extend well beyond income. When markets become more competitive, people who have to sell their labor or goods face greater uncertainty and economic insecurity that can depress well-being. Many jobs have become less secure, and many of the policy initiatives associated with liberalization, such as shifts away from pension plans offering defined benefits, reductions in unemployment benefits, and new limits on health benefits, have forced many people to bear more of the risks associated with adverse life events and economic fluctuations (Hacker 2004; Taylor-Gooby 2004; Hacker et al. 2010).

The neoliberal era has also seen the extension of market logics into ever more spheres of the lifeworld (Habermas 1985; Sennett 2006). An increasing number of organizations, ranging from firms to universities and public agencies, are now subject to more competitive pressure. Although reforms of this sort can breathe new life into old organizations, they can also put those working in them under more strain (Hochschild 2003). They often alter the normative orders embedded in organizational culture, subordinating human relationships to competitive concerns (Sauder and Espeland 2009; Streeck 2009). Even family relations have changed, as more children are subjected to competitive pressures at ever earlier ages (Hochschild 2003; Levey forthcoming).

In short, the market liberalization of the 1980s and 1990s has had wide-ranging effects on multiple spheres of life. By opening up new opportunities, foreclosing others, and subjecting people to new pressures, it is likely to have been consequential for well-being in many ways. Where can these effects be observed?

Shifts in Worldview During the Neoliberal Era

We begin by considering whether the neoliberal era has had a pervasive impact on the worldviews of ordinary people. Above all else, this era was marked by a shift in reigning ideas about the value of market competition. Underpinning them were changes in the doctrines of mainstream economics. Under the influence of rational expectations theory, economists acquired a new skepticism about the value of macroeconomic management and discovered a "natural" rate of unemployment reducible only through structural reform on the supply side of the economy (Crystal 1979; Cuthbertson 2000). Informed opinion changed in tandem with these doctrines toward the view that markets are efficient allocators of resources and government intervention likely to impede that efficiency. The implications were that people should be paid by their performance and governments should not restrict competition or equalize incomes, lest they damage the capacity of markets to produce well-being for all. By 1985, the nostrums of the new economics were working their way into politics (Blyth 2002; Prasad 2006).

One notable feature of this movement was the breadth of its influence. Although parties on the political right led the way, they were soon followed by those on the mainstream left. Figure 7-2 shows the movement, in seventeen developed democracies from 1945 to 2005, on an index reflecting party positions on eight economic issues central to neoliberalism, such as the appropriate role of state and market in economic regulation and the priority to be accorded economic efficiency relative to social protection (Cusack and Engelhardt 2002; Iversen 2006). The solid line in the middle of the figure indicates the average position on this index of the parties in these legislatures weighted by their share of seats.[1] Between 1980 and 1998, legislatures became significantly more neoliberal, as parties on both the right and left moved in that direction.

Were these shifts in worldview simply an elite phenomenon, or did they reflect changes in the beliefs of ordinary people as well? We are especially interested in three issues. Did neoliberal ideas induce changes in people's thinking about how the economy should work, how they should behave, and how economic rewards should be distributed? The latter touches on what Europeans call "social solidarity," namely, the willingness of people to see resources redistributed to those who are less well off (cf. Lane 1972; Hochschild 1981; Goldstein and Keohane 1993; Boltanski and Chiapello 1999). Unfortunately,

---

[1] The *dotted line* shows the relative balance in these legislatures between parties on the political left and right as classified by experts. We are grateful to Torben Iversen for sharing this data.

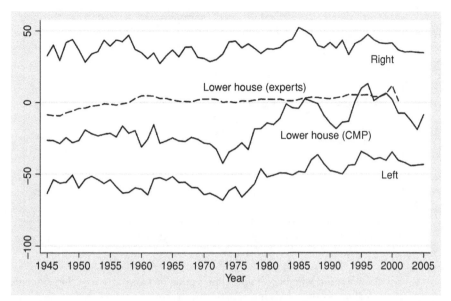

FIGURE 7-2. Change in party positions on the economic ideology index 1945 to 2005. *Notes:* The *solid middle line* indicates the common mean position (CMP) of legislators on an economic ideology index where higher values reflect more market-oriented policy positions. The *top* and *bottom lines* indicate the mean position of parties on the right and left of the political spectrum on this index. The *dotted line* indicates the balance of seats in the legislatures held by parties classified by experts as being on the left and right of the political spectrum. *Source:* Data provided by Torben Iversen. See also Iversen 2006.

long runs of relevant data are scarce, but some suggestive answers are available from the World Values Survey, which has asked a consistent series of questions of nationally representative samples at five-year intervals since 1981. Although not every country was surveyed in every wave, our observations cover eighteen OECD countries for a total sample of up to 47,890 respondents.

There is evidence that market-oriented ideas made important inroads into popular beliefs, especially during the 1980s. With regard to how the economy should operate, the inclination of people in all income groups to regard "competition" as good rather than harmful increased during the early 1990s, and although support for competition declined in the second half of the 1990s, the balance of opinion remains favorable to it (Fig. 7-3).[2] With respect to the distribution of economic rewards, consider views about what people who perform the same job with different degrees of competence should be paid. Market ideology usually specifies that people who perform better should be paid more, a view popular among those with higher incomes. As Figure 7-4

---

[2] The high income group is people with incomes at the seventieth percentile and above; low income is at the thirtieth percentile and below, and the middle income group is those in between.

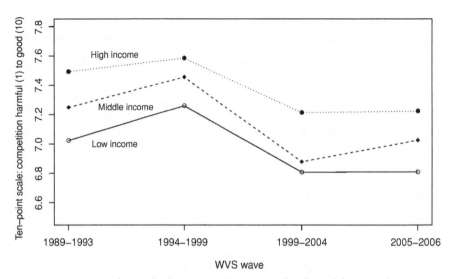

FIGURE 7-3. Views about whether competition is good or harmful across three income groups. *Note:* Values on the y-axis indicate the mean score on a scale of 1 to 10 where "harmful" is 1 and "good" is 10. *Source:* World Values Survey.

indicates, support for this position increased significantly among people at all levels of income during the 1980s, and it has remained high ever since.

Because market ideology also endorses self-interested behavior, it is notable that the proportion of people who think it can be justifiable to avoid paying a fare on public transport increased from 33 percent in 1981 to 43 percent in 2005, a 30 percent rise.[3] In broad terms at least, the market-oriented ideas popularized over the past thirty years do seem to have shifted the views of ordinary people about how the economy should function and what behavior is appropriate to it.

However, market ideas do not appear to have altered fundamental attitudes to social solidarity. Figure 7-5 indicates that people in virtually all income groups across a wide range of countries became more supportive of the views that governments should take responsibility for providing for everyone and that incomes should be made more equal in the wake of the neoliberal initiatives of the 1990s.[4] Responses in successive surveys about the role of government reflect similar trends. On a battery of questions about whether it is the government's responsibility to redistribute wealth and provide jobs for everyone

[3] It remains an open question how profound or pervasive this shift in views has been. There has been no analogous increase, for instance, in the numbers deeming it justifiable to cheat on their taxes.

[4] The countries included in the statistics given in Figure 7-5 include Argentina, Australia, Brazil, Bulgaria, Canada, Chile, China, Finland, Germany, India, Italy, Japan, South Korea, Mexico, the Netherlands, Poland, Romania, Russia, Slovenia, Sweden, the United Kingdom, and the United States.

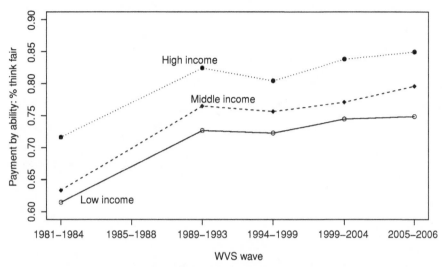

FIGURE 7-4. Percent of people who think it fair to pay the ablest more (by income group). *Note:* Figures on the y-axis are the percentage who think it is fair to give more pay to those who perform better rather than offer the same pay for the same job. *Source:* World Values Survey.

and benefits for unemployed and elderly individuals, the majorities supporting such measures in OECD countries shifted very little between 1985 and 2006, and the proportion thinking the government has a responsibility to reduce income differences between the rich and the poor increased slightly from 68 percent in 1985 to 74 percent in 2006 (International Social Survey Program 2009). Although market-oriented ideas have left their mark on the popular imagination, they do not seem to have eroded feelings of social solidarity or the belief of a majority of citizens in most OECD countries that governments bear responsibility for securing it.

Shifts in Well-Being During the Neoliberal Era

Our primary concern is with well-being. We use the term "well-being" to denote a person's welfare understood in broad terms as a multidimensional phenomenon encompassing material circumstances, health, and security. In keeping with a substantial literature, we measure it by the level of satisfaction people express with their lives (Helliwell and Barrington-Leigh 2010; Helliwell, Huang, and Harris 2010).[5] This instrument allows people to define well-being

---

[5] The relevant question asks, "All things considered, how satisfied are you with your life as a whole these days?" to which a response is given ranging from 1 (completely dissatisfied) to 10 (completely satisfied).

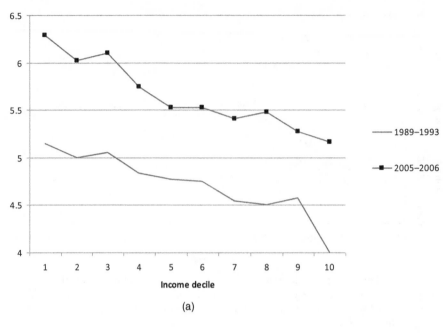

(a)

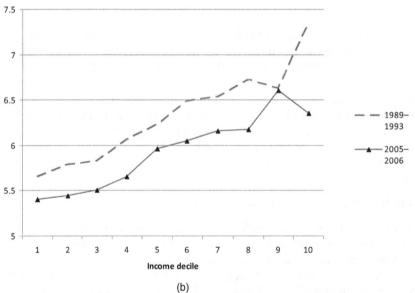

(b)

FIGURE 7-5. Views about the responsibilities of the state and income equality by income decile. (a) The state should take more responsibility for ensuring everyone is provided for (10) versus individuals should take more responsibility for providing for themselves (1) – average on a scale of 1 to 10. (b) Incomes should be more equal (1) versus there should be greater incentives for individual effort (10) – average on a scale of 1 to 10.

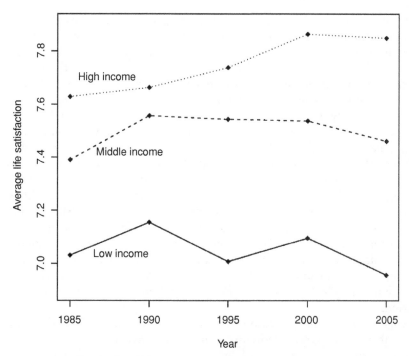

FIGURE 7-6. Level of well-being over time in three income groups. *Source:* Authors' calculations, World Values Survey.

in their own terms and, for assessing the impact of a multidimensional phenomenon such as market liberalization, it has advantages over narrower indicators that reduce a person's welfare to income (Sen 1999; Nussbaum 2001; Stiglitz, Sen, and Fitoussi 2009). In addition, this approach allows us to evaluate the impact of changes in income on well-being. Strong evidence indicates that life satisfaction is a good indicator for quality of life, reflecting common conditions across national contexts and, in our dataset, it is highly correlated with measures for other factors associated with the quality of life, such as health and the household financial situation (for reviews, see Veenhoven 1996; Diener et al. 1999; Helliwell 2008).

How did the experience of neoliberal reform affect the well-being of ordinary people? Figure 7-6 shows average well-being across eighteen developed democracies for three groups whom we will describe as the lower middle class (at or below the thirtieth percentile in the income distribution), the upper middle class (at or above the seventieth percentile), and the middle class (between the other two groups). In keeping with the view that neoliberal reforms promote prosperity, average well-being increased by a total of 3 percent between 1981 and 2005. However, that increase is modest compared with the 1.9 percent increase per year in gross domestic product (GDP) per capita for the OECD countries over this period.

More important, the distribution of well-being became significantly more unequal over the course of the neoliberal era. It is not surprising that the well-being of all three income groups improved during the 1980s, since 1981, our base year, came amid the worst global recession since 1945. During the 1990s, however, only the upper middle classes experienced increases in well-being, and the average well-being of the middle and lower middle classes fell during the 1990s and early 2000s. In short, this was an era of winners and losers. Over these twenty-five years, average well-being increased by 2 percent for the upper middle class but declined by 3 percent for the lower middle class.

Although these numbers may seem small, the gap is statistically significant ($p = .0396$) and striking given how stable national assessments of subjective well-being tend to be. As Easterlin (1974, 1995) and others have shown, those assessments do not move much even over decades of economic change, and, at the individual level, changes in subjective well-being induced, for instance, by changes in income tend to have a short half-life (Suh, Diener, and Fujita 1996; Di Tella, Haisken-De-New, and MacCulloch 2010). The gap in average well-being between the upper middle and lower middle classes in 2005 is more than twice the standard deviation in the country averages for well-being over this period.

To what extent is this increase in inequality attributable to liberalization processes that made markets more open and competitive as opposed to other developments over this period? Given limitations in the available data, this is an issue we cannot resolve definitively. Some analysts have argued that increases in income inequality were inspired by technological change, which privileged those with technical skills relative to low-skilled individuals. However, the evidence suggests that technological change accounts at best for a small portion of the rise in income inequality in the OECD over this period (Harjes 2007; cf. Autor et al. 2005). Others attribute such distributive effects to the increasing flows of trade and capital associated with globalization. By making low-skill production in the developing world more feasible, the opening of global markets intensified competition and increased relative returns to skill in the developed world (Wood 1994; Leamer 1996; Antràs, Garicano, and Rossi-Hansberg 2006). However, governments had to decide to make international markets more open, and we see the opening of global markets as one aspect of broader liberalization processes with political origins.

Many domestic policies associated with liberalization also had direct consequences for the lower middle class. Efforts to weaken trade unions were largely successful. The proportion of the OECD workforce that is unionized dropped from 33 percent in 1980 to 18 percent in 2008, and the strength of the trade union movement is closely correlated with wage levels at the lower end of the income spectrum (Card and Di Nardo 2002). Steps to reduce employment protection and encourage temporary employment contracts reduced the job security of large segments of the workforce, as increasing turnover rates indicate. At a basic level, there is a natural class bias to liberal reforms. Reforms that extend the purview of markets often enhance the aggregate "efficiency" of allocation, but they also privilege those with access to marketable resources, such as capital and high levels of skills typical in the upper middle class, relative to those without them. Intensifying market competition magnifies the distributive effects that follow from disparities in marketable resources.

By contrast, it is unlikely that increasing inequality in well-being stems from the two other socioeconomic developments most prominent in this era, namely, the entry of women into the paid labor force or the rise of service sector employment. Although entry into the labor force seems to have depressed the life satisfaction of women, women from the upper and lower middle classes enter the labor force in roughly similar proportions, and we did not find a significant gender-based class difference in our data (Blanchflower and Oswald 2004; Stevenson and Wolfers 2009). Although there is significant cross-national variation in the types of service sector jobs created, the expansion of service sector employment was also a cross-class phenomenon (Esping-Andersen 1999).

In sum, one of the most striking features of the neoliberal era has been a shift in the distribution of well-being. After narrowing slightly in the 1980s across the OECD, inequality in well-being increased markedly after 1990 as well-being rose among the upper middle classes and stagnated among other groups.

Cross-National Variation in Well-Being

Although the distribution of well-being became more unequal in most countries in our sample over the neoliberal era, that increase was much larger in some societies than others. How is this cross-national variation to be explained?

For the purposes of cross-national comparison, we construct an index of inequality in well-being that indicates, for each country at each point in time, the ratio of the average level of life satisfaction reported by people in the upper middle class (namely, in the top three income deciles) to the average level of life satisfaction reported by people in the lower middle class (in the bottom three income deciles). We compare well-being across these large groups rather than small bands at the top and bottom of the income distribution in order to capture the life situations of a majority of people and to minimize the measurement error that might arise from looking at smaller groups. In intuitive terms, a score of 110 on this index means that, for country x at time t, the average well-being of people in the upper middle classes was 10 percent higher than the level of well-being among people in the lower middle classes. To correct for the possibility that people may be culturally less inclined to express satisfaction with their life in some countries than others, this measure compares the responses of co-nationals. Thus, it provides a measure of inequality in well-being that is broadly comparable across countries and time.

Figure 7-7 shows the level of inequality in well-being in each of the OECD countries in our sample in 2005, and Figure 7-8 shows the average annual rate of change in this index between 1980 and 2000. Significant differences are visible. After two decades of the neoliberal era, the distribution of well-being

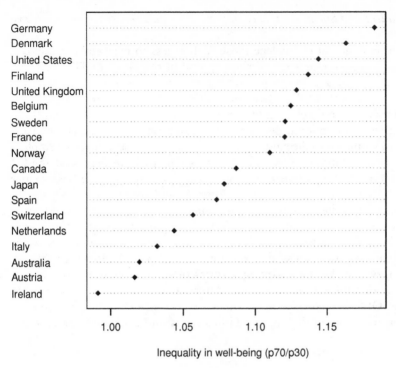

FIGURE 7-7. Inequality in well-being between the upper middle class and lower middle class in 2005.

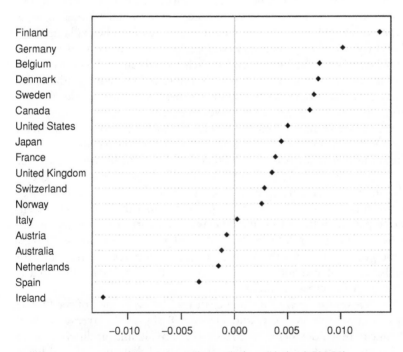

FIGURE 7-8. Average annual change in inequality in well-being, 1985 to 2005.

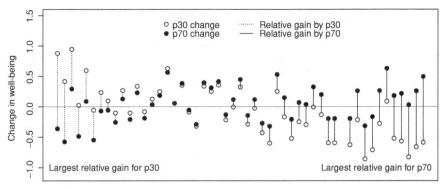

FIGURE 7-9. Changes in well-being of the lower middle and upper middle classes across each period from 1980 to 2005 in the OECD countries. *Notes:* The y-axis indicates the magnitude of change in well-being from the previous period. Figures above the line are positive and below the line negative changes. The *solid diamonds* indicate change in well-being of people with incomes at p70 and above. The *circles* indicate changes in well-being of people with incomes at p30 and below over the same period. Each *line* indicates changes in one country over one time period. *Source:* World Values Survey.

is more equal in Ireland, Australia, Italy, and the Netherlands but relatively unequal in Germany, Denmark, the United States, and Finland. To appreciate the substantive significance of these inequalities, note that, in our sample, the ratio of well-being of a full-time worker compared with that of an unemployed worker, whose well-being is typically depressed by unemployment, is 1.17, not so different from the ratio across income groups in countries where well-being is distributed most unequally (cf. Blanchflower and Oswald 2004: 1373).

Figure 7-9 reports each change in well-being in each country in our sample over all subperiods between 1981 and 2005, arrayed from left to right based on the extent to which the change marked an increase in inequality in well-being, decomposed into changes in well-being among the upper and lower middle classes. The circles show the change in well-being over the subperiod among the lower middle class and the diamonds the change among the upper middle classes. It is apparent that, where large increases in inequality took place (to the right in the diagram), they were attributable mainly to a decline in well-being among the lower middle class.

Thus, the problem becomes primarily one of explaining why the relative well-being of the lower middle class is lower in some times and places than in others. This is likely driven in fundamental ways by the economic situation of the lower middle classes. Three types of material factors might matter. The first is the level of national income: where it is higher, everyone should be better off, and this might improve the well-being of some groups more than others, although we have no ex ante expectation about which groups will benefit most. A second relevant factor is the distribution of income: where it is more equal, well-being should be more equally distributed. The third factor is the rate of unemployment. Because the incidence of unemployment is typically higher

TABLE 7-1. *The Material Determinants of Inequality in Well-Being in OECD Countries*

	Model 1	Model 2	Model 3	Model 4
(Intercept)	0.90‡	0.82‡	0.81‡	0.58‡
	0.08	*0.07*	*0.09*	*0.09*
GDP/capita (00000s)	0.14*	0.23†	0.22†	0.12*
	0.1	*0.11*	*0.13*	*0.09*
Unemployment rate	0.11‡	0.27		
	0.04	*0.39*		
Inequality (prefisc Gini)	0.37‡	0.43‡	0.52‡	1.31‡
	0.15	*0.17*	*0.21*	*0.24*
Social spending (00000s)			−0.27	
			(0.79)	
Redistributive effort				−0.93‡
				0.23
Mediterranean		−0.01	−0.02	−0.01
		0.02	*0.02*	*0.02*
Social democratic		0.03	0.04	0.12‡
		0.02	*0.03*	*0.03*
Continental		0.05‡	0.05‡	0.09‡
		0.02	*0.02*	*0.02*
n	52	52	52	52
R^2	0.14	0.35	0.35	0.53
Adjusted. R^2	0.09	0.27	0.26	0.46
Res. sd	0.05	0.04	0.04	0.04

Note: Standard errors in italics below the coefficient. Levels of statistical significance indicated as follows: * = .10, † = .05, ‡ = .001. The omitted type of welfare state is liberal. GDP = gross domestic product.

among those at lower incomes, where the level of unemployment is lower, the lower middle class may be relatively better off.

To assess these propositions, we estimate the impact of GDP per capita, the standardized rate of unemployment, and the Gini coefficient for the inequality of market income before taxes and transfers on the index for inequality in well-being using an ordinary least squares regression covering all countries and periods in our sample. Because we have few observations for each country, it is not practicable to include country-level fixed effects, but we do control for types of welfare state (Esping-Andersen 1990). The results are in models 1 and 2 of Table 7-1.[6] They suggest that, where market income inequality is higher, inequality in well-being will also be greater. Higher levels of national income

---

[6] This time-series data presents the usual problems for causal inference. For instance, inequality in the United Kingdom in 2005 is not independent of inequality in 2000. Because we have a small panel, we cannot isolate statistically significant effects when a lagged-dependent variable is included, although the point estimates retain the signs indicated in Table 7-1. Thus, the coefficients should be interpreted with caution. Using panel-corrected standard errors to allow for

may also increase inequality in well-being, suggesting that, at least in this period, higher levels of prosperity were shared unequally. Both coefficients are typically significant at the .05 level. Surprisingly, we find no systematic relationship between the rate of unemployment and inequality in well-being.[7] These results have to be treated with caution because they are not robust to the inclusion of a time trend, but they suggest that income inequality contributes to inequality in well-being, without fully determining it, as the low R^2 indicates.

The country rankings in Figure 7-7 are intriguing. Although we might expect inequality in well-being to be relatively high in countries such as the United States and United Kingdom where inequalities in income and health are significant, it is also high in countries such as Germany, Denmark, and Finland, where corresponding inequalities in income and health have long been lower and egalitarian political traditions stronger. To some extent, these figures reflect the fact that liberalizing reforms have had an important impact on relative well-being even in these countries, but they probably also reflect the way in which existing political traditions mediate the experience of such reforms. Assessments of well-being are conditioned, not only by circumstances but also by expectations, and in countries where welfare states have been relatively generous and egalitarian economic outcomes more prized, neoliberal reforms and accompanying increases in income inequality may well have depressed the sense of well-being of the lower middle class more than in countries where people were accustomed to higher levels of inequality.

This interpretation is consistent with the findings of Alesina, DiTella, and MacCulloch (2004) that income inequality reduces the subjective well-being of those in the bottom half of the income distribution more in Europe than in the United States, and it conforms to the fact that the coefficients on type of welfare state (in Table 7-1) indicate that, at any given level of income inequality, members of the lower middle class in countries with continental or social democratic welfare states are likely to feel less well off relative to members of the upper middle class than their counterparts in the liberal market economies (Esping-Andersen 1990; Hall and Soskice 2001). Similar considerations may explain why inequality in well-being did not increase in Ireland and Spain (see Figure 7-8). Both countries experienced economic transformations over this period whose fruits likely exceeded the expectations of many in the lower middle class (McGraw forthcoming).

---

panel heteroskedasticity, however, tends to reduce the standard errors and leave all substantive interpretations intact.

[7] Note, however, that higher levels of unemployment depress *average* levels of well-being, as indicated in the results of estimations of a hierarchical linear model reported in model 1 of Table 7-2. Higher levels of income inequality also have a large effect on average well-being. The movement from the highest to the lowest levels of income inequality in our sample is associated with an improvement in average well-being equivalent to that obtained by increasing per capita income by about $50,000.

Sources of Social Resilience

Many people faced challenges to their well-being during the 1980s and 1990s. Stylizing slightly, the intensification of market competition can be seen as an economic shock. The resulting dislocation put the well-being of the lower middle class at particular risk. However, the consequent levels of well-being are not simply a function of the magnitude of the shock but conditioned by the social resilience of those at risk. The core issue is how is such resilience constituted? What are the sources of social resilience on which people facing more economic insecurity, potential unemployment, and declining incomes might draw to preserve their well-being in the face of such developments? For approaches to this, we draw on two kinds of theoretical literatures.

Consider first the individual-level strategies that people can adopt. Multiple literatures suggest that, in challenging situations, individuals turn to other people for support, whether informational, emotional, or logistical, often to compensate for the material resources they lack. Studies of life under communism find that, when resources are scarce, people seek assistance from their relatives, friends, and colleagues – for help in securing goods and small services and to navigate the bureaucracy (Wedel 1986; Hann 1993). Studies in population health find that people who become ill recover more quickly if they can rely on close friends or relatives, and people who are tied into social networks enjoy better general health than those who are not (Berkman and Glass 2000; Berkman et al. 2000). Building on Link and Phelan (1995), the contributors to *Successful Societies* (Hall and Lamont 2009) describe social connectedness as a "social resource" on which people draw to enhance their capabilities for coping with life challenges. The inference is that social connectedness may be a buffer against increases in the "wear and tear" that people experience when markets become more competitive.

To assess this possibility, we estimate the effect of social connections on well-being at the individual level for everyone in our sample between 1980 and 2005, using hierarchical linear models with cross-level interactions. Several kinds of social connectedness might matter, ranging from intimate ties to family members, social connections to friends, and the relationships that come with membership in voluntary associations. Therefore, we measure social connectedness on three dimensions based on what respondents said about how important ties to family and friends were to them and the number of associations to which they belonged. The estimations contain a range of controls for the other factors that might matter to well-being, including income (measured by household income decile), type of occupation, employment status, years of education, age, and gender. We include time and country fixed effects and look where appropriate for nonlinear effects.

Table 7-2 reports the results. The material determinants of well-being all have the expected effects. Well-being increases with income but is lower among unskilled and semi-skilled manual workers relative to managers and professionals (not shown) and among unemployed individuals. With respect to age,

TABLE 7-2. *Individual-Level and Country-Level Determinants of Individual Well-Being: Hierarchical Linear Models*

	Model 1	Model 2	Model 3	Model 4	Model 5
Country-Level Variables					
Rate of unemployment	7.97†			2.63	
	3.34			3.71	
GDP/capita (000s)	0.02†			0.02	
	0.01			0.01	
Income inequality	−5.04†			−3.21*	−4.28†
	1.65			1.79	1.71
Redistributive effort					1.53*
					0.68
Density of associational Memberships			0.19*		
			0.08		
Trade union density				0.99*	
				0.41	
Individual-Level Variables					
(Intercept)	8.21†	7.13†	7.27†	7.77†	8.65†
	0.79	0.15	0.18	0.78	0.74
Associational membership	0.17†	0.07†	0.15†		0.17†
	0.02	0.01	0.01		0.02
Ties to family		0.5†			
		0.03			
Ties to friends		0.22†			
		0.02			
AM–income interaction	−0.01†		−0.01†		−0.01†
	0		0		0
Years of education	0.01	−0.01	−0.01	0.01	0.01
	0.02	0.01	0.01	0.01	0.01
Years of. Education²	0	0	0	0	0
	0		0	0	0
Unemployed	−0.73†	−0.78†	−0.79†	−0.82†	−0.77†
	0.06	0.05	0.05	0.05	0.05
Income	0.14†	0.1†	0.12†	0.12†	0.13†
	0.01	0	0	0	0.01
Female	0.02†	−0.03	0.01	0.03	0.01
	0.02	0.02	0.02	0.02	0.02
Age	−0.03†	−0.03†	−0.03†	−0.03†	−0.030
	0.0	0	0	0	
Age²	0†	0†	0†	0†	0†
	0	0	0	0	0
N obs	26966	38411	38874	31964	29044
N groups	40	54	55	48	41
AIC	107479	152724	155279	127882	116107
BIC	107684	152920	155476	128083	116306

Notes: Intercepts vary by country wave. Standard errors are in italics below the coefficient. Statistical significance indicated as follows: * = .05, † = .01. AM-Income interaction is the interaction between associational membership and income.

well-being has a U-shaped relationship, lower among the middle aged than the young but rising again later in life. However, model 2 shows that all three types of social connectedness also have a statistically significant relationship to a person's well-being in this period. Ties to family are most closely associated with well-being followed by ties to friends; membership in associations had a smaller but significant effect. Strong ties to friends improve well-being as much as a movement up two income deciles would, and strong ties to family have an effect on well-being equivalent to a movement up five income deciles. The conclusion we draw is that social connectedness has been an important source of social resilience during the neoliberal era.[8]

However, there is a distributive dimension to these results: social connectedness matters more for the well-being of the lower middle class than of the affluent. In model 3 in Table 7-2, we include a term that interacts income with membership in associations. The negative coefficient indicates that membership in associations improves well-being for people with low incomes more than for those with higher incomes.[9] By the same token, people with lower incomes suffer greater losses in well-being from lower levels of social connectedness than do affluent individuals. Moreover, social connectedness can be seen as a feature of social structure, and just as the economic structure of capitalist societies distributes material resources unequally, the social structure of those societies tends to distribute social resources unevenly. Social connectedness is stratified by social class. As Table 7-3 indicates, in virtually all OECD countries, people in higher social classes have denser networks of social connections than those in lower social classes. In sum, social connectedness is especially important to the well-being of people in the lower middle class but less available to them than to people in the upper middle class.

As Putnam (2001) and others have observed, of course, people may benefit from the density of social networks in a community in ways that are independent of their own social connections (Sampson, Morenoff, and Gannon-Rowley 2002; Schneepers et al. 2002), and we find some confirmation for this in our multilevel estimations. The average level of associational memberships in a country has a statistically significant impact on people's well-being independent of their own membership in such associations (model 3 in Table 7-2).

---

[8] An important literature in psychology argues that subjective well-being is also mediated by various features of personality. Longitudinal studies from this perspective find that subjective well-being is conditioned for some time by life events such as unemployment (Suh et al. 1996; Clark et al. 2008). Personality is unlikely to explain the variations in well-being across time in the large social groups in which we are interested. However, to control for it, in estimations not reported here, we have included a variable measuring "self-mastery," widely seen as a dimension of personality linked to well-being. We find that self-mastery has a statistically significant effect on well-being at the individual level and including it attenuates the size of our point estimates on ties to family, friends, and associational memberships, but the latter continue to have a statistically significant impact on well-being in terms substantively similar to those reported here.

[9] Conversely, low income has more damaging effects on the well-being of people with few social connections than on those who are well connected.

TABLE 7-3. *The Relationship Between Social Class and Social Connectedness*

	Ties to Friends and Family (Waves 2 and 5)	Membership in Associations (Waves 2 and 5)	Ever Feel Lonely (Wave 1)	Spend Time Socially (Wave 4)
Social Class	*Index Score*	*Mean Number*	*% Frequently or Sometimes*	*% Not at All*
Professional-managerial	5.33	2.2	28	31
White collar office workers (C1)	5.25	2.09	35	32
Skilled manual workers (C2)	5.16	1.8	33	41
Unskilled, semi-skilled manual (DE)	5.09	1.61	42	58

Notes: Higher values on the family and friends index indicate ties to family and friends are more important to the person; for details, see Barnes et al. (2010). The indicator "spend time socially" averages responses from each class to questions asking if respondents ever spend time with colleagues from work or with people at sport, cultural, or communal organizations.
Source: World Values Survey.

Broadly speaking, these results suggest that some important sources of social resilience are rooted in the structure of social relations. In some respects, however, they may reinforce, rather than even out, inequalities in well-being. If social connectedness is especially important to the well-being of people in the lower middle class, it is also usually less available to them than to members of the upper middle class, and more intense market competition can disrupt these connections, as it does, for instance, when people are forced to move to find new employment. We do not find any general decline in social connectedness over this period, but such issues deserve further investigation, as do the effects that might follow from cross-national variation in social structure (cf. Scheepers, Grotenhuis, and Gelissen 2002; Barnes, Hall, and Taylor 2010). We find that, in countries with denser networks of social connections, average well-being is higher, but where social connectedness is distributed more unequally across income groups, the relative well-being of the lower middle class may suffer.

However, people do not rely solely on individual-level strategies to cope with challenges to their well-being. These challenges can also be addressed through collective action. We consider two modes of collective action especially relevant to the challenges posed by neoliberalism, namely those that operate through the trade union movement and those that democratic governance makes possible.

The effect of trade unions on well-being is of special interest during the neoliberal era because unions were important sources of resistance to neoliberal measures that would make employment less secure, wage competition more intense, and social benefits more restrictive. A large literature suggests that trade unions can improve the well-being of their members and, as political actors, they often agitate for measures aimed at improving the well-being of the lower middle class more generally (Freeman and Medoff 1984; Hall and Soskice 2001; Radcliff 2005; Flavin, Pacek, and Radcliff 2010).

Democratic governments were also potentially important vehicles for collective response to the challenges of the neoliberal era. Some classic views portray democratic governments as instruments that harnesses advancing knowledge to a popular will in pursuit of a wider social welfare (Beer 1974; Held 2006; Hall 2010). In the neoliberal era, of course, governments were part of the problem as well as the solution: state-sponsored initiatives to deregulate markets were central to intensifying market competition. However, as Polanyi (1944) observes, the governance of markets is ultimately a double-sided affair. Governments create markets, but they also offer protection from the worst effects of market competition. A failure to do so endangers their chances for reelection, if not the stability of the social order (Pacek and Radcliff 2008; Flavin, Pacek, and Radcliff 2011).

Of course, both of these contentions are controversial. Few doubt that trade unions improved the living standards of the workforce in previous eras, but there is debate about their benefits during the neoliberal era (Rueda 2007). A sizeable literature sees the efforts of trade unions to raise wage floors, resist layoffs, and limit the reorganization of production as impediments to the well-being delivered by flexible markets (Hirsch 2003; Oswald 1985). Some analysts see democratic governments in similar terms, as sectarian agents more likely to deliver rents to their partisans than to serve the well-being of the populace as a whole (Bates 1981; Tanzi 2005; Hacker and Pierson 2010). Therefore, these issues deserve empirical scrutiny.

To assess the contention that trade unions preserved well-being in the face of the challenges of the neoliberal era, we estimate a hierarchical linear model with intercepts that vary by country wave and a wide range of controls for the determinants of well-being at the individual level. The results reported in model 4 in Table 7-2 indicate that trade union density at the national level – that is, the proportion of the national workforce belonging to unions – is positively associated with the well-being of individuals in these countries over this period and statistically significant at almost the .01 level.[10] Moreover, this effect is present even when we control for union membership at the individual level. In short, trade unions sustain the well-being of large portions of the populace, not simply of their own members (see also Flavin et al. 2010). They operate as factors of social resilience by virtue of how they defend social solidarity in the national political economy.

---

[10] The results are similar using either the Organisation for Economic Co-operation and Development measure for trade union density or a measure derived from the World Values Survey samples.

Can democratic governments have similar effects? To examine this possibility, we estimate the impact of social spending (as a share of GDP) and of the redistributive efforts of governments on the index of inequality in well-being for each of our country periods. Our expectation is that social spending will have little effect on inequality in well-being. Although it increased on average in the OECD from 16 percent of GDP in 1980 to 21 percent in 2005, social spending is a blunt instrument for addressing inequalities in well-being because many of its beneficiaries are relatively affluent recipients of retirement and other benefits. By contrast, the government's redistributive effort is much more likely to reduce inequality in well-being because it entails the redistribution of income from upper to lower income earners through taxation and transfers. As an indicator for redistributive effort, we take the difference between the Gini coefficient for household market income (before taxes and transfers) and the Gini coefficient for disposable household income (after taxes and transfers) in each period.

The results are reported in Table 7-1. As expected, aggregate social spending has no effect on inequality in well-being (model 3). However, model 4 indicates that a government's redistributive efforts reduce inequality in well-being by a substantial amount (statistically significant at the .03 level). We explore the issue further by incorporating a term for the government's redistributive effort into a multilevel model for determinants of individual well-being that controls for other factors. In Table 7-2 (model 5), the relevant coefficient is positive and statistically significant at the .05 level. Moving from the minimum to the maximum level of redistribution present in this sample increases average well-being by about as much as an increase of $30,000 in average income would. This suggests that the efforts of governments to redistribute resources during the neoliberal era improved the well-being of large segments of the population.

In other words, democratic governments can also be important sources of social resilience for the populace by virtue of their capacities to redistribute income. However, it should be noted that there is wide variation in the extent to which governments made such efforts and controversy over what drives them. Some attribute the success of redistributive coalitions to a country's electoral rules, others to its longstanding cleavage structures and political traditions, and others to the organizational power of the political left (Huber and Stephens 2001; Swank 2002; Iversen and Soskice 2006; Pontusson and Rueda 2009; see also Chapter 9 by Bouchard). Thus, there are second-order issues to this dimension of social resilience that are beyond the scope of this chapter to explore.

Conclusion

The distribution of well-being has become markedly more unequal during the neoliberal era. Although overall well-being in the developed democracies increased slightly during the 1980s, average well-being among the lower middle class was only 88 percent of its level among the upper middle class by 2005, down from 92 percent in the early 1980s; and in some countries, it fell by as much as 17 percent.

From an egalitarian perspective, this development is cause for concern. After three decades in which democratic welfare states fulfilled their promise to improve well-being for all, they have presided over three decades in which well-being increased only for those in the most privileged strata of society. The fruits of post-industrial capitalism are being distributed less equally today than they were thirty years ago, and the wear and tear of daily life has increased for many people.

However, these developments are troubling from other perspectives as well. In particular, they may be contributing to fissures that threaten intractable social conflict. One of the achievements of the postwar Keynesian welfare state was to displace class conflict from the political arena into the industrial arena, where regularized collective bargaining in the context of steady economic growth ultimately muted it (Lipset 1964; Offe 1983). Despite some resurgence in the late 1960s and 1970s, class conflict of the sort that dominated interwar politics has never returned (Crouch and Pizzorno 1978; Dalton, Flanagan, and Beck 1984). Rising in its stead, however, is increasingly bitter conflict over immigration and ethnicity. Across the developed democracies, the principal challenge to established political parties comes not from a radically egalitarian left but from a radically nationalist right, incensed to see people of different origins, ethnicities, and religions take up places in society (Kitschelt 1997). The many political reflections of this movement include the French National Front, the Austrian Freedom Party, the Swedish Democrats, and the American Tea Party movement.

This conflict is normally associated with the effects of globalization and its continental counterpart, the European Union, which have promoted increases in immigration. However, levels of immigration alone do not explain much of the variation in support for anti-immigrant parties (Lubbers and Scheepers 2000; Van der Brug, Fennema, and Tillie 2005; Swank and Betz 2002). Other factors are at work here. We suspect that one of those factors is the growing discrepancy in well-being between social classes. Those who fan the flames of ethnic division typically draw on the diffuse discontents people feel about their lives, and among the lower middle class, twenty years of stagnating well-being has provided fuel for those flames.

There is some evidence for this proposition. Resentment of immigrants has increased in the developed democracies since 1980. Although 8.5 percent of people in our sample said they would not like to have an immigrant as a neighbor in 1981, 12.2 percent said so in 2005, an increase of almost 50 percent. This trend is notably independent of broader changes in values over the period. Asked whether they would teach their children tolerance, in 2005, 83 percent of respondents said they would compared with 52 percent in 1981. Even more telling are the estimations reported in Table 7-4 in which we examine the impact of inequality in well-being at the national level on feelings of

TABLE 7-4. *The Impact of Inequality in Well-Being on Hostility to Immigrants*

	Model 1	Model 2	Model 3
(Intercept)	−0.23*	−0.21*	−0.21*
	0.15	0.15	0.15
GDP per capita (00000s)	−0.06	−0.01	−0.01
	0.10	0.01	0.01
Inequality in well-being	0.32[†]	0.27[†]	0.27[†]
	0.14	0.13	0.13
Value of tolerance			−0.00
			0.05
Mediterranean		0.00	0.00
		0.02	0.02
Social democratic		0.00	0.00
		0.02	0.02
Continental		0.03	0.03
		0.02*	0.02*
N	66	66	66
R²	.08	.15	.15

Notes: Standard errors in italics below the coefficient. Levels of statistical significance indicated as follows: * = .10, [†] = .05.

hostility to immigrants (measured by the percent of respondents who mention not wanting to have an immigrant or foreign worker as a neighbor) at five points in time between 1980 and 2005. Higher levels of inequality in well-being have a statistically significant effect (at about the .05 level) on hostility to immigrants. By contrast, generalized support for tolerance (measured by the percentage of people who say they would teach tolerance to their children) has no impact on attitudes to immigrants. Although many factors condition hostility to immigrants, including discourse in the public realm, where the gap in well-being between the lower and upper middle classes is larger, hostility to immigrants is likely be more prevalent (cf. Andersen and Fetner 2008).

In sum, rising inequality in well-being does not simply increase relative deprivation. It also threatens the social solidarity of societies in ways that portend growing social conflict. Support for measures to make incomes more equal, which is one indicator for social solidarity, has increased from 41 percent in favor in 1990 to 50 percent in 2005, but hostility to immigrants is another indicator of the limits to social solidarity, and it has remained high since 1990.

The concept of social resilience has also been central to our concerns. In the social sciences, there are two quite different literatures on resilience. One in psychology analyzes resilience as an attribute of individuals, usually acquired in childhood or adolescence as a result of experience with a caring family or role models in the local community. From this perspective, personal capacities for resilience allow a person to retain emotional health and achieve goals, such as good educational results, in the face of adversity, such as the loss of a parent or a decline in family income (Schoon 2006; Ungar 2008). A second literature in ecology sees resilience as an attribute of a physical or human system based on features that allow that system to return to a favorable equilibrium in the face of shocks engendered by climate change, plague, or other environmental developments (Adger 2000; Folke 2006).

By contrast, we construe social resilience as an attribute of social groups, whether understood as communities, nations, or social classes, that reflects the ability of the group to sustain its well-being in the face of challenges. This formulation has implications for where we look for the sources of social resilience. It directs our attention to experiences the group has in common and to the institutional or cultural frameworks that structure them. We see the factors structuring relationships within and between groups as key mediators of their response to change.

Several dimensions of these institutional and cultural frameworks have the potential to confer resilience on a social group. These include some we have not examined here, such as the collective narratives that are constitutive elements of a group's identity, the shape of a society's status hierarchy, and various features of its collective organization that condition the potential for mobilization (Cornell and Kalt 2000; Lamont 2000; Putnam 2001; Bouchard 2003; Barnes et al. 2010). Because of the data available to us, we have put special emphasis on the dimensions of social structure associated with social connectedness. Social connectedness emerges here as a crucial social resource intimately linked to social resilience. Our findings suggest that it has been especially important to the capacity of members of the lower middle class to sustain their well-being during the neoliberal era, and there would be real value in looking more closely at how it varies across countries and over time (Barnes et al. 2010).

We have also argued that trade unions and democratic governments can be significant factors of social resilience, namely, vehicles for collective response to socioeconomic challenges capable of sustaining the well-being of ordinary people. Our observations about trade unions are especially consequential in light of the dramatic losses in membership they have suffered during the neoliberal era (Baccaro and Howell 2011; Pinto and Beckfield 2011). If our findings are correct, many societies are losing one of their most important sources of social resilience. In the same vein, this analysis carries implications for how we view democratic governance. As Beer (1974) observed some decades ago, in principle, democratic governments can be vehicles for the formulation and implementation of common purposes. In many instances, they are no more efficient at this than capitalist economies are at securing economic growth, but from the standpoint of resilience, democratic governments provide a capacity for concerted response not present in other biological systems, and there is scope for exploring further the conditions under which they are indeed sources of social resilience (cf. Mayntz and Scharpf 1987).

Finally, our analysis points to the value of looking further into the distribution and determinants of well-being. Although many studies emphasize how the distribution of income changed during the neoliberal era, its initiatives conditioned well-being in other important ways. Assessments of well-being raise inevitable measurement issues, but they hold the potential for developing a better understanding of the contribution that nonmaterial, as well as material, factors make to social welfare (Stiglitz et al. 2009). There are important research agendas here worth pursuing.

Authors' Notes

We are grateful to Peter Gourevitch for inspiration for this chapter and to Jason Beckfield, Jim Ennis, Robert Fishman, John Helliwell, Lane Kenworthy, Will Kymlicka, Martin Schröder, Rosemary Taylor, and colleagues in the Successful Societies Program for helpful comments. Roberto Foa provided research assistance.

References

Adger, W. Neil. 2000. "Social and Ecological Resilience: Are they Related?" *Progress in Human Geography* 24 (3): 347–64.

Alesina, Alberto, Rafael DiTella, and Robert MacCulloch. 2004. "Inequality and Happiness: Are Europeans and Americans Different?" *Journal of Public Economics* 88 (9–10): 2009–42.

Andersen, Robert and Tina Fetner. 2008. "Economic Inequality and Intolerance: Attitudes toward Homosexuality in 35 Democracies." *American Journal of Political Science* 52 (4): 942–58.

Antràs, Pol, Luis Garicano, and Esteban Rossi-Hansberg. 2006. "Offshoring in a Knowledge Economy." *Quarterly Journal of Economics* 121 (1): 31–77.

Autor, D., L. Katz, and M. Kearny. 2005. "Trends in U.S. Wage Inequality: Re-Assessing the Revisionists." Working Paper No. 11627. Cambridge, MA: National Bureau of Economic Research.

Baccaro, Lucio and Chris Howell. 2011. "A Common Neoliberal Trajectory: The Transformation of Industrial Relations in Advanced Capitalism." *Politics and Society* 39 (4): 521–63.

Barnes, Lucy, Peter A. Hall, and Rosemary C. R. Taylor. 2010. "The Social Sources of the Health Gradient: A Cross-National Analysis." Unpublished manuscript.

Bates, Robert. H. 1981. *States and Markets in Tropical Africa: The Political Basis of Agricultural Policy*. Berkeley: University of California Press.

Beer, Samuel H. 1974. *Patterns of Government*. New York: Random House.

Berkman, Lisa and Thomas Glass. 2000. "Social Integration, Social Networks, Social Support and Health." In *Social Epidemiology*, edited by Lisa Berkman and Ichiro Kawachi. New York: Oxford University Press: 137–74.

Berkman, Lisa, Thomas Glass, Ian Brissett, and Teresa E. Seeman. 2000. "From Social Integration to Health: Durkheim in the New Millennium." *Social Science and Medicine* 51: 843–57.

Blanchflower, David G. and Andrew J. Oswald. 2004. "Well-Being Over Time in Britain and the USA." *Journal of Public Economics* 88: 1359–86.

Blyth, Mark M. 2002. *Great Transformations: Economic Ideas and Political Change in the Twentieth Century*. New York: Cambridge University Press.

Boltanski, Luc and Eve Chiapello. 1999. *Le Nouvel Esprit du Capitalisme*. Paris: Gallimard.

Bouchard, Gérard. 2003. *Raison et Contradiction: Le Mythe au Secours de la Pensée*. Québec: Éditions Nota bene/Cefan.

Card, D. and J. Di Nardo. 2002. "Skill-Biased Technological Change and Rising Wage Inequality: Some Problems and Puzzles." *Journal of Labor Economics* 20 (4): 733–83.

Cornell, Stephen and Joseph P. Kalt. 2000. "Where's the Glue? Institutional and Cultural Foundations of American Indian Economic Development." *Journal of Socio-Economics* 29: 443–70.

Crouch, Colin and Alessandro Pizzorno, eds. 1978. *The Resurgence of Class Conflict in Western Europe*. London: Macmillan.

Crystal, Alec. 1979. *Controversies in British Macroeconomics*. London: Philip Alan.

Cusack, Thomas and Lutz Englehardt. 2002. *The PGL File Collection: Computer File*. Berlin: Wissenschaftszentrum Berlin für Sozialforschung.

Cuthbertson, Keith. 2000. *Macroeconomic Policy: New Cambridge, Keynesian and Monetarist Controversies*. London: Halsted Press.

Dalton, Russell, Scott Flanagan, and Paul Beck, eds. 1984. *Electoral Change in Advanced Industrial Democracies*. Princeton, NJ: Princeton University Press.

Diener, E., E. M. Suh, R. E. Lucas, and H. E. Smith. 1999. "Subjective Well-Being: Three Decades of Progress." *Psychological Bulletin* 125: 276–302.

Di Tella, Rafael, John Haisken-De-New, and Robert MacCulloch. 2010. "Happiness Adaptation to Income and to Status in an Individual Panel." *Journal of Economic Behavior and Organization* 76: 834–52.

Easterlin, Robert. 1974. "Does Economic Growth Improve the Human Lot?" In *Nations and Households in Economic Growth: Essays in Honor of Moses Abramovitz*, edited by Paul A. David and Melvin W. Reder. New York: Academic Press: 89–125.

Easterlin, Robert. 1995. "Will Raising the Incomes of All Increase the Happiness of All?" *Journal of Economic Behavior and Organization* 27: 35–47.

Eichengreen, Barry. 2007. *The European Economy since 1945: Coordinated Capitalism and Beyond*. Princeton, NJ: Princeton University Press.

Esping-Andersen, Gösta. 1990. *Three Worlds of Welfare Capitalism*. Princeton, NJ: Princeton University Press.

Esping-Andersen, Gösta. 1999. *Social Foundations of Post-Industrial Economies*. Oxford: Oxford University Press.

Flavin, Patrick, Alexander C. Pacek, and Benjamin Radcliff. 2010. "Labor Unions and Life Satisfaction: Evidence from New Data." *Social Indicators Research* 98 (3): 435–49.

Flavin, Patrick, Alexander C. Pacek, and Benjamin Radcliff. 2011. "State Intervention and Subjective Well-Being in Advanced Industrial Democracies." *Politics & Policy* 39 (2): 251–69.

Folke, Carl. 2006. "Resilience: The Emergence of a Perspective for Social-Ecological Systems Analyses." *Global Environmental Change* 16: 253–67.

Freeman, Richard and James B. Medoff. 1984. *What Do Unions Do?* New York: Basic Books.

Gamble, Andrew. 1988. *The Free Economy and the Strong State: The Politics of Thatcherism*. Basingstoke, UK: Palgrave-Macmillan.

Glyn, Andrew. 2006. *Capitalism Unleashed: Finance, Globalization and Welfare*. Oxford: Oxford University Press.

Goldstein, Judith and Robert Keohane. 1993. "Ideas and Foreign Policy: An Analytical Framework" in *Ideas and Foreign Policy*, edited by Judith Goldstein and Robert Keohane. Ithaca, NY: Cornell University Press: 3–30.

Gottschalk, Peter and Tim Smeeding. 1997. "Cross-National Comparisons of Earnings and Income Inequality." *Journal of Economic Literature* 35 (6): 633–87.

Habermas, Jürgen. 1985. *The Theory of Communicative Action*. Boston: Beacon.

Hacker, Jacob S. 2004. "Privatizing Risk Without Privatizing the Welfare State: The Hidden Politics of Social Policy Retrenchment in the United States." *American Political Science Review* 98 (2): 243–60.

Hacker, Jacob S., Gregory A. Huber, Philipp Rehm, Mark Schlesinger, and Rob Valletta. 2010. *Economic Security at Risk: Finding from the Economic Security Index*. New York: Rockefeller Foundation.

Hacker, Jacob and Paul Pierson. 2010. *Winner Take-All Politics: How Washington Made the Rich Richer and Turned its Back on the Middle Class*. New York: Simon and Schuster.

Hall, Peter A. 1986. *Governing the Economy: The Politics of State Intervention in Britain and France*. Oxford: Polity Press.

Hall, Peter A, ed. 1989. *The Political Power of Economic Ideas: Keynesianism across Nations*. Princeton, NJ: Princeton University Press.

Hall, Peter A. 1993. "Policy Paradigms, Social Learning and the State: The Case of Economic Policy-Making in Britain." *Comparative Politics* April: 275–96.

Hall, Peter A. 2010. "Samuel H. Beer and the Possibilities of Politics." *British Politics*.

Hall, Peter A. and Michèle Lamont, eds. 2009. *Successful Societies: How Institutions and Culture Affect Health*. New York: Cambridge University Press.

Hall, Peter A. and David Soskice. 2001. *Varieties of Capitalism: The Institutional Foundations of Comparative Advantage*. Oxford: Oxford University Press.

Hall, Peter A. and Kathleen Thelen. 2009. "Institutional Change in Varieties of Capitalism." *Socio-Economic Review* 7 (1): 7–34.

Hann, Chris, ed. 1993. *Socialism: Ideals, Ideologies and Local Practices*. London: Routledge.

Harjes, Thomas. 2007. "Globalization and Income Inequality: A European Perspective." IMF Working Paper. 07/160. Washington, DC: International Monetary Fund.

Held, David. 2006. *Models of Democracy*: Cambridge: Polity.

Helliwell, John. 2008. "Life Satisfaction and Quality of Development." Working Paper 14507. Cambridge MA: National Bureau of Economic Research.

Helliwell, John and Christopher P. Barrington-Leigh. 2010. "Measuring and Understanding Subjective Well-Being." Working Paper 15887. Cambridge MA: National Bureau of Economic Research.

Helliwell, John, Haifang Huang, and Anthony Harris. 2010. "International Differences in the Determinants of Life Satisfaction." Unpublished manuscript.

Hirsch, Barry T. 2003. *What Do Unions Do for Economic Performance?* Discussion Paper No. 892. Bonn: IZA.

Hochschild, Arlie Russell. 2003. *The Commercialization of Intimate Life: Notes from Home and Work*. Berkeley: University of California Press.

Hochschild, Jennifer. 1981. *What's Fair: American Beliefs about Distributive Justice*. Cambridge, MA: Harvard University Press.

Huber, Evelyne and John D. Stephens. 2001. *Development and Crisis of the Welfare State*. Chicago: University of Chicago Press.

International Social Survey Program. *Consolidated Role of Government Surveys I to IV*. GESIS Cologne Germany ZA4700.

Iversen, Torben. 2006. "Class Politics is Dead! Long Live Class Politics! A Political Economy Perspective on the New Partisan Politics." *APSA-CP Newsletter* 17 (20): 1–6.

Iversen, Torben and David Soskice. 2006. "Electoral Institutions and the Politics of Coalitions: Why Some Democracies Redistribute More than Others." *American Political Science Review* 100 (2): 165–81.

Kenworthy, Lane and Jonas Pontusson. 2005. "Rising Inequality and the Politics of Redistribution in Affluent Countries." *Perspectives on Politics* 3 (3): 449–71.

King, Desmond. 1987. *The New Right: Politics, Markets and Citizenship*. Basingstoke: Palgrave-Macmillan.

Kitschelt, Herbert. 1997. *The Radical Right in Western Europe*. Ann Arbor: University of Michigan Press.

Krieger, Joel. 1986. *Reagan, Thatcher and the Politics of Decline*. New York: Oxford University Press.

Lamont, Michèle. 2000. *The Dignity of Working Men: Morality and the Boundaries of Race, Class and Immigration*. Cambridge, MA: Harvard University Press.

Lane, Robert E. 1972. *Political Man*. New York: Basic Books.

Leamer, Edward. 1996. "Wage Inequality from International Competition and Technological Change: Theory and Country Experience." *American Economic Review* 86 (2): 309–14.

Levey, Hilary. Forthcoming. "Raising Middle Class Children in the Competitive Culture of the United States: Parenting and Competitive Children's Activities." In *Dilemmas of the Middle Class Around the World*, edited by Katherine S. Newman.

Link, Bruce G. and Jo C. Phelan. 1995. "Social Conditions as Fundamental Causes of Disease." *Journal of Health and Social Behavior* 80–94.

Lipset, Seymour Martin. 1964. "The Changing Class Structure and Contemporary European Politics." *Daedalus* 93 (1): 271–303.

Lubbers, M. and P. Scheepers. 2000. "Individual and Contextual Characteristics of the German Extreme Right Vote in the 1990s." *European Journal of Political Research* 38 (1): 63–94.

Mayntz, Renate and Fritz Scharpf. 1987 "Politische Steuerung und gesellschaftliche Steuerungsprobleme. Anmerkungen zu einem theoretischen Paradigma." In *Jahrbuch zur Staats- und Verwaltungswissenschaft*, edited by T. Ellwein, J. J. Hesse, R. Mayntz, and F .W. Scharpf. Baden-Baden: Nomos: 89–110.

McGraw, Sean. Forthcoming. *Democracy's Choices: Irish Political Parties and the Constraining of the Political Arena*.

McNamara, Kathleen. 1998. *The Currency of Ideas*. Ithaca, NY: Cornell University Press.

Nussbaum, Martha. 2001. *Women and Human Development: The Capabilities Approach*. Cambridge, UK: Cambridge University Press.

Offe, Claus. 1983. "Competitive Party Democracy and the Keynesian Welfare State: Factors of Stability and Disorganization." *Policy Sciences* 15: 225–46.

OECD. 2008. *Growing Unequal? Income Distribution and Poverty in OECD Countries*. Paris: OECD.

Oswald, Andrew J. 1985. "The Economic Theory of Trade Unions." *Scandinavian Journal of Economics* 87(2): 160–93.

Pacek, Alexander and Benjamin Radcliff. 2008. "Assessing the Welfare State: The Politics of Happiness." *Perspectives on Politics* 6 (2): 267–77.

Pinto, Sanjay and Jason Beckfield. 2011. "Organized Labor in Europe 1960–2006: Common Decline, Continuing Differences." *Research in the Sociology of Work* 22: 153–79.

Polanyi, Karl. 1944. *The Great Transformation: Political and Economic Origins of Our Time*. Boston: Beacon Press.

Pontusson, Jonas. 2005. *Inequality and Prosperity: Social Europe versus Liberal America*. New York: Cornell University Press.

Pontusson, Jonas and David Rueda. 2009. "The Politics of Inequality: Voter Mobilization and Left Parties in Advanced Industrial States." *Comparative Political Studies* 43 (6): 675–705.

Prasad, Monica. 2006. *The Politics of Free Markets: The Rise of Neoliberal Economic Policies in Britain, France, Germany and the United States*. Chicago: University of Chicago Press.

Putnam, Robert. 2001. *Bowling Alone: The Collapse and Revival of American Community*. New York: Simon and Schuster.

Radcliff, Benjamin. 2005. "Class Organization and Subjective Well-Being: A Cross-National Analysis." *Social Forces* 84 (1): 513–30.

Rueda, David. 2007. *Social Democracy Inside Out: Government Partisanship, Insiders, and Outsiders in Industrialized Democracies*. Oxford: Oxford University Press.

Sampson, Robert J., Jeffrey D. Morenoff, and Thomas Gannon-Rowley. 2002. "Assessing Neighborhood Effects: Social Processes and New Directions in Research." *Annual Review of Sociology* 28: 443–78.

Sauder, Michael and Wendy Espeland. 2009. "The Discipline of Rankings: Tight Coupling and Organizational Change." *American Journal of Sociology* 74 (1): 63–82.

Scheepers, Peer, Manfred Te Grotenhuis, and John Gelissen. 2002. "Welfare States and Dimensions of Social Capital: Cross-National Comparisons of Social Contacts in European Countries." *European Societies* 4 (2): 185–207.

Schoon, Ingrid. 2006. *Risk and Resilience: Adaptations in Changing Times*. Cambridge, UK: Cambridge University Press.

Sen, Amartya. 1999. *Development as Freedom*. New York: Alfred A. Knopf.

Sennett, Richard. 2006. *The Culture of the New Capitalism*. New Haven, CT: Yale University Press.

Stevenson, Betsey and Justin Wolfers. 2009. "The Paradox of Declining Female Unhappiness." *American Economic Journal: Economic Policy* 1 (2): 190–225.

Stiglitz, Joseph P., Amartya Sen, and Jean-Paul Fitoussi. 2009. *Report of the Commission on the Measurement of Economic Performance and Social Progress*. Paris. http://www.stiglitz-sen-fitoussi.fr.

Streeck, Wolfgang. 2009. *Re-Forming Capitalism: Institutional Change in the German Political Economy*. Oxford: Oxford University Press.

Suh, Eunkook, Ed Diener, and Frank Fujita. 1996. "Events and Subjective Well-Being: Only Recent Events Matter." *Journal of Personality and Social Psychology* 70 (5): 1091–1102.

Swank, Duane. 2002. *Global Capital, Political Institutions and Policy Change in Developed Welfare States*. New York: Cambridge University Press.

Swank, Duane and Hans-Georg Betz. 2002. "Globalization, the Welfare State and Right-Wing Populism in Western Europe." *Socio-Economic Review* 1 (2): 215–45.

Tanzi, Vito. 2005. "The Economic Role of the State in the 21st Century." *Cato Journal* 25 (3): 617–38.

Taylor-Gooby, Peter, ed. 2004. *New Risks, New Welfare: The Transformation of the European Welfare State*. Oxford: Oxford University Press.

Ungar, Michael. 2008. "Resilience across Cultures." *British Journal of Social Work* 38: 218–35.

Van der Brug, Wouter, Meindert Fennema, and Jean Tille. 2005. "Why Some Anti-Immigrant Parties Fail and Others Succeed: A Two-Step Model of Aggregate Electoral Support." *Comparative Political Studies* 38 (5): 537–73.

Veenhoven, Ruut. 1996. "Developments in Satisfaction Research." *Social Indicators Research* 37: 1–46.

Vogel, Steven. K. 1998. *Freer Markets, More Rules: Regulatory Reform in Advanced Industrial Welfare States.* Ithaca, NY: Cornell University Press.

Wedel, Janine. 1986. *The Private Poland: An Anthropologist's Look at Everyday Life.* Oxford: Facts on File Publications.

Wood, Adrian. 1994. *North-South Trade, Employment and Inequality: Changing Fortunes in a Skill-Driven World.* Oxford: Oxford University Press.

Wood, Stewart. 2001. "Employer Preferences, State Power and Labor Market Policy and Germany and Britain." In *Varieties of Capitalism*, edited by Peter A. Hall and David Soskice. Oxford: Oxford University Press.

8

National Differences in Population Health and Development

Daniel Keating, Arjumand Siddiqi, and Quynh Nguyen

Evaluating Social Resilience: Population Health and Development Outcomes

As Evans and Sewell argued in Chapter 1, the period from around 1980 forward can be described as a "neoliberal era" during which a set of economic and political forces, underpinned by a relatively clear ideological perspective, revamped the post–World War II consensus that had coalesced around modest levels of state intervention. Although there are other aspects of a more general trend toward globalization before and during this neoliberal turn, it is fair to note that the impact on social organization and action of neoliberalism was profound. Evans and Sewell identify central features linked to this shift, including a turn toward economic and social policies that focused more on private and market-driven rather than collective or state-driven solutions to social challenges, on deregulation of market forces, and on individual responsibility rather than shared risk and public protection against negative economic events. In some countries, these policies were aligned with an explicit ideological movement that strongly affected the social imaginary – Margaret Thatcher's claim that "there is no such thing as society" comes immediately to mind – but in others the shifts were a pragmatic response to real or perceived mandates from external powerful actors, often characterized as global market forces.

A key question animating this volume is how effectively different societies responded to this set of challenges. The core construct is the notion of resilience, which draws attention to differences across societies in the quality and effectiveness of how they dealt with the neoliberal challenge. This chapter looks at important outcomes in population health and development and then examines whether such differences in population outcomes can be systematically linked to identifiable aspects of different societal responses.

The chapter is organized into the following sections: (a) theoretical and methodological considerations that frame the analytic model; (b) multiple

country comparisons of population developmental health (PDH[1]), characteristics of those PDH outcomes and their relation to a number of potentially
important features of social resilience; and (c) a case comparison of two similar
countries, the United States and Canada, to examine societal mechanisms that
characterized their responses to neoliberal challenges and the PDH outcomes
related to those responses.

Considerations in Assessing Population Health and Development

We have argued previously that maintaining and enhancing PDH is one important aspect of successful societies (Keating 2009). This may be especially relevant during periods of societal transition, which can elevate PDH risks. Ideally,
we would like to know whether societal changes are affecting PDH in real time
or as close to that as possible so that such information can enter into policy considerations. In addition to overall PDH and temporal changes in it, we
argue that it is essential to attend to the *inequality of outcomes*. Specific vulnerabilities to negative effects of neoliberal reforms are likely to be differentially
distributed across the population, and thus an examination of the average levels of PDH will not capture the full picture. Increases in inequality in PDH
outcomes may have deleterious effects on social participation and cohesion,
as well as on the aggregate population challenges and opportunities offered
by a society. Second, we argue that a focus on critical or sensitive periods of
human development is a particularly salient aspect of differences in vulnerability across populations because of the well-documented long-term effects arising
from difficulties early in development (Keating and Hertzman 1999; Boyce and
Keating 2004; Keating 2009, 2011a, 2011b).

To explore these issues empirically, we used two complementary methodologies – multiple country comparisons of PDH differences – in relation to factors
that have been proposed as sources of societal resilience that may account for
such differences and a more focused case comparison between the United States
and Canada that holds constant a number of potential factors so as to allow a
deeper probe into the relations among various features of societal resilience.

Ideally, such an analysis would include three key elements. First, a relevant
set of national-level indicators would be assembled, including (a) average health
and development, (b) the social gradient across the full population on these
indicators, and (c) specific analyses of subgroups that may be particularly
vulnerable. Second, the measurable characteristics of societal level mechanisms
would then be investigated to evaluate their potential as candidate mechanisms
for these PDH outcome measures. Third, the relationship between *changes* in
outcomes and *changes* in candidate social mechanisms should be examined to

---

[1] In this chapter, we use the construct of PDH based on prior work identifying potentially important common pathways to a wide range of outcomes, including physical health, mental health,
social competence, and cognitive and academic performance (Keating and Hertzman 1999;
Keating 2009, 2011b).

explore social resilience, which focuses on how effectively different societies have responded to the neoliberal challenge.

It is increasingly recognized that the availability of appropriate metrics to capture all these dimensions systematically is limited but improving: "It has long been clear that GDP [gross domestic product] is an inadequate metric to gauge well-being over time, particularly in its economic, environmental, and social dimensions" (Stiglitz, Sen, and Fitoussi 2009: 8). In both of the empirical approaches described in this chapter – multi-country comparisons and a two-country case study – we acknowledge these limitations. We selected indicators and databases that, in aggregate, could address the three key elements noted and suggest that these analyses illustrate the potential for more systematic studies of social resilience, whose full realization depends on progress on several fronts.

International Comparisons of Population Health and Development

There are numerous possibilities for exploring social resilience among multiple countries using the analytic model described earlier. We focus on several indicators of adolescent health and development in the developed countries described as being at the "flat end of the health-wealth curve," where overall national wealth bears little or no relationship to average health (Hertzman 1999). In those societies, socioeconomic, psychosocial, and human development factors become more prominent in accounting for differences in PDH. The focus on adolescent outcomes was guided by several considerations, including the availability of high quality databases on adolescent health (Health Behavior of School Age Children [HBSC]) and educational achievement (Programme for International Student Assessment [PISA]) that featured data collection on a repeating schedule along with information about participants' families, allowing for the estimation of social gradients.

In addition, there is a strong substantive reason for this focus. Adolescence is a critically important period of development and is potentially reflective of key features of social resilience because factors with wider social import may have an earlier and more readily detectable effect on adolescents (often described as the "canary in the mine"). Similar to early childhood (Keating 2011b), adolescence is a period during which there is increased sensitivity to experience-dependent influences that operate both behaviorally and through biological embedding (Casey and Jones 2010). Adolescent outcomes thus reflect both cumulative and contemporaneous effects of developmental histories. In addition, the life course consequences of differential experiences during adolescence are substantial in a number of critical domains of health and development.

Averages and Inequalities: Longitudinal and Within- and Between-Domain Relationships

We first examined the relationship among mean performance on the key indicators as well as inequalities in them. We selected the set of OECD countries

($n = 21$) for which the following data were available: PISA in 2000, PISA in 2009, and HBSC in 2005. We selected these two PISA administrations because their primary focus was the same, namely on reading literacy among representative samples of 15-year-old adolescents from each country. This created the opportunity to look at country-level changes in the same domain over time, for two cohorts: one born in 1985 in the earlier phase of the neoliberal era and a second born in 1994 after neoliberal reforms had become more firmly established in many of these countries. The HBSC 2005 administration was selected because an independent estimate of inequality in self-reported health symptoms among representative samples of 11- to 15-year-olds in the target countries was also available for this cycle of the HBSC (United Nations Children's Fund [UNICEF] 2010).[2]

Country means for the HBSC are available in a separate report (Currie et al. 2008). Country means for PISA are also directly reported. Using PISA data from 2000 and 2009, we computed a relative index of inequality (RII) for each country using parental education as the measure of socioeconomic status. The RII represents that country's level of socioeconomically-based inequities in literacy and is in effect a social gradient adjusted for differences in the proportion of individuals at different levels of education in different countries.

In addition, a composite measure of inequality among adolescents was computed by the Innocenti Research Centre (UNICEF, 2010) using three indicators from each of three domains, material inequality (income inequality, educational resources, living space); educational inequality (reading, math, and science, from PISA data); and health inequality (self-reported health symptoms, physical activity, and nutrition). This omnibus measure of inequality across domains is included in these analyses. Note, however, that the measures of inequality in the Innocenti report (used here for both the composite measure of inequality and for the HBSC inequality measure) are univariate rather than bivariate. They capture differences in "how far behind are children being allowed to fall?" (UNICEF 2010: 8), estimating the distance from children in the bottom decile (10 percent) to children at the median in each country. They do not capture the social gradient of that inequality as would a regression against household income, parental education, or other aspects of socioeconomic position. Univariate estimates capture the degree of absolute inequality; bivariate estimates capture the social gradient of inequality in relation to socioeconomic status. In practice, they are somewhat interdependent: countries with shallow gradients on a given dimension are unlikely to have high levels of absolute inequality and vice versa.[3]

---

[2] PISA data are publicly released for analyses soon after completion of each cycle. HBSC reserves access to its data for the principal use of HBSC investigators in participating countries. This restricted access makes it more difficult to readily carry out comparative analyses.

[3] They are mathematically independent except at the extreme low end of absolute inequality, in which case there is no variance to be captured in a bivariate correlation or regression.

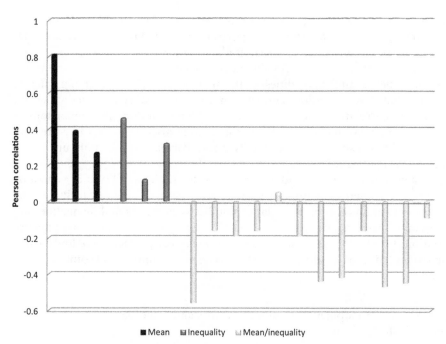

FIGURE 8-1. Correlations among national means and inequality measures for adolescent achievement and health.

In the first set of analyses, we asked several related questions. Is *average performance* on different indicators of PDH among adolescents correlated across domains (health and educational achievement) and across time (educational achievement in 2000 and 2009)? Are within-country *inequalities* in these indicators correlated across domain and across time? Finally, is average performance associated with inequalities across domains and across time? This last question arises from observations in both the developmental health literature (Keating 2009) and the adult health literature (Wilkinson and Pickett 2009) that countries with steeper social gradients tend also to have lower mean performance. This observation suggests that large outcome inequalities may be a population characteristic that reduces average population outcomes.

The results of these analyses are shown in Figure 8-1 as a chart of the relevant bivariate correlations (Pearson r's). The first three columns show the correlations among means, the next three correlations among inequality measures, and the remainder the correlations between means and inequalities on both health and achievement. The overall pattern is quite consistent.

Across these 21 countries, average health and average educational achievement (at two time points) show a positive relationship, including a quite substantial one $(r = .82; p < .01)$[4] between average scores on PISA reading literacy in 2000 and 2009. The portrait of inequality is similar: countries tend to have shallow or steep social gradients consistently across domains and time. Finally, there was a surprising degree of consistency in the relationships between means and inequalities in the predicted direction that high means are associated with shallow gradients and low inequality and vice versa. Of the twelve correlations including within- and between-domain comparisons as well as contemporaneous and longitudinal comparisons, all but one are negative (and that exception is essentially a zero correlation); half are at or near statistical significance.[5]

Taken together, these findings show considerable stability and generalizability in national indicators of average levels and inequalities in PDH. The cross-domain findings on the relationship between means and inequalities are especially intriguing, suggesting a general tendency toward a consistent inverse relationship (shallow gradients and high means, steep gradients and low means) across both time and indicators, perhaps reflecting country-level common pathways.

Population Developmental Health Indicators and Candidate Societal Mechanisms

The next step in the analysis is to examine how these population characteristics for adolescents in OECD countries are related to candidate mechanisms at the societal level. In the first set of analyses, three types of candidate mechanisms were included: (a) average wealth, measured as gross domestic product per capita, adjusted for purchasing power parity (GDP/PPP)[6]; (b) income inequality, measured as the Gini coefficient[7]; and (c) human development investment, measured here as total spending on education as a percentage of GDP. These are intended to capture key mechanisms that have been proposed to account for differences in population health and development: richer countries will outperform poorer ones (unlikely in this case because these are OECD countries residing at the "flat end of the health–wealth curve"), countries that have more equitable material distributions will perform better in other ways, and countries that invest more in human development will perform better as a result of that investment. We included estimates of each of these indicators from two time points: 1980, or the earliest available data, to capture information from the earlier period near the onset of the neoliberal era, and 2009, or the most recent available data, to capture information after neoliberal reforms were presumably

---

[4] r is the Pearson bivariate correlation between country scores on PISA or HBSC; p is the probability value of obtaining that relationship by chance at the specified level.

[5] The significance cutoff was set at $p < .10$, recognizing that statistical power is low, in that the number of countries, is highly constrained by data availability.

[6] All data for these analyses are drawn from the relevant OECD databases.

[7] A scale that runs from 0 to 1, with higher values indicating greater inequality in income.

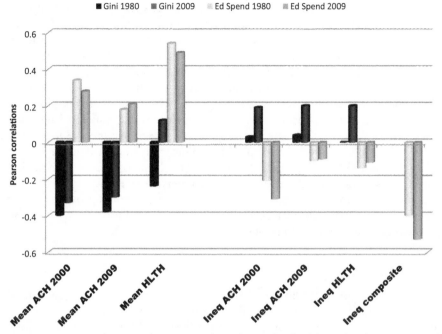

FIGURE 8-2. Correlations of means and gradients for health and achievement with income inequality and education spending.

more entrenched.[8] This also affords the possibility of looking at change over time, to which we turn in the section to follow.

The results showed, as expected, that GDP/PPP was unrelated to any of the PDH outcomes in either average performance or inequalities, and thus it was not included in subsequent analyses. The results for income inequality (Gini) and education spending are shown in Figure 8-2. The first set of results shows the association of mean health and achievement with the Gini coefficient and education spending, and the set to the right shows the associations between the latter and inequalities in health and achievement. The overall pattern is as predicted: higher levels of income inequality are associated with lower mean performance and greater inequality of outcomes. The pattern for education spending is precisely the reverse: higher education spending is associated with higher mean performance and lower inequality of outcomes. For the inequality composite (UNICEF 2010), the results show a strong and significant inverse relationship with education spending: countries with higher investment in education have significantly lower levels of inequality in PDH.[9]

---

[8] All analyses were first evaluated to ascertain whether the year from which data were drawn was associated with an outcome; no significant correlations emerged; thus, year of data collection was not examined further.

[9] The composite could not be tested against the Gini coefficient because it includes an income inequality measure, thus leading to a confounded correlation.

The pattern that emerges from these analyses is strikingly consistent and, given the data limitations, moderate to strong in magnitude. Better PDH outcomes at the country level, with respect both to mean levels and inequalities in those outcomes, are substantially related to each other, such that better mean outcomes are consistent across domain and time, as are country level social gradients. Moreover, there is substantial evidence that better mean outcomes are associated with shallower social gradients within and between domains as well as across time. In turn, these PDH outcomes are associated with the candidate societal mechanisms in the predicted directions: income inequality is associated negatively with mean performance – a finding consistent with other research (Viner et al. 2012) – and positively with outcome inequality, but higher spending on education shows the reverse pattern. The cross-domain generalizability and longitudinal consistency of these patterns provide support for a view that social characteristics at the country level give rise to common pathways, leading in turn to population outcomes.

Social Resilience

The preceding analyses, however, do not speak directly to the question of resilience, which by definition implies a consideration of change over time – in this case, over a period during which neoliberal reforms were being implemented, albeit differently in different countries. To explore resilience directly, we looked at changes in PDH outcomes associated with changes in candidate societal mechanisms. It should be noted that such analyses of change are constrained by how much change exists. As noted earlier, reading literacy mean scores from PISA 2000 to PISA 2009 were highly correlated ($r = .82$, accounting for 67 percent, or two-thirds, of shared variance). Similarly, PISA inequality (measured as RII) was significantly correlated at the two time points ($r = .46$, accounting for 21 percent of shared variance). This is also true of the candidate societal mechanisms: the correlation across the two points in time for the Gini coefficients was $r = .82$ and for education spending was $r = .43$. Thus, associations of changes in population outcomes with changes in societal mechanisms can be tested only in the context of substantial longitudinal consistency in both.

To deal with the issue of low statistical power, arising from longitudinal consistency and small sample sizes because countries are the units of analysis, we developed a proxy measure of social resilience. Change scores in the Gini coefficient (from 1980 to 2009, or their nearest approximations) were standardized, and countries were given a 0 if above the median (i.e., the change in income inequality was comparatively higher) and 1 if below the median (i.e., the change in income inequality was comparatively lower). A similar operation was applied to education spending as a percent of GDP except that a score of 0 showed lower increases (or actual decreases) in education spending and a score of 1 showed larger increases. We added a third candidate mechanism for which a change score was not available but that we regard as theoretically compelling:

a coordination index, indicating the degree of market coordination in a country, derived from a principal component analysis across a number of indicators for both corporate governance and labor relations (Hall and Gingerich 2009). From a "varieties of capitalism" perspective, the index distinguishes between more coordinated market economies (CMEs) and less coordinated liberal market economies (LMEs). Using that index, countries below the median were assigned a 0, and those above the median were assigned a 1. This component taps institutional characteristics that may be relevant to the coordination of responses to the neoliberal challenge. As Hall and Gingerich (2009) observe, "While LMEs sharpened market mechanisms, many CMEs cushioned their citizens against the effects of market adjustment with increases in benefit entitlements" (478–9). Although a time-variant coordination index was not available, it is worth noting that the relative differences across time in the underlying components of this index, where these were available, for LMEs versus CMEs remained quite stable (Hall and Gingerich 2009).

We combined information across these three median splits into a resilience index, such that countries with a total score of three were above the median on decreases in income inequality, increases in education spending, and closer to the CME pole of the coordination index; countries with a total of zero were at the opposite end of the three median splits. For simplicity and to enhance the power of the contrast, we grouped countries with a two or three together ($n = 12$) and those with a zero or one together ($n = 7$).[10] We then calculated standardized scores on the PISA 2000 and PISA 2009 for both means and inequalities (i.e., the RII), and the change in both indicators from 2000 to 2009 was then calculated and standardized.

The results showed that countries which were low on the resilience index had significantly greater decreases in average PISA scores from 2000 to 2009 compared with countries higher on that index ($t_{17} = 2.21; p < .05$). Differences in the PISA gradient from 2000 and 2009 were unrelated to the resilience index ($t_{17} = 0.76$, NS). In Table 8-1, we show the twelve countries at the high end and seven countries at the low end of the resilience index. It is interesting to note that all but one of the low resilience countries is of Anglo-Saxon heritage or has a U.K. colonial history. Although somewhat speculative given the limitations of the current analyses, this observation points to the possibility that there may be some longer term path dependence operating here (Pierson 2000), such that certain kinds of institutional arrangements intertwined with cultural predispositions and social imaginaries yield unexpected consistencies of response when countries confront challenges such as those of the neoliberal era. This parallels a pattern noted some time ago by Urie Bronfenbrenner (1992), who observed a distinctive style of "child care in the Anglo-Saxon mode."

To test whether these findings generalize beyond changes in educational achievement, we also included a measure of adolescents' participation in society: the proportion of individuals from age fifteen to nineteen years actively

[10] Introducing the coordination index reduced our overall *n* from 21 to 19.

TABLE 8-1. *Countries High and Low on the Resilience Index*

High Resilience	Low Resilience
Austria	Australia
Belgium	Canada
Denmark	Ireland
Finland	Netherlands
France	New Zealand
Germany	United Kingdom
Italy	United States
Norway	
Portugal	
Sweden	
Spain	
Switzerland	

attending school or working. This indicator was derived from the OECD (2008: 14), which provided average annual growth rates for activity and inactivity from 1995 (or earliest year available) to 2004.[11] This trend line was divided into quartiles, moving from the greatest decreases in adolescent inactivity to the greatest increases. The correlation between this measure of change and the Resilience Index was +.35 ($p < .10$).

Interestingly, these changes in adolescent activity and inactivity were substantially correlated with the changes in PISA mean scores ($r = .50$; $p < .02$). To enhance the comprehensive nature of a change index in adolescent PDH, we performed a principal component factor analysis of the three measures of outcome changes (PISA means, PISA RIIs, and activity or inactivity).[12] This yielded one factor with an eigenvalue greater than one; on that factor, PISA mean change and increase in school or work activity had strong positive loadings, and PISA inequality change had a weak negative loading. As predicted, standardized factor scores derived from this analysis were significantly correlated with the resilience index ($r = .39$; $p < .10$). Taken together, the evidence that changes in societal mechanisms and in PDH are correlated is substantial, reflecting significant consistencies at the country level across outcomes and time.

This is not to say that countries at the high or low end of our resilience index are identical to each other. One complementary method for delving more deeply into the sources of social resilience is to compare how otherwise similar countries responded to the neoliberal challenge. In the next section, we report such a case study of the United States and Canada, countries that are similar

[11] This, however, reduced the country sample size to fifteen, further reducing statistical power. Statistical significance was accordingly assessed with one-tailed tests.

[12] This is below the recommended rule of thumb to have at least ten cases per variable in a principal component analysis, but we proceeded because of the illustrative goals of these analyses.

in many ways beyond their location on our resilience index. Any connections found between differences in outcomes in these otherwise similar countries and differences in the social mechanisms that might explain them are likely to be informative about the nature of social resilience at a more fine-grained level of analysis.

A Case-Based Analysis of Population Developmental Health: The United States versus Canada

In this section, we adopt a two-country comparative case study approach to understanding social resilience in terms of PDH, building on the multi-country analysis we have just described. We examine the United States and Canada to provide a closer examination of the candidate societal mechanisms that appear to be linked to greater resilience. We explore how resilience may result from the blocking or muting of pathways leading from neoliberal reforms to worse PDH outcomes. Prior research emphasizes that these pathways function in a manner that compromises the ability of individuals and families (particularly at the lower end of the socioeconomic spectrum) to acquire the goods and services required for health and development (e.g., health care, education, safe living conditions). Neoliberalism does so by (a) reducing their capacity to purchase these resources privately and (b) creating policies that link the availability of these resources to individual or family socioeconomic position rather than providing them as a right of citizenship (see Chapter 2).

From this perspective, a comparison of the United States and Canada affords a particularly instructive case study. Institutional typologies often group these countries together, and the empirical data from our multi-country comparison supports this generic typology. Indeed, both countries were on the low end of the resilience index. However, as we will see, the United States and Canada exhibited substantial differences in average levels and inequalities in PDH outcomes during the neoliberal era. We argue that the institutions of these societies also displayed marked differences – in sociocultural, market, and governmental domains – which may be sources of resilience in PDH outcomes in Canada relative to the United States during the period of neoliberalism.

We begin our analysis during the 1980s – the decade during which neoliberalism in many of its forms began to secure strong footholds in the global economic, political, and social consciousness – and we examine the subsequent three decades. We note that neoliberalism became a strong current in policymaking more than a decade later in Canada than in the United States. In Canada, neoliberalism penetrated the policy sphere more tepidly than in the United States, and it did not have nearly as much influence over the nation's social imaginary. We argue that Canada secured greater resilience in at least three ways: (a) by avoiding a socially divisive rhetoric that named the "welfare class" as the source of the country's economic distress and enacting policies that encouraged greater social integration of ethnic minorities and social cohesion among Canadian citizens; (b) by maintaining lower levels of income inequality;

and (c) by building on its legacy of greater universality to ensure that access to public goods such as health care, education, and quality living conditions was not marketized. In the United States, by contrast, (a) the divisive ideological aspects of neoliberalism were more deeply embedded, in large part because of their consonance with ideologies of racism, individualism and competition of long historical standing; (b) income inequality rose at a more rapid rate over this period; and (c) the privatization and marketization of public goods was widespread and intense. We argue that these factors meant that few features of American society offered refuge from neoliberalism in all its forms.

Capturing all the relevant factors that may condition resilience is not easy. We argue that there are multiple sources of societal resilience, including cultural assumptions that render social divisions more or less likely to be salient to people, longer term policies that mitigate or exacerbate increases in the distribution of income or wealth, and aspects of the collective imaginary that characterize social safety net policies as charitable contributions rather than citizenship rights. In this sense, for resilience, societies draw on longstanding sets of cultural factors and institutional arrangements that are intertwined. From this perspective, the delay before neoliberal reforms were adopted in Canada may in itself be viewed as a form of "resistance" to external pressures and thus as an indirect indicator of resilience. Cross-national differences in these sources of resilience offer an explanation for the better PDH outcomes in Canada during a period in which both nations undertook substantial neoliberal reforms. In the section that follows, we describe the unfolding of these processes. We start by establishing the basis for comparison between these two societies.

The United States and Canada: Societal Similarities

In his institutional comparison of the United States and Canada, Lipset noted that " . . . overall these two people probably resemble each other more than any other two nations on earth . . . [yet] there are consistent patterns of difference [between] them. . . . " (Lipset 1986). Their many similarities make them potentially strong sources for counterfactuals in causal terms. Both are amongst the world's wealthiest nations, with GDP rankings of fourth (the United States) and twelfth (Canada). Both nations have economies with a free-market orientation and have undergone similar economic transformations over time, and both now have economies dominated by the service sector. Both countries are liberal market economies in which the role of the market figures prominently in resource allocation (Hall and Gingerich 2009). Although their political systems are somewhat dissimilar, both are longstanding democracies.

Moreover, among their peer nations, the United States and Canada both have a long tradition of accommodating large and diverse immigrant populations. Documented immigrants comprise 12 percent of the population in the United States and 20 percent of the population in Canada. Immigration laws and reforms have been similar over time in both countries. Both also exhibit high levels of racial and ethnic diversity. The 2006 Canadian Census suggests

16.2 percent of the population consider themselves to be a member of a visible minority; 22.9 percent of people in the United States reported being in a category other than white in the 2000 Census (Siddiqi, Zuberi, and Nguyen 2009; Siddiqi and Nguyen 2010).

The unfolding of neoliberalism in the United States and Canada was by no means identical, and that will be addressed later. For the moment, however, the question is whether there were sufficient similarities in their experience of neoliberalism to provide a useful comparison. We argue that there were. The effects of neoliberalism on policies affecting workers during this period appear most similar in these two nations. The pro-market, anti-entitlement features of neoliberal policies and their American expression have been described by Evans and Sewell (see Chapter 1). The legislation that perhaps best typifies American neoliberalism is the 1996 Personal Responsibility and Work Opportunities Reconciliation Act (PRWORA). This law ratcheted down the benefits the government provided to unemployed individuals and ratcheted up their dependence on the labor market. Hallmark elements of the reforms included the introduction of ongoing work requirements for receipt of benefits, a five-year limit on those benefits, and the devolution of funding and authority over the program to the state level.

Canada entered its neoliberal period, slightly after the United States, in 1984. From this point forward, there were increasing changes to social legislation in Canada that began to mirror those in its southern neighbor. By the mid 1990s, in the name of deficit reduction, Canada's governing Liberal party had implemented massive cuts to welfare benefits for most single workers and frozen benefits for most others. Similar to the United States, Canada reduced federal transfer payments for social programs to its provinces (by a hefty 14 percent) (Mauldin 2010) and decentralized decision making regarding these programs (Jackson 2010). Before asking whether there were meaningful differences in the societal responses to neoliberalism, we first consider whether there were differences in the ultimate outcomes in PDH.

The United States and Canada: Population Health and Development Differences

Despite notable similarities in the characteristics and implementation of neoliberal policies in the United States and Canada, the health and developmental status of their populations displayed significant differences. Because it is administratively collected at the national level, life expectancy and the related measure of mortality rates constitute the most complete data we have available for detailed tracking of changes (Fig. 8-3). The overall pattern suggests that Canada opened up and sustained approximately a two-year advantage in life expectancy over the United States during this period. This gap in both female and male life expectancies was principally driven by differences in adult mortality; a two-year gap in life expectancy corresponds to a 30 to 50 percent higher rate of death for any given age group in the United States than in

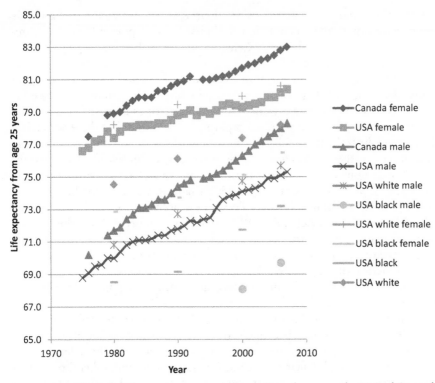

FIGURE 8-3. Changes in longevity, 1975 to 2009, Canada versus the United States by gender and race.

Canada (Siddiqi and Hertzman 2007). Beginning in the 1980s, Canada held an approximately 1.5-year advantage in life expectancy. By the 1990s, this gap had grown to approximately two years, and, during the 2000s, it continued to widen, such that for the last years of available data, the gap was 2.6 years for women. These gaps in life expectancy were a result of relatively larger and steadier increases in Canada compared with smaller increases and more fluctuations in the United States.

A significant part of the explanation for higher average levels of health in Canada seems to be connected to lower levels of social and economic inequalities in health status. Although neither country systematically monitors national health inequalities, studies using nationally representative samples from the 1990s and early 2000s demonstrate that although the United States showed significant health disparities based on race (Siddiqi and Nguyen 2010), immigrant status (Siddiqi et al. 2009), and social class (Eng and Feeny 2007), these disparities were comparatively muted or absent in Canada. Despite the dearth of population-based social inequality data, we have life expectancy statistics by race in the United States (see Fig. 8-3), and these statistics demonstrate striking disparities. The black–white male life expectancy gap in the United States is particularly stark: in 1980, the racial gap was 6.7 years (white male life expectancy of 70.8 years versus black male life expectancy of 64.1). By 1990, this gap had increased to more than eight years. In 2000, the gap declined to 1980 levels, and by 2006 it was, at six years, still very large. Although no directly comparable Canadian trend data are available, analysis of a 2003 to 2004 nationally representative survey shows far fewer disparities between whites and non-whites in Canada than the United States (Siddiqi and Nguyen 2010).

Barnes and Hall (see Chapter 7) find that although there was inequality in self-reported well-being between the upper middle class and the lower middle class in almost all OECD nations, its magnitude was far greater in the United States, which ranked sixteenth of eighteenth countries in level of inequality; Canada ranked ninth. Even within racial and socioeconomic groups, the health of Canadians was better than in the United States. Based on survey data from the 1990s and early 2000s, compared with Canadian whites, whites in the United States demonstrated significantly worse outcomes (Siddiqi and Nguyen 2010), and the health of the poorest 20 percent of Canadians was comparable to that of Americans at average income levels (Singh and Siahpush 2001).

As we have noted, many PDH outcomes are not well monitored at the national level. During the 1990s and in 2000, however, there have been international assessments of adolescent and adult literacy. In 1999, eighth graders in the United States placed eighteenth in science literacy and nineteenth in mathematics literacy; in Canada, they placed fourteenth and tenth, respectively (Mullis et al. 2004). In 2000, a survey of reading literacy among 15-year-olds ranked Canada sixth and the United States eleventh (Siddiqi et al. 2007). As with health outcomes, evidence is emerging that lower average performance is, in part, a function of higher social and economic inequalities (Siddiqi et al. 2007; UNICEF 2010), a pattern confirmed in these analyses.

What Explains Differential Outcomes Despite Social Similarities?

Our analysis suggests that the United States and Canada are comparable societies that underwent a period of similar neoliberal policy reforms during the past three decades but experienced divergent trends in population health and development, with Canada faring better on a variety of PDH metrics, including on inequalities of PDH. This raises the question: how was Canada able to better maintain the well-being of its citizenry amid neoliberal reforms? What factors made Canadian society more resilient in terms of PDH outcomes than American society during the neoliberal era?

Our analysis of the sources of resilience focuses on the potential means through which Canada was more successful than the United States at providing health-related resources for its citizenry, particularly for the most disadvantaged members of society. We suggest, first, that neoliberalism appeared earlier and had a greater influence over American than Canadian society in large part because of differences in the socio-historical contexts of these two nations. The result was a shorter and weaker brand of neoliberalism in Canada. We then demonstrate that as neoliberal policies took hold, Canadian institutions made health resources more available by maintaining lower levels of income inequality and by sustaining investment in policies that provided these resources as a right of citizenship.

In essence, we attempt to show in the following sections that Canada resisted the neoliberal trend longer, implemented neoliberal reforms less forcefully, adopted them with fewer pejorative allusions to the personal attributes of those less favored by market outcomes (hence placing social cohesion at less risk), and could rely on more social reserves in the form of policies such as universal health insurance. We argue that these societal mechanisms – based on resistance, lower social divisiveness, and greater institutional reserves – conferred on Canada a greater social resilience.

Social Cleavages and the Manifestation of Neoliberalism

In this section, we discuss the factors – which we view as sources of resilience – that may have delayed the onset and reduced the intensity of neoliberalism in Canada compared with the United States. We hypothesize that the socio-historical context of class- and race-based fissures primed American society to embrace neoliberalism both as an ideology and as a set of social policies to a greater extent than corresponding conditions did in Canada.

In Canadian discourse, support for neoliberalism seemed to turn far less on a rhetoric of individual responsibility. Neoliberal policies seem to have been enacted in Canada during the 1990s primarily as a pragmatic response to deficits (Fourcade-Gourinchas and Babb 2002), and they occurred within the context of a collective imaginary that continued to attach value to social policy seen as a right of citizenship and to ideals of egalitarianism and universality (Jenson and Saint-Martin 2003). On this dimension, Lipset (1990) underlines the contrast with the United States, writing that " . . . the American social structure and values foster an emphasis on competitive individualism, an orientation that is not congruent with class consciousness, support for socialist or social democratic parties. . . . " Thus, in the United States, neoliberal policies appeared against a historical, cultural, and political backdrop that positioned the society to accept legislation eroding this kind of "basic guarantee" (Myles and Pierson 1997) and embedded neoliberalism more deeply into the economic ideology and collective imaginary of the nation.

Lamont and colleagues (see Chapter 4) describe how the notions of self-reliance and competitiveness are deeply embedded even in the repertoires of African Americans, a population that has undergone institutional disadvantage throughout their history in the United States. They suggest that " . . . these responses [to discrimination] exist independently of neoliberalism as they are central to the American creed. . . . " This context helps to explain why the United States was blanketed with an anti-statist, pro-privatization rhetoric during the Reagan era much more forceful than the rhetoric of the contemporaneous Mulroney regime in Canada (see Jenson and Levi, Chapter 2).

In both the United States and Canada, ethnic and racial diversity has been an integral axis along which to understand social cohesion and its intersection with economic inequality. Indeed, in the United States, much of the opposition to the notion of a basic guarantee of social rights stems from the racial antagonism that remains a central organizing feature of society (Myles and Pierson 1997). The salience of this antagonism was epitomized in the imagery evoked early by Reagan and disseminated widely by the media of a mythical "welfare queen" living undeservedly off the largesse of society – and not coincidentally an African American mother (Hancock 2004). Bloemraad (2007) describes the United States as having a "laissez-faire" approach to civic citizenship in which race, ethnicity and other sociocultural aspects of identity are "... legitimate terms of debate in public fora...." Groups are free to use their own resources for such purposes, but public investment in the promotion and maintenance of cultural expressions is largely absent.

By contrast, in Canada, during this time of economic austerity, "... there is little evidence of attempts to exclude minorities from social programs... and welfare recipients and the poor more generally are not socially distinctive in Canada: they do not stand out in linguistic, ethnic, or racial terms" (Banting and Kymlicka 2003). This is reflected in the modest to strong support (55 to 70 percent), for multicultural policies in Canada (Banting and Kymlicka 2003). The multicultural policies established there in the 1980s "... [were meant] to strengthen equality rights in the Canadian Charter, to strengthen hate-speech laws, to strengthen employment equity legislation... to lobby for historical redress agreements...." and to give "... civic voice for historically excluded and oppressed people... [and buttress] their claims for inclusion and respect...." (see Kymlicka, Chapter 3). Canada's approach to civic citizenship, known as "multiculturalism," charges the government and broader society to "... actively recognize cultural diversity and make accommodations for the needs of cultural minorities...." These accommodations are not seen as special privileges but factors "... facilitating the survival and vitality of cultural communities is a matter of fairness, justice, and equality...."

The relative absence of neoliberal ideology in the national Canadian social imaginary was paralleled at the regional and local levels. As Bouchard describes in Chapter 9, in Québec, there was strong adherence to the values of "... equality, solidarity, deliberative democracy, and the quality of life...." Though these were under some attacks during the neoliberal era... [the majority of Quebecers] flatly rejects neo-liberalism and supports the 'Quebec model,' particularly state intervention, egalitarianism, networking, and social participation.... Social-democracy is deeply rooted in Quebec psyche...." By contrast, in the United States, the neoliberal rhetoric at the national level was mirrored by declines in social trust and civic engagement in communities (Putnam 2000) and in lack of public support for social welfare programs, as the latter became associated with racial divisions, particularly between whites and African Americans (Gilens 1999).

These cross-national differences in the social imaginary affected the severity and support for neoliberal policies in these two countries. Nevertheless, as we have noted, Canadian policy also moved in neoliberal directions during the 1990s, which raises the question: given those neoliberal reforms, how did Canada manage to maintain its PDH while the United States did not in the context of parallel reforms? We will argue that in Canada, a smaller increase in income inequality and the less emphasis on marketization and privatization of health resources protected the PDH of Canadians.

Income Inequality

Both the United States and Canada saw an overall increase in income inequality during the neoliberal period. However, there were several differences in their experience. We focus on data for the working-age population (18–65 years), whose health was most affected during this time (Siddiqi and Hertzman 2007). First, the United States began the era with a higher level of inequality (1980 posttax, posttransfer Gini coefficient for the United States = 0.33; for Canada = 0.29). Over the subsequent three decades, the United States income gap rose slowly and steadily, reaching a Gini coefficient of 0.37 by the mid 2000s. By contrast, Canada was able to maintain the existing level of inequality until 2000, when its Gini coefficient jumped to 0.33, the approximate level also recorded in the mid 2000s (OECD 2011).

Second, there was a stark difference in the extent to which the two nations used tax and transfer policies to redistribute market-based income, a phenomenon that can be observed by comparing pre- and posttax and transfer measures of income inequality. In the United States, the decline in the Gini coefficient after taxes and transfers was 0.05 in the mid 1980s and in 1990, 0.07 in the mid 1990s and in 2000, and 0.06 in the mid 2000s. By contrast, Canadian tax and transfer policy redistributed income to a much greater extent, especially before 2000. In the mid 1980s and 1990, the decline in the Gini coefficient after taxes and transfers were applied was 0.08, 0.11 in the mid 1990s; and 0.09 in 2000 and the mid 2000s (OECD 2011).

In sum, the ability of individuals, particularly those at the lower end of the socioeconomic spectrum, to purchase health-related resources through market mechanisms, including health care, education, quality housing, and adequate nutrition, was compromised in both countries by growing income inequality, but it was compromised far earlier and to a greater extent in the United States. Income inequality in the United States started high and stayed high, but it did not rise until 2000 in Canada, a function of Canadian tax and transfer policies that redistributed market-based income much more aggressively than such policies did in the United States.

Several other aspects of these trends are noteworthy in the context of resilience. Increasing income inequalities were mitigated more significantly in Canada than in the United States via two mechanisms, one direct (less inequality in market incomes, arriving later, as shown in the changes in the basic Gini), and the other indirect (more mitigation via social transfers in Canada than in the United States). These factors affected access to health care but also other health-supporting and health-promoting resources, such as better nutritional balance, as well as the potential psychosocial effects of falling farther behind in comparative terms (Marmot 2004).

Public Provision of Health-Related Resources

During this time, there were also large differences in the extent to which health resources were publicly provided in these two nations. In the United States, at the same time that the incomes of those in the lowest socioeconomic strata were stagnating, social spending was low (~13 percent of GDP) and stayed within one percentage point of that figure until the end of the 1990s, but Canada sustained a higher level of social spending (~18 percent of GDP) throughout this era (OECD 2011).

However, it is not only the extent of spending but the coverage and ways in which it is distributed that matter (Meyers, Gornick, and Peck 2001). Whereas Canada maintained its tradition of providing more services as a universal right of citizenship, the United States focused on targeting benefits during this era even as these were being reduced. As Lipset (1990) notes, even Brian Mulroney, the prime minister who ushered in the neoliberal era in Canada, described welfare provisions as a "sacred trust." Perhaps the most notable of these provisions came in the domains of health care and education.

In the United States, health care insurance, which was (and remains) primarily employer based, is tied to one's position in the labor market (Siddiqi et al. 2009). Those who are employed in stable middle and high-wage jobs are likely to have consistent health insurance, although often with substantial premiums and user fees, particularly for those with families. The poorest of the population also may have insurance through targeted public programs – such as Medicaid and, more recently, State Children's Health Insurance Program (SCHIP) for children – although these offer more sparse and low-quality services than employer-based insurance (Foraker et al. 2008). The number of uninsured –who fall between these two groups – amounts to roughly 20 percent of the adult population and 10 percent of children (Institute of Medicine 2009).[13] By contrast, Canada has a universal system of health care, which has been in place since 1971.

There are differences, again, in the manner in which education – which is also extremely influential for health status– is provided in the United States and Canada. On the one hand, the United States maintains a more privatized system. Although data are sparse for the whole neoliberal era, during the 1990s, 10 percent to 12 percent of primary and secondary students in the United States were enrolled in private schools compared with 6 percent to 8 percent in Canada (UNESCO 2011). Some of this difference can be explained

---

[13] These figures are slated to change as the provisions of the Affordable Care Act (ACA) come gradually on line. Analyses of the rhetoric of ACA opponents would likely confirm the argument here in that the idea of a citizenship right to health care was clearly rejected by them.

by the later and still-incomplete transition in Canada from state-supported Catholic schools to a private system. On the other hand, even more salient here than differences between the private schooling systems of these nations, which accommodate a rather small proportion of children, are differences in their public schooling systems.

In the United States, public schools are funded largely through local property taxes that remain local. In wealthier locales, schools are better resourced; in the poorest locales, resources are, at best, extremely limited. This funding strategy results in an intimate tie between schooling quality and the position of parents in the housing market. Whereas those who can afford homes in richer areas are able to access well-resourced schools for their kids, the children of those who cannot are relegated to low-quality schools. Compounding this effect is the presence of high levels of economic and racial segregation, which increase the economic distance between locales (neighborhoods) and thus between schools and deliver poorly resourced schools to those on the lower end of the income spectrum and racial minorities (Massey and Denton 1993). By contrast, although Canadian schools are also funded through local property taxes, these funds are aggregated at the provincial level and generally distributed more or less equally on a per pupil basis across each province. Effectively, such a policy serves to sever much of the link between school quality and one's place in the housing market.

Basic resources for PDH were linked to income far more closely in the United States than in Canada. But disparities in the distribution of resources across communities were also wider in the United States, a phenomenon driven by two interrelated factors. First, the level of residential segregation by race and socioeconomic class differed drastically across these nations. Data from the late 1980s demonstrate that blacks and Asians in Canadian cities experienced segregation that has been described as minimal compared with the pervasive segregation that characterized the United States (Massey and Denton 1993; White, Fong, and Cai 2003). Second, compared with the United States, the urban planning policies of provinces and municipalities ensured that key elements of community infrastructure, such as schools, community centers, parks, and transportation, were maintained at a high level across all neighborhoods, not just in the wealthier neighborhoods (Zuberi 2006). Thus, greater attention to providing equality of resources across neighborhoods combined with neighborhoods that were more economically and racially mixed in Canada to provide people with access to high levels of resources irrespective of their individual characteristics or their neighborhood of residence.

Case Study Summary

Our analysis highlights three sources of social resilience that helped Canada to maintain fewer inequalities in PDH outcomes and thus stronger overall PDH outcomes than the United States. We argue that the late onset and more moderate form of neoliberalism in Canada followed from culturally rooted institutional efforts to minimize social divisions and create a sense of social cohesion in Canadian society that were a basis for social resilience. Canada did not escape neoliberalism altogether. Nonetheless, during a period of neoliberal policy reforms, Canada was able to maintain lower levels of income inequality, particularly among working-age adults, than the United States. Ross and colleagues (2000) find that there was no significant association between metropolitan- and provincial-level income inequality and health (measured in terms of mortality rates) in Canada, but there was such an association in the United States (Ross et al. 2000). Their study highlights the strength of this effect among the working-age population.

Second, a principle of universality underpinning some key areas of Canadian policy (e.g., health and education) buffered the effects of income inequality in Canada even when it did rise. The health of insured Americans at the higher end of the socioeconomic spectrum mirrors that of Canadians; it is among the uninsured and those at the lower end of the socioeconomic spectrum that cross-national health differences emerge (Sanmartin et al. 2006). We see this as a source of social resilience that might be described as a societal reserve capacity, a set of institutional capabilities established more or less as insurance against potential threats to PDH.

Although we were unable to find systematic data on the health effects that follow from the distribution of resources across neighborhoods and communities in Canada, there is a large literature on this subject in the United States. A large body of evidence suggests that high levels of economic and racial segregation (themselves highly correlated) are associated with poorer health in a variety of domains, including physical health, mental health, and health behaviors (Acevedo-Garcia et al. 2008). The nexus of individual-level economic and social resource stressors with community-level stressors, exacerbated in the United States by high levels of residential segregation, should be seen as a dynamic system of related processes.

In broader terms, dynamically related societal mechanisms – greater social cohesion, lower overall inequality, and more societal buffers against the effects of income inequality in the form of universal policies – played significant roles in moderating the adverse effects of neoliberalism on population health and development outcomes in Canada compared with the United States. Differences in these mechanisms made Canada more resilient than the United States during the neoliberal era, as assessed in part through their PDH outcomes.

Implications and Limitations

Considering the findings that emerge from taking two different methodological approaches – multi-country comparisons of PDH and a detailed case comparison of two otherwise similar countries that affords a more detailed look at social processes – it is hard not to be struck by the fractal-like quality of the findings on social resilience. Similar factors at multiple levels – regarding material inequality, investment in human development, and social coordination and cohesiveness – appear in both analyses to be jointly responsible for differences in PDH outcomes across several domains and age groups. Evidence for this comes from the broader analysis, which leverages the similarities between the United States and Canada and the detailed case study in which their differences are explored. Moreover, it appears to be the convergence of these factors and the responses to challenges associated with them, rather than any single factor, that stand out. In even more fine-grained analyses, Bouchard (see Chapter 9) describes Québec's response as even more protective on these factors than the rest of Canada, and Hertzman and Boyce (2011; also see Hertzman and Siddiqi, Chapter 10) extends this analysis to the level of within-province differences in British Columbia, reflecting characteristics across communities that differentially support PDH.

As noted earlier, there are significant limitations to these analyses arising from issues of data quality, availability, and comparability. We note this both as a limitation and as an agenda essential to future policy research (Stiglitz et al. 2009). More power to differentiate and evaluate social resilience could be secured if more countries did regular monitoring of key PDH indicators, linked to demographic characteristics. The power of such analyses increases with both sample size and occasions of measurement, and such improvements allow for higher signal-to-noise trajectory analyses.

The policy implications from this and future research are likely to vary depending on which level is considered but also according to the particular cultural and institutional characteristics of countries, many of which may be highly path dependent (Pierson 2000). Appeals to collective rights or to expectations of care may be highly effective in some countries or communities but not in others. In countries with a stronger affinity for individualism (e.g., the Anglo-Saxon grouping noted in Table 8-1), appeals to support human development as a wise *investment* strategy may be more effective, but such appeals may be counterproductive in other settings. The contextualized study of social resilience, we argue, will be especially crucial for policy analysis during an era of current and forthcoming challenges.

References

Acevedo-Garcia, Dolores, Theresa L. Osypuk, Nancy McArdle, and David R. Williams. 2008. "Toward a Policy-Relevant Analysis of Geographic and Racial/Ethnic Disparities in Child Health." *Health Affairs (Millwood)* 27 (2): 321–33.

Adler, N. and J. Ostrove. 1999. "Socioeconomic Status and Health: What We Know and What We Don't." *Annals of the New York Academy of Sciences* 896: 3–15.

Baker, J. L., L. W. Olsen, and T. I. Sørensen. 2008. "Weight at Birth and All-Cause Mortality in Adulthood." *Epidemiology* 19 (2): 197–203.

Banting, K. and W. Kymlicka. 2003. *Do Multicultural Policies Erode the Welfare State?* Luxembourg Income Study Working Paper Series.

Bloemraad, I. 2007. "Unity in Diversity? Bridging Models of Multiculturalism and Immigrant Integration." *Du Bois Review* 4 (2): 317–36.

Boyce, W. T. and D. P. Keating. 2004. "Should We Intervene to Improve Childhood Circumstances?" In *A Life Course Approach to Chronic Disease Epidemiology*, edited by S. Ben-Shlomo and D. Kuh. Oxford: Oxford University Press.

Bronfenbrenner, U. 1992. "Child Care in the Anglo-Saxon Mode." In *Child Care in Context*, edited by M. E. Lamb, K. J. Sternberg, C. G. Hwang, and A G. Broberg. Hillsdale, NJ: Erlbaum: 281–91.

Bureau of Labor Statistics. 2011. *Union Members Summary*.

Casey, B. J. and R. M. Jones. 2010. "Neurobiology of the Adolescent Brain and Behavior: Implications for Substance Use Disorders." *Journal of the American Academy of Child and Adolescent Psychiatry* 49 (12): 1189–201.

Currie, C., S. Nic Gabhainn, E. Godeau, C. Roberts, R. Smith, D. Currie, W. Pickett, M. Richter, A. Morgan., and V. Barnekow, eds. 2008. *Inequalities in Young People's Health: HBSC International Report from the 2005/06 Survey*. Health Policy for Children and Adolescents, No. 5. Copenhagen, Denmark: WHO Regional Office for Europe.

Dowd, J. B., A. M. Simanek, and A. E. Aiello. 2009. "Socio-Economic Status, Cortisol and Allostatic Load: A Review of the Literature." *International Journal of Epidemiology* 38 (5): 1297–309.

Eng, K. and D. Feeny. 2007. "Comparing the Health of Low Income and Less Well Educated Groups in the United States and Canada." *Population Health Metrics* 5 (10).

Esping-Andersen, G. 1990. *The Three Worlds of Welfare Capitalism*. Princeton, NJ: Princeton University Press.

Foraker, R. E., K. M. Rose, E. A. Whitsel, C. M. Suchindran, J. L. Wood, and W. D. Rosamond. 2008. "Neighborhood Income, Health Insurance, and Prehospital Delay for Myocardial Infarction: The Atherosclerosis Risk in Communities Study." *Archives of Internal Medicine* 168 (17): 1874–9.

Ford, E. S., R. K. Merritt, G. W. Heath, K. E. Powell, R. A. Washburn, A. Kriska, and G. Haile. 1991. "Physical Activity Behaviors in Lower and Higher Socioeconomic Status Populations." *American Journal of Epidemiology* 133 (12): 1246–56.

Fourcade-Gourinchas, M. and S. L. Babb. 2002. "The Rebirth of the Liberal Creed: Paths to Neoliberalism in Four Countries." *American Journal of Sociology* 108 (3): 533–79.

Geronimus, A. T. 1992. "The Weathering Hypothesis and the Health of African-American Women and Infants: Evidence and Speculations." *Ethnicity and Disease* 2 (3): 207–21.

Geronimus, A. T., M. Hicken, D. Keene, and J. Bound. 2006. "'Weathering' and Age Patterns of Allostatic Load Scores Among Blacks and Whites in the United States." *American Journal of Public Health* 96 (5): 826–33.

Gilens, M. 1999. *Why Americans Hate Welfare: Race, Media, and the Politics of Anti-Poverty Policy*. Chicago: University of Chicago Press.

Hall, P. A. and D. W. Gingerich. 2009. "Varieties of Capitalism and Institutional Complementarities in the Political Economy: An Empirical Analysis." *British Journal of Political Science* 39 (3): 449–82.

Hall, P. A. and D. Soskice. 2001. "An Introduction to Varieties of Capitalism." In *Varieties of Capitalism: the Institutional Foundations of Comparative Advantage*, edited by P. A. Hall and D. Soskice. New York: Oxford University Press.

Hancock, A.-M. 2004. *The Politics of Disgust: the Public Identity of the Welfare Queen.* New York: NYU Press.

Hertzman, C. 1999. "The Biological Embedding of Early Experience and Its Effects on Health in Adulthood." *Annals of the New York Academy of Sciences* 896: 85–95.

Hertzman, C. and T. Boyce. 2010. "How Experience Gets Under the Skin to Create Gradients in Developmental Health." *Annual Review of Public Health* 31: 329–47.

Institute of Medicine. 2009. *America's Uninsured Crisis: Consequences for Health and Health Care.* Washington, DC.

Jackson, A. 2010. *The Canadian Austerity Model.* http://www.globalresearch .ca/index.php?context=va&aid=18928.

Jenson, J. and D. Saint-Martin. 2003. "New Routes to Social Cohesion? Citizenship and the Social Investment State." *Canadian Journal of Sociology* 28 (1): 77–99.

Kawachi, I. and L. F. Berkman, eds. 2000. *Social Cohesion, Social Capital, and Health. Social Epidemiology.* New York: Oxford University Press.

Keating, D. P. 2009. "Social Interactions in Human Development: Pathways to Health and Capabilities." In *Successful Societies: Institutions, Cultural Repertoires and Population Health,* edited by P. Hall and M. Lamont. New York: Cambridge University Press.

Keating, D. P., ed. 2011a. *Nature and Nurture in Early Child Development.* New York: Cambridge University Press.

Keating, D. P. 2011b. "Society and Early Child Development: Developmental Health Disparities in the Nature-and-Nurture Paradigm." In *Nature and Nurture in Early Child Development,* edited by D. P. Keating. New York: Cambridge University Press.

Keating, D. P. and C. Hertzman, eds. 1999. *Developmental Health and the Wealth of Nations: Social, Biological, and Educational Dynamics.* New York: Guilford Press.

Keating, D. P. and S. Z. Simonton. 2008. "Developmental Health Effects of Human Development Policies." In *Making Americans Healthier: Social and Economic Policy as Health Policy,* edited by J. House, R. Schoeni, H. Pollack, and G. Kaplan. New York: Russell Sage: 61–94.

Krieger, N. 2000. "Discrimination and Health." In *Social Epidemiology,* edited by L. Berkman and I. Kawachi. New York: Oxford University Press.

Lipset, S. M. 1986. "Historical Traditions and National Characteristics: A Comparative Analysis of Canada and the United States." *Canadian Journal of Sociology* 11 (2): 113–55.

Lipset, S. M. 1990. *Continental Divide: The Values and Institutions of the United States and Canada.* New York: Routledge.

Marmot, M. 2004. *The Status Syndrome.* New York: Holt.

Massey, D. and N. Denton. 1993. *American Apartheid.* Cambridge, MA: Harvard University Press.

Mauldin, J. 2010. "O Canada!" http://www.investorsinsight.com/blogs/john_mauldins_ outside_the_box/archive/2010/10/18/o-canada.aspx.

Meyers, M., J. Gornick, and L. R. Peck. 2001. "Packaging Support for Low-Income Families: Policy Variation Across the United States." *Journal of Policy Analysis and Management* 20 (3): 457–83.

Mullis, I., M. Martin, et al. 2004. *TIMSS 2003 International Mathematics Report: Findings from IEA's Trends in International Mathematics and Science Study at the Fourth and Eighth Grades.* Boston: Boston College.

Myles, J. and P. Pierson. 1997. "Friedman's Revenge: The Reform of "Liberal" Welfare States in Canada and the United States." *Politics & Society* 25: 443–72.

Newman, K. S. 1999. *No Shame in My Game: The Working Poor in the Inner City.* New York: Russell Sage Foundation.

OECD. 2008. *Women and Men in OECD Countries.*

OECD. 2011. "OECD Social Expenditure Database (SOCX)."

OECD. 2011. "OECD Statistics Portal."

Pierson, P. 2000. "Path Dependence, Increasing Returns, and the Study of Politics." *American Political Science Review* 94 (2): 251–67.

Putnam, R. 2000. *Bowling Alone: The Collapse and Revival of American Community.* New York: Simon & Schuster.

Rose, D. 1999. "Economic Determinants and Dietary Consequences of Food Insecurity in the United States." *Journal of Nutrition* 129 (2S Suppl): 517S–520S.

Ross, N. A., M. C. Wolfson, J. R. Dunn, J.-M. Berthelot, G. A. Kaplan, and J. W. Lynch. 2000. "Relation Between Income Inequality and Mortality in Canada and in the United States: Cross Sectional Assessment Using Census Data and Vital Statistics." *British Medical Journal* 320 (7239): 898–902.

Sanmartin, C., J. M. Berthelot, E. Ng, K. Murphy, D. L. Blackwell, J. F. Gentleman, et al. 2006. "Comparing Health and Health Care in Canada and the United States." *Health Affairs* 25: 1133–42.

Siddiqi, A. and C. Hertzman. 2007. "Towards an Epidemiological Understanding of the Effects of Long-Term Institutional Changes on Population Health: A Case Study of Canada versus the USA." *Social Science & Medicine* 64 (3): 589–603.

Siddiqi, A., I. Kawachi, L. Berkman, S. V. Subramanian, and C. Hertzman. 2007. "Variation of Socioeconomic Gradients in Children's Developmental Health Across Advanced Capitalist Societies: Analysis of 22 OECD Nations." *International Journal of Health Services* 37 (1): 63–87.

Siddiqi, A. and Q. C. Nguyen. 2010. "A Cross-National Comparative Perspective on Racial Inequities in Health: the USA versus Canada." *Journal of Epidemiology & Community Health* 64 (1): 29–35.

Siddiqi, A., D. Zuberi, and Q. C. Nguyen. 2009. "The Role of Health Insurance in Explaining Immigrant versus Non-immigrant Disparities in Access to Health Care: Comparing the United States to Canada." *Social Science and Medicine* 69 (10): 1452–59.

Singh, G. K. and M. Siahpush. 2001. "All-Cause and Cause-Specific Mortality of Immigrants and Native Born in the United States." *American Journal of Public Health* 91 (3): 392–9.

Statistics Canada. 2009. "Perspectives on Labour and Income." Statistics Canada. 10.

Stiglitz, J. E., A. Sen, and J. Fitoussi. 2009. *Report by the Commission on the Measurement of Economic Performance and Social Progress.* Paris: Commission on the Measurement of Economic Performance and Social Progress.

UNESCO. 2011. *UNESCO Statistical Database.*

UNICEF. 2010. *The Children Left Behind: A League Table of Inequality in Child Well-Being in the World's Rich Countries.* Florence, Italy: Innocenti Research Centre.

Viner, R. M., E. M. Ozer, S. Denny, M. Marmot, M. Resnick, A. Fatusi, and C. Currie. 2012. "Adolescence and the Social Determinants of Health." *Lancet* 379 (9826): 1641–52.

White, M. J., E. Fong, and Q. Cai. 2003. "The Segregation of Asian-Origin Groups in the United States and Canada." *Social Science Research* 32: 148–67.

Wilkinson, R. and K. Pickett. 2009. *The Spirit Level.* New York: Bloomsbury Press.

Zuberi, D. 2006. *Differences That Matter: Social Policy and the Working Poor in the United States and Canada.* Ithaca, NY: Cornell University Press.

PART IV

COMMUNITIES AND ORGANIZATIONS AS SITES
FOR SOCIAL RESILIENCE

9

Neoliberalism in Québec

The Response of a Small Nation Under Pressure

Gérard Bouchard

Introduction[1]

The general question that drives this analysis of Québec relates to the capacity – or lack thereof – of a society to recover after a trauma or to face a serious challenge that can threaten its very foundations, cultural as well as material. In keeping with the focus of this book, I will use the concept of resilience to denote the capacity of a society to cope with a challenge or a "shock." For a society, this can be achieved in at least three ways: (a) by successfully opposing and resisting the external assault in such a way as to return to the former state (or "equilibrium"); (b) by adapting to the new situation through adjustment, negotiation, and compromise; and (3) by seizing on the occasion to respond creatively to the challenge and to reinvent oneself through major innovations and progressive changes – in other words, to thrive in adversity and, in the process, "do better than expected" (see Chapter 5; Cyrulnik 1999).[2] In each of these scenarios, through different strategies, the society energetically reacts and manages to maintain its basic institutions and to restore its ways of life.[3] Accordingly, one could talk of three forms of resilience: conservative, adaptive, and progressive. It follows that a nonresilient society will flatly renounce or fail to fight for its primary ideals and goals, for the institutional setting that

[1] I wish to thank Pierre Fortin, Benoît Lévesque, Camil Bouchard, Nancy Neamtan, Frédéric Lesemann, Yves Vaillancourt, François Vaillancourt, Luc Godbout, Alain Noël, Simon Langlois, Diane-Gabrielle Tremblay, Alain Roy, François Fournier, and Catherine Audet for their invaluable help. The chapter has also tremendously benefited from the comments offered by the Successful Societies group's members. As usual, final responsibility lies with the author. The research supporting this chapter has been made possible thanks to grants from the Canada Research Chair Program and the Canadian Institute For Advanced Research (CIFAR).
[2] The second and third ways could be likened to what has been termed secondary and primary coping by Compass et al. (2001).
[3] Indirectly, of course, this implies that the set of values, traditions, and ideals that underlie the social fabrics are restored or preserved as well.

they inform, and for its ways of life. It will also prove to be unable to take advantage of the new context.

It should be understood that the response can be orchestrated at the local or community level as well as at the macro-social and national level by individual and collective actors. Yet, at the micro level, the perspective differs insofar as a particular social group or category of citizens is less likely to bring about major societal changes. A progressive form of resilience at this level may consist in a redefinition of the interactions of that group with its social environment. Therefore, as shown by the literature in this field, one must be aware of the variety of forms resilience can assume and the variety of ways it can be pursued. That encourages prudent utilization of this highly polysemous concept.[4]

A major part of my analysis is empirical, focusing on the manifestation of resilience in the recent past of Québec. It also includes an attempt to identify the sources of resilience (where and how a society finds the strength to overcome adversity), which is the most critical as well as the most difficult part. One reason is that the challenge or so-called shock to be dealt with may alter the very resources that are thought to be the source of resilience. For instance, old national myths, robust repertoires, and local solidarities ("social capital") can be weakened or broken by globalization, leaving very little with which to mount a vigorous response.[5]

Similar to most societies of the world, Québec had to face the surge of neoliberalism and globalization in the 1970s. Those two trends unfolded hand in hand, and it is not easy to establish a clear distinction between them. Theoretically, neoliberalism refers to a wide range of economic policies and practices inducing major political, social, and cultural changes. Some of them are unquestionably negative (e.g., deteriorating health or increased social inequality), some are positive (more efficient governance, widening of communication networks, individual freedom), and others are ambivalent or controversial (on this, see Chapter 1).

For its part, globalization can be seen as a more encompassing notion, one that highlights the spectacular enlargement of the scope of social life, affecting ways of thinking, interpersonal relations, networks of information, patterns of consumption, traveling, and so forth (Tomlinson 1999; O'Meara et al. 2000). Overall, it is fair to say that neoliberalism and globalization have fed off each other in many ways. In the first parts of this chapter, because I intend to target Québec's economic and social spheres, I will mostly refer to neoliberalism. The globalization framework will become more salient in the last parts where I discuss the cultural thread.

In line with the theoretical frame of this chapter, the emergence of neoliberalism will represent the external "shock" that has shaken Québec from the 1970s. I will consider three particularly sensitive areas of impact and response:

---

[4] For an insightful discussion from the field of psychology, see Ungar (2008).
[5] One also thinks of the weakening of the trade unions in the United Sates in the 1960s and 1970s (Fantasia and Voss 2003).

economic (destructuration–restructuration processes), social (state involvement in welfare policies, citizens' initiatives, the evolution of several indicators pertaining to education, criminality, health, and so on), and cultural (primarily the response to new waves of immigration and cultural patterns brought on by neoliberalism and globalization). The analysis will primarily focus on the years 1975 to 2000, corresponding to the emergence and the golden age of neoliberalism, that is, the period during which its impact is most likely to be seen. The post-2000 years, possibly a turning point, will be examined separately.

Overall, the analysis suggests the image of a resilient society, mostly progressive (in the sense of the typology above), insofar as Québec has (a) cashed in on neoliberalism to diversify and to grow economically, (b) managed to preserve and even expand its social net, and (3) opened up and is exploring new promising ways to reinvent itself in the face of ethno-cultural diversity. As for the sources of the resilience, I will highlight the major role of some institutions and new social actors. But I will mostly direct the analysis toward the area of collective imaginaries and national myths that have acted as powerful symbolic engines of resistance and invention.[6] Finally, I will hypothesize that, to a large extent, the future of the Québec model will depend on the dynamics of its old national myths, which are also facing unprecedented challenges today.

First, a word about Québec. Although one of ten provinces of Canada, Québec is considered as a nation in and of itself, a status that the Canadian Parliament officially recognized in November 2006. Of course, this recognition is restricted to a sociological meaning. Québec is a collectivity with a government endowed with truncated but still significant powers,[7] a large territory, a population of 8 million (82 percent Francophone),[8] a strong identity, a set of distinct institutions, and a sense of its own history and destiny (French immigrants were the first Europeans to settle in the present Canadian territory at the beginning of the seventeenth century). This qualifies Québec as a separate object of study within the Canadian federation. But it is worth noting that the distribution of jurisdictions between Québec and Ottawa often lacks clarity, which fosters constant disputes. Indeed, there is a fair amount of overlap between the two levels of government (e.g., two charters of rights, two

---

[6] Broadly construed, collective imaginaries must be understood as the whole set of representations (meanings, dreams, memory, and so on) that constitute the symbolic foundation of a society or a nation (Bouchard 2003). A collective imaginary institutes a set of basic relationships to space (a homeland, a cradle, an historical site, landscapes), to self and other (an identity dynamics of inclusion and exclusion), to the past (narratives), to the future (a world mission, utopias), and so on. However, the core of a collective imaginary is largely made up of myths. (I will come back to this notion later on.)

[7] Québec has total or wide control in various fields such as education, health, welfare, immigration, culture, public works, agriculture, and police. It also exercises several taxation powers that allow for a significant impact on economic life.

[8] The Québécois are a cultural minority, accounting for around 23% of the Canadian population and 2% of the North American population. Thus, Francophones are both a strong majority in Québec and a tiny minority in their continental environment. Among all the characteristics of Québec, this double status is paramount.

different approaches to ethno-cultural diversity, two languages policies, two justice systems, two departments of the environment, and so forth). This, of course, must be taken into account when analyzing Québec per se and, when needed, mention will be made of federal policies that weigh on Québec's society. Overall, though, the powers wielded by Québec within Canada, its strong national identity and specific traits, and the long and rich tradition of Québec studies warrant the focus of this chapter.

The Québec Economy: Resisting and Capitalizing on Neoliberalism

From the Quiet Revolution of the 1960s[9] onward, Québec has taken a number of initiatives, most often spearheaded by the government, to modernize its economy and to secure a continuous growth. At that time, Québec was a poorly developed society compared with many parts of North America, and the private sector was unable to provide the huge amount of capital needed to initiate and sustain the required overhaul. However, the public debt was almost nonexistent, so the state took over and grew much more active than before. What ensued was the emergence of a development model relying heavily on governmental programs and parapublic (government-owned or controlled) institutions, close cooperation with the private sector, and constant consultation and coordination with major collective actors (unions, school management, the business class, the Church, youth organizations, community representatives, and so on). What came to be called the Québec model was characterized at the outset by a strong reliance on the state, an emphasis on the social dimension of economic development along with a democratic mode of decision making.

One of the hallmarks of the model is the primacy put on coordinated action that has led to the periodic organization of "Sommets" or Estates-General (national assizes) at which, for several days, representatives from all sectors of society try to build a consensus on major issues through deliberation and negotiation. How can we account for this feature of Québec's governance approach based on collective bargaining? Five factors will be called upon. First, those coordinating practices, relying on partnership and social democracy, bear the hallmark of a small nation with a long history of decolonization and fighting for cultural survival that has generated a strong sense of togetherness. Second, they reflect the confidence that Quebecers had developed toward the state since the 1960s and their willingness to rely on that institution that they entrusted with major social, economic, and cultural responsibilities (see later discussion). Third, the practice also stems from a new ideological landscape created during the Quiet Revolution in the 1960s, a landscape that lent itself to the building of a wide social consensus. Fourth, something of the Quiet Revolution's spirit survived into the 1990s, that is, a sense of urgency, the concern that this

---

[9] In Québec, the so-called Quiet Revolution refers to a major historical watershed. The 1960s was a period of deep change consisting in a rapid economic, social, and cultural modernization with the state as the leading collective actor (Thomson 1984).

minority, fragile society should not be imperilled, that the stakes were too high and a joint effort beyond particular interests was required. Finally, as often with Québec, nationalism was no stranger to those feelings. All those factors combined have made possible the national and regional "Sommets" and wide-ranging collective bargaining practices.

Overall, as it was taking shape, the Québec model aimed to implement a form of capitalism in keeping with the core values of this society (equality, solidarity, deliberative democracy, and the quality of social life). According to Vaillancourt (2002), the model has enabled Québec to move "away from the hierarchical conceptions specific to the entrepreneurial state in the Keynesian and Fordist vein, without opening the door to privatization and dismantling of the welfare state" (5). It also reflects a willingness to empower usually neglected social actors (e.g., community groups, women, elderly). But at the same time, Vaillancourt also maintains that the model was heterogeneous, making room for various, sometimes contradictory logics (2002: 15–18).

To an extent that is hard to ascertain, there is no doubt that under neoliberalism, the Québec economy has changed, and sometimes for the worse, in recent decades. Multinational companies that felt no social commitments to the fate of local populations have closed plants without notice in Montréal and in several economically vulnerable regions where mill towns abound. Since 1975, the average net salary (i.e., the purchasing power) as a proportion of gross domestic product (GDP) has remained stable at 75 percent (but the profits of enterprises followed a similar pattern, hovering around 17 percent of GDP).[10] As is true in Canada as a whole, part-time, undeclared work and precarious employment have risen, mostly at the expense of young people and women. For a growing number of workers, job security disappeared, and the unions themselves proved unable or unwilling to protect the interests of their young members. Several big corporations engaged in outsourcing (e.g., Bombardier in Mexico, CGI in India). The forest industry suffered from market deregulation (although other causes have contributed to its downfall). There are also signs that individualism has been on the rise, particularly among the youths, a noteworthy phenomenon in a small nation known for its strong collectivist tradition.[11] This coincides with the expansion of a "consumer culture."[12] Finally, echoing a world trend, foreign trade and the circulation of capital were deregulated (a change initiated by the Canadian government, which legislates on those matters).

Interestingly, on the other hand, Québec society has also managed to resist many changes induced by neoliberalism. As noted earlier, throughout the period, the workers' share of profit in the national income has not diminished. Changes in public spending (as a proportion of GDP) between 1981

---

[10] Fortin (2010a: 12–13); Boivin et al. (2008).

[11] According to Béland and Leclerc (2003), this is the most striking change that has occurred in Québec since the 1990s.

[12] The proportion of credit card holders among young Quebecers (19–24 years old) jumped from 25 percent in 1986 to 57 percent in 2001 (Brochu and Young 1986; Léger Marketing 2001).

and 2000 show no significant shrinkage of the state, although the size of the civil service has decreased from 28 to 24 percent of total salaried employment (Statistics Canada, 2010, Table CANSIM 282-0012; Guay and Marceau 2004: 76-8). Contrary to a widespread perception, the total tax burden of private companies seems to have increased in recent decades (Godbout et al. 2006).[13] The proportion of the unionized workforce (union density) has hovered around 40 percent since the 1990s (it had increased from 25 to 40 percent between 1965 and 1990). It is still the highest in North America (Canada: 31.4 percent; United States: 11 percent).[14] The average unemployment rate, traditionally high in Québec, stood at around 12 percent between 1975 and 1990 and declined from 13 to 8 percent between 1991 and 2008 (Langlois 2008: 67–68; Joanis, Godbout, and Aubry 2009: 40). Fortin (2009a: 291, Figure 2) has also shown that the rate of employment of the working-age population declined between 1955 and 1982 and has risen steadily until now. Québec labor laws, which have the reputation of treating workers generously, have survived unscathed. In terms of enrollment the private component of the school system rose from 8.0 to 17.2 percent between 1973 and 1993, but has not expanded since then, while access to public higher education doubled at the undergraduate level and tripled at other levels between 1976 and 2007 (Gingras 2010). Finally, an effort by the Québec (Liberal) government to implement a broad program of neoliberal policies in the late 1980s came to naught, thwarted by massive public opposition.

Québec has similarly avoided a wave of denationalization in the electricity, alcohol, lottery, insurance, water supply, and other sectors.[15] According to numerous polls, so-called social-democracy (state intervention, egalitarianism, networking, and social participation) is deeply rooted in the Québec psyche.[16] Those and other polls have consistently shown that a majority of the population rejects neoliberalism. At the cultural level, Québec has nevertheless witnessed a celebration of the entrepreneur class and of the entrepreneurship mentality; however, this narrative was not tied to neoliberalism per se but to the Quiet Revolution and its drive to promote the affirmation of Francophones in the economic sector.

Interestingly, not only has Québec resisted to a large extent the negative changes usually associated with neoliberalism, but it has also capitalized on them. On average, between 1981 and 2008, Québec's real per capita GDP increased by 1.43 percent annually compared with 1.36 percent for Ontario, 1.57 percent for Canada excluding Québec, and 1.91 percent for the United States. During the same period, the unemployment rate declined (more significantly than in Ontario or the rest of Canada). Since the early 1990s, thanks

[13] That report, which draws on a solid and compelling analysis, contradicts the conclusions of an earlier study published by Bernard et al. (2006).
[14] Fortin (2010a: 12, 34), Langlois (2008: 71–72), and Roy (2010b).
[15] All of these areas fall under Québec's jurisdiction.
[16] See, for example, the comparative findings presented in Noël (2010).

to the opening of international markets and particularly the free trade agreement between Canada and the United States in 1988 (later expanded into the North American Free Trade Agreement in 1994 and the Canada/US Accord on our Shared Borders in 1995), Québec exports to other countries have more than doubled (from 20 percent to more than 40 percent of GDP). The level of trade with the United States has been even more spectacular with a threefold increase between 1988 and 2001.[17] As a result, Québec is now a major producer in several areas, including aeronautics, where it ranks sixth in the world.

Globalized entrepreneurship has flourished with the emergence of major multinational corporations founded and controlled by Francophones. New major ventures have also emerged, spearheaded by immigrant entrepreneurs. In the 1990s, the pace of economic growth was such that, between 1991 and 2004, Québec's GDP outstripped that of Canada, the United States, and the average for the Organisation for Economic Co-operation and Development (OECD) and G7 countries (Lisée 2003). Finally, despite the adverse effects of neoliberalism and several recessions, the portion of the Québec economy owned or controlled by Francophone Quebecers has continued to grow throughout recent decades (47.1 percent in 1961, 54.8 percent in 1978, and 67 percent in 2003) (Vaillancourt and Vaillancourt 2005: 34–6).

The foregoing discussion does not provide a complete picture of the Québec economy between 1975 and 2000, which was not the objective. And one should not overlook the well-known dark sides of this period (precarious employment, relatively slow growth in GDP, soaring public debt, low productivity, brutal plant closures, and so on). However, this summary brings to light major gains that have been made despite or possibly thanks to neoliberalism.

Overall, it is fair to say that between 1975 and 2000, Québec's economic response to neoliberalism was positive in that unemployment decreased and, more generally, the economy kept growing without eroding major pillars of the so-called Québec model, including an active state and a pattern of coordinated planning and joint endeavors. Finally, as noted earlier, Québec has largely avoided the wave of privatization that occurred in other nations such as England, France, Germany, New Zealand, and Australia.

Preserving the Social Fabric: Expanding the Social Net

An examination of the social dimension yields an even more impressive picture, at odds with the features commonly associated with neoliberalism. In this regard, four elements stand out in Québec's recent past: (a) a new approach to economic development, (b) the emergence of new social actors from below, (c) the expansion of social policies, and (d) several remarkable achievements.

---

[17] Since the 1980s, Québec, in contrast with English Canada, has strongly supported free trade, particularly with the United States. By 2001, it had become that country's seventh trading partner.

With respect to the first point, Québec has a long history of community initiatives (cooperatives, "mutuelles," savings groups, associations of all sorts).
Until the 1970s, the cooperative movement and the mass of community associations consisted of very small entities operating locally and dedicated to mutual
aid. Changes began to take place in the 1970s and culminated in the early
1980s as a response to the North American economic crisis and to the surge
of neoliberalism. That was the origin in Québec of what is known today as
the social economy (or social entrepreneurship). From then on, a very different
approach took shape, sustained by a vast coalition of micro actors, a number of which belonged to the informal economy (D'Amours 2006). The era of
top-down decision making by the state was over.

The social economy movement in Québec, still a booming initiative nowadays, defines itself in terms of values and rules such as social equity, collective
ownership, profit sharing, the primacy of personal and community needs over
strict capital rationality, deliberative decision making, autonomous functioning (at arms' length from the state), and sustainability. Operating between
and beyond the state and the market (but in close cooperation with both of
them), social entrepreneurship explicitly conveys the willingness to carve out a
new model of development and to bring about social transformations both at
the societal and community levels. The overall objective is to structure "civil
society" as a powerful third sector.[18]

As a result, new actors have emerged in the social and the political arena
that cannot be overlooked. In addition to those just mentioned, the labor
unions deserve attention for their original involvement in the new economy.
The Fédération des travailleurs et travailleuses du Québec (which has more
than 500,000 members) engaged in a pioneering initiative in 1983 by creating the *Fonds de solidarité des travailleurs* (Québec workers' solidarity
fund), which had half a million shareholders as of May 2010 and whose
$7.3 billion in assets are invested as venture capital in "socially responsi-
ble" Québec enterprises in accordance with a philosophy of social capitalism.
This gesture was soon to be replicated in English Canada and other countries. The second largest Québec trade union (the *Confédération des syndicats
nationaux*, which has 300,000 members) followed suit in 1996 by creating
Fondaction. Together with all the other organizations linked to the social
economy, these form a new coalition of stakeholders who, working with
the state and the private sector, have contributed to changing the model of
governance in Québec. This economic involvement by the unions is all the
more remarkable because they had to reconcile such involvement with their
fairly radical anticapitalist stance. Since then, they have come to terms with

---

[18] On the foregoing, there is a vast literature available. Among many other titles, see Chantier
de l'économie sociale (2004), Larose et al. (2004, 2005), Vaillancourt (2002, 2006, 2008),
Vaillancourt et al. (2009), Bouchard et al. (2005), Neamtan (2006), Lévesque (2008), and
Jetté (2008). Another valuable source is the website of the Chantier de l'économie sociale
(http://www.chantier.qc.ca), which is headed by Nancy Neamtan.

neoliberal pressure and have redefined themselves in a way that has allowed them to act as partners while still pursuing their social agenda (Rouillard 2008).

A broad consensus in most segments of Québec society has enabled it to preserve its social safety net. Throughout the period, the main social programs have been maintained (universal public health care, family allowances, long-term unemployment benefits, public education,[19] and so forth). Even more remarkable is the general expansion and reinvention of the safety net in the wake of the 1996 October "Sommet" on the economy and employment:[20] universal drug insurance, universal early childhood daycare centers, a new home-care network, a new parental leave program (up to one year for the mother and five weeks for the father, the most generous program in North America), a gender pay equity policy (an unprecedented measure in the Western world), lower taxes for female single parents, the creation of new social networks, social housing programs, increased provincial family allowances, the poverty reduction policy, and so forth. At the same time, the minimum wage has steadily increased. It now stands at $9.50, equivalent to 46 percent of the average wage (again, among the highest ratios in North America). The curve of public social spending, already ascending since the 1970s, reflects those innovations, with a sharp increase after 1998, while spending in other sectors remained stable (Joanis et al. 2009: 141–2).

All told, these measures amounted to a bold and innovative reengineering of Québec's social programs that went well beyond traditional forms of assistance. The new orientation consisted in redefining welfare policies in such a way that it could serve general goals such as children's development, parental employment, and the emancipation of women in a spirit of equality and social citizenship. The daycare centers policy, for instance, allowed a lot of unemployed women, recipients of welfare payment, to join the workforce. Moreover, these reforms clearly stemmed from political choices informed by values averse to neoliberalism.

For that and other reasons, Québec is often characterized as a social-democratic or even leftist nation (or as "a socializing enclave"[21]). What really matters, however, is the efficiency of these initiatives in terms of individual and collective well-being. Here are a few relevant facts and figures. Over the period, poverty has steadily declined in Québec. In 2007, it enjoyed the lowest level of

---

[19] Québec's postsecondary tuition fees have traditionally been the lowest in North America. During the winter and spring of 2012, an attempt made by the Québec government to raise the fees has been defeated by a strong opposition in the population, thousands of people taking to the streets for weeks on end across the province which had not witnessed such a turmoil since decades.

[20] It was followed in 1998 by another province-wide summit conference on social development, thirteen regional forums, and seventy local forums (see Vaillancourt 2006).

[21] *Le Devoir*, August 2, 2010, p. A6 ("La nouvelle définition des élites"). According to Clement and Myles (1994: 234), Quebecers "have the most progressive social space" in North America. Along the same line, see also Adams (2003: 86–7).

child poverty in Canada.[22] Québec has become the province where there are fewer poor people and where the wealthy are the most heavily taxed (Fortin 2010b). A similar picture emerges from the data on social inequality. Several studies relying on various indices (including the Gini index) have turned up convergent conclusions: inequalities have been remarkably contained in recent decades, although they have increased lately. They remain below the Canadian and the U.S. levels, thanks partly to a more progressive tax structure. In 2007, the ratio of the earnings of the 1% wealthiest to the average earnings of the population was 18.5 in the United States, 11.0 in Canada, and 9.1 in Québec.[23]

Still in terms of social performances, a few more insights may be of interest:

- Women's living conditions have significantly improved since the 1990s, mainly as a result of the reduction of poverty and the pay equity policy. The gender salary gap has narrowed; female unemployment has decreased; and, in education, female students have steadily advanced in terms of enrollment and performance.
- The crime rate, especially homicides and other violent crimes, has remained low (the homicide rate, for instance, has been declining since 1974). In this respect, Québec stands apart in North America, with a lower rate than most of the Canadian provinces, Canada as a whole, and the United States.[24]
- The health record has improved. The sharp drop in the infant mortality rate continued between 1971 and 2008 (from 17.3 0/oo to 4.2), and life expectancy rose dramatically (for men, from 68.0 to 78.3 years; for women, from 75.0 to 83.0) years.[25]
- Civic participation (the level of voting in general elections) has remained strong throughout the period, exceeding the threshold of 80 percent on several occasions between 1970 and 2000, for an average of 76.5 percent. A decline has been observed since the mid 1990s, replicating a general trend in industrialized nations – although the level of voting in the 2012 September elections was close to 75%.[26]
- Québec has a mixed record in the field of education with both exceptional and poor performance on various indicators, such as the remarkable achievement of its students in OECD tests[27] or the level of instability and anxiety generated by many reforms. Be that as it may, according to data provided

[22] Findings reported in Noël (2010: 102).
[23] On the foregoing, see Bouchard (1998), Langlois (2004: 172–173; 2008: 81–4), Joanis et al. (2009: 62), Saez and Veall (2005), Guay and Marceau (2004: 78–79), Crespo (2007, 2008), Fortin (2009b), Fortin (2010b: 1), Noël (2010: 101–2), and Fortin (forthcoming).
[24] From Guay and Marceau (2004: 79–80); Ouimet (2001: 5; 2004: 80), Human Resources and Skills Development Canada (http://www.rhdcc.gc.ca), and others.
[25] Choinière et al. (2007), Alix and Choinière (2008), Bouchard (2009: 193–5), and Fournier (2010a).
[26] Data compiled from government sources by Roy (2010a) and Fournier (2010b).
[27] For instance, see on the OECD website the findings of the studies conducted through the Program for International Student Assessment (PISA). Dubuc (2006: 186–7) summarizes the findings of these and other international competitions.

by the Québec Department of Education, Recreation, and Sports (2010), the drop-out rate at the secondary level declined dramatically between 1979 and 2008 (the graduation rate jumped from 57 to 87 percent). The average education level (the total number of years in school) among the 25- to 34-year-old cohort was 9.5 in 1961 (11.0 in Ontario; 12.2 in the United States) and 14.4 in 2001 (14.7 in Ontario; 13.1 in the United States). From the perspective of this chapter, what matters is the steady progress throughout the period and the sustained increase in government spending.[28]

- Québec has maintained its efforts to stimulate research and development. Public investment in this sector (measured as a proportion of GDP) steadily increased between 1980 and 2002, from $200 million to $1.3 billion (Gingras 2010: 85).

Overall, the foregoing discussion clearly reveals that Québec has succeeded in preserving and expanding its safety net in recent decades. Moreover, it has been able to respond to a context of instability by changing its approach, even its mode of governance, and by implementing innovative policies. This is particularly true for the years 1997 to 2000 when numerous politicians and other leaders became aware of the threat posed by difficult economic conditions. It is also noteworthy that the two major landmarks in the development of social programs in the early 1980s and late 1990s coincide with economic slumps that led to budget cuts.[29] However, in each instance, a consensus was achieved to preserve and even bolster the social safety net to ensure that the less privileged would not bear the brunt of the crisis. There was a willingness to invent new ways to cope with economic constraints and to do better with the available resources. All in all, Québec validates the major conclusions of Chapter 1 concerning (a) the marked national variations in responses to neoliberalism, (b) the mediating role played by the state and local institutions, and (c) the capacity of the state and society's to make choices that alleviate and sometimes even eliminate the effects of neoliberalism.

In fact, attempts to promote a neoliberal agenda in Québec were simply going against the grain, due to Quebecers' strong attachment to their core values of equality, solidarity, and participatory democracy inherited from their colonial past. This is clearly a case in which a reluctant collective imaginary has largely defeated an aggressive brand of market-oriented policies. Traditionally, individualism has always been contained in this closely knit society, where a sense of fragility, collective discrimination and material deprivation have nurtured a collectivist predisposition and a vibrant nationalism. The fact that the American dream (or a Québec version of it) has never been salient in the elite's discourse reflects the same spirit. It is no coincidence that the strongest resistance to neoliberalism and major initiatives in terms of social programs has

---

[28] On the foregoing, see a short statistical compilation by Roy (2010c).

[29] In the early 1980s: the fight against North American recession. In the late 1990s: the fight against the public deficit and exacerbation of fiscal imbalance resulting from a new federal policy of equalization payments at the expense of the provinces.

come from the nationalist, sovereignist Parti Québécois. Similarly, the biggest trade unions and cooperative institutions are known both for their social and nationalist commitment (if not their sovereignist sympathies). By contrast, the Liberal (federalist and more business-oriented) Party has been more inclined to promote individualism and neoliberal values. The foregoing clearly highlights a major fact of recent Québec history, that is, the close association of nationalism and progressive social policies.

In other words, neoliberal myths have been too weak to seriously impact this society. They have been unable to connect with deep-rooted traditions and, until recently, they have been widely rejected. It is also noteworthy that, over the years, the Québec model has become a part of national identity, embodying the Francophone "difference" in Canada and in North America, another connection with a key facet of Québec's national imaginary.

That said, although the previous sections have emphasized the negative side of neoliberalism, one cannot help perceiving its overall impact in a more positive light. More precisely, it could be argued that neoliberalism has contributed to Québec's successful response, at least in two ways. First, Québec society and its economy have benefited directly from the deregulation of international trade, which has encouraged massive exports and allowed several corporations to expand globally. Second, the spectacular growth of the social economy, regardless of its anticapitalist stance, is not alien to the spirit of community entrepreneurship also promoted – quite paradoxically – by neoliberalism. In other words, one should be wary of a simplistic, one-sided account of the relationship between Québec and neoliberalism. Obviously, a complex trade-off has been unfolding, amazingly replicating a dynamic that was at work at the micro-level between regional authorities and Québec's government (Dionne and Klein 1995).

Likewise, English Canada has been quite successful in preserving its safety net, which speaks to values surprisingly similar to Québec's but drawing on a very different historical grounding.

The Cultural Challenges of Neoliberalism and Globalization

Changes in Québec's cultural sphere in recent decades suggest a slightly different picture in that a remarkable dynamism has been combined lately with expressions of insecurity and soul searching. In this area again, a number of success stories are associated with globalization.[30] Québec artists and other performers have been very successful on the international scene. Statistics also show that, in various ways, Quebecers have taken full advantage of the new facilities for communications and travel that the globalized world offers (internet utilization, publications in foreign journals, international research collaboration, and so forth). Overall, they have been very active in finding ways to cash in on globalization.

[30] As mentioned earlier, because the focus of this chapter is now shifting to culture, I will use the concept of globalization more often than neoliberalism.

Another question is how did Québec, as a minority culture, respond to the local impact of globalization? The latter has been and is still a matter of concern among a majority of Quebecers insofar as it enhances the influence of English as the new *lingua franca* through many channels. Moreover, globalization is associated with powerful trends and patterns that often compete with and weaken the set of deep-seated values, traditions, and myths that for a long time have sustained the collective identity. As a consequence of the deregulation and growing mobility associated with the rise of neoliberalism and globalization, immigration in particular has become a major channel through which new cultural (and religious) inputs are imported. How has Québec managed this very sensitive issue?

From the 1960s to the late 1990s, through various policies, Québec displayed a noticeable consistency in its effort to adapt to the diversification brought about by growing immigration.[31] One major step was the adoption in 1975 of a charter of rights. Another one was Bill 101, which, in 1977, established French as the official language of Québec in public life, thus enabling immigrants to access full citizenship, including easier employment and social mobility. Along the way, the French Canadians began to redefine themselves as Quebecers to assert their new modern mindset, and they dismissed religion as a major feature of the new collective identity. The pre-1960 conservative nationalism was overhauled and suffused with progressive facets such as liberal values, equality, secularization, human rights, openness to the world, and so on. After rejecting Canadian multiculturalism policy (1971) as unsuitable for Québec, the government set out to craft its own model – interculturalism – to manage growing ethno-cultural diversity (Bouchard 2012).

In the realm of ethno-cultural diversity as in many others, the formula has proved successful. Indeed, the integration of immigrants has proceeded rather smoothly, which seems all the more noteworthy because, as a result of a long-established pattern, close to 90 percent of the newcomers live in the Montréal region. It is also significant that with respect to nondiscrimination (real or perceived) and positive attitudes toward immigrants, Québec has usually ranked well in polls and annual reports by monitoring bodies in the Jewish and other communities (including SOS-Racisme).[32] Among the major Canadian cities, Montréal, Québec, and Trois-Rivières still have the lowest hate crime rates (Walsh and Dauvergne 2009; Lisée 2010). Moreover, protest about immigrants stealing jobs was – and is still – virtually unheard of in Québec.

By the late 1990s, however, tensions began to build up. The causes are manifold, but it is no coincidence that a first heated controversy in 1995 focused on a religious issue (the wearing of the hidjab in the public classrooms). Soon another polemic arose around the wearing of the kirpan in school. Subsequent

---

[31] For more detailed accounts, see Labelle (2000), Juteau (2002, 2004), Bouchard and Taylor (2008: 116–22), Rocher et al. (2008), and Gastaut (2009).

[32] For example, an analysis based on the 2002 Canadian Ethnic Diversity Survey shows that the rate of self-reported discrimination was lower in Québec than in the rest of Canada (Reitz and Banerjee 2009: 131).

debate in the years that followed involved numerous similar demands of accommodation for religious purposes in public institutions.[33] Growing discontent, widely fuelled by the media, could be observed, which in 2007 led the government to establish a public consultation commission co-chaired by the author of this chapter and the political philosopher Charles Taylor.[34] Essentially, the Commission concluded that (a) accommodation practices designed to protect the rights of minorities were commonplace in public institutions but reasonable guidelines were applied and, overall, the situation was under control; (b) the media have persistently aroused popular discontent by giving overblown accounts of a few cases of unreasonable demands that had been granted, thus contributing to distorted public debate; and (c) in large segments of the population, these erroneous accounts connected with a preexisting climate of insecurity about the future of Québec's identity and Francophone culture, especially its so-called core values.

This uneasiness persists. Polls reveal that a majority of Quebecers oppose religious accommodations (although support for immigration remains strong). Interculturalism, suspected of excessive permissiveness toward immigrants, particularly toward Muslims, is now questioned. Immigration has significantly increased, reaching an annual average of 40,000 over the past decade (54,000 in 2010, a little less in 2011), as opposed to 23,550 during the 1980s. The newcomers are now recruited from all continents, and the issue of managing ethno-cultural (and especially religious) diversity has grown more sensitive than ever.

However, although sometimes heated, the ongoing debate is open and creative, and it is proceeding in a remarkably disciplined and democratic way. It has enriched the public thought about ethno-cultural diversity and that, in itself, is another sign of dynamism and resilience. Ultimately, lively debate over the future of this society, beyond all kinds of divides and boundaries, may be what matters most. As Laitin (1986) reveals, ideological, religious, and cultural differences can be argued out in a way that prevents open conflicts and engenders dynamism rather than stagnation.

The 2000s Watershed

As the preceding discussion suggests, the current cultural landscape is moving in several directions as Québec searches for a new consensus on basic issues (e.g., integration, core values, citizenship, collective identity). This situation must be considered in tandem with what is taking place in the social and economic realms, where a new tendency has emerged in the past decade. The Québec model is now on trial, and the neoliberal stream is gaining momentum.

---

[33] For a detailed account, see Bouchard and Taylor (2008: chapter II).

[34] Consultation Commission on Accommodation Practices Related to Cultural Differences (it has come to be known as the Bouchard-Taylor Commission). Its report was released in May 2008. See: www.accommodements.qc.ca.

To a large extent, the shift coincided with the election of the Charest Liberal government in 2003 and the defeat of the sovereignist Parti Québécois, a strong advocate of welfare policies. Indeed, the new government has succeeded in implementing significant elements of a neoliberal agenda (tax reduction on business, privatization in a few areas, budget cuts to some social programs, and so on). However, several of these initiatives have been met with widespread protests (Bordeleau 2010) and uneven success, suggesting that support for the Québec model is still strong. The Charest government has actually been compelled to extend expensive social policies initiated during the 1980s and toward the end of the 1990s (e.g., the fight against poverty, pay equity, parental leave). It has even introduced new policies, including a fertility-assisted program.

Nevertheless, the business class has become more active in denouncing the Québec model. According to the counter-discourse, priority should be given to reducing the public debt (presently at the level of most of the OECD countries), the burden of social policies, and the size of the state. It is also said that Quebecers are overtaxed and that the mode of governance based on a deliberative democracy between the state, the business class, and "civil society" prevents the achievement of consensus, stalls the decision-making process at the highest levels, and impedes entrepreneurship. Values that underpin the Québec model (solidarity, equality, participation, and so on) are also accused of hindering economic development and making it impossible to produce enough wealth to rescue the model: once an asset, as the discourse goes, these values have become a liability.[35] Other, more radical voices assert that the path that Québec has followed in recent decades (if not since the 1960s) was the wrong one. It is said to have led to a deep cultural crisis; what is needed now is a bold policy of *tabula rasa* and a whole new beginning drawing on the conservative traditions foolishly destroyed by the Quiet Revolution.[36] Finally, the vigorous fight for French language, in the face of globalization, is blamed for missed business opportunities that need an increased use of English, specially in the Montréal area.

To understand such a shift, it is important to highlight the context of this new debate, a context characterized by a growing sense of collective insecurity feeding on various sources. Among them, an ageing population structure resulting from a very low fertility rate is a widespread source of concern. In addition, major economic difficulties face Québec, including slow productivity growth, a lagging investment rate, declining exports, an increasing level of state indebtedness, skyrocketing health care costs, and a growing specialized labor shortage. According to a widespread view, the state, financially strained, can no longer be the major provider that has driven Québec society since the 1960s.

---

[35] For an expression of those views, see, for instance, Dubuc (2006), McMahon (2003), Bertrand (2006), and *Focus stratégique* (2010). For a defense of the Québec model, see Lisée (2003), Guay and Marceau (2004), and Venne (2006).

[36] This mindset has been well expressed by a think tank of young intellectuals in a collective essay written by Bédard (1998). In a similar vein, among others, see Grand'Maison (1979), Dumont (1997), Paquet (1999), Bédard (2003, and P.-E. Roy (2010).

And needless to say, the traditional pillars of Francophone Québec (the family, the Catholic Church, the high fertility rate that used to sustain strong population growth, the sense of belonging to a Francophone nation that stretched from coast to coast – with significant extensions into the United States) belong to an old past, and none of these has been replaced.

In the same vein, as noted earlier, the linguistic integration of immigrants remains an uncertain challenge, and globalization is an additional threat to the French language. Immigrant groups as a whole are often perceived as conveying a traditional culture that is at odds with Québec's core values, such as gender equality and secularism. Québec nationalism itself seems to be in a deadlock – according to most analysts, it is seeking a second wind.[37] As a result, the national issue ("la question nationale") is still seen as an unfinished business, and as long as it remains so, it will bear heavily on public debate on major questions, including the integration of immigrants and the management of ethno-cultural diversity. Finally, there is a widespread suspicion of corruption in Québec public administration, a suspicion that has lead to the creation, in October 2011, of a governmental commission of inquiry.

All told, these concerns feed uncertainty and generate a depressed mood among many Quebecers that displays itself in various ways.[38] Harsh criticism of the elites, disenchantment, and cynicism along with a sense of powerlessness are spreading. Many lament the loss of traditions and ideals, the "résignation tranquille."[39] Some advocate a "re-foundation," but the periodic calls for another Quiet Revolution have so far remained fruitless. According to a recent poll, 85 percent of Quebecers believe that Québec is going in the wrong direction.[40] In another poll, 87 percent of respondents characterized themselves as disheartened or put off.[41] A third poll revealed that Quebecers are the most pessimistic among Canadians.[42]

Québec at a Crossroads

This chapter has shown that, for a long time, Québec successfully withstood most of the negative effects of neoliberalism. In terms of the typology outlined

[37] This view is supported by the downfall of the Bloc Québécois in the last Canadian elections and by the crisis that has rocked the Parti Québécois in 2011. The latter has won the 2012 September elections but few people believe that it will be able to reignite the fight for sovereignty. It is also meaningful that during the electoral campaign, national issues took a back seat.

[38] In books, polls, radio talk shows, interviews, letters to newspapers, and so forth. According to Lisée (2003: 47), public discourse in Québec is dominated by a strange despondency ("une étrange sinistrose"). Against this background, one is puzzled by the findings of a recent Canadian survey (by the Centre for the Study of Living Standards [CSLS]) according to which Quebecers were as happy in 2008 as they had ever been since 1981 (see Dubuc 2006: 63–4; CSLS 2009).

[39] Benoît Pelletier, a former minister in the Québec Liberal government, coined the expression (*Le Devoir*, October 6, 2010, p. A9).

[40] Léger Marketing, *Journal de Montréal*, November 22, 2010 (p. 5).

[41] Angus Reid, *La Presse*, May 7, 2010 (p. A6). On the same topic, see a detailed survey based on a sample of intellectuals in Bouchard and Roy (2007).

[42] Poll conducted for Franklin Templeton Investments, *Le Devoir*, February 3, 2010 (p. B1).

at the outset of this chapter, I would characterize as progressive the kind of resilience exhibited by this society between the 1970s and the late 1990s. In various ways, not only has it been able to adapt to the new environment created by the surge of neoliberalism, but to a large extent, it has reinvented itself (a new mode of governance that makes room for a "third sector," innovative social engineering, expansion of welfare programs, union involvement as a partner in the capitalist economy, emphasis on international trade, and so on). As underscored by Kymlicka in Chapter 3, Québec has relied on its cultural and social resources to block some neoliberal reforms entirely while rerouting others in unexpected directions. It has also evinced flexibility in integrating elements of neoliberalism: nationalism, for example, has not prevented Québec from admitting high numbers of immigrants and opening its economy to the world market.

However, similar to many other small nations, Québec is now at a cross-roads, and one wonders if the remarkable resilience displayed in recent decades might merely have delayed the negative impact of neoliberalism. If so, decisive battles and choices loom ahead, such as: To shore up the Québec model? To carve out a streamlined version? To turn to a different, neoliberalized model? With various levels of commitment, it is fair to say that the major components of Québec society – including the business class – have pulled together between the 1970s and the end of the century. But that is no longer the case. This being said, whatever direction Québec chooses, a new flow of collective energy will be required to dispel the current sullenness and the growing sense of helplessness and to tackle the challenges that unquestionably lie ahead.

Because this kind of strength is usually found in culture, I will now focus my inquiry on the realm of collective imaginaries, and in this particular case, national myths.[43] What is the state of national myths in Québec? First, a few words about the concept of myth are in order. Contrary to a widespread view, myths are not only lies or manipulations, and they are not always harmful. In general, they are powerful collective, socially produced representations that convey values, beliefs, and ideals (beneficial or detrimental). Mixing reality and fiction, veracity and falseness, they are also a combination of emotion and reason wherein the former overrides the latter. But their most salient characteristic is that they enjoy an authority that draws on a sacredness of sorts, hence their enduring quality and their social efficacy. A characteristic of full-fledged myths is to possess a taboo status that makes them largely immune to criticism and to overt rejection (myths of freedom, peace, gender and racial equality, and the dignity of human life come to mind).

Another feature of full-blown myths is that they escape cold, rational scrutiny and debate; again, they are emotionally driven. Because they are usually taken for granted, one tends to forget that originally they were just ideas, among others, with limited purchase and that they had to travel a complex journey to acquire their extraordinary power. Present in all societies at all

---

[43] As noted earlier, myths are the most powerful component of collective imaginaries, which explains why they must be jointly addressed.

times, they address basic symbolic needs by generating meanings, feeding identities, and providing visions of the future as well as the past. Another major trait of myths is their capacity to mobilize a society on behalf of common goals, to persuade individuals to sacrifice their interests (and sometimes their lives), to unleash energy, and to foster resilience (Bouchard 2003; forthcoming-a). Myths operate in various venues (e.g., organizations, churches, communities), but they are mostly visible at the national level.[44]

The emotional dimension of myths is central. I assume that in the past of every collectivity or society, a few particularly meaningful events or episodes took place (e.g., military victories or defeats, oppression, collective humiliation, natural disasters, remarkable collective achievements), leaving a deep imprint (or feeling) in the psyche. Oftentimes, they are painful experiences that feed a narrative of suffering perpetuated by rituals of commemoration. Officially or apparently designed to heal the scars of the past, these rituals actually accentuate the imprints, reopen the wounds, reactivate the suffering, and reinforce the myths. What matters (for the sake of this analysis) is that somehow the feelings associated with the painful episodes are progressively translated into values (or an ethos). For instance, colonialism will inspire a deep yearning for freedom and democracy, a humiliating defeat will inspire a dream of recovery and reconquest, a regime of privileges will foster an ideal of equality and social justice, and so forth. This configuration (defining episodes → imprints → narratives → ethos) largely driven by emotion and promoted by social actors within a structure of power relations is what I call a myth. One understands why the questioning or the rejection of a full-blown myth sparks an emotional response – it is primarily received as the denial of a suffering or of a glorious accomplishment. Again, that combination accounts for the power of a myth. It also makes clear that a myth cannot be created only through a top-down endeavor; rather, it has to connect with a past episode that resonates with ordinary people and the challenges that they face.

Illustrations of this symbolic configuration abound in contemporary history. The racial equality myth feeds on the suffering of bondage, apartheid, and other forms of discrimination based on skin color. Gender equality taps into a long past of male domination. Popular sovereignty is a legacy of various kinds of enduring totalitarianism. Pluralism, as a philosophy advocating the rights of every individual and the respect of diversity, is a byproduct of multiple experiences of atrocities linked to ethnicism and genocides. The green ideal mostly lives on the fear of environmental destruction associated to past or anticipated catastrophes partaking of dystrophies.

The foregoing also instantiates what I call the mythification process. In each case, one can figure out an initial idea or view that is framed by intellectuals and then strongly promoted by social actors who use it to advance their agenda.

---

[44] From the foregoing, one can see how much I depart from C. Levi-Strauss's approach, which ignores the emotional part of myths, downplays their social and historical nature, emphasizes their symmetric architecture, and mostly locates them in premodern societies.

Subsequently, through a connection with a painful or heartening experience emotionally framed, it results in an unquestioned, widely endorsed value or ideal. This is a complex process in which the last and most defining step occurs when emotion takes over from reason. It coincides with an intriguing cognitive shift that allows for the sacralization of the representation that has now become a full-fledged myth.

Let's come back to Québec. A frequently voiced diagnosis of the present state of Québec's national myths asserts that in the 1960s and 1970s, Québec had vibrant national myths (based on modernity, Francophone self-assertion and emancipation, equality, refoundation, and so on) but that these have subsided without being replaced, thus creating a pernicious vacuum. I do not share this view. True, except for political sovereignty, equality, and democracy, the 1960s myths have faded away but simply because they have exhausted their potential for change. In addition, many observers seem to downplay the fact that new powerful symbolic forces have emerged subsequently, rooted in ecology and sustainability, respect for human rights, pluralism, global thinking, anti-globalization, individual self-promotion through career-achievement, and so on. Still, the feeling of a loss lingers on. What, then, is the problem with the new myths? Why this strong sense of a void?

My answer is threefold. First, all of these new myths share a characteristic that restricts their purchase: they have been brought into Québec through the channels of globalization, so they are not intrinsically the products of Québec history; they are not part of the collective self-script and, to that extent, they do not speak to the nation and to its multisecular narratives (survival, reconquest, and so forth). Moreover, to some extent, they clash with those narratives (e.g., globalization vs. French language). As a result, they do not enjoy widespread emotional endorsement (at least among the Francophones descended from New France's settlers, who now account for 72 to 75 percent of the population), and they are less likely than home-grown myths to generate collective energy and capabilities. Second, they do not coalesce nor do they feed off each other; they operate simply as loose fragments. By contrast, the myths of the Quiet Revolution were closely connected, revolving around one core idea: the affirmation of Francophones in a conjuncture that required a collective catching up. In this kind of configuration, each myth is reinforced by its complementary relationship to the others. Being aligned with each other, they form together what I call an archemyth, a phenomenon that rarely occurs in the history of a society and, not surprisingly, no longer exists in Québec. However, its absence is (wrongly) perceived as a tragic emptiness or a deficit that should urgently be remedied. Third, the new myths have been promoted mostly by experts, marginal groups, leftist intellectuals, and activists with a strong base in academia and among young educated people. As a result, they have yet to percolate into more conventional centers and channels of influence and to get more deeply and emotionally embeded in the mainstream culture.

The analysis of national myths provides another insight into contemporary Québec. I think that, at the core of every collective imaginary, are two sets of myths. The first one consists in a few basic tenets that structure the symbolic foundation of a society and act as a matrix. These tenets are rooted in the so-called imprint, and they express the deepest feelings, fears, values, and aspirations from which people make sense of their lives. I call them master myths. In the case of Québec, one immediately thinks of (a) the old sense of being a fragile cultural minority in North America, compelled to constantly fight for its survival, and (b) the longing for a reconquest as well as a full emancipation nurtured on the experience of colonial domination since 1763[45] and social exploitation endured under both the colonial rule and the Catholic clergy (along with its allies within the professional bourgeoisie). These are obviously at the core of Québec nationalism.

The master myths change very slowly: their structuring power ensures their durability. In turn, they are periodically translated into derivative (or secondary) myths, that is, sets of beliefs, values and ideals that are designed to deal with the ever-evolving anxieties and dreams of a society (anchored in its imprints) and to meet the particular challenges of a given time. Consequently, the structure of a collective imaginary may be seen as a pyramidal architecture comprising a layer of rather stable master myths and a layer of transient derivative myths that may sometimes coalesce into an archemyth.

It can also be anticipated that the replacement of derivative myths will be associated with a period of instability and uncertainty. If so, one can imagine that a substitution at the level of the master myths will be even more distressing. Needless to say, societies are reluctant to engage in that kind of perilous and most destabilizing endeavor, and they tend to defer the dreaded deadline of an overhaul at that profound level.

The master and the derivative myths account overall for a puzzling, double characteristic of myths as we know them in that they are both short lived and durable. Derivative myths provide a society with the means to constantly adapt and change, sometimes through radical ruptures, while thanks to master myths, it still keeps a sense of continuity and stability essential for its survival.

By applying this framework to the history of Québec since the 18th century, it is easy to identify several junctures at which such translations took place, the most recent occurring in the 1960s (Bouchard forthcoming-b). The same approach leads to posit that Québec is now experiencing another of these junctures. So far, however, it has been unable to carry out the transition to a new set of derivative myths that would efficiently address the current challenges in keeping with its master myths. One simply assumes that it is in the process of doing so, beneath the divisions and the sometimes confusing structure of public debate.

But there may be much more at stake. It cannot be precluded that some major adjustments may be underway as well at the very level of the old master myths. Several indicators point in this direction. Understandably seduced by

---

[45] That year, New France became part of the British Empire following the military defeat on the Plains of Abraham (now part of Québec City).

the globalized world, a number of young Quebecers have begun to distance themselves from Québec's master myths. The watering down of national history in the school curriculum (now the topic of heated debate) might also have chipped away at the national imaginary and identity. A number of Québec's leaders (mostly but not only from the business class) now openly question the relevance of the master myths, accusing them of being more of an impediment than an asset.[46] Even among the baby boomers, some sign of weariness can be perceived. In this regard, the recent election of the soveregnist Parti Québécois may be misleading. It has been elected only as a minority government even though the Liberal Party after ten years at the helm of the state had become exceptionally unpopular amid accusations of deep corruption and collusion with multinational corporations. Moreover, the idea of a new referendum on sovereignty is rejected by a strong majority of Quebecers.

One may realistically speculate that the major changes that have taken place in the wake of the Quiet Revolution (increased material security, equality, education, and freedom) have eroded among the Francophones the old sense of victimization and the longing for social emancipation and reconquest. Consequently, over the years, Quebecers have grown more receptive to the new cultural patterns monitored by the World Values Survey (the search for personal development, happiness, self-expression, and the like). Be that as it may, if the hypothesis of a movement at the master myths level were borne out, then Québec would undoubtedly be in for a rough ride. For the time being, however, this is mere conjecture, and one ought to avoid jumping hastily to conclusions. Contexts can change rapidly in an unpredictable way, and it would not be the first time in Québec history that a sullen mindset gives way to the regained faith and optimism that leads to a collective jumpstart.[47]

Still, a huge question is waiting for an answer: Will Québec be able to adapt or redefine its national myths in such a way that they unify and mobilize most of its citizens, as the old myths did? For one thing, as of now, the spirit of the Quiet Revolution, which was a dramatic example of a bold, deep, and peaceful collective overhaul, is definitely gone. Then, what will follow?

Concerning the source of resilience, this analysis seeks to stress the defining role of myths and collective imaginaries more generally, as key factors in the way a society or a nation defines and manages itself for better or for worse. That is why I believe we should pay closer attention to them. As for Québec, it is obvious that from the 1970s to the late 1990s, community organizations and social actors were at the forefront of the fight for the Québec model. But beyond that, it is no less obvious that Quebecers have found in their symbolic

---

[46] A Léger Marketing poll conducted in October 2010 revealed that according to 27% of respondents, Québec should cast aside the national debate, a proportion unthinkable only fifteen years ago.

[47] Among other examples, the dark aftermath of the 1980 referendum on political sovereignty comes to mind. Just a few years later, Québec was back on a new wave of collective action that ultimately led to the 1995 referendum.

capital (i.e., their old master myths that foster a vibrant collective identity and provide a sense of their "difference" to be preserved in North America) the motivation and strength to withstand the assault of neoliberalism and to fight for their institutions and social values inherited from the past.[48] This is what has traditionally nurtured Québec nationalism and driven Francophone Quebecers.

Such a response has been consonant with the heart of their historical legacy. Having been a threatened minority for more than two centuries, plagued by poverty and inequality and seeking emancipation, has sown the seeds of a deep sense of belonging, solidarity, equality, and freedom, as well as a willingness to chart their own destiny. It has also provided the collective energy to mobilize and to act creatively, which is what myths often do. One is reminded that those are the values carried by the master myths, and they had been deeply internalized by the popular groups that have been so active in shoring up the social safety net. Likewise, the elites that have championed this fight were heirs of the Quiet Revolution, itself driven by the old master myths (Bouchard forthcoming-b).

As noted earlier, the neoliberal agenda was on a collision course with the old cultural fabric of this society. In other words, not only actors and ideas matter but also the mythical framework that underlies any collective imaginary. That being said, one should not rule out the possibility that these very sources of progressive resilience in Québec are now being eroded by new economic challenges and globalization – although this statement might call for qualification in the light of the widespread social protest that took place during the first half of 2012 against the neoliberal policies of the government, namely an attempt to significantly raise the tuitions fees at the university level (see note 19).

References

Adams, Michael. 2003. *Fire and Ice: United States, Canada and the Myth of Converging Values*. Toronto: Penguin.

Alix, Carolyne and Robert Choinière. 2008. "La santé en chiffres." In *L'État du Québec 2009*, edited by Miriam Fahmy. Montréal: Fides.

Bédard, Éric. 1998. *Le pont entre les générations*. Montréal: Les Intouchables.

Bédard, Éric. 2003. "La fracture morale." In *Justice, démocratie et prospérité: L'avenir du modèle québécois*, edited by Michel Venne. Montréal: Québec Amérique.

Béland, Claude and Yvon Leclerc, eds. 2003. *La voie citoyenne*. Montréal: Plurimedia.

Bernard M., L.-P. Lauzon, M. Hasbani, and G. Ste-Marie. 2006. *L'autre déséquilibre fiscal. Le développement du fardeau fiscal des compagnies vers les particuliers au cours des dernières décennies*. Montréal: Chaire d'études socio-économiques de l'UQAM.

---

[48] In this book, Lamont et al. (Chapter 4) highlight the role of a strong collective identity as a source of empowerment and resilience and as a buffer against adversity. Other chapters (e.g., Chapter 7 by Barnes and Hall) underscore the positive impact of social connectedness (within families, social classes, nations, and so on) on well-being and resilience.

Bertrand, Françoise. 2006. *Pour sortir le Québec de l'immobilisme et raviver le dynamisme de l'activité économique.* Montréal: Fédération des Chambres de commerce du Québec.

Bordeleau, Christian. 2010. "Partenariats public-privé : chronique d'un échec." In *L'état du Québec 2010*, edited by Miriam Fahmy. Montréal: Boréal.

Bouchard, Gérard. 1998. "Economic Inequalities in Saguenay Society, 1879–1949: A Descriptive Analysis." *Canadian Historical Review* 79 (4): 660–90.

Bouchard, Gérard. 2003. *Raison et contradiction. Le mythe au secours de la pensée.* Québec: Nota Bene/Cefan.

Bouchard, Gérard. 2009. "Collective Imaginaries and Population Health: How Health Data Can Highlight Cultural History." In *Successful Societies: How Institutions and Culture Affect Health*, edited by Peter A. Hall and Michèle Lamont. Cambridge, UK: Cambridge University Press.

Bouchard, Gérard. Forthcoming-a. "Towards a Sociology of Myth. A Blueprint."

Bouchard, Gérard. Forthcoming-b. "The Small Nation with a Big Dream. Québec National Myths (18th–20th centuries)." In Gérard Bouchard (ed), *National Myths. Constructed Pasts, Contested Presents.* London, Routledge (in press).

Bouchard, Gérard. 2012. *L'interculturalisme. Un point de vue québécois.* Montréal: Boréal.

Bouchard, Gérard and Alain Roy. 2007. *La culture québécoise est-elle en crise?* Montréal: Boréal.

Bouchard, Gérard and Charles Taylor. 2008. *Building the Future. A Time For Reconciliation, Québec Government.* Report of the Consultation Commission on Accommodation Practices Related to Cultural Differences. Québec Government.

Bouchard, Marie J., Benoît Lévesque, and Julie St-Pierre. 2005. *Modèle québécois de développement et gouvernance: entre le partenariat et le néolibéralisme?* Montréal: Chaire de recherche du Canada en économie sociale, Université du Québec à Montréal.

Bovin, Jean, Pierre Fortin, and Marc Van Audenrode. 2008. ≪Créer plus de richesse pour mieux la répartir ensuite≫. *Le Devoir* (16 mai): A9.

Brochu, M., and L. Young. 1986. *Les habitudes de consommation des jeunes Québécois de 19 à 24 ans.* Québec: Office de la Protection du consommateur.

Centre for the Study of Living Standards. 2009. *New Estimates of the Index of Economic Well-Being for Canada and the Provinces, 1981–2008.* Ottawa:

Chantier de l'économie sociale. 2004. *Une économie à valeurs ajoutées. Outil de sensibilisation à l'économie sociale.* Montréal: Chantier de l'économie sociale.

Choinière, Robert, Carolyne Alix, Laurie Paquette, and Brahim Belhocine. 2007. *La mortalité au Québec en 2001. Une comparaison internationale.* Québec: Institut national de santé publique du Québec.

Clement, Wallace and John Myles. 1994. *Relations of Ruling: Class and Gender in postindustrial Societies.* Montréal: McGill-Queen's University Press.

Compass, B. E., J. K. Connor-Smith, H. Saltzman, A. H. Thomsen, and M. E. Wadsworth. 2001. "Coping with Stress During Childhood and Adolescence: Progress, Problems, and Potential in Theory and Research." *Psychology Bulletin* 127: 87–127.

Crespo, Stéphane. 2007. *L'inégalité de revenu au Québec 1979–2004: les contributions de composantes de revenu selon le cycle économique.* Québec: Institut de la statistique Québec.

Crespo, Stéphane. 2008. *Annuaire de statistiques sur l'inégalité de revenu et le faible revenu.* Québec: Institut de la statistique du Québec.

Cyrulnik, Boris. 1999. *Un merveilleux malheur*. Paris: Odile Jacob.

D'Amours, Martine. 2006. *Le travail indépendant: un révélateur des mutations du travail*. Sainte-Foy: Presses de l'Université du Québec.

Dionne, Hugues and Juan-Luis Klein. 1995. "Les villages face à l'État: de la révolte territoriale au développement local." In Alain Gagnon and Alain Noël, *L'espace québécois*. Montréal, Québec Amérique.

Dubuc, Alain. 2006. *Éloge de la richesse*. Montréal: Éditions Voix parallèles.

Dumont, Fernand. 1997. *Récit d'une émigration: mémoires*. Montréal: Boréal.

Fantasia, Rick and Kim Voss. 2003. *Des syndicats domestiques. Répression patronale et résistance syndicale aux États-Unis*. Paris: Raisons d'agir.

Focus stratégique. 2010. "Pour un Québec 3.0." *Montréal: Focus stratégique Québec 2010*. http://www.focusstrategique.com.

Fortin, Pierre. 2009a. "Six observations sur la croissance québécoise à la manière de Gilles Paquet." In *Gilles Paquet: homo hereticus*, edited by Caroline Andrew, Ruth Hubbard, and Jeffrey Roy. Ottawa: University of Ottawa Press.

Fortin, Pierre. 2009b. "Quebec's Surprising Economic Performance: The Myth of a Lagging Quebec Doesn't Stand up to the Facts," *Inroads* Winter/Spring: 108–115.

Fortin, Pierre. 2010a. "La Révolution tranquille et l'économie: où étions-nous, qu'avons-nous accompli, que nous reste-t-il à faire?" Public lecture, Grande Bibliothèque. Montréal, May 11.

Fortin, Pierre. 2010b. "Quebec Is Fairer: There Is Less Poverty and Less Inequality in Quebec." *Inroads: A Journal of Opinion* 26: 58–65. Fortin, Pierre. Forthcoming. « Income Inequalities in United States, Canada and Québec ».

Fournier, François. 2010a. *Les indicateurs de mortalité générale au Québec: perspectives comparées dans le temps et l'espace*. Document I-E-34. Chicoutimi: Chaire de recherche du Canada sur la dynamique comparée des imaginaires collectifs.

Fournier, François. 2010b. *La participation électorale au Québec: perspectives comparées*. Document I-E-37. Chicoutimi: Chaire de recherche du Canada sur la dynamique comparée des imaginaires collectifs.

Gastaut, Yvan. 2009. "La diversité culturelle au Québec: enjeux identitaires d'une histoire complexe au XXᵉ siècle." *Migrance* 34: 4–28.

Gingras, Yves. 2010. "Trente ans de recherche universitaire au Québec. Les chiffres." *Découvrir* May–June: 80–8.

Godbout, Luc, Pierre Fortin, and Suzie St-Cerny. 2006. "La défiscalisation des entreprises au Québec est un mythe: Pour aller au-delà de la croyance populaire." In *Document de travail* 2006/03. Sherbrooke: Chaire de recherche en fiscalité et en finances publiques.

Grand'Maison, Jacques. 1979. *La nouvelle classe et l'avenir du Québec*. Montréal: Stanké.

Guay, Alain and Nicolas Marceau. 2004. "Le Québec n'est pas le cancre économique qu'on dit: Les écarts avec le reste du Canada s'effacent progressivement depuis 25 ans." In *L'annuaire du Québec 2005*, edited by Michel Venne. Montréal: Fides.

Jetté, Christian. 2008. *Les organismes communautaires et la transformation de l'État-providence: Trois décennies de coconstruction des politiques publiques dans le domaine de la santé et des services sociaux*. Québec: Presses de l'Université du Québec.

Joanis, Marcelin, Luc Godbout, and Jean-Pierre Aubry. 2009. *Le Québec économique 2009: le chemin parcouru depuis 40 ans*. Québec: Les Presses de l'Université Laval.

Juteau, Danielle. 2002. "The Citizen Makes an Entrée: Redefining the National Community in Quebec." *Citizenship Studies* 6 (4): 441–58.

Juteau, Danielle. 2004. "'Pures laines' Québécois: The concealed ethnicity of dominant majorities." In *Rethinking Ethnicity: Majority Groups and Dominant Minorities*, edited by Eric P. Kaufmann. London and New York: Routledge.

Labelle, Micheline. 2000. "La politique de la citoyenneté et de l'interculturalisme au Québec: défis et enjeux." In *Les identités en débat: intégration ou multiculturalisme*, edited by H. Greven and J. Tournon. Paris: L'Harmattan.

Laitin, David D. 1986. *Hegemony and Culture: Politics and religious Change among the Yoruba*. Chicago: University of Chicago Press.

Langlois, Simon. 2004. "Le Québec en profonde mutation." In *L'annuaire du Québec 2005*, edited by Michel Venne. Montréal: Fides.

Langlois, Simon. 2008. "Québec 2008: Portrait social." In *L'état du Québec 2009*, edited by Miriam Fahmy. Montréal: Fides.

Larose, Gérald, Yves Vaillancourt, Genevière Shields, and Muriel Kearney. 2004. "Contributions de l'économie sociale au renouvellement des politiques et des pratiques dans le domaine de l'insertion socioéconomique au Québec, de 1983 à 2003." *Cahiers du LAREPPS*. Montréal: Université du Québec à Montréal.

Larose, Gérard, Yves Vaillancourt, Geneviève Shields, and Muriel Kearney. 2005. "Contributions of the Social Economy to the Renewal of policies and practices in the area of welfare to work in Quebec during the years 1983–2003." *Canadian Journal of Career Development* 4 (1): 11–28.

Léger Marketing. 2001. *Les Canadiens et les cartes de crédit*. Québec: Léger Marketing.

Lévesque, Benoît. 2008. "Le potentiel d'innovation et de transformation de l'économie sociale: quelques éléments de problématique." *Interaçoes-Revista Internacional de Desenvolvimento local* 9 (2): 193–216.

Lisée, Jean-François. 2003. "Un mauvais procès au modèle québécois. Étude des pièces à conviction." In *Justice, démocratie et prospérité. L'avenir du modèle québécois*, edited by Michel Venne. Montréal: Québec Amérique.

Lisée, Jean-François. 2010. "Pour fuir la haine nord-américaine." *L'Actualité* June 17.

McMahon, Fred. 2003. "Quebec Prosperity: Taking the Next Step." Vancouver: Centre for Budgetary Studies, The Fraser Institute.

Neamtan, Nancy. 2006. *L'économie sociale au Québec: au coeur de l'innovation et des transformations sociales*. Public lecture, Bank of Montréal April 4.

Noël, Alain. 2010. "Quebec." In *The Oxford Handbook of Canadian Politics*, edited by John C. Courtney, and David E. Smith. New York: Oxford University Press.

O'Meara, Patrick, H. D. Mehlinger, and K. Matthew, eds. 2000. *Globalization and the New Challenges of a New Century: A Reader*. Bloomington: Indiana University Press.

Ouimet, Marc. 2001. "Réflexions sur la baisse de la criminalité au Québec." Paper presented at the annual conference of the Société de criminologie du Québec, May 23.

Ouimet, Marc. 2004. "État de la criminalité au Québec." In *L'annuaire du Québec 2005*, edited by Michel Venne. Montréal: Fides.

Paquet, Gilles. 1999. *Oublier la Révolution tranquille: Pour une nouvelle socialité*. Montréal: Liber.

Québec Government. 1990. *Vision: A Policy Statement on Immigration and Integration*. Québec: Ministère des Communautés culturelles et de l'Immigration.

Québec Government. 2010. *Indicateurs de l'éducation*. Québec, Department of Education, Recreation and Sports (www.mels.gouv.qc.ca).

Reitz, Jeffrey G. and Rupa Banerjee. 2009. "Racial Inequality and Social Integration." In *Multiculturalism and Social Cohésion*, edited by J. G. Reitz, R. Breton, K. K. Dion, K. L. Dion. New York: Springer.

Rocher, François, Micheline Labelle, Ann-Marie Field, and Jean-Claude Icart. 2008. *Le concept d'interculturalisme en contexte québécois: généalogie d'un néologisme.* Research report no. 3. Montréal: Bouchard-Taylor Commission.

Rouillard, Jacques. 2008. *L'expérience syndicale au Québec.* Montréal: VLB.

Roy, Alain. 2010a. *Note sur la participation démocratique au Québec et au Canada.* Document I-E-33. Chicoutimi: Chaire de recherche du Canada sur la dynamique comparée des imaginaires collectifs.

Roy, Alain. 2010b. *Note sur le taux de syndicalisation.* Document I-E-35. Chicoutimi: Chaire de recherche du Canada sur la dynamique comparée des imaginaires collectifs.

Roy, Alain. 2010c. *Note sur le niveau de scolarité.* Document I-E-38. Chicoutimi: Chaire de recherche du Canada sur la dynamique comparée des imaginaires collectifs.

Roy, Paul-Émile. 2010. *Le mouvement perpétuel. Itinéraire d'un Québécois candide dans la modernité.* Montréal: Bellarmin.

Saez, Emmanuel and Michael R. Veall. 2005. "The Evolution of High Incomes in Northern America: Lessons from Canadian Evidence." *American Economic Review* 95 (3): 831–49.

Statistics Canada. 2010. *Education Indicators in Canada: An International Perspective.* Ottawa: Catalogue 81-604-X.

Thomson, Dale C. 1984. *Jean Lesage and the Quiet Revolution.* Toronto: Macmillan.

Tomlinson, John. 1999. *Globalization and Culture.* Chicago: University of Chicago Press.

Ungar, Michael. 2008. "Resilience Across Cultures." *British Journal of Social Work* 38: 218–35.

Vaillancourt, François and Luc Vaillancourt. 2005. *La propriété des employeurs au Québec en 2003 selon le groupe d'appartenance linguistique.* Québec: Conseil supérieur de la langue française.

Vaillancourt, Yves. 2002. "Le modèle québécois de politiques sociales et ses interfaces avec l'union sociale canadienne." *Enjeux publics* 3 (2): 2–52.

Vaillancourt, Yves. 2006. "Le développement social: Un enjeu fondamental pour le bien-être des communautés." In *Le développement social: Un enjeu pour l'économie sociale*, edited by Marielle Tremblay, Pierre-André Tremblay, and Suzanne Tremblay. Québec: Presses de l'Université du Québec.

Vaillancourt, Yves. 2008. *L'économie sociale au Québec et au Canada: configurations historiques et enjeux actuels.* Cahiers du LAREPPS no. 08–07. Montréal: Laboratoire de recherche sur les pratiques et les politiques sociales (LAREPPS/UQAM).

Vaillancourt, Yves, Christian Jettè, and Philippe Leclerc. 2009. *Les arrangements institutionnels entre l'État québécois et les entreprises d'économie sociale en aide domestique: une analyse sociopolitique de l'économie sociale dans les services de soutien à domicile.* Montréal: Éditions Vie Économique.

Venne, Michel. 2006. "Le mythe de l'immobilisme." In *L'Annuaire du Québec 2007*, edited by Michel Venne, and Miriam Fahmy. Montréal: Fides.

Walsh, Phil and Mia Dauvergne. 2009. "Police-reported hate crime in Canada, 2007." *Juristat* 29 (2): 1–9.

Can Communities Succeed When States Fail Them?

A Case Study of Early Human Development and Social Resilience in a Neoliberal Era

Clyde Hertzman and Arjumand Siddiqi

Early human development matters. By school age, the experiences children have had in the places where they have grown up, lived, and learned have influenced their level of development, that is, understanding and expressing language, sense of belonging, capacity for empathy and self-control, and ability to focus on complex tasks (Barker 1994; Bronfenbrenner 1979; Wadsworth 1997). Some children grow up in warm, responsive environments that protect them from inappropriate disapproval and punishment and where there are opportunities to explore their world, to play, and to learn how to speak and listen to others (Ramey and Ramey 1998). But others do not. Although abuse and neglect are serious matters, these relatively subtle differences in children's day-to-day environments accumulate into large developmental effects. For example, the number of words a child can recognize and express by age three years varies by more than threefold among otherwise normally developing children. This is because receptive and expressive language skills improve in a "dose-response" fashion with the number and variety of words spoken directly to them, and the forms in which language is used, during those three years (Hart and Risley 1995a). By the time they reach school age, the American child who has heard the most language has actually heard approximately 30 million more words than the child who has heard the least (Hart and Risley 1995b)!

Early experiences, and the state of development they produce, go on to influence health, well-being, learning, and behavior across the balance of the life course. By the second decade of life, early experiences influence the risk of school failure, teen pregnancy, and criminality. By the third and fourth decades of life, early life influences obesity, blood pressure, and depression; by the fifth and sixth decades, coronary heart disease and diabetes; and by late life, premature aging and memory loss (Harkonmäki et al. 2007) Social factors, from the most intimate experiences within the family to the most global, influence early human development in tangible and highly interdependent ways.

Taken together, these factors function similar to complex adaptive ecological systems in nature.

Accordingly, this chapter asks the question: can local communities succeed in promoting the early stages of human development when public provision, and the senior governments that provide it, fail? This question goes to the sources and character of social resilience because, as we shall see, questions about social resilience are especially salient at the meso level of society that exists between the level of the individual and the state. Social resilience is bound up in whether or not, and how, people and institutions interacting daily with children succeed or fail in fostering healthy development in the face of broader social and economic forces that may be hostile to families; occurring during an era when traditional public provision approaches are in retreat.

Social resilience is a function of the adaptive qualities of the "complex system" that produces or undermines early human development. This chapter addresses the theme of social resilience by exploring whether local communities in British Columbia, Canada, have been able to successfully support early human development in the face of emerging challenges arising from social and economic forces operating at broader levels of society during a neoliberal era, such as the changing gender roles and demands of the labor market that are occurring in a context of increasing levels of family socioeconomic inequality. It shows that only a small minority of local communities has been able to succeed under these conditions. Successful communities provide important lessons in social resilience, showing that it is *possible* for strength at some levels of society to substitute for weakness at others. Most important, success depended on a process of evidence-based coalition formation. As we shall see when we discuss "trend-bucker communities," effective coalitions had to be *intersectoral* in character and provide *durable* resources to families with children in both human and material terms. Although certain exceptional communities succeeded in this process, in the absence of ongoing support from the senior levels of government, most failed. In general, neoliberal reforms at senior governmental levels, in effect, defeated initiatives at the local level.

Successfully supporting the earliest stages of human development is a significant challenge to our collective capacities and is hard to achieve. In Canada, the proportion of children reaching kindergarten "vulnerable"[1] (i.e., behind where they need to be to get full benefit from school) in one or more domains of development (physical, social, emotional, language and cognitive, or communication skills) varies from fewer than 5 percent in some neighborhoods to as much as 70 percent in others (Forum for Early Child Development Monitoring 2011). Yet at birth, no more than 5 percent of children have clinically diagnosable limitations to their development. Our studies of neighborhood variations in vulnerability across Canada show that vulnerability at or below 5 percent is

---

[1] The validity of measurements of vulnerability has been well established and is presented in the section that discusses the Early Development Instrument.

rarely achieved, but 10 percent is a practical target for Canadian society *because it has been achieved* in a range of neighborhoods across the country. Therefore, with vulnerability currently standing at 29 percent in British Columbia, approximately two thirds would be avoidable if its de facto complex ecological system for early human development were better adapted. Because vulnerability rates greater than 10 percent are, in principal, avoidable, a tremendous amount of "excess vulnerability" emerges in Canada before school age.[2]

Excess vulnerability, in the sense described here, is important for society as a whole, not just the individual child. In British Columbia, vulnerability data have been linked to school achievement data on an individual basis. These, in turn, have been linked to "end of school qualifications" and then to models of the economic returns to end of school qualifications. For every 1 percent that vulnerability can be reduced in a given school entry cohort, the model predicts that there will be a 1 percent increase in gross domestic product (GDP) over that cohort's working life after discounting for inflation (Kershaw et al. 2009). In the case of British Columbia, the cost to reduce vulnerability from 29 to 10 percent is estimated at $3 billion per year in a jurisdiction with approximately 200,000 children ages 0 to 5 years. But the prospects of a 19 percent increase in GDP over the working lifetime of the beneficiaries translates into a $6 return for each new dollar spent in the early years on quality learning, development, parenting, and care programs. This is the argument for considering early child development (ECD) spending an investment. Moreover, it has the largest potential economic return to society of any new conceivable investment even after accounting for the years and decades it takes for children to grow up (Carneiro and Heckman 2003) and much greater than a marginal new dollar spent on grades one to twelve or, for that matter, at the postsecondary level.

Developing policies and programs that actually improve ECD at the level of the population is not straightforward because ECD is influenced in different ways by a wide range of interdependent factors, some programmatic and others not. To understand the nature of this challenge and its implications for social resilience in a neoliberal era, we present the Total Environment Assessment Model of Early Child Development (TEAM-ECD; Fig. 10-1) (Irwin, Siddiqi, and Hertzman 2007). Working from micro to macro, it features interacting and interdependent spheres of influence that affect ECD outcomes: the individual; family and dwelling; residential and relational communities; civil society; programs and services; and regional, national, and global environments.

The Determinants of Early Human Development: TEAM-ECD

TEAM-ECD suggests that human development is an emergent property of multiple levels of a complex adaptive ecological system. Yet the determinants of early human development (herein, we use ECD, or early child development,

---

[2] At present, Canada and Australia are the only countries to produce comparable population-based data to make such inferences. Australia's patterns of vulnerability are similar to Canada's.

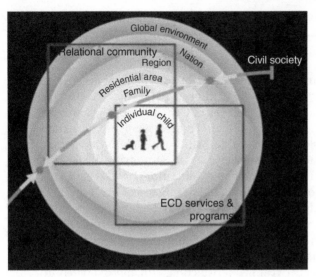

FIGURE 10-1. The Total Environment Assessment Model of Early Child Development.

as an acronym) are commonly treated as factors that operate independently of one another or, at most, as factors operating simultaneously in multiple spheres. What is often neglected is the extent to which the level and effect of relevant factors in any one sphere depends on factors normally thought to belong to other spheres. The following description of the levels shows both their special character and the qualities of interdependence that need to be taken into consideration.

The Individual Child
The links between individual development and population health have only been understood for the past fifteen to twenty years. We now know that disparities emerge early in life in children's physical, social and emotional, and language and cognitive development that are largely attributable to systematic differences in the nurturant qualities of their early environments, including nutrition, bonding and attachment, stimulation, and opportunities for participation (Mayall 1994; Grantham-McGregor et al. 1997; Boyden and Levison 2000; Irwin and Johnson 2005; Irwin 2006). A dense, hierarchically connected series of sensitive periods occurs in brain and biological development during those years, such that early environments can embed themselves in brain circuitry and other biological systems (Hertzman and Boyce 2010). Within the past five years, it has become clear that early experiences penetrate to the deepest levels of human biology; changing the way that genes express themselves (Hertzman and Boyce 2010). These emerging understandings are important because they call for changes in the causal beliefs of key actors at all levels of society, ones that demand new coalitions for policy and action to better

manage the complex ecosystem of early human development (Jenkins-Smith and Sabatier 1994).

The Family

Families provide most stimuli for children, define the social and economic resources available to children, and largely control children's contact with the wider environment and the terms upon which it occurs (Shonkoff and Phillips 2000; Richter 2004; United Nations Children's Fund [UNICEF] 2007). Social resources include parenting skills and education, cultural practices and approaches, intrafamilial relations, and the health status of family members. Economic resources provide material goods (e.g., healthy foods and adequate dwelling conditions) and help to reduce stress for parents, which in turn supports nurturing relationships between family members and with children. As one goes from the bottom to the top of families in terms of social and economic resources, child developmental outcomes, on average, improve. This is the "gradient effect," which is a principal source of modifiable inequality in ECD (Houweling et al. 2005). Gradients mean that the fraction of vulnerable children *gradually* increases *without a threshold* as one goes from the most privileged to the least privileged families. Children in the least privileged families have the greatest chance of lacking resources and therefore of being vulnerable. However, from the perspective of society, *the largest number* (i.e., the numerical majority) of vulnerable children is spread more thinly across the (much more numerous) middle class. Although material deprivation is not, typically, a feature of middle class childhood, parental time pressures; postpartum maternal depression; inconsistent, detached, or authoritarian parenting styles; and mediocre childcare are thought of as significant sources of vulnerability for middle class children. A key characteristic of a society that is successfully supporting ECD is gradient flattening, that is, children from lower socioeconomic backgrounds reaching school age at a similar level of physical, social-emotional, and language and cognitive development as those from more privileged backgrounds.

Residential and Relational Communities

Socioeconomic, social capital, physical, and service characteristics of *residential* communities influence ECD (Kawachi and Berkman 2003). Socioeconomic inequalities among residential communities are associated with inequalities in children's development, but there are important caveats. Children from low socioeconomic families living in economically mixed neighborhoods often do better in their development than low socioeconomic children living in poor neighborhoods (Kohen et al. 2002). There is an inverse association between the socioeconomic status of a community and the chances that its residents will be exposed to toxic or otherwise hazardous exposures such as wastes, air pollutants, poor water quality, excessive noise, residential crowding, or poor housing quality (Evans and Katrowitz 2002). Physical spaces accessible to children create both opportunities and constraints for play-based learning and exploration, which is critical for motor, social and emotional, and cognitive development (Irwin 2006). Access to high-quality services, including learning and recreation, childcare, medical, transportation, food markets, and opportunities for employment, often varies according to community socioeconomic status (Leventhal and Brooks-Gunn 2000). Child development is also influenced by the quality of community social capital (Putnam 2001; Carpiano 2006; Drukker et al. 2006).

The *relational* community is the group that gives children and families their primary identity and is often how outsiders identify them. It is also a source of information regarding child-rearing practices and norms of child development. The relational community may be defined by language, religion, ethnicity, geography (e.g., rural), or the occupational status of the parents. It is a primary source of prospects for social inclusion or exclusion, sense of self (e.g., efficacy, self-worth, self-esteem), and gender norms. The extent to which adults and children in communities are linked to one another, whether there is reciprocated exchange (of information, in-kind services, and other forms of support), and whether there is informal social control and mutual support is, in part, a function of the relational community. A complementary dimension is the bridge between the relational community and the broader society through inclusive definitions of citizenship. When inclusiveness is successful, it serves to break down barriers of access to social resources outside the relational community that can facilitate ECD, especially for ethno-racial minorities.

Civil Society
In British Columbia, similar to other places around the world, governments have tried to address the challenges of ECD in a neoliberal era through a civil society approach. Civil society is called upon to organize strategies at the local level that provide families and children with effective delivery of ECD services, improve the safety and cohesion of residential environments, and increase the capacity of local and relational communities to better the lives of children. They have supported local "intersectoral coalitions" (see later discussion) and called upon them to address the needs of families with children when public funding and provision are lacking. As we shall see, however, trying to replace public provision with civil society rather than building systems that bring the public and the civic together is a failing strategy. Much of the reason for this is bound up in the character of effective ECD programs and services.

Early Child Development Programs and Services
When they are of high quality, ECD programs promote the development of human capital, that is, individuals' competencies and skills for participating in society and the workforce (Knudsen et al. 2006). The competencies and skills fostered through quality ECD programs are not limited to the cognitive domain but also include physical, social, and emotional development.

Accordingly, ECD programs – which incorporate and link health-promoting measures (e.g., good nutrition, immunization) with nurturance, participation, care, stimulation, and protection – offer the prospect of sustained improvements in physical, social, emotional, language, and cognitive development. More specifically, ECD programs usually address one or more of the following key issues: breastfeeding, developmental monitoring, early childhood care and education, nutrition, parenting, community strengthening, or institutional capacities such as training. A prime example of a comprehensive approach is Sweden's. Its system provides high-quality, high-coverage prenatal care associated with low low-birth-weight rates; near-monthly developmental monitoring in the first 18 months of life such that all vision, hearing, speech and language, and dental problems are identified and addressed before children start school; universal, noncompulsory access to publicly funded high-quality programs of early learning and care (which 80 to 90 percent of preschool age children attend) run by university educated staff that are funded and monitored nationally but organized and delivered locally; and, finally, a gradual transition from play-based to formal learning at school age that serves to avoid privileging January babies and girls and disadvantaging December babies and boys. These programs and services are complemented by an incomes policy that brings virtually all families with young children above the poverty line, as well as up to 18 months of paid parental leave with incentives for the father to take some of it.

Programs such as this are expensive to provide (absorbing ~1.5 percent of GDP) (Organisation for Economic Co-operation and Development [OECD] 2006) and are most effective when they are organized in a way that coordinates diverse sectors (e.g., health, education, family support, childcare, town planning). This is why regional and national governments, with their taxing authority and broad policymaking powers, are essential supports for local agencies and institutions trying to deliver effective programs.

Regional and National

Regions (i.e., subnational political jurisdictions) and nations are important for their capacity to provide, or deny, families access to societal resources. Although child development tends to be more successful in wealthy than in poor countries, the priority given to children in social policy can overcome national poverty by enabling families to make positive choices and decisions in the best interests of their children. Kamerman et al.'s (2003) review of family policies across countries identified five domains that make a difference: income transfers (cash and tax benefits), employment policies, parental leave and other policies to support maternal employment, early childhood education and care services, and prevention and other interventions related to teen pregnancy. At the regional level, factors that support or undermine family capacity include the physical environment (e.g., transportation, local accessibility of programs and services, family friendliness of housing market), the degree to which the labor market accommodates families' needs for income and time flexibility, and the policy priority placed on investments in the early years. Absent these resources, children born into low-resource families are more likely to be exposed to conditions that are adverse for development, such as homelessness, crowding, slum living conditions, and unsafe neighborhoods (DiPietro 2000; Dunn and Hayes 2000), as well as a variety of forms of parental psychological distress, including negative self-worth and depression (NICHD Early Child Care Network 2002; Patel, DeSouza, and Rodrigues 2003).

The Global Environment

The global environment influences ECD through its effects on economic and social conditions within nations. Heymann's (2006) research on children and families in resource-poor countries demonstrates the importance of access to quality childcare for families the world over. Because of increased female participation in the global workforce, millions of children worldwide are being left home alone, left in informal childcare (often by other children), or being brought to work and exposed to unsafe working conditions. The global environment is also characterized by international treaties, such as the United Nations Convention on the Rights of the Child (UN-CRC), that affirm the rights of children (UN General Assembly 1989) and of the principal caregivers of children, women (UN General Assembly 1979). In particular, General Comment #7, a rider attached to UN-CRC, called "Implementing Rights in Early Childhood" (UN Committee on the Rights of the Child [CRC] 2006), creates an opportunity to hold signatory countries responsible for the physical, social and emotional, and language and cognitive development of young children.

Implications of the TEAM-ECD Model

There are four principal implications of the TEAM-ECD model for social resilience in a neoliberal era. First, there is the imperative to address the non-dramatic elements of daily experience that drive early development, which are hard to influence effectively without strong working ties between public funders and local providers. Second, it makes clear the degree of interdependence of the social determinants of ECD. Although strong families or strong programs can make a difference, action on any one determinant, absent the others, may have limited long-term effect *at the level of the population*. Thus, TEAM-ECD meets the basic criterion for a complex system, such that insights about adaptivity and resilience in other complex systems could prove instructive (Homer-Dixon 2006). (These are discussed in the trend-bucker section later.) One key indicator of the health of this particular complex adaptive system is the steepness of the socioeconomic gradient in ECD such that the flatter the gradient the more healthful the ecosystem. This leads to the third implication. Because of the statistical properties of gradients, showing gradually increasing rates of vulnerability as one goes down the socioeconomic spectrum, no special population can be targeted – by income, race, ethnicity, immigration, birth weight, gestational age, family psychosocial risk status, or adverse neighborhood circumstances – that will include a majority of the children who will be developmentally vulnerable by the time they reach school age. This is counter to the notion that public provision matters for poor kids but not rich kids. For example, the argument goes, if we provide free summer programs for poor children, then families that are most disadvantaged will be able to make up for not being in school, but privileged families will find ways to create stimulating summer experiences without public provision. The evidence, instead, predicts that the "public provision for the poor and private resources for the rich" will be ineffective when it comes to improving ECD across the whole population. Fourth, pursuing policies that flatten gradients would appear to have the best chance of improving overall societal outcomes. For example, in the advanced capitalist nations, differences in average levels of reading literacy seem to be driven by differences in socioeconomic inequality in reading literacy; smaller socioeconomic inequalities result in higher averages. Moreover, cross-national differences in socioeconomic inequalities themselves result from differences in the literacy of those at the lower end of the socioeconomic spectrum, but across countries, those at higher ends of the spectrum perform similarly well (Siddiqi et al. 2007).

Case Study: The Province of British Columbia

British Columbia provides a useful case study because it is a jurisdiction where civil society initiatives for ECD were widely encouraged by the provincial government, concurrent with neoliberal federal and provincial policies that were limiting public spending and provision. In other words, British Columbia presents a natural experiment wherein the mesolevels of society, at which issues of social resilience are most salient, were directly put to the test. Luckily, British Columbia has also created the world's best population-based system for monitoring ECD outcomes over time. These data allow us to directly evaluate social resilience by tracking how the state of ECD changed in different communities across the province from 2000 to 2010.

Population-based measurement of ECD at kindergarten (age five years) began in 2000 using the Early Development Instrument (EDI) and has been repeated every few years, such that by 2010, four rounds of population-wide data had been collected. The EDI (Janus and Offord 2000) is a checklist-style questionnaire that is filled out by kindergarten teachers on each child in February of the kindergarten year when they know each child well enough to provide reliable, valid answers. The EDI has five scales that encompass the key domains of children's early development: physical, social, emotional, language/cognitive, and communication skills. Each scale has an established vulnerability cut-off with known predictive validity (Janus et al. 2007) such that children who are designated "vulnerable" on one or more EDI scale are, on average, at higher risk of failing to gain benefit from their school years. At first, the fact that the EDI is teacher rated gave rise to concerns about its validity and reliability compared with direct assessments. However, these concerns have been laid to rest through studies showing that the EDI outperforms direct assessments in predicting school success (Forget-Dubois et al. 2007; D'Anguilli et al. 2009). In contrast to direct assessment, kindergarten teacher reporting is inexpensive enough to allow all children in a jurisdiction to be included; allowing for a population-based assessment of the state of ECD and its determinants.[3] British Columbia, however, is the only jurisdiction with four rounds of data, allowing assessment of trends in ECD over time.

By 2004, all school districts in British Columbia had completed the EDI at least once. Developmental vulnerability had been mapped according to the province's 59 geographic school districts[4] and the 484 residential neighborhoods within them. Neighborhood boundaries relevant to ECD were created through research team consultation with local intersectoral coalitions for ECD, which had either been directly set up and funded by the province (the Children First program) or indirectly funded through the United Way/Credit Unions of British Columbia (the Success by Six program). Overall, 26.1 percent of kindergarten children demonstrated vulnerability on one or more EDI scales, with a range across school districts from 14 to 37 percent and a greater range, of less than 10 to greater than 60 percent, across neighborhoods. The magnitude of the gradient can be expressed by saying that approximately 50 percent of the variation in vulnerability rates was "explained," in a statistical sense, by variations in neighborhood socioeconomic status. These data were widely circulated around the province through community and in camera presentations, newspaper articles, and web-based distribution. As a result, an astonishing amount of activity was initiated; at least 500 initiatives – the vast majority of them local – were inspired, in whole or in part, by these data. Initiatives ranged from expanding parenting support programs to decisions on where to place new community centers, to new capital spending on childcare. Moreover, initiatives could be found in virtually all parts of the province (Mort 2004).

Between 2004 and 2007, a second province-wide round of EDI measurement was completed. Because of all of the ECD initiatives started in the interim, hopes were high that things had improved, that is, that vulnerability rates would be down and neighborhood socioeconomic gradients would be reduced. Sadly, neither of these things happened. The overall vulnerability rate increased to 29.6 percent; the school district range of vulnerability widened to 12 to 54 percent, and the number of neighborhoods classified as "high" vulnerability (i.e., greater than one third of the children vulnerable on one or more domain of development) increased from 86 to 142. Furthermore, on the third (2007–2009)

---

[3] Currently, the EDI is the population-based measure of choice in Canada and Australia. It has been introduced in more than a dozen other countries and is being considered for widespread use in the United States, Scotland, Sweden, and China.

[4] School districts were used as a unit of geography. Children were mapped according to the geographic school district where they lived regardless of where they went to school.

and fourth (2009–2010) rounds of data collection, by which time many of the local initiatives to support ECD had matured, vulnerability remained stuck between 28.5 and 30.0 percent. To summarize: over one decade, vulnerability rose by 10 to 15 percent in relative terms, such that, by the 2009 to 2010 school year in a jurisdiction with 40,000 births annually, approximately 1200 "extra" vulnerable children were starting school each year compared with the school years 2000 to 2001 to 2003 to 2004. This occurred despite health promotion messaging and widespread local initiatives for ECD.[5]

The Sources of Decline in Healthy Child Development

Why did developmental vulnerability rise despite commitment and action to support ECD, found in all communities in the province? A natural impulse is to look for an explanation that is unique to British Columbia. However, enough trend data from the EDI were available from other jurisdictions in Canada to show that rising vulnerability was a national pattern and not confined to British Columbia. This observation was crucial because it took the issue from the provincial to the national level, requiring a Canada-wide explanation. The search for an explanation began with insights from previous work on Canada–United States comparisons of trends in health status (Siddiqi and Hertzman 2007), an example that led us to look for institutional trends in public provision that might drive declining human development outcomes by gradually undermining family, local, and regional capacity to support children in their earliest years.

The precedent, from comparisons of Canada–United States trends in health status, goes as follows. The last three decades of the twentieth century, a period of relative economic stagnation and higher unemployment in Canada compared with the United States, nonetheless saw the health status of Canadians increasingly surpass that of their American counterparts (Siddiqi and Hertzman 2007). Life expectancy in Canada grew faster than in the United States, creating a gap of 2.2 years by 1996, which represented 30 to 40 percent lower mortality rates in the working years 25 to 64 years. During this period, the socioeconomic gradient in health status remained stable in Canada such

---

[5] When the overall increase in EDI vulnerability is disaggregated by scale, it shows that there had been some *declines* in vulnerability in language and cognitive development, which had been offset, in the aggregate, by larger increases in vulnerability in physical, social, and emotional development and communication skills. Within the EDI, most of the traditional measures of "readiness for school" are concentrated in the language and cognitive development scale (e.g., knowledge of letter and number facts). A pattern of decline in vulnerability on this scale, in conjunction with increases in the others, is consistent with a prospect that widespread interest in the importance of the early years may have led parents and their local institutional partners to trade off the goals and values of holistic early development against a more narrowly defined, academically competitive notion of "readiness for school." This trend occurred despite extensive evidence that noncognitive traits and behaviors may be equally, if not more, important for long-term socioeconomic success (Farkas 2003).

TABLE 10-1. *Diverging Trends of Life Expectancy Versus Mortality in Infancy and Childhood*

Outcome	Canada	United States	Sweden
Life Expectancy (years)			
1996	78.2	76.0	79.0
2008	81.0	78.4	81.2
Infant Mortality Rate (%)			
1996	5.6	7.3	3.8
2008	5.7	6.7	2.3
Under-Five Mortality Rate (%)			
1996	7.0	9.0	4.6
2008	6.4	7.8	3.0

World Bank, 2010.

that, over the twenty-five-year period from 1971 to 1996, each income quintile experienced roughly equal gains in life expectancy (Wilkins, Berthelot, and Ng 2002). In the United States, by contrast, the highest income quintiles gained life expectancy at a *significantly* faster pace than the lowest quintile (Singh and Siahpush 2002). By the end of the twentieth century, the poorest 20 percent of Canadians enjoyed the same life expectancy as Americans of average income (Singh and Siahpush 2002; Wilkins et al. 2002), and infant mortality among the poorest 20 percent of Canadians was lower than infant mortality for the United States as a whole.

Institutional factors such as mechanisms for income distribution and redistribution, as well as public provision of other health-related resources, dominated the explanation for this trend. In contrast, levels of health care spending, economic growth, and unemployment proved counterfactual because, as the Canadian health advantage emerged, the American economy grew more rapidly than Canada's, unemployment stayed lower, and health care spending grew much more rapidly. Public provision seemed to act as a buffer, providing resources that supported better health in what were relatively challenging economic times in Canada. Moreover, this historic example reinforced the importance of the macro-spheres of public policy – those that are under the control of senior governments with the primary taxing and spending authority in supporting the health and well-being of the population.

In retrospect, however, 1996 turned out to be a watershed year, after which time trends for Canadian life expectancy began to diverge, in dramatic fashion, from infant and under-five mortality. Table 10-1 shows that Canada's life expectancy continued to climb from 1996 to 2008, both in absolute terms and relative to the United States and Sweden. By 2008, Canadian life expectancy was within rounding error of the longest in the Western world. In contrast, the infant mortality rate in Canada did not fall at all, and the under-five mortality rate fell only marginally over this twelve-year period, but both continued to fall in the United States and Sweden. The under-five mortality rate is particularly instructive here. By 1992, Canada had caught up and matched Sweden that, at the time, had the lowest under-five mortality rate in the world. But as Table 10-1 shows, by 2008, Canada's rate was more than double Sweden's, and Canada's infant mortality rate was 2.5 times Sweden's.

These observations are salient for the present case study because EDI data collected from 2000 to 2010 come from cohorts of children born between 1995 and 2005 – during the decade of non-improvement in child survival that followed decades of declines going back to the 1920s. In other words, the trend toward no improvement – and even increases – in vulnerability on the EDI occurred among the same birth cohorts that did not experience declines in infant mortality rate.

The pattern of divergence between infant mortality and life expectancy, unobserved in other wealthy countries, requires an explanation. It emerged concurrently with changes in public provision that were not aimed directly at ECD but nonetheless worked their way into ECD because of the ways in which multiple social determinants interact. There are two key examples here. First, in the early 1990s, rule changes in entitlement led to the proportion of unemployed people in Canada who received unemployment insurance payments declining dramatically, from more than 70 percent in 1990 to 1991 to less than 40 percent by 1997. In other words, in a six-year period, Canada switched its unemployment protection program from something that matched coordinated market economies (e.g., Germany) to something that matched the most liberal of liberal market economies (e.g., United States). Because of the influence of seniority on job security and entitlement, these changes disproportionately affected young workers of childbearing age. Second, in 1996, under pressure from the International Monetary Fund, the Federal government took decisive action against its ballooning deficit and the highest debt-to-GDP ratio in the OECD by changing the rules governing transfer payments to the provinces for health and social programs, in effect capping them. This saved billions of dollars for the federal government because the previous formula permitted growth in transfers that it could not control. The effect, however, was to transfer the federal fiscal crisis to the provinces, which provide most of the services to families with children.

From the standpoint of ECD, the federal policy and program changes occurred during a time of radical change in the character of Canadian families. From 1945 to the end of the century, birth rates had fallen by more than half; the proportion of women in the labor force, the incidence of lone-parent families, and the share of indigenous people in the population had tripled; divorces had increased by a factor of six; and the share of immigrants from Europe or the United States had fallen from 94 to 22 percent (Jenson 2004).

These federal program changes of the mid 1990s were neoliberal in character. Reducing unemployment benefits aimed to increase Canadian competitiveness by reducing employment protection while capping federal–provincial transfers was meant to increase Canada's international standing in ways that would attract investment in an increasingly competitive global environment (see Chapter 7). Although not meant to adversely affect families with children, their circumstances nonetheless started to deteriorate markedly. Starting in 1996, family income inequality in Canada, which had remained unchanged over the period 1976 to 1996, increased sharply over the following several years and re-equilibrated at a higher, more unequal, level. Age differences in the trend in the Gini coefficient for income inequality, after taxes and transfers, are revealing. For Canadians ages 18 to 65 years (who may have families with children), the Gini coefficient rose from 0.29 in the mid 1990s (where it had been since the late 1970s) to 0.32 by the middle of the first decade of this century. In contrast, for those older than age 65 years, the Gini coefficient actually dropped from 0.35 in the 1970s to 0.26 to 0.27 in the 1990s and early 2000s, with no inflection point in the mid 1990s (OECD 2011).

By 2005, Canadian children stood seventeenth of twenty-four OECD countries on the UNICEF index of inequality of material well-being, such that the inequality gap in family income was far above the average among wealthy nations (UNICEF 2010). The fraction of female lone-parent heads of families in the labor force rose from 62 percent in 1996 to 85 percent by 2005, and the fraction of two-earner couples with children increased from 76 to 85 percent over the same period (in both cases, there had been declines from 1988 to 1995) (The Vanier Institute of the Family 2010). Families with children began to make up an increasingly larger proportion of those at the lowest end of the Canadian income distribution. Trends in income inequality were not just about cash but served as a marker for a host of capabilities and resources. For example, the number of hours per year that parents needed to work to maintain a given economic level increased sharply. By 2005, it stood at 300 hours more than a decade earlier, taking precious evening and weekend time away from their children (Yalnizyan 2007). By 2008, 20 percent of Canadian teenagers between the ages of 15 and 19 years were no longer pursuing a formal education; higher than the average of 15 percent across the 31 countries of the OECD. The OECD proportion was down from 20 percent in 1998 despite remaining stable at 20 percent in Canada (CBC News 2010). Although proposals to fund a national childcare program were floated in the 1970s and 1980s, these never came about. Thus, the reforms of the mid 1990s seemed to unmask the underlying weakness in Canada's traditional family policies. ECD investments were low, and when the policies changes of the 1990s came along, there was no system in place to buffer them.

Having opted for a neoliberal program of fiscal constraint, how did Canada respond to the emerging knowledge about the importance of the early years and the changing gender roles that put the majority of mothers back in the labor force by the time their children were two years old? The primary policy turning point came in 1997 with the adoption of a new, social investment focus on children. The federal, provincial, and territorial governments first agreed to target child poverty, with the National Child Benefit (NCB) announcement in the 1997 Speech from the Throne (Dobrowolsky and Saint-Martin 2004). This was followed by the National Children's Agenda (NCA), which was meant to institutionalize the social investment focus by revitalizing the movement toward a pan-Canadian childcare system. Under the NCA, the federal government began to offer funds to the provinces in several different packages in an attempt to entice them to make a strong commitment to ECD and education (Mahon and Phillips 2002: chapter 8). For example, a small federal–provincial program to support local ECD initiatives was implemented in 2001. Funding for Children First and Success by Six, described earlier, came from this transfer program. The NCB and the NCA were founded on a different policy logic from that of the male breadwinner and female caregiver. All parents were to be in the labor market, and governments targeted income support toward children so as to fight child poverty. Accordingly, between 1995 and 2005, single-parent recipients with one child saw their incomes drop by 5 to 30 percent (Jenson 2009: chapter 1). At the same time, the federal government expanded parental leave, under the employment insurance program, to one year. A series of programs to support child development among the indigenous population – both on and off reserve – began. Finally, federal–provincial transfer funds were provided to support the educational needs of immigrant families with children. All of these investment programs were relatively small and did not fully compensate families for the cuts in benefits from traditional programs such as unemployment insurance and social assistance. By 2005, Canada was identified (OECD 2006) as the wealthy world's lowest investor in "early learning and care" (at less than 0.5 percent of GDP compared with 1.5 to 2.0 percent in the Nordic countries). In 2006, the Liberal government, following negotiations with each province, initiated a new transfer program for early learning and care. This was meant to be the beginning of publicly provided universal access to quality, developmentally appropriate childcare. But after the 2006 election, it was canceled by the Conservative government. By 2008, Canada scored last among 26 wealthy countries on its index of early learning and care, meeting only one of ten benchmarks. In contrast, Sweden met ten of ten (UNICEF 2008).

Despite the move to a social investment policy in 1997, Canada (outside Québec[6]) has clearly not moved from investing the least in the early years to a comprehensive approach like Sweden's. Calls for public investment and collective responsibility taking in the early years have been met by emotional rhetoric, insisting that such proposals are a totalitarian intrusion on the prerogatives of the family. This rhetoric is reported by both national newspapers in English-speaking Canada, neither of which has provided editorial support for public provision of early learning and care programs. Finally, in its 2006 election campaign, the Conservative Party vowed to eliminate a new

---

[6] 1997 was the year that the Parti Québécois government announced a new family policy, redesigning family allowances and other income supports, as well as introducing universal and affordable childcare to fight poverty, encourage labor-market attachment, and provide quality preschool and out-of-school childcare (Jenson 2009).

federal–provincial transfer program for early learning and care and replace it with cash transfers to families with children. The party leader used the slogan "Don't trust the experts . . . we have two experts and their names are mom and dad!" Promises of cash to families proved popular, and the federal–provincial transfer program was duly canceled after the election. This example, in which a problem requiring strengthening Canada's collective capacities was reduced to a tax expenditure program, illustrates the way in which a neoliberal policy approach managed to change the emphasis to individualism, market mechanisms, and the privatization of risk.[7]

Since the 2006 election, there have been renewed attempts to find ways to recast ECD in terms that will have appeal in a neoliberal climate. These focus on ECD programs as part of a more progressive social investment strategy to help households harmonize work and family obligations and train the population in the kinds of skills that postindustrial society demands (see Chapter 2). The use of made-in-Canada, population-based data sources rather than reliance on economic inferences drawn from foreign studies of high-risk populations, has proven popular. The research described on page 295 of this chapter was published by the BC Business Council and is drawing widespread attention in economic circles traditionally committed to neoliberal approaches. This receptivity highlights an important question addressed elsewhere in this volume (see Chapter 2): does the reemergence of support for public provision as an investment in human potential, rather than as a right of citizenship, represent a progressive response to neoliberalism?

Trend-Buckers at the Community Level

We have shown that changes in the broad policy environment were associated with a range of negative changes in the resources available to families with children and by declines in ECD in a jurisdiction (i.e., British Columbia) where this could be tracked. But these trends only indirectly help to understand how the policy environment might influence what happens at a local level, where the raising of children actually takes place. Here we approach this issue by looking at communities that did manage to limit ECD vulnerability in the neoliberal era. To do this we examine a handful of places in British Columbia – either clusters of neighborhoods or small geographic school districts – where vulnerability across all EDI scales dropped in a sustained manner over four rounds of data collection. These places also offer an opportunity to understand social resilience in the sense that a significant outcome of human

---

7 The transformation of the "Tiger Economies" of Southeast Asia from resource-poor, low life expectancy to resource-rich, high life expectancy societies was accomplished, partly through investment in children from conception to school leaving (Siddiqi and Hertzman 2001; Hanushek and Woessman 2008). Here, the declining birth rate was "harvested" to provide increased resources per child during their early and school years. This is an example of a social investment strategy that was not diverted by neoliberal ideology despite the image of the Southeast Asian Tigers as neoliberal in character.

well-being – ECD – was sustained and improved in the face of a predominantly negative societal trend.

As the first and second waves of EDI data were being analyzed, one of the authors (CH) toured the province and presented local EDI results back to every community. Presentations included a thorough discussion of the importance of the early years, the social determinants of ECD, and a comparison of local EDI results to other places in British Columbia with a similar socioeconomic character. Each presentation contained a key organizational message: the principal domains of ECD – language and cognitive, social and emotional, and physical – were diffuse and did not have existing institutions designed to support them. Therefore, progress would require new leadership coalitions and collective action across a wide range of actors. More than one hundred community visits took place in a five-year period, with most places being visited twice. Thanks to funding from the Ministry of Child and Family Development and the United Way (which, in turn, came from the small federal–provincial ECD transfer program), virtually all British Columbia communities had a part-time community coordinator for ECD who reported to a committee of agencies that served young children. These groups hosted the EDI presentations and were considered to be the primary clients for the results. Thus, both trend-bucker and non–trend-bucker communities began with similar information on ECD and with funding for a similar community coordination infrastructure.

Even though the number of trend-bucker communities was small (less than 10), they were diverse in their geopolitical and sociodemographic characteristics. Two examples are highlighted here. Community 1 is a small rural school district of approximately 10,000 people in the western Rocky Mountains. It is geographically circumscribed by the mountains and has an economic base that is relatively stable by interior of British Columbia standards. The population is primarily of European origin, and a working knowledge of English is universal. Educational levels among parents are average for the province, and child poverty and the proportion of lone parent families was slightly below average. In community 1, EDI vulnerability dropped from 23 percent on wave 1 to approximately 10 percent on the next three consecutive waves. Community 2 is a neighborhood of approximately 15,000 people in a working class suburb of Vancouver. Its population is overwhelmingly made up of new immigrants from a wide range of non–English-speaking countries around the world (with no dominant group), where approximately 20 percent of the adult population has virtually no working knowledge of English or French. The rate of household turnover is more than 20 percent per year. Family poverty, levels of parental education, and the proportion of lone parent families were all average for the province. On waves 1 and 2, EDI vulnerability in community 2 stood at 46 to 48 percent but fell to approximately 26 percent on the following waves of data collection.

Interviews with key informants were carried out in these and other trend-bucker communities (as well as comparison communities) to determine what made them different, that is, what kind of social resources were brought to bear that effectively addressed the challenge of supporting ECD in the face of adverse society-wide socioeconomic and policy influences (Mort 2004). Several characteristics were shared among trend-buckers that were not found among other communities. These characteristics, described later, highlight the extent to which outcomes can be shaped by coalition formation and collective action. This case study suggests that social resilience is a function of the capacities that produce something we will call "collective implementation goods." Collective implementation goods are outcomes that depend on durable networks capable of coordinating to perform a variety of tasks requiring inputs from multiple actors.

The key capacities were:

- Consistent with the insights of Sabatier and his colleagues (Jenkins-Smith and Sabatier 1994), the willingness of local leaders to translate core under- standings about the importance or challenges of ECD into a new and durable policy coalition. In practice, this took the form of a strong, stable, broadly based intersectoral coalition. That is to say, the community coordi- nation funds described earlier were exploited to create a planning table that included both traditional child-serving agencies and nontraditional actors in the municipal and economic sector. This table emerged as the local gover- nance body for ECD over time and played a key role in getting a wide range of key individuals on board with an ECD agenda.

- Senior leaders from local government and key tax-funded institutions (e.g., regional health authorities, which are provincially funded but locally run) stayed with the coalitions rather than "delegating downward" over time, bringing resources and credibility to the table. In particular, leaders in the public school system played prominent roles, bringing the cachet of "uni- versality" (i.e., schools represent an investment in human development that is for everyone rather than presenting ECD programs as something to target at high-risk populations), offering high-quality physical spaces, stabilizing temporary community ECD coordinator jobs with long-term support, and aligning ECD programs with the schools.

- The EDI outcomes were used in workshop contexts for strategic planning to focus program choices on the key domains of development and where the neighborhood variations in vulnerability on these domains were found. Thus, leaders mobilized people to both create new programs and alter exist- ing ones.

- To keep the focus on all children and not just high-risk groups, a "barriers of access" approach was taken. That is, all children can be put on a con- tinuum based on the number and intensity of barriers of access that stand between them and opportunities to support their development. For middle class children, the principal barrier is time pressure on their parents, but as one goes down the socioeconomic spectrum, other barriers emerge (e.g., cost of program, transportation, time of day offered, distrust and social distance between parents and would-be caregivers,[8] language barriers, no effective advocate for the child). By identifying and addressing barriers in a systematic fashion, communities were able to finesse the challenge of the gradient in ECD (described earlier), wherein the highest vulnerability populations do not include the majority of vulnerable children, who are spread more thinly across the more populous middle class.

- A willingness to sacrifice institutional prerogatives to create program coordination or integration that increased parental choices while reducing fragmentation of program opportunities.
- Collaborative or coordinated fundraising (often through creating "second-tier cooperatives") that mitigated competition among service providers for funding opportunities. In practice, these communities have also been able to attract more funding directly from senior governments (provincial and federal) because of their unity and credibility and their capacity to align local priorities with provincial and national ones.

In community 1, the most notable element was the role of the school district superintendent, who made it the intersectoral coalition's business to have contact with all families with young children 0 to 4 years old and ensure that they had unfettered access to community resources. The school superintendent in community 1 had high stature before the EDI data became available and had been looked to for matters related to children's development and well-being. Thus, community 1 is consistent with the insights of Tsai (2006) wherein local authorities created collective implementation goods on the strength of their existing reputation and used reputational mechanisms to hold intersectoral coalition partners accountable for providing the coordination that secured access for all families in the community. Community 1 also fits with the assertion of Ostrom (1990) that it is easiest to produce social capital in small communities that have tight networks.

Yet what is needed for ECD is not quite the same as what is needed to resolve Ostrom's common pool access problems, and community 2 is an example counter to the notion that collective goals are difficult to pursue in large communities where informal trust is hard to generate. In community 2, the most notable element was collaboration among provincial, municipal, and local actors to create a new multicultural community center that served as the

---

[8] This is particularly salient for the Indigenous community in British Columbia that, because of high fertility levels, produces approximately 10 percent of the childbirths per year in the province. For example, when ECD programs are set up in certain buildings, many indigenous people simply say, "That is not a place I am welcome" and do not go there with their children. Moreover, as pointed out elsewhere in this volume (see Chapter 4), indigenous people, as members of stigmatized group, live with the expectation that they will be overscrutinized misunderstood, and disrespected as parents and caregivers. The barriers that apply to indigenous peoples often apply to language-culture minorities as well, although our experience in British Columbia shows that each language-culture group is different in this regard.

focal point for family support and early years programming. There the policy coalition included individuals from the provincial ministry that had control of the federal–provincial transfer funds to support educational success among new immigrant families. These individuals saw support of early childhood as part of their mandate. In community 2, no preexisting community leadership was evident, but the broader municipal intersectoral coalition was able to identify individuals within each ethnic enclave that had some status among their group. Following the insights of Swidler (see Chapter 11) on the cultural sources of traditional authority, when these individuals became convinced that ECD was important and community capacity building was necessary, support for collective action on ECD followed. This helped to create a community identity organized around the notion that "we take care of our most vulnerable members" (see Chapter 9). The successes of community 2 in reducing vulnerability are consistent with insights on the importance of immigrant welcoming institutions supporting the transformation to citizenship in Canada, as well as the longstanding image of Canada of being a caring society (Bloemraad 2006).

Our investigations showed that trend-bucking depended, most of all, on a process of coalition formation. To be effective, these coalitions had to have certain features. They had to be *intersectoral* because no single agency or institution touches the early childhood environment broadly enough to have a major impact on its own. They had to provide *durable* resources in both human and material terms. The emergence of strong, stable intersectoral coalitions, dominated by key agency leaders, demonstrated that governments were far from the only source of social resources and that other actors with some measure of cultural authority could be crucial to the collective capacities of communities. The performance of strong, stable intersectoral coalitions to support ECD in trend-bucking communities also helped illustrate how institutional redundancies may operate. Intersectoral coalitions that have mobilized resources from multiple sectors and mounted flexible responses to local challenges show that traditional family functions can be successfully augmented by the community. Although public provision alone is not enough, the viability of the intersectoral coalitions depended on public provision in the first instance and their capacity to attract new public resources over time. This latter is entirely consistent with the interdependent nature of the social determinants of ECD and helps explain why families and even communities cannot support ECD alone even though the primary experiences that drive ECD occur in the most intimate environments. Also striking is how closely these observations match those from entirely different lines of inquiry on what makes complex systems adaptive and resilient (Homer-Dixon 2006):

- The individual elements that make up the system are highly diverse and "detachable" in the sense that if one element fails, the others do not fail. At the same time, there must be sufficient redundancy in function of the elements (and funding sources) to allow the system to operate when some are taken out of action.

- Decision making is distributed across the system's elements.
- The system is unstable enough to produce unexpected outcomes but orderly enough to learn from failures and successes.

Stepping back, what have we learned about effective support for ECD? The overall strategic approach needs to be one that addresses the interdependent social determinants of ECD in ways that produce de facto universal access to environments that will minimize vulnerability and support healthy child development. This in turn requires some straightforward goods that are publicly supplied, such as family benefits, notably for how they address income inequality, and some standard public goods, such as affordable early childhood education and care. But when it comes to effective ECD, community and state are not alternatives. The necessity for highlighting collective implementation goods begins with a simple fact: what people who interact with children do matters, and what society does to support or undermine these people also matters. The evidence shows that effective ECD involves multiple kinds of interventions, from multiple agencies or institutions, which work better when they are coordinated. They are providing collective goods in the sense that they are meant to benefit all families and children, but their implementation depends on effective interaction among key players in positions of potential influence in the local community. Accordingly, we need to be concerned not only whether local communities can play host to traditional public goods but also whether their officials and agencies can do something else of equal importance (and sometimes lower cost), namely, coordinating with each other to enhance the ways each of the programs they supervise feed into a common objective, in this case ECD, and sometimes devising – and building political support for funding – further dimensions of those programs.

Conclusion

Canada's having the weakest public funding and provision for ECD in the wealthy world generally trumped local community efforts to reduce developmental vulnerability in the earliest years of life. In most places in British Columbia, the state of early human development measurably declined despite a wide range of community initiatives to support it. Even though some exceptional communities managed to buck the trends, it has proven especially hard to do so in the absence of adequate ongoing support from senior governments. On the plane of economic and social policy, the case study provides an illustration of how shifts in public policy in line with the market ideologies of the neoliberal era led to families bearing a greater burden for coping with the life risks that pose serious challenges to their children's development and well-being. It turns out that it is much harder to secure ECD when basic levels of material inequality are higher. But the story does not end with the failure of senior governments. By virtue of seeing the environment for ECD as a social ecology of multiple layers, we can see that effective policies for ECD require local provision of collective implementation goods. This directs our attention to the conditions under which these are likely to be supplied, reminding us that government spending and support is crucial but is far from the only thing that is needed.

Finding trend-bucking communities and discovering commonalities in their approach to the early years has raised the prospect that other communities could learn useful lessons and produce better outcomes for young children without new initiatives from senior governments. Yet many of the elements of success listed earlier in this chapter are collective implementation goods in the sense that they involve cooperation for joint supply but are not public goods, which are nonexcludable. In other words, access to the de facto benefits of growing up in a trend-bucking community cannot simply be mandated. Most of the trend-buckers identified to date are either small communities or single urban neighborhoods rather than large urban agglomerations. Even if legislation and policy were designed to encourage local communities to imitate the trend buckers, many of the characteristics that have made them successful may depend on the individual character of local leaders; the nature of local institutional structures; cultural practices available to specific relevant local actors; and their recognition by families, communities, and senior government officials *as leaders*. It is very difficult to imagine that it will be possible to bring vulnerability in early childhood down from 29 to 10 percent in a place like British Columbia by depending exclusively on community capacities.

The Advocacy Coalition Framework (ACF) (Jenkins-Smith and Sabatier 1994) for understanding the policy process is particularly useful here. The profound new insights into the importance of the early years call for a change in the policy core beliefs of key actors in society, inside and outside of government. In response, new policy subsystems need to emerge that collectively understand the need to transform the traditional approach to the early years – ensure survival, then provide health care and education – into one that focuses directly on the principal domains of development – physical, language and cognitive, and social-emotional – and has the capacity to transform institutions in light of what it takes to optimize these domains. Ecological approaches to complex systems and what allows them to move to new, improved equilibrium states transcend simple causation or simple intervention approaches and support a new policy subsystem, *pace* Sabatier, that would be committed to producing the collective implementation goods necessary to manage the complex adaptive ecosystem of early childhood. (In this context, the EDI has started to gain credibility as an indicator of the "health" of this ecosystem.) The new subsystem would need to connect national or provincial policymakers and their treasuries to local actors (in a position to improve the daily lives of young children) in a common framework of understanding and action. As the ACF approach would predict, such a transformation takes considerable time, measured in years and decades. In the case of British Columbia, some elements of this transformation have taken place, but others have not, and the result so far has been highly variable ECD outcomes across local communities.

References

Barker, J. P. David. 1994. *Mothers Babies and Disease Later in Life*. London: BMJ Publishing Group.

Bloemraad, I. 2006. *Becoming a Citizen: Incorporating Immigrants and Refugees in the United States and Canada*. Berkeley: University of California Press.

Bronfenbrenner, U. 1979. *The Ecology of Human Development: Experiments by Nature and Design*. Cambridge, MA: Harvard University Press.

Boyden, J. and D. Levison. 2000. "Children as Economic and Social Actors in the Development Process." Working paper for Expert Group on Development Issues. Stockholm, Sweden.

Carneiro, P. and J. J. Heckman. 2003. *Human Capital Policy*. IZA discussion paper, No 821. http://papers.ssrn.com/sol3/papers.cfm?abstract_id=434544.

Carpiano, M. R. 2006. "Toward a Neighborhood Resource-Based Theory of Social Capital for Health: Can Bourdieu and Sociology Help?" *Social Science and Medicine* 62 (1): 165–75.

CBC News. 2010. *20 Percent of Canadian Teens Not in School in 2008*. http://www.cbc.ca/canada/story/2010/09/07/statscan-.html.

D'Angiulli, A., W. Warburton, S. Dahinten, and C. Hertzman. 2009. "Population-Level Associations between Preschool Vulnerability and Grade-Four Basic Skills." *PLoS One* 4(11), e7692.

DiPietro, J. A. 2000. "Baby and the Brain: Advances in Child Development." *Annual Review of Public Health* 21: 455–71.

Dobrowolsky, A. and D. Saint-Martin. 2004. "Agency, Actors and Change in a Child-Focused Future: 'Path Dependency' Problematised." *Commonwealth and Comparative Politics* 43 (1): 1–33.

Drukker, M., C. Kaplan, J. Schneiders, F. J. M. Feron, and J. van Os. 2006. "The Wider Social Environment and Changes in Self-Reported Quality of Life in the Transition from Late Childhood to Early Adolescence: A Cohort Study." *BMC Public Health* 6 (133): 1–11.

Dunn, J. R. and M. V. Hayes. 2000. "Social Inequality, Population Health, and Housing: A Study of Two Vancouver Neighbourhoods." *Social Science and Medicine* 51 (4): 563–87.

Evans, G. W. and E. Katrowitz. 2002. "Socioeconomic Status and Health: The Potential Role of Environmental Risk Exposure." *Annual Review of Public Health* 23: 303–31.

Farkas, G. 2003. "Cognitive Skills and Noncognitive Traits and Behaviors in Stratification Processes." *Annual Review of Sociology* 29: 541–62.

Forget-Dubois, N., J. P. Lemelin, M. Boivin, D. Ginette, J. R. Séguin, F. Vitaro, and R. E. Tremblay. 2007. "Predicting Early School Achievement with the EDI: A Longitudinal Population-Based Study." *Early Education and Development* 18(3): 405–26.

Forum for Early Child Development Monitoring. 2011. Pan-Canadian EDI mapping pages. http://www.childdevelopmentmonitoring.net/population-measures

Grantham-McGregor, S. M., S. P. Walker, S. M. Chang, and C. A. Powell. 1997. "Effects of Early Childhood Supplementation With and Without Stimulation on Later Development in Stunted Jamaican Children." *American Journal of Clinical Nutrition* 66 (2): 247–53.

Hanushek, A., A. Eric, and L. Woessman. 2008. "The Role of Cognitive Skills in Economic Development." *Journal of Economic Literature* 46 (3): 607–68.

Harkonmäki, K., K. Korkeila, J. Vahtera, M. Kivimäki, S. Suominen, L. Sillanmäki, and M. Koskenvuo. 2007. "Childhood Adversities as a Predictor of Disability Retirement." _Journal of Epidemiology and Community Health_ 61: 479–84.

Hart, B. and T. R. Risley. 1995a. _Meaningful Differences in the Everyday Experience of Young American Children_. Baltimore: Brookes.

Hart, B. and T. R. Risley. 1995b. "The Early Catastrophe: The 30 Million Word Gap by Age 3." _American Educator_ 27 (1): 4–9. http://www.treehouselearning.com/pdf/The_Early_Catastrophe_-The_30_Million_Word_Gap_by_Age3.pdf.

Hertzman, C. and T. Boyce. 2010. "How Experience Gets Under the Skin to Create Gradients in Developmental Health." _Annual Review of Public Health_ 31: 329–47.

Heymann, J. 2006. _Forgotten Families: Ending the Growing Confrontation Children and Working Parents in the Global Economy_. New York: Oxford University Press.

Homer-Dixon, T. 2006. _The Upside of Down: Catastrophe, Creativity, and the Renewal of Civilization_. Washington DC: Island Press.

Houweling, T. A. J., A. E. Kunst, C. W. N. Looman, and J. P. Mackenbach. 2005. "Determinants of Under-5 Mortality Among the Poor and the Rich: A Cross-National Analysis of 43 Developing Countries." _International Journal of Epidemiology_ 34 (6): 1257–65.

Irwin, L. G. 2006. "The Potential Contribution of Emancipatory Research Methodologies to the Field of Child Health." _Nursing Inquiry_ 13 (2): 94–102.

Irwin, L. G. and J. Johnson. 2005. "Interviewing Young Children: Explicating Our Practices and Dilemmas." _Qualitative Health Research_ 15 (6): 821–31.

Irwin, L. G., A. Siddiqi, and C. Hertzman. 2007. "Early Childhood Development: A Powerful Equalizer." _Coordinators' Notebook_ 29: 29–34.

Janus, M., S. Brinkman, E. Duku, C. Hertzman, R. Santos, M. Sayers, J. Schroeder, and C. Walsh. 2007. "The Early Development Instrument: A Population-Based Measure for Communities." In _A Handbook on Development, Properties and Use_. Hamilton: Offord Centre for Child Studies, McMaster University. http://www.offordcentre.com/readiness/pubs/publications.html.

Janus, M. and D. Offord. 2000. "Reporting on Readiness to Learn in Canada." _ISUMA Canadian Journal of Policy Research_ 1: 71–5.

Jenkins-Smith, H. C. and P. A. Sabatier. 1994. "Evaluating the Advocacy Coalition Framework." _Journal of Public Policy_ 14 (2): 175–203.

Jenson, J. 2004. _Canada's New Social Risks: Directions for a New Social Architecture. Canadian Policy Research Network Social Architecture Papers: Research Report_. F(43) Ottawa: Canadian Policy Research Family Network.

Jenson, J. 2009. "Writing Gender Out: The Continuing Effects of the Social Investment Perspective." In _Women and Public Policy in Canada Neo-liberalism and After?_ edited by A. Dobrowolsky. New York: Oxford University Press: 25–47.

Kamerman, S. B., M. Neuman, J. Waldfogel, and J. Brooks-Gunn. 2003. "Social Policies, Family Types, and Child Outcomes in Selected OECD Countries." _OECD Social, Employment, and Migration Working Papers_, No. 6. Paris: OECD Publications.

Kawachi, I. and L. F. Berkman. 2003. _Neighborhoods and Health_. New York: Oxford University Press.

Kershaw, P., L. Anderson, W. Warburton, and C. Hertzman. 2009. _15 by 15: A comprehensive framework for early human capital investment in BC_. Report to the Business Council of British Columbia Opportunity 2020 Project. Vancouver: Human Early Learning Partnership.

Knudsen, E. I., J. J. Heckman, J. L. Cameron, J. P. Shonkoff. 2006. "Economic, Neurobiological, and Behavioral Perspectives on Building America's Future Workforce." *Proceedings of the National Academy of Sciences* 103 (27): 10155–62.

Kohen, D. E., J. Brooks-Gunn, T. Leventhal, and C. Hertzman. 2002. "Neighbourhood Income and Physical and Social Disorder in Canada: Associations with Young Children's Competencies." *Child Development* 73 (6): 1844–60.

Leventhal, T. and J. Brooks-Gunn. 2000. "The Neighborhoods They Live In: The Effects of Neighborhood Residence on Child and Adolescent Outcomes." *Psychological Bulletin* 126 (2): 309–37.

Mahon, R. and S. Phillips. 2002. "Dual-Earner Families Caught in a Liberal Welfare Regime? The Politics of Child Care Policy in Canada." In *Child Care Policy at the Crossroads: Gender and Welfare State Restructuring*, edited by S. Michel and R. Mahon. New York: Routledge: 191–218.

Mayall, B. 1994. *Children's Childhoods: Observed and Experienced*. London: Farmer Press.

Mort, J. N. 2004. *The EDI (Early Development Instrument) Impact Study. BC School Districts: Embracing Young Children and Their Families*. Vancouver, British Columbia: Human Early Learning Partnership. http://www.earlylearning.ubc.ca/resources/help-publication-archive/.

NICHD Early Child Care Network. 2002. "Early Child Care and Children's Development Prior to School Entry: Results from the NICHD Study of Early Child Care." *American Educational Research Journal* 39: 133–64.

OECD. 2006. *Starting Strong II: Early Childhood Education and Care*. Paris: OECD Publications.

OECD. 2011. StatExtracts. http://stats.oecd.org/Index.aspx?QueryId=26067.

Ostrom, E. 1990. *Governing the Commons: The Evolution of Institutions for Collective Action*. New York: Cambridge University Press.

Patel, V., N. DeSouza, and M. M. C. Rodrigues. 2003. "Post-natal Depression and Infant Growth and Development in Low Income Countries: A Cohort Study from Goa, India." *Archives of Disease in Childhood* 88: 34–7.

Putnam, R. D. 2001. "Foreword." In *Social Capital and Poor Communities*, edited by S. Saegert, J. P. Thompson, and M. R. Warren New York: Russell Sage Foundation: xv–xvi.

Ramey, C. T. and S. L. Ramey. 1998. "Prevention of Intellectual Disabilities: Early Interventions to Improve Cognitive Development." *Preventive Medicine* 27 (2): 224–32.

Richter, L. 2004. *The Importance of Caregiver Child Interactions for the Survival and Healthy Development of Young Children: A Review*. Geneva: Department of Child and Adolescent Health and Development, World Health Organization.

Shonkoff, J. and D. A. Phillips, eds. 2000. *From Neurons to Neighborhoods: The Science of Early Childhood Development*. Washington, DC: National Academies Press.

Siddiqi, A. and C. Hertzman. 2001. "Economic Growth, Income Equality and Population Health Among the Asian Tigers." *International Journal of Health Services* 31: 323–34.

Siddiqi, A. and C. Hertzman. 2007. "Towards an Epidemiological Understanding of the Effects of Long-Term Institutional Changes on Population Health: A Case Study of Canada versus the United States." *Social Sciences and Medicine* 64 (3): 589–603.

Siddiqi, A., I. Kawachi, L. Berkman, S. V. Subramanian, and C. Hertzman. 2007. "Variation of Socioeconomic Gradients in Children's Development Across Advanced

Capitalist Societies: Analysis of 22 OECD Nations." *International Journal of Health Services* 37 (1): 63–87.

Singh, G. K. and M. Siahpush. 2002. "Increasing Inequalities in All-Cause and Car-diovascular Mortality Among US Adults Aged 25–64 Years by Area Socioeconomic Status, 1969–1998." *International Journal of Epidemiology* 31 (3): 600–13.

Tsai, L. 2006. *Accountability Without Democracy: Solidarity Groups and Public Goods Provision in Rural China*. New York: Cambridge University Press.

UNICEF. 2007. *State of the World's Children 2007, Women and Children: The Double Dividend of Gender Equality*. New York: UNICEF.

UNICEF. 2008. *The Childcare Transition: A League Table of Early Childhood Edu-cation and Care in Economically Advanced Countries*. Innocenti Report Card 8. Florence: Innocenti Research Centre.

UNICEF. 2010. *The Children Left Behind: A League Table of Inequality in Child Well-Being in the World's Rich Countries*. Innocenti Report Card 9. Florence: UNICEF, Innocenti Research Centre.

UN General Assembly. 1979. *Convention on the Elimination of All Forms of Discrim-ination Against Women*. United Nations, Treaty Series 1249: 13. http://www.unhcr. org/refworld/docid/3ae6b3970.html.

UN General Assembly. 1989. *Convention on the Rights of the Child*. United Nations Treaty Series 1577:3. http://www.unhcr.org/refworld/docid/3ae6b38fo.html.

UN Committee on the Rights of the Child (CRC). 2006. *CRC General Comment No. 7 (2005): Implementing Child Rights in Early Childhood*. CRC/C/GC/7/Rev.1. http://www.unhcr.org/refworld/docid/460bc5a62.html.

The Vanier Institute of the Family. 2010. "Families Count: Family Economic Security and Caring Part II – Canada's Families: Economic Security." *Transition* 40 (3): 4–7.

Wadsworth, M. E. 1997. "Health Inequalities in the Life Course Perspective." *Social Science and Medicine* 44 (6): 859–69.

Wilkins, R., J. M. Berthelot, and E. Ng. 2002. *Trends in Mortality by Neighbourhood Income in Urban Canada from 1971 to 1996*. Ottawa: Health Reports/Statistics Canada, Canadian Centre for Health Information, 82–003:S13.

World Bank. 2010. Data Catalog. http://data.worldbank.org/data-catalog.

Yalnizyan, A. 2007. *The Rich and the Rest of Us. The Changing Face of Canada's Growing Gap*. Toronto: Canadian Centre for Policy Alternatives.

Cultural Sources of Institutional Resilience

Lessons from Chieftaincy in Rural Malawi[1]

Ann Swidler

One of the great challenges of the neoliberal era is that of institutional capacity: the capacity of collectivities – from communities, to states, to transnational bodies – to create or sustain resilient social forms that embody collective purposes, enforce rights and obligations, and have the capacity to organize collective action.[2] Neoliberalism, both as ideology and as policy, has a love–hate relationship with institutions. On the one hand, as Evans and Sewell (see Chapter 1) make clear, neoliberal ideology has been defined by an attack on government – both public provision of welfare services and government regulation of the economy. Globally, one of the signature policies of the neoliberal era was structural adjustment, which forced government retrenchment and drastic cutbacks in government services throughout the Global South (Stiglitz 2002). At the same time, however, the collapse of the Soviet Union and attempts to establish functioning market economies in many formerly socialist states

---

[1] I would like to thank Gabi Abend, Eleni Arzoglou, Jane Collier, Arlie Hochschild, Louise Lamphere, Michelle Poulin, Lily Tsai, and Susan Watkins and seminar participants at Harvard, Yale, New York University, Princeton, Boston University, Brown, and Northwestern for helpful responses to earlier versions of this paper. I am indebted to Tom Pessah for valuable research assistance. I am also grateful to my colleagues in the Successful Societies Program, especially Peter Hall and Michèle Lamont, for their continuing advice and help.

[2] The question of how to define "institution" is complex. W. Richard Scott (2008) devotes several chapters to explicating this definition (8): "Institutions are comprised of regulative, normative and cultural-cognitive elements that, together with associated activities and resources, provide stability and meaning to social life." I discuss alternative conceptualizations below, but here it suffices to say that most authors see institutions as stable structures, precisely in Sewell's (1992) sense, in that they are continually reproduced as people instantiate cultural schemas using resources that in turn reproduce the schemas. In this sense, the enduringness of institutions is precisely a kind of resilience – the reproduction of an underlying pattern despite changes (see Jepperson 1991). Although some authors treat any stable forms as institutions, along with Scott, I hark back to an older tradition of institutional theory, associated with the work of Philip Selznick (1957) among others, that associates successful institutionalization of social forms – from marriage, to the university, to the nation state – with their ability to embody shared purposes and thus to evoke both loyalty and compliance.

have highlighted the need for effective institutions, both legal institutions to make markets work (Fligstein 2001) and government institutions capable of restraining ethnic antagonisms and providing social stability.[3]

Even as neoliberal theorists have decried excessive government, the neoliberal era has produced a welter of new or newly empowered institutions through which the world's business is supposed to get done. Indeed, the neoliberal era has fostered wide-ranging institutional innovation (Fukuyama 2004; Slaughter 2004). Alongside the frayed authority of nation states[4] and high-modernist Weberian bureaucracies have emerged more heterogeneous institutional forms: the profusion of nongovernmental organizations (NGOs), and transnational social movements that address human rights or the AIDS epidemic (Keck and Sikkink 1998; Callaghy, Kassimir, and Latham 2001; Calhoun 2008; Hammack and Heydemann 2009; Watkins, Swidler, and Hannan 2012); initiatives for decentralization and participatory governance (Baiocchi, Heller, and Silva 2008); and new or enhanced international organizations that regulate global trade, provide peacekeeping, or attempt to establish and enforce human rights (de Waal 2009; Sikkink 2009).

Contemporary thinking about institutions reflects many assumptions characteristic of the neoliberal era. Although economists, political scientists, and sociologists have become increasingly interested in institutional orders and where they come from (Skocpol 1979; North 1990; Hall and Taylor 1996; Thelen 2004; Streeck and Thelen 2005; Greif 2006, among many others), most of the discussion centers on how the interests of actors lead them to commit themselves to binding rules. Often lost or overlooked is the role of institutions in producing collective goods, a crucial facet of all societies.[5]

I use the term "collective goods" rather than the economists' preferred term "public goods." Public goods are those – such as national defense or clean air – from which people cannot be excluded even if they fail to contribute and therefore that government may legitimately provide or require. The term "collective goods," as I use it, has a very different emphasis. It also refers to benefits that serve a whole community and from which it would be difficult or impossible to exclude people. But the reference of the term "collective goods" is wider. The term serves as a reminder of general interdependence, the degree

---

[3] In Africa, we come back to Samuel Huntington's (1965) insight about the barriers to economic development: without political development, most efforts at other sorts of development are likely to fail. Pritchett, Woolcock, and Andrews (2010) have recently raised this issue again, talking about "capability traps" that make the implementation of global policy initiatives impossible because governments lack the "capability" to implement them.

[4] Although the political assault on the authority and prestige of government has probably gone further in the United States than elsewhere, confidence in government has fallen across the modern democracies (Nye, Zelikow, and King 1997; Dalton 2005).

[5] For a notable exception, see the work of Elinor Ostrom and her collaborators (Ostrom 1990; Gibson et al. 2005; Brondizio, Ostrom, and Young 2009; Poteete, Janssen, and Ostrom 2010), who examine the institutional arrangements groups develop to regulate common pool resources such as water for irrigation.

to which we all depend on groups and organizations that require more of us and benefit us in ways that cannot be precisely measured, monitored, and rewarded.

Neoliberalism, in both theory and practice, has tried to narrow and monetize interdependencies, using markets to charge for externalities, for example, or advocating that individuals pay the full costs of their education, conceived as benefitting only themselves, rather than also benefitting the larger society. A focus on collective goods emphasizes a very different understanding of the human condition: that all of social life, from the informal ties in a workgroup; to the solidarities among neighbors or family members; to loyalty to professions or employers, nations, or religious communities, is infused with meanings and commitments to larger collective purposes. People contribute more than can be measured or monitored even as they depend on the help and support of their fellows.

The neoliberal view of interdependence embraces volunteering to help neighbors and friends even while it presses a skeptical view of institutions (see Margaret Thatcher's rhapsodic embrace of volunteering in the speech quoted by Jenson and Levi in Chapter 2). But volunteers cannot replace institutions: created by human groups but coming to stand over and outside those groups, infusing their members with a sense of meaning and purpose, sanctioning cooperation so as to sustain it. But in the neoliberal era, scholars of market economies have reduced the idea of institutions to the enforceable rules within which transactions take place. This flattened understanding of what institutions are leaves mysterious the question of how institutions are created, how they acquire their authority and their power over the imagination, and how they can be rebuilt or revised when they no longer serve collective purposes. This chapter draws on research on African chiefdoms to derive a richer set of answers to these questions.

African Chieftaincy

In this chapter, I attempt to broaden the conceptual frame for thinking about institutions by analyzing the remarkably resilient institution of chiefs[6] or

---

[6] I use the terms "chiefdom" and "chieftaincy" interchangeably to refer to the chief systems that came to characterize much of Africa under colonial rule. These systems were in some places imposed; elsewhere they were the remnants of more formal, hierarchical polities after the indigenous rulers were defeated or subdued. In yet other places, there was considerable continuity between pre-colonial and post-independence chiefdoms. The classic treatment of pre-colonial African political systems, Fortes and Evans-Pritchard's *African Political Systems* (1940) differentiates pre-colonial African political systems into "primitive states" versus "stateless societies." In primitive states, a chief is the administrative and judicial head of a given territory, often with final economic and legal control over the land within his boundaries. Everybody living within these boundaries is his subject, and the right to live in this area can be acquired only by accepting the obligations of a subject. He is the embodiment of the political unity of the society. In stateless or "acephalous" societies, on the other hand, people may compete for status and prestige in the lineage system through performance of ceremonial obligations, but there is no formal law or

chieftaincy (or sometimes elders, headmen, or simply "traditional leaders") in many parts of Africa,[7] focusing especially on Malawi. I explore the ways culture in the broadest sense contributes to the functioning of the institution of chieftaincy in Malawi in order to explore the more general question of how culture sustains institutional forms, especially institutions that provide collective goods.

In doing so, however, I walk a fine line both empirically and theoretically. I do not argue that chiefs or other traditional leaders, or the institution of chieftaincy, provides the "best" system of governance for rural Malawians or other African villagers even though – given the current alternatives – villagers in many parts of Africa in fact prefer chiefs to legislators or government officials and repose more trust in them.[8] If they had wider choices, however, Malawian villagers like most Africans, would probably prefer to live in a modern nation state that provided physical security; rule of law; and basic social services such as schooling, health care, clean water, roads, and reliable electricity. (That does not mean that they would immediately adopt the notion that they or their relatives should behave in disinterested, universalistic ways rather than taking care of those to whom they have obligations of kinship, clan, or ethnicity [see Chabal and Daloz 1999; Chabal 2009]). They would almost certainly prefer paid employment in a functioning market economy to the unremitting toil and pervasive insecurity of subsistence farming. Nonetheless, the remarkable resilience of chiefdoms in contemporary Africa demonstrates the complex ways cultural meanings and practices are implicated in the effective functioning of institutions. The institution of chieftaincy recommends itself to close examination not only because it still plays such a vital role in Africa but also because

---

political authority, and no one person defines the political unity of the group. As Mamdani (1996) has pointed out, colonial systems imposed something resembling indirect rule everywhere, imposing what he calls a "decentralized despotism," in which – within the authority of the formally dominant colonial state – a hierarchy of chiefs (or in West Africa, elders, marabouts, or other traditional leaders) effectively exercised – locally and only over native inhabitants – the forms of authority that Fortes and Evans-Pritchard describe for "primitive states," but grounded in lineage ties that legitimated the chief's rule. See, for example, Colson (1986) for Zambia or Geschiere (1993) for Cameroon on the ways colonial rule homogenized systems of chiefly rule.

[7] Although I focus only on African chiefdoms, the problem of understanding polities whose origins are kin, clan, or lineage based is a very general one (see Charrad 2001). American involvement in "nation building" in places such as Iraq and Afghanistan, as well as its difficulties in dealing with political systems such as those of Pakistan or Yemen, indicates how limited are the intellectual resources for thinking about what creates effective institutions in states where strong ethnic and kin-based groups challenge the formal sovereignty of nation states (Migdal 1988, 2001).

[8] Surveys reported in Dionne (2012) for Malawi, Abotchie et al. (2006) for Ghana, Baldwin (2009) for Zambia, and Logan (2011) for several African nations show that villagers in various parts of Africa have more confidence in chiefs than in other political figures and that they believe that on the whole chiefs act on behalf of their people. Dionne (2012) also shows that the policy preferences of Malawian chiefs and village headmen correspond closely to those of villagers. Logan (2009) analyzes Afrobarometer data from across Africa to argue that most Africans do not see a conflict between rule by traditional authorities and democratic governance.

thinking about chiefdoms allows us to think about institutional resilience more generally.[9]

Institutions

In a now classic paper, Hall and Taylor (1996) distinguish three varieties of "new institutionalism": historical institutionalism, rational choice institutionalism, and sociological institutionalism. In this chapter, I focus on the limitations of much of the rational choice institutionalism that predominates in political science and economics, which analyzes institutional arrangements largely as if they were products of agreements by self-interested actors about the larger structure of rules, sanctions, and rewards that would facilitate exchange and (sometimes) cooperation.[10] Although I also see institutions as systems of rules and practices that specify rights and obligations, regulate conduct, and facilitate both exchange and cooperation, I follow the historical institutionalists in arguing that social groups do not produce institutions through agreements but almost always inherit them with a rich embedding in complex cultural meanings and that the meanings embedded in institutions themselves define identities and shape interests.

Chieftaincy is not an institution inherited unchanged from an ageless past (no more than "bureaucracy" or any other institutional form can be abstracted from the concrete context of struggles for power, interest, and advantage) but a set of deeply embedded cultural schemas that people draw on in complex

---

[9] Of course, chiefdoms and other related institutions often compete with and undermine, rather than strengthen, modern states. Joel Migdal (2001) makes the simple but essential point that "the very purposes for which leaders employ the state – seeking predominance through binding rules – automatically thrust it into conflict with other organizations over who has the right and ability to make those rules." (65). Thus, tribes, clans, village elders, and so on compete to be the ones able to provide predictable answers to local people's desire for secure rules that ensure their claims on resources (e.g., who enforces that this goat is really yours), people (e.g., who enforces that this husband or child is yours or who can give you a divorce), opportunity (e.g., who or what can get you a job, get your child into school), and reliable help.

[10] The emphasis on rational agreement among autonomous, self-interested actors that is so central to rational choice institutionalism is, I would argue, a projection of the deeply entrenched Western (particularly American) cultural imagination in which social life is produced by the voluntary choices of autonomous individual actors (Bellah et al. 1985; Fischer 2010; Henrich, Heine, and Norenzayan 2010; Markus and Schwartz 2010). These assumptions impair even the most ambitious current work on institutions. A recent paper in the *American Economic Review* by Fearon, Humphreys, and Weinstein (2009), for example, analyzes a field experiment – run by an NGO and randomized to villages in post-conflict Liberia – designed to increase social capital. In the authors' view, the greater willingness of villagers in the experimental villages to contribute the maximum in a public goods game demonstrates that "brief, foreign-funded efforts *to build local institutions* [can] have positive effects on local patterns of cooperation" [288, emphasis added]. Even though Liberia was recovering from a devastating civil war, however, the authors' findings suggest that local institutions – chiefdoms – had survived the civil war and that it was the effectiveness of chiefs in pressing their villagers to contribute, not some newly implanted institutional capacities, that accounted for the experiment's "success."

ways, creating and recreating a seemingly familiar form to serve new purposes (Sewell 1992).[11]

African chieftaincy is especially fascinating not because it has endured unchanging but precisely because it has proved so adaptable and resilient. As recent observers note, "Since the beginning of the 1990s, a wave of what has been called 're-traditionalisation' seems to have reversed the previous policy of containing the chiefs as negative forces. In a large number of Sub-Saharan African countries, if not all, this wave has been expressive of a gradual resurgence and enlargement of the formal role of chiefs in local governance and development" (Kyed and Buur 2006: 1).

In Malawi, as in much of the rest of Africa, despite the distortion of the institution by colonial systems of indirect rule (Mamdani 1996), chiefs still retain much of their "traditional" legitimacy. The debate between those, such as Mamdani, who are most critical of postcolonial chiefdom, and those, such as Collier (2004) or Oomen (2008) who stress the institution's resilience and its continuing ability to produce collective goods, rests in large part on how they assess Mamdani's claim that "from African tradition, colonial powers salvaged a widespread and time-honored practice, one of a decentralized exercise of power, but freed that power of restraint, of peers or people. Thus they laid the basis for a decentralized despotism" (48).[12] Collier and Oomen share Mamdani's understanding of the logic of chieftaincy but stress that the authority of chiefs is still very much dependent on "peers" and "people." Even in places such as the South African homelands, where chiefs were seen as collaborators with the apartheid regime, in the postapartheid period, chiefly systems have rebounded, growing in importance and influence (for South Africa, see Oomen 2000, 2008 and Ntsebeza 2008; for Mozambique, West and Kloeck-Jenson 1999; for Ghana, Abotchie et al. 2006; for Zambia, Baldwin 2009).

What Do Chiefs Do?

In Malawi, as elsewhere, chiefs play a central role in the provision of collective goods. If villagers are to act collectively in their own behalf, the chief typically organizes that cooperation. If a village's paths need to be repaired (in Tanzania, "brushed," meaning cleared of brush), the chief calls villagers together and

---

[11] Rudolph and Rudolph (1967) made a similar argument about caste systems, and John Mohr and Harrison White (2008) have recently reinforced the point. See Oomen (2000; 2008) for a thoughtful, empirically grounded analysis of the changing vicissitudes of chieftaincy in South Africa.

[12] Mamdani (1996: 50) goes on to say that "European rule in Africa came to be defined by a single-minded and overriding emphasis on the customary ... [which] was stretched to include land.... Just as matters like marriage and inheritance were said to be customarily governed, so procuring basic sustenance required getting customary access to communal land. With this development, there could be no exit for an African from the world of the customary." But as Collier (2004) emphasizes, it remains true in much of Africa that "a chief does not rule land; he rules people." A bad chief is thus in danger of losing his people or of being forced out ("destooled" in Ghanaian parlance; "deposed" in Malawi).

requires them to contribute a day's work to the collective task. The same is true if the village needs to provide bricks or labor to attract an NGO project, to build a house for a Peace Corps volunteer, to repair a communal well, or to repair a school building.[13]

Anyone who has worked in an NGO project, in the Peace Corps, or for a faith-based organization in sub-Saharan Africa will recognize that one cannot even begin a project without clearing it with the local chief (or in West Africa, perhaps with the Président des Jeunes, the leader of the adult men), and it is the chief who calls the villagers together for a public meeting at which the benefits of the project, the procedure for electing leaders, or any other features of the project will be laid out. NGOs, development workers, and even government officials simply cannot get access to the village community without going through the chief.

Second, the chief, or the "royal family," literally embodies the name that gives the village its collective identity. In Malawi, the village does not exist as a village except insofar as it has a chief. In this sense, the chief is something like a Durkheimian totem, symbolically embodying in his (or occasionally her) own person the very existence of the community. In Malawi, the sentence "Traditional Authority Zulu [person] is the Traditional Authority [official title] of Traditional Authority Zulu [administrative unit]" is a perfectly coherent sentence, true by definition.[14] The village, or the group of villages, or the

---

[13] Chiweza (2007: 69–70) writes of chiefs in Malawi: "The planning system's stress on projects having 'community contributions' of at least 25 percent has been interpreted by village chiefs and many state officials as their having to have a cache of bricks to show when the project team arrives, so that they can be considered fit for funding." In a study of "town chiefs" in Malawi (who are less important and influential than rural village chiefs), Cammack, Kanyongolo, and O'Neil (2009: 18) describe the traits sought in a chief, suggesting that chiefs are chosen for their ability to provide collective goods:

> Town chiefs are consistently chosen for having certain characteristics. Specifically, they are reportedly of 'good character', 'hard working', 'respectable' and 'quiet' people of 'good standing', who know 'how to stay with people', 'should understand the problems of the people', will 'help them', be 'good to them' and 'keep them well'. They have 'lived there a long time' and are well settled in an area, often making them 'homeowners'. They are neither quarrelsome, nor known 'drunkards' or 'womanisers'. They appear to be among the local economic elite – that is, they 'are self-reliant' or 'self-sufficient'. For instance, they are (retired) civil servants, teachers, civil society leaders (and heads of churches) or are businessmen (e.g., a building contractor, a restauranteur, a money-lender, a kiosk owner). Interestingly, we found that several town chiefs who were (s)elected are also members of (hereditary) chiefly families in their home areas, though they claim that their 'royal' status was likely unknown to those who chose them to lead in town – a claim that deserves further investigation.
>
> . . . .
>
> TCs are selected because they can represent the interests of their communities – that is, they are good 'public speakers' and 'influential'.

[14] David Maxwell (1999) notes the same taken-for-granted reality on the first page of his classic study of the Hwesa of Zimbabwe: "The territory which, like the dynasty and its chief, is also known as Katerere is the stage for an extraordinary social history" (1). Writing of southern

Traditional Authority (a key administrative unit) has its existence – and its name – because of its chief (and, of course, the chief has his name because it is the name of the administrative unit). Southern Malawi is largely matrilocal, and I once asked a youngish village-level chief whether he would move to his wife's village when he married. His cousin, standing next to him, cried out in horror, "Move? Move! He can't move! No chief, no village! No chief, no village!"

Third, chiefs may adjudicate disputes in chiefly courts, advising, cajoling, and sometimes deciding matters ranging from marriage and divorce, to a lost or stolen goat, to inheritance claims. The power of chiefs to some degree rests on their role in chief's courts and the absence or expense of other legal routes for resolving disputes.[15] To varying degrees chiefs may also have authority over land, especially where land remains under communal control rather than having become alienable private property.

Chiefs, Status, and Collective Goods

Chiefs also operate as reservoirs of pooled collective obligations and as informal account keepers, reinforcing the ties of reciprocal interdependence that are so central to African societies (Kaler and Watkins 2001; Swidler and Watkins 2007; Chabal 2009). The indirect ways that chiefs contribute to collective goods are thus even more important than their direct, formal roles. This indirect

---

Malawi (then Nyasaland) in the 1940s, J. Clyde Mitchell (1956: 110) remarks that "... the village headman is a representative of a corporate group, the village."

[15] Baldwin (2007: 7–8) describes the role and powers of chiefs in Zambia:

> The power of chiefs stems from their control of land and law. Chiefs are the "custodians" of the land in Zambia: they are responsible for overseeing the distribution of customary land within their chiefdoms and they must give approval before land can be converted from customary tenure to leasehold tenure (Cap 83(8)(2)). In addition, they play an important role in law enforcement: they are empowered to "take reasonable measures to quell any riot, affray or similar disorder which may occur" (Cap 287(11)(1)) and to have their assistants "arrest without warrant any person upon reasonable suspicion of his having committed an offense in connection with [a] riot, affray or disorder and detain any person so arrested until he can be delivered into the custody of a police officer or brought before a competent jurisdiction to be dealt with according to law" (Cap 287).

> In addition to these officially sanctioned powers, chiefs have a number of unofficial sources of influence. For example, almost every chief in Zambia has a traditional court to settle disputes between subjects. Although these courts are not officially recognized within the Zambian legal system, they are tolerated because the formal court system does not have the capacity to deal with all cases. In addition, the officially recognized courts are geographically and financially inaccessible to most rural residents, who have no real alternative but to take disputes to the chief's court. Finally, chiefs have influence in their communities by virtue of the trust people have in them. According to the 2003 Afrobarometer survey, 52% of Zambians trust traditional leaders a lot or a great deal; in contrast, only 32% of Zambians have this degree of trust in the ruling party and only 18% have this amount of trust in opposition parties. Furthermore, this figure masks the degree of trust in chiefs in some rural areas; for example, in Eastern and Luapula Province, more than 75% of people trust traditional leaders a lot or a great deal.

management of collective obligations continually recreates the link between a chief's status, his spiritual powers, and the well-being of the community.

Chiefs reward those who contribute to community life, and informally, they keep the accounts about who has (or has not) been public spirited. Chiefs then redistribute both spiritual and material goods to reward those who have helped their fellows (Collier 2004). Chiefs thus reinforce the general obligation of those who have more to redistribute to those who have less. I was told by the director of a Zambian AIDS hospice, for example, that when the hospice asked families to take in AIDS orphans, their requests succeeded only when the chief made the request. Taking in a relative's child may be obligatory, but it is the chief who often enforces, and perhaps later rewards, performance of that taken-for-granted obligation. A villager in southern Malawi, who had a modest cash income to supplement her subsistence farming, was asked by her chief to found a youth club to discuss AIDS. When, later, the chief had government-subsidized fertilizer coupons to distribute, he gave this widow not one but two.

A different example of how a chief indirectly provides public goods comes from northern Malawi. A young Malawian villager – intelligent, cheerful, and with good mastery of English – was asked by his chief first to be the liaison to a group of Peace Corps volunteers and later to volunteer to form a community-based organization (CBO), which was able to attract donor funding. After the chief realized "the goodness of CBOs," he asked the young man to help other villages to found their own CBOs, bringing in badly needed donor money (Swidler and Watkins 2009). When, later, the young man's mother died and he went to his uncle to ask for land, his uncle was very generous, giving him five hectares to farm. His chief declared that "it was a very good thing [his] uncle had done." So, in Malawi as elsewhere, "what goes around, comes around," and the chief provides a critical link in that process.

The chief recirculates the collective capacity for creating collective goods partly by recirculating status or honor. When a chief speaks at a funeral, for example, he can praise the deceased as having been a "worthy" man or woman, or indeed, as one informant described it, he can make a point of giving the funeral oration himself – rather than sending an underling – and thus communicate the deceased person's prestige (and thereby descendants' continuing claims on the community). Chiefs thus "store" and redistribute status and prestige, and they do so in proportion to contributions to the community.

Chiefs and the Sacred

Chiefs also store up – and in some sense embody – sacred power. Their sacred power is connected to what are, or were, at least in the indigenous systems, specific ritual roles in communicating with the ancestors or ensuring the fertility of land, animals, and people (Mitchell 1956; Collier 2004). It is difficult, however, to distinguish a chief's prestige, which comes in part from traditional cultural roles, from his sacred or spiritual powers, which in turn both reflect and protect the strength and health of his community. Chiefs' prestige in turn depends on their ability to access and contain sacred powers.

Chiefs in Malawi control burial grounds and thus connections to ancestors, where ancestors are a source of both danger and help. Indeed, to be forbidden to bury one's kin in the village graveyard would in essence mean having to leave the village. The intertwining of the chief's practical responsibility for funerals and his spiritual responsibility for protecting the community against witchcraft and other malevolent spiritual forces is evident in Cammack, Kanyongolo, and O'Neill's (2009: 23) description of "Town Chiefs" in Malawi:

The funereal tasks [chiefs] perform are social and economic in nature – they announce the death to the community and other chiefs, they 'open the graveyard' and have the grave dug, they permit mourning to begin and ensure funds and ufa (maize flour) are collected for the wake.

Historically death has been perplexing, and blamed on the intervention of malevolent spirits. It is partly this continuing belief in the inexplicable nature of death that makes funerals so important. Specifically, it is generally believed that the spirit (mzimu) of the dead survives the body and can cause misfortune for survivors. Therefore, 'funeral rites are designed to make the mzimu depart so that the living may forget the dead'. Immediately after a death the family reports to the chief. He will send young men to inform the population. No one is allowed to eat meat till after the burial as witches are thought to eat the flesh of the dead, so not eating meat is a way to show others you are not a witch. The chief must give permission for the body to be prepared for the grave, and he will lead discussions about the circumstances of the death. Is there anyone who caused the death? If relatives had not warned the chief that there was a serious illness in their family, a case might be brought and the burial cannot take place until the case is settled. A 'diviner' can be brought in to determine if the person was killed through witchcraft, though this happens less frequently nowadays since practicing witchcraft is against the law. Only when the case is settled will the chief order the body to be buried.

Without the chief, a death cannot be dealt with practically – arranging the burial, spiritually – avoiding the potential danger that comes from the spirits of the dead, or intellectually – resolving what caused the death. Because village chiefs also control the burial grounds, their role in funerals and in managing the critical relations with ancestors more generally is of paramount importance for the village community.[16]

In Botswana, I attended a rural funeral, and as three pastors from different denominations conducted the burial service, the chief three times interrupted the funeral, cutting off the pastors in midsentence, to have his headman, speaking through a megaphone attached to his small white truck, demand that

---

[16] Clyde Mitchell, in *The Yao Village* (1956), describes how the founding of a new village in what is now southern Malawi depended on the chief's communication with the ancestors and on the chief's own sexual substance and how the ritual for installing a new chief involved the symbolic "reincarnation" of the former chief, with the "important implication that the headman is immortal. He shares this characteristic with the group of which he is the leader" (121).

the assembled mourners press more closely around the graveside to comfort the bereaved mother, then that they sing with more verve, and finally that they stop gossiping and pay greater attention to the proceedings. Although the pastors conducted the funeral ritual, the chief was responsible for the cohesion of the community, which, at least symbolically, took priority.

Finally, a chief also protects his community against witchcraft – an ever-present danger. In part, this is direct: I was told that if a chief lacks spiritual power, his people will be more subject to witchcraft from surrounding villages. But the chief also contains witchcraft by trying to resolve sources of envy and resentment and damp down conflict within the community. Because witchcraft is particularly likely when there are unresolved sources of envy and resentment or when people have failed to live up to their obligations to one another, the chief's role in trying to avoid or smooth over conflict is critical to the overall health of the community.

The chief's prestige – his control of spiritual and material resources (Collier 2004) – plays both practical and sacred roles. Indeed, these cannot really be separated because a chief who does not watch out for the practical well-being of his community loses some of his spiritual power as well as his prestige. A chief who does not accumulate control over material and spiritual resources becomes less "sacred," less prestigious, and thus less able to provide collective goods for his community, both in the material and spiritual realms.

Why Can Chiefs Create Collective Goods?

What can we learn from the specifics of the ways chiefs operate in Malawi about why culture matters for the ways institutions function? Why are chiefs able to coordinate the provision of public goods, but other authorities, not grounded in local cultural traditions and practices, are not able to do so? Chiefs have substantial sanctioning power: they are often responsible for allocating small benefits, such as coupons for a government fertilizer subsidy program or blankets that an NGO provides for orphans; chiefs' courts may adjudicate local disputes about marriage and divorce and conflicts over property or petty crimes; chiefs also have residual control over communal lands; and in extreme cases, a chief can drive a recalcitrant villager out of the village. On the other hand, most chiefs try to govern by consensus, and chiefs who behave in selfish, corrupt, or morally reprehensible ways can be deposed.

Apart from their control over concrete rewards and sanctions, chiefs' authority over funerals is also a source of substantial power. In societies where relations to ancestors are important and also potentially dangerous and where lineage relations define identities and thus the obligations of one person to another, chiefs' authority over burials reinforces relationships of inheritance and continuing obligations among the living. A chief's ability to define when a witchcraft accusation is legitimate and how it should be dealt with is also a source of both practical and cultural power. In a world where witchcraft is a pervasive danger and therefore no one can feel safe either from witchcraft itself or from the possibility of a witchcraft accusation, even the chief's ability to treat an accusation as meriting serious attention is significant.[17]

Given some sanctioning power, however, what keeps the chiefs committed to the welfare of their communities? First, some chiefs are not. Some take advantage of the perquisites of their status; their reputations, their ability to win cooperation from their people, and the community's ability to produce collective goods suffer accordingly. Nonetheless an Afrobarometer survey across a number of countries in Africa finds that although levels of support vary, traditional leaders are trusted more than either government officials or elected politicians (Logan 2011). Many chiefs thus appear to maintain considerable commitment to securing public goods for their people (see also Baldwin 2007, 2009).[18] Malawians sometimes offer a simple explanation. When asked, for example, why fertilizer coupons distributed by the chiefs mostly reached their intended recipients, although a similar program in which extension agents from the ministry of agriculture distributed the coupons resulted in almost all of the coupons being stolen, their answer was simple: the chiefs live in the village, so they have to see the villagers every day.

Chiefs have high status, and their sense of what enhances their own status is a major goad to public spiritedness. The ability of institutions to confer status honor is probably a general mechanism that helps institutions produce public goods. Lily Tsai (2007a, 2007b) studied public goods provision in more than 300 Chinese villages. She found minimal influence of village wealth or village governance structure (top-down bureaucratic controls or formally democratic village institutions) on the provision of collective goods such as roads, elementary school classrooms, and running water. What predicted public goods provision was instead whether or not the village had a traditional cultural association – a village temple committee or a village-wide lineage group – that both "encompassed" and "embedded" village officials. Tsai's argument is that these traditional cultural associations provided a place where officials could receive status for accomplishments that benefitted the village as a whole, and this status in turn provided resources with which to win cooperation from other members of the village community for collective projects.

---

[17] Adam Ashforth (1998, 2005) has written of the "spiritual insecurity" that characterizes African life: a world in which malevolent forces – never predictable, never tameable – are a constant danger. Witchcraft does not follow rules, and it cannot be definitively diagnosed or reliably prevented; witches always deny their deeds, and the only evidence is the illness or death they have caused.

[18] Chiefs' responsibility to provide public goods can conflict with their responsibility to help the poor in their communities, as in the following story from my field notes, related by a colleague: "One of the S – chiefs laughed with his interviewer about the fact that GoM [Government of Malawi] instructed him to distribute fertilizer subsidies to the poorest households, making the point to the interviewer (something like), 'But who is going to help you build a school when you need him to?', meaning, you need to take care of the labor force (and those who are better off) in your village."

Tsai's findings about rural China echo those of Steve Cornell and Joseph Kalt (1997, 2000) on American Indian tribes. Using systematic data on 225 tribes and more focused case studies of 67 of those tribes, Cornell and Kalt (2000) show that the economic well-being of American Indian groups is unrelated to their natural resources or local labor market conditions but depends instead on how well governed they are. Good governance in turn is most strongly related to the "cultural match" between tribes' current governing institutions and the structures of their governing institutions at first recorded contact with European settlers. Thus, Cornell and Kalt, like Lily Tsai, find that something about cultural continuities affects the effective functioning of social institutions and thus the provision of collective goods.

As in rural China or in American Indian groups, status allocation in chieftaincy systems keeps their incumbents focused on public goods provision, especially where chiefs must compete for status. In Malawi, village headmen, group village headmen, traditional authorities, and paramount chiefs do not simply "have" status. Rather, chiefs are also always competing to increase their status – by becoming one of the counselors to a higher chief, by moving up in the hierarchy of chiefs, or by being granted one of the symbols of chiefly prestige (in the traditional Yao system in what is now southern Malawi, for example, marks of rank such as the size of one's entourage, the right to hold certain initiation ceremonies, or the right to wear a scarlet headband [Mitchell 1956: 90–107]). Jane Collier (2004) has described the perpetual competition for power, prestige, and rank in the lineage hierarchy (because genealogies are continually revised to reflect current prestige) as fundamental to chiefdom systems. And a chief increases his rank by drawing followers to himself and increasing the number and the well-being of his followers.

In a set of ingenious experiments, Willer (2009) has shown how status rewards provide a solution to collective action problems. By simulating varying levels of contribution to a group task, Willer shows that higher contributions are perceived by other members of the group as representing greater commitment to the group and are rewarded with status. Members perceived as higher status can also elicit greater cooperation and eventually are also treated more generously by others. In turn, "status rewards for contribution to collective action encourage greater giving in the future" (Willer 2009: 37). Willer notes that status allocation provides at least one answer to the question of how societies and social institutions manage to exist despite the many temptations to purely self-seeking behavior. He notes:

The status solution fits the collective action problem well in a few ways. The status incentive system does not require central, formal organization. The incentives rest in the regard members have for one another. This means that the system is not easily destroyed or undermined and does not require any explicit management or leadership to be maintained. Also, status incentives, unlike material ones, increase as the collective action becomes more difficult. As tasks require greater sacrifice from group members, contributing indicates even greater concern for the group (40).

The awarding and the receipt of status are fundamental to the ways institutions work. In some ways, this point is obvious – as anyone who has taken on extra obligations, performed onerous committee work, or accepted a demanding but prestigious position in the academic profession will recognize. Bourdieu and his followers (Bourdieu 1986, 1996; Bourdieu and Passeron 1990; Bourdieu and Wacquant 1992) see status as valuable because it can be converted into other kinds of "capital," but an equally good argument can be made that status is an end in itself – providing the emotional energy at the end of "interaction ritual chains" (Collins 2004) and, as Hall and Taylor (2009: 93) argue, enhancing people's "capabilities" by serving as "an all-purpose social lubricant conditioning the cooperation one receives from others" and providing the "social recognition" that is an important source of self-esteem, confidence, and "self-efficacy." Status is thus one of the major rewards collectivities offer those who are seen as contributing to the group's purposes, and the sense of what one's own status requires is both a goad to effort and an inhibitor of certain sorts of selfish or destructive behavior.

Legitimacy and Norms

One of the most obvious but also most theoretically unfashionable arguments about culture and institutions is that institutions function best where they are legitimate and where institutional actors are both motivated and constrained by norms that support the institution. Such arguments have long been out of favor in the social sciences, not because anyone really doubts that legitimacy and norms make a difference but because there seem to be so many counter examples where social groups maintain patterns of behavior that they themselves claim to regard with disapproval (see Smith 2006 on corruption in Nigeria and Hirsch et al. 2009 on marital infidelity in Africa) or where individuals seem to find a way to justify even reprehensible behavior as normative. Indeed, there are so many problems with the concept of "norms" that many sociologists abandoned the idea.[19] Nonetheless, if the concept of norms is moved from the arena of subjective, internally sanctioned behavior to the public social arena of agreements about what behavior will be seen as wrong, discrediting, or worthy of sanction, the idea of norms again gathers force.[20]

---

[19] Cancian (1975) analyzes one of the basic difficulties: if norms are the ideals that people articulate verbally, then there is very little correlation between norms and action. If, on the other hand, norms can be read from actual behavior, then norms can hardly be said to be the cause of that behavior. Because one of the important aspects of norms is that they are socially shared, it becomes even more difficult to separate the idea of what is normative from some idea of what is normal or typical.

[20] Various more systematic ways of treating norms have emerged in recent scholarship. These salvage the idea of norms by relocating them from inner subjective states that regulate individual conduct by comparing it to an internalized ideal, instead seeing norms as community standards backed by the (potentially measurable) willingness of a community to enforce those standards (see, e.g., Sampson, Morenoff, and Gannon-Rowley 2002 on "collective efficacy" and Greif

In chiefdoms, as in other governance institutions where face-to-face relationships play a major role, norms matter. Good leaders are expected to be civil and respectful and to consult with their influential followers even as they exercise authority over them (Collier 2004; see also Karlström 1996 on contemporary Uganda and Schaffer 1998 on Senegal). Mamdani (1996: 44) offers a wonderful example of the mutual incomprehension about the nature of African chiefs' authority as officials from the Cape Native Laws and Customs Commission in 1881 questioned a former Zulu king:

144. As the king of the Zulus, was all power invested in you, as king, over your subjects?

– In conjunction with the chiefs of the land.

145. How did the chiefs derive their power from you as king?

– The king calls together the chiefs of the land when he wants to elect a new chief, and asks their advice as to whether it is fit to make such a man a large chief, and if they say "yes" the chief is made.

146. If you had consulted the chiefs, and found they did not agree with you, could you appoint a chief by virtue of your kingship?

– In some cases, if the chiefs don't approve of it, the king requires their reasons, and when they have stated them he often gives it up. In other cases he tries the man to see whether he can perform the duties required of him or not.

147. In fact, you have the power to act independently of the chiefs in making an appointment, although you always consult them?

–No; the king has not the power of electing an officer as chief without the approval of the other chiefs. They are the most important men. But the smaller chiefs he can elect at his discretion.

Chiefs in Malawi are expected by their followers to represent the community and to act on its behalf. Behaving unfairly, failing to redistribute goods that flow into the community, or failing to act when village projects are needed subject a chief to gossip, grumbling, public repudiation, and the possibility of being deposed.

A village headman who was driven out of his village in a particularly humiliating way – the women of the village surrounded his hut jeering and hurling insults – was described by an informant as someone who if the roads needed repairing would say he saw no need, but if there were a training in the nearby district capital for which he would receive a per diem, "he would be there at nine sharp." As dissatisfaction with the chief's leadership grew, he retaliated by expanding the village graveyard so that it encroached on a dissident family's land. This unjust use of his powers precipitated his being deposed and driven from the village.

2006:143–52 on norms and rule enforcement). By this logic, as Harding (2010) has argued, norms are less effective where there is "cultural heterogeneity."

The effects of norms can be understood as simply raising the cost – internal and external sanction – of less socially acceptable behaviors. Avner Greif (2006) has tried to model exactly how much likelihood of sanction is needed to enforce a practice like the repayment of debts in a trading network. But in functioning institutions, the whole point is that internal sanction, public disapproval, and the possibility of actual sanction – such as getting a reputation as a bad person from whom others withdraw cooperation – are interconnected and tied to the purposes of the institution. Indeed, much of what we normally think of as "morality" – from fidelity in marriage, to honesty in business dealings, to evaluating academic peers in terms of their scholarly competence – makes sense only in terms of the meanings that organize institutions.

Chiefs in Malawi talk as if they feel, or know that they are supposed to feel, an internal sanction to care for their people's welfare. They repeatedly insist that they "love" their people and "care for them," providing examples of how they go out of their way to help those in need and to divide benefits so as to spread the wealth and reduce the chances of envy or conflict.

Cornell and Kalt (1997, 2000) see one effect of normative legitimacy as discouraging "destructive rent seeking": "When political culture – as described by these four normative dimensions [the structure, scope, location, and source of authority] – supports institutions as legitimate, the private rewards and penalties of the 'social sentiments' are triggered by the social networks within which individuals are embedded in ways that inhibit free riding and defection vis-a-vis those institutions. Numerous examples from fieldwork in Indian Country illustrate the 'policing' role of culturally founded legitimacy" (Cornell and Kalt 1997: 265).

Ritual and Narrative

Status can motivate contributions to collective well-being, but shared cultural traditions provide the ritual occasions and the face-to-face contexts where status can be awarded and where the links between status and collective purposes can be publicly articulated. At funerals, as I have described, chiefs praise the worthy and reinforce communal ideals by articulating what behaviors are praiseworthy. Chiefs and other leaders can also use funerals to criticize unworthy behavior, as when a village headman and a sheikh each used the funeral of a well-known prostitute who had died of AIDS to warn against sexual immorality (see Watkins and Swidler 2009: 15).

This role of funerals in chiefdoms suggests a larger role of ritual in institutional resilience. Shared cultural traditions provide recognized ritual occasions at which prestige is bestowed (or withheld) and the virtues of valued members praised.[21] Ritual occasions vary in texture and in the richness of the

---

[21] Theorists such as Sewell (1996) analyze the role of powerful ritual moments in the transformation of social structures, and classical anthropology saw ritual as crucial for the preservation of social patterns. In the villages Tsai (2007a, 2007b) studied, traditional cultural associations

shared meanings they carry. Sometimes the assertion of rank seems to constitute the entire meaning of the ritual, as when a meeting between African chiefs and NGO officials turns out to be, from the point of view of the chiefs, mainly about the short speeches each chief offers in reverse order of precedence. Other rituals, such as weddings or funerals, may be freighted with many layers of meaning, but even so, the ritual itself will provide many opportunities to enact who is near or distant kin, who is deferred to in seating arrangements or opportunities to speak, or who is important enough to play central ritual roles. Indeed, one of the uncomfortable things about rituals is that they are so semiotically rich – they both permit and require manifesting in publicly visible ways who matters to whom and how. In our own society – and indeed in many of our own work lives – annual banquets, award ceremonies, or prizes demonstrate the role that shared cultural meanings play in the status processes that tie individuals to institutional purposes and reward their commitment.

Considering an organization's annual banquet, a sports team's award ceremonies, or even a typical retirement party immediately suggests another way ritual occasions promote institutional resilience. Ritual occasions highlight and often magnify contributions to the collective good, and they also, crucially, reinforce a narrative about the value of the collectivity and the efforts those honored are making on its behalf. Such narratives not only suggest that those contributing to collective purposes are worthy and perhaps merit as-yet-unspecified reciprocity in the future. They also reinforce an image that others are contributing to the collectivity, reducing defections and free riding by highlighting those who are cooperating. The whole cultural complex involved in granting, symbolically affirming, and celebrating status reinforces the understanding that the collective good exists, that others are contributing to it, and that one's own contributions will be noticed and acknowledged.

Rituals also, as Michael Chwe (2003) has noted, provide the occasions when commitments, alliances, and loyalties can be publicly acknowledged and rehearsed. Thus, a shared repertoire of cultural forms, such as those that govern funerals, public meetings, and celebrations, can provide a ready way of generating common perceptions, including perceptions of the enthusiasm, obedience, or cooperativeness of others (Wedeen 1999). Such knowledge in turn facilitates the coordination of collective action. When a chief calls a meeting – to announce a government program, to resolve a dispute, or to remind people of an obligation – the simple presence of villagers at the meeting is a token of their willingness to accept his authority and to participate in collective tasks.

were vital for creating the "virtuous circle" in which village authorities' contributions to collective goods could be rewarded with status, which in turn encouraged the production of more collective goods. In a very different context, Zhou and Bankston (1998) make a very similar point when they explain the high academic performance of very poor Vietnamese American high school students in part by the pressure Vietnamese immigrant parents feel at the community banquets where parents receive awards for the academic achievements of their children.

When a chief announces a decision that is greeted with laughter, ululating, and delighted clapping (as when a group village headman in southern Malawi announced that he had removed a corrupt headman), the shared emotional response reinforces the common knowledge that facilitates coordinated action, as does the indifferent silence that greets less welcome announcements. But the entire array of ritual occasions – from funerals, which are major occasions in Malawi and throughout Africa, to dances, to the now rare but still known rituals in which chiefs lead villagers in beseeching ancestors for rain – provide the cultural resources that make chiefdom a resilient institutional form.

Resilience and Collective Action Schemas

How "shared" does culture need to be in order to sustain resilient institutional forms? Economists and political scientists have long argued that social communities produce more public goods when they have fewer ethnic, religious, or communal divisions.[22] But what is striking about chieftaincy in much of Africa – and suggestive for broader theories of institutions – is that chieftaincy is often a solution to problems of conflict and cultural heterogeneity, resilient far outside the confines of small, homogeneous villages. The development of "town chiefs" in areas of heterogeneous in-migration, far removed from the village context, shows the way a culturally recognized institutional form can be transposed and reconstituted to serve new functions in new contexts. In Malawi, Cammack et al. (2009: 36) describe town chiefs as a "hybrid" social form:

Firstly, traditional chieftaincies are themselves an institutional hybrid as a result of the historical process of state formation. Secondly, institutions similar to those of traditional chiefs may underpin town chiefs, but these are being adapted to urban conditions (e.g.

---

[22] The classic study showing that ethnic fragmentation reduces public goods is Easterly and Levine (1997). Alesina, Baqir, and Easterly (1999) find a similar negative effect of ethnic fragmentation on public goods for U.S. cities and counties. Lieberman's (2009) analysis of national responses to the AIDS epidemic shows that sharp ethnic boundaries reduce national effort to combat AIDS. Recent research has, however, added complexity to the argument. Lieberman (2009) argues that it is not underlying ethnic or racial differences, but the cultural strength of boundaries that matters, so that, for example, "in Brazil . . . the weakly institutionalized category of race was not politicized for most of the history of AIDS, making possible a politics of national solidarity," but in South Africa, "discussions of risk, and a politics of blame and denial, broke down along racial lines, lowering demand for a supply of aggressive AIDS policies" (22). Miguel (2004) reports that cultural and institutional efforts to strengthen national identification can weaken the effects of ethnic divisions: villages in Kenya and neighboring Tanzania have similar variations in ethnic fragmentation, and in Kenyan villages, ethnic heterogeneity is indeed associated with poorer provision of public goods. In Tanzania, in contrast, policies of active nation building have eliminated the tendency of ethnic heterogeneity to reduce public goods provision. Recent research by Baldwin and Huber (2010) also shows that between-group economic inequality reduces public goods, but cultural fractionalization and ethno-linguistic fractionalization unrelated to economic inequalities do not.

absence of state recognition, cultural heterogeneity, etc.) and to specific demands arising in each locality. The hybrid nature of town chiefs is further influenced by the complexity of parchment institutions arising from legal innovations and inconsistencies and their various interpretations. Town chiefs are best described as hybrid governance modes resulting from an indigenous adaptation of an existing hybrid institution to a modern environment.

. . . .

Town chiefs, therefore, help groups to overcome collective action problems through being supported by overlapping norms that: (i) enable them to bridge and create a sense of belonging and cohesion amongst disparate individuals; and (ii) endow them with authority and effective sanctions to impose rules. This enables town chiefs to contribute to the provision of important public goods, [including]: (i) justice and reconciliation; and (ii) security and order (mundane and spiritual). Both are fundamental public goods that are particularly important for generating belonging and cohesion in urban settlements where the lack of planning and funds, and weak state capacity lead to unmet needs.

From the other side of the continent, Sandra Barnes (1986), in a classic study of a suburb of Lagos, Nigeria, with more than one million in-migrants, shows that when new urban residents sought political recognition they adapted the chiefdom form, creating a system of chieftaincy that helped them access such necessities as "jobs, housing, schooling, loans." The suburb's political leaders sought and eventually won political recognition in the form of "chieftaincy titles" (184–200). Barnes explains the "anachronism" of a chieftaincy system arising between the 1950s and the 1970s as having both "cultural and pragmatic" sources:

So far as culture was concerned, Yoruba-speaking peoples dominated the privileged stratum from which local leadership emerged. Despite the fact that the structure of chieftaincy systems varied widely throughout Yorubaland, the one element of political culture most of Mushin's leaders held in common–the one element which, despite foreign rule and the rise of an educated ruling class, remained open to ordinary citizens, be they educated or uneducated, rich or poor–was chiefship and the idea that certain political rights and opportunities in the wider community could be derived from holding a title. The models for a chieftaincy system surrounded the new District of Mushin, and thus, when its leaders were in a position to bring cultural content to political aspiration, chiefship was a logical choice.

In pragmatic terms, politicians wished to secure the support of chiefs in political campaigns. Each title-holder was the centre of a political arena consisting of kinsmen, clients, friends, and followers, and therefore each one presided over a natural and organised constituency from which politicians could seek votes and other forms of political backing. Politicians also saw personal benefits in the institution of chieftaincy. Titles gave legitimacy to political action, security of tenure, access to the centre, and, last but not least, honour and renown. Titles were not simply hollow markers of status, but resources which could be used profitably in the quest for political power and advancement (pp. 97–8).

Chieftaincy, like other resilient institutions, provides a very general model that people can use to organize diverse aspects of social life.[23] Precisely because establishing patron–client ties and using those ties to claim chiefly title can be tried in many situations, with a variety of supporters, and to achieve varied purposes, the structure keeps reemerging. Patron–client structures have tended to erode formal democratic and bureaucratic governance in much of Africa (Chabal and Daloz 1999; Chabal 2009). Nonetheless, others argue that "developmental patrimonialism" in Africa has sometimes led to better economic outcomes than the more "orthodox" good-governance strategies insisted on by Western experts (Kelsall and Booth 2010; Booth and Golooba-Mutebi 2011). Similarly, many NGO and donor programs in sub-Saharan Africa "work" precisely because they provide resources that can be converted into patron–client ties (Smith 2003; Swidler 2009; Swidler and Watkins 2009), often by chiefs, who are crucial intermediaries in such programs.

In *Talk of Love* (Swidler 2001), I argued that societies' collective schemas for understanding the way action is organized – such as the American myth of "voluntarism" (that social groups emerge from freely chosen cooperation of individuals pursuing common goals) and its correlative assumption of the autonomous individual actor – endure for a reason. I called these myths "collective action schemas," arguing that they retain their cultural power precisely because they embody the shared "default option" for solving collective problems: what everyone knows that everyone else knows about how social action can be organized. Such collective myths – really formulas or codes for describing group formation – are very hard to change even in the face of repeated failure or other contradictory experience because it takes powerful, shared collective experience – a cathartic convulsion or a collective ritual transformation in Sewell's (1996) formulation – to enact an alternative vision and constitute a new myth, to signal publicly that everyone knows that everyone knows that there is now a new basis on which people can act together to address collective problems. Michael Chwe (2003) has made a similar argument in rational-choice terms, pointing to the importance of ritual occasions in allowing everyone to see that everyone else has seen that a pattern of collective action is intact or has changed.

---

[23] Richard Biernacki (1995) offers another example of the resilience of even nearly moribund social forms. In explaining why "labor" became commodified very differently in Germany versus England, Biernacki asks what institutional frameworks were available in each country at the time industrialists were creating textile factories and recruiting labor, constituting labor as a commodity. German industrialists, when they needed to recruit factory labor, modeled their understanding of what labor was on the corvée labor systems of feudal agriculture and thus saw themselves as paying for labor time or effort directly because they did not have the developed commodity and labor markets that made labor-as-embodied-in-the-product seem the natural way to structure payments to workers. British employers, who already had developed commodity and labor markets, saw labor as embodied in the product, paying laborers not for their labor time or effort directly but for cloth of varying density and complexity of weave.

Such a formulation would pick up on elements of arguments by Frank Dobbin (1994) and others about how certain approaches to solving policy questions keep reappearing in national contexts because they reinforce collective understandings of how the nation has solved important problems in the past. Beliefs about what has "worked" in the past, of course, depend not simply on actual history but on various forms of collective memory. Collective memory of capacities for collective action may be retained as historical narrative, but it can also be retained in more general forms as people, institutional forms, and general images of collective life are imbued with a sense of the sacred (Feierman 1999). Clifford Geertz (1968: 44) argued that enduring institutional forms embody differing conceptions of "the mode in which the divine reaches into the world" – through the holy charisma of an individual leader in Moroccan Islam or through the ordering of an "exemplary center" in Java's "theater state." This capacity of culture to "store" and "release" collective energies in the form of sacred power is very evident in the case of Malawian chiefs. This is not simply a matter of belief in legitimacy or of beliefs about whether it is right or obligatory to obey one's chief. Even a Malawian who despised her chief and ignored his wishes would see chieftaincy as embodying powerful, if dangerous forces. This sense of sacred power – in the Durkheimian sense in which the collectivity embodies the sacred – is another reason why embedded cultural meanings and practices encode collective capacities without which it is difficult for institutions to succeed in engaging their members and sustaining the provision of collective goods.

Conclusion

Awareness of interdependence is inevitably greater in a very poor country such as Malawi, with its underdeveloped labor and credit markets, unpredictable rainfall, and sometimes feckless government (Swidler and Watkins 2007). There people cannot maintain even the illusion that their achievements are all their own doing; that their resources belong exclusively to them; and that they depend on no one but themselves for security, opportunity, and purpose. But the lessons from Malawi very much apply in the advanced economies as well. The ability to manage complex markets, the interdependencies between, for example, educational, welfare, employment, and retirement systems depend on effective, resilient institutions (Hall and Soskice 2001). As the challenges of global interdependence grow, with an interlinked global economy and looming ecological crisis, the question of how to maintain the vitality of existing institutions and build new ones has never been more urgent. Although I have not presented anything like a complete theory here, I have emphasized the ways cultural meanings contribute to resilient institutions. Status rewards sustain the meanings that evoke commitment from an organization's members; rituals enact and reproduce those meanings; narratives of shared purpose reduce defections and make more extensive cooperation possible. Institutions are justified by claims about the larger collective purposes they serve, and they remain resilient as long as the reward systems they generate reinforce rather than subvert their claims to purpose and their assessments of value (White and White 1965). It is precisely in the irreducible interdependencies of social life that the capacity of institutions to evoke commitment resides. For institutions to be infused with meaning and purpose, they must also be seen to serve collective ends. Collective goods – from social peace to functioning markets to effective climate policies – are both the product of resilient institutions and their raison d'être. We neglect those goods at our peril.

References

Abotchie, Chris, Albert Awedoba, Irene K. Odotei, et al. 2006. "Perceptions of Chieftaincy." In *Chieftaincy in Ghana: Culture, Governance and Development*, edited by Irene K. Odotei and Albert K. Awedoba. Legon, Accra, Ghana: Sub-Saharan Publishers: 103–144.

Alesina, Alberto, Reza Baqir, and William Easterly. 1999. "Public Goods and Ethnic Divisions." *Quarterly Journal of Economics* 114 (4): 1243–84.

Ashforth, Adam. 1998. "Reflections on Spiritual Insecurity in a Modern African City: Soweto." *African Studies Review* 41 (3): 39–68.

Ashforth, Adam. 2005. *Witchcraft, Violence, and Democracy in South Africa*. Chicago: University of Chicago Press.

Baiocchi, Gianpaolo, Patrick Heller, and Marcelo Kunrath Silva. 2008. "Making Space for Civil Society: Institutional Reforms and Local Democracy in Brazil." *Social Forces* 86 (3): 911–36.

Baldwin, Kate. 2007. "Bringing Traditional Patrons Back into the Study of Patronage: Chiefs and Politics in Zambia." Paper presented to the African Studies Association, New York: October 18–21.

Baldwin, Kate. 2010. "Big Men and Ballots – The Effects of Traditional Leaders on Elections and Distributive Politics in Zambia." Doctoral dissertation, Department of Political Science, Columbia University.

Baldwin, Kate and John D. Huber. 2010. "Economic versus Cultural Differences: Forms of Ethnic Diversity and Public Goods Provision." *American Political Science Review* 104 (4): 644–62.

Barnes, Sandra T. 1986. *Patrons and Power: Creating a Political Community in Metropolitan Lagos*. Bloomington, IN: Indiana University Press.

Bellah, Robert N., Richard Madsen, William Sullivan, Ann Swidler, and Steven M. Tipton. *Habits of the Heart: Individualism and Commitment in American Life*. Berkeley: University of California Press, 1985.

Béné, Christophe, Emma Belal, Malloum Ousman Baba, Solomon Ovie, Aminu Raji, Isaac Malasha, Friday Njaya, Mamane Na Andi, Aaron Russell, and Arthur Neiland. 2009. "Power Struggle, Dispute and Alliance over Local Resources: Analyzing 'Democratic' Decentralization of Natural Resources through the Lenses of Africa Inland Fisheries." *World Development* 37 (12): 1935–50.

Biernacki, Richard. 1995. *The Fabrication of Labor: Germany and Britain, 1640–1914*. Berkeley: University of California Press.

Bourdieu, Pierre. 1986. "The Forms of Capital." In *Handbook of Theory and Research for the Sociology of Education*, edited by John Richardson. New York: Greenwood: 241–258.

Bourdieu, Pierre. 1996. *The State Nobility: Elite Schools in the Field of Power*. Stanford: Stanford University Press.

Bourdieu, Pierre and Jean-Claude Passeron. 1990. *Reproduction in Education, Society and Culture*, second edition. London: Sage Publications.

Bourdieu, Pierre and Loïc J.D. Wacquant. 1992. *An Invitation to Reflexive Sociology*. Stanford: Stanford University Press.

Booth, David and Frederick Golooba-Mutebi. 2011. "Developmental Patrimonialism? The Case of Rwanda." In *Africa Power & Politics Working Paper No. 16*. London: Africa Power and Politics Programme, Overseas Development Institute.

Brondizio, Eduardo S., Elinor Ostrom, and Oran R. Young. 2009. "Connectivity and the Governance of Multilevel Social-Ecological Systems: The Role of Social Capital." *Annual Review of Environment and Resources* 34: 253–78.

Calhoun, Craig. 2008. "The Imperative to Reduce Suffering: Charity, Progress, and Emergencies in the Field of Humanitarian Action." In *Humanitarianism in Question: Politics, Power, Ethics*, edited by Michael Barnett and Thomas G. Weiss. Ithaca, NY: Cornell University Press: 73–97.

Callaghy, Thomas M., Ronald Kassimir, and Robert Latham, eds. 2001. *Intervention and Transnationalism in Africa: Global-Local Networks of Power*. Cambridge, UK: Cambridge University Press.

Cammack, Diana, Edge Kanyongolo, and Tam O'Neil. 2009. "'Town Chiefs' in Malawi." *Africa Power and Politics Working Paper No. 3*. London: Africa Power and Politics Programme, Overseas Development Institute.

Cancian, Francesca M. 1975. *What Are Norms?: A Study of Beliefs and Action in a Maya Community*. Cambridge, UK: Cambridge University Press.

Chabal, Patrick. 2009. *Africa: The Politics of Suffering and Smiling*. London: Zed Books.

Chabal, Patrick and Jean-Pascal Daloz. 1999. *Africa Works: Disorder as Political Instrument*. Bloomington, IN: Indiana University Press.

Charrad, Mounira M. 2001. *States and Women's Rights: The Making of Postcolonial Tunisia, Algeria, and Morocco*. Berkeley: University of California Press.

Chiweza, Asiyati Lorraine. 2007. "The Ambivalent Role of Chiefs: Rural Decentralization Initiatives in Malawi." In *State Recognition and Democratization in Sub-Saharan Africa: A New Dawn for Traditional Authorities?* edited by Lars Buur and Helene Maria Kyed. New York: Palgrave Macmillan: 53–78.

Chwe, Michael Suk-Young. 2003. *Rational Ritual: Culture, Coordination, and Common Knowledge*. Princeton, NJ: Princeton University Press.

Collier, Jane Fishburne. 2004. "A Chief Does Not Rule Land; He Rules People (Luganda Proverb)." In *Law and Empire in the Pacific: Fiji and Hawai'i*, edited by Sally Engle Merry and Donald Brenneis. Santa Fe, NM: School of American Research Press: 35–60.

Collins, Randall. 2004. *Interaction Ritual Chains*. Princeton, NJ: Princeton University Press.

Colson, Elizabeth. 1986. "Political Organization in Tribal Societies: A Cross-Cultural Comparison." *American Indian Quarterly* 10 (1): 5–19.

Cornell, Stephen and Joseph P. Kalt. 1997. "Successful Economic Development and Heterogeneity of Governmental Form on American Indian Reservations." In *Getting Good Government: Capacity Building in the Public Sectors of Developing Countries*, edited by Merilee S. Grindle. Cambridge, MA: Harvard University Press: 257–96.

Cornell, Stephen and Joseph P. Kalt. 2000. "Where's the Glue? Institutional and Cultural Foundations of American Indian Economic Development." *Journal of Socio-Economics* 29 (5): 443–70.

Dalton, Russell J. 2005. "The Social Transformation of Trust in Government." *International Review of Sociology* 15 (1): 133–54.

de Waal, Alex. 2009. "Mission Without End? Peacekeeping in the African Political Marketplace." *International Affairs* 85 (1): 99–113.

Dobbin, Frank. 1994. *Forging Industrial Policy: The United States, Britain and France in the Railway Age.* Cambridge, UK: Cambridge University Press.

Dionne, Kim Yi. 2012. "Local Demand for a Global Intervention: Policy Preferences in the Time of AIDS." *World Development.* doi: 10.1016/j.worlddev.2012.05.016.

Easterly, William and Ross Levine. 1997. "Africa's Growth Tragedy: Policies and Ethnic Divisions." *Quarterly Journal of Economics* 112 (4): 1203–50.

Fearon, James D., Macartan Humphreys, and Jeremy M. Weinstein. 2009. "Can Development Aid Contribute to Social Cohesion after Civil War? Evidence from a Field Experiment in Post-Conflict Liberia." *American Economic Review: Papers & Proceedings* 99 (2): 287–91.

Feierman, Steven. 1999. "Colonizers, Scholars, and the Creation of Invisible Histories." In *Beyond the Cultural Turn*, edited by Victoria E. Bonnell and Lynn Hunt. Berkeley: University of California Press: 182–216.

Fischer, Claude S. 2010. *Made in America: A Social History of American Culture and Character.* Chicago: University of Chicago Press.

Fligstein, Neil. 2001. *The Architecture of Markets: An Economic Sociology of Twenty-First-Century Capitalist Societies.* Princeton, NJ: Princeton University Press.

Fortes, Meyer and E. E. Evans-Pritchard. 1940. *African Political Systems.* London: Oxford University Press.

Fukuyama, Francis. 2004. *State-Building: Governance and World Order in the Twenty-First Century.* Ithaca, NY: Cornell University Press.

Geertz, Clifford. 1968. *Islam Observed: Religious Development in Morocco and Indonesia.* New Haven: Yale University Press.

Geschiere, Peter. 1993. "Chiefs and Colonial Rule in Cameroon: Reinventing Chieftaincy, French and British Style." *Africa* 63 (2): 151–76.

Gibson, Clark C., Krister Andersson, Elinor Ostrom, and Sujai Shivakumar. 2005. *The Samaritan's Dilemma: The Political Economy of Development Aid.* New York: Oxford University Press.

Greif, Avner. 2006. *Institutions and the Path to the Modern Economy: Lessons from Medieval Trade.* Cambridge, UK: Cambridge University Press.

Hall, Peter A. and David Soskice. 2001. *Varieties of Capitalism: The Institutional Foundations of Comparative Advantage.* New York: Oxford University Press.

Hall, Peter and Rosemary C. R. Taylor. 1996. "Political Science and the Three New Institutionalisms." *Political Studies* 44: 936–57.

Hall, Peter A. and Rosemary C. R. Taylor. 2009. "Health, Social Relations, and Public Policy." In *Successful Societies: How Institutions and Culture Affect Health*, edited by Peter A. Hall and Michèle Lamont: 82–103.

Hammack, David C. and Steven Heydemann, eds. 2009. *Globalization, Philanthropy, and Civil Society: Projecting Institutional Logics Abroad.* Bloomington, IN: Indiana University Press.

Harding, David J. 2010. *Living the Drama: Community, Conflict, and Culture among Inner-City Boys*. Chicago: University of Chicago Press.

Henrich, Joseph, Steven J. Heine, and Ara Norenzayan. 2010a. "The Weirdest People in the World?" *Behavioral and Brain Sciences* 33 (2–3): 61–83.

Hirsch, Jennifer S., Holly Wardlow, Daniel Jordan Smith, Harriet M. Phinney, Shanti Parikh, and Constance A. Nathanson. 2009. *The Secret: Love, Marriage, and HIV*. Nashville: Vanderbilt University Press.

Huntington, Samuel P. 1965. "Political Development and Political Decay." *World Politics* 17 (3): 386–430.

Jepperson, Ronald L. 1991. "Institutions, Institutional Effects, and Institutionalism." In *The New Institutionalism in Organizational Analysis*, edited by Walter W. Powell and Paul J. DiMaggio. Chicago: University of Chicago Press: 143–63.

Kaler, Amy and Susan Cotts Watkins. 2001. "Disobedient Distributors: Street-Level Bureaucrats and Would-Be Patrons in Community-Based Family Planning Programs in Rural Kenya." *Studies in Family Planning* 32 (3): 254–269.

Karlström, Mikael. 1996. "Imagining Democracy: The Political Culture and Democratisation in Buganda." *Africa* 66 (4): 485–506.

Keck, Margaret and Kathryn Sikkink. 1998. *Activists Beyond Borders: Transnational Advocacy Networks in International Politics*. Ithaca, NY: Cornell University Press.

Kelsall, Tim and David Booth with Diana Cammack and Frederick Golooba-Mutebi. 2010. "Developmental Patrimonialism? Questioning the Orthodoxy on Political Governance and Economic Progress in Africa." *Africa Power & Politics Working Paper No. 9*. London: Africa Power and Politics Programme, Overseas Development Institute.

Kyed, Helene Maria and Lars Buur. 2006. "Recognition and Democratisation: 'New Roles' for Traditional Leaders in Sub-Saharan Africa." Copenhagen: Danish Institute for International Studies, DIIS.

Lieberman, Evan S. 2009. *Boundaries of Contagion: How Ethnic Politics Have Shaped Government Responses to AIDS*. Princeton, NJ: Princeton University Press.

Logan, Carolyn. 2009. "Selected Chiefs, Elected Councillors and Hybrid Democrats: Popular Perspectives on the Co-Existence of Democracy and Traditional Authority." *Journal of Modern African Studies* 47 (1): 101–28.

Logan, Carolyn. 2011. "The Roots of Resilience: Exploring Popular Support for African Traditional Authorities." Afrobarometer Working Paper No. 128.

Mamdani, Mahmood. 1996. *Citizen and Subject: Contemporary Africa and the Legacy of Late Colonialism*. Princeton, NJ: Princeton University Press.

Markus, Hazel Rose and Barry Schwartz. 2010 "Does Choice Mean Freedom and Well-Being?" *Journal of Consumer Research* 37: 344–55.

Maxwell, David. 1999. *Christians and Chiefs in Zimbabwe: A Social History of the Hwesa People*. Westport, CT: Praeger.

Migdal, Joel S. 1988. *Strong Societies and Weak States: State-Society Relations and State Capabilities in the Third World*. Princeton, NJ: Princeton University Press.

Migdal, Joel S. 2001. *State in Society: Studying How States and Societies Transform and Constitute One Another*. Cambridge, UK: Cambridge University Press.

Miguel, Edward. 2004. "Tribe or Nation? Nation-Building and Public Goods in Kenya Versus Tanzania." *World Politics* 56: 327–62.

Miller, Peter and Nikolas Rose. 2008. *Governing the Present: Administering Economic, Social and Personal Life*. Cambridge, UK: Polity.

Mitchell, J. Clyde. 1956. *The Yao Village: A Study in the Social Structure of a Nyasaland Tribe*. Manchester, UK: Manchester University Press.

Mohr, John W. and Harrison C. White. 2008. "How to Model an Institution." *Theory and Society* 37 (5): 485–512.

Ntsebeza, Lungisile. 2008. "The Resurgence of Chiefs: Retribalization & Modernity in Post-1994 South Africa." In *Readings in Modernity in Africa*, edited by Peter Geschiere, Birgit Meyer, and Peter Pels. Bloomington: Indiana University Press: 71–79.

North, Douglass C. 1990. *Institutions, Institutional Change and Economic Performance*. Cambridge, UK: Cambridge University Press.

Nye, Joseph S., Jr., Philip D. Zelikow, and David C. King, eds. 1997. *Why People Don't Trust Government*. Cambridge, MA: Harvard University Press.

Oomen, Barbara. 2000. *Tradition on the Move*. Amsterdam: Netherlands Institute for Southern Africa.

Oomen, Barbara. 2008. "Chiefs! Law, Power & Culture in Contemporary South Africa." In *Readings in Modernity in Africa*, edited by Peter Geschiere, Birgit Meyer, and Peter Pels. Bloomington, IN: Indiana University Press: 80–84.

Ostrom, Elinor. 1990. *Governing the Commons: The Evolution of Institutions for Collective Action*. Cambridge, UK: Cambridge University Press.

Poteete, Amy R., Marco A. Janssen, and Elinor Ostrom. 2010. *Working Together: Collective Action, the Commons, and Multiple Methods in Practice*. Princeton, NJ: Princeton University Press.

Pritchett, Lant, Michael Woolcock, and Matt Andrews. 2010. "Capability Traps? The Mechanisms of Persistent Implementation Failure." Working Paper 234. Washington, DC: Center for Global Development (December).

Rudolph, Lloyd I. and Susanne Hoeber Rudolph. 1967. *The Modernity of Tradition: Political Development in India*. Chicago: University of Chicago Press.

Sampson, Robert, Jeffrey D. Morenoff, and Thomas Gannon-Rowley. 2002. "Assessing Neighborhood Effects: Social Processes and New Directions in Research." *Annual Review of Sociology* 28: 443–78.

Schaffer, Frederic C. 1998. *Democracy in Translation: Understanding Politics in an Unfamiliar Culture*. Ithaca, NY: Cornell University Press.

Scott, W. Richard. 2008. *Institutions and Organizations: Ideas and Interests*, 3rd ed. Thousand Oaks, CA: Sage Publications.

Selznick, Philip. 1957. *Leadership in Administration: A Sociological Interpretation*. New York: Harper & Row.

Sewell, William H., Jr. 1992. "A Theory of Structure: Duality, Agency, and Transformation." *American Journal of Sociology* 98: 1–29.

Sewell, William H., Jr. 1996. "Historical Events as Transformations of Structures: Inventing Revolution at the Bastille." *Theory and Society* 25: 841–81.

Sikkink, Kathryn. 2009. "From State Responsibility to Individual Criminal Accountability: A New Regulatory Model for Core Human Rights Violations." In *The Politics of Global Regulation*, edited by Walter Mattli and Ngaire Woods. Princeton, NJ: Princeton University Press: 121–50.

Skocpol, Theda. 1979. *States and Social Revolutions: A Comparative Analysis of France, Russia, and China*. Cambridge, UK: Cambridge University Press.

Slaughter, Anne-Marie. 2004. *A New World Order*. Princeton, NJ: Princeton University Press.

Smith, Daniel Jordan. 2003. "Patronage, Per Diems and 'the Workshop Mentality': The Practice of Family Planning Programs in Southeastern Nigeria." *World Development* 31 (4): 703–15.

Smith, Daniel Jordan. 2006. *A Culture of Corruption: Everyday Deception and Popular Discontent in Nigeria*. Princeton, NJ: Princeton University Press.

Streeck, Wolfgang and Kathleen Thelen. 2005. *Beyond Continuity: Institutional Change in Advanced Political Economies*. Oxford, UK: Oxford University Press.

Stiglitz, Joseph E. 2002. *Globalization and Its Discontents*. New York: W.W. Norton.

Swidler, Ann. 2001. *Talk of Love: How Culture Matters*. Chicago: University of Chicago Press.

Swidler, Ann. 2009. "Dialectics of Patronage: Logics of Accountability at the African AIDS-NGO Interface." In *Globalization, Philanthropy, and Civil Society: Projecting Institutional Logics Abroad*, edited by Steven Heydemann and David C. Hammack. Bloomington: Indiana University Press: 192–220.

Swidler, Ann and Susan Cotts Watkins. 2007. "Ties of Dependence: AIDS and Transactional Sex in Rural Malawi." *Studies in Family Planning* 38 (3): 147–62.

Swidler, Ann and Susan Cotts Watkins. 2009. "'Teach a Man to Fish': The Sustainability Doctrine and Its Social Consequences." *World Development* 37 (7): 1182–96.

Thelen, Kathleen. 2004. *How Institutions Evolve: The Political Economy of Skills in Germany, Britain, the United States and Japan*. Cambridge, UK: Cambridge University Press.

Tsai, Lily L. 2007a. "Solidary Groups, Informal Accountability, and Local Public Goods Provision in Rural China." *American Political Science Review* 101 (2): 355–72.

Tsai, Lily L. 2007b. *Accountability without Democracy: Solidary Groups and Public Goods Provision in Rural China, Cambridge Studies in Comparative Politics*. Cambridge, UK: Cambridge University Press.

Watkins, Susan Cotts and Ann Swidler. 2009. "Hearsay Ethnography: Conversational Journals as a Method for Studying Culture in Action." *Poetics* 37 (2): 162–84.

Watkins, Susan Cotts, Ann Swidler, and Thomas Hannan. 2012. "Outsourcing Social Transformation: Development NGOs as Organizations." *Annual Review of Sociology* 38: 285–315.

Wedeen, Lisa. 1999. *Ambiguities of Domination: Politics, Rhetoric, and Symbols in Contemporary Syria*. Chicago: University of Chicago Press.

West, Harry and Scott Kloeck-Jenson. 1999. "Betwixt and Between: 'Traditional Authority' and Democratic Decentralization in Post-War Mozambique." *African Affairs* 98 (393): 455–84.

White, Harrison C. and Cynthia White. 1965. *Canvases and Careers: Institutional Change in the French Painting World*. New York: John Wiley and Sons.

Willer, Robb. 2009. "Groups Reward Individual Sacrifice: The Status Solution to the Collective Action Problem." *American Sociological Review* 74: 23–43.

Zhou, Min and Carl L. Bankston III. 1998. *Growing up American: How Vietnamese Children Adapt to Life in the United States*. New York: Russell Sage Foundation.

The Origins and Dynamics of Organizational Resilience

A Comparative Study of Two French Labor Organizations[1]

Marcos Ancelovici

Since the late 1990s, in the wake of John Sweeney's election as president of the American Federation of Labor-Congress of Industrial Organizations (AFL-CIO) in the United States, the study of labor revitalization has become a small industry. Although this industry (e.g., Frege and Kelly 2004; Milkman and Voss 2004; Turner 2005) has identified many external (e.g., employer hostility, unfavorable legal framework, outsourcing, neoliberalism, globalization) and internal (e.g., disconnected leadership, bureaucratic inertia, fear of change, inter-union competition) factors that can shape trade unions' decision to engage in revitalization strategies, it has given a secondary status, if any at all, to culture.[2] In doing so, these studies have neglected the cognitive constraints and symbolic work that underpin the diagnoses of trade unions and have thus failed to explain how labor activists come to believe that revitalization is necessary in the first place and furthermore, devise a strategy for achieving that goal.

This chapter attempts to fill this gap by comparing the political-cultural processes behind the divergent outcomes of two French labor organizations: the French Democratic Confederation of Labor (CFDT) and the General Confederation of Labor (CGT). Whereas the former reacted relatively quickly to decline and demonstrated resilience, the latter proved incapable of responding adequately to decline and drifted for a long period before it finally tried to change course. What is most puzzling in the case of the CGT is that it lost approximately 65 percent of its membership between 1977 and 1990 without acknowledging that it was undergoing a crisis and therefore without substantially attempting to take a new course. Only in the early 1990s did it finally recognize that dramatic changes were required, and it took another ten years to engage in recruitment campaigns to try to attract new members. How can

---

[1] I wish to thank the editors, Peter Hall and Michèle Lamont, for very helpful comments and suggestions and Sara Hall for editing the text.
[2] For an exception, see Lopez (2004).

we make sense of such drift? How can we explain the contrast between the CFDT and the CGT? Why has the CFDT proven more resilient than the CGT? More generally, why are some organizations more resilient than others?

I propose to treat organizational resilience as the capacity of organizations to cope with and bounce back from unfavorable changes in their environment (Bégin and Chabaud 2010). As Hall and Lamont state in the Introduction to this volume, "At issue is the capacity of individuals or groups to secure favorable outcomes... under new circumstances and, if need be, by new means." The capacity of a given trade union to engage successfully in recruitment and organizing campaigns in an unfavorable context, such as neoliberalization, can thus be considered an instance of organizational resilience. Although it touches on issues of organizational survival, the population ecology approach (Hannan and Freeman 1977, 1984) is not very helpful for answering the questions I raised earlier because it focuses on entire organizational sectors of society – what they call populations of organizations sharing some unit character – rather than looking at a single organization at a time. This approach would thus attempt to explain the "mortality rate" of the entire trade union population in a given country rather than account for the divergent trajectories of some unions within that population (see Hannan and Freeman 1988).

In contrast, this chapter builds on the political approach developed by scholars such as, from different standpoints, Lindblom (1959), Pfeffer and Salancik (2003 [1978]), Kitschelt (1994), and Levitsky (2003) in the tradition of rational adaptation theory; it stresses internal political struggles and incremental change (for an overview, see Demers 2007). However, it diverges from this approach by taking into account the cognitive and cultural dimensions of these political struggles and acknowledging their unintended consequences. This combination of political and cognitive/cultural processes distinguishes my perspective from both a strict political approach and a cognitive approach à la Karl Weick that would focus almost exclusively on collective sense-making (see Weick 1988 and Demers 2007: 61–73). In that respect, my perspective is close to Neil Fligstein's "political-cultural" approach (cf. Fligstein 1987, 1996).

This chapter treats the crisis of trade unions fostered by the neoliberalization of the labor regime as a phenomenon akin to a critical juncture during which a substantial reorientation can take place and divergent long-term pathways are established (cf. Pierson 2004; Slater and Simmons 2010). Divergent outcomes in terms of organizational resilience exemplify such potential pathways. In the case of the two labor organizations under scrutiny in this chapter, I hypothesize that organizational resilience, or lack thereof, was the product of three overlapping processes: *narration* (how actors make sense of their environment and insert their representation in a causal chain of events unfolding over time and pointing to a particular path), *learning* (how organizations produce and encode knowledge into routines that guide behavior), and *institutionalization* (how the leadership imposes and infuses with value a particular narrative and strategy within the organization). Insofar as these processes are intertwined with power relations and involve conflict, they are fundamentally political.

I also hypothesize that these three processes were conditioned by a combination of cultural (repertoires) and organizational (centralization and leadership autonomy) factors; these factors constitute antecedent conditions that shape the range of options available to organizations and thereby shape their agency. Organizations endowed with a heterogeneous repertoire are more likely to be resilient than organizations endowed with a homogeneous repertoire. Heterogeneous repertoires offer a wider variety of frames and scripts to organizations and thereby foster a friction that can potentially feed adaptability and innovation.[3] In contrast, homogeneous repertoires contribute to the institutionalization and taken-for-grantedness of the goals and strategy of organizations and reduce the scope of cultural materials that actors have on hand for making sense of changes in their environment and devising creative solutions and new strategies.

But having a heterogeneous repertoire is not enough to be resilient. The structure of the organization is also a critical factor in two respects. First, it shapes the ability of the leadership to have access to information to assess the external environment of the organization. Second, it affects the implementation capacity of the leadership; the more centralized the organization and autonomous the leadership, the more a new strategy is likely to be successfully implemented and institutionalized after it has been devised. A decentralized organization that lacks an autonomous leadership could generate creative solutions but fail to implement them.

Therefore, I argue that when faced with dramatic membership losses in the late 1970s and early 1980s, the CFDT benefited from having a heterogeneous repertoire, a centralized structure, and autonomous leadership that allowed it to learn from its environment, narrate the situation in a way conducive to change, and implement and institutionalize a new strategy of action that fostered the maintenance of the organization. In contrast, the CGT was hindered by a more homogeneous repertoire, a decentralized structure, and a dependent leadership that prevented it from assessing and acknowledging the extent of the crisis it was facing and from formulating and implementing a new strategy of action that could potentially foster resilience.

To make this case, this chapter first outlines the problems and challenges that the CFDT and CGT faced in the late 1970s and 1980s in the context of the neoliberalization of the French labor regime. Next, it presents their respective repertoires and structures as a set of antecedent conditions and traces how the three processes identified above unfolded over time to generate divergent pathways that had dramatic implications for the resilience of these organizations.

---

[3] An organization can innovate without necessarily inventing something new in absolute terms. As Mohr (1969: 112) remarks: "Invention implies bringing something new into being; innovation implies bringing something new into use."

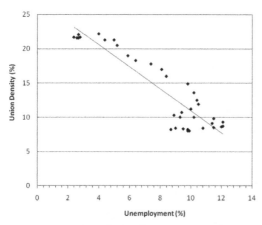

FIGURE 12-1. Correlation between unemployment and union density in France (1970–2005). *Source:* OECD, "OECD.StatsExtracts." *Note:* Each dot represents a year.

The Neoliberalization of the Labor Regime as an Exogenous Shock

Labor regimes refer to the institutional rules, productive arrangements, and understandings that shape the identification, problem definitions, claims making, and prevailing strategies of workers and employers.[4] Starting in the late 1970s and accelerating in the 1980s during the Socialist presidency of François Mitterrand, the neoliberalization of the French labor regime shook the institutionalized strategies of action of trade unions. It involved, first, a massive reorganization of production that brought about high unemployment. This process began in the late 1970s with the restructuring of the French steel industry (cf. Ross 1982) and deepened subsequently in 1983 by the replacement of Keynesian demand stimulus with austerity budgets, the abandonment of wage indexation, and tight monetary policy (Levy 2005: 105); the fight against inflation became the priority at the expense of employment. Similarly, the state disengaged from the direct supervision of the economy by demanding that state firms focus on profitability, so as to eventually privatize them, and that private firms raise their own capital rather than depend on state subsidies even if that entailed waves of bankruptcies (Levy 2005: 106). The unemployment rate thus went from 2.4 percent in 1970 to 4 percent in 1975, 6.4 percent in 1980, and 10.2 percent in 1985 and has remained between 9 and 12 percent since then.

This restructuring of production, as well as macro-economic policies and the unemployment they caused, greatly contributed to a dramatic decrease in union density: from 22.2 percent in 1975 to 13.6 percent in 1985 and below 10 percent since 1992. The rise of unemployment is indeed strongly correlated with the decline of union density (Fig. 12-1). Moreover, in the cases of both the CGT and the CFDT, the greatest membership collapse happened in the

[4] My definition of labor regimes is a paraphrase of Jenson's definition of citizenship regimes (Jenson 2007).

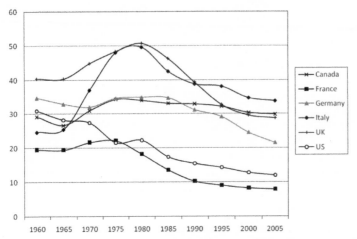

FIGURE 12-2. Union density in Organisation for Economic Co-operation and Development Countries (%). *Source:* OECD, "OECD.StatsExtracts."

metalworkers' federation, thereby indicating the impact of the reorganization of production in traditional manufacturing sectors. France is not an isolated case, and most developed countries have experienced similar trends (Fig. 12-2). However, the fact that unions fared better in other countries despite comparable levels of unemployment suggests that the latter is not the only – and maybe not even the most important – factor that matters. National institutions also make a difference (Western 1997; Ebbinghaus and Visser 1999; Scruggs and Lange 2002). I touch on here the second dimension of the neoliberalization of the French labor regime.

Neoliberalization also involved a substantial process of institutional change to redefine the rules in favor of capital and at the expense of labor. The government lifted restrictions on layoffs (Levy 2005: 106–7) before that, and more importantly, rewrote about a third of the French labor code with the introduction of the Auroux Laws in 1982. These laws deepened the decentralization of collective bargaining by increasing the role of work councils in firms and establishing compulsory annual bargaining – but not agreement – at the firm and branch level. They required strong local unions to yield results, but beyond the legal recognition of union delegates and access to greater resources (experts, time off for union duties, office space), little was done to strengthen them (Howell 1992). This reform contributed to the neoliberalization of the French labor regime not only because it decentralized collective bargaining and thereby isolated workers at the firm level while undermining the leverage that they could have derived from industry-wide bargaining but also because it opened the door to bypassing unions by focusing on work councils. As Howell (1992: 175) points out, the Auroux Laws undermined unions at the firm level by giving the power to engage in collective bargaining and sign agreements to work councils in lieu of unions.

These structural and institutional changes associated with the neoliberalization of the French labor regime were accompanied by a substantial shift in understandings that legitimated the firm and the market, as well as a decline in working-class identification, trade union legitimacy, and strike activity.[5] For example, in a major review of public opinion surveys on class identification since the 1960s, Michelat and Simon (2004: 142) remark that class belonging[6] dropped from 61 percent in 1966 to 53 percent in 2002. The decline intensified in the early 1980s. More significantly, identification with the working class dropped from 23 to 14 percent in the same period. This shift in subjective identification, or in class consciousness, did not simply reflect changes in social stratification (i.e., working-class affiliation declines because there are, proportionally, fewer blue-collar workers today than in the 1960s). Even among blue-collar workers, working-class identification dropped: in 1966, one of two objectively "hard-core working-class individuals" (*très ouvrier*), defined by the number of their working-class attributes (manual job, working-class family background, and so on), identified with the working class compared with one of four in 1993 and one of five in 2001 (Michelat and Simon 2004: 145). In other words, working-class affiliation among blue-collar workers dropped from 50 percent in 1966 to 20 percent in 2001. In addition to this shift away from working-class identification, Lallement (2006: 65) notes that an increasing number of workers did not identify with their union and attempted instead to address disputes with employers through labor courts (the "*Prud'hommes*").

All of these factors and processes converged toward a dramatic decline of union density in France. At one point in the mid 1980s, the hemorrhage of members was so intense that unions seemed on the verge of simply disappearing (Fig. 12-3). This chapter argues that whether and how unions responded to this situation and engaged on the path to resilience depended on their cultural repertoires, how they used these, and how they implemented their new strategy of action.

Antecedent Conditions: The Repertoires and Structures of French Unions

Although the neoliberalization of the labor regime outlined earlier sets the problems that all French trade unions face, their respective organizational structures and cultural repertoires shape how they make sense of these problems and go about trying to solve them. These two factors are antecedent, or initial, conditions of the processes contributing to resilience. The notion of antecedent conditions stresses that the interpretations and choices of actors in moments

---

[5] It is worth stressing, however, that the French state was not dismantled but redeployed (cf. Levy 2005). Although neoliberalization was taking place, other new social policies were being implemented. Therefore, we should not conclude that the neoliberalization of the labor regime goes hand in hand with neoliberalization at large.

[6] Class belonging is measured by the rate of positive answers to the question, "Do you have the impression of belonging to a social class?" without specifying a particular class.

FIGURE 12-3. Total membership of the General Confederation of Labor (CGT) and the French Democratic Confederation of Labor (CFDT). *Note:* The CGT(a), CFDT(a), and CFDT(b) series are based on nine monthly payments a year of union dues. However, between 1995 and 2003, nine-monthly-payments series are not available for the CGT (Andolfatto and Labbé 2007: 3). The CGT(b) series are thus based on "FNI" dues; because the latter are estimated to be, on average, 10 percent higher than the nine-monthly-payments series (cf. Andolfatto and Labbé 2007: 3), I deducted 10 percent from the FNI series so as to make them comparable to the CGT(a) and the CFDT series. *Sources:* CGT(a), Andolfatto and Labbé 1997: 233; CGT(b), my calculations based on Andolfatto and Labbé 2007: 3; CFDT(a), Visser 2000: 276–77; CFDT(b), Andolfatto and Labbé 2007: 12.

of crisis or critical juncture are rooted in prior events and processes; it is a way to take into account the legacies upon which actors build. It also implies a particular manner to divide and organize the seamless flow of history to avoid the problem of infinite regress (Mahoney 2001: 7–8). Antecedent conditions are neither the mere context of action nor competing causal factors (Slater and Simmons 2010: 889–90). Context by itself does not tell much about outcomes and can be causally irrelevant; similarly, if antecedent conditions were competing causal factors, they would make the study of the three processes that I introduced earlier unnecessary. The repertoires and structures of organizations do not bring about the outcome by themselves, but nonetheless condition the ways in which the three processes producing this outcome interact and become causally significant. As Salter and Simmons (2010: 891) put it, antecedent conditions "predispose (but do not predestine) cases to diverge as they ultimately do."

Here I treat the repertoires and structures of organizations as given and do not account for them. I discuss the concept of repertoire in more detail because I believe it requires more elaboration and description, and then turn to organizational structure.

Repertoires

Repertoires refer to the relatively stable – but not necessarily coherent – cultural materials available to actors to make sense of the world and engage in it (Swidler 1986; Lamont and Thévenot 2000: 8; Hall and Lamont 2009: 12). These materials play the role of both *lenses* to interpret social reality and *resources* to act upon this reality. Thus, repertoires both enable and constrain collective action and limit the range of possible developmental pathways: "people are unlikely to engage in an action unless the strategy to perpetrate it is part of their repertoire" (Small, Harding, and Lamont 2010: 16). To paraphrase Marx, people make their own history but not with repertoires of their own choosing. The relationship between actors and their repertoires is not strictly instrumental and strategic because actors cannot conceive the world and calculate the cost and benefit of using the different materials of their repertoire without relying on their repertoire and habitual behavior. Even when they use their cultural resources, they do so in a cultured way; they cannot step out of culture. Therefore, repertoires provide simultaneously models *of* past reality and models *for* future reality (cf. Geertz 1973: 93), and the actors' relationship to them is as much dispositional as instrumental.

Existing studies relying on the concept of repertoire have essentially treated repertoires as properties of polities or countries (cf. Tilly 1995; Lamont and Thévenot 2000; Tilly 2008) rather than organizations. Such a perspective is congruent with institutional claims about varieties of labor regimes: the repertoire of unions is shaped by the (national) labor regime in which these unions are embedded. However, I contend that the repertoires of unions are not simple reflections of national repertoires. The latter resemble a language rather than an individual consciousness, as Tilly (1995: 30) rightly points out, but not all individuals speak the same language. The repertoires of organizations stem from their distinct trajectories, as past events and interpretations are institutionalized and turned into organizational sediments that shape the new layers on the surface (cf. Berger 1974). Put differently, repertoires do not include whatever ideas or options people hear about; rather, they include symbolic elements that directly stem from an individual's past experience. For example, dancing is not part of your repertoire because you know that it is possible to dance or that some people dance; instead, it is part of your repertoire only insofar as you have danced in the past.[7] Repertoires become effective thanks to know-how generated over time and transposable to other situations. Insofar as unions have a distinct know-how, experience, and history, they have distinct repertoires.

The repertoires of the CFDT and the CGT reflect their respective trajectories and are constituted by different arrays of symbolic materials. Here I focus on two types of symbolic elements of their repertoires that are particularly relevant for explaining how the two organizations made sense of, and responded to,

---

[7] Thanks to Ann Swidler for drawing my attention to this dimension.

TABLE 12-1. *The Repertoires of the French Democratic Confederation of Labor (CFDT) and the General Confederation of Labor (CGT)*

	Ideological Traditions	Frames	Scripts
CFDT	Christian-democracy	Antimaterialism	Vanguard
	Social-democracy and Fabianism	Antistatism	Militant
	Anarcho-unionism	Anticommunism	Self-management
		Class struggle	Apolitical
		Firm as community	Social dialogue
CGT	Anarcho-unionism	Patriotic class struggle	Vanguard
	Communism	Statism	Militant
	Nationalism		Protest

the neoliberalization of the labor regime: frames and scripts. *Frames* refer to cognitive lenses and sets of categories that make possible but also simplify our perception of social life. "Frames define horizons of possibilities, individual life projects, or what is thinkable" (Small et al. 2010: 15). *Scripts* are learned routines that provide cultural templates or models of expected behavior that actors enact in given situations; "They are akin to Swidler's 'strategies of action' in that they prescribe how to solve problems or achieve goals" (Harding 2010: 142). Frames and scripts can be combined and recombined in different ways as actors make sense of the world and engage in problem solving. As they do so, they do not simultaneously and equally use all the constitutive elements of their repertoire. As Swidler (1986: 277) puts it: "All people know more culture than they use." In the episode that this chapter addresses, some frames and scripts played a more central and pervasive role than others. In what follows, I outline the repertoires of the CFDT and the CGT in turn (Table 12-1) and then explain why having a more heterogeneous repertoire can foster resilience. My brief mapping of their respective repertoires is based on their confederal archives since the 1970s, semistructured interviews with union staff members, and secondary sources.

The French Democratic Confederation of Labor

Created in 1964, the CFDT is an offshoot of the French Confederation of Christian Workers (CFTC). Its repertoire has historically drawn from three different traditions: the Christian-democratic tradition,[8] social democracy and English socialism as expressed in Fabianism, and revolutionary anarcho-trade unionism (Rosanvallon 1980: 9–10). These traditions underlay a denunciation

---

[8] Tixier (1992: 243–60) argues that the Christian heritage of the CFDT also stemmed from the influence that the "personalist" thought of Emmanuel Mounier and his review *Esprit* had on Paul Vignaux and the "Reconstruction" group that led the transition from the CFTC to the CFDT. On social Catholicism in France, see Berger (1987) and Hazareesingh (1994).

of the market with strong moral – as opposed to just political and economic – overtones but also fed a forceful critique of the state that departed from the statist Jacobin tradition of the French left. They involved anti-authoritarianism and a refusal of rigid hierarchies, a belief in local and decentralized forms of collective action (e.g., subsidiarity), and faith in the self-organizing capacity of civil society. One of the logical consequences of this antistatism was a preference for contractual relations between employers and workers rather than state intervention through the law. These traditions also implied a deep suspicion toward communism – hence the CFDT's insistence on *democratic* socialism and *democratic* planning as an alternative to the statist Leninist model promoted by the communist left. Furthermore, in contrast to the latter but in accordance with its Christian roots, the CFDT stressed the moral needs of individuals. This meant serious attention to the cultural consequences of capitalism, particularly materialism and alienation, and the claim that real social change could not happen without cultural change (Groux and Mouriaux 1989: 164–5). In other words, social progress required not only quantitative but also qualitative demands.

The repertoire of the CFDT initially included three primary frames: *antistatism* (contractual relations, the self-organizing capacity of civil society, subsidiarity), *anticommunism* (the primacy of democratic liberties and individual rights), and *antimaterialism* (a moral critique of the market based on Christian ethics and focused on qualitative issues). In the late 1960s, as the CFDT was trying to gain its leftist credentials to compete against the CGT and as a new cohort of members influenced by the events of May 1968 joined in, the *class struggle frame* became omnipresent and enriched the repertoire of the CFDT. Later on, while the CFDT was distancing itself from socialism in the 1980s, the *firm as community frame* was resurrected from the Christian-democratic tradition to rehabilitate the firm and legitimate its priority given to collective bargaining; it gradually became one of the cornerstones of the CFDT's new strategy of action.

The CFDT also had a wide range of available scripts: the vanguard script, the militant script, the self-management script, the apolitical script, and the social dialogue script. The *vanguard script* was shared by the CFDT and the CGT and was a direct product of the history and configuration of the French labor regime; enacting it implied claiming to have a clear vision of what the working class *will* want and need when it becomes aware of its objective interests. The *militant script* was also shared by the CFDT and the CGT; it stressed the ideological and activist conception of union membership. The *self-management script* expressed a faith in the self-organizing capacity of civil society and emphasized qualitative demands at work to counter alienation; it was recast in socialist terms so that the CFDT could represent itself as radical while simultaneously distinguishing itself from both its past, Christian self, and its communist competitor (the CGT). Enacting self-management often involved occupying and managing factories or applying the logic of self-management in other organizational settings. Inspired by the Christian-democratic tradition, the *apolitical script* was gradually articulated in the late 1970s as the CFDT distanced itself from electoral politics and initiated a redeployment of its resources toward collective bargaining (what would be known as "recentering" or "reunionization"). This script was closely intertwined with a nonmilitant conception of membership that first appeared in the early 1970s (Bévort 1994). Finally, the *social dialogue script* emerged in the 1980s together with the firm as community frame. Benefitting from the support of the French government and the European Commission headed by Jacques Delors – who was close to the CFDT – this script, tied to the CFDT's Christian roots, quickly became a central element of the CFDT's repertoire.

The General Confederation of Labor

Created in 1895, the CGT is France's oldest labor organization. Its repertoire originally drew from three distinct and yet complementary traditions: anarcho-unionism, communism, and nationalism. Although the influence of the latter two is still felt today, the mark of anarcho-unionism lies primarily in the decentralized structure of the CGT.[9] The communist tradition took hold with the rise of the French Communist Party (PCF) and entailed a lasting influence of Marxism-Leninism and a widespread presence of the communist political culture at all levels of the organization. Starting in 1936 and throughout much of the twentieth century, the CGT thus defined itself as a mass and class-based trade union (*"syndicat de masse et de classe"*). The CGT's repertoire also drew from French nationalism – not the ethnic nationalism that came to the forefront of public debates during the Dreyfus affair in the 1890s and subsequently supported the Vichy Regime during WWII but the civic and collectivistic nationalism of the French Revolution (Jacobinism) and the resistance against the Nazis.[10] The CGT first drew from this tradition during World War I, when it decided to support the French war effort. However, during the 1930s and particularly, during World War II, this tradition acquired a lasting influence on the CGT's repertoire, as the CGT began to interpret social life through the lenses of the *patriotic class struggle frame*. The CGT gradually developed a pervasive narrative in which French blue-collar workers, embodying the nation and general interest, relentlessly struggled against "cosmopolitan capital," thereby suggesting an opposition between rooted French workers and rootless capitalists. Capitalism had – and still has – to be opposed not only because it undermined the interests of the working class but also because it was antinational. At a practical level, the CGT strongly supported the reconstruction efforts and the

---

[9] As an ideological current inside the CGT, anarcho-unionism was marginalized between the two world wars as communists became the dominant faction of the CGT. Similarly, there was a reformist faction, but it did not leave a deep imprint on the repertoire of the CGT and left the organization in 1947 with the beginning of the Cold War to create Force ouvrière (CGT-FO).

[10] On the distinction between civic-collectivistic nationalism and ethnic nationalism, see Greenfeld (1992).

nationalization of leading firms after World War II,[11] denounced the Marshall Plan and later European integration as a product of capitalism and American imperialism, and campaigned in favor of French consumption ("Buy French" campaigns) and production ("Made in France" campaigns) in the late 1970s and early 1980s (Mouriaux 1982: 186). Similarly, the logic of the patriotic class struggle frame implied that the state had to be seized not only because it was a necessary step toward socialism but also because it was the only instrument that could supervise economic development for the benefit of the country rather than a single class. The patriotic class struggle frame thus contributed to the emergence of the *statist frame*. The latter quickly became central and the CGT turned nationalizations – and later the defense of public monopolies and state intervention – into the cornerstone of its participation in public debates.

In addition to these frames, the repertoire of the CGT included three scripts that its members regularly enacted. Whereas the *vanguard script* persuaded militants and leaders that they knew better than ordinary workers, the *militant script* prevented the CGT from taking decreasing membership seriously and from devising new recruitment strategies. Finally, the *protest script* had been guiding the public performances of the CGT for the past century. It was closely intertwined with the political strategy of the PCF and aimed at politicizing industrial conflict so as to pressure the state and turn workers' discontent into electoral support for the PCF. In contrast to the social dialogue script enacted by the CFDT, at the *national* level, the CGT thus rejects social partnership as class collaboration and cultivates its enduring preference for confrontation, national protest days, and strikes.[12]

The Benefits of Heterogeneity

The respective repertoires of the CFDT and the CGT varied in two respects. First, they included different constitutive elements that would lead to very different diagnoses and prognoses of similar problems and thus to diverging horizons of possibilities. These differences went beyond the particular traditions that fed these repertoires to include a different relation to change itself. Whereas the CFDT had been constantly redefining itself and thus saw change as a constant, the CGT had been relatively stable since the late 1940s and had dealt with change by marginalizing its advocates.

Second, the repertoires of the two organizations were characterized by different levels of heterogeneity. As I have shown, the repertoire of the CFDT was

---

[11] The CGT did not originally advocate nationalizations; it started doing so during its involvement in the Resistance (Groux and Mouriaux 1992: 247).

[12] This contentious preference is present at the industry or national level but not necessarily at the firm or local level (Andolfatto and Labbé 2009: 73). At the firm or local level, there is not much difference between the actual behavior of the CFDT and the CGT; it is at the national level that the difference emerges, with the confederal leadership of the CGT being more politicized and contentious than that of the CFDT.

quite heterogeneous, which is consistent with Minkoff's claim that organizations that have undergone several changes and substantial reorientations in the recent past are more likely to have a heterogeneous repertoire (Minkoff 1999: 1677). The repertoire of the CFDT entailed contradictions and tensions – between, for example, the firm as community frame and the class struggle frame – but also a wide array of dormant or latent resources that could turn into a substantial advantage. That is the case of the apolitical and the social dialogue scripts. In contrast, the CGT had a more coherent repertoire that involved a lower level of heterogeneity; although this coherence limited internal conflict, it also restrained the range of symbolic resources to which the CGT could turn to cope with uncertainty or crisis.

This chapter contends that higher heterogeneity fosters innovation capacity and adaptability and thereby organizational resilience. I am not alone in making such a claim (e.g., Ganz 2000; Crouch and Farrell 2004; Pierson 2004; Crouch 2005; Stark 2009). For example, Marshall Ganz (2000) argues that the successful organizing campaign of the United Farm Workers (UFW) in the 1960s was the result of higher creativity and innovation that he calls "strategic capacity." According to Ganz (2000: 1013), the latter stems from diverse personal experiences, diverse staff, diverse networks, diverse repertoires, open processes of deliberation, heterogeneous resource flows, and diverse forms of local accountability. Population ecologists have made similar claims at the aggregate, societal level and argue that societies with a diversity of organizational forms are more likely to adapt to changed environmental conditions (Hannan 1986: 85, quoted in Stark 2009: 178).

However, some authors have questioned the value of cultural heterogeneity. For example, David Harding (2010) argues that in culturally heterogeneous, poor inner-city neighborhoods, youths do not do as well as they do in more culturally homogeneous neighborhoods. Harding defines cultural heterogeneity as the presence of socially supported competing and conflicting cultural models in a given organization or neighborhood; in the Boston neighborhoods that he studied, cultural heterogeneity implied the coexistence of mainstream and alternative cultural models. Harding (2010: 156–8) argues that such cultural heterogeneity is harmful for youths because it makes it more difficult to figure out what option is best, it lowers the level of commitment to any given option ("model shifting"), it makes it more unlikely that people will have enough information to follow through ("dilution"), and it can paralyze youths by confronting them with two conflicting models simultaneously ("simultaneity").

Harding (2010: 156) assumes that there is one best option to solve a given problem. But in situations of uncertainty, such as the one that unions have been facing in France since the late 1970s, there is no best solution for people who are still trying to figure out what the problem is. In situations of uncertainty, the organizations with the capacity to innovate and adapt – and, thereby, the organizations that are more likely to be resilient – are the ones with multiple different frames, scripts, and models of evaluation so that friction among them will foster recombination. According to Stark (2009: 180), "Diversity matters not because it preserves already-known solutions at hand. Instead, it contributes to adaptability by preserving a more diverse organizational 'gene pool,' increasing the likelihood of possibly fruitful *recombinations* in times of unpredictable change." Cultural heterogeneity contributes to adaptability and resilience precisely for the reasons that Harding depicts as negative: it provides conflicting models simultaneously and fosters model shifting. The friction that heterogeneity generates prevents frames, scripts, goals, and the general orientation of the organization from becoming fully institutionalized and taken for granted. The social carriers – be they the confederal leadership, some dissenting faction, or challengers – of the different elements of the repertoire compete against one another for institutionalizing the frames and scripts they hold and in so doing have to spell out what goes without saying and justify their stance. This friction narrows the space of what is taken for granted and widens actors' sense of limits and thereby expands their agency and reduces the likelihood of inertia.

Organizational Structures

Similar to their respective repertoires, the organizational structures of the CFDT and CGT predisposed but did not predestine them to take different paths; it conditioned their potential transformation rather than directly brought it about. Organizational structures have many different dimensions; here I want to emphasize the degree of centralization and the (internal and external) autonomy of the leadership. But first, let us clarify what labor confederations are.

The CFDT and the CGT are labor confederations similar to the AFL-CIO. Confederations concentrate political, lobbying, legal, training, and research activities and are led by an executive commission that implements the broad orientations voted on in the confederal congress. In this chapter, when I refer to the confederal leadership, I mean the executive commission. Each confederation is composed of workers' federations such as the textile-apparel workers' federation, the health workers' federation, or the metalworkers' federation, that are comparable to international unions such as the Service Employees International Union (SEIU) in the United States. Each workers' federation is in turn constituted by local unions organized at the workplace level. Although confederations are organized by sector of activity, there is also a geographical dimension to them, with Regional Units (*union départementales*, UD) coordinating trade union action at the level of the *département* administrative units.

The CFDT has a formal and informal centralized structure. It inherited the centralized collection and management of union dues that the CFTC established in 1963; this financial centralization was further reinforced and legitimized with the creation of a financial chart in 1973 (Bévort and Labbé 1992: 102–14). Put simply, the confederal leadership held the purse. Furthermore, despite all the talk about statutes and democratic procedure, after 1970, power became informally centralized in the hands of a small core around Secretary

General Edmond Maire to the extent that in the 1976 confederal congress, internal challengers started denouncing the "presidential regime" of the CFDT (Bévort and Labbé 1992: 65). As a result, the confederal leadership was not strongly constrained from within by lower subunits and the rank and file. The CFDT was also, and still is, completely independent from any single political party: there were no formal linkages between the confederation and labor or left-wing parties, and the segments of its membership that were politically active participated in a large spectrum of parties and organizations so that not a single one could claim a substantial membership overlap that would put it in a hegemonic position. This formal centralization of finance, informal centralization of authority, and organizational independence entailed that the confederal leadership enjoyed a relatively high degree of autonomy that increased its room for maneuvering.

Despite its historical ties with the French Communist Party (PCF) and its reputation of orthodoxy, the CGT is actually quite decentralized, and the confederal leadership has limited means to impose its decisions to local unions and rank-and-file members (cf. Piotet 2009). In contrast to the CFDT, until 2006 the collection and management of union dues were controlled at the local level and unions as well as workers' federations could hand only a small portion of their revenues to the confederation or simply withhold them.[13] Furthermore, local unions and rank-and-file members often ignored the priorities and national campaigns of the confederal leadership to the extent that one scholar recently described the CGT as a form of "organized anarchy" (Piotet 2009). However, the fact that so many members of the CGT, at all levels of the organization, were active members of the PCF narrowed the range of options that even potential internal challengers were willing to consider. Similarly, the confederal leadership was highly coherent, and its members were all top members of the PCF as well, which substantially shaped the priorities of the CGT at the peak level. The space that a decentralized structure could have opened for bottom-up innovation and change was deeply curtailed by the overwhelming organizational and ideological influence of the PCF inside the CGT.[14] Therefore, organizational decentralization and a low level of internal and external autonomy implied that the confederal leadership of the CGT had a very low capacity for implementing changes and was predisposed – but not predetermined – to stick with its past routines as well as to fail to keep up with changes in its environment.

Now that we have outlined the repertoires and structures of the CFDT and CGT, we need to look at the ways in which these conditioned the three processes that I introduced earlier: narration, learning, and institutionalization.

---

[13] Interview with Gérard Alezard, confederal secretary in charge of economic affairs at the CGT from 1982 to 1995, May 2008.

[14] According to Gérard Alezard, confederal secretary in charge of economic affairs at the CGT from 1982 to 1995, the weight of the communist culture inside the CGT was so great that formal linkages were irrelevant. Interview with author, May 2008.

Different combinations of these processes generated diverging pathways, one leading to resilience and the other leading to stagnation. I now trace these two pathways in turn.

The Pathway to Resilience: The Case of the French Democratic Confederation of Labor

The crisis that the neoliberalization of the French labor regime brought about represented a strong impetus to change, although change was not inevitable. The repertoire and organizational structure of the CFDT favored change, but the new strategy of action still had to be generated through three overlapping processes.

Narration

The CFDT started losing members in 1976 to 1977 (Fig. 12-3). At first, the confederal leadership did not pay much attention because membership had been progressing since the foundation of the organization in 1964 and because of the stable performance of the CFDT in professional elections, one of the main indicators of union strength in France. Furthermore, although the overall unionized population was decreasing in most traditional industrial sectors, the CFDT's share of unionized workers remained stable and even increased in some sectors. However, in the early 1980s, all indicators pointed in the same direction. The financial situation of the CFDT was in very bad shape as fewer and fewer union dues were coming in, a growing number of training sessions for union delegates were being canceled because not enough people were registering, and entire local union sections were being wiped out overnight. The organizational structure of the CFDT conditioned the first step toward acknowledging the problem because the centralized collection of union dues, in particular, allowed the confederal leadership to measure the magnitude of the changes that were taking place. In 1983 and 1984, the CFDT finally realized the extent of the crisis it was facing.

Two competing narratives emerged to make sense of the situation and propose solutions; both drew primarily upon the antistatist frame of the CFDT's repertoire. Because the antistatist frame stressed the self-organizing capacity of civil society and subsidiarity, it was closely intertwined with the self-management and apolitical scripts; it entailed that unions should not invest resources in electoral politics because the solution to their problems would not come from political parties and the state. Nonetheless, despite this shared basis, actors used the antistatist frame differently. Moreover, the high heterogeneity of the CFDT's repertoire allowed the competing narratives to build on additional, contradictory frames and scripts; each narrative was articulated and supported by different factions and alliances.

The first narrative, upheld by the confederal leadership, emerged in the late 1970s as membership was just beginning to fall in order to counter the influence of leftist militants inside the CFDT. It used the antistatist frame to blame the CFDT's involvement in politics for membership losses. This narrative first appeared in a report presented by CFDT National Secretary for Political Affairs Jacques Moreau in January 1978. The "Moreau Report" asserted that the CFDT had invested too many resources and hopes in electoral politics and that its strategy no longer fit the national and international context: "We must ask ourselves if this practice [of privileging politics and governmental action] is relevant with the analysis of the emergence, role, functions, consequences, of multinational corporations and of industrial restructuring to which capitalism has been proceeding these last few years."[15] According to Moreau, the CFDT's investment in electoral politics led it to focus on opposing the right-wing electoral majority at the expense of obtaining concrete gains through collective bargaining and negotiation. Moreau claimed that such political strategies were partly responsible for the weakness of trade unions and collective bargaining in France.

Henceforth, salvation lay in social compromise: "Obtaining concrete results, giving hope, requires necessary compromises with those that lead the economy and social life."[16] Such a conception implicitly reconsidered the role of firms in a more positive light and emphasized the subsidiarity element of the antistatist frame: to solve its membership problem, the CFDT had to engage in direct dialogue with firms rather than the state. Moreau claimed thus that the CFDT had to "recenter" its resources on collective bargaining rather than protest and make recruitment a priority, which in turn required abandoning the traditional conception of membership as ideological commitment so as to expand the pool of potential members. This narrative initiated a shift away from the militant script toward a more orthodox apolitical script and announced the firm as community frame as well as the social dialogue script that became prevalent in the late 1980s.

Similarly, for CFDT Secretary General Edmond Maire, the issue was not simply building a more legitimate and stronger organization to engage in collective bargaining but also following the social evolution of society: "We remain a trade union organization dominated by a single masculine-industrial cultural model whereas the tertiary sector gathers 57 percent of workers, including 40 percent of women."[17] "Recentering" (*recentrage*) and adjustment to the new structure of the labor market were presented as two sides of the same coin. If the CFDT did not endorse them and stuck instead with its previous strategy, the argument went, it would suffer substantial damage. In advocating such reorientation, Moreau and Maire were not only recombining several frames and scripts of the CFDT's repertoire but also laying the groundwork for an intensification of friction and conflict when membership started to seriously collapse in 1983.

---

[15] Jacques Moreau, "Rapport de situation générale," Conseil national, CFDT, sessions of January 26–28, 1978, p. 9. Unless otherwise noted, all translations are mine.
[16] Moreau, "Rapport de situation générale," p. 10.
[17] Edmond Maire, "Présentation du rapport général," 38th Congress, CFDT, May 8, 1979, p. 3.

The second narrative, articulated essentially by the textile-apparel workers' federation, the postal and communication workers' federation, and the health workers' federation, challenged Moreau and Maire's position and "recentering" as a conservative abdication to capitalism. It further claimed that membership decline actually stemmed not from an overpoliticization of the CFDT but from the very strategy that the confederal leadership had begun to implement. Building on the class struggle frame, this narrative targeted "recentering" as the real culprit because it abandoned socialism and favored negotiations with employers at the expense of rank-and-file mass mobilization.[18] This interpretation became recurrent in internal debates. For example, in 1984, the textile-apparel workers' federation intervened in a meeting of the CFDT's National Council and stated:

The current de-unionization [*désyndicalisation*] comes in great part from the CFDT's change in orientation of the CFDT.... In our reflection on the causes of de-unionization, it has become clear that the lack of action was one of the causes of the workers' loss of confidence... we see that many militants are demobilized by the current change of orientation. They no longer identify with the CFDT. They have doubts, ask questions, and that undermines unionization.[19]

What is striking here is that this second narrative also built on the antistatist frame of the CFDT but this time combined it with the class struggle frame so as to reassert the socialist self-management script and the militant script. It thus called for the mobilization of rank-and-file workers in the workplace against both employers and the state. In contrast to the first narrative, which presented apolitical membership as part of the solution, this second narrative celebrated ideologically driven militants as the key ingredient to tip the power balance in favor of unions.[20]

Learning
The friction generated by the heterogeneity of the CFDT's repertoire entailed that actors needed more information to support their claims, reduce uncertainty, and justify the formulation of a new strategy of action. They needed to invest resources into understanding why and how their organization was losing so many members and then encode the knowledge produced into new routines that would guide the behavior of the different subunits of the organization (cf. Levitt and March 1988: 320). This learning process required first the establishment of a new organizational subunit that would put in place a new information system. As Pfeffer and Salancik (2003 [1978]: 78) remark, "Those

[18] Interview with Léon Dion, secretary general of the textile-apparel workers' federation of the CFDT from 1977 to 1986, April 2003.
[19] Hacuitex-CFDT. 1984 "Extraits de notre intervention sur l'adaptation du syndicalisme au Conseil national du 25 au 27 avril 84." *Hacuitex* 375: 14.
[20] Interview with Léon Dion, former secretary general of the textile-apparel workers' federation of the CFDT, April 2003.

that do not develop new, appropriate information systems are less likely to survive."

Thus, in 1984, the confederal leadership secretly put together a team of four men to travel around France and interview rank-and-file members so as to understand membership decline. This group was called the Action Group for Unionization (*Groupe d'action pour la syndicalisation* [GAPS]). It came out in the open during the 1985 confederal congress of the CFDT, when unionization officially became a top priority.[21] Although GAPS produced a relatively consensual diagnosis, it argued that the militant script – according to which only activist members mattered but ordinary and nonmilitant members were useless to the union – undermined mobilization and advocated instead a "membership unionism" (*syndicalisme d'adhérents*) aimed primarily at collective bargaining.[22] GAPS thus contributed to a shift from the militant to the apolitical script; it was able to do so precisely because the latter script had been part of the repertoire of the CFDT since the early 1970s. The new emphasis on the apolitical script was not innocent because an unofficial motive of GAPS was to try to change the demographic balance between supporters of the confederal leadership and supporters of dissenting factions by fostering the recruitment of apolitical members in local unions controlled by the far left.[23] Recruitment thus became a central battleground for both the existence of the CFDT and its political orientation.

Institutionalization

As these internal struggles unfolded over time, the confederal leadership managed to gradually implement a new strategy of action that departed from the previous one. The "recentering" initiated in 1979 entailed the articulation and then consolidation of the firm as community frame and of the apolitical and social dialogue scripts. The implementation of this reorientation was made possible by the organizational structure of the CFDT.

The internal autonomy of the confederal leadership allowed it to bypass the workers' federations and the rank and file of the CFDT to secretly create GAPS in 1984. At the 1985 confederal congress, GAPS recommended the training and deployment of "professional" recruiters (the *développeurs*). What it had learned from the experience of local unions was turned into new routines that were adopted by all the workers' federations of the CFDT, including the ones controlled by opponents of the confederal leadership. New recruits were also socialized into this model and made it their own. This model was infused

---

[21] CFDT, "Histoire d'une courbe," March 20, 1998, p. 10.
[22] CFDT, "Histoire d'une courbe," March 20, 1998, p. 25, and interview with GAPS member Michel Lenoir, April 2003. The idea of a *syndicalisme d'adhérents* is closely intertwined with the apolitical script; it was first introduced during the 1973 confederal congress of the CFDT but remained symbolic. In 1973 as in 1985, the goal was not simply to increase the membership but also to consolidate the control of the organization (Bévort 1994: 122).
[23] Interview with GAPS member Michael Lenoir, April 2003.

with value to the extent that recruitment almost became a goal in itself; these professional recruiters are still in place today, and the capacity of the CFDT to renew its membership level to that of its peak in the mid 1970s is a clear indicator of their effectiveness.[24]

Furthermore, the confederal leadership increased the formal and informal centralization of the organization. It regularly bypassed organizational layers and subunits where dissenters were present and tried to contain debates and decisions within an Executive Commission that no longer included representatives of all the largest workers' federations (Bévort and Labbé 1992: 51). Similarly, it reformed internal rules in 1988 so that only local unions rather than departmental unions and workers' federations – more likely to be controlled by opponents – could speak during confederal congresses (Defaud 2009: 46). The confederal leadership took advantage of the growing power of the CFDT to marginalize internal opponents: some critical staff members were replaced; some dissenting local unions were dismantled or excluded; and in 1988, Pierre Héritier, the only dissenting voice in the confederal leadership, was expelled from the CFDT's Executive Commission (see, for example, Hamon and Rotman 1984 [1982]: 289 n2; Groux and Mouriaux 1989: 91;). Such marginalization reduced the social support for certain elements of the CFDT's repertoire.

Thus, the institutionalization of the new strategy of action involved not only infusing with value certain practices and turning the confederal narrative into a taken-for-granted discourse that came to define the very collective identity of the organization but also the relative marginalization of the social carriers of frames and scripts that had historically been part of the CFDT's repertoire. Without such social support, these frames and scripts stopped being cultivated and enacted by the organization. Therefore, institutionalization had the unintended effect of reducing the scope of the CFDT's repertoire and making it more homogeneous.

The Pathway to Stagnation: The Case of the General Confederation of Labor

The case of the CGT shows that change does not necessarily – or at least, not immediately – stem from a crisis. The latter may expand the agency of actors by loosening certain constraints without leading to a significant departure from past practices and strategies. This divergent outcome is not simply the result of the antecedent conditions – homogeneous repertoire, decentralized structure, and dependent leadership – described earlier. In what follows, I explain how the processes of narration, learning, and institutionalization took a different form inside the CGT, thereby producing different effects and leading to stagnation rather than resilience.

---

[24] Having said that, although the absolute numbers are comparable, the union density is not because the total workforce has increased since then.

Narration

After reaching a peak in the early 1970s, the CGT's membership began to decrease systematically and between 1977 and 1990, the organization lost more than one million members (see Fig. 12-3). However, the CGT's decentralized organizational structure made it difficult to have a clear sense of the situation. In contrast to the CFDT, in the CGT local unions and workers' federations controlled the collection of dues and transferred only a portion of these to the confederal level; the amount transferred varied depending on the financial needs of local unions and workers' federations. Therefore, the confederal leadership lacked accurate and reliable indicators of the state of the membership.[25] The CGT was losing members, but it was very difficult to assess the magnitude of the losses and connect them to specific union practices or strategies. Such uncertainty opened a space for diverse interpretations and solutions. However, as I show below, the homogeneous repertoire and the organizational structure of the CGT greatly limited the range of options considered.

The initial response of the CGT's confederal leadership was surprisingly more self-critical than one would have expected. As the organization began to lose members, CGT Secretary General Georges Séguy argued that the CGT had to look in the mirror and recognize that it was a closed organization suffering from a limited internal democracy with an ideologically homogeneous leadership that did not reflect the diversity of its membership. According to Séguy, such organizational characteristics pushed workers away from the CGT.[26] Similarly, Jean-Louis Moynot (1982: 65–6), a member of the Confederal Bureau of the CGT from 1967 to 1981, expanded this narrative in the early 1980s to denounce the subordination of the CGT to the political strategy of the PCF at the expense of real gains for workers and the CGT. Although he was himself a member of the PCF, Moynot directly challenged the vanguard and protest scripts of the CGT. According to Moynot (1982: 74), the difficulties of the CGT stemmed from a mistaken strategy that rested on a mythic conception of working-class struggle. In a move that brought him close to the perspective advocated by Moreau and Maire at the CFDT, Moynot argued that the CGT should focus on pragmatic negotiations and propositions to incrementally gain benefits for workers. In so doing, he was implicitly attempting to introduce the social dialogue script into the CGT. The fact that Moynot had a Catholic background and had been active in Christian labor organizations before joining the CGT (Berger 1987: 39) could maybe explain this convergence.

However, such borrowing beyond the repertoire of the CGT did not resonate within the organization, and the efforts of Séguy and Moynot soon hit a wall. The lack of autonomy of the confederal leadership vis-à-vis the PCF here was

---

[25] In 2006, the CGT took a step toward a more centralized structure by giving the responsibility of managing union dues to the confederal leadership.

[26] Georges Séguy, "La bataille du recrutement est lancée: La CGT partout et pour tous." *Le Peuple* No. 984, February 25–29, 1976, p. 5–6; Georges Séguy, "Rapport d'ouverture," 40th confederal congress of the CGT, November 26–December 1, 1978, p. 31–33.

obvious. In 1981, as a result of significant pressure from the PCF, Séguy backed down and agreed to step down from his position for the benefit of a loyal supporter of the PCF line, Henri Krasucki (see Andolfatto and Labbé 2006: 330; Séguy 2008: 187–95). Similarly, that same year, Moynot and several other members that had criticized the CGT's orientation resigned from the organization's Confederal Bureau.[27] Henceforth, the confederal leadership of the CGT would be even more homogeneous and cohesive and would rule out any substantial challenge to its alliance with the PCF or to its mobilization strategy.

After 1982, the CGT continued to lose members at an alarming pace, but the confederal leadership reasserted its traditional frames and scripts in a very orthodox manner. It relied on its patriotic class struggle frame and blamed the economic crisis and anti-CGT campaigns for its situation: the economic crisis had brought about mass unemployment and growing flexibility, thereby feeding increased competition between workers that made it more difficult for them to realize that they shared class interests opposed to those of capitalists (Magniadas 1987: 135).[28] This narrative also contended that the CGT was the most affected labor organization in France because it was the most active opponent of capital.[29] Membership losses were depicted as an indirect indicator of a strong militant base. Thus, the narrative told by the confederal leadership rejected the very existence of a membership crisis: "There is no crisis of our 'struggle unionism' [*syndicalisme de lutte*] . . . ; there is on the other hand a CGT that is well grounded in a hard battle without mercy against a powerful and seasoned class adversary that is all the more aggressive as it feels threatened."[30] In other words, being at the vanguard of the struggle against capitalism had a cost, but it was not a crisis; only reformist unions were experiencing a crisis.[31] The situation of the CGT was thus not only interpreted through the patriotic class struggle frame but was also used to consolidate the vanguard and militant scripts. As Gérard Alezard, member of the Confederal Bureau of the CGT from 1982 to 1995, explains:

We thought we could avoid the crisis. . . . Implicitly, we thought that a union like the CGT was protected from such problem; we also told ourselves . . . that in France the labor movement relied on militants rather than members. . . . It's better to have "quality

---

[27] The other resignations included René Buhl, Jacqueline Lambert, and Christiane Gilles (Andolfatto and Labbé 2006: 330).

[28] Although here I refer specifically to the analysis of Jean Magniadas, member of the Executive Commission of the CGT in the 1980s and director of its Center for Economic and Social Studies, this assessment came up in numerous internal bulletins of the CGT in the 1980s.

[29] Henri Krasucki, "Rapport du bureau confédéral," 42nd confederal congress of the CGT, November 24–29, 1985, p. 13.

[30] Alain Obadia, "La bataille idéologique aujourd'hui." *Le Peuple* No. 1239, April 9, 1987, p. 11. Magniadas (1987: 131–32) stated that the expression "crisis of unionism" attacked "the very foundations of unionism by presenting it as archaic, useless, even harmful."

[31] Gérard Alezard, member of the Confederal Bureau of the CGT and confederal secretary from 1982 to 1995. Interview with author, May 2008.

than quantity." It's better to have very active members that act as spokespersons of the CGT and animate the labor movement than members that are only paying dues.[32]

Furthermore, the consolidation of strong linkages between the confederal leadership of the CGT and the PCF after Henri Krasucki became secretary general in 1982 entailed that the possibility that the CGT's involvement in electoral politics, through its support for the PCF, might have contributed to membership losses was categorically ruled out. In line with its statist frame and protest script, the confederal leadership believed that only state intervention and, therefore, seizing state power through the PCF could have a significant impact on the fate of workers' lives. In 1982, a year after Mitterrand was elected president, it reasserted that the electoral victory of the left would create a very favorable context for a rise in membership that would compensate for the losses of the past few years.[33] Although the statist frame was not questioned, such enthusiasm for the electoral victory of the left did not last. In 1984, after leaving the coalition government led by the Socialist Party (PS), the PCF began to attack the PS as a sell-out to capitalism and used the CGT to organize protest campaigns to express workers' discontent. The CGT thus consistently enacted its protest and militant scripts throughout the 1980s; it did so not only to support the PCF's strategy but also with the belief that it would attract new members.

However, this strategy proved inefficient and even damaging for the PCF and CGT. The former lost a substantial part of its vote in the 1980s, and the latter kept losing members at a dramatic rate. As a result of its inability to introduce significant changes, the confederal leadership was letting the CGT, the main and oldest organization of the French labor movement, drift toward its potential disappearance.

The Challenge of Learning
In contrast to the CFDT, the CGT did not create a subunit or new information system that would allow it to collect information about membership losses and thereby improve its understanding of its environment; it neither produced new knowledge nor developed new routines that would guide the behavior of the organization. In fact, during the 1980s, the inability of the CGT to learn from its environment and the experience of other unions contributed to its continued decline.

The CGT did try to do something to stop its decline. In March 1985, the confederal leadership launched a three-month fundraising campaign called "CGT Emergency" ("*Urgences CGT*"); the goal was not simply to raise funds that would compensate for the decline of union dues but also to talk to workers

---

[32] Interview with author, May 2008.
[33] CGT, "Document d'orientation," 41st confederal congress of the CGT, June 13–18, 1982, p. 787–88.

about the necessity of joining the CGT. Although the campaign raised a substantial amount of money, it did not manage to attract a significant number of new members.[34] The CGT's difficulty in devising new strategies was not simply the product of the PCF's hegemony. It was also the result of the CGT's homogeneous repertoire. The latter limited internal friction and conflict, and consequently, its constitutive elements were more fully institutionalized and taken for granted than in the CFDT. Thinking outside the box was very difficult, if not almost impossible.

The leaders of the CGT could not envision the world through different lenses: they could not think beyond their patriotic class struggle and statist frames. They thus invested their resources in doing more of the same rather than analyze how changes in the economy – deindustrialization, outsourcing, the rise of precarious work, flexibility, the increasing role of women and migrant workers, and so on – were redefining the role and prospects of trade unions. As Alezard explains: "We weren't that blind... but it took us a long time to perceive these mutations. We had a really hard time modifying our analytical frameworks; we were using analytical frameworks developed in the 1950s and 1960s whereas we were in 1980 or 1990."[35] Such a pattern fits common arguments about the constraining effects of legacies. For example, Pfeffer and Salancik (2003 [1978]: 78) claim that "the organization is, in a sense, always lagging. Its attentional processes are inevitably focused on what *had been* important in the past." Similarly, Bourdieu's concept of *hysteresis* stresses "the structural lag between opportunities and the dispositions to grasp them which is the cause of missed opportunities and, in particular, of the frequently observed *incapacity to think historical crises in categories of perception and thought other than those of the past*" (Bourdieu 1977 [1972]: 83; emphasis added).

Organizational learning is shaped by institutionalized frames, scripts, and routines (Dodgson 1993: 383). The homogeneity of the CGT's repertoire made the effects of these legacies even more constraining. The CGT took the path to stagnation rather than resilience because it was unable not only to learn but also to *unlearn* unsuccessful past practices and strategies (cf. Dodgson 1993: 385).

Partial De-Institutionalization and Failed Institutionalization

Although the CGT did not learn from its environment and failed to develop new routines that would guide its behavior, two parallel events that took place in the 1980s fostered a process of de-institutionalization and led it to recognize that survival required significant organizational changes. First, the failure of the Common Program partially implemented by the PS-PCF coalition government

---

[34] Gérard Alezard, member of the Confederal Bureau of the CGT and confederal secretary from 1982 to 1995. Interview with author, May 2008.

[35] Ibid.

1981 to 1983 and the subsequent austerity policy of the PS, led many members of the CGT to question whether an electoral victory of the left, including the PCF, was the best way to support workers' interests (Giraud 2008: 41–5). Second, the decline of the PCF (in terms of membership and electoral support) undermined the grip of the PCF over the CGT. In 1992, Henri Krasucki was replaced with Louis Viannet at the head of the confederal leadership. Although Viannet was faithful to the PCF, in 1993 he stopped calling CGT members to vote for the PCF in national elections. Then in 1996, Viannet resigned from the Political Bureau of the PCF (but not from its National Committee, formerly known as the Central Committee), and in 1999, the CGT refused to officially support a national protest day organized by the PCF. Finally, in 2001, the CGT announced that it would henceforth forbid its confederal officials from taking leading positions in the PCF (Andolfatto and Labbé 2006: 332–5). The linkage between the CGT and the PCF did not disappear. It continued to shape the CGT, if only through the logic of overlapping memberships, but it was no longer as strong and determinant as it had been in the past. Accordingly, the external autonomy of the CGT's confederal leadership increased, providing the latter with more room for maneuvering.

As a result of these questionings and newly gained autonomy, the confederal leadership began to distance itself from its previous practices and strategies. In the 1989 confederal congress the CGT committed to greater transparency with the hope that it would improve its image among workers and facilitate the retention and recruitment of members. This commitment entailed regularly making public the actual membership and financial situation of the organization.[36] In 1992, the confederal leadership underscored both the contextual (e.g., the economic crisis, the transformation of the organization of production, and anti-CGT campaigns) and the internal (e.g., the lack of transparency and democracy) factors behind membership losses.[37] Insofar as objective factors were difficult to correct, the CGT had to introduce organizational changes and new strategies that would allow it to attract workers anew. One of these strategies rehabilitated collective bargaining as a means to obtain benefits for workers without having to rely on electoral politics and emphasized the development of a counter-expertise that could be used as leverage and as a source of credibility (Giraud 2008: 46–51).

However, this departure from previous practices and strategies has not been institutionalized yet. It is neither infused with value nor taken for granted. The new strategy mentioned earlier does not represent the enactment of the social dialogue script cultivated by the CFDT because the CGT combines the rehabilitation of collective bargaining with its protest and militant scripts. It still sees the power of the streets and ideologically driven members as quintessential

---

[36] Pierre Koehler, "Rapport financier," 43rd confederal congress of the CGT, May 21, 1989, p. 249.
[37] CGT, "Document d'orientation," 44th confederal congress of the CGT, January 26, 1992, p. 478.

elements of success. For example, according to Christian Larose, secretary general of the textile-apparel workers' federation of the CGT from 1982 to 2003: "The issue is not to get members for the sake of members. If you recruit members, it is to carry out a battle, a struggle, not just to get money [i.e. union dues].... The issue is to recruit members to organize the resistance."[38] Even after the extent of membership losses had been acknowledged, the problem redefined in a different light, and a new strategy of action outlined, the CGT did not invest massive resources in recruitment (Béroud 2009). In line with its protest script, it has instead attempted to participate in new coalitions with social movements such as the global justice movement (Béroud 2005) and the migrant workers' movement (Barnier and Perrin 2009). Although these efforts have contributed to the public visibility of the CGT, so far they have not led to an increase in membership. The hold, coherence, and homogeneity of the CGT's repertoire make the elaboration of a pathway to resilience very difficult and even unlikely.

Conclusion

In this chapter, I have tried to show that the varying resilience of trade unions stems from a political-cultural process conditioned by the repertoire and structure of organizations and shaped by the particular combination of three overlapping processes: narration, learning, and institutionalization. The comparison of the CFDT and the CGT illustrates the extent to which a heterogeneous repertoire coupled with leadership autonomy and centralization can foster creative adaptation and innovation and thereby increase the likelihood of organizational resilience. In contrast, a homogeneous repertoire on top of a dependent leadership and a decentralized structure undermines innovation and thereby decreases the likelihood of resilience. Heterogeneity matters insofar as it feeds friction and collective reflexivity; leadership autonomy and centralization matter insofar as they facilitate the implementation and institutionalization of innovations. Thus, although the approach developed here does not allow us to make predictions such as "if x then y," it does permit us to predict which developments are extremely unlikely (cf. Pierson 2004: 160–1).

The comparison of the CFDT and the CGT also suggests that the effects of the repertoire and structure of organizations depend on the context. In this respect, the CFDT benefited from the relative compatibility between its repertoire – particularly the antistatist and firm as community frames and the apolitical and social dialogue scripts – and the evolution of the French labor regime. Even the self-management script, despite its apparent radicalism, was compatible with certain elements of neoliberalism. For example, as Pierre Rosanvallon (1976: 45) points out, "The self-management proposition, based on the social property of the means of production and democratic planning, resonates with the liberal project of limiting state power and fostering civil

---

[38] Interview with author, April 2003.

society."[39] Similarly, Howell (1992: 170) remarks that after being deprived of its socialist character, self-management entailed treating the firm as a community and opened the way to a justification of flexibility. The role that the CFDT played in the elaboration of the Auroux Laws, which led to the decentralization of collective bargaining and undermined unions, also points to the compatibility between the CFDT's repertoire and the evolution of the French labor regime. In this specific instance, the CFDT not only responded to changes in its environment but also directly contributed to shaping them.

Finally, the comparison of the CFDT and CGT shows that the capacity to be resilient is not a static feature. The institutionalization of the CFDT's new strategy involved the marginalization of certain elements of its repertoire and thereby a narrowing of the range of options available and a decrease in heterogeneity. Organizational resilience had the unintended effect of homogenizing the CFDT's repertoire. In so doing, it decreased the future capacity of the CFDT to be resilient. Successful adaptation in the short term can thus undermine adaptive capacity in the long term.

References

Andolfatto, Dominique and Dominique Labbé. 1997. *La CGT: Organisation et audience depuis 1945*. Paris: La Découverte.

Andolfatto, Dominique and Dominique Labbé. 2006. *Histoire des syndicats (1906–2006)*. Paris: Seuil.

Andolfatto, Dominique and Dominique Labbé. 2007. "La syndicalisation en France: Essai de dénombrement des effectifs de la CGT et de la CFDT (1990–2006)." Paris and Grenoble.

Andolfatto, Dominique and Dominique Labbé. 2009. *Toujours moins! Déclin du syndicalisme à la française*. Paris: Gallimard.

Barnier, Louis-Marie, and Évelyne Perrin. 2009. "La grève des sans-papiers d'avril 2008 et la CGT." In *Quand le travail se précarise, quelles résistances collectives?*, edited by Sophie Béroud and Paul Bouffartigue. Paris: La Dispute: 289–304.

Bégin, Lucie and Didier Chabaud. 2010. "La résilience des organisations: Le cas d'une entreprise familiale." *Revue française de gestion* 200: 127–42.

Berger, Suzanne. 1974. *The French Political System*. New York: Random House.

Berger, Suzanne. 1987. "Religious Transformation and the Future of Politics." *European Sociological Review* 1 (1): 23–45.

Béroud, Sophie. 2005. "La CGT, entre soutien distancé et refondation de l'activité internationale." In *L'Altermondialisme en France: La longue histoire d'une nouvelle cause*, edited by Eric Agrikoliansky, Olivier Fillieule, and Nonna Mayer. Paris: Flammarion; 291–316.

Béroud, Sophie. 2009. "Organiser les inorganisés. Des expérimentations syndicales entre renouveau des pratiques et échec de la syndicalisation." *Politix* 22 (1): 127–46.

Bévort, Antoine. 1994. "Le syndicalisme français et la logique du recrutement sélectif: le cas de la CFTC-CFDT." *Le Mouvement Social* 169: 109–36.

Bévort, Antoine and Dominique Labbé. 1992. *La CFDT: Organisation et audience depuis 1945*. Paris: La Documentation française.

---

[39] My translation.

Bourdieu, Pierre. 1977 [1972]. *Outline of a Theory of Practice*. Cambridge, UK: Cambridge University Press.

Crouch, Colin. 2005. *Capitalist Diversity and Change: Recombinant Governance and Institutional Entrepreneurs*. New York: Oxford University Press.

Crouch, Colin and Henry Farrell. 2004. "Breaking the Path of Institutional Development? Alternatives to the New Determinism." *Rationality and Society* 16 (1): 5–43.

Defaud, Nicolas. 2009. *La CFDT (1968–1995): De l'autogestion au syndicalisme de proposition*. Paris: Presses de Sciences Po.

Demers, Christiane. 2007. *Organizational Change Theories*. Thousand Oaks, CA: Sage.

Dodgson, Mark. 1993. "Organizational Learning: A Review of Some Literatures." *Organization Studies* 14 (3): 375–94.

Ebbinghaus, Bernhard and Jelle Visser. 1999. "When Institutions Matter: Union Growth and Decline in Western Europe, 1950–1995." *European Sociological Review* 15 (2): 135–58.

Fligstein, Neil. 1987. "The Intraorganizational Power Struggle: Rise of Finance Personnel to Top Leadership in Large Corporations, 1919–1979." *American Sociological Review* 52 (1): 44–58.

Fligstein, Neil. 1996. "Markets as Politics: A Political-Cultural Approach to Market Institutions." *American Sociological Review* 61 (4): 656–73.

Frege, Carola and John Kelly, eds. 2004. *Varieties of Unionism: Strategies for Union Revitalization in a Globalizing Economy*. Oxford, UK: Oxford University Press.

Ganz, Marshall. 2000. "Resources and Resourcefulness: Strategic Capacity in the Unionization of California Agriculture, 1959–1966." *American Journal of Sociology* 105 (4): 1003–62.

Geertz, Clifford. 1973. *The Interpretation of Cultures*. New York: Basic Books.

Giraud, Baptiste. 2008. "L'affrontement au pouvoir politique transfiguré par les logiques de l'action syndicale: Le cas de la CGT." In *Pour une gauche de gauche*, edited by Bertrand Geay and Laurent Willemez. Bellecombe-en-Bauges, France: Éditions du Croquant: 37–55.

Greenfeld, Liah. 1992. *Nationalism: Five Roads to Modernity*. Cambridge, MA: Harvard University Press.

Groux, Guy and René Mouriaux. 1989. *La CFDT*. Paris: Economica.

Groux, Guy and René Mouriaux. 1992. *La CGT: crises et alternatives*. Paris: Economica.

Hall, Peter A. and Michèle Lamont. 2009. "Introduction." In *Successful Societies: How Institutions and Culture Affect Health*, edited by Peter A. Hall and Michèle Lamont. New York: Cambridge University Press: 1–22.

Hamon, Hervé and Patrick Rotman. 1984 [1982]. *La deuxième gauche: Histoire intellectuelle de la CFDT*. Paris: Editions du Seuil.

Hannan, Michael T. and John Freeman. 1977. "The Population Ecology of Organizations." *American Journal of Sociology* 82 (5): 929–64.

Hannan, Michael T. and John Freeman. 1984. "Structural Inertia and Organizational Change." *American Sociological Review* 49 (2): 149–64.

Hannan, Michael T. and John Freeman. 1988. "The Ecology of Organizational Mortality: American Labor Unions, 1936–1985." *American Journal of Sociology* 94 (1): 25–52.

Harding, David J. 2010. *Living the Drama: Community, Conflict, and Culture among Inner-City Boys*. Chicago: University of Chicago Press.

Hazareesingh, Sudhir. 1994. *Political Traditions in Modern France*. Oxford, UK: Oxford University Press.

Howell, Chris. 1992. *Regulating Labor: The State and Industrial Relations in Postwar France*. Princeton, NJ: Princeton University Press.

Jenson, Jane. 2007. "The European Union's Citizenship Regime. Creating Norms and Building Practices." *Comparative European Politics* 5: 53–69.

Kitschelt, Herbert. 1994. *The Transformation of European Social Democracy*. New York: Cambridge University Press.

Lallement, Michel. 2006. "New Patterns of Industrial Relations and Political Action since the 1980s." In *Changing France: The Politics that Markets Make*, edited by P. D. Culpepper, P. A. Hall, and B. Palier. Houndmills, UK: Palgrave: 50–79.

Lamont, Michèle and Laurent Thévenot. 2000. "Introduction: Toward a Renewed Comparative Cultural Sociology." In *Rethinking Comparative Cultural Sociology: Repertoires of Evaluation in France and the United States*, edited by Michèle Lamont and Laurent Thévenot. New York: Cambridge University Press: 1–22.

Levitsky, Steven. 2003. *Transforming Labor-Based Parties in Latin America: Argentine Peronism in Comparative Perspective*. New York: Cambridge University Press.

Levitt, Barbara and James G. March. 1988. "Organizational Learning." *Annual Review of Sociology* 14: 319–40.

Levy, Jonah. 2005. "Redeploying the State: Liberalization and Social Policy in France." In *Beyond Continuity: Institutional Change in Advanced Political Economies*, edited by Wolfgang Streeck and Kathleen Thelen. Oxford, UK: Oxford University Press: 103–26.

Lindblom, Charles E. 1959. "The Science of 'Muddling Through.'" *Public Administration Review* 19 (2): 79–88.

Lopez, Steven Henry. 2004. *Reorganizing the Rust Belt: An Inside Study of the American Labor Movement*. Berkeley: University of California Press.

Magniadas, Jean. 1987. *Le syndicalisme de classe*. Paris: Messidor/Éditions sociales.

Mahoney, James. 2001. *The Legacies of Liberalism. Path Dependence and Political Regimes in Central America*. Baltimore, MD: The Johns Hopkins University Press.

Michelat, Guy and Michel Simon. 2004. *Les ouvriers et la politique: Permanence, ruptures, réalignements*. Paris: Presses de Sciences Po.

Milkman, Ruth and Kim Voss, eds. 2004. *Rebuilding Labor: Organizing and Organizers in the New Union Movement*. Ithaca, NY: Cornell/ILR Press.

Minkoff, Debra. 1999. "Bending with the Wind: Strategic Change and Adaptation by Women's and Racial Minority Organizations." *American Journal of Sociology* 104 (6): 1666–703.

Mohr, Lawrence B. 1969. "Determinants of Innovation in Organizations." *American Political Science Review* 63 (1): 111–26.

Mouriaux, René. 1982. *La CGT*. Paris: Éditions du Seuil.

Moynot, Jean-Louis. 1982. *Au milieu du gué: CGT, syndicalisme et démocratie de masse*. Paris: Presses Universitaires de France.

Pfeffer, Jeffrey and Gerald R. Salancik. 2003 [1978]. *The External Control of Organizations: A Resource Dependence Perspective*. Stanford, CA: Stanford University Press.

Pierson, Paul. 2004. *Politics in Time: History, Institutions, and Social Analysis*. Princeton, NJ: Princeton University Press.

Piotet, Françoise. 2009. "La CGT, une anarchie (plus ou moins) organisée?" *Politix* 22 (85): 9–30.

Rosanvallon, Pierre. 1976. *L'âge de l'autogestion*. Paris: Seuil.

Rosanvallon, Pierre. 1980. "L'identité CFDT." *Esprit* 40: 9–14.

Ross, George. 1982. "The Perils of Politics: French Unions and the Crisis of the 1970s." In *Unions, Change and Crisis: French and Italian Union Strategy and the Political Economy, 1945–1980*, edited by P. Lange, G. Ross, and M. Vannicelli. London: George Allen & Unwin.

Scruggs, Lyle and Peter Lange. 2002. "Where Have All the Members Gone? Globalization, Institutions, and Union Density." *Journal of Politics* 64 (1): 126–53.

Séguy, Georges. 2008. *Résister, de Mauthausen à Mai 68*. Paris: l'Archipel.

Slater, Dan and Erica Simmons. 2010. "Informative Regress: Critical Antecedents in Comparative Politics." *Comparative Political Studies* 43 (7): 886–917.

Small, Mario Luis, David J. Harding, and Michèle Lamont. 2010. "Reconsidering Culture and Poverty." *Annals of the American Academy of Political and Social Science* 629: 6–27.

Stark, David. 2009. *The Sense of Dissonance: Accounts of Worth in Economic Life*. Princeton, NJ: Princeton University Press.

Swidler, Ann. 1986. "Culture in Action: Symbols and Strategies." *American Sociological Review* 51 (2): 273–86.

Tilly, Charles. 1995. "Contentious Repertoires in Great Britain, 1758–1834." In *Repertoires and Cycles of Collective Action*, edited by Mark Traugott. Durham, NC: Duke University Press: 15–42.

Tilly, Charles. 2008. *Contentious Performances*. New York: Cambridge University Press.

Tixier, Pierre Éric. 1992. *Mutation ou déclin du syndicalisme? Le cas de la CFDT*. Paris: Presses universitaires de France.

Turner, Lowell. 2005. "From Transformation to Revitalization: A New Research Agenda for a Contested Global Economy." *Work and Occupations* 32 (4): 383–99.

Visser, Jelle. 2000. "France." In *The Societies of Europe: Trade Unions in Western Europe since 1945*, edited by Bernhard Ebbinghaus and Jelle Visser. London: Macmillan: 237–77.

Weick, Karl E. 1988. "Enacted Sensemaking in Crisis Situations." *Journal of Management Studies* 25 (4): 305–17.

Western, Bruce. 1997. *Between Class and Market: Postwar Unionization in the Capitalist Democracies*. Princeton, NJ: Princeton University Press.

Index

Note to index: A *b* after a page number indicates a box; an *f* after a page number indicates a figure; an *n* after a page number indicates a note; a *t* after a page number indicates a table.